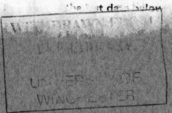

MUḤAMMAD
and
THE COURSE OF ISLÁM

By the same author

A TRILOGY ON THE FOUNDERS OF THE BAHÁ'Í FAITH
EDWARD GRANVILLE BROWNE AND THE BAHÁ'Í FAITH

In Persian

THE STORY OF THREE SISTERS (the Brontës)
HALF-BROTHERS
(Collection of short stories translated from English)
WORDS IN ENGLISH DERIVED FROM PERSIAN

سورة البقرة مدنية ٢٨٦
بسم الله الرحمن الرحيم
بنام خدای بخشاینده مهربان
الم ذلك الكتاب لا ريب فيه
این کتاب شکی نیست در آن
هدى للمتقين الذين يؤمنون
راهنمای پرهیزکارانست کسانیکه گرویدند
بالغيب ويقيمون الصلوة ومما
بنادیده یعنی خدا و روز قیامت و برپا میدارند نماز را و پاره از آنچه
رزقناهم ينفقون والذين
روزی داده ایم بایشان نفقه میکنند و کسانی که
يؤمنون بما انزل اليك وما انزل
گرویده اند بآنچه فرستاده شده بسوی تو و آنچه فرستاده شد
من قبلك وبالاخرة هم يوقنون
پیش از تو و بروز قیامت ایشان جزم میدارند

MUḤAMMAD
and
THE COURSE OF ISLÁM

by

H. M. Balyuzi

GR

GEORGE RONALD
OXFORD

First published by
George Ronald
46 High Street, Kidlington, Oxford, OX5 2DN

ISBN 0 85398 060 8

Set in 11 on 12 point Garamond
and printed in Great Britain
by Richard *Clay (The Chaucer Press), Ltd,*
Bungay, Suffolk

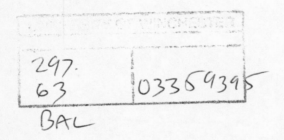

This is the Book, undoubtedly, a guidance to the God-fearing, who believe in the world unseen, who render the prayer ordained, who give alms from what We have bestowed upon them, who believe in the Revelation sent down to thee, who believe in the life hereafter.

SÚRAT AL-BAQARAH
Opening verses from the
second súrah of the Qu'rán

Contents

PART I

The Founder of Islám

PART II

The Course of Islám

List of Illustrations

Foreword

THIS book has been about a decade in writing, not continuously but at intervals. It took the best part of 1974 to complete it. My sources have in the first place been works in Arabic and Persian, and secondly books written in the West on the Founder of Islám and the course of His Faith. I have studiously avoided giving copious references to my sources for two good reasons. Firstly, the general reader finds it boring and cumbersome, as I do myself, when I encounter miles of print containing just numbers of pages. Secondly, of some books more than one edition exists, and in a number of cases the edition which I owned or had access to is rare and unobtainable. Such was the case with my edition[1] of the life of the Prophet by Ibn-Hishám (d. A.D. 833) which, unfortunately, some Western authors still refer to as the book by Ibn-Isḥáq (d. A.D. 768). That earliest biography of the Prophet does not exist and *Síratu Rasúli'lláh* is its recension by Ibn-Hishám. Again, the excellent history by 'Izzi'd-Dín Ibn al-Athír, *al-Kámil fi't-Táríkh*, on which I have relied to a great extent, I own in a six-volume edition printed[2] in Cairo. There is an earlier edition of this book, in fourteen volumes, published in Leyden and Upsala.[3]

I have consulted all the books detailed in my bibliography. There are other works, scholarly and otherwise, from which I have gained much knowledge and understanding, but the cramming of a bibliography can be as tedious for the reader as filling footnotes with too many references.

To my cousin, Abul-Qasim Afnan, I am particularly grateful for having kept me provided, over the years, with a wide variety of books. I wish to record my sincere thanks to Shahab Zahrai, who, having heard that I was engaged in writing this book,

[1] Traubner, London, 1873.
[2] 1290 A.H. (A.D. 1873–74).
[3] 1851–76.

kindly sent me a recent Arabic publication: *'Abdu'lláh Bin Sabá Wa Asáṭír Ukhrá* ('Abdu'lláh Bin Sabá and other Myths) by Murtaḍá al-'Askarí.[4] The author, powerfully and almost convincingly argues his case that 'Abdu'lláh Ibn Sabá—a man said to have been of Jewish origin and to have achieved notoriety by proclaiming the divinity of 'Alí, the cousin and son-in-law of the Prophet, losing his life in the bargain for such blatant blasphemy—had never really existed. But, no matter how mythical the person of 'Abdu'lláh Ibn Sabá, the fact remains that a firm belief in the divinity of 'Alí has persisted down the centuries in diverse forms.

I am profoundly grateful to my old friends Abul-Qasim Faizi and Professor Zeine N. Zeine for reading my manuscript and making valuable suggestions.[5] I have also to thank Geoffrey Nash most sincerely for a last-minute checking of much of the text. But whatever error is contained in the book is entirely mine. My grateful thanks also go to Rustom Sabit and Denis MacEoin for assisting in reading the proofs.

My debt of gratitude to Marion Hofman is truly immense for putting this book into its present shape ready for publication. And finally my wife's encouragement, suggestions and patience have been unfailing, helping me through to the end.

London
August 1975

[4] Published in Beirut, 1968.

[5] Professor Zeine kindly sent me the facsimile of a document, purported to be the Prophet's letter to the ruler of Írán. This document is in Beirut and has been put on exhibition. If genuine this would be a find of prime importance. But it is not within my competence to express any opinion.

A Note on Transliteration

THE system of transliteration used in this book is on the whole the same favoured by orientalists of an earlier generation, including two occupants of Sir Thomas Adams's Chair of Arabic at the University of Cambridge: Edward Granville Browne and Reynold Alleyne Nicholson. They did not, however, put a line under 'ch', 'dh', 'kh', 'sh', 'th' and 'zh'; it has been done here to show that these combinations of two letters indicate a single letter in the original script. But the accenting here used is the same, and indicates the following pronunciation of vowel sounds: 'á' as long 'a' in 'ah' or 'father'; the unaccented 'a' is short as in 'band' or 'ran'. 'Í' represents a vowel sound as in 'meet' or 'feet'; the unaccented 'i' represents a simple 'e' sound as in 'met' or 'set'.[1] 'Ú' indicates 'oo' as in 'boot' or 'root'; the unaccented 'u' serves as 'o' as in 'port' or 'sort'.

As for the consonants, 'zh' has the same sound as 'j' in French; an English 's' conveys it in 'pleasure', as does 'g' in words borrowed from the French, such as 'barrage' and 'garage', or 'z' in words like 'azure'. Although the sounds of 'kh' and of 'gh' are not easy for English-speaking people to utter, they are not uncommon in the West. 'Ch' in 'loch' has the same sound as 'kh', which is also a familiar sound in German. The French give utterance to the sound of 'gh' when they speak of 'Paris'. 'Q' has a sound which cannot be described in writing, and the same is true of 'ḍ' 'dh' and 'ẓ', as spoken in Arabic, when they have distinct modes of pronunciation, although in Persian they all sound as 'z'. I am conscious that this description of sounds cannot apply to words in Turkish. An Arab or a Persian says 'Muḥammad' where a Turk would have it as 'Mehmet'. This is why in earlier times the name of the Prophet appeared as 'Mahomet' in

[1] In two cases I have broken the rule and have used accents reluctantly when not warranted, by accenting the 'i' in Mu'áwíyah and Zíyád because, I believe, it will make it easier to pronounce these names.

English; it had come from the Turks and Turkish. Later, when it was realized that the letter is 'd' not 't', 'Mahomed' replaced 'Mahomet'.

Throughout this book I have tried to give the Arabic version where Arabic names and words are concerned, and have treated Persian names and words in the same manner. But pitfalls are many. Arabs say 'Khadíjah' and 'Fáṭimah'. Persians say 'Khadíjih' and 'Fáṭimih'—these names having found a secure home in Persian. Take the reverse side of the coin. The word *Dastúr* is a Persian word which has more than one meaning, but its meaning in modern Arabic is not one of them. Today an Arab uses *ad-Dustúríyyah* or *ad-Dustúrí* to connote Constitutional Government, and his pronunciation does not accord with the Persian's. *Mashrúṭih* is the Persian's word for 'Constitutional'; it is of Arabic origin and pronounced as *Mashrúṭah* in Arabic, to convey the meaning of 'conditional'. In the Indian sub-continent, *Dastúr* is the designation which the Pársís have given to their priests, and their pronunciation of the word is subtly different.

Arabic has no 'v' (that is why Victoria has become Fictoria in Arabic) and Persian has no 'w'. The name of a certain province and city in Transoxania always appears as 'Khwárizm' in the writings of orientalists, for which there is no justification, unless they regard it as purely Arabic. Persian has many words containing a 'v'—*váv* (Persian), *wáw* (Arabic)—which is not at all pronounced, and 'Khárazm' is one of them. In recent years, attempts have been made, unsuccessfully, to drop this unpronounced letter altogether in spelling. Khívih is the modern name for Khárazm, and it should not be written as 'Khíwah', unless it is stated at the same time that this is how an Arab would speak of that city.

Arabic has no letter to correspond to 'ch'. It also lacks such sounds as are conveyed by 'p', 'zh', and a hard 'g'. Egyptians have turned the soft 'g' ('jím') into a hard one, and speak of 'Gamál' although it is written as 'Jamál'.

Khárazmí, or Khwárizmí (in the version of orientalists), is the name of a very great scientist of the Islamic civilization, who was certainly not an Arab, but wrote in Arabic because it was the common language of learning and the learned, as Latin was in Europe of the Middle Ages, even into the days of Copernicus and Newton. Khárazmsháh was the generic title of the rulers of two dynasties who were based on Khárazm. The second of these dynasties, which eventually went down before the Mongols, had a flourishing and extensive kingdom.

When Arabic words and phrases poured into Persian, to enrich it immeasurably and make it a much more expressive language, the Persians accepted the alphabet of the Arabs, but added to it four letters with sounds corresponding to those of 'p', 'c͟h', hard 'g' and 'z͟h'. They also had to accept letters that are represented in our system of transliteration by 't͟h', 'ḥ', 'ṣ', 'ḍ', 'ṭ', 'ẓ', ' ' ' and 'q', but their pronunciation, as one finds with Arabs, is not followed today. 'T͟h' and 'ṣ' sound in Persian like a plain 's'; 'ḍ' and 'ẓ' are indistinguishable from 'z'; 'ḥ' and 'ṭ' are treated as 'h' and 't' without the dot, ' ' ' (a sound impossible to convey in writing) and 'q' are greatly softened.

Now it only remains to point out a sad lapse on the part of popular writers, notably reporters and journalists; and to show how unrealistic a particular practice of the orientalists has been. Ever since the time of Sulṭán 'Abdu'l-Ḥamíd of Turkey (or perhaps even earlier), who was objurgated as 'Abdul the Damned', certain writers have assumed that 'Abdul' by itself is a first name. It is nothing of the sort. It means 'the Servant of the', and is a part of a name. It would not have mattered very much, apart from displaying ignorance, if this lack of understanding did not have more serious implications. To imagine that a man named 'Abdu'l-Qayyúm has 'Abdu'l as his first name and Qayyúm as his surname is grossly erroneous; and then referring to him as Mr. Qayyúm borders on offensive sacrilege, because Qayyúm means 'Self-Subsistent', and for a devout Muslim it can only denote God.

And for some years, orientalists have insisted on reproducing the Arabic definite article 'al' exactly as it is, no matter if it is pronounced or not. Now Arabic letters are of two kinds: the Solar (*as͟h-S͟hamsíyyah*) and the Lunar (*al-Qamaríyyah*). When the article 'al' is placed before a word that has a solar letter as its first letter, the 'l' of 'al' is not enunciated and becomes a replica of that solar letter, as in *as͟h-S͟hams* (sun) itself. But not so with words that begin with a lunar letter. 'Al' before such words has its 'l' fully enunciated as in *al-Qamar* (moon) itself. Why, one is entitled to ask, do a host of orientalists insist on writing that 'al' exactly as it is, in such instances when its 'l' is transmuted into something else? No less an authority than the late Professor Arberry has time and again written the name of the great mystic Persian poet, Rúmí, as Jalál al-Dín, although it is pronounced Jaláli'd-Dín or Jalála'd-Dín or Jalálu'd-Dín. Should an unsuspecting English-speaking lover of oriental poetry tell an Íránian that he knew of the great Jalál al-Dín, the Íránian would put it down, at best, to downright crass ignorance and, at worst, would feel insulted and consider it a stupid attempt to have fun at his expense. Fortunately, in more recent times a number of orientalists have reversed the process and reproduced their definite articles realistically. But what can one do when renowned works of reference perpetuate the error.

One final word to underline the fact that words of Arabic origin which have found a home in Persian are not necessarily bound by grammatical rules that originally governed them. The same might be said for words of Persian origin which have found a niche in Arabic, but whereas Arabic grammar is as complex as Latin, Persian grammar is as simple as English.

Acknowledgements

The author acknowledges with sincere thanks the permission to quote extracts from works in copyright which the following persons and publishers have kindly granted:

Judge W. Ameer-Ali and Chatto and Windus Ltd, from *The Spirit of Islam*, and Macmillan, London and Basingstoke, from *A Short History of the Saracens*, both titles by Syed Ameer Ali; George Allen & Unwin Ltd, from *Oriental Essays* and from *The Koran Interpreted*, with acknowledgement also to Barnes & Noble Inc. for the latter, both titles by A. J. Arberry; Peter Davies Limited, from *Akbar*, by Laurence Binyon; Cambridge University Press, from *A Literary History of Persia* (vols. I and IV) by E. G. Browne, from *A Literary History of the Arabs* by R. A. Nicholson, and from *A History of the Crusades* by Steven Runciman; the Estate of Robert Byron, from *The Road to Oxiana*, this extract also reprinted by permission of A. D. Peters and Co. Ltd; Hodder and Stoughton Limited, from *The Life and Times of Muhammad* by John Bagot Glubb; George Allen & Unwin Ltd and Aldine Publishing Company, from *Classical Islam, A History 600–1258* by G. E. von Grunebaum; the Gibb Memorial Trust, from *The Kashf Al-Maḥjúb* by Al-Hujwiri, translated by R. A. Nicholson; Philip K. Hitti, from his book *The Arabs: A Short History*; Macmillan, London and Basingstoke, and St. Martin's Press, Inc., from *History of the Arabs* by Philip K. Hitti; The University of Minnesota Press, Minneapolis, as originating publisher, from *Islam, A Way of Life* by P. K. Hitti, © Copyright 1970 by the University of Minnesota, all rights reserved; George Allen & Unwin Ltd, from *The Persian Ṣūfis* by Cyprian Rice, O.P., and from *Christians in Persia* by Robin E. Waterfield, with acknowledgement also to Barnes & Noble Inc. for the latter title; Hutchinson University Library, from *The Arabs in History* by Bernard Lewis; Longman Group Limited, from *What Is Islam?* by W.

Montgomery Watt; also, from W. M. Watt's *Muhammad, Prophet and Statesman*, © Oxford University Press 1961, by permission of the Oxford University Press, Oxford; from *A Study of History* by Arnold Toynbee, published by Oxford University Press under the auspices of the Royal Institute of International Affairs, reprinted by permission; Edinburgh University Press, from *The Islamic Dynasties*, by C. E. Bosworth. The Authorised Version of the Holy Bible is Crown Copyright and extracts used are with permission.

Maps are by Roy Mole: plates II, III, VI, VII and p. 231.

SOURCES OF ILLUSTRATIONS

Horst Kolo: Frontispiece photography
Radio Times Hulton Picture Library: Plate I
Elek Books Ltd: Plate IV
A. F. Kersting: Plates V, IX, X, XI
Trustees of the British Museum: Plate XIII
A Survey of Persian Art by Arthur Upham Pope and Phyllis Ackerman, published by Oxford University Press; and Jay Gluck, Japan: Plates XIV, XV
Robert Harding: Plates XII, XVI

Introduction

THERE is no lack of books in English on Muḥammad and the Faith which He founded. We have very learned tomes as well as light chronicles. In spite of a few notable and brilliantly outstanding exceptions, such as *The Preaching of Islam* by Sir Thomas Arnold, *The Spirit of Islam* by Syed Ameer Ali, and in our day the works of Professors Arberry, Bernard Lewis and Montgomery Watt, the majority fail to do full justice to their theme.

This inadequacy among Western authors may be traced to a fundamental lack of appreciation of the full claims and mission of the Prophet. However greatly impressed by His achievements, character and even doctrines, their judgement of Muḥammad Himself and their evaluation of His Faith cannot be other than suspect when their fundamental conviction was that He was a deluded impostor. Witness George Sale's meticulous and scholarly introduction to his translation of the Qur'án. This comment, by a famous Dean of Durham, exemplifies a similar approach:

'Nor can it be doubted that Mohammed, to whom, in an historical sense, most of our troubles in the Near East are due, might well have been won to Christianity had the representatives of the faith whom he encountered been in any sense worthy of their name. On Trinity Sunday it is worth while for us to remember that if, instead of a zeal for arid disputations on the mysteries of the faith, they had shown an unmistakable zeal for righteousness, that titanic power might have been enlisted in the Christian cause, and the God of Mohammedan worship, instead of being the God of Power, might have been the God of Love whom Jesus Christ proclaimed.'[1] As recently as the year 1971, Lord Soper, another famous churchman, stated in a radio programme that Islám, like Communism, was a 'Christian heresy'.

Then there are renowned scholars: Alfred Guillaume, Émile Dermenghem, A. S. Tritton, to name a few, who, despite their

[1] Dr. C. A. Alington in the *Daily Telegraph and Morning Post* of 11 June 1938.

intense admiration for Muḥammad and their ready admittance that the Prophet of Arabia sincerely believed in His divine mission, cannot accept the Qur'án as the 'Word of God'. They consider Him to have been a very remarkable man, a very great man, but go no further. Either they have a religious persuasion that precludes the recognition of Muḥammad as a Messenger chosen by God, or none at all.

Thirdly, we have had popular writers whose portrait of Muḥammad is grotesquely distorted. The Arabian Prophet is not so much the Founder of a Theophany, a new Dispensation but a leader of men in the mould of a successful chieftain, courageous and bold and generous, but also full of human foibles. Some borrow from the writings of those Muslim apologists from the East, whose outlook was primitive, who related stories of angels assuming human form to take part in bloody combats, of jinn (genii) holding converse with the Prophet, and who expatiated on how Muḥammad literally cleft the moon in twain. At the time of the Apollo 15 exploration of the moon, an organization in London, which called itself the Moslem Educational Bureau, was reported to have issued a statement asserting the literal fact of the cleavage of the moon and expressing its certainty that the astronauts of the Apollo 15 would find in the Hadley Rille (a crack on the surface of the moon) the positive proof of the performance of that miracle. An enterprising British journalist in one of the national dailies (known as a quality newspaper), blew up this incredible statement into a sensational story, which occupied a prominent place in a centre page under the heading: 'Mohammed's Moonshot'. It would have been laughable, were it not insulting to one of the major Faiths of mankind. Those Eastern chroniclers and theologians, who gave currency in the past to such stories, bear a heavy burden of responsibility for lowering the Arabian Prophet in the eyes of the West. Today, fortunately, their extravagances are discounted.

These two paragraphs from a work by Professor Montgomery Watt show clearly the standpoint of a Western admirer of Muḥammad and His Faith:

'We have to allow a large measure of truth to the Islamic vision, not merely for what it has achieved in the lives of Muslims, but also for what we ourselves may learn from it. At the same time we cannot fully accept the standard Islamic view that the Qur'ān is wholly true and the criterion of all other truth; for in the strictly historical field we cannot hold that the Qur'ān may override the usual canons of historical evidence. The solution of this problem would appear to be most likely of attainment through some expansion of the diagrammatic conception of truth. Other points have to be taken into consideration, however, in finding a consistent formulation of those mentioned, so that the whole operation properly belongs to the province of theology and cannot usefully be discussed further here.

'Finally a personal word may be in order. Critics of my books on Muḥammad have accused me of not stating my views clearly. Presumably they meant that I did not state a view obviously concordant with their own, or else one they could easily denounce as false. I may have fought shy of a decision, but the matter is difficult when one is writing for a great variety of readers who will understand the key concepts in many different ways. May I put my position as follows? I am not a Muslim in the usual sense, though I hope I am a *muslim* as "one surrendered to God"; but I believe that embedded in the Qur'ān and other expressions of the Islamic vision are vast stores of divine truth from which I and other occidentals have still much to learn.'[2]

The present writer believes in the God-given mission of Muḥammad. Islám and its Holy Book, the Qur'án, he believes to have represented God's purpose and guidance for mankind. The power of Muḥammad, he believes, did not reside in human ingenuity, not in the production of supernatural feats, nor in the arraying of angels on the battlefield, but in the fundamental fact of His being the chosen Messenger of God, the vehicle of the Logos. He could and did re-create the lives of men. He brought them the gift of second birth. On the basis of His teachings and by virtue of the enlightenment of His followers, there arose a civilization and a culture, which, though monotheistic, did not preclude pagan thought; which brought within their pale the philosophy and the science of ancient Greece, without giving the heritage of the past a supernatural aura and sanction. Even more, this civilization and this culture were not wrought by Arabs alone or by Muslims alone. People of other creeds and many nations were partners in this great adventure. Tolerance was engendered by the Faith of the Muslims and was practised. 'Those who have

[2] Watt, *What is Islam?*, p. 21.

believed, the Jews, the Christians and the Sabeans, who believe in God and the Day of Judgement, and do righteously, have their reward with their Lord; neither is there fear for them, nor are they to grieve'—so unequivocal was the pronouncement of the Qur'án (ii, 59). The warning and the promise, which the following verse contains, should also be noted: 'Do not revile them who worship others besides God, lest they, moved by malice and ignorance revile God; thus have we adorned every nation with their own works, and unto God shall they hereafter return, and He shall inform them of that which they have done.' [3] (vi, 108.)

Over a vast area of the world, extending from the heart of Asia and the boundaries of the Pacific to the shores of the Atlantic, the power of Islám raised men to a high level of achievement and ennobled their lives. Only prejudice can ignore these facts.

This book is not intended for scholars nor yet for those little acquainted with the general background of history. Scholars have the great tomes of the orientalists to read, and the works of the great Arab historians, such as Ibn-Khallikán, Ibn-Khaldún and Ibn-al-Athír, to consult. To have attempted to cater for those with little knowledge of history would have made it impossible to put within the compass of a single manageable volume all that the author had set out to do.

There is nothing new that we can learn about the life of Muḥammad. No archaeological find can add to our knowledge. No lost record or forgotten document is expected to come to light which can tell us more about events and actions already known to history. All that remains is to interpret, and here is another attempt at interpretation.

[3] Translations of Arabic and Persian texts are by the author unless otherwise attributed. (Ed.)

PART I

The Founder of Islám

Prologue

THE Founder of Islám was an Arabian. He was born, grew up, received His mandate, preached, fought against odds, achieved staggering, almost unbelievable triumphs and died in Arabia. And Arabia was, and still is, a forbidding land. To the best of our knowledge, there are areas in its vastnesses that no human foot has ever touched. To obtain a picture of its immensities and its frightening solitude one should read *Arabia Deserta*, the classic work of that prince of travellers: Charles Doughty. The prodigious stores of oil that lie deep, deep under its scorching soil betoken a time, scores of millions of years ago, when lush vegetation covered Arabia. But in the days of the Founder of Islám, and for a long, long time before them, as today, Arabia was arid and barren, torrid and parched. Rainfall was, and is, scarce. There were, and are, times when not a single drop falls from the skies throughout the year. And there were, and are, times when the skies open and torrents descend and the dry river-beds, called wadis, bubble with water. At these times even the desert blooms; lovely flowers, particularly the red anemone, blossom and herbiage appears. But it is all short-lived. The water seeps through the earth and river-beds dry up and the desert becomes forlorn once again. Here and there the nomads have dug deep wells to reach the water and here and there water comes to the surface to give life to an oasis. These wells and oases feature prominently in the story of the Arabian Prophet.

Although there had been nomads eking out a poor existence in parts of the interior, settled life was possible only along the peripheries of the peninsula. No townships could flourish in the heart of Arabia. The most advanced of these settled regions were Ḥírah in the north and Yemen (Yaman) in the south. They could boast of being kingdoms, and of their rich, ancient civilizations. Neither of them, however, experienced the impact of the mission of Muḥammad until the closing years of His life. The regions with which Muḥammad was principally concerned, throughout His ministry, were Ḥijáz and parts of Najd. These regions were backward and barbaric, and possessed no culture or learning, apart from the traditions and the lore of the Jews, who lived in settlements of their own and were aliens in Arabia. There was no law to be observed, other than the law of necessity and certain tribal customs and taboos, and there was no recognized authority to enforce any law. Therefore the prescript of vendetta prevailed, every clan (subdivision of a tribe) used its strength to give protection to its members, and powerful men of each clan also indulged in extending protection[1] to whomever it pleased them to take under their wing. However, the peoples of Arabia had one great asset: their language, an important branch of the Semitic tree. Arabic was and remains a marvel. No one has ever been able to explain how this disparate group of people, whose past is buried in legend and myth, managed to develop such a poetic, mellifluous, highly expressive and extremely malleable language, endowed with vast potentialities. Much that has been written about the early history of Arabia, and of the nomads of later times and their brethren settled in Mecca (Makkah), Yat͟hrib and aṭ-Ṭá'if, is purely conjectural. 'Until we can dig for history in Arabia, as we have dug in Egypt, Palestine and Mesopotamia,' writes Professor Bernard Lewis, 'the early centuries of Arabia will remain obscure, and the searcher in the field will have to pick his way warily among the debris of half-erected and half-demolished hypotheses which the historian, with the scanty equipment of fact he now possesses, can neither complete nor raze to the ground.'[2]

Southern Arabia had a civilization, a legacy of the times of antiquity, and a language with a script of its own, close to the Ethiopic; but the language which finally held sway over the whole of the peninsula was the Arabic of further north. And strange it is that although inscriptions have been found in Yemen and elsewhere in Southern Arabia, no book of any kind has come down from the ancient civilization of that region. Arabic being the language that it is, poetry ranked high amongst the Arabs. This poetry, luxuriantly rich in imagery and hyperbole, cared little for the abstract. Because Muḥammad presented the Qur'án, with

[1] *Jiwár* or *juwár*.
[2] *The Arabs in History*, p. 22.

its stunning terseness and fluidity, its enchanting eloquence, as His greatest proof, His detractors said of Him that He was a poet, which He immediately disavowed: He had not composed a single line of poetry in His life.

Contemporary with Muḥammad were poets of high repute and a number of them were extremely antagonistic to Him. They used their undoubted talent to lampoon the Prophet and pour scorn over Him. Jewish poets were particularly guilty in this respect. The greater the extension of the Prophet's work became, the more strident became the invective of hostile poets. This type of satire and contempt had a visible and deleterious effect on the body-politic which was emerging from Muḥammad's mission, for the Arabs were susceptible to the bewitchments of poetry. Muḥammad could no longer ignore the barrage of abuse and derision, as he had done in days past, no matter how wounding the lashing of tongues. He had to condemn the offending poets in the strongest terms. That was why Ka'b Ibn al-Ashraf, the prominent Jewish poet, lost his life; and Ka'b Ibn Zuhayr, the most eloquent poet of his time, would have lost his had he not hurried to seek the Prophet's pardon.

Poets, with their heroics and panegyrics, were no less instrumental in fanning the embers of feuds and vendettas which set man against man, clan against clan and tribe against tribe. Except for four months of the year when taboos barred all fighting, murder and raid and treachery, ravishing and plundering constituted the normal mode and pattern of life, in a land where the struggle for existence was hard and bitter. Islám was born in this inhospitable milieu and survived to become a world religion.

I

The Homeland of Muḥammad and His Early Years

ACCOUNTS of the life of Muḥammad generally open with a description of Arabia, its forbidding deserts, its scorching sun and paucity of rainfall, its caravan routes and oases, its nomads and town-dwellers and settlements of Jews and Christians. A knowledge of the geography of the peninsula and the background against which Muḥammad lived His life is, of course, essential. But too often the emphasis is misplaced. The starkness of the desert was there; so was the poverty of existence and the perpetual feuds and barbarous ways. Muḥammad was, certainly, keenly aware of them. He undoubtedly came in contact with the monotheists of the peninsula and beyond, and came to know their creeds. It has been suggested that what He gleaned from their lore was garbled. No doubt Jews did not speak with one voice, nor did the Christians. Nestorian influence was very strong in and around Arabia. The Monophysites of Ethiopia had attempted the conquest of Mecca, the birth-place and home of Muḥammad. Both these Christian sects had been declared heretical by oecumenical councils (Ephesus, A.D. 431; Chalcedon, A.D. 451). But it was not the topography and the climate, the environment and the conflicting versions of faith and practice that awakened a chord in the mind of Muḥammad and fired His soul to action. He was sensitive and discerning, honest and upright. Years before He came forth with a Message, He was called al-Amín—the One to be Trusted. But His call came to Him from God, and He responded to that call.

There is a saying ascribed to Muḥammad: 'I was born during the reign of the just king'; that king was Chosroes I (Khusraw Anúshirván), the Sásánid monarch.[1] It has also long been held

[1] Reigned A.D. 531–79.

that Muḥammad was born in the 'Year of the Elephant', supposed to have been either A.D. 570 or 571. Recent research has tended to predate it by two years.[2] The 'Year of the Elephant' witnessed the assault on Mecca by the Ethiopians, who came with elephants and were seemingly invincible. Abrahah or Abraham, the Ethiopian ruler of Yemen, was seeking to destroy Mecca and its shrine, the Ka'bah, which housed idols. A short súrah (chapter) of the Qur'án (cv), entitled the 'Súrah of the Elephant', relates what befell them: 'Hast thou not seen how thy Lord dealt with the people of the elephant? Did He not make their stratagem to lead them to error and send against them flocks of birds that hit them with stones of baked clay? Then He turned them into the likeness of munched straw.' Professor Hitti states that the Ethiopians were destroyed by an epidemic of small-pox.

How was it that the Ethiopians had come to rule over Yemen? The occasion was the attempt by the Jewish king, Dhú-Nuwás,[3] to break up the Christian community of Najrán. The Ethiopians came to their defence, and were encouraged by Byzantium to undertake the conquest of South Arabia. Although the Ethiopians, being Monophysites, were heretics in the eyes of the Byzantines, the latter were glad to see them established in Yemen. The Íránians, however, could not tolerate any extension of Byzantine influence, and the already inflamed situation was aggravated by Ethiopian tyranny. Sayf, the son of Dhú-Yazan, a descendant of the Ḥimyarite kings, led an expedition against them with Persian aid. The Ethiopians were slaughtered and the control of Yemen passed into Persian hands. But this dominance was short-lived, for Bádhán, the Íránian viceroy, and those of his countrymen who had settled in Yemen, embraced Islám shortly before the passing of the Prophet.

These ebbs and flows of fortune in Yemen during the sixth century A.D., besides registering a trial of strength between contending creeds, were a strong pointer to the intense and ruinous antagonism between the Mazdean (Zoroastrian) Sásánid Empire and the Christian Byzantine. On the northern frontiers of Arabia the Íráno-Roman conflict was even more in evidence, and had forced vassal Arab principalities to be arrayed in opposing camps. The Ghassánids were Christians and bound to Byzantium. The

[2] This view is not, however, universally accepted.
[3] He was the last Ḥimyarite king.

Lakhmids, who ruled over Ḥírah, were also Christian, but they owed allegiance to Írán. Ghassán was Monophysite, Ḥírah Nestorian. The court of Ḥírah was renowned for its patronage of culture. Imru'-al-Qays and Nábighih,[4] the greatest of the poets of pre-Islamic Arabia, were Christians of the north.

But for the Arabs who worshipped idols, Mecca was the focal point. And Mecca was in the hands of the Quraysh, the great tribe into which Muḥammad was born. They took their name from Fihr, surnamed Quraysh, a remote ancestor of the Prophet. The tribe was divided and subdivided, with an even greater number of clans. Quṣayy, another ancestor of Muḥammad, nearer to Him in time, who lived in the middle of the fifth century, succeeded in gaining control over Mecca, and possibly over almost the whole of Ḥijáz, that area of western Arabia in which Mecca and Medina are situated. Holding the reins of power, he set about rebuilding Mecca and its shrine. Quṣayy was an able administrator and shrewd planner. People thronging to worship at the Ka'bah required food and water; a system had to be devised to supply their needs. This he devised. The city, no longer an assortment of mean huts, had to have a worthy building to serve as its seat of administration. This he provided. By the sixth century the face of Mecca had changed.

The grandsons of Quṣayy fell out among themselves. Wrangling over who should exercise authority, they decided in the end to divide it. Sons of 'Abda'd-Dár, a son of Quṣayy, became the custodians of the Ka'bah and the keepers of the city standard. 'Abd-Shams, the son of 'Abd-Manáf (another son of Quṣayy) took over the administration of the revenue and the water supply. From him these powers passed to his brother Háshim, another man of outstanding ability and enterprise. This transference of authority was destined to affect profoundly the course of Islám.

Háshim was a merchant. He saw clearly that Mecca, in order to maintain its paramount position, needed trade, and on a considerable scale. To obtain it, he instituted two annual treks. One caravan, large and well-equipped, travelled northwards in summer to Syria. Another took the road to the south and Yemen, in the winter season. Both were highly profitable. Háshim also realized that trading could not be safely conducted without the

[4] Of Banú-Dhubyán.

goodwill of neighbours. He made overtures to the Ethiopians in Yemen, to the Arab principalities in the north, to the Byzantine and Sásánid officials on the periphery of the peninsula, and concluded agreements with them.

Háshim died about A.D. 510, and his brother Muṭṭalib took his place. But Muṭṭalib's tenure of office was not long, and on his death Háshim's son, Shaybah, better known as 'Abdu'l-Muṭṭalib, succeeded him. Shaybah was the grandfather of Muḥammad. Under his roof, Muḥammad, when orphaned, was to spend some years of His childhood. By then the descendants of 'Abda'd-Dár were getting restive, and Umayyah, a son of 'Abd-Shams, chafed under a sense of grievance. He was the progenitor of the Umayyads, who, in the following century, came to wield power in the Empire of Islám, having wrested it from the House of the Prophet. They were eventually overthrown by the scions of the House of Háshim.

Notwithstanding opposition from his relatives, 'Abdu'l-Muṭṭalib remained the virtual ruler of Mecca for almost sixty years. He was helped by the elders and avoided ruinous dissensions in the sacred city. 'Abdu'l-Muṭṭalib achieved further renown by rediscovering the waters of Zamzam, that legendary fountain which was believed to have welled forth at the heels of the infant Ishmael, saving him and his mother, Hagar, from death. In the course of centuries Zamzam had disappeared under layers of sand. 'Abdu'l-Muṭṭalib guessed aright that the well must have been close to Ka'bah. The water was brackish, but was a great boon to pilgrims.

This great patriarch had ten sons. Five of them are well remembered: 'Abdu'lláh, the youngest, because he was the father of Muḥammad; Abú-Ṭálib, because he inherited his father's position, and in his house Muḥammad grew to manhood; Ḥamzah, for his heroic devotion to the cause of his Nephew; 'Abbás, for his superb feat of sitting on the fence for so long, and because his descendants, in the eighth century A.D., overthrew the detested Umayyads; and Abú-Lahab, who gained notoriety by his implacable hatred of his Nephew, and because of the injuries which he and his equally vituperative wife inflicted upon Him. Abú-Lahab is the sole kinsman of the Prophet whose name appears in the Qur'án. Thus runs the súrah cxi: 'Perish shall the hands of Abú-Lahab and perish shall he. His riches profit him not, neither what he hath gained. In flaming fire shall he be burned, also his wife bearing faggots, having on her neck a cord of palm-fibres.'

The city of Mecca, at the time of Muḥammad's birth, enjoyed pre-eminence in Arabia. It had a fairly efficient system of administration, wealth and a flourishing trade. The aristocracy lived in good houses, in the neighbourhood of Ka'bah, in a quarter called Baṭḥá, a name which has, at times, been applied to Mecca itself. On the edge of the town were hovels peopled by the dregs of humanity, also houses of pleasure and entertainment, and parasites swarmed there for whom a place of pilgrimage, such as Mecca, provided the right milieu for their activities.

The climate of Mecca was far from salubrious. The heat was intense, the water unwholesome and difficult to come by, and the landscape bleak and barren. Medina, then known as Yathrib, presented a vivid contrast. Its air was kinder, good water was abundant, and there were orchards and varieties of fruit. Mostly it was peopled by the tribes of Aws and Khazraj, while close by were large and powerful settlements of Jews. And it had an effective system of administration.

Not far from Mecca was aṭ-Ṭá'if, with lush orchards, water and fruit in plenty. This fair oasis features prominently in the story of the life of the Prophet.

Mecca, Ṭá'if, Yathrib, Jewish and Christian settlements, Yemen and northern principalities did not, however, make a nation. Over vast tracts of the peninsula only brutal lawlessness held sway. Tribes battled and pillaged mercilessly, except during four months of the year, which by the sanction of custom were free from fighting. During this period of truce people went on pilgrimage, and gathered at great fairs, such as 'Ukáẓ, to recite and listen to poetry. Their poetry was rich and pictorial, but its range was limited and abstract thought had no place in it. Although very hospitable, people were also treacherous. Their manners were uncouth and they paid scant attention to cleanliness and hygiene. They also had the habit of walking into one another's homes unbidden and unannounced, even when a man was closeted with his wife. Muḥammad Himself suffered from this discourtesy. People scaled the walls of His house, broke in upon His privacy and called out to Him, 'O Muḥammad! Talk to us'. Later, the Prophet would counsel them not to enter anyone's house before knocking at the door. Yet another custom was sometimes to bury

I THE KA'BAH AT MECCA

Arabia's most holy shrine and the Qiblih of Islám, which contains the Black Stone reputedly brought to Abraham by the Angel Gabriel. A drawing from the first photograph ever taken.

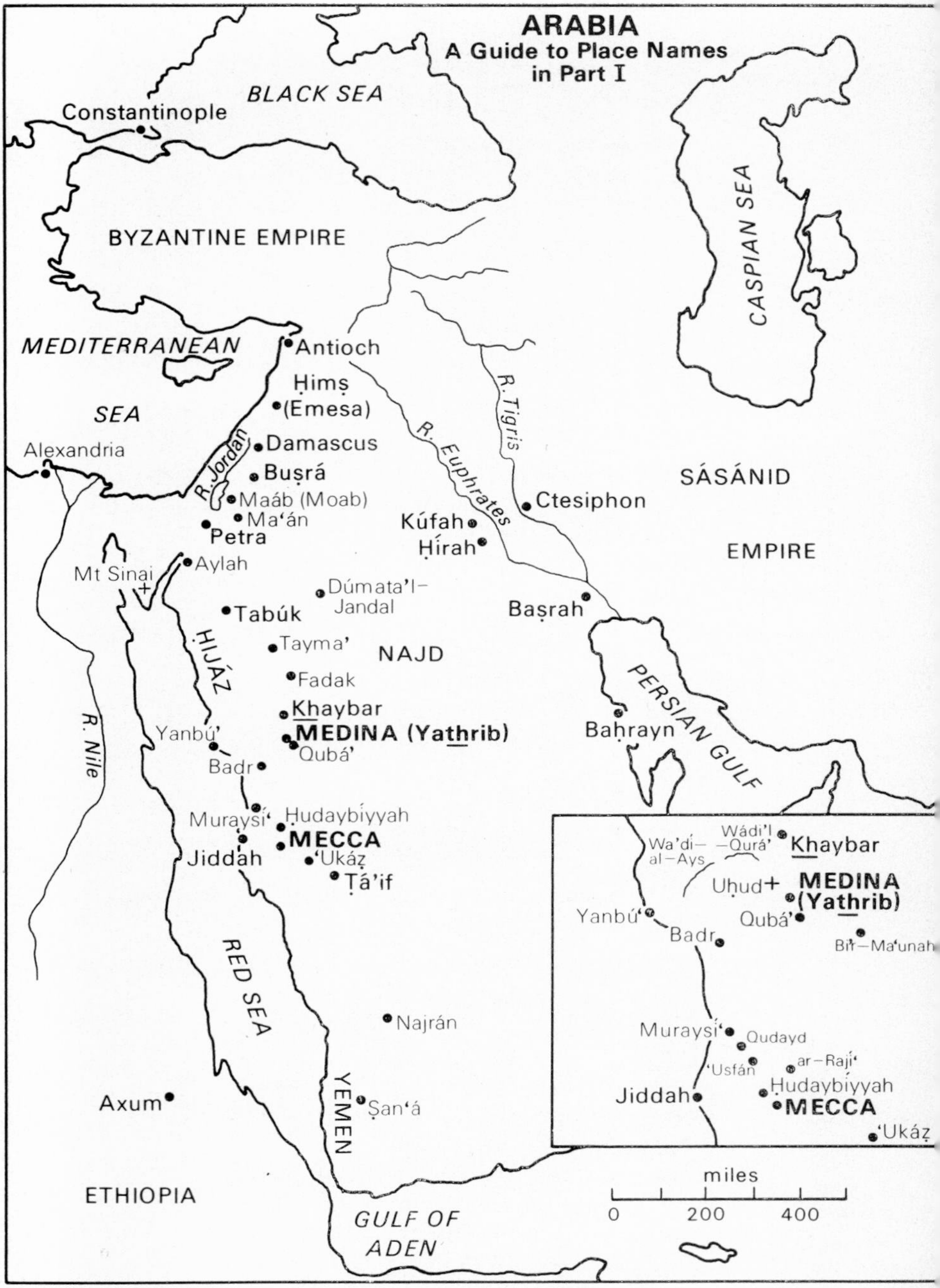

ARABIA
A Guide to Place Names in Part I

The Lineage and Kinsmen of Muḥammad

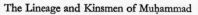

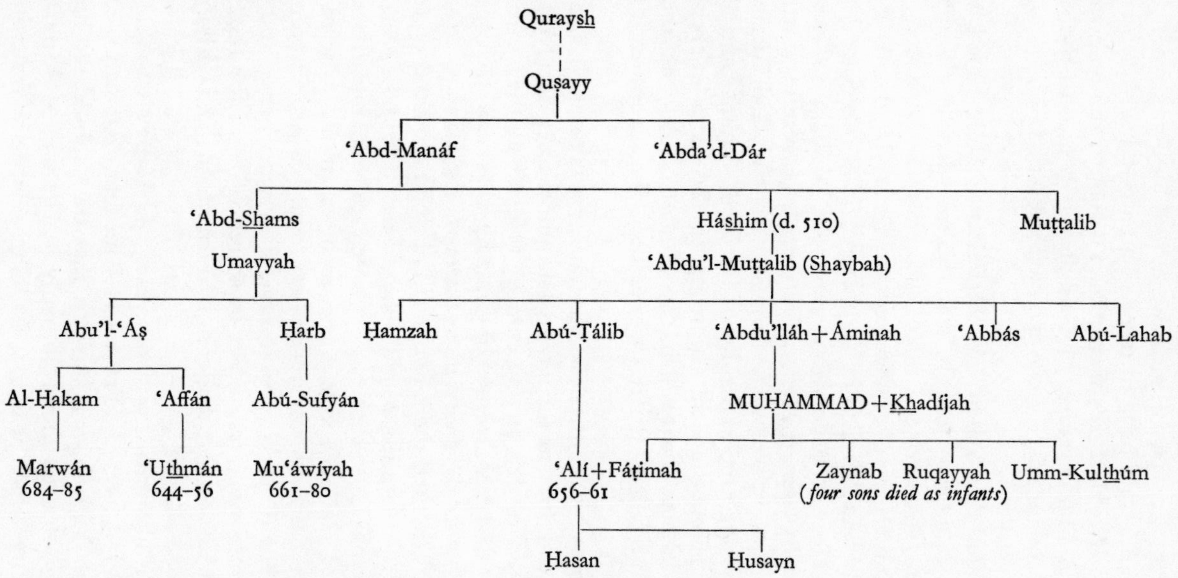

The first two Caliphs, members of the Quraysh, are not included above: Abú-Bakr of Banú-Taym (632–34), 'Umar of Banú-'Adí (634–44). Four later Caliphs are included. A.D. dates are of their reigns.

infant girls alive, since girls were not highly prized. Indeed, Muḥammad would have to teach them a good deal.

Such was Arabia when Muḥammad was born and such were His forbears. A Manifestation of God always comes to the darkest, dreariest land, amidst people who are degraded.

It is related that 'Abdu'lláh, the father of Muḥammad, was the old patriarch's favourite son. It is also said that he was strikingly handsome. He married Áminah, the daughter of Wahab, of the clan of Zuhrah, a subdivision of the Quraysh. Shortly after his marriage 'Abdu'lláh died in Yathrib, where he had gone in pursuit of trade. He was twenty-five years old. Muḥammad was born some months later in Mecca. We cannot be certain whether the year was A.D. 570 or 571. August 20th and also August 29th have been suggested as the day of His birth. Sunnís [5] and Shí'ahs [6] differ regarding the date according to the lunar calendar. The former celebrate the twelfth day of Rabí'al-Awwal, the latter consider the felicitous day to have been the seventeenth of that month.

Muḥammad was fatherless, His mother was not rich, and the air of Mecca did not suit the infant. His grandfather decided that the child should be left in the care of a foster-mother, away from Mecca. At that time, women of nomadic tribes used to come to the holy city to offer their services as foster-mothers. It was an arrangement that benefited them financially, helped the children to grow up in healthier conditions and relieved rich parents of some pressing problems. The woman into whose care Muḥammad was given was named Ḥalímah. She was a member of the tribe of Banú-Asad. Her husband was a shepherd, and his people were more concerned with seeking pasturage than with battle and booty. They roamed over the desert in search of food for their flocks and herds, and at that tender age Muḥammad lived with them the life of a nomad.

When Muḥammad was six years old Ḥalímah took Him to Mecca and delivered Him to His mother. Áminah, who had relatives in Yathrib, was anxious that they should see her child and they journeyed there. So, early in His life, Muḥammad first saw the city which was to offer Him safety and fealty in future

[5] Upholders of the elective principle in the matter of succession to the Prophet.
[6] Legitimists upholding the rights of the House of the Prophet.

years. Their stay in Yat͟hrib was short, and within weeks they were once again crossing the desert. Áminah succumbed to its hardships and was buried at a place named Abwá. Her son was taken to Mecca and handed over to His grandfather, the renowned patriarch. But 'Abdu'l-Muṭṭalib was an old man and within two years he too was dead. Before he died he gave the charge of Muḥammad to his son, Abú-Ṭálib. Muḥammad was then barely eight years old.

Abú-Ṭálib succeeded to his father's office. He traded and led caravans, but he was not a rich man and the size of his family taxed his resources. Muḥammad had no inheritance of His own and did not grow up in circumstances of affluence. When no longer a child He accompanied His uncles on their expeditions: Abú-Ṭálib leading trading caravans to Syria; az-Zubayr heading forays into hostile territory.

In the northern limits of Arabia was the town of Buṣrá, a flourishing and important centre of commerce on the caravan route, where merchants from Byzantium came to exchange goods. All around were Christians, and near by lived a Christian monk of Nestorian persuasion named Baḥírah. On one occasion he saw Abú-Ṭálib's young nephew and saw in Him the Christ. He urged the Meccan chief to take particular care of the youth.

Very little is known of the childhood and youth of Muḥammad. Stories are told in which supernatural beings are involved—jinn, angels, heavenly hosts, Lucifer and his hordes. There is the story that Pushkin has made the subject of a poem, concerning the time when Muḥammad lived with His foster-mother in the desert. One day while out with His playmates, Muḥammad, it is said, was snatched away by angels, His chest was opened and His human heart was replaced by one celestial. Some of these stories spring from interpretations placed upon Qur'ánic verses, some have a symbolic import, some are the fabrications of an age different from ours. Their counterparts abound in the writings of the Fathers of the Church.

There are other accounts and anecdotes which concern the affairs of this world and describe Muḥammad's bearing and conduct in His years of young manhood. His integrity shines through them. People trusted Him and called Him al-Amín: the One who was honest and in whom they could repose their confidence, a quality illustrated by the following story.

Ka'bah, the most holy shrine of Arabia, was (and is) a solid cubic structure. In a corner of it is the most revered object, the *Ḥajara'l-Aswad* (*al-Ḥajar al-Aswad*—the Black Stone). This is the stone which, it is said, the Angel Gabriel brought to Abraham from Paradise. Ravages of time and the elements necessitated extensive repairs to the cubic masonry. The Black Stone was removed, the structure was renovated, and then a furious argument began about the replacement of the sacred stone. The honour was coveted by all. Who was to do it? They turned to Muḥammad for judgement. He spread His cloak on the ground and told them to put the stone on it. Then He invited them all to take hold of the cloak, lift it up and carry the stone to the spot where it was to be placed. Thus they were all participants in the act and were equally honoured. An ugly clash was averted by His wisdom and tact, and the respect which people already had for Him was heightened.

Muḥammad has been referred to as a camel-driver. The connotation is obscure. If it is meant that Muḥammad was a groom, it is palpably false. If it is to indicate that He, like His uncle, led caravans carrying merchandise, it is correct. And what Arab would not tend a camel?

At this time there lived in Mecca a lady twice widowed, who commanded considerable wealth, named Khadíjah Bint[7] Khuwaylid. Trading was her concern and she was seeking someone to whom she could entrust the management of her flourishing business. Her choice fell on Muḥammad. But here a digression is necessary.

It has become fashionable among writers of popular histories and apologists of Faiths to transpose the modes of speech, thought and practice current in the present day to their portrayal of the past, in order to make the events of bygone ages easier to understand. A classic example is provided by the late Dorothy Sayers's admirable and moving radio serial on the life of Christ, *The Man Born to Be King*. This brave attempt to make situations foreign to modern experience more comprehensible is indeed worthy, but it should be done within definite limits. Otherwise a picture is presented which is not true: the Arabian fair at 'Ukáẓ would be seen as a present-day Eisteddfod, the Meccan mart as Leadenhall Street, the bewildered, infuriated and toiling masses of

[7] '*Bint*' means 'daughter of'.

Judea of twenty centuries ago as men of today contesting the merits of their football teams or dazed by the awful doom of the hydrogen bomb. Certainly, basic human instincts and emotions produce recurring patterns. In that sense history repeats itself. It is obvious, too, that man is always presented with a choice of alternatives. But man's domain of knowledge at any given time, be it scientific or traditional, intellectual or esoteric, mystical or superstitious, profoundly affects his condition and his reactions. Cruelty is never commended, always condemned. But what one age fails to see as cruel another does. And how many are there today in the Western world who, whenever an eclipse occurs, talk for days and weeks with dread and terror of the attempt made by the dragon to swallow the moon or the sun, and try to put the monster to flight by beating their copper pots and pans? Yet this was how the generality of men once behaved in the East when dark shadows fell over these celestial bodies. The fear of the dragon might be equated with the fear of the bomb. But the ways men in different ages have talked of their fears and reacted to them are different.

Having made this digression, let it be stated at once that Muḥammad, as a merchant or as a trading agent for a widow in Mecca, should not be equated with a tea trader or a metal merchant of today. His approach to His problems and the very nature of the problems would have been different. We ought to be able to stretch our imaginations to encompass the past, not try to see the past entirely in terms of the present. Perhaps until three or four decades ago, one could still find, here and there in the East, merchants whose styles might have approximated to the style of the merchants of sixth-century Arabia. The present writer recalls times not too far past, the years of his own childhood, so unlike today when a commercial agent flies in and out of a country with a brief-case of samples and glossy literature. Then agents took long sea journeys, with several trunks of goods and wares and voluminous matter-of-fact catalogues. The outlook of those sellers and their customers of a few decades ago could not have been like ours today. Therefore, when writers speak of business concerns and banking arrangements in Mecca in the days of Muḥammad, one ought to be on one's guard not to fall into the trap of a closed imagination.

Our knowledge of Muḥammad during the years that He traded

on behalf of Khadíjah Bint Khuwaylid is meagre. We do know that Khadíjah was much His senior in age. Historians have averred that there was a difference of fifteen years between them. Were it so, she was forty years old when she herself proposed marriage to Muḥammad, for the Prophet's age, we know, was twenty-five at the time He married. According to Ibn-al-Athír, eight children were born to them, four sons and four daughters. None of the sons—Qásim, 'Abdu'lláh, Ṭáhir and Ṭayyib—lived beyond infancy. The four daughters—Zaynab, Ruqayyah, Umm-Kulthúm and Fáṭimah—reached womanhood and married, but all died before the age of thirty. Only Fáṭimah outlived her father, and that by six months. Zaynab was married to Abu'l-'Áṣ, the son of Rabí', of the clan of 'Abd-Shams. The mother of Abu'l-'Áṣ was a sister of Khadíjah and had a great affection for her nephew Muḥammad. Ruqayyah was married to 'Uqbah, a son of Abú-Lahab, but he was made to divorce her when opposition to the Prophet became fierce. Ruqayyah was subsequently wedded to 'Uthmán, the son of 'Affán, of the clan of Umayyah. After her death, Muḥammad gave His third daughter, Umm-Kulthúm, in marriage to 'Uthmán. She also died childless. The fourth daughter, Fáṭimah, became the wife of 'Alí, the son of Abú-Ṭálib.

Muḥammad, as we have seen, grew up in the house of Abú-Ṭálib, His uncle. And now to make the burden of supporting a large family less onerous for that uncle, Muḥammad took 'Alí into His own care. Another member of His household was Zayd, the son of Ḥárithah. Zayd, a Christian from the north, had been captured during a raid and sold into slavery. A nephew of Khadíjah bought him and gave him to his aunt, who in turn presented the boy to her husband. Eventually Zayd's father traced his son to Mecca and came to buy him. Muḥammad gave Zayd the choice of accompanying his father to Syria, but Zayd preferred to remain in Mecca. Whereupon Muḥammad freed him from slavery and adopted him as His own son. 'Alí, though Muḥammad's cousin, was also young enough to be His son. It was a happy household, and Muḥammad, much devoted to His wife and children, His adopted son and His cousin, went on His way as a merchant, quietly engaged in trade and commercial transactions. And during the lifetime of Khadíjah, Muḥammad did not take a second wife.

It is related that one day, on a journey north, He took shelter from the blazing sun under the shade of a tree. A Christian monk happened by and seeing Him exclaimed that none but a Prophet had ever sat under that tree. Christian monasticism pioneered by St. Anthony in the wilderness of Egypt, in the year 285, had reached its peak in the years that Muḥammad had grown into manhood.

As Muḥammad's years increased, tradition has it that He became more reflective, taking Himself to the bleak hills round Mecca for longer and longer periods of quiet meditation. A particular resort, favoured by Him, was a cave in Mount Hirrá'.

2

'Read in the Name of Thy Lord'

THE vehicle of the Revelation which came to Muḥammad on Mount Hirrá' has been traditionally described as the Angel Gabriel. He held up a Tablet to Muḥammad to read. But Muḥammad was untutored and He could not read. Again He was told to read and again He pleaded ignorance. A third time the Angel told Him to read, and once again Muḥammad said that read He could not. Then the words of revelation reached Him: 'Read in the Name of thy Lord Who created; Who created Man of blood congealed. Read, thy Lord is the Most Beneficent; Who taught by the Pen; Who teacheth Man what he knoweth not.'[1] Muḥammad was so overcome that He would have hurled Himself down a precipice. Then, the clear voice rang out again, in the stillness of the lone hillside, to tell Muḥammad that God had chosen Him to be His Messenger to mankind. The weight of revelation was too great to bear, and Muḥammad, now aware of His awesome mission to proclaim the Oneness of the Godhead, fled to His home, not more than three or four miles away, and asked Khadíjah, His wife, to cover Him with His mantle. Muḥammad said, on this occasion, that as He lay covered He felt that His soul had left His body for a while. It is related that it became His wont to seek the cover of His mantle, at the approach of a fresh revelation.

There are two súrahs in the Qur'án, the seventy-third and the seventy-fourth—*al-Muzammil* ('The Enwrapped') and *al-Mudaththir* ('The Covered'), both Meccan (revealed in Mecca)—that spotlight the inauguration of the ministry of Muḥammad. Scholars have been busy speculating about them, some even suggesting that the very first intimation of His prophethood was given to Muḥammad by the seventy-fourth:[2]

[1] *Súrat al-'Alaq*—'The Congealed Blood', xcvi, 1–5.

[2] 'The Covered', according to Sale; 'The Immantled', according to Montgomery Watt; 'Shrouded', according to Arberry.

O thou covered!
Rise and warn.
Thy Lord magnify.
Thy garments purify.
Abomination flee.
Give not as to gain more.
And be patient unto thy Lord.
(vv. 1–7.)

It is claimed that, at the outset, Muḥammad's prime task was to 'warn' His people. He is referred to in the Qur'án as *Nadhír* (He Who Warns), and as *Bashír* (He Who Gives Glad Tidings).

Muḥammad's wife, Khadíjah, was the first to believe in Him. She had no doubt at all that her husband's experience on Mount Hirrá' was truly a call from God. She had a cousin named Waraqah, son of Nawfal, who was Christian, probably a Nestorian or a Monophysite, believed to have translated the Gospels into Arabic and to have been learned in Christian traditions. Khadíjah went to him and related what her husband had experienced in the cave overlooking Mecca. Waraqah listened intently and then exclaimed with joy that *Námús*[3]—the Spirit of God witnessed by Moses on Mount Sinai—had descended upon Muḥammad. Indubitably, he said, Muḥammad was the chosen Messenger of God.

All accounts agree that then a long hiatus followed, during which no revelation reached Muḥammad. He was in despair until at length He was assured, by being reminded of God's benefactions in the past:

By the bright forenoon,
And the brooding night.
Thy Lord hath not forsaken thee, nor doth He hate thee.
Verily the life hereafter shall be better for thee than the life in this world.
And ere long shall thy Lord reward thee, whereby thou shalt be pleased.
Did He not find thee an orphan and give thee shelter?
Did He not find thee erring and give thee guidance?
Did He not find thee in need and provide for thee?
As to the orphan, do not oppress him.

[3] This word is of Greek origin (*nomos*), meaning 'Law'.

As to the beggar, do not turn him away.
And declare the goodness of thy Lord.
(Súrah xciii, *Aḍ-Ḍuḥá*—'The Forenoon'.)

The duration of that hiatus has been a matter of conjecture. Some[4] have put it as long as three years, others as low as ten days to a fortnight. Whatever the case, the first three years of the ministry of Muḥammad are relatively obscure. All we know for certain is that from the year 610 to 613 there was no public announcement of His mission, that His followers could be counted on one's fingers, and that the people of Mecca were unaware that God had chosen one of themselves—a man well known—to be His Messenger to them.

The fifty-third súrah of the Qur'án, *an-Najm*—'The Star', gives a vivid account of the moment the Prophet was made aware of His mission and destiny. But this súrah was revealed when Meccans, having learnt of Muḥammad's claims, were ridiculing Him:

By the star when it waneth,
Your companion erreth not, nor is he led astray.
Neither doth he speak of his own caprice.
This is naught but a revelation revealed.
Taught him by one of great might
And of great strength. He stood poised
On the highest level of the horizon.
Then He approached [Muḥammad] and drew near to him,
At the distance of two-bows' length, or nearer.
Then He revealed to His servant what He revealed.
His heart lieth not of what he saw.
Would ye dispute with him concerning that which he saw?
(vv. 1–12.)

The second to believe in Muḥammad, with unsurpassed devotion, was His cousin 'Alí, the son of Abú-Ṭálib, who was only nine or ten years old. He and Zayd Ibn Ḥári<u>th</u>ah, the next to acknowledge the prophethood of Muḥammad, were, as we have seen, members of His household. There is no doubt that Abú-Bakr Ibn Abí-Quḥáfah, of the Quray<u>sh</u> clan of Banú-Taym, was the fourth Muslim. He was younger than Muḥammad by some two or

[4] Amongst them the great historian, Muḥammad Ibn Jarír aṭ-Ṭabarí (d. A.D. 922).

three years, and was a man of substance. Gaining his allegiance was a signal victory because he was much respected in Mecca, but we know nothing of the circumstances of his conversion. Abú-Bakr's name was 'Atíq; Muḥammad gave him the name of His own father, 'Abdu'lláh.

Another early convert was Khálid Ibn Sa'íd, whose father was one of the richest men in Mecca and remained an unbeliever. Khálid was a much younger man and was a descendant of Umayyah. We have already noted that there was much bitterness in the relationships between the rival and kindred Houses of Umayyah and Háshim. Therefore his conversion, which was followed, not long after, by that of 'Uthmán Ibn 'Affán, another member of the House of Umayyah, was particularly significant. Islám overrode feuds of families and clans. As previously mentioned, Muḥammad gave two of His daughters (one after the death of the other) in marriage to 'Uthmán, who rose to be the third successor to the Prophet. A modern scholar has expressed surprise that Khálid did not attain prominence in later years. Perhaps a reason lies in events immediately following the Prophet's death, when Khálid, who was in charge of a region in Yemen, hurried to Medina and promptly declared that succession to Muḥammad rightly belonged to 'Alí. He refused to transfer his allegiance to Abú-Bakr.

Another youthful member of the group of fifty, whose names have come down to us as the first Muslims, was Zubayr Ibn al-'Awwám, cousin of the Prophet, whose mother 'Átikah was a daughter of the patriarch 'Abdu'l-Muṭṭalib. And so was Sa'd Ibn Abí-Waqqáṣ, then seventeen years old, who was destined to humble the might of the Sásánian Empire. How many of them acknowledged the prophethood of Muḥammad in the first three years of His ministry is a problem unresolved.

It must be borne in mind that those men who gave their allegiance to Muḥammad in the inaugural years of His ministry were called primarily to renounce the worship of their idols, to acknowledge the existence of one God, supreme over all, and to accept Muḥammad as His Prophet and Messenger. There was no other obligation. But the renunciation of idols by a Meccan was no easy matter. The life of Mecca revolved round the four-square shrine of Ka'bah which housed al-Lát and al-'Uzzá, Manát and Hubal and Ṭághút and other idols which Arabs came from near and far to worship. To become a Muslim meant cutting oneself away from a social milieu which was all one's native town could offer.

The idea of monotheism was not a novelty. The clans and tribes of Arabia had rubbed shoulders with Jews and Christians for centuries. Waraqah, the cousin of Khadíjah, was a Christian, and there were others similarly inclined. We are told of a man named Zayd Ibn 'Amr who could no longer believe in his idols. Judaism, Christianity and even Islám passed him by, while he lamented that he did not know how to worship the one true God. Men who were monotheists or had monotheistic tendencies were known as *ḥaníf*s. A man so styled is supposed to have been a follower of the religion of Abraham, whatever that might have been.[5] But all the *ḥaníf*s in Mecca and its neighbourhood had had little or no influence on the mould of thought of the people of that town. It was Muḥammad who shook Mecca to its foundations.

[5] The term *ḥaníf* has also been and is applied to Islám itself and also to Muslims.

3

Public Declaration

MOST of the early Muslims were young men, some very young, less than twenty years old. With a few exceptions they came from humble walks of life. Their conversion to Islám posed no serious threat to the confraternity of merchants, heads of clans and attendants of the Ka'bah, who held power in Mecca. Yet they did not remain immune from rejection and various degrees of ill-treatment. Khálid Ibn Sa'íd, for example, brought upon himself such fury from outraged parents that, for a period of time, he had to seek shelter in the house of the Prophet Himself. Slaves, who had become Muslims, were particularly harassed and even tortured by their masters. One such was an Ethiopian named Bilál Ibn Ribáḥ. His master, Umayyah, the son of Khalaf of the clan of Banú-Jumaḥ, made him lie down every day in the blistering sun, with a huge piece of rock laid on his chest. This torment did not daunt the Ethiopian. Eventually Abú-Bakr rescued him from his plight, by exchanging a slave of his own for Bilál, and promptly giving him his freedom. Later, Bilál gained the distinction of becoming the first *mu'adhdhin* (muezzin) in Islám. Abú-Bakr spent a fortune buying and freeing slaves, who, because of their newly-found Faith, were suffering at the hands of their masters. The exact dates of these events cannot now be ascertained. It may be that they belong to the time when Muḥammad had made the Meccans at large aware of His claim to be the Messenger of the one true God.

Some time in the fourth year of His ministry, or thereabouts, Muḥammad received a revelation bidding Him give the tidings of His mission to His kith and kin:

> So, call not upon another god, with God, lest thou be of those who are chastised.

And warn thy clan, thy nearest kin.
And lower thy wing to those who follow thee, being believers.
Should they disobey thee, then say: I am quit of what ye do.
And put thy trust in the All-Mighty, the All-Compassionate:
Who sees thee when thou standest,
And when thou turnest about amongst those who bow and prostrate in worship.
Verily, He is the All-Hearing, the All-Knowing.

(*Súrat ash-Shu'ará'*—'The Poets', xxvi, 213–20.)

We have differing accounts, but there is general agreement that Muḥammad invited the descendants of Háshim to a repast to tell them that God had chosen Him to be His Messenger. It is impossible to believe that many of them (and particularly His uncle, Abú-Ṭálib) had not already sensed the change in Him. We are told of a time when Abú-Ṭálib came upon Muḥammad, with 'Alí and Zayd, when they were occupied with their daily devotions. Abú-Ṭálib, astonished by their genuflexions and prostrations, demanded an explanation of this strange behaviour; whereupon Muḥammad apprised him of His mission.

At the repast to which 'Alí had invited their kinsmen, on behalf of the Prophet, nothing of any consequence happened. Abú-Lahab, Muḥammad's uncle, the wealthiest son of the patriarch 'Abdu'l-Muṭṭalib, with much derision and jest sent the guests away before Muḥammad could speak to them. Abú-Ṭálib, who had already told his Nephew that he was too old to change his beliefs, was, as usual, mild and understanding.

There was a further gathering of the House of Háshim. One account has it that the Prophet called all the Meccans to meet Him on Mount Ṣafá, and His kinsmen came with the rest. At this second gathering, either of Banú-Háshim alone, or of the Meccans at large, Muḥammad made a public declaration of His mission, summoning them to the worship of the one true God, Invisible, Transcendent, Supreme. Abú-Lahab, according to the eminent historian, aṭ-Ṭabarí, made himself the spokesman of denial. He complained scornfully that Muḥammad had wasted their time dragging them to a gathering, in order to speak of sweet nothing. He then advised them to go away, mind their own business, and not listen to Muḥammad, who had taken leave of His senses. His wife, Jamílah, a sister of Abú-Sufyán, the leading man of the House of Umayyah, was no less abusive. Abú-Lahab to his dying day remained an implacable enemy of his Nephew.

Whereas before this public declaration Muḥammad and the handful of His followers could worship at ease, and in their own manner, within the enclosure of the Ka'bah, now it became increasingly difficult for them to do so. Hardly a day passed without overt attacks being made on them. An opponent, no less determined and vitriolic than Abú-Lahab, was Abú-Jahl,[1] a member of the powerful Quraysh clan of Banú-Makhzúm. On the other hand, al-Arqam, a wealthy man of the same clan, said to have been under twenty-five years of age, threw open his large house, which was not far from the Ka'bah, as a meeting-place for the Prophet and His followers. Muḥammad's 'entry into the house of al-Arqam' became a landmark in the course of His ministry. From that time, probably about the year 614, opposition to the Prophet intensified, while the number of Muslims increased. Two men, who gave their allegiance to Muḥammad in this period, brought great strength to the still weak and defenceless Muslim community. One was Ḥamzah, the hunter uncle of the Prophet; the other was 'Umar, the son of al-Khaṭṭáb, a prominent member of the Banú-'Adí clan of the Quraysh.

One day, on his return from a hunting expedition, Ḥamzah was told that Abú-Jahl had maltreated Muḥammad in a most offensive manner. Aroused, he rushed to the Ka'bah where he found Abú-Jahl seated amongst his friends. Ḥamzah made a dash for him and hit him with his bow. How dared Abú-Jahl abuse Muḥammad when he, Ḥamzah, was a follower of the Faith that his Nephew was preaching? Some of the Banú-Makhzúm who were present rose to oppose the hunter, but Abú-Jahl, confessing his exceeding vindictiveness in his treatment of Muḥammad, restrained them and bloodshed was averted. Ḥamzah had not professed Islám before this incident, but he never went back on his word. There is another version of his sudden and impetuous espousal of the cause of his Nephew but, however it happened, Ḥamzah remained an ardent Muslim and met his death, years later, on the battlefield. Verse 122 of the sixth súrah, *al-An'ám* ('The Cattle'), refers to Ḥamzah and Abú-Jahl: 'Shall the dead, whom We have quickened, and for whom We have ordained a light

[1] Abu'l-Ḥakam 'Amr Ibn Hishám. Abú-Jahl means 'father of ignorance'. He is known by this epithet because of his stubborn opposition to the Prophet.

whereby he may walk among men, be like him, whose likeness is in the darkness, whence he will not come forth? So it is decked out fair to the unbelievers the things they have done.'

'Umar's conversion took place under equally dramatic circumstances. He was well known for his quick, fiery temper and proneness to sudden outbursts. Hearing one day that Muḥammad was in the house of al-Arqam with His followers, he flew into a rage and decided to go straight there, disperse the gathering and slay Muḥammad. On his way he met a member of his own clan, who, hearing what 'Umar intended, retorted that he had better look first to his own kindred. To his horror and astonishment, 'Umar heard that his sister Fáṭimah, and her husband Sa'íd, had become followers of Muḥammad. 'Umar, carrying his sword, now rushed to his sister's home where, at that moment, Fáṭimah and Sa'íd had a visitor, a literate slave named Khabbáb, who had brought the twentieth súrah of the Qur'án to read to them. 'Umar heard the sound of Khabbáb's voice, and his imprecations, heralding his arrival, made Khabbáb seek hiding, since, as a slave, he could easily be cut down by 'Umar. Beside himself with rage, 'Umar would have struck his brother-in-law, but Fáṭimah shielded her husband and received the full force of the blow, which drew much blood from her face. This cooled 'Umar's temper and, instead of subjecting his sister and Sa'íd to further torments, he asked to be shown what was being read. But Fáṭimah told him that he was a worshipper of idols, unclean, and was not fit to handle the sacred text. Strangely enough, 'Umar went meekly away, washed himself and returned. On reading the opening verses of the súrah of *Ṭá-Há*, he marvelled at their excellence and was overcome with remorse.

We have not sent down the Qur'án unto thee that thou shouldst grieve.

But for an admonition unto him who feareth God, being a revelation from Him Who created the earth and the lofty heavens.

The All-Merciful sitteth on His throne.

To Him belongeth whatsoever there is in the heavens and on the earth, and whatsoever there is between them, and whatsoever there is neath the soil.

And shouldst thou raise thy voice, He assuredly knoweth all that is secret and all that is yet more hidden.
God—beside Whom there is no other God, and to Whom belongeth the Names most excellent. (xx, 1–7.)

'Umar left his sister's home to seek Muḥammad once again in the house of al-Arqam. Muslims gathered there, noticing his approach, were perturbed, but Ḥamzah told them not to fear, for he could deal with 'Umar single-handed. It was Muḥammad Himself who met 'Umar at the door. 'How much longer art thou going to persecute me?' he asked. And 'Umar, contrite and abashed, replied: 'O Messenger of God! I have come to offer thee my allegiance.'

4

Migration to Ethiopia

SOME time in the year 615, a number of Muslims, men, women and children, went to Ethiopia. Some returned within a few years, others stayed in Africa for more than a decade, and at least one of them became a Christian there. These are the bare facts. However, Western scholars have posed problem after problem in the context of this migration. Why did these Muslims leave Mecca? Why did they choose to go to Ethiopia? Why did some return earlier and some much later? Was there the danger of some kind of schism within the relatively minute Muslim community? These are some of the questions they have been asking, and since there is no way of getting detailed answers in histories written by Muslims themselves, they have resorted to conjecture. But perhaps there are simple answers to these questions.

The opposition to the Prophet was increasing, but so was the number of Muslims. Even the person of Muḥammad Himself was no longer immune from attack, for His adversaries, no longer content with verbal abuse, would strike Him, throw ashes over Him, and strew thorns in His path. His followers—particularly slaves and young members of well-known families—likewise suffered persecution. What could be more natural than to get a number of them away from the seething cauldron of Mecca. But where would they go? Not yet to Yat͟hrib, where they could not be certain of their reception. On the northern confines of the peninsula, Persians and Byzantines and their respective clients were at each other's throat. Yemen in the south was in Persian hands. Over the years, however, there had been traffic between Arabia and Ethiopia, and the Negus (or the Najás͟hí as the Arabs called him) was known to be a humane and benevolent monarch.

Those Muslims who went to Ethiopia came from a variety of clans and from many backgrounds. There were 'Ut͟hmán Ibn

'Affán and the youthful Khálid Ibn Sa'íd, both of the clan of 'Abd-Shams of the House of Umayyah; Ja'far Ibn Abí-Ṭálib, a brother of 'Alí, of the House of Háshim; 'Uthmán Ibn Maẓ'ún of the clan of Banú-Jumaḥ; 'Amr Ibn Suráqah of Banú-'Adí, the clan to which 'Umar Ibn al-Khaṭṭáb belonged; Abú-'Ubaydah, the son of al-Jarráḥ of the clan of al-Ḥárith; 'Ayyásh Ibn Abí-Rabí-'ah of Banú-Makhzúm, a powerful clan. These few names suffice to show their diversity.

Yet nowhere can one find any evidence of schism. The whole Muslim community was under attack, was too small to split apart, and, above all, gave total and unreserved allegiance and devotion to the Prophet. Had there been any danger of a rift, would the Prophet have allowed a large number of Muslims to take themselves off to a distant land for an indefinite period, totally bereft of His guidance? That is inconceivable.

We shall never know on what basis the choice of emigrants was made, or exactly how many they were. Ibn-Hishám, in his life of the Prophet (*Síratu Rasúli'lláh*), has recorded eighty-three names, but the number has been put as high as one hundred and nine. They could not have attempted to move out of Mecca in one group; their adversaries would have blocked their departure. So, in small numbers, they quietly slipped away, without such men as Ḥamzah, Abú-Bakr and 'Umar, who would not take the road to self-imposed exile. When the leaders of the Meccans learned of the Muslims' exodus, they took fright, and sent two men to the Negus to ask for the return of the emigrants. One of these was 'Amr Ibn al-'Áṣ, whom we shall encounter frequently in the course of this book. The other has been named variously as 'Abdu'lláh, the son of Abú-Rabí'ah, and 'Ammárah, the son of Walíd.

It was the wily 'Amr who acted as the spokesman for the aggrieved leaders of the Quraysh. 'Amr, destined to become the conqueror of Egypt, whether as pagan or Muslim had always a sweet tongue and was master of the art of beguilement. The two envoys took with them an appreciable supply of leather goods, for which the craftsmen of Mecca were famous, to smooth their way into the favour of the officials and courtiers at Axum, the capital city of Ethiopia. When received by the Negus, 'Amr protested that these emigrants were renegades who had brought disgrace to their town and clans; they had abandoned the religion of their forefathers, had not adopted the religion which the Negus followed, but instead had contrived a pernicious religion of their own. He besought the Negus not to keep such mischief-makers in his realm, but to send them back to Mecca where they could be contained. Courtiers, well primed and bribed, added their voices to his pleas. However, as the emigrants had rightly surmised, the Negus was a just man and would not be swayed by ‘Amr Ibn al-‘Áṣ, or by his own courtiers. He summoned the emigrants to appear before him, and they chose Ja‘far Ibn Abí-Ṭálib, the cousin of the Prophet, to speak for them. When questioned by the Negus, Ja‘far replied: ‘O King! Ask these men whether we have been guilty of theft or murder.’ They could only answer in the negative. Then Ja‘far told the Negus that they had been idolaters leading a life of lustful extravagance; they had been cruel to the weak and totally unmindful of their deeds, until God gave them a Prophet, whose name was Muḥammad Ibn ‘Abdi’lláh. Their Prophet, Ja‘far said, had taught them the worship of the one true God, and had guided them to shun evil ways. Then the Negus asked to hear some of this Prophet’s sayings. Ja‘far had with him either the whole or a part of the nineteenth súrah of the Qur’án—the Súrah of Maryam or Mary—in which the story of Zachariah and John the Baptist and Mary and Jesus is told, and wherein it is related that the infant Jesus said, while in his cradle: ‘Peace be upon me, the day I was born, and the day I die, and the day I am raised up alive’ (v. 34). The ruler of Ethiopia was well satisfied, and declared that the emigrants could stay in his country and live amongst his people as long as they wished.

‘Amr, although crest-fallen, would not admit defeat. He thought of a ruse which he was certain would enmesh the Muslims. A day or two later, he once again sought an audience with the Negus. The Muslims, he suggested, should be interrogated on how they viewed the person of Christ. Ja‘far was again sent for and questioned. His answer was that Christ, in the words of their Prophet, was the Servant of God, His Apostle, His Spirit and His Word, born of Mary, the Blessed Virgin.

‘Amr had lost.

5

Boycott of the House of Háshim

MUḤAMMAD was now left in Mecca with a reduced following, and seemed more defenceless than ever. But His vehemence in denouncing the worship of idols did not abate. On the contrary it gained in vigour. He had indeed risen to be the *Nadhír*—He who warns. The man who was now increasingly the spearhead of opposition to Muḥammad was Abú-Jahl ('Amr Ibn Hishám) of the Banú-Makhzúm. The failure of the Meccans' envoys to Ethiopia made His opponents even more determined to quash His Faith, which was gaining ground so alarmingly. They arranged to meet visitors to Mecca, mostly those who had come to worship al-'Uzzá and al-Manát and the other idols in the Ka'bah, and tell them that Muḥammad was an accomplished magician, who had, by His art of magic, succeeded in breaching family loyalties. For Arabs, family ties and the sense of kinship were of paramount value, not to be trifled with. (This was particularly evidenced in the case of Muḥammad Himself, when all His relations, with the exception of His uncle, Abú-Lahab, stood by Him, even though most of them were not Muslims.) The leaders of the Quraysh were certain that these grave charges of assaulting family bonds and of practising magic, which their tradition abhorred, would make any visitor approached by Muḥammad and His followers recoil in horror. When 'Abdu'lláh Ibn Mas'úd, who was a freedman, tried to recite verses from the Qur'án in public, he was stoned and driven away.

As the Muslims, in general, came to feel more and more the burden of rejection, even Abú-Bakr, a highly-respected figure in the society of Mecca, could not but sense that he was becoming isolated from the merchants who ordered the affairs of the town. He had bought a number of slaves, fellow Muslims, in order to free them, and had given financial aid to the emigrants. Now his business was dwindling and he was growing poorer all the time. At last even his life was threatened, and the Prophet bade him leave Mecca and find a place of safety. Reluctantly he left the town, bewildered as to where to go. His own clan, the Banú-Taym, was not powerful enough to give him adequate protection. Ibn-Hishám tells us that in the desert Abú-Bakr came upon Ibn-ad-Dughunnah (or al-Dughaynah), of the clan of Banu'l-Ḥárith Ibn ‘Abd-Manát, who was also the head of a confederacy called al-Aḥábísh. This man knew Abú-Bakr well, and enquired what he was doing there in the middle of the desert. On learning of Abú-Bakr's plight, he took him back to Mecca and announced to the people that Abú-Bakr was under his *jiwár* or ‘protection', and that none should presume to molest him.

Since no degree of ill-treatment, no amount of calumny or persecution could either discredit Muḥammad or silence Him, the leaders of the Quraysh tried fresh tactics. They chose a deputation to attend upon Abú-Ṭálib and appeal to him to restrain His Nephew. Included in that deputation were Abú-Jahl; Abú-Sufyán, the son of Ḥarb, the leading man of the House of Umayyah; ‘Utbah, the son of Rabí‘ah, and his brother, Shaybah, of the clan of ‘Abd-Shams—all wealthy and influential merchants of Mecca. Abú-Ṭálib managed to pacify them, but the Prophet's denunciation of all the polytheists of previous generations stung the leaders of the Quraysh to the quick, and a second deputation went to Abú-Ṭálib complaining bitterly. They stated that their patience was exhausted, and that if the head of the House of Háshim did not act soon to put an end to Muḥammad's activities, or to disown him, both he and his Nephew would suffer the consequences.

Yet a third time a deputation visited Abú-Ṭálib. Still the Prophet would not yield an inch to the idolaters' demands, nor would Abú-Ṭálib withdraw his protection from Muḥammad. By then the leaders of the Quraysh had reached the end of the road. They decided to impose a boycott on the Houses of Háshim and Muṭṭalib. A formal declaration was drawn up and placed in the Ka‘bah. It banned marriage with any member of the two Houses, and forbade all transactions with them: nothing was to be bought from them, nothing sold to them. This boycott was imposed sometime in the year 616 and lasted for three years. With the exception of Abú-Lahab all the Háshimites and the Muṭṭalibites, most of whom were not Muslims, moved into the valley adjacent to Mecca, where Abú-Ṭálib had his abode. Muḥammad could still frequent the heart of the town and converse with the people. Muslims of other clans, not being under a similar interdict, had no need to move, but they suffered enormously and some of them had to seek protectors.

While most of the historians and chroniclers have glossed over the events of those three years of the boycott, some exaggerated accounts do exist which bear no relation to the facts. It is simply not true that Muḥammad and his people went hungry and thirsty, that they lived the life of pariahs in barren caves. The interdict voiced by the leaders of the Quraysh in Mecca had no binding effect on other clans and tribes who dwelt around Mecca. And roads into the town were not barred either to the members of the two Houses or to non-Meccans who traded with them. It is interesting to note that during this very period a number of the emigrants returned from Ethiopia.

But all that being said, the embarrassments, hardships and tribulations of those three years ought not be underestimated. Abú-Jahl and Abú-Sufyán and the other vociferous and inveterate adversaries of Muḥammad had achieved a good measure of success. And when the boycott ended, because of its ineffectiveness in ridding the Meccan merchants of the towering personality of the Prophet, and because of the diminishing interest of the bulk of the population which balked at its enforcement and clamoured for its repeal, the Prophet was suddenly overwhelmed by such stark tragedies and tyrannies as put His life at risk, causing Him to say: 'No Prophet has ever suffered as I'.

6

Darkest Days

NO sooner had the boycott ended than Khadíjah died. For twenty-five years she had been Muḥammad's mainstay and support. She it was who gave Him an occupation and provided Him with means of livelihood. She it was who gave Him a home of His own. She it was who in the hour of doubt gave Him assurance. She it was who prior to anyone else gave Him unreserved allegiance. As long as Khadíjah lived Muḥammad took no other wife, although she was advanced in years when He was still in the prime of His manhood. Now she had gone from Him and the sense of desolation must have been immense. The woman He married, a year later, was Sawdah, widow of one of the emigrants to Ethiopia; her father, Zam'ah, was a man of influence in Mecca. Sawdah's son by her late husband became a charge of the Prophet.[1]

Hard upon the heels of the loss of His wife, Muḥammad suffered another bereavement: the death of Abú-Ṭálib, which deprived Him of His protector and led to His loss of security. When Abú-Ṭálib was on his death-bed, the leaders of the Quraysh visited him and asked him to send for Muḥammad, so that they could come to terms and make their peace. Muḥammad's response was that they should say, 'There is no God but God and Muḥammad is the Messenger of God', and then all would be well. These hardened idolaters would never admit that, and the chasm between them and Muḥammad remained as wide as ever. The man who succeeded Abú-Ṭálib as the head of the House of Háshim was that same inveterate foe who, in the three years of the boycott, had cut himself off from all his kinsmen, but now had the right of seniority. Abú-Lahab, it being expected of him, at first gave his protection to Muḥammad, but soon he found a pretext

[1] This was 'Abda'r-Raḥmán, who was killed in the battle of Jalúlá, the second great battle which the Arabs fought with the forces of the Sásánid Empire.

to reverse his decision, withdraw that protection and disown his Nephew. He tried to make the Prophet compromise Himself by withdrawing His condemnation of their idolatrous ancestors, a step which Abú-Ṭálib had never taken. Being left without the protective arm of one's clan had very serious consequences in Arabia. Muḥammad's life was now imperilled, and He decided to leave Mecca. Alone and unaided He made His way to Ṭá'if, although some chroniclers have stated that He was accompanied by Zayd Ibn Ḥári<u>th</u>ah, His freedman and adopted son.

Ṭá'if, peopled by the Banú-<u>Th</u>aqíf, was some fifty miles south-east of Mecca, and stood in vivid contrast to it. Being well endowed with water, Ṭá'if was far more salubrious and was a place of verdure and trees. Many wealthy merchants and notables of Mecca possessed orchards and vineyards there, to which they resorted occasionally. Thus the influence of the Quray<u>sh</u> was much felt in Ṭá'if.

According to Ibn-Hi<u>sh</u>ám there were three brothers in Ṭá'if, sons of 'Amr Ibn 'Umayr, who held the reins of power: 'Abd-Yálíl, Mas'úd and Ḥabíb. The Prophet sought them out and told them of His mission. But they rejected Him. One of them said, 'Could not God find someone other than thee to send us as His Messenger?' and another exclaimed: 'Should God have sent thee He would have torn away the covering of the Ka'bah,' while the third brother made this plea: 'If thou art a Messenger of God as thou sayest, then thou art too great a person to talk to me, and if thou art lying, it is not seemly for me to speak to thee.' Muḥammad was taken aback by their levity and shallowness and sensed that with such men at the head of the town, it was futile to tarry any longer with the Banú-<u>Th</u>aqíf. He asked them not to mention to anyone what he had told them, but the three brothers laughed and invited the people to mock and taunt him. Muḥammad had to make His escape followed by the mob who pelted Him with stones.

Wounded and bruised in body and spirit, the Prophet found refuge in a vineyard which belonged to the brothers, 'Utbah and <u>Sh</u>aybah, sons of Rabí'ah, who had been members of the first deputation that attended Abú-Ṭálib to ask him to restrain his Nephew. Both brothers were in their vineyard and noticed the state to which Muḥammad had been reduced. Even they were moved to pity for Him and gave their Christian slave, 'Addás, a plate of grapes to take to Muḥammad. Before eating, the Prophet said, '*Bismi'lláh*'—'In the Name of God'. The Christian slave was greatly astonished and, looking intently at Muḥammad, said: 'By God,this is not the kind of word spoken by the people of these parts.' Muḥammad asked him: 'Of which land art thou a native and what is thy Faith?' 'I am a Christian from Nineveh,' 'Addás replied. The Prophet said, 'The home of Jonah, son of Matthew.' 'Addás, even more astonished, asked Muḥammad: 'And what dost thou know of Jonah?' 'He was my brother, a Prophet,' replied Muḥammad, 'and I am a Prophet.' Then, Ibn-Hishám tells us, 'Addás kissed the head and hands and feet of the Messenger of God, and his masters, seeing him do this, berated him. But 'Addás said: 'My masters! in the whole world nothing can be better than this, because He spoke of something which none but a Prophet can know,' to which the sons of Rabí'ah rejoined: 'Do not abandon thy religion for his, for thine is a better one.'

It was there in Ṭá'if that the Prophet, rebuffed and insulted by its headmen and stoned by its people, prayed thus: 'O God! I grieve before Thee for the feebleness of my powers and the insignificance of my being amongst men. O God, the Most Merciful! Thou art the Lord of the weak and Thou art my Lord.'

This was the darkest hour. Muḥammad was isolated, insecure everywhere in the land of His birth, where He had been reared and had lived all His life. Cast out of Ṭá'if, He could return to Mecca only if He could find a powerful chieftain to provide Him with *jiwár* (protection). He appealed to Akhnas Ibn Shurayq, the head of the Banú-Zuhrah, but was rejected. Then He turned to Suhayl Ibn 'Amr, who also refused to stand by Him. Al-Muṭ'im Ibn 'Adí, chief of the Banú-Nawfal, agreed, in the end, to extend his protection to Muḥammad. How harrowing it must have been for the Prophet to set foot in His native town under the umbrella of a chieftain not of His own clan, and an inveterate idolater to boot.

When the Prophet reached Mecca the fair and the annual markets were in full swing, and many tribes had come to render homage to the idols of the Ka'bah and participate in various ceremonials. Muḥammad approached them to gain their adherence, while Abú-Jahl and Abú-Lahab and Abú-Sufyán went about telling these visiting Bedouins not to heed Muḥammad, for He had taken leave of His senses. The first tribe to reject Him out of hand was the Banú-Ḥanífah. The leading man of Banú-

'Ámir Ibn-Ṣa'ṣa'ah, would have entered into an alliance with Him with the object of establishing his own dominion over the whole of Arabia. But he found the Prophet completely unresponsive to such overtures. Then Ṭufayl Ibn 'Amr of the clan of Banú-Daws recognized and accepted the mission of Muḥammad. However, the Prophet chose to remain in Mecca and not to commit Himself to an uncertain reception by the Banú-Daws. It is said that sixteen clans and tribes gave a negative answer to Muḥammad's call. It was at this time that the Prophet had an experience which is known as the *Mi'ráj* or the Ascent.

The first verse of the seventeenth súrah, the *Baní-Isrá'íl* ('The House of Israel'), reads:

> Glory be to Him, who carried His servant by night
> from the Holy Mosque to the Further Mosque
> the precincts of which We have blessed,
> that We might show him some of Our signs.
> He is the All-hearing, the All-seeing.[2]

This verse is the basis for the account of the Prophet's 'Night Journey' from Mecca to Jerusalem, and the 'Ascent' from Jerusalem to Heaven. Émile Dermenghem relates the full story of the *mi'ráj* in his book, *The Life of Mahomet*. The world of Islám has accepted the literal fact of this Night Journey, just as Christendom has accepted the literal fact of the Resurrection and the Ascension of Christ. However, voices have been raised, here and there, to assert that the *mi'ráj* of the Prophet was not an actual physical occurrence but a profound spiritual experience. Shaykh Aḥmad-i-Aḥsá'í (1743–1826) and Siyyid Káẓim-i-Rashtí (1793–1843), founders of the Shaykhí school, took this stand openly, for which they were severely criticized and even vehemently denounced.

A full decade had passed since the day Muḥammad received His call in the wilderness of the hills overlooking the House of Ka'bah. Still the idols stood around the Ka'bah, and Muḥammad was tolerated in His native town only by the fiat of an idolatrous chieftain, unrelated to His own clan. At the end of that decade, in the summer of A.D. 620, an event occurred, at first apparently insignificant, which was to open the way to the total triumph of Muḥammad's ministry.

[2] A. J. Arberry's translation. He calls this súrah 'The Night Journey'.

7

Converts in Yat_h_rib

IN the pilgrim season of A.D. 620 Muḥammad focused His attention on visitors from Yat_h_rib. This was the town where His father had died in the prime of manhood and near which he was buried. In His childhood, Ámínah, His mother, had taken Him to Yat_h_rib where she had relatives. Conditions in this town differed from those at Mecca. The existence of three strong Jewish colonies—the Banú-Qaynuqá', the Banu'n-Naḍír and the Banú-Qurayẓah—enriched the life and widened the outlook of the people, who were mostly tillers of the soil and keepers of orchards, unlike Meccans who were men of the mart and trade. They belonged in the main to two tribes, the Aws and the K_h_azraj, each with its own subdivisions and clans. Civil war in or around 615 had disturbed the calm of Yat_h_rib. At the battle of Bu'át_h_, the Aws, with the aid of the Jewish Banú-Qurayẓah and Banu'n-Naḍír, had defeated the K_h_azraj.

Muḥammad, in that summer of 620, met and conversed with several men from Yat_h_rib, six in number according to Ibn-His_h_ám and seven according to Ibn-al-At_h_ír. Their names have been recorded.[1] They listened to Muḥammad and accepted Him. Then they returned home with the good news that a Prophet had risen amongst the Arabs.

Speculation regarding these first converts of Yat_h_rib and their motives is fruitless. All of them were men of the K_h_azraj, the beaten and subdued tribe. None of them, with the possible exception of As'ad Ibn Zurárah, were of particular eminence amongst their compatriots. On the whole, the people of Yat_h_rib were poverty-ridden as compared with the merchants of Mecca, for the

[1] They were As'ad Ibn Zurárah, 'Awf Ibn al-Ḥárit_h_, Ráfi' Ibn Málik, Quṭbah, the son of 'Ámir, and 'Uqbah, the son of another 'Ámir, Jábir Ibn 'Abdu'lláh, and 'Ámir Ibn 'Abd-Ḥárit_h_ah.

money, skills and good properties of Yathrib belonged to the Jewish colonies. Yathrib was not a compact township. It consisted of a number of fortified villages within which the various clans dwelt, cultivating the palm groves and orchards which separated them.

The few men who accepted Muḥammad had nothing to gain, but were genuinely convinced that He was indeed what He claimed to be—the Messenger of God and His Apostle. The following year five of them came back to Mecca, bringing seven others to whom they had imparted His message. We do not know in what manner they conveyed that message. Nor do we know what Muḥammad did in Mecca during that year, from one summer to the next. He does not seem to have attracted any more Meccans to His Faith. It is said that the idolater Muṭ'im gave Him protection, on the understanding that He did not engage in public debate. Whatever the reason, it looks as if Muḥammad, by this time, had turned His back on the people of Mecca.

In a mountain pass, the 'Aqabah, close to Mecca, the Prophet met the twelve men of Yathrib, and they pledged their fealty to Him. The Meccans, of course, had no inkling of what was happening between Muḥammad and these men. In addition to the seven newcomers, five had come to Mecca for a second time.[2] According to Ibn-Hishám, 'Ubádah, the son of Ṣámit, related that at night they repaired to the 'Aqabah and made the pledge that they would never join partners with God,[3] would refrain from theft, adultery, murder of their offspring and calumny, and would obey the Prophet in all things. This pledge was called the *Bay'at an-Nisá'*—the Pledge of Women—because, although embracing loyalty and fidelity, it did not include a promise to fight. When the time came for them to depart, Muḥammad sent Muṣ'ab Ibn 'Umayr with them to teach and instruct them. Muṣ'ab was a descendant of 'Abd-Manáf, the great-great-grandfather of the Prophet. Before long he gained a signal victory by winning the

[2] The seven newcomers are named as: 'Uwaym Ibn Sá'idah, 'Ubádah Ibn Ṣámit, Abu'l-Haytham Ibn Tayyihán (or Tayhán), 'Abbás Ibn 'Ubádah, Yazíd Ibn Tha'labah, Dhakwán Ibn 'Abd-Qays, and Mu'ádh Ibn al-Ḥárith, a brother of 'Awf, who had responded the previous year to Muḥammad's call and had come once again. In addition to 'Awf, the four others who came a second time were: As'ad Ibn Zurárah, Ráfi' Ibn Málik, 'Uqbah and Quṭbah.

[3] This expression means putting oneself on a par with the one God, Who is supreme over all.

allegiance of Sa'd Ibn Mu'á<u>dh</u>, the chieftain of the tribe of Aws, and Usayd Ibn Ḥuḍayr, another prominent figure of the same tribe.

And now once again a curtain falls upon the events in Mecca. There is no report of further opposition to Muḥammad, no report of any new converts to Islám. But in Ya<u>th</u>rib Muṣ'ab was forging ahead with remarkable success, for in the pilgrim season of the following year, A.D. 622, seventy-two men and three women came to Mecca to present themselves to the Prophet. In the dead of night, when Mecca and the visitors to Mecca slept, those seventy-five Muslims of Ya<u>th</u>rib quietly made their way to the same mountain pass, the 'Aqabah. Muḥammad came, accompanied by his uncle, 'Abbás, who, although still an idolater, kept an eye on the interests of his Nephew. 'Abbás wished to be assured of their unswerving loyalty to Muḥammad, were He to make His home with them and entrust to them His all. He spoke first, followed by Muḥammad, who recited to them portions from the Qur'án. Muṣ'ab had done his work well. These Muslims of Ya<u>th</u>rib were firm, determined, unwavering. They made it plain that they would stand by the Prophet through thick and thin.

According to Ibn-Hi<u>sh</u>ám, the recognized leader of the group, al-Bará' Ibn Ma'rúr, spoke for all when he said that they would protect the Prophet with their arms. Thus they gave their word that, should necessity arise, they would not hesitate to fight under the banner of the Prophet. Abu'l-Hay<u>th</u>am now posed the question whether Muḥammad would in future ever leave them to their fate and return to His native town. The Prophet smiled at this and gave a categorical declaration: 'Your blood will be my blood, and your cause my cause. Ye are mine and I am of you. I shall fight whoever shall fight you, and shall keep peace with whoever is at peace with you.' Then 'Abbás Ibn 'Ubádah addressed his compatriots, asking whether they were absolutely certain in their hearts as to what they were committing themselves. Whoever had any doubts, he said, should go, for there would be no turning back later; but should they give their allegiance to Muḥammad, it would benefit them forevermore. With one voice they gave their assent and expressed their conviction: they believed in Muḥammad. They accepted Him as the Messenger of God. Then they filed past Him, one by one, touching His hand which was their way of swearing fealty. Then the same 'Abbás Ibn 'Ubádah asked the Prophet for His word of command that they might, on the morrow, set upon the idolaters and disperse them. Muḥammad replied that God had not sanctioned such action and that they should go in peace.

Twelve men were now chosen to be the *Nuqabá'*—the leaders—nine from the <u>Kh</u>azraj and three from the Aws. Muḥammad told them that they stood in the same relation to Him as the Apostles to Jesus; they were to be the shepherds of His flock. The nine <u>Kh</u>azrajites were: Asa'd Ibn Zurárah, Sa'd Ibn Rabí', 'Abdu'lláh Ibn Rawáḥah, Ráfi' Ibn Málik, al-Bará' Ibn Ma'rúr, 'Abdu'lláh Ibn 'Amr, 'Ubádah Ibn aṣ-Ṣámit, Sa'd Ibn 'Ubádah, Mun<u>dh</u>ar Ibn 'Amr; and the three from the Aws were: Usayd Ibn Ḥuḍayr, Sa'd Ibn <u>Kh</u>ay<u>th</u>amah and Abu'l-Hay<u>th</u>am Ibn Tayhán.

Their pledge given and the compact made, the Muslims of Ya<u>th</u>rib went back quietly to their encampment, but the movement of such a large number did not go unnoticed. The leaders of the idolaters of Mecca became aware that something had passed between Muḥammad and some of the pilgrims from Ya<u>th</u>rib. They sent their men to investigate, but those responsible for the contingent from Ya<u>th</u>rib denied any knowledge of the affair, as indeed they had none. The Ya<u>th</u>ribites were allowed to depart, but the conviction grew at Mecca that all was not well and that Muḥammad had had some dealing with these people. A body set out in pursuit of the pilgrims from Ya<u>th</u>rib, who had already covered a good distance. Sa'd Ibn 'Ubádah, one of the twelve *nuqabá'*, who was some way behind his compatriots, fell into the hands of the Meccans. He was beaten and dragged back to Mecca, and would most probably have met his death at their hands, had he not invoked the *jiwár* of Jubayr Ibn Muṭ'im, which he enjoyed. Jubayr was the son of that Muṭ'im who had given the Prophet his protection.

Muḥammad now counselled His followers in Mecca to betake themselves to Ya<u>th</u>rib, but they were not to go in a mass exodus because it would enrage the idolaters. This meant total uprooting, abandoning homes, businesses, property, although many of them had little to leave behind. But what the heads of clans and families most resented, as they had already shown when they had asked the Negus to send away the Muslim emigrants, was the total disregard of blood ties and kinship which Muslims displayed, and which the idolaters of Mecca considered to be a deliberate and unforgivable insult. 'Umar Ibn al-Khaṭṭáb and his brother, Zayd, found little difficulty in quitting Mecca, but some of the younger men were less fortunate. Two of them, Hishám Ibn al-'Áṣ and 'Ayyásh Ibn Abí-Rabí'ah, were held and chained, but were eventually rescued. Ṣuhayb Ibn Sinán was another Muslim who found himself prevented from leaving Mecca; but he was wealthy and could buy his way out. It is thought that verse 203 of the second súrah of the Qur'án, *al-Baqarah* ('The Cow'), refers to him: 'And there are those amongst men who sell themselves to attain the good pleasure of God, and God is kind to His servants.'

Within a short time Mecca was almost denuded of its Muslims, and the idolaters were not only outraged but sorely frightened. However, Muḥammad was still there, and so were the first Muslims: 'Alí and Zayd and Abú-Bakr.

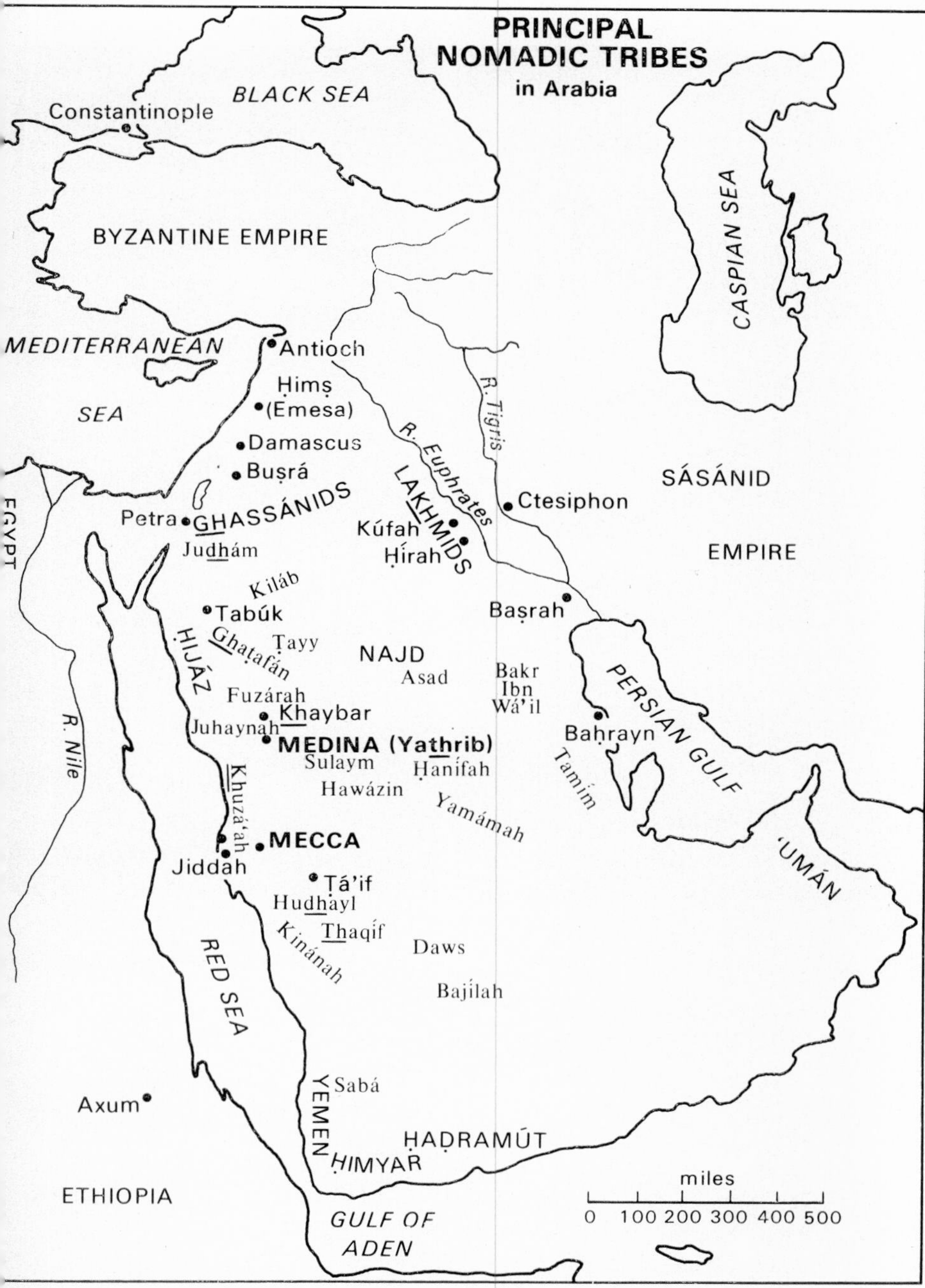
PRINCIPAL NOMADIC TRIBES in Arabia
BLACK SEA
Constantinople
BYZANTINE EMPIRE
CASPIAN SEA
MEDITERRANEAN SEA
Antioch
Ḥimṣ (Emesa)
Damascus
Buṣrá
R. Tigris
R. Euphrates
LAKHMIDS
SÁSÁNID EMPIRE
Ctesiphon
EGYPT
Petra
GHASSÁNIDS
Judhám
Kúfah
Ḥírah
Kiláb
Tabúk
Baṣrah
ḤIJÁZ
Ghaṭafán
Ṭayy
NAJD
Asad
Bakr Ibn Wá'il
PERSIAN GULF
Fuzárah
Khaybar
Juhaynah
R. Nile
MEDINA (Yathrib)
Bahrayn
Sulaym
Ḥanífah
Hawázin
Tamím
Yamámah
Khuzá'ah
MECCA
Jiddah
'UMÁN
Ṭá'if
Hudhayl
Thaqíf
Kinánah
Daws
RED SEA
Bajílah
Sabá
YEMEN
Axum
ḤAḌRAMÚT
ḤIMYAR
ETHIOPIA
miles
0 100 200 300 400 500
GULF OF ADEN

IV VIEW FROM THE CAVE IN MOUNT HIRRÁ'

A favoured retreat of Muḥammad's, in the bleak hills a few miles from His home, where Revelation first reached Him.

8

The Idolaters' Plot

THE leaders of the Quraysh, now thoroughly aroused to future possibilities, held a conclave to decide what action they should take against the person of Muḥammad. It may be diverting to read a historian writing solemnly of Satan coming into that conclave in the guise of a benign old gentleman from Najd. But Satan or no Satan, the purpose of those leaders of the Quraysh was truly satanic. They intended to find the most convenient way of destroying the Prophet. Of course Abú-Jahl and Abú-Sufyán were there, and so were 'Utbah and Shaybah, sons of Rabí'ah; Umayyah and Ubayy, sons of Khalaf; Abu'l-Bakhtarí Ibn Hishám and al-'Áṣ Ibn Wá'il—all seasoned opponents. Some forty of these men had assembled in the council chamber which Quṣayy had built, taking care to exclude the members of the House of Háshim and their confederates. The conclusion they reached was that Muḥammad should be murdered, not by a solitary assassin, but with all the clans participating in the act, each to provide one man for the purpose. Thus the Banú-Háshim would be faced with the fact that there was not just one murderer, whose clan they could engage in a blood-feud, and they would rest content with receiving blood-money, to be provided by all the clans. Verse 30 of the eighth súrah, *al-Anfál* ('The Spoils'), refers to this consultation of the idolaters of Mecca: 'And when the unbelievers were plotting against thee, to put thee under restraint, or to slay thee, or to expel thee, they were plotting and God was plotting and God is the best of plotters.'

About this time Abú-Bakr was preparing to depart for Yathrib, but Muḥammad asked him to wait a while so that they could go together. Abú-Bakr was overjoyed that he would be travelling in the company of the Prophet, and undertook all the arrangements for the journey. By then the idolaters were keeping watch over Muḥammad's house. One noon in June 622 (September has also been suggested), the Prophet left His home in such a manner that He was not noticed and went to the house of Abú-Bakr. That night 'Alí slept in the Prophet's bed, but the idolaters did not recognize him. They thought that the sleeper was Muḥammad Himself and watched and waited for the daylight. In the meantime, the Prophet and Abú-Bakr, under cover of darkness, left Mecca and withdrew to a hiding-place in a cave on Mount Thawr, about three miles from the town, in the opposite direction from Yathrib. Abú-Bakr had bought two camels and left them in the charge of 'Abdu'lláh Ibn Arqaṭ (or Urayqaṭ) of the clan of Banú-Dayl (a branch of the Kinánah), who was not a Muslim but was trusted by Abú-Bakr. A freedman of Abú-Bakr, a Muslim named 'Ámir Ibn Fuhayrah, had been commissioned to take them milk every evening and to bring his sheep to the mouth of the cave, so that footprints would be obliterated by their hooves. 'Abdu'lláh, a son of Abú-Bakr, was to convey to them news of what the leaders of the Quraysh were doing. Abú-Bakr had only five thousand dirhams left of his riches, which he carried with him. The Prophet, it seems, had no money to carry.

In the morning when the idolaters discovered the identity of the sleeper they were naturally furious, and one of them, Abu'l-Bakhtarí, would have murdered 'Alí, but Abú-Jahl prevented him: Muḥammad had gone and no purpose would be served by 'Alí's death. They set out in search, coming close to the entrance of the cave. Hearing footsteps, Abú-Bakr was greatly agitated, but the Prophet told him that God was with them and they had nothing to fear. 'If ye do not help him, God did verily help him, when he was driven out by the unbelievers; when the two were in the cave, and the second of the two told his companion: "Sorrow not, for God is surely with us"; and God sent down on him His Shechinah,[1] and aided him with unseen hosts; and degraded the word of the unbelievers to the uttermost, and God's word is that which attaineth the heights, and God is the All-Mighty and the All-Wise.' (Súrah ix, 40, entitled *at-Tawbah*—'The Repentance'.) Legend has it that a shrub grew at the mouth of the cave and threw out its tendrils, doves came, built a nest and laid their eggs, and spiders wove their webs; when searchers wanted to enter the

[1] A Hebrew word meaning 'calmness': *Sakínah* in Arabic.

cave, Umayyah, the son of Khalaf (who used to expose his slave, Bilál, to the blaze of the midday sun), told them not to waste their time since no one could have gone into that cave without disturbing the doves and the spiders' webs, adding jocosely that the spiders seemed to have been at work long before the birth of Muḥammad. The idolaters, not finding any trace of Muḥammad and His companion, announced a reward of a hundred camels (another version gives two hundred) for anyone who would bring them Muḥammad, dead or alive.

After three days, 'Abdu'lláh, the son of Abú-Bakr, reported that the uproar in Mecca had subsided and the Meccans had given up hope of finding the fugitives in the precincts of the town. His sister, Asmá', brought food for the journey, a lamb roasted whole and wrapped in a leather spread. In order to fasten the bundle of food and the water-gourd, two lengths of cord were needed, and since they had none, Asmá' took off her girdle and tore it into halves, earning the appellation of *Dhát an-Niṭáqayn* (Possessor of Two Girdles), which has come down throughout history. Then 'Abdu'lláh Ibn Arqaṭ brought the two camels. Muḥammad and Abú-Bakr rode one, and 'Ámir and 'Abdu'lláh the other. They needed the son of Arqaṭ, although a polytheist, to act as their guide through the unbeaten tracks of the desert. Before long they were overtaken by Suráqah Ibn Málik of the Banú-Mudlij, who was after the reward offered by the leaders of the Quraysh. However, a mishap to his horse forced him to appeal to the Prophet for help, which being granted he gave up the pursuit and went back to tell the Quraysh that he had tried but could not find Muḥammad anywhere in the desert.

The next encounter was with Buraydah of the Banú-Aslam, who had an escort of seventy riders. Such was the power and eloquence of Muḥammad's speech that, enthralled and overwhelmed, Buraydah exclaimed: 'Who art thou?' to which the Prophet replied: 'I am Muḥammad, the son of 'Abdu'lláh the son of 'Abdu'l-Muṭṭalib, the Messenger of God—the Lord of all the worlds.' Buraydah instantly affirmed: 'I bear witness that there is no god but God, and Muḥammad is verily the Messenger of God.' His riders followed their master's example and ranged themselves behind the Prophet. Buraydah asked Muḥammad to let him be His host in Yathrib, to which Muḥammad replied that He would allow His camel to go wherever it wished; where it stopped there He would take His abode. But Buraydah, afire with the zeal of his newly-found Faith and wishing to perform a spectacular deed, took off his turban, fixed it on his lance, and rode in front of the cavalcade as the standard-bearer of the Prophet.

Az-Zubayr Ibn al-'Awwám, the cousin of the Prophet, was the next person met with on the road. By then, Muḥammad was well away from the danger zone. Az-Zubayr, returning from a trading journey to Syria, had white robes with him which the Prophet and Abú-Bakr donned. Muḥammad advised him to go on to Mecca, settle his business transactions, and then join Him in Yathrib.

The question naturally arises, why did not some of the idolaters of Mecca themselves set off in pursuit of Muḥammad, to gain the reward of a hundred or two hundred camels, rather than leaving it entirely to the men of the desert? We shall never know. They had a sufficient number of young and agile men in their ranks, who were fiercely opposed to the Prophet. There were 'Ikrimah, the son of Abú-Jahl; Ṣafwán, the son of Umayyah the son of Khalaf; and Khálid Ibn al-Walíd. Abú-Jahl closely questioned 'Abdu'lláh and Asmá', who had helped their father to escape. He slapped Asmá' so hard in the face that her earring came loose and fell off. But there it all ended and no further effort was made by the Meccans to trace the whereabouts of the Prophet.

Meanwhile, the Muslims of Yathrib had received news of the Prophet's departure from Mecca. Each day they went to the outskirts of the town, taking shelter from the sun under overhanging rocks, to scan the horizon for a sign of the Prophet; and when the midday sun began to wane, they returned to their homes, anxious and perplexed. On June 28th (other versions are July 2nd and September 24th), after the Muslims had gone home, a Jew, looking over the wall of his settlement, saw the Prophet approaching the oasis on his camel, named al-Quswah. He called out to the Muslims that He whom they awaited had come; and Muslims, some five hundred men and many women and children, poured out of the town singing and shouting: 'The Prophet of God has come, the Messenger of God has come.' It is reported that a Jew, whether the same one who had announced the arrival of the Prophet or not, bitterly complained to a co-religionist that these accursed Arabs had just then gathered round a man from Mecca, who claimed to be a Prophet. That was how the celebrated Salmán al-Fárisí[2]—Salmán, the Persian—working in the palm grove of his master, first heard about Muḥammad.

[2] The Persians would call him Salmán-i-Fársí.

9

Medina—the City of the Prophet

WITH the arrival of Muḥammad, Ya<u>th</u>rib changed its name and the old name was soon forgotten. It was now the City of the Prophet—al-Madínat an-Nabí. In the course of years that was shortened to al-Madínah[1]—the City, and the City it has remained.

When the Prophet reached Ya<u>th</u>rib He alighted at Qubá' on the edge of the oasis, where the clan of Banú-'Amr Ibn 'Awf lived. He was very tired after the hardships of His hurried exit from Mecca. Kul<u>th</u>úm Ibn Hidm, who was not as yet a Muslim, invited Muḥammad to rest in his house for a while, which the Prophet accepted. How long He stayed in Qubá' is uncertain—three days, four days, five, fourteen, even twenty-two days have been mentioned. What is certain is that He stayed long enough for 'Alí to join Him, and for a mosque to be built on a piece of land owned by Kul<u>th</u>úm, opposite his house. 'Alí had remained in Mecca for a few days to pay Muḥammad's creditors and return all the goods consigned to Him. He had then started on foot for Ya<u>th</u>rib, arriving there in a state of exhaustion. Yet soon he was at work, helping to build the mosque at Qubá'—the first house of worship in the realm of Islám. Muḥammad purchased the land from Kul<u>th</u>úm, and all the Muslims gave a hand in constructing the mosque. Muḥammad Himself could be seen carrying earth and making mud bricks. Verse 109 of the Súrah of Repentance (ix, *at-Tawbah*) is said to refer to the mosque of Qubá':

> A mosque that was founded
> upon godfearing from the first day is worthier
> for thee to stand in; therein are men who love
> to cleanse themselves; and God loves those
> who cleanse themselves.[2]

[1] Medina is the form used in English, just as Mecca has come current for al-Makkah.
[2] Translated by A. J. Arberry.

At last the day came when the Prophet mounted His camel again to continue into the heart of Medina. The route lay through a quarter where the clan of Banú-Sálim Ibn ‘Awf lived. Here the Muslims had a place for worship, and it being a Friday, Muḥammad halted there to greet and talk to them. It was the first sermon He gave in His city.

Once more on His camel, Muḥammad was surrounded on all sides by people who pleaded with Him to make His home with them. ‘Itbán Ibn Málik and Nawfal Ibn ‘Abdi’lláh of the Banú-Sálim took hold of the halter of the camel to persuade the Prophet to stay in their quarter. But Muḥammad gave them the same answer He had given to Buraydah in the desert: He would let His camel decide and take Him where it wished. Thus He went through the quarters of the Banú-Sá‘idah and the Banú-Ḥáriṯẖ Ibn al-Ḵẖazraj, until He reached that of the Banú-‘Adí Ibn an-Najjár. Abú-Salíṭ of that clan reminded Muḥammad that the Banú-‘Adí were His uncles; it was meet that He should reside with them. And Silmá, the mother of the patriarch ‘Abdu’l-Muṭṭalib came from this clan. But the Prophet went His way. As He passed by the house of ‘Abdu’lláh Ibn Ubayy, the latter turned aside, saying: ‘Go to the people who deceived thee and brought thee to this town.’ Sa‘d Ibn ‘Ubádah (one of the twelve *nuqabá’*) intervened to inform the Prophet that the son of Ubayy was now a frustrated, resentful man, moved by envy, and should be ignored; subsequent to the miseries of their civil war people had agreed to hail him as their ruler, but the advent of the Prophet had blocked his path to power.

On a piece of land, barren and empty save for a few palm trees, the camel stopped and knelt. There the Prophet would make His abode, but there was no house on that site. Close to it, however, lived Ḵẖálid Ibn Zayd, known as Abú-Ayyúb, and he took the Prophet’s baggage into his house. When another invitation was pressed on Him, Muḥammad replied that a man should always stay with his baggage. He lodged in the house of Abú-Ayyúb for several months.

The land, where the camel had stopped, belonged to two orphans, Sahl and Suhayl, who would happily have made a present of it to the Prophet. As‘ad Ibn Zurárah, one of the first Muslims of Medina and one of the twelve *nuqabá’*, was their guardian and supported their suit, but Muḥammad desired them to accept payment. This was made by Abú-Bakr. A mosque was built on that site and, next to it, a house for the Prophet. Eventually other houses were built on the periphery of the mosque which was then of simple construction. When Muḥammad gave His first sermon there, He leaned against the trunk of a palm tree. And there today beside the mosque stands the tomb of the Prophet.

As'ad Ibn Zurárah died shortly afterwards. His clan, an-Najjár, asked Muḥammad to appoint a *naqíb* (singular of *nuqabá'*) for them, to take office in succession to As'ad. The Prophet, whose great-grandmother belonged to this clan, offered Himself as their *Naqíb*.

So here was Muḥammad established in Medina. But large numbers of the inhabitants of the town were still either idolaters or feigned a belief in Muḥammad which was far from genuine. And the Jews of the three settlements, who had hoped that Muḥammad, preaching monotheism as fervently as He did, would naturally gravitate towards them, began to draw back and even turn hostile, when they realized that Muḥammad was calling them to testify to His Faith. However, one of their outstanding men, Ḥusayn Ibn Salám, to whom the Prophet gave the name of His own father, sought the company of Muḥammad, and was eventually won over to Him. Other Jewish leaders kept their distance.

Muḥammad named the emigrants from Mecca *al-Muhájirún* (which means exactly that—the Emigrants), and gave the Muslims of Medina the appellation of *al-Anṣár*, the Helpers. Then He established ties of brotherhood between individuals of the two groups, and likewise joined a number of Meccans together in the same relationship. 'Alí He chose as His own brother. His uncle Ḥamzah, whom Ibn-Hishám designates as Asadu'lláh—the Lion of God, and the Lion of His Apostle—became a brother to Zayd Ibn Ḥárithah, the freedman of the Prophet and His adopted son. Abú-Bakr and 'Umar He pronounced brothers; and then He joined Abú-Bakr to Khárijah Ibn Zayd of the Khazraj, and 'Umar to 'Itbán Ibn Málik, also of the Khazraj. 'Abda'r-Raḥmán Ibn 'Awf and 'Uthmán Ibn 'Affán, both Meccans, were allied together as brothers, and then 'Uthmán was given a brother from the Anṣár in the person of Aratt Ibn Thábit, while 'Abda'r-Raḥmán was joined to Sa'd Ibn ar-Rabí'. Sa'd offered to share with 'Abda'r-Raḥmán everything he had (including two wives, one of whom he offered to divorce for 'Abda'r-Raḥmán to marry, the choice being left to the brother-emigrant), but all that 'Abda'r-Raḥmán wanted was a small loan, and to be shown the way to the market. He was not a Meccan for nothing. Beginning most probably as a pedlar, he went on to become a prosperous merchant. 'U<u>th</u>mán had salvaged his possessions in Mecca, and in Medina he added to his considerable wealth, which he spent freely in the interests of the Faith he professed. But many of the Muhájirún were not as lucky as 'U<u>th</u>mán or even 'Abda'r-Raḥmán. They depended entirely on the generosity of their fellow believers in Medina, who were not themselves endowed with an abundance of worldly goods. Ḥamzah, the uncle of the Prophet, was penniless, and had to manage with what his Nephew could give him. There were times when the Prophet Himself had not a morsel of food in the house, and there were times when He had to pawn His armour. 'Alí had to earn his living, at one time, drawing water from a well to irrigate an orchard belonging to a Jew. There were a number who were homeless. Muḥammad arranged some kind of a sleeping-place for them in the mosque, a *ṣuffah* (bench); hence they came to be known as al-Ahl aṣ-Ṣuffah—the People of the Bench.

The peasants of Medina shared their cultivated land with their brother-emigrants, but these Meccans, born and bred in arid areas, were not used to lush fields and stagnant water. They fell ill and, for some time, were useless as workers. It took them many long months to become acclimatized. 'U<u>th</u>mán Ibn Maẓ'ún of the Banú-Ma<u>kh</u>zúm, a foster-brother of Muḥammad, who had also been an emigrant to Ethiopia, died and was buried in the cemetery of Baqí', which achieved fame because many of the descendants of the Prophet and a multitude of early Muslims lie buried there.

The *A<u>dh</u>án*, the Call to Prayer, was instituted during those initial months in Medina. The Prophet asked the advice of His followers as to how it should be done. Someone suggested that the system of blowing a horn, which the Jews had, could be adopted, but the Prophet was averse to it. Next the bell-ringing of the Christians was mentioned and again the Prophet felt this not suitable. Lighting a bonfire was the third choice presented to the meeting, but Muḥammad rejected this because of its identification with the practices of the Magians. Incidentally, it was about this time that Salmán the Persian, who was in all probability a Mazdean (Zoroastrian), embraced the Faith of Muḥammad. Finally 'Umar proposed a vocal call, which was hailed as the ideal way, and was accepted by the Prophet. Bilál, the Ethiopian, was installed in the office of *mu'adhdhin*.[3]

Muḥammad's daughters, Fáṭimah and Umm-Kulthúm, and his wife, Sawdah, were still in Mecca. He sent Zayd Ibn Ḥárithah and Ráfi', another of His freedmen, to bring them to Medina. The leaders of the Quraysh did not prevent their departure, and Zayd was able to bring away His own family as well. 'Abdu'l-láh, the son of Abú-Bakr, also succeeded in moving out of Mecca, accompanied by his mother, Umm-Rúmán, and his two sisters, Asmá' and 'Á'ishah. Asmá', married to az-Zubayr Ibn al-'Awwám, the cousin of the Prophet, was with child, and her famous son, 'Abdu'lláh, was born as soon as they reached Qubá'. 'Abda'r-Raḥmán, another son of Abú-Bakr, still bitterly opposed to his father and to the religion of Muḥammad, remained in Mecca, as did Abú-Quḥáfah, the father of Abú-Bakr, who was very old and blind. Not long after the arrival of Abú-Bakr's family, Muḥammad married 'Á'ishah, who was then nine years old. There was no wedding feast, but Sa'd Ibn 'Ubádah, as 'Á'ishah herself has narrated, sent them a bowl of fresh milk. 'Á'ishah was the first child born in Islám.[4]

The number of Muslims in Medina was steadily increasing, and the Jews, who had cold-shouldered the Prophet, came to realize that the coming of Muḥammad was not just a passing phase in the life of their town, and that they needed a working arrangement with Him. There is uncertainty regarding the form and manner of negotiation between Muḥammad and the Jewish leaders, who have been named as Ka'b Ibn Asad of the Banú-Qurayẓah, Ḥuyy Ibn Akhṭab of the Banu'n-Naḍír, and Mukhayrayq of the Banú-Qaynuqá'; but it is certain that in the charter which the Prophet gave to all the inhabitants of the oasis, forming one body-politic out of its diverse elements, Jews were accorded freedom to practise their own Faith. Their security was guaranteed under the protection of Islám. They were not to be molested or affronted.

[3] This word usually appears as muezzin in English. It denotes one who gives the call to prayer.

[4] 'Á'ishah, Muḥammad's third wife, was a daughter of Abú-Bakr, the fourth Muslim, Muḥammad's companion on the journey to Medina and the provider of the means of escape, whose dwindling assets were always at the service of the Prophet and the Muslim community. Abú-Bakr expected to be thus honoured.

Their enemies were not to be aided. Should Medina be attacked Jews would share in its defence, and were they ever to fight on the side of the Muslims, they would contribute financially as well. No group in the oasis was to engage in a war or enter into any alliance without the sanction of the Prophet. Mutual trust and loyalty were the keynotes of the Prophet's charter.

10

Badr and Uḥud

THE Muslim calendar dates from the Prophet's Hijrah[1]—Emigration. 'Umar Ibn al-Khaṭṭáb, when caliph, instituted this calendar, and made the month of Muḥarram its starting-point, though the Prophet's journey from Mecca to Medina took place in the month of Rabí' al-Awwal, which is the second month after Muḥarram.

When the first year of Hijrah reached its conclusion Muḥammad was the virtual master of Medina. The Muslim community, within that oasis, was growing rapidly, and on the surface all was calm. But, metaphorically, Medina was the only oasis of calm in all Arabia, and even within Medina anger smouldered in the Jewish settlements and the *Munáfiqún* caused constant annoyance. These people, condemned more than once in the Qur'án, have had their name rendered into English as 'Hypocrites'. But as Sir John Glubb points out, this 'translation does not completely convey the sense'. The Munáfiqún, at whose head stood the bitterly disappointed 'Abdu'lláh Ibn Ubayy, were dissemblers who paid lip service to the Faith of Muḥammad but derided it at every possible opportunity. On one occasion their own kinsmen could no longer tolerate them and threw them out of the mosque.

Prior to the Prophet's arrival on the scene, the Jews outshone the peasants of the Aws and the Khazraj. Spiritually, culturally, financially, they were the giants; but now, a year after the coming of Muḥammad, they felt humbled and dwarfed, and were therefore resentful and angry. Even the gentle Abú-Bakr could, one day, no longer stand their taunts, and was violent to a Jew who mocked the collecting of alms; their God must be in a dreary state to need alms, he had observed.

[1] Some writers in the West have translated Hijrah as 'Flight'. For this there is no justification. (Variants in English are hegira, hejira, hejra, hijra.)

The Meccans, too, although further enriched at the expense of the Muslims by confiscating everything they had perforce left behind, were smarting under the shame of being thwarted. Muḥammad had slipped from their hands, at the very time when His destruction was assured, and was building a bastion for Himself to the north of them, not far from the route their caravans took to Syria; He would, they believed, undoubtedly come forth in future to challenge them.

Bedouins were no less disturbed. They were rapacious and valued the freedom of the desert. The Prophet was kind and considerate to them. He wished them to give up the life of nomads, and, once Muslim, to live in Medina and forget their boorish ways. One day a Bedouin was found urinating in the mosque. Naturally, the Medinites were furious, but the Prophet told them to leave him alone: 'Let him produce a bucketful if he wants'. Muḥammad went to such lengths to tame the fierce men of the desert.

The Prophet knew that sooner or later a clash must come with the unruly forces straddling Arabia. The second pledge of 'Aqabah, which bound seventy-two men of Ya<u>th</u>rib to His person, carried with it a promise to fight for Him if needed. Within three years that promise would be put to the test.

A year and a half had passed since the Prophet's arrival in Medina, when, suddenly and without any previous intimation, He changed the Qiblih (the point towards which the Muslim turns his face while saying his daily obligatory prayers) from the direction of Jerusalem to the direction of Mecca. Western scholars have contended that Muḥammad had originally chosen Jerusalem in order to ingratiate Himself with the Jews, but later, finding them unresponsive, had veered round from Jerusalem to Mecca. However, there is no evidence in support of this theory—quite the contrary. *Ṣalát*, the daily obligatory prayer, was instituted by Muḥammad in the opening years of His ministry, when the number of Muslims could be counted on finger-tips. In fact, he did not come into contact with the Jews, in any appreciable number, for at least another decade. There is no record anywhere to show that Muḥammad had spoken of His mission to any Jew. Certainly, before Muḥammad reached Ya<u>th</u>rib, He had not a single follower from the Jewish fold. Then, what reason would He have to ingratiate Himself with the Jews? Muslims for years had been turning in prayer towards Jerusalem, when there was no Jew in sight or on the horizon.

Western scholars apart, it looks strange to see in the *Násikhu't-Tavárikh*, the work of Lisánu'l-Mulk-i-Sipihr, a Persian historian of the nineteenth century, the same allegation that, by turning towards Jerusalem, Muḥammad intended to 'soften the hearts of the Jews'. Even more preposterous is the statement by Sipihr that all the while the Prophet was sad at doing this and told the Angel Gabriel that He wished God would sanction turning towards Mecca, which was also the point of adoration of Abraham, His forbear. This ridiculous story is taken a step further by affirming that Gabriel maintained his own helplessness in the matter and advised the Prophet to pray and beseech God for the desired dispensation. This state of affairs, according to Sipihr, went on until the day Gabriel brought, with great joy, the revelation which authorized Muḥammad to change the Qiblih. The vapidity of Sipihr's story, which he must have culled from the writings of one as gullible as himself, is past belief.

This is the verse which permitted Muḥammad to change the Qiblih:

> We have seen thee turning thy face about
> in the heaven; now We will surely turn thee
> to a direction that shall satisfy thee.
> Turn thy face towards the Holy Mosque; and
> wherever you are, turn your faces towards it.
> Those who have been given the Book know it is
> the truth from their Lord; God is not heedless of
> the things they do.[2]

The Jews and the idolaters were equally contemptuous of the alteration. Verse 136 of the same súrah counters their jejune objections:

> The fools among the people will say,
> 'What has turned them from the direction
> they were facing in their prayers aforetime?'
> Say:
> 'To God belong the East and the West;
> He guides whomsoever He will
> to a straight path.'[2]

[2] Translation by A. J. Arberry. Súrah ii, vv. 139 and 136, *al-Baqarah*—'The Cow'.

The 109th verse also alludes to the question of the Qiblih, and the cavillings of the opponents of the Prophet:

> To God belong the East and the West;
> whithersoever you turn, there is the Face of God;
> God is All-embracing, All-knowing.[3]

The ordinance of fasting throughout the entire month of Ramaḍán was also instituted during the second year of the Hijrah. Instructions regarding the fast are contained in verses 179–83 of the same súrah, *al-Baqarah*.

Also in that second year, Fáṭimah, the youngest daughter of Muḥammad, was married to ʻAlí. This wedding, too, was a simple affair. ʻAlí was poor and so was Muḥammad, and feasts could be costly. To provide His daughter with a few necessities, Muḥammad had to sell a coat of armour. It was bought by ʻUthmán Ibn ʻAffán, whose affairs were flourishing. Abú-Bakr was entrusted with the money and sent to the market-place. It is said that when Muḥammad saw the goods that had been purchased, He was so moved by their paucity that tears welled up in His eyes and He said: ʻO God! bless Thou those whose wares are mostly made of clay.'

It was sometime in the same year that a series of raids and skirmishes began, culminating in the battle of Badr and its sequel, the battle of Uḥud. These struggles were to assume ever wider scope and greater intensity, until the whole of Arabia would acknowledge the Faith of Islám. At Badr, Meccans suffered a disastrous defeat, and at Uḥud, Muslims were vanquished. Generally, Western writers have maintained that the first steps towards a passage of arms were taken by Muḥammad. They have not been unsupported. There were Muslim writers who believed that the mandate to wage war against the idolaters, contained in verse 40 of the twenty-second súrah (*al-Ḥajj*—ʻThe Pilgrimage'), was a command to attack and destroy the enemy. That verse and the following one read: ʻPermission is given to those who would fight, because they were wronged, and God is verily able to aid them—they who were unjustly driven out of their homes because they say, "God is our Lord". And if God had not repelled people, some by the means of others, monasteries and churches and synagogues and mosques, where the name of God is much mentioned,

[3] Translation by A. J. Arberry.

would have been destroyed. And, verily, God will give victory to whosoever gives Him victory, for God is the All-Strong, the All-Glorious.'

But scholars such as Sir Thomas Arnold, the author of *The Preaching of Islam*, and Syed Ameer Ali have pointed out that the aggressive and menacing attitude of the idolaters forced Muḥammad to action, because He was no longer only a *Nadhír* and a *Bashír*,[4] but the ruler of a large oasis with specific duties towards its inhabitants. He had to ensure the safety and the security of the people of Medina and, within the oasis itself, He had to guard against the half-hearted and the traitorous who would betray their fellow citizens. Syed Ameer Ali writes:

'He who never in his life had wielded a weapon, to whom the sight of human suffering caused intense pain and pity, and who, against all the canons of Arab manliness, wept bitterly at the loss of his children or disciples, whose character ever remained so tender and so pathetic as to cause his enemies to call him womanish,—this man was now compelled, from the necessities of the situation, and against his own inclination, to repel the attacks of the enemy by force of arms, to organise his followers for purposes of self-defence, and often to send out expeditions to anticipate the treacherous and sudden onslaughts. Hitherto, Arab warfare consisted of sudden and murderous forays, often made in the night or in the early morn; isolated combats or a general mêlée, when the attacked were aware of the designs of the attacking party. Mohammed, with a thorough knowledge of the habits of his people, had frequently to guard against these sudden onslaughts by sending forth reconnoitring parties.'[5]

Expeditions led by the Prophet Himself are called *ghazwah* and others are known as *saríyyah*. Many of them did not lead to encounters. Professor Montgomery Watt believes that in some cases the reason why nothing came of them was espionage on the part of Muḥammad's adversaries in Medina, who sent news of His intentions to the Meccans. There is no agreement regarding the number of the *ghazwahs*. Some have said as high as twenty-seven, but in only nine did an actual contest take place. Regarding the *saríyyahs*, too, there have been diverse opinions.

According to one account, the first expedition was a *ghazwah*;

[4] See p. 23.

[5] *The Spirit of Islam*, p. 61.

according to another, a *saríyyah*. The first has it that Muḥammad with sixty men went as far as Abwá, a village situated between Medina and Mecca; there the headman of the village, Muthanná Ibn 'Amr, a chieftain of the Banú-Ḍamrah, came out in peace. Muḥammad stayed for fifteen days in Abwá and no fighting occurred. The first *saríyyah* was led by Ḥamzah, the uncle of the Prophet, who, with thirty men, went nearly to the sea, deep into territory held by the clan of Juhaynah. Abú-Jahl was near by with some three hundred men. Majd Ibn 'Amr of the Juhaynah intervened and prevented a clash of arms. Subsequently the Prophet praised the perspicacity of Majd. But when Abú-Jahl reached Mecca, he roused its citizens to immediate action against Muḥammad, assembling a fighting force with 'Ikrimah, his son, in command. The news soon reached Medina, and the Prophet sent sixty men of the Emigrants, under 'Ubaydah Ibn al-Ḥárith, to meet the Meccans. Two men in the ranks of the idolaters, who had thus far succeeded in concealing their conversion, found it an opportune moment to join their brother Muslims. 'Ikrimah was infuriated by their desertion and ordered an immediate attack. Arrows were exchanged. The first arrow aimed at the Meccans was shot by Sa'd Ibn Abí-Waqqáṣ, destined for resounding fame in future years. Just what happened next is doubtful. It appears that the Meccans took fright and abandoned the field. In any case, there were no casualties. These abortive expeditions were followed by others equally abortive. At Dhu'l-'Ushayrah, near the seaside town of Yanbú', Muḥammad found no trace of the Quraysh, who had been reported as in the neighbourhood, but His sojourn there provided an opportunity to talk peace with some of the chiefs of the Banú-Mudlij.

The Quraysh next made a furtive sortie and carried away, from their pasturage, camels and cattle belonging to the people of Medina. Muḥammad took a number of the Emigrants with Him and gave chase, going as far as the vicinity of Badr, but the idolaters had made good their escape. However, the following expedition, a *saríyyah*, had consequences which could have been very grave. 'Abdu'lláh Ibn Jaḥsh, a cousin of the Prophet, was sent by Him with twelve men to reconnoitre. They encountered a Meccan caravan, returning from Ṭá'if with merchandise. There was a skirmish at Banú-Nakhlah. 'Amr Ibn al-Ḥaḍramí of the Quraysh was killed and two of his compatriots fell into Muslim hands, together with rich booty. But, as it happened, that day was the last of Rajab, one of the four months in which warfare was forbidden. As the news spread that Muslims had engaged in an armed attack in the month of Rajab, recriminaton came from all sides. Even Jews joined in. The Muslims were crest-fallen. Muḥammad forbade the sharing out of the captured goods. For days 'Abdu'lláh Ibn Jaḥsh and his companions repined and felt greatly apprehensive. But to the relief of all, there came a revelation to Muḥammad, which announced:

'They will question thee concerning the holy month and fighting therein. Say: "Fighting therein is reprehensible, it bars the way to God and is negation of faith; but in the sight of God, more grave is the expulsion of the people from the Holy Mosque, and *fitnah*[6] is more offensive than slaying.' (Súrah ii, 214.)

Now the ground was prepared for the first battle with the idolaters—the great battle of Badr.

BADR

In the autumn of the second year of the Hijrah (623), Abú-Sufyán took the annual caravan of the Meccans to Syria. A fairly large number of prosperous Meccan merchants travelled with him. They were due to return in the spring. Muḥammad sent two men to discover the whereabouts of the caravan, but they lost their way and came back to Medina without news. Muḥammad then sent two other men to reconnoitre, who were successful, but their presence in the neighbourhood of Badr was discovered by Abú-Sufyán. He immediately stopped in his tracks and turned back towards Syria whence he had come. He also dispatched a messenger to Mecca to raise the alarm. Then, with the aid of 'Amr Ibn al-'Áṣ, he made a detour, touched the sea by Jiddah, and led the caravan safely to Mecca. In the meantime Muḥammad had come out of Medina with a force composed of 314 men, and the Meccans had sallied forth to protect their caravan.

Until then, participants in the expeditions mounted by the Prophet had been exclusively from the ranks of the Emigrants, but, on this occasion, there were only 83 of these and almost three times as many of the Helpers: 61 Awsites and 170 Khazrajites. These figures are given by Ibn-Hishám. Between them they had only two horses and seventy camels. It was the month of

[6] This word has been variously rendered as 'schism', 'sedition', 'persecution'.

Ramaḍán, and Muḥammad broke His fast as soon as they were encamped outside the city. But many of His men did not follow His example. The next day He sent out a crier amongst them to announce: 'O ye the disobedient! I have broken my fast, do ye the same.'

A few stages out of Medina, two of the Medinites who were not Muslims joined them. Muḥammad wished to know what had prompted this action. They stated frankly that they were after booty. The Prophet said: 'He who is not of our Faith does not march with us.' Khubayb Ibn Yasáf became a Muslim and stayed. Qays Ibn al-Ḥárith would not and went back, only to change his mind when the Muslims returned in triumph. Qays died at Uḥud.

Ḍamḍam Ibn 'Amr, the messenger whom Abú-Sufyán had dispatched to raise the alarm in Mecca, reached there in record time and called the people to hurry to the rescue of their caravan. Some of the prominent men among the Meccans, such as Abu'l-Bakhtarí and al-Ḥárith Ibn 'Ámir, detested going out with an expedition; while others, such as Abú-Jahl and Ṭu'aymah Ibn 'Adí and Ḥanẓalah, the son of Abú-Sufyán, vigorously set about collecting men and arms. All the clans joined in, except that of 'Adí Ibn Ka'b who refused to fight Muḥammad. At this juncture Abú-Lahab fell ill and deputed al-'Áṣ Ibn Hishám to go in his stead. The latter owed Abú-Lahab a large debt which he discharged by replacing him, but al-'Áṣ died at Badr.

Umayyah, the son of Khalaf, was another recalcitrant. He was too old and obese, he protested, to go to war. But Abú-Jahl and 'Uqbah, the son of Abú-Mu'ayṭ, bitterly reprimanded him. The latter, who in years past had, at the instance of Umayyah, spat on the face of Muḥammad, came to him with an incense-burner. 'Stay at home and perfume thyself like women,' he mocked. And so Umayyah went, to meet his death at Badr.

'Abbás, the uncle of the Prophet, still sitting on the fence, made no preparations to fall in with the others. To 'Uqbah's remonstrances he replied that he was an old man, incapable of fighting, and would send his sons, 'Abdu'lláh and 'Ubaydu'lláh, Faḍl and 'Uthmán. Abú-Jahl was incensed and threatened, on their return, to expel from Mecca all the remaining members of the House of Háshim, as they were at heart partisans of Muḥammad. Other elders of Mecca concurred. Thus, 'Abbás too began to prepare. He was so furious that he refused to have anyone with him except a slave. But his nephews, Nawfal, Ṭálib and 'Aqíl (the last two brothers of 'Alí), being concerned that his age would tell against him, accompanied him.

The Quraysh encamped outside Mecca with 950 men, one hundred horses and seven hundred camels, in glaring contrast to the Muslims' strength. The rich elders—Abú-Jahl and 'Utbah, Shaybah and Zam'ah, and eight others—took it in turn to provide the daily fare of the army. 'Addás, that Christian slave who had taken grapes to Muḥammad in Ṭá'if, warned his masters that the man they were setting out to fight was, in truth, the Messenger of God; they were sure to come to grief. The brothers 'Utbah and Shaybah were killed at Badr.

Doubts lingered in both camps. The second pledge of 'Aqabah had assured the Prophet of the support of the people of Medina, but whether they were bound to defend Him in the desert remained a moot point. Sa'd Ibn Mu'ádh, the Awsite leader, promised that the Anṣár would march with Him to any danger. The Quraysh, having moved out of Mecca to fight Muḥammad, received word from Abú-Sufyán that their caravan was safe. Now, whether they should return to Mecca, since the *casus belli* had disappeared, led to serious questioning. Abú-Jahl, making a highly emotional appeal to the elders of Mecca, persuaded the Quraysh not to be faint-hearted. 'Abdu'lláh, the brother of 'Amr Ibn al-Ḥaḍramí—he who was murdered by the Muslims in the skirmish on the last day of Rajab—was brought in with garments rent, crying out for revenge. 'Utbah and Shaybah, who preferred to give up and return to Mecca, were silenced. But the clan of Zuhrah, as well as Ṭálib, the brother of 'Alí, refused to go on and returned home. Both sides were by now sending out scouts to determine how far the other had advanced.

On approaching the wells of Badr, Muḥammad called a halt. Ḥubáb Ibn al-Mundhir asked Him whether by the writ of a revelation He had chosen that particular spot, or was it His personal choice? When Ḥubáb learned that they had bivouacked there on Muḥammad's own judgement and not by command of a revelation, he strongly objected and urged that they go forward and take possession of the wells, thus denying water to the Quraysh. Muḥammad accepted his advice and changed their position, just as the Quraysh advanced towards them over the hill.

In the early morning of March 15th (624), Muḥammad received

a revelation: 'Should they incline to peace, do thou likewise; and put thy trust in God; He is verily the All-Hearing, the All-Knowing.' (Súrah viii, 63.) He sent 'Umar ahead to parley with the Quraysh. Muḥammad, 'Umar told them, did not wish to fight against them, for they were His own kith and kin. 'Utbah Ibn Rabí'ah, who had all along tried hard to prevent a clash, now went into the ranks of the Meccans and begged them to listen to the words which 'Umar had brought from Muḥammad. He himself, 'Utbah declared, would give them the equal of all the merchandise they had lost to the Muslims at Banú-Nakhlah, and would pay the blood-money to 'Abdu'lláh Ibn al-Ḥaḍramí. But Abú-Jahl, Muḥammad's inveterate enemy, intervened once again, fanned the ire of the Quraysh, and openly accused 'Utbah of cowardice. There was no drawing back now and battle had to be joined.

'Utbah, smarting under the insults hurled at him by Abú-Jahl, stepped forward with his brother Shaybah and his son al-Walíd, and challenged the Muslims to single combat. Three of the Anṣár went to meet them, but 'Utbah declared that although he acknowledged the valour of these adversaries, they wished to fight with men related to themselves. Thereupon the men of the Anṣár withdrew, and Muḥammad sent 'Alí, Ḥamzah and 'Ubaydah Ibn al-Ḥárith (of the House of Muṭṭalib) to fight the three champions of Mecca. The Meccans were killed, but 'Ubaydah also was fatally wounded. They carried him to the Prophet for whom a shelter of palm fronds had been constructed. Abú-Bakr was with the Prophet, while in front of His shelter Sa'd Ibn Mu'ádh and a few others stood guard, and behind, camels were tethered to carry Him away should the day go against Him. 'Am I not a martyr?' asked the dying 'Ubaydah. And Muḥammad replied, 'Indeed thou art.' Then, weeping over 'Ubaydah, Muḥammad cried out: 'O God! Fulfil what Thou hadst promised me, fulfil what Thou hadst promised me, fulfil what Thou hadst promised me. Were this band of Muslims to perish, none would be left on earth to worship Thee.'

Muḥammad had tried to avert the battle and had failed; and strangely, the first to fall in the ranks of the Quraysh were those men who also had pleaded for peace. Now, Muḥammad went out amongst His people to put heart into them. Their opponents numbered three times as many, and were better mounted and better equipped. A youth, 'Umayr Ibn al-Ḥimám, standing near the Prophet, was idly eating dates when he heard Muḥammad's appeal. He threw away his dates, shouted that between him and Paradise stood only death, and the death of a martyr he would seek. He plunged into the mêlée and was cut down.

And the leading men of Quraysh fell—one after the other: Ṭu'aymah, the son of 'Adí; Ḥanẓalah, the son of Abú-Sufyán; Zam'ah, the son of al-Aswad, and his brother, al-Ḥárith. This Zam'ah was the father of Sawdah, whom the Prophet married after the death of Khadíjah. Abú-Bakr saw his own son, 'Abda'r-Raḥmán, fighting against the Muslims and called out to him in bitter reproach, but received only a dusty answer. Two brothers of the Anṣár, named Mu'ádh and Ma'údh, were seeking Abú-Jahl, whom they knew to have been an unrelenting enemy of the Prophet, harming Him gravely over the years. Staying close to 'Abda'r-Raḥmán Ibn 'Awf, they asked him to identify Abú-Jahl, whereupon they attacked and brought him down. At that instant 'Ikrimah came upon the scene and, to avenge his father, dealt Mu'ádh a blow which almost severed his arm. Mu'ádh, unconscious of the terrible injury he had sustained, went on fighting, until the weight of the arm hanging by the skin became unbearable, when he put it under his foot and tore it off. Strangely, he recovered and lived for many years, but his brother Ma'údh was killed.

'Abdu'lláh Ibn Mas'úd, also one of the Anṣár, found Abú-Jahl in his death-throes. By then the Quraysh were in full flight, throwing away their armour to facilitate escape, and leaving behind seventy dead, seventy-four prisoners and rich booty. The Muslims had lost only fourteen men—six from the Muhájirún, and eight from the Anṣár. The dying idolater asked to whom the victory had gone. 'Abdu'lláh answered: 'To God and His Prophet.' But Abú-Jahl was still defiant. 'Abdu'lláh gave him the *coup de grâce* and carried his head to the Prophet. Muḥammad gazed at it long before saying: 'This man was the Pharaoh of our people'.

'Abda'r-Raḥmán Ibn 'Awf discovered Umayyah Ibn Khalaf sitting helpless among the dead. Umayyah was too old and corpulent, as he had himself protested in Mecca, to run away. Nor was there a steed available for him to ride to safety. His son, 'Adí, unable to leave him to his fate, was also stranded, and could save neither himself nor his father. 'Abda'r-Raḥmán and Umayyah were not strangers. They had been friends in a past which now seemed remote. 'Abda'r-Raḥmán formally took Umayyah and 'Adí as his prisoners, but just then the Ethiopian, Bilál, who as Umayyah's slave had suffered torments at his hands, came upon them and, espying his former master, denounced him so violently that 'Abda'r-Raḥmán's protest was of no avail; both Umayyah and 'Adí were slain.

Abu'l-Bakhtarí had, at the time of the boycott of the House of Háshim, intervened on their behalf. The Prophet ordered that his life be spared. It was not to be, for Abu'l-Bakhtarí would not be parted from a companion, and fighting they both met their death. An-Naḍr Ibn al-Ḥárith and 'Uqbah Ibn Abí-Mu'íṭ were executed because of their evil deeds. These men had done everything possible to belittle Muḥammad and His creed. An-Naḍr used to follow Muḥammad in the streets of Mecca, ridiculing His words and telling improbable Persian tales, which he claimed were as good as Muḥammad's. 'Uqbah had never failed to insult the Prophet.

The dead of the Quraysh were interred together in one large grave. Muḥammad approached the gaping pit and spoke these words: 'O people of the pit! Did you find what your god promised you to be true? I have found what my God promised me to be true.' Abú-Ḥudhayfah, the son of 'Utbah, visibly moved when he saw his father's corpse laid in that pit, told the Prophet that his father was a sagacious, kindly and cultured man; he was saddened to see him die an unbeliever. 'Utbah indeed had shown both compassion and a love of peace.

The question of dealing with the prisoners raised some debate. 'Umar was for putting them all to death. Among them were 'Abbás and his nephews, and Abu'l-'Áṣ, the husband of the Prophet's daughter, Zaynab. Abú-Bakr, wise and generous, suggested that they should be ransomed. Muḥammad agreed, and word was sent to the Meccans to redeem their kinsmen. 'Abbás pleaded that he was a Muslim and should not be made to pay a ransom. But he had fought in the ranks of the idolaters, and the Prophet knew that His uncle, as a very rich man, was trying to have the best of both worlds. In the end, 'Abbás had to ransom himself and also his nephews, who were poor. Zaynab sent a valuable necklace which had been her mother's to obtain her husband's freedom. The sight of Khadíjah's necklace made the

Prophet weep, and the Muslims decided not to put that piece of jewellery in the common pool. Abu'l-'Áṣ had been a favourite nephew of Khadíjah, but he would not accept the Prophet and, when he reached Mecca, sent Zaynab to Medina as he had promised. His story, however, had a happy ending. Some years later he did become a Muslim and was reunited with Zaynab. Ruqayyah, another daughter of Muḥammad, had died during the Prophet's absence from Medina. Her husband, 'Uthmán Ibn 'Affán, had remained with her. Nevertheless, Muḥammad included 'Uthmán among the warriors of Badr. Those prisoners who could not raise the ransom money were freed, on their promise never again to bear arms against the Muslims. Before their release they were kept busy teaching the Medinites how to read and write. The merchants of Mecca were far more literate than the peasants of Medina.

In Mecca the sense of desolation was great. Abú-Lahab could not believe the tidings of disaster when they reached him, and hurried out as fast as his racked, corpulent body could take him, to the well of Zamzam where many had gathered. He could not outlive the shock of defeat and died a week later. Mecca had lost almost all its elders, and now Abú-Sufyán rose to pre-eminence, resolved that the dead of the Quraysh would be avenged. A number of the Meccans decided to prevent the departure of Zaynab, the Prophet's daughter, but she had already gone. Abú-Sufyán joined them to ride out in pursuit. Habbár Ibn al-Aswad and Náfi' Ibn 'Abdi'l-Qays overtook Kinánah, the brother of Abu'l-'Áṣ, who was leading the camel which bore the howdah of Zaynab. Habbár raised his spear to attack her, but Kinánah, who was a master of archery, would have shot Habbár and his associates had not Abú-Sufyán come up in time to intervene and prevent bloodshed. However, terrified by Habbár's assault, Zaynab, who was with child, suffered miscarriage. We shall hear of Habbár once again.

One of the prisoners in Medina was a man called Wahb. His father, 'Umayr, was poor and could not ransom his son. Ṣafwán, the son of Umayyah Ibn Khalaf, made a secret pact with 'Umayr to look after his family and pay his debts, if the latter would go to Medina, ostensibly to implore Muḥammad for the release of Wahb, actually to murder the Prophet when an opportunity presented itself. But Muḥammad found him out, and both 'Umayr and his son embraced Islám. Muḥammad sent them back to Mecca to guide the Muslims through the desert, whenever needed.

The battle of Badr constitutes a landmark in the history of mankind. It assured survival to Islám. Had the Muslims been routed that day the whole polity of Medina would have broken down, and Muḥammad would have had nowhere to establish a base. Those chroniclers who have written,with gusto, of hosts of angels descending to mow down the idolaters at Badr have indeed belittled the achievement of that day.

The assassination of a Jewess, named 'Aṣmá, soon after the episode of Badr, and the expulsion of the Jews of the Banú-Qaynuqá', some two months later, were indications of the weaknesses which the Prophet's base at Medina still sustained. 'Aṣmá, the daughter of Marwán and a poetess of fame, continuously satirized Muḥammad and His Faith. Arabs, as a people, had (and have) a penchant for poetry, and were much influenced by it, especially when recited with bravado and panache. Muḥammad suffered a good deal at the hands of hostile poets; he was much disturbed when He Himself was accused of being just another poet (and a mediocre one at that) whom other poets could excel. A blind Medinite named 'Umayr Ibn 'Adí resolved, entirely on his own, to rid the Muslims of the caustic tongue of 'Aṣmá. The traditional account of this murder is most extraordinary. It is said that he, although blind, managed one night to make his way into the house of 'Aṣmá, where he found her in bed with her children, one of whom she was suckling. Pushing the children aside, he pressed his dagger hard upon the chest of 'Aṣmá until she was transfixed. But why did 'Aṣmá make no effort to defend herself or run away? It is an unbelievable tale. Another Jew, Abú-'Afak, also a poet holding Muḥammad up to ridicule, was assassinated soon after; as he was a very old man, said to have been one hundred and twenty years of age, Sálim Ibn 'Umayr, the assassin, would have had little difficulty in overpowering him.

The expulsion of the Banú-Qaynuqá', according to Ibn-Hishám, had its origin in an affront to a Muslim woman, committed by a Jew in the market-place of that clan. A Muslim, who witnessed the event, murdered the Jew on the spot and was, in turn, immediately set upon and killed by the Jews. Muḥammad sent for the elders of the Banú-Qaynuqá' and reminded them of

His pact with them, but they reacted with scorn and went off, confident that they could easily defy Him. However, a fortnight's siege convinced them of the necessity of submission. 'Ubádah Ibn aṣ-Ṣámit, of the Aws, who had ties of confederacy with the Banú-Qaynuqá', renounced them, while 'Abdu'lláh Ibn Ubayy, of the Khazraj, would not. Muḥammad ordered their expulsion from Medina, and 'Ubádah, their one-time ally, was given the task of removing them. They went north to join their co-religionists, their quarters and goods becoming the property of the Muslims. It is strange that the other two Jewish clans of Medina, the Banu'n-Naḍír and the Banú-Qurayẓah, made no attempt to come to their aid.

Once the contest was joined between Medina and Mecca, it must have been obvious that, given the conditions and circumstances of Arabia, there could never be unbroken peace between these contestants. Within Mecca there was rage and an intense desire for revenge. Within Medina there were still a large number of people who were either half-hearted or positively antagonistic to the Prophet, and who kept up a clandestine traffic with the Quraysh; they would have had no hesitation in rendering any help in their power to weaken the position of Muḥammad. The Prophet, too, had His men in and around Mecca who sent Him news of the activities of the Quraysh and their allies. We read of several sorties and *ghazwahs* during the months following the battle of Badr. On one occasion Abú-Sufyán reached the vicinity of Medina in a lightning raid, killed a man or two, destroyed some houses and palm trees and quickly withdrew. Muḥammad set out in pursuit, but Abú-Sufyán was well beyond reach. This expedition of the Prophet has been called the *ghazwah* of Sawíq, because in his haste to reach safety, apparently Abú-Sufyán told his men to discard their sacks of *sawíq* (toasted wheat or barley) that they might travel faster, and their pursuers collected them. Next the Prophet heard that men of the Banú-Sulaym and Ghaṭafán were lurking close to Medina, ready to deal a blow on behalf of the Quraysh. But they fled precipitately when apprised of the Prophet's decision to march out to meet them. On this occasion a large number of camels were captured and brought to Medina.

Not long after, some of the Banú-Tha'labah gathered at Dhú-Amr, hoping to take the Medinites by surprise. Muḥammad went out once again in person, at the head of four hundred and fifty men, to deal with them. He did not encounter them because, having heard of the Prophet's approach, they had taken up a position on cliff-tops. The life of the Prophet was imperilled on this expedition when the chieftain of a hostile clan found Him alone and unarmed. Muḥammad, however, overcame him and sent him back to his people. That was in June 624; in August came news that a number of the men of Banú-Sulaym had foregathered at Baḥrán to the east of Medina. But they too dissolved into the desert as soon as they learned that Muḥammad had set out to meet them.

Zayd, the adopted son of the Prophet, soon after led an expedition to intercept a caravan of the Quraysh which was taking a circuitous route to Syria. Since the battle of Badr the Meccans had decided not to let their caravans come too close to Medina. One of the leaders of this particular caravan was Ṣafwán, who, after the death of his father, Umayyah Ibn Khalaf, at Badr, had attained prominence in Mecca. Zayd was successful, for leaders of the caravan fled and abandoned all their merchandise.

In the opening months of the third year of the Hijrah, two other prominent Jews, Ka'b Ibn al-Ashraf and Sallám (also known as Abú-Ráfi') Ibn Abi'l-Ḥuqayq, were assassinated, the first by the Awsites and the second by the Khazrajites. Ka'b was another poet, half-Jewish, who reviled Muḥammad and eulogized His enemies. After the battle of Badr, he hurried to Mecca to condole with the Quraysh and to incite them to retaliation. As he lived close to Medina with the Jews of Banu'n-Naḍír, his presence in the proximity of Medina was a constant menace to the safety and the tranquillity of the city. One day the Prophet was heard to exclaim: 'Who will deliver me of Ibn-al-Ashraf?' Whereupon Muḥammad Ibn Maslamah concerted a plan with Abú-Ná'ilah, a foster-brother of Ka'b. They won the poet's confidence, lured him out of his stronghold and stabbed him to death. The next day Ka'b's relations came to the Prophet to ask why He had tolerated the assassination of their kinsman. Muḥammad detailed to them Ka'b's unceasing efforts to undermine His position and disrupt utterly the life of Medina with his vituperative but eloquent poetry, which had cast its baneful influence over a wide region. Having no answer to the charges laid at the door of Ibn-al-Ashraf, they went quietly away.

Men of Aws had struck down a powerful and implacable foe; now the men of Khazraj resolved to match that deed with one of their own. The obvious choice was Abú-Ráfi', a wealthy merchant who possessed a castle close to the Jewish settlement of Khaybar in the north. An inveterate enemy of the Prophet, he was perpetually striving to arouse hostility to Muḥammad among his co-religionists, as well as in the neighbouring tribe of Ghaṭafán. Because Abú-Ráfi' lived far from Medina, it was neither easy to reach him nor to gain entry to his castle. Moreoever, an intruder unfamiliar with its plan and the habits of its dwellers could quickly become lost and entrapped. 'Abdu'lláh Ibn 'Atík, choosing four others to support him, went north without arousing suspicion. By a ruse he managed to get into the castle, just at sunset as the gate-keeper was about to shut and lock the gate for the night. The gathering dusk saved him from being discovered as he sought a hiding-place, where he could keep a sharp eye on the domestic arrangements within the castle. Abú-Ráfi' met the same fate as Ka'b. In his haste to get away, 'Abdu'lláh fell down a ladder and broke his ankle, but he had purloined the great key of the castle and succeeded in rejoining his companions.

UḤUD

Abú-Sufyán, since his swift raid on the outskirts of Medina, had been preparing for decisive action, collecting money and men and trying to weld alliances with the clans of the desert. In the spring of 625, all was ready to steal a march on Medina. 'Abbás, the uncle of the Prophet, sent a messenger post-haste to warn his Nephew of the impending attack. Muḥammad called a council of war. His own view was that they should not go out of the city to meet the enemy, but should rather see to their defences and await the arrival of the Meccans. But the young men of Medina, anticipating a repetition of the victory at Badr, insisted that they ought to face the Quraysh in the open. Muḥammad acceded to their wish. When the Prophet had put on His armour and the men had gathered, there were only a thousand of them and they had no more than two horses and two hundred cuirasses. Doubts were expressed whether, with that showing, it would not be wiser to remain entrenched in Medina. Muḥammad refused to change plans at this eleventh hour, and told His men that once a Prophet had drawn His sword, it would be unedifying were He to put it back in its sheath, out of fear.

The army of Mecca presented a splendid sight: five thousand

men with three thousand camels, two hundred horses, seven hundred cuirasses, fifteen howdahs in which sat the wives of notables and chiefs. The women had come to encourage the men to greater effort, with their songs and poems; but the fact of bringing them out of Mecca and exposing them to the hazards of war was a display of supreme confidence. At the head of the Meccan army stood Abú-Sufyán, supported (apart from a few of the old guard) by a younger generation such as Ṣafwán, 'Ikrimah (whose fathers had died at Badr) and Khálid Ibn al-Walíd, a brilliant master of both tactic and strategy, whose rise to eminence, with the passage of years, was to be truly remarkable.

Two days out of Medina and approaching Mount Uḥud, the Muslim army was suddenly depleted of three hundred men. 'Abdu'lláh Ibn Ubayy and those attached to him deserted the Prophet because He had not listened to their advice to stay in Medina. By following the foolish counsel of a number of immature youths the lives of many were unnecessarily endangered, they felt, which entitled them to withdraw from the contest. These verses in súrah iii of the Qur'án—*Ál-'Imrán* ('The House of 'Imrán')—refer to Uḥud and the desertion of the three hundred:

'When thou went out at dawn from thy people to place the believers in their positions for the battle—and God is the All-Hearing, the All-Knowing; and when two factions amongst you became faint of heart, though God was their protector—and in God should the believers put their trust. God did verily give you victory at Badr, when ye were utterly abject; so fear God that perchance ye will be thankful.' (vv. 117–19.)

'And whatever visited you on the day the two parties clashed, it happened by God's leave, that He might know the believers, and that He might also know the dissemblers. And when they were told, "Come and fight in the path of God, or defend", they said, "If only we knew how to fight, we would have followed you". That day they were nearer to denial than to belief. They let their tongues utter what was not in their hearts. And God knoweth well what they conceal.' (vv. 160–1.)

Muḥammad stationed His men so that they faced Medina, with Mount Uḥud at their back and Mount 'Aynán (or 'Aynayn) to their left. Fifty archers, under the command of 'Abdu'lláh Ibn Jubayr and 'Abdu'lláh Ibn 'Amr, took up a position in the gorge of Mount 'Aynán, to protect the flank of the army and repel assaults from the Meccan cavalry. The Prophet expressly ordered them not to move out of the gorge, under any circumstances, and no matter what happened elsewhere. On arriving at the scene, the Meccans wheeled round and barred the way to Medina. They had their idol, Hubal, with them, and a semblance of an altar was set up, round which the women gathered to sing and play their instruments, shouting encouragement to their warriors. Hind, the wife of Abú-Sufyán, whose hatred of the Muslims was overwhelming, was one of these women; she had lived for this day to see her father, 'Utbah, her uncle, Shaybah, and her brother, al-Walíd, avenged. As Ḥamzah, the uncle of Muḥammad, had killed her father at Badr, she had engaged an Ethiopian slave named Waḥshí to slay Ḥamzah with his javelin. Waḥshí was promised his freedom should he accomplish this task.

The descendants of 'Abda'd-Dár held the hereditary office of standard-bearer of Mecca. Now, one of them, Ṭalḥah Ibn 'Abdi'l-'Uzzá, was holding the banner of the Quraysh. Noting this, Muḥammad gave His own banner into the charge of Muṣ'ab Ibn 'Umayr, who was also of the House of 'Abda'd-Dár. Abú-'Ámir, known as ar-Ráhib (The Hermit), a renegade from Medina, was in the ranks of the Quraysh. He had inclined towards Islám at one time, but then broke with Muḥammad and transferred to Mecca with fifty of his kinsmen. He had assured the Quraysh that when the Medinites beheld him battling on their side, they would renounce Muḥammad and come over to them. But his appearance at Uḥud evoked only jeers and ridicule from the Anṣár. Covered with shame, Abú-'Ámir tried to redeem himself by raining arrows at the Muslims. 'Ikrimah, guarding the left flank of the Meccans, attempted a general assault which failed. At this juncture, Zubayr Ibn al-'Awwám mounted an attack on the right flank of the Quraysh, which was led by Khálid Ibn al-Walíd. Khálid, unable to contain the attack, was on the point of giving way when Abú-Sufyán moved to his rescue. Zubayr had to retreat. Then came the turn of Ṭalḥah, the standard-bearer of the Quraysh, to challenge the Muslims. 'Alí struck him down and, as he fell, his brother Muṣ'ab snatched the banner and held it aloft. 'Alí slew him too. Then the next brother, 'Uthmán, grasped the banner and was killed by Ḥamzah. Another brother, Abú-Sa'íd, next raised the Meccan banner and an arrow shot by Sa'd Ibn Abí-Waqqáṣ, an accomplished archer, laid him low. Sa'd was standing near the

Prophet, who was handing him his arrows. It was now the turn of Musáfi', the son of Ṭalḥah, to bear the banner of the Quraysh. 'Áṣim Ibn Thábit let fly an arrow at him. The dying Musáfi' was taken to his mother, Suláfah. She cried out that whoever brought her the head of 'Aṣim would be rewarded with a hundred camels, and of the skull she would make a drinking-vessel. The brothers of Musáfi', al-Ḥárith and Kiláb, followed him to hold the banner of the Quraysh and went down with it. Five more of the House of 'Abda'd-Dár died, in the attempt to hold aloft the banner, one after the other, until no one was left of that proud House to bear the standard of Mecca. Suwáb, a slave of the fallen scions of 'Abda'd-Dár, leapt into the foray and raised it from the dust. When 'Alí hacked off his right hand, Suwáb took it in his left, and when he lost that hand too, he held the banner pressed against his chest and cried out: 'O sons of 'Abda'd-Dár, are ye pleased with me?' Finally a woman, 'Amrah, the daughter of 'Alqamah carried the banner and was left alone.

The Prophet had a sword on which these words were engraved: 'Cowardice carries its stigma and venturing forth proves the man's mettle; and whoever turns away with fear cannot escape his destiny.' Muḥammad called out to his men: 'Who will take this sword from me and do justice to it?' 'Umar and Zubayr stepped out to take it, but the Prophet refused it to them and gave it to Abú-Dujánah, one of the Anṣár. Wrapping a red kerchief round his head which bore the slogan, 'Help is from God and victory is at hand', Abú-Dujánah charged into the serried ranks of the enemy and scattered the men of Quraysh in all directions, until he reached the spot where the idol, Hubal, rested on a camel's back, the women circling around it. Hubal was overturned, the women fled, and Abú-Dujánah found himself facing Hind, the wife of Abú-Sufyán. He raised his sword to smite her, but remembered in time that it belonged to the Prophet and should not be stained with a woman's blood.

Ḥamzah, who had followed Abú-Dujánah into the thick of the battle, had broken into the heart of the enemy's formations. Now Waḥshí, the Ethiopian slave of Jubayr,[7] found his chance, took aim and hurled his javelin at the towering figure standing near by. It struck Ḥamzah in the loins. He wavered and fell, and Waḥshí,

[7] The son of Muṭ'im, whose uncle Ṭu'aymah had died at Badr. Ibn-Hishám states that it was Jubayr who had directed Waḥshí to slay Ḥamzah in return for his freedom.

as he himself used to say in later years, rushed forward, pulled out his javelin from the body of the dying Ḥamzah and ran away to freedom.

Now came an assault by the Muslims before which the Quraysh visibly quailed. They began to retreat while the Muslims fell upon them. But at that moment, the archers whom Muḥammad had stationed in the cleft of Mount 'Aynán with strict orders not to move, seeing their fellow believers helping themselves to the booty abandoned by the Meccans, broke ranks and joined the mêlée. 'Abdu'lláh Ibn Jubayr endeavoured to stop them but failed. Khálid Ibn al-Walíd and 'Amr Ibn al-'Áṣ took note of the unprotected flank of the Muslim army, came up with two hundred men, killed 'Abdu'lláh who had remained at his post, raced past the spot where Muḥammad stood, and attacked the advancing Muslims from the rear. The Muslims were caught almost in a vice, and in trying to disentangle themselves caused total confusion, so that friend was fighting friend. Ḥudhayfah could not save his father, al-Yamán, from the blows of his fellow Muslims and saw him die.

As at Badr, Abú-Bakr espied his son, 'Abda'r-Raḥmán, fighting for the idolaters. He drew his sword to engage him, but Muḥammad would not allow it. 'Put back thy sword,' He said; 'come hither and keep us company.' Thirty men stood in front of the Prophet to shield Him from the enemy. As the day wore on, their number was gradually reduced until only fourteen remained.[8] Ubayy Ibn Khalaf, who was one of the prisoners ransomed after the battle of Badr, now came at full gallop to slay Muḥammad, as he had promised to do. The Prophet had asked His men to caution Him as soon as they sighted the son of Khalaf. Ubayy hurtled on, reviling the Prophet and shouting that nothing could save Him now. As he drew near, Muḥammad took a weapon from Zubayr and threw it at the arrogant Meccan. Ubayy received a wound in the neck which made him turn aside and, in the end, proved fatal.

Muḥammad was holding His ground, although His army was in disarray. Muṣ'ab of the renowned House of 'Abda'd-Dár, so many of whose members had fallen that day for the glory of Hubal,

[8] These heroic men were 'Alí, Abú-Bakr, 'Abda'r-Raḥmán Ibn 'Awf, Sa'd Ibn Abí-Waqqáṣ, Ṭalḥah Ibn 'Ubaydu'lláh, az-Zubayr Ibn al-'Awwám and Abú-'Ubaydah Ibn al-Jarráḥ, of the Muhájirún; Ḥubáb Ibn al-Mundhir, Abú-Dujánah, 'Áṣim Ibn Thábit, Sahl Ibn Ḥaníf, Usayd Ibn Ḥuḍayr, Sa'd Ibn Mu'ádh and al-Ḥárith Ibn Ṣimmah, of the Anṣár.

was holding aloft the Prophet's banner. Four idolaters came forward to attack Muḥammad. As Abú-Dujánah disposed of 'Abdu'l-láh Ibn Ḥamíd, Muḥammad exclaimed: 'O God! Be thou pleased with the son of Kharashah,[9] as I am pleased with him.' Mughayrah Ibn al-'Áṣ, adept at stone-throwing, hit Muḥammad on the hand which made Him drop His sword. 'I have killed Muḥammad,' he cried, but 'Álí shouted back: 'Thou liest'; so Mughayrah took aim again and wounded Muḥammad in the forehead. At that moment 'Ammár Ibn Yásir rushed up and struck Mughayrah down. Just then 'Abdu'lláh Ibn Qami'ah approached Muḥammad with sword drawn. Muṣ'ab, His standard-bearer, barred his way. When Ibn-Qami'ah struck off his right arm, Muṣ'ab is said to have spoken words later revealed to Muḥammad, which constitute verse 138 of the third súrah (*Ál-'Imrán*) of the Qur'án: 'Muḥammad is naught but a Messenger; and verily, other Messengers have passed away before him. Should he die or be killed would ye turn around on your heels; and he who turns round on his heels, nothing would ever harm God; and God will recompense the thankful.' Muṣ'ab now held the banner in his left hand, but that too was struck off by Ibn-Qami'ah. Once more Muṣ'ab repeated the words he had just uttered, and Ibn-Qami'ah brought him down with his lance, thinking him to be Muḥammad Himself. He gave a loud yell that he had at last rid them of Muḥammad. The cry was taken up by others—'Muḥammad is dead'. On hearing this cry, the Muslims, who had torn apart the ranks of the Quraysh, were suddenly seized with panic and abandoned the field. As they came rushing past the Prophet, He called out to them: 'I am the Messenger of God. I am here and alive; come back,' but they seemed not to hear or heed. Anas Ibn an-Naḍr attempted to stop the stampede: the more reason now to fight the idolaters, he cried out. But it was of no avail. Anas himself turned round and charged again into the massed forces of the enemy. After the battle, fifty wounds were found on his body, and he could be recognized only by his fingers.

In the meantime, Ibn-Qami'ah, realizing it was not Muḥammad he had slain, renewed his attack on the Prophet, striking His forehead with a stone so that blood poured down His face. 'Abdu'lláh Ibn Shibáb wounded Muḥammad in the arm, and 'Utbah—the brother of Sa'd Ibn Abí-Waqqáṣ who was defending

[9] The father of Abú-Dujánah.

the Prophet—aimed another stone at His mouth and knocked out two of His teeth. Sa'd would later say that in that moment his brother seemed in his sight the most evil person in the whole of mankind, the one he most ardently wanted to destroy. According to Ibn-Hishám, Muḥammad exclaimed: 'How can a people attain salvation who cause blood to flow over the face of their Prophet, whilst He is calling them to God?' And at that instant, with blows raining upon Him, Muḥammad received a revelation:

> No part of the matter is thine, whether He turns
> towards them again, or chastises them; for
> they are evildoers.[10]

And He raised His hands and repeated the words which Jesus had used on the Cross: 'O God! forgive my people, for they know not.'

Once more Ibn-Qami'ah attacked the Prophet, this time with his sword. Muḥammad's coat of mail saved Him from injury, but He lost His balance and fell from His horse into one of the pits which, according to Ibn-Hishám, Abú-'Ámir had dug to discomfit the Muslims. Ṭalḥah Ibn 'Ubaydu'lláh, who had put forth his bare hand to protect Muḥammad from the sword-thrust, leapt into the pit despite his injury, and with 'Alí's aid Muḥammad was raised to His feet and helped out. Abú-Bakr brought some water for the Prophet. Muḥammad directed him to succour the unconscious Ṭalḥah, whom He praised. Accounts differ, but one version gives these as His words: 'Whoever wishes to see someone walking in this world, who is an inmate of Paradise, let him gaze at Ṭalḥah Ibn 'Ubaydu'lláh.'

The Muslims were now in full flight, and the enemy was relentlessly pressing its advantage. Wahb Ibn Qábús and his nephew, al-Ḥárith Ibn 'Uqbah, came hurrying from Medina where the rout of the Muslims had already been reported. Both were cut down. So was Ḥanẓalah, the son of Abú-'Ámir, who, with the Prophet's permission, had remained in Medina for his marriage. He rose from his nuptial bed, put on his armour, and raced to Uḥud and to death. Mukhayríq (or Mukháriq), a Jew, and Asayrim al-Ashhalí, an idolater, both of Medina, also rushed to Uḥud when the news of the disaster reached them, fought the Quraysh and fell on the battlefield. Mukhayríq was very rich; before departing

[10] Translation by A. J. Arberry. Súrah iii, 123.

for Uḥud, he told his co-religionists that should he die, all his wealth must be handed over to Muḥammad. 'Abdu'lláh Ibn Jaḥsh, a cousin of the Prophet and one of the early Muslims, was another casualty of Uḥud.

Muḥammad and the few standing with Him now climbed to the top of Mount Uḥud. Muḥammad was too weak to climb unsupported but, once more, Ṭalḥah came to His aid, ensuring his abode in Paradise, the Prophet said. Henceforth, Ṭalḥah came to be known as *aṭ-Ṭalḥata'l-Khayr*—Ṭalḥah the Good. The women of Quraysh now went onto the battlefield to ravish the bodies of the slain. They sliced off organs, tore open abdomens, and made bracelets and necklaces of noses, ears, livers and genitals. Hind tried to eat Ḥamzah's liver, but found it hard to chew. She is still remembered as 'Hind, the Eater of Liver'.

At last Abú-Sufyán decided that the time had come to disengage and go home. He rode to the foot of the Mount and called in turn the names of Muḥammad, Abú-Bakr and 'Umar. The Prophet told His men not to answer. Then, addressing his own people, Abú-Sufyán triumphantly exclaimed that all these three were dead. 'Umar could not resist shouting at him: 'Thou liest, O enemy of God and His Messenger. God hath kept them alive to thy detriment.' Abú-Sufyán's parting shot was to call out that they would find their dead mutilated; it had not been by his orders but he was not displeased; they would fight again at Badr in the coming year. The dead of the Quraysh, on the day of Uḥud, were some thirty in number. Muslims lost seventy-four men: four from the Muhájirún and the rest from the Anṣár. It was a reversal of Badr.

As the Meccans left the field, Muḥammad sent Sa'd Ibn Abí-Waqqáṣ to follow them to see whether they had taken the road to Mecca or intended to make for Medina. Should they attempt to raid Medina, He said, He would hasten to fight them despite His wounds and fatigue. But Abú-Sufyán, at the end of the day, desired nothing better than to seek rest and comfort in his native town. From the direction of Medina came a group of women, anguished and distressed by the news that the Prophet had been killed. Among them were His daughter, Fáṭimah, and 'Á'ishah, his wife. Muḥammad came down from the mountain to reassure them and to attend to the burial of the dead. As his wounds were still bleeding, Fáṭimah burnt a piece of straw matting and covered them with the ashes.

The Prophet did not know that Ḥamzah was dead and being unable to find him kept repeating: 'How has my uncle, Ḥamzah, fared; how has Ḥamzah fared?' Al-Ḥárith Ibn Ṣimmah went in search of Ḥamzah but did not return, being too pained to give Muḥammad the tidings of His uncle's death. In the end 'Alí took the news to Him. When Muḥammad saw the desecrated body of Ḥamzah, His grief was uncontrollable. 'O Ḥamzah, O uncle of the Messenger of God, O Lion of God and the Lion of His Messenger,' He cried out; 'O Ḥamzah, O author of righteous deeds; O Ḥamzah, O remover of sorrows.' He vowed to avenge Ḥamzah, whereupon a revelation came to Him which constitutes the last two verses of the sixteenth súrah—*an-Naḥl* ('The Bee'): 'Were ye to inflict chastisement on anyone, do it in the measure of what was done to you; but if ye be patient, well shall it be with those who practise patience. Be patient, and thy patience shall be the bestowal of God to thee. Do not grieve over them, and do not be sad at heart because of what they devise. Verily, God is with those who fear Him, and they are the people of good deeds.' Muḥammad did atonement for the vow He had taken in haste, and affirmed that He would be patient.

'Do not consider as dead those who have died in the path of God. Indeed they are living with their Lord, partaking of His bounties, rejoicing in what God hath bestowed upon them by His grace, joyful for those who have remained and shall come after them. No fear is there for them and no sorrow shall touch them'.[11] Such was the verdict on the martyrs of Uḥud, as revealed in the Qur'án.

Uḥud had a sequel. On the way to Mecca, Abú-Sufyán began to doubt whether they had been wise to turn back so quickly. Had they not missed the chance to put Muḥammad out of action for all time? 'Ikrimah, Khálid Ibn al-Walíd and 'Amr Ibn al-'Áṣ were of the same mind, that they ought to have made their victory complete. But other leading men, notably Ṣafwán Ibn Umayyah, disagreed. So the Meccans tarried for a while at Rawḥá', to debate the issue and determine their next step.

In Medina, too, Muḥammad felt uneasy. Were the Quraysh really returning to Mecca? Should they not be thwarted at once, if they were planning to steal a march back to Medina? And so

[11] Súrah iii, 163.

He called on all who had been at Uḥud to prepare to go out with Him in pursuit of the Quraysh. Although so many of them, Muḥammad included, were wounded and exhausted, they went as far as Ḥamrá' al-Asad, some eight miles from Medina. Ma'bad of the tribe of Khuzá'ah, who was on his way to Mecca, stopped to express his sympathy to the Prophet. He was not a Muslim, but his tribe and another, the Juhaynah, had become allied to the Muslims; whereas the Banú-Kinánah were confederates of the Quraysh and some had fought at Uḥud under Abú-Sufyán. Continuing his journey, Ma'bad met the Quraysh at Rawḥá' and informed them that Muḥammad had left Medina with a large force and would soon overtake them. Ṣafwán Ibn Umayyah, who was totally opposed to a resumption of hostilities, felt vindicated and advised his fellow Meccans to start immediately for home. Ma'bad sent word to the Prophet that the Meccans, induced by Ṣafwán, were well on their way. 'Ṣafwán had rightly guided them, whilst he himself was not of the rightly guided,' was the Prophet's comment.

On the road to Mecca, the Quraysh met men of the clan of Banú-'Abd-i-Qays, who were going to Medina in quest of provisions. Abú-Sufyán engaged one of them, Na'ím Ibn Mas'úd, with the promise of high reward, to frighten the Muslims with tales of the Quraysh strength, that they might hasten back to their stronghold. Na'ím did as he was told but the Muslims retorted: 'God is sufficient unto us and He is the best Protector'. Súrah iii, 167–8 of the Qur'án refers to this incident:

'Those who were told by some people that people had gathered against you, and you ought to fear them, it caused their faith to increase, and they said, "God is sufficient unto us and He is the best Protector". Then they returned, favoured with the grace and the bounty of God, untouched by evil. They followed the good pleasure of God, and God's bounty is great.'

11

The Investment of Medina

REPERCUSSIONS of the Battle of Uḥud continued into the following months and into the fourth year of the Hijrah (13 June 625 to 2 June 626). The first was an ugly incident fraught with treachery and bad faith. We saw in the last chapter that Suláfah, the mother of Musáfi' Ibn Ṭalḥah, offered a substantial reward to whoever would bring her the head of 'Áṣim Ibn Thábit at whose hands Musáfiḥ had met his death. 'Áṣim survived Uḥud, but the offer of that reward stood and was even renewed.

When the Meccan army returned victorious from the battlefield of Uḥud, some men of the tribe of Hudhayl, which was allied to the Quraysh, came to present their felicitations. Amongst them was a member of the Banú-Liḥyán clan of the Hudhayl, named Sufyán Ibn Khálid. He had heard of the heavy losses which the House of 'Abda'd-Dár had sustained at Uḥud, and the reward of a hundred camels announced by Suláfah. Thereupon he concocted a plan for gaining that reward. This was to send seven men chosen from the clans of 'Aḍal and Qárih to Medina, who would profess Islám and ask the Prophet to send teachers to convert and teach them. They were to ensure that 'Áṣim Ibn Thábit was included in the group. Muḥammad chose six men to accompany the conspirators, including 'Áṣim. At ar-Rají', in the vicinity of Mecca, Sufyán Ibn Khálid, leading some two hundred warriors of the Banú-Liḥyán, attacked the small Muslim contingent. 'Áṣim and two of his companions were killed, and the others were captured. Although 'Abdu'lláh Ibn Táriq managed to sever the cord which tied his hands, he had no chance to escape and fell fighting his captors. The other two, Khubayb Ibn 'Adí and Zayd Ibn al-Dathinnah, were taken to Mecca and sold. Khubayb was bought by a daughter of al-Ḥárith Ibn 'Ámir, whose father had died at Badr. Zayd was sold to Ṣafwán Ibn Umayyah. It was the month of Dhu'l-Qa'dah, in which fighting was forbidden. So, Khubayb and Zayd were kept in bonds for two months, before being led to Tan'ím, away from the precincts of the House of Ka'bah, to be executed. Khubayb asked to be allowed to say a prayer of two *rik'ahs* (prostrations), and this became a tradition; in future, Muslims about to be executed would make the same request. They tied Khubayb to a cross but offered to spare him if he would renounce Muḥammad. This he spurned and laid a curse upon them. So strong were his words that they made the Quraysh tremble. Abú-Sufyán was there with Mu'áwíyah, his younger son, who would recall, when caliph, that his father threw him on the ground, as it was believed that the evil effects of a curse would pass by one lying prone. Sa'íd Ibn 'Ámir, later governor of Ḥimṣ in Syria, was subject to occasional swooning fits. On one occasion 'Umar Ibn al-Khaṭṭáb (then the second caliph) asked him what had come over him. Sa'íd replied that he was present at Khubayb's death; whenever he remembered that scene and Khubayb's words: 'O God! count them all, slay them all and let none be spared,' he would lose consciousness. Khubayb was speared to death, exclaiming before he died: 'O God! For me there is no Apostle save Muḥammad, upon whom be peace. And bear, my God, my salutation unto Him.' Zayd was decapitated by Naṣṭás, a slave of Ṣafwán, to avenge the death of Ṣafwán's father at Badr.

According to Ibn-al-Athír, Muḥammad sent two men to Mecca to assassinate Abú-Sufyán, but they were recognized and failed in their mission. It is also related that the Meccans kept the mangled body of Khubayb on the cross and watched over it. Muḥammad asked for volunteers to go to Mecca to rescue his body. Zubayr Ibn al-'Awwám (a Meccan, well known in his native town) and Miqdád Ibn al-Aswad volunteered and succeeded. 'Abdu'l-láh Ibn Anas was given the task of eliminating Sufyán Ibn Khálid, who not only had incited men of 'Aḍal and Qárih to go on a false errand to Medina, thus causing the death of six Muslims, but was now reported to be gathering a force to raid Medina.

Following the tragedy of ar-Rají', another disaster of even greater dimensions overtook the Muslims. 'Ámir Ibn Málik, the head of the clan of Banú-'Ámir Ibn Ṣa'ṣa'ah, who was known as Abú-Bará', came from Najd to Medina to renew his acquaintance with Muḥammad. He was a man advanced in years and wished to become a Muslim, but he was concerned about the reaction of his clan. Perhaps the Prophet would send teachers to propagate His Faith in Najd. But Muḥammad was reluctant to do this because of what had happened recently not far from Medina; Najd was more remote and the desert-dwellers there had shown no inclination towards Islám. Abú-Bará', however, was insistent and assured the Prophet that the Muslims would come to no harm, as they would be under his protection. Muḥammad sent forty men, according to Ibn-Hishám; seventy, according to aṭ-Ṭabarí. 'Ámir Ibn Ṭufayl, nephew to Abú-Bará', was sorely displeased at his uncle's initiative, but finding his own people loyal to the pledge of protection, he incited the clansmen of Banú-Sulaym to destroy the emissaries of Muḥammad. *En route*, the Muslims bivouacked by the side of a well, known as Bi'r-Ma'únah, about fifty miles from Medina. The men of Banú-Sulaym set upon them in force, and all were killed save two: 'Amr Ibn Umayyah and Ka'b Ibn Zayd. Making his way back to Medina, 'Amr came upon two men of the Banú-'Ámir Ibn Ṣa'ṣa'ah and killed them, although they were ignorant of the treachery of their chief's nephew. When the Prophet was apprised of 'Amr's hasty action He was angry and paid blood-money to their clan, because the murdered men were under His protection. Ka'b, the other Muslim who escaped, was severely wounded and left for dead, but he recovered sufficiently to reach Medina. A casualty of Bi'r-Ma'únah was 'Ámir Ibn Fuhayrah, the freedman of Abú-Bakr, who had emigrated with the Prophet and his former master from Mecca to Medina.

Within a matter of months, the Prophet had received three grievous setbacks,[1] and the effects in Medina were discernible. The Munáfiqún (Dissemblers) jeered openly at the misfortunes which had befallen the Muslims. Jews also were jubilant. According to Ibn-Hishám, the Jews of Banu'n-Naḍír plotted to murder Muḥammad. The occasion was a controversy between the Banu'n-Naḍír, who are said to have numbered a thousand, and the Banú-Qurayẓah, whose numbers have been estimated at seven hundred. An agreement between them had been repudiated by the latter, who maintained it to be at variance with the Law of the Torah. 'Abdu'lláh Ibn Ubayy, the chief man amongst the Munáfiqún, was allied to the Banu'n-Naḍír and championed their case. He went to Muḥammad and spoke in a haughty manner

[1] Uḥud (March), ar-Rají' (May), Bi'r-Ma'únah (July).

which offended the Prophet. Two verses in the Qur'án refer to this episode:

'O Messenger, let them not cause thee sorrow, who hasten to infidelity, either of those who say, "We believe" with their mouths, but whose hearts believe not, or the Jews who listen to lies and to other people, who have not come to thee. They pervert the words [of the Law] from their places and say: "If this is brought to thee, receive it; but if it be not brought to thee, then take heed [beware of receiving aught else]"; and for whomsoever God wisheth to bring low, thou shalt obtain naught from God. They whose hearts God doth not intend to cleanse shall suffer humiliation in this world, and severe chastisement in the next—they who listen to lies and consume the forbidden. Should they come to thee, judge betwixt them, or turn away from them. If thou turnest away nothing shall harm thee. But shouldst thou judge between them, judge justly, for verily God loves the just.' (vv. 45–6: *Súrat al-Má'idah*—'The Table'.)

Muḥammad found that the Banú-Qurayẓah were justified in their complaint and gave His verdict accordingly. But the Banu'n-Naḍír were resentful and considered it a deliberate affront. Ḥuyy Ibn Akhṭab, a vindictive opponent of the Prophet, dwelt with the Banu'n-Naḍír and persuaded them to attempt the life of Muḥammad. One day, Muḥammad had gone to the settlement of this Jewish clan to carry out certain transactions. Finding Him resting against their wall, they were about to hurl down a piece of rock to crush Him, when He suddenly got up and walked away. Traditionalists say that the Angel Gabriel informed Him of their evil intent. In any case, the Banu'n-Naḍír were foiled.

Muḥammad soon came to the conclusion that the presence of a large colony of Jews, smouldering with hate and discontent, and backed by a relatively powerful body of Dissemblers, constituted a permanent menace to the peace of Medina. He was also aware that the Banu'n-Naḍír had clandestine dealings with the idolaters. And so an ultimatum was delivered to them to leave Medina and seek a home elsewhere. Of course 'Abdu'lláh Ibn Ubayy was furious and, at the risk of offending the Prophet yet again, tried hard to obtain concessions for his Jewish allies. He went so far as to encourage them to reject the ultimatum and resist the Prophet with all their strength, promising that he and his men would come to their aid. Súrah lix of the Qur'án—

Súrat al-Ḥashr ('The Mustering')—foreshadows and casts light on the course of events:

'Hast thou not observed the Dissemblers telling their brethren —the people of the Book—who are unbelievers: "If ye are expelled, we shall go forth with you, and we shall never obey anyone in regard to you; and if they fight you, we shall rise to aid you." And God bears witness that verily they are liars. Should those be expelled, they will not go out with them, and should those be fought, they will not aid them. And even if they give aid to them, they will turn their backs on them, and then those will be left unaided.' (vv. 11–12.)

The Banu'n-Naḍír defied the Prophet, but after a fortnight's siege they realized that resistance was useless. 'Abdu'lláh Ibn Ubayy did not come to their aid; their fellow believers of the Banú-Qurayẓah held aloof, for they had been the aggrieved party in their contentions and Muḥammad had ruled in their favour. The Banu'n-Naḍír now tried to negotiate favourable terms. But Muḥammad would allow them to take of their goods and chattels only what they could load on their camels. They asked for additional concessions, but the Prophet promptly refused and, in the end, they had to accept the terms offered in the first instance. They left Medina with an outward appearance of joy and jubilation, their minstrels playing and singing as they rode out of their oasis. But two of them, named 'Imrán and Binyámín (Benjamin), became Muslims and remained in possession of their property. After the departure of the Banu'n-Naḍír, Muḥammad told the Anṣár that, if they agreed, He would turn over their houses and groves to the Muhájirún, who would then cease to be a burden to them. Sa'd Ibn Mu'ádh and Sa'd Ibn 'Ubádah, the chiefs of the Aws and the Khazraj, respectively, gave consent, and even stated that the Muhájirún could still share with them everything they had. Muḥammad gave utterance to this prayer: 'O God! Show mercy to the Anṣár, and the sons of the Anṣár, and the sons of the sons of the Anṣár.' The *Súrat al-Ḥashr* ('The Mustering') commends and illumines the generous ways of the Anṣár:

And those who made their dwelling in
the abode, and in belief, before them,
love whosoever has emigrated to them,
not finding in their breasts any need

> for what they have been given, and
> preferring others above themselves, even
> though poverty be their portion. And
> whoso is guarded against the avarice
> of his own soul, those—they are
> the prosperers.[2]

However, Muḥammad gave a portion to two of the very poor Anṣár: Abú-Dujánah (the hero of Uḥud) and Sahl Ibn Ḥaníf. The expulsion of the Banu'n-Naḍír took place in September 625.

Abú-Sufyán, it will be recalled, threatened Muḥammad at Uḥud with another encounter at Badr in the coming year. In April 626, the Prophet took a force of fifteen hundred men to meet the Quraysh, but the Meccans did not come. Instead, the Muslims, who had also brought merchandise with them, participated in the annual fair held in the month of Dhu'l-Qa'dah at Badr, and returned home much richer than before, having sold all their goods.

In that same year, the fourth of the Hijrah, the Prophet forbade the use of wine.[3] An earlier revelation, contained in súrah xvi, 69—*Súrat an-Naḥl* ('The Bee')—had not forbidden the use of intoxicants and seemed even to have commended them:

> And of the fruits of the palms and the vines, you take
> therefrom an intoxicant
> and a provision fair.
> Surely in that is a sign for a people who understand.[2]

But because Muslims sometimes attended to their daily prayer while inebriate, hardly conscious of what they were saying, a warning was given to them, as conveyed in súrah iv—*an-Nisá'* ('Women'): 'O true believers, come not to prayers when ye are drunk, until ye understand what ye say . . .' (v. 46.)[4] However, the situation remained unresolved and probably chaotic until the Prophet pronounced His interdiction. 'They will ask thee concerning wine and arrow-shuffling;[5] say, "In both there is great sin and profit for the people, but their sinfulness is greater than their profit."' (Súrah ii, 216: *al-Baqarah*—'The Cow'.)

[2] Translation by A. J. Arberry. (lix,9.)
[3] Some commentators have put the date as much as four years later.
[4] Translation by George Sale.
[5] A kind of gambling.

Not long after the battle of Badr, Muḥammad married Ḥafṣah, the widowed daughter of 'Umar Ibn al-Khaṭṭáb, whom 'Umar himself requested the Prophet to marry. Ḥafṣah's husband was one of the fourteen Muslims who fell at Badr. Following the battle of Uḥud, Muḥammad was wedded to Zaynab Bint Khuzaymah, another such widow. Zaynab had only a few more months to live. Umm-Salamah, who, together with her husband, Abú-Salamah, had emigrated to Ethiopia and was another widow of Uḥud, became Muḥammad's sixth wife. But it is Muḥammad's marriage to Zaynab Bint Jaḥsh, in March 627, that has invited harsh criticism from Western scholars. Zaynab, sister to 'Abdu'lláh who died at Badr, was also a cousin of the Prophet. She had been married against her wishes to Zayd, the adopted son and a freedman of Muḥammad. It is suggested that this marriage was distasteful to her because of Zayd's inferior status. There is an improbable story that one day Muḥammad called on Zayd, who was not at home; finding Zaynab not fully dressed and seeing her thus, it is said that Muḥammad fell in love with her, and when Zayd heard of it he divorced his wife that Muḥammad might marry her. It must be remembered that being Muḥammad's cousin and married to his adopted son, she had been known to Him over many years. Certainly, it could not have been 'love at first sight'. Moreover, Zaynab's youth had long passed and she was only two or three years short of her fortieth year. Apparently, 'Abdu'lláh Ibn Ubayy and people of his kind in Medina looked askance at this marriage of the Prophet, chiefly because Zaynab had been married first to His adopted son. Several verses (36–40) in the thirty-third súrah—*al-Aḥzáb* ('The Confederates')—shed light upon the circumstances of this marriage, and the position of the Prophet in relation to the Muslim community:

> It is not for any believer, man or
> woman, when God and His Messenger
> have decreed a matter, to have the choice
> in the affair. Whosoever disobeys
> God and His Messenger has gone astray
> into manifest error.

> When thou saidst to him whom God had blessed
> and thou hadst favoured, 'Keep thy wife to thyself,

and fear God,' and thou wast concealing
within thyself what God should reveal,
fearing other men; and God has better right
for thee to fear Him. So when Zaid[6] had accomplished
what he would of her, then We gave her in marriage
to thee, so that there should not be any fault
in the believers, touching the wives of their
adopted sons, when they have accomplished
what they would of them; and God's commandment
    must be performed.
There is no fault in the Prophet, touching what
God has ordained for him—God's wont with those
who passed away before; and God's commandment
    is doom decreed;
who were delivering the Messages of God,
and were fearing Him, and fearing not any one
except Him; and God suffices
    as a reckoner.
Muhammad is not the father of any one
of your men, but the Messenger of God,
and the Seal of the Prophets; God has knowledge
    of everything.

(Translation by A. J. Arberry.)

A Muslim was allowed no more than four wives, but a special dispensation granted to Muḥammad alone permitted Him to exceed that number. It is contained in the same súrah—*al-Aḥzáb*: 'O prophet, we have allowed thee thy wives unto whom thou hast given their dower, and also [the slaves] which thy right hand possesseth, of the [booty] which God hath granted thee; and the daughters of thy uncle, and the daughters of thy aunts, both on thy father's side and on thy mother's side, who have fled with thee [from Mecca], and any [other] believing woman, if she give herself unto the prophet; in case the prophet desireth to take her to wife. [This is] a peculiar privilege [granted] unto thee, above the rest of the true believers.'[7] (v. 49.)

Sir John Glubb points out that 'It is, however, worthy of note that of all his wives, only Aisha was a virgin when he married

[6] Zayd is the only Muslim mentioned by name in the Qur'án.
[7] Translation by George Sale. Words which Sale italicized are not in the text, and are here shown in brackets.

her. Zainab bint Jahash was a divorced wife and all the rest were widows, some of them, it would seem, not particularly attractive. Moreover, the Apostle had married Khadija when he was twenty-five and she was a widow considerably older than he was. He had remained completely faithful to her for twenty-four years until her death.'[8] And Sir John further states: 'It is noticeable that the Apostle, when a young man, had six children by Khadija, yet he had no children by the twelve women who followed her, except for a son by Mary, the Egyptian concubine. Most of his wives, though not in their first youth, were capable of bearing children. In Medina, Muhammad had less and less leisure time and must often have been mentally and physically exhausted, especially as he was in his fifties and latterly over sixty. These are not the circumstances under which men are interested in the indulgence of extreme sexuality.'[9]

Professor Montgomery Watt's comment is: 'Most of Muḥammad's own marriages, as well as those he arranged for his daughters and close associates, are found to have political reasons of one kind or another.'[10]

A personal loss for the Prophet in the fourth year of the Hijrah was the death of a grandson—'Abdu'lláh, the son of 'Uthmán Ibn 'Affán. He was six years old. His mother was Ruqayyah, the first of the two daughters of Muḥammad married to 'Uthmán. Some three months later, in January 626, Muḥammad had another grandson: Ḥusayn was born to 'Alí and Fáṭimah.

The fifth year of the Hijrah (2 June 626–22 May 627) witnessed the investment of Medina. But prior to that event, which shattered the morale of the Meccans and assured their total defeat, there were expeditions, led by the Prophet Himself, that had remarkable effects. In June 626 Muḥammad set out on a punitive expedition against the Ghaṭafán, whose hostility remained unabated. He went as far as Dhát-ar-Riqá' in the Ghaṭafán territory, some sixty miles from Medina. But the nomads had no heart for a pitched battle and melted away. The Muslims returned home with large booty. The next expedition, in August, to Dúmata'l-Jandal (the present-day al-Jawf) was of particular significance. This oasis is some four hundred miles to the north of Medina.

[8] *The Life and Times of Muhammad*, p. 237.
[9] ibid., p. 239.
[10] *Muhammad, Prophet and Statesman*, pp. 102–3.

The news that robbers infested it was the cause of the Prophet's leading an army of a thousand men all that distance from his base, although never before had he mounted an expedition to such a remote place. The strength of his position was demonstrated by his confidence that he could venture so far from His city, in order to suppress lawlessness and ensure the safety of the trade route. The intelligence He had received proved to be correct and the robbers were put to flight.

Apart from achieving its objective, this expedition made a deep impression on the nomads of those northern reaches of Arabia. Within three months the tribe of Muzaynah came to offer its allegiance, as one body, to the Prophet.

The investment of Medina, which took place in April 627, towards the end of the fifth year of the Hijrah, marked the last effort of the Meccans to break the power of Muḥammad. The previous year they had failed to meet the Prophet at Badr, but now they were goaded into action by the dislodged Jewish leaders of the Banu'n-Naḍír and others of their co-religionists, who feared that the remnants of their colonies in Arabia might soon be overwhelmed; particularly active among them were Ḥuyy Ibn Akhṭab, Kinánah Ibn ar-Rabí' and Sallám Ibn Abi'l-Ḥuqayq. Some twenty of these Jewish leaders travelled to Mecca and foregathered with a number of prominent Qurayshites in the House of Ka'bah, where they made a pact to fight Muḥammad to the bitter end. Next they visited the intractable Ghaṭafán and promised them a good share of the date crop of Khaybar, should they join an expedition against Muḥammad. The Ghaṭafán readily agreed to fall in with their plans. Further alliances were sought and made with the Banú-Asad, the Banú-Murrah, the Banú-Ashja', the Banú-Aslam and the Banú-Sulaym.

Abú-Sufyán came out of Mecca with four thousand men, and as he led the Meccans towards Medina contingents from various tribes came to join his army, until together they numbered ten thousand. The strength of the confederates was staggering. Had Muḥammad marched out of Medina to engage them in battle, it is likely the confederates would have won the day. As it was, time was too short for the Prophet to seek aid from friendly clans and He had to rely entirely on the resources of His own city. He took counsel with His followers. 'Abdu'lláh Ibn Ubayy, who was present, gave the same advice he had given before the battle of Uḥud, and this time Muḥammad complied with it. He decided not to leave Medina, but to stay within and fortify the city against attack. Next, Salmán the Persian presented a scheme for defence. Persians, he said, dig moats or trenches around their towns to check the advance of an enemy. For the Arabs this was a novel idea, but they speedily got down to the task. Muḥammad Himself worked along with His followers. Implements were borrowed from the Banú-Qurayẓah. That side of Medina which was flanked by this Jewish settlement was left unguarded, because Muḥammad counted on the Jews to observe strict neutrality.

It was the month of Ramaḍán and, although it was springtime, under the circumstances of hard physical labour fasting was onerous. One day the Prophet, enfeebled and exhausted, was lying prone in the mosque, when He was informed by Salmán that in a part of the trench they had come upon a stone which resisted all their efforts. Bará' Ibn 'Ázib of the Anṣár, who at the time was no more than fifteen years old, has related that the Prophet came, took a pickaxe and, with three strokes, demolished the stone. According to Ibn-Hi<u>sh</u>ám, Muḥammad told Salmán that, at the first stroke, He was given dominion over Yemen; at the second, Syria and the lands beyond in the West were opened up to Him; and at the third, He reached out to the kingdoms of the East. His followers, He promised, would achieve these wonders after Him, and would conquer these realms. Dissemblers, hearing that, chuckled and said: 'Listen to this man! He is cornered in Ya<u>th</u>rib, is digging a ditch to take refuge behind, but boasts of mastery over Yemen and the dominions of Kisrá (Chosroes) and Qayṣar (Caesar).'

Even as the Dissemblers scoffed and sneered at the Prophet, in this period of rising doubt and uncertainty, He was revealing the following: 'Say, "O God, the Lord of the Kingdom! Thou givest the Kingdom to whomsoever Thou willest, and Thou takest away the Kingdom from whomsoever Thou willest; and Thou exaltest whomsoever Thou willest, and Thou abasest whomsoever Thou willest. In Thy hands Thou holdest that which is good. Verily, Thou holdest dominion over all things." ' (Súrah iii, 26: *Ál-'Imrán*—'The House of 'Imrán'.)

One incident, which occurred in the very early days of digging the moat, was indicative of the revived hopes of those within

Medina who yearned for the Prophet's downfall. He had placed the women and children in a quarter of the city which was well fortified and protected. As soon as He went with His army of three thousand men to take positions under Mount Sal', a man named Najdán ran into the quarter of the Banú-Ḥárithah, where these women and children had been lodged, and ordered them out at sword-point. It was an ugly situation as a motley crowd was gathering, but the intervention of a certain Ẓáfir Ibn Ráfi' saved the day. The intruder was cut down.

There is a story told by Jábir of those days of trench-digging that echoes the story of Jesus and the loaves. Many traditions are traced back to Jábir of the Anṣár, whose father, 'Abdu'lláh Ibn 'Amr, died at Uḥud. One day, he related, he saw such clear signs of hunger on Muḥammad's face that he hurried home, killed a goat which he had, and told his wife to cook it and to bake some bread; he was going to ask the Prophet to have His evening meal with them. At the close of the day, when the work was over and the men were dispersing, Jábir approached the Prophet to invite Him to his home, together with a few others. But Muḥammad called out to the thousand men who had been engaged in digging and told them that Jábir had prepared a feast for them. All went, they were all fed, and still some food remained, which the Prophet said should be taken to the people who had not been there.

The task of digging the moat was completed before the confederates arrived at Medina on March 31st. They must have been amazed by what they saw—something no Arab had hitherto experienced; a deep moat barred their way and, on the other side of it, archers prepared to shoot whoever dared to jump into the trench, where trespassers would be at total disadvantage and helpless. Abú-Sufyán's thousand camels and three hundred horses were now of no use to his four thousand men. Indeed, they were encumbrances. The idolaters had no choice but to set up camp and lay siege to Medina. But that proved their undoing. It is one thing to keep a large body of men and beasts constantly on the move, only halting for a foray; but quite another to hold them in one place, over a period of time, with insufficient provisions and no way of obtaining food and fodder in adequate quantities. They settled down facing Muḥammad and his men, not knowing what next to do. The easy task of overrunning Medina was now a dream.

In the meantime, Ḥuyy Ibn Akhṭab, the Jewish leader before

mentioned, presented himself at the gate of the stronghold of the Banú-Qurayẓah. Ka'b Ibn Asad, the chief of that settlement, shouted at him to take himself off, for he was a man of ill omen who had already led the Banu'n-Naḍír into disaster. Furthermore, Ka'b reminded him, the Banú-Qurayẓah had a pact with Muḥammad, had no quarrel with Him, and had always found Him just, truthful and loyal. But Ḥuyy would not go away. He had come, he declared, with great tidings—a large army of confederates had arrived who had it in their power to overthrow Muḥammad and efface all traces of His work. Such an opportunity should not be missed. Still Ka'b would have no truck with him until Ḥuyy resorted to ridicule, attributing his reluctance to open the gate to the thought of having another mouth to feed. Thus chided and riled, Ka'b let the son of Akhṭab enter the settlement and, by so doing, sealed the fate of his own people, which was to be grim indeed.

It was this Ḥuyy who had gone to Mecca with a number of like-minded Jews to scheme the destruction of Muḥammad. When the idolaters of Mecca had asked whether their religion was superior to Muḥammad's, the Jews, although monotheists, had replied that it was. Their abominable statement receives severe condemnation in the fourth súrah of the Qur'án—*an-Nisá'* ('Women'): 'Hast thou not observed those to whom a Book was allotted, expressing belief in Jibt and Ṭághút, telling the infidels they are better guided in the path than those who are believers. These are accursed by God, and for whomsoever God hath cursed, there shall be no helper.' (vv. 54–5.)

Despite vigorous protests by such men as Zuhayr Ibn Báṭá and Yásín Ibn Qays, leading figures among the Jews of the Banú-Qurayẓah, Ka'b Ibn Asad yielded to the blandishments of Ḥuyy, decided to repudiate his pact with Muḥammad, and threw in his lot with the idolaters. When Muḥammad was apprised of Ḥuyy's visit to the stronghold of the Banú-Qurayẓah, He sent the two Sa'ds, one the son of Mu'ádh, the head of the Aws, and the other the son of 'Ubádah, the head of the Khazraj, to warn Ka'b and counsel him not to break his word. They were accompanied by three other prominent men of the Anṣár, but returned to say that the Banú-Qurayẓah had gone the way of the 'Aḍal and the Qárih. Those clans, it will be recalled, betrayed the Muslims at ar-Rají'. The defection of the Banú-Qurayẓah was not a light matter. Relying on their loyalty, Muḥammad had left that side of the city totally undefended. He had to find a way—some way—to counter whatever evil designs their chief had in mind. Would Ka'b give the besiegers a passage into Medina through his settlement? Would he mount an attack on the Muslims? These were imponderables, but for the time being it seemed that Ka'b was doing no more than seeing to his own defences.

A man of the Ghaṭafán, named Nu'aym Ibn Mas'úd, had been converted to Islám only a few days before the arrival of the confederate army outside Medina. Neither the Jews nor the idolaters knew this, and the Prophet accepted Nu'aym's offer to make use of this fact to cause a rift between them. Nu'aym went first to the Banú-Qurayẓah; winning their confidence, he suggested that to obtain continued support from the idolaters, particularly the Meccans, and to ensure their own safety, they should ask for hostages from the Quraysh, who would not then abandon them to their fate. Then Nu'aym went to the confederate camp and warned them to be on guard against the trickery of the Jews. They would ask the Quraysh for hostages, he said, but would hand them over to Muḥammad in order to ingratiate themselves with Him and avert His vengeance. In due course the Banú-Qurayẓah were told to attack the Muslims on the south side of the oasis; they asked first for hostages and their demand was rejected. Mutual suspicion, engendered by Nu'aym, kept the Quraysh and the Banú-Qurayẓah apart and the latter out of the war.

The Prophet offered the Ghaṭafán one-third of the date product of Medina should they break away from the Quraysh and return home. Their leaders asked for half the harvest. At this point Sa'd Ibn Mu'ádh intervened to enquire whether this was a command from God or the Prophet's own idea to buy off the Ghaṭafán. On learning that it was Muḥammad's own, Sa'd said that when they were idolaters, the Ghaṭafán paid for their requirements; they would not now receive them free.

The whole episode of the investment of Medina—the Ghazwah of the Trench (*Khandaq*), or the Ghazwah of the Confederates (*al-Aḥzáb*), as Muslim historians have it—lasted only twenty-five days, but they were laborious days because nothing conclusive seemed to happen. Almost no casualties resulted from the activities of the archers, and the circumstances of the siege and the inability of either side to bring the other to its knees were frustrating. The Muslims had to be constantly on the defence, poised for action to repel attacks. The confederates could not sustain a general assault, continuous enough to be effective, nor could they find any way to penetrate into Medina.

One day ʻAmr Ibn ʻAbduwud, a giant of a man, accompanied by four other prominent warriors of the Quraysh, managed to make their horses jump the trench at a narrow section. There was much tumult and great consternation. ʻAlí induced the son of ʻAbduwud to dismount and fight him in single combat. ʻAmr was worsted and his companions fled, one of whom was Hubayrah, the husband of Umm-Hání, ʻAlí's sister. Nawfal Ibn ʻAbdi'l-láh could not make a getaway, was pelted with stones by the Muslims, and begged to be put out of his misery. ʻAlí gave him the *coup de grâce*. ʻIkrimah, the son of Abú-Jahl, made good his escape. It was on this occasion that Saʻd Ibn Muʻádh, the chief of the Aws, was wounded in the arm by an arrow; it was a wound which eventually caused his death. Like his namesake, the chief of the Khazraj, Saʻd was a pillar of society in Medina and his death was to be a severe blow to the Muslim community.

The total casualties of the Ghazwah of the Trench were only nine: six of the Anṣár and three of the Quraysh.

It was the inclemency of the weather which finally shattered the great confederacy against Muḥammad. Already unseasonably cold, one night a tempest raged and played havoc in their camp. Without hope of action on the part of the Banú-Qurayẓah, and having no way to replenish their dwindling food stocks, the Ghaṭafán gave up. Despite opposition by such leaders as ʻIkrimah, Abú-Sufyán raised the siege and led his men back to Mecca. The last attempt of the Quraysh to destroy Muḥammad had failed.

The confederates had gone, but the Banú-Qurayẓah were still there and secure in their stronghold. Guilty of betrayal, they could easily have wrecked the work of the Prophet if a subtle stratagem had not paralysed their will to act. The course they might take in future contingencies was highly problematical. What was certain was that they had proved fickle and could not be trusted; the security of Medina demanded their expulsion. Muḥammad turned His attention to them as soon as He was assured by intelligence brought to Him that the confederates had gone for good and that their alliance had dissolved. The Banú-Qurayẓah soon became aware of their predicament. It was either Ḥuyy Ibn

Akhṭab, their evil genius, or Ka'b Ibn Asad, their chief, or the two together, who presented the clan with three possible courses of action: to submit to Muḥammad and become converts to His Faith; to defy Muḥammad and fight to the last, first killing their women and children to spare them slavery in case of defeat; or to rush out of their fastness on the morrow, which was a Sabbath, and fall upon the Muslims around them. None of these proved acceptable. They would not profess belief in Muḥammad, they could not put to death their women and children, and they found action on the Sabbath abhorrent. In the old days, the Banú-Qurayẓah had been allied to the Aws, and now they asked Muḥammad to send a man of the Aws, named Abú-Lubábah, to visit them. It is related that this Abú-Lubábah indicated to them, by some gesture, that if they came out of their stronghold Muḥammad would exterminate them; then, realizing his disloyalty to the Prophet, he hurried to the mosque and tied himself to a pillar, to do penance. (He was forgiven before long.) However, there is a contradiction here with the facts as they emerged later, because, as we shall see, the extermination of the male members of the Banú-Qurayẓah was not decreed by Muḥammad but by the dying Sa'd Ibn Mu'ádh.

The Banú-Qurayẓah sat behind their walls and the Muslims maintained a siege. Although chroniclers speak of fighting, there do not seem to have been many casualties. Neither side could achieve victory, but the position of the Banú-Qurayẓah was much the weaker, because they were hemmed in and lacked the resources which Medina enjoyed. At last, they offered to leave Medina as the Banu'n-Naḍír had done. But Muḥammad would have no conditions attached to their surrender. Finally they agreed to come out and abide by the judgement of an arbiter named by Muḥammad. The Prophet appointed Sa'd Ibn Mu'ádh, the chief of the Aws, to decide their fate. He had been an ally and a supporter of these Jews. Now a dying man and too feeble to move, as the result of his recent wound, Sa'd was mounted on a donkey and held by two men. Thus he was brought to the mosque. Men of the Aws beseeched him to be gentle in his judgement. But stern and unbending, Sa'd pronounced the sentence of death on the male members of the Banú-Qurayẓah. Their women and children were to be sold as slaves, and their property divided among the Muslims. Estimates vary as to the number who perished in that mass execution; it may have been about seven hundred. An old man, Zubayr Ibn Báṭá, had once saved the life of Thábit Ibn Qays Ibn al-Shammás, a follower of the Prophet. Thábit asked Muḥammad to spare Zubayr for his sake and the Prophet granted his wish, but Zubayr preferred to die. Muḥammad married one of the women of the Banú-Qurayẓah, named Rayḥánah Bint 'Amr.

Professor Montgomery Watt comments thus on the fate of the Banú-Qurayẓah:

'Some European writers have criticized this sentence for what they call its savage and inhuman character . . .

'In the case of the Muslims involved in the execution what was uppermost in their minds was whether allegiance to the Islamic community was to be set above and before all other alliances and attachments . . . Those of the Aws who wanted leniency for Qurayẓah seem to have regarded them as having been unfaithful only to Muḥammad and not to the Aws. This attitude implies that these men regarded themselves as being primarily members of the Aws (or of some clan of it) and not of the Islamic community. There is no need to suppose that Muḥammad brought pressure to bear on Sa'd ibn-Mu'ādh to punish Qurayẓah as he did. A far-sighted man like Sa'd must have realized that to allow tribal or clan allegiance to come before Islamic allegiance would lead to a renewal of the fratricidal strife from which they hoped the coming of Muḥammad had delivered Medina. As he was being led into Muḥammad's presence to pronounce his sentence, Sa'd is said to have made a remark to the effect that, with death not far from him, he must consider above all doing his duty to God and the Islamic community, even at the expense of former alliances.'[11]

Professor Montgomery Watt further remarks:

'After the elimination of the Qurayẓah no important clan of Jews was left in Medina, though there were probably several small groups. One Jewish merchant is named who purchased some of the women and children of Qurayẓah! . . .

'The continuing presence of at least a few Jews in Medina is an argument against the view sometimes put forward by European scholars that in the second year after the Hijrah Muḥammad adopted a policy of clearing all Jews out of Medina just because they were Jews, and that he carried out this policy with ever-increasing severity. It was not Muḥammad's way to have policies of this

[11] *Muhammad, Prophet and Statesman*, pp. 173–4.

kind. He had a balanced view of the fundamentals of the contemporary situation and of his long-term aims, and in the light of this he moulded his day-to-day plans in accordance with the changing factors in current events. The occasions of his attacks on the first two Jewish clans were no more than occasions; but there were also deep underlying reasons. The Jews in general by their verbal criticisms of the Qur'ānic revelation were trying to undermine the foundation of the whole Islamic community; and they were also giving political support to Muḥammad's enemies and to opponents such as the Hypocrites. In so far as the Jews abandoned these forms of hostile activity Muḥammad allowed them to live in Medina unmolested.'[12]

[12] ibid., pp. 174–5.

12

The Truce of al-Ḥudaybíyyah

WITH the abject failure of the confederates and the elimination of the Banú-Qurayẓah, the Islamic community of Medina attained a degree of security not known before. It seemed certain that never again would a hostile combination pose a menace to the City of the Prophet. But within the city itself Dissemblers, although now bereft of massive support, still jeered and snarled. Muḥammad left them severely alone to follow their forlorn course; they could no longer harm the community. He looked well beyond Medina to areas where other antagonists lurked. Thus in the sixth year of the Hijrah (23 May 627 to 10 May 628), in the month of July, He set out to punish the Banú-Liḥyán for their treachery at ar-Rají'. But the Banú-Liḥyán disappeared into the hills and there was no meeting in the field. Muḥammad visited His mother's grave on this occasion.

During the following months there were a number of expeditions led by such prominent men as 'Alí, Zayd, Muḥammad Ibn Maslamah, 'Ukkáshah Ibn Muḥṣin, 'Abda'r-Raḥmán Ibn 'Awf and Abú-'Ubaydah Ibn al-Jarráḥ, with varying degrees of success and also setbacks. The one in which Muḥammad Himself was involved had a small beginning: it has been called the Ghazwah of Dhí-Qarad. 'Uyaynah Ibn Ḥiṣn, the Ghaṭafán chieftain to whom, in the days of the Trench, Muḥammad had offered a third of the date harvest of Medina, feeling aggrieved that his onslaught on Medina, in the company of the Quraysh, had brought him no gain or advantage, came on a lightning raid and carried away a number of camels that belonged to the Prophet. In the skirmish some of the herdsmen were killed. When the news reached Medina a few men hurried to the scene of action and the Prophet followed with a small force. There was no pitched battle, but in the course of the hit-and-run tactics employed, 'Abda'r-Raḥmán, the son of the chieftain, and three others of the Ghaṭafán were killed. A Muslim was also slain. Although a number of the camels were retrieved, the raiders escaped with the rest. The Prophet stopped at a well called Dhí-Qarad—hence the appellation of *ghazwah*. A Muslim woman, who had been abducted with the camels, escaped her captors. When she reached the camp of the Prophet she approached Him with the plea that she had vowed to sacrifice the camel which she rode, should she ever reach safety. Muḥammad told her, with a smile, that she was relieved from her vow because the camel was His, not hers to sacrifice, and moreover it was a poor requital for a camel that had brought her safely home.

Zayd seems to have been particularly active in that sixth year of the Hijrah. He led a trading caravan to Syria—the first ever to start out from Medina. He also led a successful raid on a Meccan caravan. In that Meccan party was Abu'l-'Áṣ, husband of Zaynab, a daughter of the Prophet. We have seen that Abu'l-'Áṣ was taken prisoner at Badr and ransomed. As he had promised, he sent his wife to Medina. And now he managed to reach Medina to seek her help. Zaynab hurried to her father, before the Prophet had any intelligence of the arrival of a stranger, to say that she had given *jiwár*—protection—to her husband. Her word was honoured and Muslims returned the goods belonging to Abu'l-'Áṣ. On this, he went to Mecca, gave his clients the merchandise that was theirs, settled his affairs, and then returned to Medina to give his allegiance to the Prophet. His conversion must have gladdened Muḥammad greatly, for not only was Abu'l-'Áṣ his son-in-law, but he had been a favourite nephew of Khadíjah.

Zayd's own Syrian caravan met with disaster. The Banú-Badr, a clan of the Ghaṭafán, intercepted it, killed a number of the Muslims and carried away the merchandise. Zayd, himself, fled to Medina. Muḥammad put a force under his command to seek out the raiders. At Wádi'l-Qurá', Zayd overtook them and avenged his rout.

An expedition led by 'Abda'r-Raḥmán Ibn 'Awf is particularly worthy of note. His destination was the oasis of Dúmata'l-Jandal, where the Prophet Himself had gone the previous year to flush out robbers. The people of the Banú-Kiláb received him in peace. He stayed three days with them, during which Aṣbagh, their chief, who was a Christian, together with a number of his clansmen, espoused Islám. The rest agreed to pay *jizyah* or 'tithes'. 'Abda'r-Raḥmán married a daughter of the chieftain and returned to Medina with his force untouched by warfare.

In December 627, Muḥammad came to hear that al-Ḥárith Ibn Abí-Ḍirár, the chief of the Banu'l-Muṣṭaliq, a clan of the Khuzá'ah, was gathering a force and seeking allies to attack Medina. There appears to have been some uncertainty regarding his plans, however, and Buraydah, who had ridden into Medina with the Prophet's standard on the day He arrived there, volunteered to discover the intentions of the chief. He approached al-Ḥárith, pretending that he had come to join forces with him for the battle against Muḥammad. Al-Ḥárith was overjoyed and told Buraydah of his preparations, who, in turn, hastened to inform the Prophet. Muḥammad took His army to the area of al-Muraysí', a well which served the people of the Banu'l-Muṣṭaliq. Their resistance was soon overcome, and large numbers were taken prisoner, including a daughter of al-Ḥárith. Her captor, a certain Thábit Ibn Qays, led her to the Prophet to discuss her ransom. Once in the presence of Muḥammad, she announced that she had become a Muslim. Muḥammad offered to pay her ransom, gave her the name of Juwayríyah, and married her. Seeing that the daughter of al-Ḥárith was now a wife of the Prophet, Muslims felt that her relatives, whom they had captured, ought not to be kept in bondage and freed them all. Next, al-Ḥárith himself came to the Prophet and declared his belief in Him. Muḥammad gave Juwayríyah the option of returning to her clan with her father or of going to Medina with Him. She gladly chose the latter.

On the way back to Medina, two events occurred which were of considerable import. While the Muslims were bivouacked by a well, a Ghifárí man in the service of 'Umar and a man related to the Anṣár both came to draw water, and there arose a dispute between them. Sinán, the Juhaní ally of the Anṣár, was wounded and called on the Medinites to come to his aid. And finding himself in peril, 'Umar's groom solicited help from the Muhájirún. Some of the chroniclers say that the two parties fought each other and, even more serious, that blood was shed. Others make no mention of a passage of arms between the Muslims of Meccan origin and the Anṣár of Medina. They speak only of a man named Ji'ál who was creating such a disturbance that a clash seemed inevitable, but others begged Sinán to forgive the aggressive Ghifárí groom, which he did. The matter would have rested there had it not been for ʻAbdu'lláh Ibn Ubayy, who took Jiʻál to task and was rude to him. Jiʻál would not bear meekly the lashes of ʻAbdu'lláh's tongue and retorted in kind. Whereupon, the Dissembler became exceedingly angry and told his compatriots that they were now reaping what they had sown: they had let these Meccans into their town, shared their possessions with them, and provided them with houses and occupations, only to make them insolent and arrogant. 'Fatten your dog,' he said, 'just to devour you.' And he uttered a veiled threat that he would expel Muḥammad from Medina. Zayd Ibn Arqam, a youth of the Anṣár, apparently under fifteen years of age, heard ʻAbdu'l-láh's threat, and reported his words to the Prophet. Muḥammad was disinclined to accept them as true and told Zayd that he might have misheard what the son of Ubayy had said. But Zayd was adamant, although a number of Medinites reprimanded him severely for having accused so unashamedly an eminent man of his people. ʻUmar Ibn al-K͟haṭṭáb, impetuous as ever, asked permission to behead the dissembling ʻAbdu'lláh. Muḥammad refused his request and waited. Then He received a revelation which testified to Zayd's veracity. By now ʻAbdu'lláh was protesting his innocence, and his own son was offering to rid the community of his troublesome father. Muḥammad, however, would not sanction it. Yet in spite of his loud protestations, ʻAbdu'lláh soon found another opportunity to deride and belittle the Prophet.

Whenever Muḥammad led an expedition, He was usually accompanied by one (and sometimes two) of His wives. During this *g͟hazwah* against the Banu'l-Muṣṭaliq both ʻÁ'is͟hah and Umm-Salamah were with the Prophet. On the return journey, at the last halt before Medina, ʻÁ'is͟hah lost a necklace and went in search of it. When she came back the army had moved on. As the curtains were drawn round her howdah, her absence had gone unnoticed. All that ʻÁ'is͟hah could do, under the circumstances, was to sit by the wayside and wait for help. It being still before daybreak ʻÁ'is͟hah fell asleep. In the meantime a handsome youth, Ṣafwán Ibn Muʻṭal, was lingering in the area where the army had bivouacked. On the instructions of the Prophet, he was keeping an eye on any property left behind, to be collected and restored to its owners. As Ṣafwán came up, he noticed what seemed to be a bundle, and on approaching the spot, to his astonishment he realized it was a woman sitting on the ground, and of all women it was 'Á'ishah, the wife of the Prophet. Although highly embarrassed, he had no alternative but to make his camel kneel, dismount and let 'Á'ishah ride it. Holding the halter of the camel, he guided it safely home, to the surprise of the beholders.

Again the matter would have ended there, if gossip-mongers had not been at work—and chief among them was 'Abdu'lláh Ibn Ubayy. 'Á'ishah herself was blissfully unaware of the monstrous insinuations, and could not understand Muḥammad's aloofness. When she learned of them from the mother of Misṭaḥ, whose own son had had a hand in spreading rumours, she asked for permission to retire to her father's house. Muḥammad granted her request. The sneers of 'Abdu'lláh Ibn Ubayy were particularly wounding. Muḥammad was sad and withdrawn and the situation was tense. The two main branches of the Anṣár, the Aws and the Khazraj, almost took to arms, because 'Abdu'lláh the Dissembler was of the Khazraj, and still wielded some power among his people. Abú-Bakr, highly respected figure as he was, felt deeply hurt and was incapable of any action to clear his daughter's name because of the Prophet's studied silence. 'In the days when we were idolaters,' he said, 'no one dared level such accusations against our House, how much less should they hazard it now that our hearts are illumined by our belief in the one true God.' But still there was no word from the Prophet, until He received a revelation which established 'Á'ishah's innocence, admonishing and censuring her accusers:

> Those who came with the slander are a
> band of you; do not reckon it evil
> for you; rather it is good for you.
> Every man of them shall have the sin
> that he has earned charged on him; and
> whosoever of them took upon himself
> the greater part of it, him there awaits
> a mighty chastisement.
> Why, when you heard it, did the believing
> men and women not of their own account
> think good thoughts, and say, 'This is
> a manifest calumny'?
> Why did they not bring four witnesses
> against it? But since they did not

bring the witnesses, in God's sight
they are the liars.
But for God's bounty to you and His mercy
in the present world and the world to come
there would have visited you for your mutterings
a mighty chastisement. When you received it
on your tongues, and were speaking with your mouths
that whereof you had no knowledge, and
reckoned it a light thing, and with God it
was a mighty thing—
And why, when you heard it, did you not
say, 'It is not for us to speak about
this; glory be to Thee! This is
a mighty calumny'?
God admonishes you, that you shall
never repeat the like of it again, if
you are believers.[1]

The fourth verse of the same súrah ordains the administration of eighty strokes of the whip to anyone who slanders a married woman and cannot produce four trustworthy witnesses to support the contention. Now, Muḥammad brought in the ringleaders and had them whipped. One of these was Ḥassán Ibn Thábit, the chief poet of the Anṣár; another was Misṭaḥ Ibn Utháthah, a cousin of Abú-Bakr. Some have maintained that 'Abdu'lláh Ibn Ubayy was not chastised, but that seems improbable, since no one could or would commit himself, in this instance, to his defence. It is related that the poet satirized Ṣafwán, the handsome youth whose name had been coupled with 'Á'ishah's, and Ṣafwán was so enraged that he stabbed the poet; whereat Qays Ibn Thábit got hold of Ṣafwán to punish him, but 'Abdu'lláh Ibn Rawáḥah, a prominent man of the Anṣár, intervened and took them all to the Prophet. Muḥammad asked the poet to forgive Ṣafwán for his rash act. Ḥassán complied and the Prophet settled some property on him.

Misṭaḥ had been a poor orphan dependent on the generosity of his cousin, Abú-Bakr. As he grew up, Abú-Bakr continued to support him, but now that he had so blatantly wronged 'Á'ishah, his cousin was loath to keep up that support, and swore to with-

[1] Translation by A. J. Arberry, *Súrata'n-Núr* ('Light') xxiv, 11–16.

draw it. However, he restored to Misṭaḥ all his past favours when he heard the verdict of revelation on his decision—a decision rooted in bitterness:

> Let not those of you who possess bounty
> and plenty swear off giving kinsmen
> and the poor and those who emigrate
> in the way of God; but let them pardon
> and forgive. Do you not wish that God
> should forgive you? God is All-forgiving,
> All-compassionate.[2]

Misṭaḥ was a kinsman of Abú-Bakr, poor and an emigrant.

The Jewish opponents of the Prophet, who were now all gathered in their stronghold of Khaybar, to the north of Medina, had not ceased inciting the tribesmen. They were still dreaming of a concerted effort to overthrow the Prophet. The formation of a new confederacy, directed against Muḥammad, was no longer possible, but their petty intrigue continued unabated. Al-Ḥárith of the Banu'l-Muṣṭaliq had, in all probability, received encouragement and backing from the emissaries of Khaybar. Sallám Ibn Abi'l-Ḥuqayq, a man expelled from Medina, was one of those inveterate enemies of the Prophet. Early in 628 he was assassinated. Muslim historians agree that, having become a very dangerous adversary, the Prophet sanctioned his elimination.

One night Muḥammad dreamt that He had gone on pilgrimage to Mecca. On the morrow, He declared that He would immediately undertake this journey and called on His followers to join Him. They would go to Mecca, He announced, as pilgrims, not as warriors equipped for battle. Every man would have only his sword and no other weapons, when they approached the precincts of Mecca. This, however, was the month of Dhu'l-Qa'dah, preceding the month of Dhu'l-Ḥijjah in which the rites of *ḥajj* (pilgrimage) take place. Therefore, this journey of the Prophet could be only for the *'umrah*, which is the lesser pilgrimage. On 13 March 628, accompanied by some sixteen hundred men, Muḥammad set out for Mecca. He had put on white cloth, the garment of a pilgrim, and had seventy camels to offer for sacrifice. A number of His followers had found good reasons not to take

[2] ibid., v. 22.

part in this pilgrimage. This was not *jihád* against idolaters. It was not a *ghazwah* led by the Prophet. The end of the trail was uncertain. But a group of the Khuzá'ah tribesmen, some of whom may not have been Muslims, accompanied the Prophet. At 'Usfán, Busr Ibn Sufyán of the Banú-Ka'b informed the Prophet that the Quraysh had decided to prevent His entry into Mecca. They could not believe that Muḥammad had come for a peaceful purpose. A body of horsemen, under the command of the intrepid Khálid Ibn al-Walíd, took positions at Kurá'-al-Ghamím to halt His progress. But the Prophet took a different route and reached al-Ḥudaybíyyah, only a few miles distant from Mecca. There He stopped and awaited developments.

Shortly, Budayl Ibn Warqá', a man of standing amongst the Banú-Khuzá'ah, arrived at al-Ḥudaybíyyah to make searching enquiries and report back to the Quraysh. The Prophet told him what he had already told His followers: it was not His intention to fight, He had come as a pilgrim. Budayl believed Him; and so did al-Ḥulays Ibn 'Alqamah, a man of the Banú-Kinánah, who came to al-Ḥudaybíyyah on a similar errand. Whereas the Banú-Khuzá'ah had been friendly and well disposed towards Muḥammad, and Budayl was so inclined, the people of Kinánah had allied themselves to the Quraysh and had taken part in the investment of Medina. Al-Ḥulays was therefore deeply hurt when the Meccans rejected his report as coming from an ignorant Bedouin —he, who had served the Quraysh so well in the past. Another emissary of the Meccans, Mikraz Ibn Ḥafṣ, a Qurayshite himself, brought back the same news, that Muḥammad had not come to fight and wished only to visit the House of Ka'bah. But the Quraysh were dissatisfied and rattled. The thought oppressed them that Muḥammad, with a sizeable force, was no more than a few miles distant. It was obvious, too, that they had no zest for fighting. There was a man of the Banú-Thaqíf living in Mecca, named 'Urwah Ibn Mas'úd, of high repute and highly respected. He offered to go and meet Muḥammad. When talking with Muḥammad, his lofty attitude was so patronizing that, according to Ibn-Hishám, Abú-Bakr, always wise and sober in his speech, made a retort which was obscene. As he spoke, 'Urwah kept pulling the beard of the Prophet; and al-Mughayrah Ibn Shu'bah, who was standing behind Him, kept hitting 'Urwah's hand with the scabbard of his sword. 'Urwah's visit solved nothing, but the man was so impressed by what he saw that, on his return to Mecca, he informed the Quraysh that, though he had been to the courts of Chosroes, Caesar and the Negus, nowhere had he seen the like or equal of the reverence which Muslims rendered to Muḥammad.

There was deadlock. Meccans were uncertain and tremulous, Muslims fretful and ill at ease. At last, Muḥammad took the initiative. He sent 'Uthman Ibn 'Affán, His son-in-law, to parley with the Quraysh. According to Ibn al-Athír, Muḥammad intended to give this commission to 'Umar Ibn al-Khaṭṭáb. 'Umar, however, pleaded that he would no longer carry any weight in Mecca, and as there were hardly any of his clan, the Banú-'Adí, left there, his life would be in jeopardy. He suggested that 'Uthmán should go instead, because he belonged to the influential House of Umayyah and was a cousin of Abú-Sufyán. 'Uthmán went, and for a while there was no news of him. The Muslims were worried and greatly concerned since rumour had it that 'Uthmán had been put to death. Muḥammad could not ignore the fear and doubt creeping into His camp, and asked His followers to renew their pledge of fealty to Him, in the same manner as the men and women of Yathrib had done at 'Aqabah, six years before. He stood under the shade of a tree, and they came, one by one, to touch His hand and affirm their faith and belief and loyalty. 'Uthmán was conspicuously absent. Muḥammad raised His right hand, declared that it would serve as 'Uthmán's and touched His other hand. This renewal of fealty is known as the *Bay'at-ar-Riḍwán*—the pledge of Riḍwán (Good Pleasure). Verse 19 of súrah xlviii—*al-Fatḥ* ('Victory')—recalls it:

> God was well pleased with the believers
> when they were swearing fealty to thee
> under the tree, and He knew what was
> in their hearts, so He sent down the
> Shechina[3] upon them, and rewarded them with
>   a nigh victory
> and many spoils to take; and God is ever
>   All-mighty, All-wise.[4]

But 'Uthmán did return. And Suhayl Ibn 'Amr came from Mecca, on behalf of the Quraysh, to negotiate with the Prophet.

[3] See p. 48n.
[4] Translation by A. J. Arberry.

He was one of their leading figures, who had been captured at Badr and ransomed. When it came to drawing up an agreement, and 'Alí, who was acting as scribe, wrote to the Prophet's dictation: 'This is what Muḥammad, the Apostle of God, has agreed with Suhayl Ibn 'Amr,' Suhayl immediately objected: 'If we had recognized thee as the Apostle we would not have barred your way to Mecca'. The Prophet wished to make peace, and calmly told 'Alí to write: 'Muḥammad Ibn 'Abdi'lláh' instead of 'Muḥammad, the Apostle of God'. The terms of the agreement were such that they caused dismay amongst the Muslims. 'Umar, bewildered and shaken, went to Abú-Bakr to express his discomfiture. Abú-Bakr, serene and unperturbed as usual, advised him to speak to the Prophet Himself. And to 'Umar's expostulations the Prophet replied that He would not deviate from what God had commanded: He would not fight the Meccans, He would seek peace.

Muḥammad had agreed to a ten-year truce with the Quraysh, and to send back to Mecca anyone coming to Him from that city professing Islám, without demanding reciprocal action. Thus, a refugee from Medina could remain safe and secure in Mecca. Tribes would be free to join either side in alliance and would enjoy the immunities of the ten-year truce. The only concession on the part of the Meccans was to allow Muḥammad and His followers to come the following year to Mecca, armed only with sheathed swords, and to remain three days to perform the rites of '*umrah*. It is not to be wondered that Muslims felt forlorn and disheartened. But they had just renewed their pledge of fealty to Muḥammad. It was then that Abú-Jandal, the son of Suhayl Ibn 'Amr himself, arrived from Mecca in rags, dragging the fetters fastened to his legs. Because he wished to be a Muslim, this cruel treatment had been meted to him. Now he had broken loose and had managed to reach a haven, but it was not to be for long. His father intervened and demanded that his son be returned to him, in accordance with the agreement just signed. Muḥammad asked Suhayl to make an exception in the case of Abú-Jandal, but Suhayl refused to grant the Prophet His request. Abú-Jandal, crushed by his plight, appealed to the Muslims, who could only stand round, abashed, helpless and enraged. Muḥammad told Abú-Jandal to be patient, God would ease his path; and a member of the Meccan party promised that Abú-Jandal would not be maltreated a second time. 'Umar walked away with the young man, holding tightly to his sword for Abú-Jandal to see, whispering to him that all these Meccans were polytheists and to shed their blood was of no consequence. Abú-Jandal took the point, but refrained from acting on it.

As soon as Suhayl Ibn 'Amr and his associates had returned to Mecca, Muḥammad instructed his people to shave their heads (part of the rites of pilgrimage) and offer their sacrifice. He had to repeat this command a second and a third time, and still the Muslims, dazed and disheartened, failed to respond. When Muḥammad complained to Umm-Salamah, His wife, that nothing seemed to move them to action, she suggested that only His own example would have the desired effect. She had correctly appraised the situation. After performing part of the rites of '*umrah* at al-Ḥudaybíyyah, the Prophet took the road back to Medina. But the Muslims were still dejected and felt themselves humiliated. Half-way between the two cities, the *Súrat-al-Fatḥ* ('Victory') was revealed to the Prophet. Its opening line is: 'Verily, We have granted thee a conspicuous victory'. (xlviii, 1.) Muḥammad rejoiced, but the Muslims could not understand what it meant and remained deep in gloom.

Before long, it became evident that the truce of al-Ḥudaybíyyah was indeed a remarkable victory. A ten-year truce meant that the Muslim and the idolater could now meet in peace. This unrestrained association caused men to develop the highest regard for Muḥammad, and greatly weakened the position of the Quraysh. Within months Meccans of such calibre as Khálid Ibn al-Walíd and 'Amr Ibn al-'Áṣ were deserting Mecca to embrace Islám. And how were they allowed to remain in Medina despite the terms of the agreement of al-Ḥudaybíyyah? The story is soon told. Muḥammad had hardly reached Medina when Abú-Baṣír—'Utbah Ibn Usayd of the Banú-Thaqíf—dashed out of Mecca and covered the distance between the two cities in seven days. Hard on his heels came two men to take him back to Mecca. The Prophet handed him over, in accordance with the pact He had concluded. On the way to Mecca, Abú-Baṣír killed one of the guards with the man's own sword. The other guard fled to Medina to seek protection. Abú-Baṣír also returned to Medina, but knowing that the Prophet would not allow him to stay, he took himself to Wádí-al-'Ayṣ, close to the sea and on the trade route. Ere long Abú-Jandal and many others made good their escape from Mecca and joined him. Their number rose to seventy and probably more. Some authorities have even mentioned the figure as three hundred. There they became the scourge of Meccan trade. The Quraysh, perforce, sent a deputation to Medina and asked Muḥammad to drop from their agreement that item which made the return of Meccan fugitives compulsory, to which Muḥammad gave gladly His consent. Abú-Baṣír was on his death-bed when He received the Prophet's letter, informing him that he could now come to Medina. Abú-Jandal buried him, built a mosque over his grave and went triumphantly with his companions to Medina. God had eased the path of Abú-Jandal, as Muḥammad had promised him. The truce of al-Ḥudaybíyyah, although dispiriting at the start, had proved, in the end, a boon to the cause of Islám and a mighty victory.

13

The Call to the Kings

ALL Muslim historians agree that Muḥammad wrote to the rulers of the neighbouring lands, calling them to recognize Him as the Messenger of God. Historians in the West, on the other hand, have cast doubts on the entire truth of this assertion. Of course, the archives of the Sásánians of Írán, the Emperors of Byzantium, the Prelates of Egypt, the Amharic Kings of Ethiopia are lost beyond retrieval. No evidence can be forthcoming from those sources. And apart from the fact that hardly any contemporary historical work has survived, no historian would have thought to mention a letter from an unknown man dwelling in an insignificant Arabia. Furthermore, by this time the two giants straddling Eastern Europe, Western Asia and Northern Africa had bled each other white. The Íránians and the Byzantines had been locked in mortal combat for almost a generation. When their twenty-four-year war began, the Persians had won victory after victory, swept over Palestine, Syria and Asia Minor, raced on to Alexandria, and laid siege to Constantinople. Then Heraclius, the Byzantine Emperor, had made a supreme effort and rolled back the invaders to the foot-hills of the Íránian plateau. Khusraw Parvíz (Chosroes II), the Sásánian monarch, who had wantonly prolonged the war when he could have had good terms for peace and had, in his rage, put his defeated generals to death, was dethroned and murdered in A.D. 628. In lands so ravished and devastated, any chronicler would have turned to the events of the day: defeats and triumphs, miseries and reliefs, rather than to a letter from an obscure Arabian, which would have seemed to him of no significance.

The final victory gained by Heraclius was foreshadowed in the Qur'án. If the Persians and the Byzantines had little or no interest in the affairs of Arabia (even the Persian colony in Yemen seems to have been forgotten and left to its own devices), the Meccans, for whom trade was a matter of life and death, had a keen interest in all that transpired in the Byzantine and Sásánian realms. It is related that when Muḥammad's letter reached Heraclius, the Emperor was in Emesa [Ḥimṣ] to attend to the ravages wrought by the Persians, and Abú-Sufyán was also there to attend to his trade. Tradition has it that the enormous successes achieved by the Sásánian arms, prior to the rapid reversal of their fortunes, had made the idolaters of Mecca mock at Muḥammad, because the followers of Jesus, whom the Qur'án had extolled, were being soundly beaten and humbled. It was then, it is said, that the *Súrat-ar-Rúm* (xxx) was revealed:

'Rúm [the Byzantines] were defeated in the near land. They, after their defeat, shall be victorious, in a few years. Command belongs to God, before and after; and on that day the believers shall rejoice in God's aid. God will aid whomsoever He willeth. And He is the All-Mighty, the Merciful. The promise of God: God faileth not to fulfil His promise, but most men do not know it.' (vv. 1–5.)

Among the potentates addressed by Muḥammad, the Negus, called Najáshí by the Muslim historians, was the only ruler familiar with his story. The emissary of the Prophet to the Negus was a man named 'Amr Ibn Umayyah. (Here one may wonder why a special envoy was dispatched, since there were still Muslims in Ethiopia who had emigrated more than a decade before.) The Negus, it is related, bore witness to the prophethood of Muḥammad and sent his own son with three or four score men to attend the Prophet; but the ship bearing the Ethiopian prince to Arabia sank in the Red Sea and there were no survivors. This may be a legend. What is certain, however, is the fact that the Negus had friendly feelings towards the Prophet. Acting upon His request, the Negus arranged marriage to Him, by proxy, of a daughter of Abú-Sufyán, and enabled her to return to her homeland. This daughter of Muḥammad's bitter enemy was Umm-Ḥabíbah, the widow of 'Ubaydu'lláh Ibn Jaḥsh. The latter was a brother of that 'Abdu'lláh who fell at Badr, and of Zaynab, whose marriage to the Prophet caused controversy. While in Ethiopia, 'Ubaydu'l-láh abandoned his allegiance to Muḥammad and became a Christian, but Umm-Ḥabíbah did not follow her husband. By this marriage Muḥammad cemented further His ties with the

House of Umayyah. Some other Muslims also returned from Ethiopia, one of whom was Ja'far, the son of Abú-Ṭálib and a brother of 'Alí.

'Abdu'lláh Ibn Ḥudháfah was the bearer of Muḥammad's letter to Khusraw Parvíz (Chosroes II), who was reeling under defeat. It is related that the Sásánian monarch was enraged, tore up Muḥammad's letter and wrote to Bádhán, his governor in Yemen, to lay hold upon Him and send Him to Ctesiphon. The Prophet, when apprised of the reaction of the Sásánian, foretold his downfall, or prayed for it. Bádhán commissioned two of his trusted men to travel to Medina to inform Muḥammad of the orders of Chosroes. Should Muḥammad refuse to submit, they declared, Chosroes would force His submission and reduce His city. The Prophet kept them for a while, until, when they asked for a definite answer, He informed them that Chosroes was no more: the night before, his son, Shírúyih, had murdered him. The story goes that Bádhán marvelled at the message brought by his emissaries, and embraced Islám as soon as news from Ctesiphon verified the words of the Prophet. There can be no doubt that the Persian ruler of Yemen did embrace Islám.

The story told of Heraclius by no less a historian than Ibn-al-Athír is indeed hard to credit. It is averred that when Heraclius received the Prophet's letter he expressed his belief in the truth of Muḥammad's claim, questioned Abú-Sufyán, who (as previously stated) happened to be in the same city, regarding the antecedents, the status and the character of Muḥammad, and advised Muḥammad's envoy to go to Rome and summon the Pope to Islám. Even more strange is the assertion that this Pope, who can be identified as Honorius I of Campania (A.D. 625–38), testified to the prophethood of Muḥammad, but was rejected by the people. Heraclius, according to this account, was afraid to make public his faith, lest his subjects repudiate him. It is all very improbable.

The reaction of the ruler of Egypt, whom Muslim historians name as Maqawqis, was apparently equivocal. He sent back the emissary, Ḥáṭib Ibn Abí-Balta'ah, with presents for the Prophet. Included in Maqawqis's offerings were two female slaves, Máríah (Mary) and her sister, Shírín. Muḥammad took Máríah as His wife, and they had a son whom the Prophet named Ibráhím (Abraham). The child died in infancy. Maqawqis also sent a white mule, named Duldul, and a donkey named Ya'fúr. Tradition has it that Muḥammad often rode the mule; then it passed to 'Alí and from 'Alí to Ḥasan, his son. Duldul, it is assumed, lived many a year; but Ya'fúr, it is said, died within a few years.

Shujá' Ibn Wahb of the Banú-Asad was the bearer of the Prophet's letter to al-Ḥárith Ibn Abí-Shimr, the Ghassánid prince in Damascus. Al-Ḥárith was infuriated, and would have raised an army to march against Medina. Heraclius seems to have dissuaded him. The Prince of Yamámah, Hawdhah Ibn 'Alí, was a Christian and he received the Prophet's envoy, Salíṭ Ibn 'Amr of the Banu-'Ámir, with warmth and open arms. But what Hawdhah really desired was to share power with Muḥammad; he died soon after. Of all the envoys sent by the Prophet, the one truly successful was al-'Alá Ibn al-Ḥaḍramí. Mundhir Ibn Sáwí, who held Baḥrayn on behalf of the Sásánian monarch, and most of the islanders, according to Ibn al-Athír, gave their allegiance to Muḥammad.

Apart from a host of doubts, the time of the dispatch of these emissaries has been in dispute. Ibn al-Athír terminates his chronicle of the events of the sixth year of the Hijrah with the account of missions to rulers; when he reaches the end of their story, he writes: 'Opened the year seven'.

14

Jews and Christians of the North

THE seventh year of the Hijrah, which opened on 11 May 628 and closed on 30 April 629, saw the reduction of the last Jewish stronghold in Arabia. Muḥammad had now entered into a ten-year truce with the Meccans, which was proving, in every way, advantageous to Him. The Quraysh, who had persecuted and spurned Him and forced Him to flee His native town, had, by concluding this truce, explicitly conceded to Him the position of an equal. The free association of idolaters and Muslims, now made possible, was working to the detriment of the Quraysh. Their inferiority was becoming much too evident. The important centres of resistance and opposition to Muḥammad had almost ceased to function, with one glaring exception—Khaybar, the large Jewish settlement to the north of Medina. The hostility of the Jewish leaders in Khaybar was relentless. They tried by every available means to injure Muḥammad and bring Him into disrepute, cavilling at His words, mocking His utterance, encouraging whoever was bold enough to fight Him. The situation of this settlement—being on a route to the north beyond the peninsula, and in proximity to the tribal areas of the Ghaṭafán and the Banú-Asad—made the inimical attitude of the Jewish leaders even more dangerous. It has been suggested by Western writers that Muḥammad embarked on the expedition to Khaybar in order to mollify those of His followers who had accompanied Him on the intended '*umrah*, and to 'compensate' them for having come back empty-handed. In reasoning thus they point to the fact that the invasion of Khaybar followed very closely their return from al-Ḥudaybíyyah, and that Muḥammad allowed only those Muslims who had been with Him there to take part in the expedition to Khaybar. But there are other factors of equal significance to be taken into consideration when searching for Muḥammad's motive. At the time Muḥammad set out on the journey which ended short of Mecca, He had plainly and openly declared that the object of the journey was the performance of the rites of the *'umrah*, and at Dhu'l-Ḥulayfah had made His men divest themselves of all fighting accoutrements except their swords. And when He prepared to march on Khaybar He announced that whoever would come in the hope of gaining booty should stay at home. Obviously the conquest of Khaybar would result in obtaining considerable spoils—that needs no argument. But the Prophet's object was to destroy a focal point of opposition.

Some Muslim historians, who would lay at the door of the dissembler 'Abdu'lláh Ibn Ubayy every manner of covert treachery, have claimed that he sent word to the Jews of Khaybar of the Prophet's designs, urging them not to shut themselves up in their strongholds but to come out and fight in the open. If 'Abdu'lláh Ibn Ubayy did commit such treachery, it would seem very strange that Muḥammad should have, in person, recited the prayer for the dead, facing his bier. The same historians tell us that when Muḥammad's army appeared before the oasis, the Jews, engaged in their usual occupation of farming, were mightily astonished and ran back into their fortified homes. Muḥammad had moved from Medina to Khaybar in easy stages; if the Jews had been forewarned of an intended attack, why in reason's name were they unconcernedly busy with their pails and spades in open fields rather than seeing to their defences, especially since their good friends and neighbours, men of the Ghaṭafán, who lived only a few miles away, had not been in a hurry to come to their aid. An improbable story relates that 'Uyaynah Ibn Ḥiṣn, the Ghaṭafán chief (whom we have encountered before), had responded to appeals for help from Khaybar, hastening there with his men, but a voice from heaven had warned that their own territory was in peril and so they had hurried away. Perhaps 'Uyaynah had come but had fallen out with the Jews. From past events, we know that this Bedouin chieftain was both greedy and unreliable.

Khaybar did not consist of one large fortress surrounded by fields and palm groves. There were at least five fortified areas which housed the farmers of Khaybar. Muḥammad reduced these forts, one after the other, within a period of less than a month. It is estimated that the population of the oasis might have been in the region of twenty thousand. This may be an exaggeration, but numerically the Jews had the advantage. Muḥammad's army was small, only some fourteen hundred of the men who had been at al-Ḥudaybíyyah with Him. There were casualties on both sides, but they were not heavy. A few of the Jewish leaders lost their lives in single combat, of whom Marḥab, a man renowned for his bravery and strength, was one. He was slain by 'Alí. By all accounts 'Alí, though ailing, evinced very great bravery at Khaybar. But miraculous feats ascribed to him, such as wrenching away the iron gate of a fort, using it as a shield, and then holding it as a bridge over the moat for the Muslim warriors to pass over into the fortress, are obvious fabrications. Indeed it is both deplorable and amazing to read in works that claim to be histories that the Angel Gabriel told the Prophet that, fearing lest 'Alí's mighty blows in the battle should pierce the earth and cut in half the ox that holds it up, he sustained the weight of those blows himself to lessen their impact. It is ridiculous stories such as these which lower the reputation of Islám. Equally absurd is another incident which, it is alleged, also occurred during the campaign for Khaybar. Muḥammad, it is related, was lying down with His head on 'Alí's lap, when His countenance indicated the approach of a revelation. 'Alí, noticing this, did not move. In the meantime the sun set and 'Alí had no chance to say the prayer prescribed for late afternoon. Whereupon Muḥammad prayed for the return of the sun, which did come back, and 'Alí was thus enabled to say the required obligatory prayer. Authority after authority is quoted in support of this grotesque tale. Men who originally wrote nonsense of this description had little idea what the retreat of the earth on its orbit meant. To repeat it in modern times is unpardonable.

It is certain that a number of the Jews of Khaybar acted as informers for the Muslims. A Jew it was who showed Muḥammad how to capture one of the forts by turning off its water supply. It was also a Jew who disclosed the whereabouts of the stores of Kinánah Ibn Abi'l-Ḥuqayq, a leading man of Khaybar, who was solemnly declaring in concert with his confrères that their treasures of gold and jewels had been spent. Because the Jews had surrendered accepting the conditions laid down by the Prophet, and had agreed not to hide any of their possessions, this discovery made the death of Kinánah inevitable. His wife, Ṣafíyyah, the daughter of Ḥuyy Ibn Akhṭab—Muḥammad's implacable enemy of yore, who brought about the annihilation of the Banú-Qurayẓah—was claimed by a Muslim. Muḥammad ransomed her, she became a Muslim and was married to the Prophet. Bilál the Ethiopian, while guiding Ṣafíyyah to the safety of the Prophet's quarters, led the way close to a spot where Jews had fallen. On hearing this, Muḥammad reprimanded Bilál for his hard-heartedness. Muḥammad was also distressed when Ṣafíyyah told Him tearfully that His wives had contemptuously called her a Jewess. 'Aaron was my father, and Moses my uncle,' He declared.

Jews were now allowed to remain in Khaybar and follow their pursuits; but a half of what they produced went to the Muslims. Fadak, Wádi'l-Qurá', and Taymá', three other oases belonging to the Jews, in the neighbourhood of Khaybar, also capitulated on terms. The Jews remained in their former strongholds, leading peaceful lives as farmers, until the days of the caliphate of 'Umar, who compensated them fully and sent them out of Arabia. By June 628, Muḥammad had wrested power completely from the Jews of the north.

A Jewish woman, Zaynab Bint al-Ḥárith, whose husband, Sallám Ibn Mishkam, had died at Khaybar, tried to kill the Prophet by poisoning. Learning that Muḥammad was fond of shoulder of meat, Zaynab roasted a goat, smeared it with poison particularly in the region of the shoulder and made Him a present of it. The Prophet invited several of His followers to partake with Him of that roasted meat for their evening meal. The taste of the first morsel was so repellent that Muḥammad spat it out and declared that the food was poisoned; but Bishr Ibnu'l-Bará', one of the Medinites eating with Him, was less fortunate and eventually died of the effects of the poison, apparently a year later. Zaynab readily confessed to the felony. She did it, she said, because her relatives had died at the hands of the Muslims. What happened to Zaynab is not certain, but the strong probability is that she was pardoned.

The rest of the year 628 Muḥammad spent in mounting a number of minor expeditions, some of them wholly punitive in nature. But He did not accompany any of them. Zayd was sent to villages around Fadak, for the purpose of inviting their inhabitants to embrace Islám. A man named Mirdás took to the hills with his family and his sheep. Usámah, the son of Zayd, chased them. When nearly overtaken, Mirdás turned round and uttered the words of profession to Islám: 'There is no God but God, Muḥammad is His Apostle.' But Usámah took no notice of his declaration of faith and felled him with a lance. Muḥammad censured Usámah for this rash deed: 'Thou hast murdered a man who professed to the Oneness of God and to my apostleship.' Usámah's lame defence was that Mirdás had made that declaration to save his life. 'How didst thou know?' Muḥammad retorted. 'Didst thou open his heart to read what it contained?'

'O ye who believe! When ye go out in the path of God, do not act with haste and do not, in the hope of gaining spoils, reject anyone as an unbeliever who salutes you in the way of faith. With God there is an abundance of spoils. Such were ye too aforetime. And God was bounteous unto you. Then be discerning. God knoweth well your actions.' (Súrah iv, 96: *an-Nisá'*—'Women'.) This is the verdict of the Qur'án on Usámah's impetuosity. Ibn al-Athír states that the *saríyyah*, in which Usámah murdered Mirdás, was led by Ghálib Ibn 'Abdu'lláh al-Laythí against the Banú-Murrah. Another *saríyyah* was led by Abú-Bakr to a place called Ḍaríyyah in the vicinity of Najd, but nothing came of it.

In February 629, Muḥammad set out, accompanied by those who had been at al-Ḥudaybíyyah, to perform the deferred rites of the *'umrah*. Some historians have put the number of pilgrims at two thousand. If so, obviously others had joined the Prophet for this journey. Sixty camels went with them, specified for sacrifice. The Quraysh, on being apprised of the Prophet's approach, evacuated Mecca. In all probability not everyone left the city. We know for certain that 'Abbás, the uncle of the Prophet (presumably a Muslim by this time) and his family, together with others of the descendants of 'Abdu'l-Muṭṭalib, remained in Mecca. One of these was a daughter of Ḥamzah (martyred at Uḥud), named 'Amárah and entitled Amatu'lláh (The Handmaiden of God). 'Alí and Fáṭimah took her with them to Medina. Subsequently there arose a dispute between 'Alí, his brother Ja'far and Zayd, each of them claiming the right to give her protection. 'Alí and Fáṭimah had brought her from Mecca; her father and Zayd had been tied as brothers by the Prophet; Ja'far was her cousin and the husband of her maternal aunt. Muḥammad had to settle the issue and decided in favour of Ja'far.

During the three-days sojourn in Mecca, 'Abbás arranged another marriage for the Prophet. The woman concerned was a widow named Maymúnah, the sister of a wife of 'Abbás. When the three days specified by the terms of the truce had passed and Muḥammad had shown no sign of moving out, the leaders of the Quraysh sent Ḥuwayṭib Ibn 'Abdi'l-'Uzzá, a well-known figure in Mecca, to ask the Prophet to leave. Muḥammad asked what harm it would do if He tarried a while longer to prepare a wedding feast to which they would all be invited. Ḥuwayṭib replied: 'We don't need your food. Leave the city.' There was no alternative but to depart.

In the days of *jáhilíyyah* (ignorance), before the advent of Muḥammad, it was customary at the time of pilgrimage for people, while still clad with the single sheet of *iḥrám*, not to use the door of the house for exit or entrance. Instead, they climbed to the roof and descended from there, and Bedouins used the rear of their tents and not the front. Whoever broke this rule was reckoned to have sinned. However, the Quraysh, the Khuzá'ah, the Kinánah, the Judaylah, the Banú-'Ámir and the Banú-Thaqíf were excepted from this rule, being of the brave who need not observe the restriction. One day during this *'umrah*, a man of the Anṣár, Rifá'ah Ibn 'Amr, followed the Prophet out of the street door. Immediately the cry went up that he was a *fájir*—a sinner. Muḥammad asked Rifá'ah why he had broken the rule, pointing out that He himself was a man of the *Ḥums* (The Brave) and could disregard the restriction. The Medinite replied: 'I am thy follower and I do as thou doest. If thou art of the *Ḥums* so must I be.' Then came a revelation which abrogated that rule of the days of Ignorance: 'It is not piety to come to the houses from the back of them; but piety is to be God-fearing; so come to the houses by their doors, and fear God; haply so you may prosper.' (Súrah ii, 185: *al-Baqarah*—'The Cow'.)

On his return to Medina, Muḥammad prepared to take action against the Christian Arabs in the far north, the region which is now Jordan. Al-Ḥárith Ibn'Umayr, a Muslim on a peaceful mission to the Governor of Buṣrá, had been wantonly killed by Shuraḥbíl, a Ghassánid prince. The news naturally spread and Muḥammad could not let this deliberate and grave insult go unredressed. He gathered a force of three thousand men, placed it under the command of Zayd, and specified that Ja'far, the brother of 'Alí, would assume command should Zayd fall, and after him,

'Abdu'lláh Ibn Rawáḥah of the Anṣár. This army marched away in September 629 (in the eighth year of the Hijrah), and covered over six hundred miles to reach Ma'án. There the Muslims learned that Heraclius had dispatched a large force to oppose them. Ibn-Hishám mentions that the Byzantine army comprised two hundred thousand men, an impossible number. Apart from the Greeks, we are told, there were large contingents from the Christian Arab tribes of Lakhm, Judhám, al-Qayn, Bahrá' and Ballí, all under the command of Málik Ibn Záfilah. The Byzantine army was centred at Maáb (Moab of biblical fame). Even if its numbers have been grossly exaggerated, it was certainly a force too great for the Muslims to face. They thought of sending to Medina to seek both aid and guidance, but it was evident that the journey of twelve hundred miles there and back would take much too long. 'Abdu'lláh Ibn Rawáḥah told his compatriots that all they could and should do was to go forth fearlessly to meet the inevitable—martyrdom. At a village called Mu'tah, near Ma'án, the opposing armies met. Zayd, Ja'far and 'Abdu'lláh went down in quick succession, and it fell to Khálid Ibn al-Walíd, with his superb generalship, to rescue the Muslim side from total annihilation and lead the men back to Medina. Despite the attempt made by some historians to denigrate the incomparable Khálid and belittle the part he played, it is plainly obvious that, without his strategy and tactics, all the Muslims would have perished in a terrain unfamiliar to them and amidst hostile hosts. Khálid, being a latecomer into the fold of Islám, did not wish to undertake the task, but once it was given to him by his fellow believers, he fulfilled it with astonishing ability. When the Muslim army came home, battered and beaten, Medinites were ashamed, and scorned and scolded the brave men who had suffered so much and now felt deeply their humiliation.

But Muḥammad was not displeased either with them or with Khálid. He praised and comforted them and referred to Khálid as one of the swords of God. Henceforth that valiant warrior became known as Sayfa'lláh—The Sword of God. It is related that Ja'far had both arms hacked off while holding aloft the standard. He is called Ja'far-aṭ-Ṭayyár—Ja'far the Flier—for he is supposed to have been given wings to take the place of his arms. However, sober commentators have stated that 'wings', in his case, were not such as birds possess, but indicated powers of the spirit. What is surprising is the smallness of the number of Muslim casualties recorded. Ibn-Hishám names only eight, and the utmost number given elsewhere is fourteen.

At Medina, Muḥammad went to the homes of His fallen commanders, embraced their children and wept bitterly with their families.

Before the eighth year of the Hijrah reached its end on 19 April 630, there were a number of other expeditions led by 'Amr Ibn al-'Áṣ, Abú-'Ubaydah Ibn al-Jarráḥ, Abú-Bakr and others. All were of a minor character. 'Amr Ibn al-'Áṣ, leading a Muslim force for the first time since his conversion, went as far as a well called Dhát-as-Salásil, in the vicinity of Wádi'l-Qurá', where some Christians of the Banú-Quḍá'ah and Banu'l-Qayn had foregathered and been joined by local Bedouins, for what purpose is not known. There were skirmishes, but nothing substantial was either gained or lost. 'Amr, it seems, was for some reason chary of headlong clashes, although the Prophet had sent him reinforcements at his request.

15

Mecca and aṭ-Ṭá'if Fall

THE rout of the Muslims at Mu'tah was unexpected—a blow but not a hard one. It did not halt the steady march of Islám. Rather, it increased the fame of Muḥammad, that His army could now operate so far from its base and in alien territory. And, furthermore, this expedition pointed the way—until then scarcely, if at all, discernible—to future conquests in those vast regions to the north of the peninsula. But for the time being it was within Arabia itself that the climax was slowly and inevitably approaching; and the most brilliant triumph for the cause of Islám was almost within sight.

The truce of al-Ḥudaybíyyah had been undertaken for ten years. One adjustment, agreeable to both sides, had been made, as we have seen. The Prophet had now performed the rites of the *'umrah*. Neither Mecca nor Medina had, in any way, made a breach of the truce. But the Quraysh had not reckoned with the irresponsible and undisciplined behaviour of their Bedouin allies, and the erratic ways of some of their own leaders. The Kinánah, allied to the Quraysh, and the Khuzá'ah, allied to the Prophet, nurtured feuds of old. The truce of al-Ḥudaybíyyah imposed a cessation of hostilities on the tribes that had chosen alliance with either Mecca or Medina. A quarrel flared up between a man named Anas, of the Banú-Bakr, a clan of the Kinánah, and a youth of the Khuzá'ah. Anas had composed a poem, satirizing the Prophet, and insisted on declaiming it in public. The Khuzá'ah youth told him to stop, but Anas would not, and he was beaten by the angry young man. Subsequently some of the Banú-Bakr decided to teach the Khuzá'ah a lesson. Thus they reactivated ancient feuds. They applied to another clan, the Banú-Mudlij, for help, but as no aid was forthcoming from that quarter, they went to the Quraysh for backing. A number of the embittered among the Meccans, such as Ṣafwán Ibn Umayyah and 'Ikrimah Ibn Abí-Jahl, were foolish enough to take up arms in support of the Banú-Bakr. The people of Khuzá'ah had gathered around a well called al-Watír, close to Mecca, which belonged to them. The men of Kinánah and the hot-heads of the Quraysh fell upon them, killing twenty. The Khuzá'ah, worsted and dislodged, fled fighting to the gate of the Ka'bah. There they met Nawfal Ibn Mu'áwíyah, the chief of the Banú-Bakr, and appealed to him to call off his men that the sacred precincts should not be desecrated. But Nawfal, in his turn, accused the Khuzá'ah of theft in the environs of the Ka'bah.

Clearly, Meccans and their allies had broken the truce of al-Ḥudaybíyyah. 'Amr Ibn Sálim, of the Banú-Ka'b clan of the Khuzá'ah, hurried to Medina to inform Muḥammad of these events and to ask for justice. Badíl Ibn Warqá', who was also of the Khuzá'ah and lived in Mecca, did likewise. Meccans were now alarmed by the fear of what Muḥammad might do. They had no heart for fighting and, of late, both their power and their prestige had dwindled. To raise a large army to go into battle with Muḥammad was a gigantic task. They were essentially merchants, good at taking caravans to Syria and Yemen. The truce had given them a breathing space and the chance to carry on their trade. Giving surreptitious aid to the Kinánah against the Khuzá'ah was almost a sport, but to equip an army was an expensive and burdensome undertaking. And so Abú-Sufyán set out for Medina with a heavy heart. The action of Ṣafwán and 'Ikrimah and others like them was not at all to his taste. He had had no previous knowledge of it and he would certainly not have sanctioned it. He hoped that Muḥammad was not too offended and would agree to a renewal of the truce.

Reaching Medina, Abú-Sufyán made his way to the home of Umm-Ḥabíbah, his daughter, who was now married to the Prophet. After so many years Umm-Ḥabíbah was not at all pleased to see him, nor would she let him sit on the carpet which was the Prophet's own. 'On this rug,' she said, 'sits the best of men and thou art an unclean polytheist.' Abú-Sufyán left her in disgust and went straight into the presence of the Prophet. But Muḥammad gave no ear to his plea. Abú-Bakr and 'Umar refused in turn to intercede for him. Next he sought the aid of Fáṭimah, the daughter of Muḥammad, but there, also, he drew a blank. Would either of her sons, he asked Fáṭimah, plead his case before their grandfather, and by so doing bring such a boon to the Quraysh as would be gratefully remembered by generations to come? Fáṭimah replied that her sons were under age and could not help him. However, 'Alí, while declining personal initiative, showed him a way which might gain him some respite. But when Abú-Sufyán left Medina and turned his face homewards he knew that he had failed. Indeed, the Quraysh suspected him of treason because his absence from Mecca had been unduly prolonged. Western writers have also suggested that, in all probability, Abú-Sufyán had obtained guarantees for his own safety and had arrived at a secret understanding to ease the Prophet's way into Mecca. This is pure surmise and there is no vestige of evidence to support it. From all that the historians and chroniclers, from Ibn-Hishám onwards, have recorded, the opposite can be concluded. Those who present this thesis of collusion maintain that almost all the early histories were composed at a time when the 'Abbásids were occupants of the seat of authority, and nothing but the odious could safely be attributed to Abú-Sufyán and to his descendants. This argument is not totally devoid of virtue; and though circumstances can be so interpreted as to point to Abú-Sufyán's possible double role, we can be certain that Abú-Sufyán was a perplexed and unhappy man when he returned to Mecca.

Muḥammad, in the meantime, had resolved to march on Mecca. He told Abú-Bakr of this and set the seal of silence on his lips. Calmly, preparations for an expedition were put in hand. Quietly, emissaries went out to friendly Bedouins inviting them to muster their forces and join the Prophet. In order to divert attention Muḥammad sent a man of the Anṣár at the head of a small contingent to deal with a small clan. No one had rightly guessed what was afoot, with one exception. This was the same man who had been the Prophet's envoy to Maqawqis of Alexandria. He wrote a letter to the Quraysh to inform them of the Prophet's intention, and gave it to a woman to carry to Mecca. Named Sárah, she had wandered from Mecca to Medina some two years after Badr, but had remained an idolater. Sárah now left in stealth for Mecca with Ḥáṭib's letter concealed in her tresses. Muḥammad sent 'Alí and six others (one of whom was 'Umar) to intercept her. 'Alí, under the threat of death, forced her to give up the letter. In His mosque at Medina, Muḥammad told the congregation that one of those present had written to the Meccans to forewarn them.

Twice He made that announcement but no one owned up. When He repeated it a third time, Ḥáṭib rose to confess. He had not recanted, he said, and was still a believer, but not being of the Quraysh and having relations and property in Mecca, he had hoped to ensure their safety in this manner. 'Umar was enraged and asked Muḥammad to allow him to behead the traitor. However, the Prophet forgave Ḥáṭib, because he had been at Badr, and because of a revelation indicating that Ḥáṭib had retained his faith:

'O ye who believe! Do not take My enemy and your enemy as friends, displaying affection towards them. They verily repudiated the truth which came unto you, and expelled the Apostle and you, because you believe in God, your Lord. If ye go out to labour in My path and obtain My good-pleasure, and show them affection in secret, I am well aware of what ye hide and what ye do in the open. And whosoever of you acts in that way, he has verily strayed from the straight path.' (Súrah lx, 1: *al-Mumtaḥanah*—'The Tested'.) In that verse Ḥáṭib is considered as one who believes and is addressed as such.

The Prophet moved out of Medina on the first day of the year 630. As He approached Mecca, contingents of the Bedouins joined His army, until the number exceeded ten thousand. The Banú-Sulaym, who had given the Prophet a good deal of trouble in the past, were represented by a thousand lancers. It was the month of Ramaḍán, and the Prophet was fasting until He reached 'Usfán or al-Qudayd, where He called for a bowl of water and broke His fast. Being told that some of His men were still observing the fast, Muḥammad said they were in the wrong. At Juḥfah, He encountered His uncle 'Abbás, who was journeying towards Medina, accompanied by the members of his family. Muḥammad told him: 'You are the last of the Emigrants as I am the last of the Prophets.' 'Abbás remained with his Nephew, while his family proceeded on their way to Medina. Further on, at Nayq-al-'Uqáb, two others of the relatives of the Prophet, with their families, arrived at His encampment. Both had been extremely hostile to Muḥammad in times past. One of them, Abú-Sufyán Ibn al-Ḥárith, a grandson of 'Abdu'l-Muṭṭalib, used to satirize his Cousin in poems that he composed and read to the crowds. The other, 'Abdu'lláh Ibn Umayyah, of the Banú-Makhzúm, was also a grandson of 'Abdu'l-Muṭṭalib through his mother, and brother to Umm-Salamah, a wife of the Prophet. At first Muḥammad turned away from them, but now they were truly penitent and declared that should the Prophet refuse to receive them they would go into the wilderness, to perish from thirst and hunger. Umm-Salamah pleaded their case; and so they too ranged themselves behind their Kinsman in His triumphal march towards Mecca.

Muḥammad went steadily forward until He reached Marr-aẓ-Ẓahrán, some twelve miles from Mecca. There the army bivouacked. Muḥammad ordered His men to light bonfires across the plain. Meccans had no intelligence of the movements of the Prophet, and being incapable of gathering a force to engage in combat, were extremely worried. On this particular evening, Abú-Sufyán in the company of Ḥakím Ibn Ḥizám, a noted man of the Quraysh, and Budayl Ibn Warqá', the Khuzá'ah ally of the Prophet, had come out of Mecca to reconnoitre. As they ascended a hillock they saw before them the whole plain ablaze with bonfires: this could only be the army of Muḥammad. Abú-Sufyán ventured forward and, as his luck held, he encountered 'Abbás, who was also feeling uneasy for the fate of the Meccans. Had Abú-Sufyán ventured further alone, undoubtedly he would have met his death at the hands of 'Umar Ibn al-Khaṭṭáb, who was in charge of the watch. But 'Abbás put Abú-Sufyán under his own protection, and conducted him to the tent of the Prophet, followed by 'Umar who was sorely displeased. Muḥammad asked 'Abbás to take Abú-Sufyán to his own tent until the morning.

At dawn the army was astir; the voice of Bilál the Ethiopian rang through the plain calling men to prayer. Abú-Sufyán was amazed and his amazement was boundless when he noticed how the Muslims would not let a drop of water, with which Muḥammad made his ablutions, reach the ground. Not even at the courts of the Sásánians and the Byzantines had he seen such devotion.

The morning prayer over, 'Abbás led Abú-Sufyán into the presence of the Prophet. Muḥammad asked him whether the time had not come for him to acknowledge the One True God. Abú-Sufyán's wonderment was overwhelming. He had done so much to harm Muḥammad and now Muḥammad was addressing him with such gentleness. He admitted that there could be but one God, the Eternal, the Ancient of Days, for otherwise, had there been deities such as he had believed in, he and the Quraysh would have received their blessings. And then, Muḥammad asked Abú-Sufyán, again gently, whether the time had not come to recognize Him as the Apostle of God. Abú-Sufyán seemed to hesitate, but 'Abbás guided him to say: 'I bear witness that verily there is no God but God, and I bear witness that verily Muḥammad is the Apostle of God.' At long last Abú-Sufyán, the bitter enemy of Muḥammad, the leader of the House of Umayyah, was safe and secure within the fold of Islám.

Now 'Abbás once again spoke for Abú-Sufyán, to remind his Nephew that, as a proud man, he should be accorded some distinction among the Quraysh. And Muḥammad said: 'Whoever enters the house of Abú-Sufyán in the upper regions of Mecca, and whoever enters the house of Ḥakím in the lower regions of Mecca, he shall be secure; and whoever lays down his arms, he shall be secure; and whoever shuts himself behind his own door, he shall be secure; and whoever enters the Masjid-al-Ḥarám [the Sacred Mosque, i.e., the Ka'bah], he shall be secure.' Abú-Sufyán was on the point of making his way back to Mecca, when a thought passed through the mind of 'Abbás: Abú-Sufyán should be shown the might of the Muslim arms, lest, once in Mecca, he should be tempted to revert to idolatry. The Prophet agreed, and as the army broke camp to march into Mecca, 'Abbás stood beside Abú-Sufyán, in a defile, and showed him the transformation which had taken place within the course of two years.

First came the formidable contingent of the Banú-Sulaym, at whose head rode Khálid Ibn al-Walíd. This Khálid was once a bright star in the firmament of the Meccans. So much and so many of their hopes had resided in his youth, his valour, his mastery of the arts of warfare. Then these contingents came and passed, one after the other: the Banú-Ghifár, the Banú-Aslam, the Banú-Ka'b, the Muzaynah, the Juhaynah, the Banú-Layth, the Banú-Sa'd Ibn Bakr of the Kinánah, and many more. The Banú-Sa'd Ibn Bakr were the very people who, but a short while before, had attacked the Khuzá'ah, thus breaking the truce of al-Ḥudaybíyyah; now they marched under the banner of Islám. Then Muḥammad and His escort came within sight. That formation, at whose heart the Prophet rode, was called *al-Qubbat-al-Khaḍrá'* —the Green Dome—because the green of the men's coats of arms glistened in the sun. Abú-Bakr rode at the right side of the Prophet, he who had been His companion in His migration from Mecca;

and Usayd Ibn Ḥuḍayr, one of the twelve Medinites who had pledged their fealty to Muḥammad at ʻAqabah, rode on His left. At the head of the Green Dome Saʻd Ibn ʻUbádah, another of those twelve *nuqabá'*, carried the standard of the Anṣár. Saʻd was so overcome by emotion when he saw Abú-Sufyán that he thundered at him: 'O Abú-Sufyán, this is the day of blood-letting, the day when God shall abase the Quraysh.' Abú-Sufyán trembled with fear and begged Muḥammad, when the Prophet drew level with him, not to change His mind but to be compassionate towards His people, His kindred. Muḥammad assured him that Saʻd had spoken in haste: 'O Abú-Sufyán, nay, today is the day of mercy. Today God shall exalt the Quraysh.'

Abú-Sufyán, well assured, hurried towards Mecca to inform its bewildered populace of the approach of this invincible army. He described to them how and where to seek their safety. His wife, Hind, was beside herself with rage when she heard of her husband's return and his tidings. She found unbearable the news that Abú-Sufyán had brought, and rushed out of their house to rain blows on him, intending that the people should kill this 'old, decrepit fool'. But Abú-Sufyán had not lied, and all could see the thick dust from the hooves of the steeds as the Muslim army drew closer, and the sheen of their armour glinting in the sun.

At Dhí-Ṭuwá, outside Mecca, Muḥammad called a halt. He put His head on the saddle and gave thanks for the unparalleled, bloodless victory which God had given Him. Eight years before, a fugitive from His home, He had looked back at the city of His forefathers and exclaimed: 'God knoweth that I love thee. Had not thy people expelled me, never would I have chosen any other city above thee, nor exchanged any other city for thee. Separation from thee grieves my heart.' Now, unbelievably triumphant, He was about to enter His beloved Mecca, not as a vengeful conqueror but as a humble son come home. It was in a cave overlooking this city that He had heard the call which shook the fibre of His being and sent Him running, terror-stricken, down the hill to His home, to His wife to cover Him with His cloak. He had been told that God had chosen Him to be His Messenger to mankind, and it was too great a wonder to contemplate, too great a burden to bear. He was to proclaim the all-encompassing sovereignty of the one All-Mighty God, supreme over all. But when He had spoken, taunts and jeers and insults, beyond human endurance, had met Him. Now He was coming into the Parthenon of Idolatry, to cleanse it, to hurl down Hubal and Ṭág͟hút and al-Lát from their pedestals in the House of His Father, Abraham.

Muḥammad rendered His thanksgiving, raised His head from the saddle and ordered the entry of His men into Mecca. Az-Zubayr Ibn al-'Awwám and his contingent of the Emigrants were told to enter by the upper regions in the north. K͟hálid Ibn al-Walíd, with the Bedouins of the Sulaym, the Juhaynah and the Muzaynah and the rest, were directed to make their entrance by the lower regions. Abú-'Ubaydah Ibn al-Jarráḥ was to lead a number of unarmed men, both of the Muhájirún and the Anṣár. Sa'd Ibn 'Ubádah, whose threats had alarmed Abú-Sufyán, had been told to hand over the banner of the Anṣár to his son, Qays, who was now to ride at the head of the main body of the Medinites. The Prophet and His escort, composed of both Meccans and Medinites, moved in by the way of Ad͟hák͟hir, in the upper part of Mecca. K͟hálid was the only commander to meet with resistance. 'Ikrimah Ibn Abí-Jahl, Ṣafwán Ibn Umayyah, Sahl Ibn 'Amr and some others of the irreconcilables gave battle and K͟hálid had to fight them. It is said that when Muḥammad heard that K͟hálid was slaughtering the Qurays͟h, He immediately sent him an order to desist; but somehow his messenger, instead of telling K͟hálid: '*Irfa' 'anhumu's-sayf*' ('Take off the sword from them') said: '*Ḍa' fíhimu's-sayf*' ('Put the sword on to them'). However, the irreconcilables, having suffered heavy casualties, were soon subdued and their ringleaders fled.

In the meantime, the Prophet, after a period of rest, mounted His horse and, flanked again by Abú-Bakr and Usayd Ibn Ḥuḍayr, rode to the entrance of the Ka'bah. This was not a pilgrimage, and He had not donned the required garb, but was fully clad in His coat of mail. He had come to end the reign of the idols in that holy place. It is related that three hundred and sixty idols were ranged around the court of the Ka'bah. As the Prophet moved from one to the other, to hurl them down, He exclaimed: 'Truth has come and the false has departed, indeed the false has truly gone.' This was the climax, the supreme moment of the mission of Muḥammad.

Then Muḥammad entered the structure of the Ka'bah. Inside were human representations on the walls. He ordered them to be effaced except for those of the Virgin Mary and the Infant Jesus.

The House of 'Abda'd-Dár had the custodianship of the Ka'bah and the Prophet now returned the key of the building to 'Uthmán Ibn Ṭalḥah and confirmed the right of his House to that custodianship, although 'Abbás coveted that honour. The Meccans, almost assured that the Prophet did not intend to harm them, came out of their houses and made their way to the Ka'bah. Among them was Suhayl Ibn 'Amr, he who at al-Ḥudaybíyyah had refused to allow the Prophet to call Himself the Apostle of God in the document establishing a truce. To Muḥammad's query as to what was passing through their minds and how they thought He would treat them, Suhayl replied that their thoughts turned to His goodness. He implied that as Joseph had forgiven his brothers, Muḥammad would forgive them. Muḥammad was greatly moved by Suhayl's words and it is related that He wept. After reminding the Meccans of the wrongs they had done to the Prophet, He forgave them and let them go in peace. Mecca itself He placed under immunity from all manner of transgression.

Next Muḥammad went up Mount Ṣafá. There He had a clear view of the Ka'bah. And Meccans crowded there to pledge Him their fealty. Abú-Bakr led his blind father, Abú-Quḥáfah, to the Prophet, and the old idolater touched the hand of Muḥammad to establish his loyalty. He had held out for a score of years, whereas his son had been the fourth to embrace the Faith of Muḥammad. At that moment, súrah cx of the Qur'án—*Súrat-an-Naṣr* ('Help') —was revealed: 'When comes the help of God and victory; and thou seest people entering God's religion in multitudes, then render thou praise and thanks unto thy Lord, and beseech His forgiveness; for verily He is the Forgiving.' The Prophet had been so generous to the people of Mecca and had so extolled their city that the Medinites felt anxious lest He choose to reside there. Muḥammad had to hasten to assure the Anṣár that He would never abandon them, that Medina would remain His home.

Of the Meccans, there were eleven men and six women whose lives the Prophet had declared forfeit. Four of these men and three of the women were put to death, but the rest were saved either by their own efforts or by the intercession of a Muslim. The reasons for the outlawing of these Meccans were mainly of two kinds: accepting Islám and then recanting subsequent to gross misdemeanour, and injuring the reputation of the Prophet by word or deed. One of them, 'Abdu'l-'Uzzá Ibn Hilál (whom Muḥammad had named 'Abdu'lláh after his conversion), had murdered his Muslim companion while on a mission for the Prophet and had then fled to Mecca, taking with him the animals consigned to his care for the Muslim community. He met his death. Another outlaw was 'Abdu'lláh Ibn Sa'd, a foster-brother of 'Uthmán Ibn 'Affán. While engaged as the Prophet's amanuensis, 'Abdu'lláh would add to or subtract from the verses dictated to him. Once this erratic behaviour became known, he ran away to Mecca where he declared that Muḥammad was not cognizant of what He was saying, and that he, 'Abdu'lláh Ibn Sa'd, had written down what was the correct revelation. Now, he took refuge with his foster-brother. After the lapse of a few days, 'Uthmán led him to the Prophet who forgave him. 'Abdu'lláh, however, was incorrigible. As we shall see, in future years he was to have a disastrous spell of misgovernment in Egypt. A third outlaw, whose life was spared, was Habbár Ibn al-Aswad, who had caused a miscarriage for Muḥammad's daughter, Zaynab, by attacking her with his spear.[1]

The three most famous of these outlaws were 'Ikrimah Ibn Abí-Jahl, Ṣafwán Ibn Umayyah and Ka'b Ibn Zuhayr, a giant amongst the poets of Arabia. 'Ikrimah and Ṣafwán, as we have already noted, fought against Khálid Ibn al-Walíd on the day the Prophet entered Mecca. They escaped to the coast, intending to take ship to some other land, but 'Ikrimah's wife who had, in the meantime, pledged her loyalty to the Prophet, followed her husband and brought him back to Mecca. Muḥammad announced that 'Ikrimah was returning an avowed Muslim, and forbade people to speak abusively of his father, Abú-Jahl, although the latter had been an unrelenting enemy of Muḥammad. Ṣafwán was a cousin of the Prophet, highly regarded by the people of the Banú-Jumaḥ. He too was pardoned by the Prophet through the intercession of a kinsman. But Ṣafwán remained an idolater, until the day of the battle leading to the fall of Ṭá'if. Ka'b Ibn Zuhayr, regarded as a peer of the celebrated poet Imru'-al-Qays,[2] had for long years satirized the Prophet and held Him up to ridicule. He fled Mecca, but nowhere finding peace of mind, he took the road to Medina and sought out Abú-Bakr to lead him to the Prophet.

[1] See p. 70.

[2] He was the most renowned and the most eloquent Arab poet of pre-Islamic times.

Two others of those who escaped the sentence passed on them were Hind, the wife of Abú-Sufyán, and Waḥshí, who slew Ḥamzah at Uḥud. Waḥshí lived to a ripe old age in Syria. When, after the passing of Muḥammad, Musaylimah, the false prophet, rose up in Yamámah to claim the right of lordship over the Arabians, it was Waḥshí who killed him during the battle, just as he had slain Ḥamzah. And having dispatched Musaylimah, Waḥshí exclaimed: 'In the days of ignorance I slew the best of men, and in the arms of Islám I slay the worst of men.'

> Say: 'O my people who have been prodigal
> against yourselves, do not despair of
> God's mercy; surely God forgives sins
> altogether; surely He is the All-forgiving,
> the All-compassionate.'[3]

That verse, the 54th of Súrah xxxix—*Súrat-az-Zummar* ('The Companies')—was revealed when Waḥshí, having come to the Prophet, despaired of ever being forgiven. Muḥammad, it is related, commented later that for this one verse of the Qur'án He would not exchange the entire world and all that it contained—'Do not despair of God's mercy; surely God forgives sins altogether'. 'Alí also commented on this verse, saying, 'In the whole of the Qur'án there is no verse more far-reaching than this.'

The idols of Ka'bah destroyed, Muḥammad turned His attention to the pagan temples in the vicinity of Mecca. Khálid Ibn al-Walíd and 'Amr Ibn al-'Áṣ were sent to demolish them. Then, on a second mission, Khálid put some of the people of the Banú-Jadhímah, a clan of the Kinánah, to the sword, although they professed Islám. Muḥammad was aghast when the news reached Him and wept. He called out: 'O God! I am innocent of what Khálid has wrought', and sent 'Alí to compensate the bereaved most generously. Khálid's flagrant act was in settlement of a blood-feud arising many years before, when men of this clan had murdered his uncle. A moving story is told of the sufferings of the Banú-Jadhímah. Among those whose hands were tied behind their backs was a youth who begged to be taken close to the tent which sheltered the women of the clan. Here he bade farewell to Ḥubayshah, whom he loved, after which he was led away and decapitated. Ḥubayshah ran out of the tent, threw herself on his

[3] Translation by A. J. Arberry.

body and died on the spot. Muḥammad, when told of this episode, exclaimed: 'Wasn't there one, merciful, amongst you?'

The people of the Hawázin and the Thaqíf, who lived to the south-east of Mecca, were alarmed by the Prophet's successes and decided to challenge Him in the field. Their evil genius was Málik Ibn 'Awf, the head of the Banú-Naṣr clan of the Hawázin. Qárib Ibn al-Aswad, the chieftain of the Thaqíf, and 'Abd-Yálíl, another prominent man of the same tribe, gathered their forces to join Málik and his men. There was an old and blind man of the Hawázin, named Durayd Ibn aṣ-Ṣimmah, whose years have been recorded as one hundred and sixty. In his younger days he had been a mighty raider and warrior. Now they brought him in a litter, fastened on the back of a camel. Durayd objected to Málik's tactics. Why, he enquired, had the women and the children, the cattle and the sheep, come with a fighting force? Málik replied that their presence would put heart into his men and make them more determined to win. Durayd answered that this was a recipe for total disaster. They were encumbrances and, should the day go against the Hawázin, their families and their property would be irretrievably lost. Málik thought that Durayd's extreme age had clouded his judgement. When the Hawázin were beaten and took to flight, Durayd, sitting in his litter, was abandoned on the battlefield. A Muslim chanced upon him and struck to behead him. But the old man's skin was too leathery and the Muslim's sword was blunt. Durayd begged his assailant to take the sword hanging in his litter and relieve him of his misery.

Muḥammad soon learned of the dispositions of the Hawázin and the Thaqíf. He had brought ten thousand men with Him, and now Mecca provided Him with two thousand more. No more than two or three weeks had passed since His entry into Mecca, but Muḥammad saw that immediate action was required to crush the alliance of the two great tribes and thus prevent their attracting more adherents. Although a number of the clans had refused to throw in their lot with the adversaries of the Prophet, there was no telling which clans might waver and make an attack. The Banú-Sa'd, amongst whom Muḥammad had lived in the desert in His infancy and early childhood, had, for that very reason, turned a deaf ear to the pleas of Málik Ibn 'Awf. A contingent from that clan, however, had already yielded to Málik's blandishments. Muḥammad borrowed a hundred coats of arms and weapons of different sorts from Ṣafwán Ibn Umayyah, who was still an idolater. To carry them, Ṣafwán also placed his camels at the disposal of Muḥammad and accompanied Him to the valley of Ḥunayn. Málik, reaching there before Muḥammad, had laid an ambush in the surrounding hills.

The vanguard of the Muslim army approached Ḥunayn at early dawn with no idea that it was almost surrounded by the enemy. When the attack came the Muslim ranks were broken. Men turned back in panic and, in their headlong rush to safety, nearly overwhelmed their companions advancing behind them. The Prophet and His immediate entourage[4] extricated themselves from the mêlée and secured a position by the side of the valley. Abú-Sufyán, the Umayyad, according to Ibn-Hishám, expressed the view that this chaotic flight could only end at the sea. Ṣafwán upbraided his half-brother for his glee at the prospect of Muḥammad's defeat. Shaybah Ibn 'Uthmán, of the House of 'Abda'd-Dár, felt that he had now the opportunity to murder Muḥammad, thus avenging the death of his father at Uḥud.

The day of Ḥunayn might well have wrecked all that the Prophet had achieved, had not the thunderous voice of 'Abbás come ringing through the valley, telling the Muslims that their Prophet had stood His ground and was calling for their help. They responded and came back, shaken and ashamed, bent on redeeming themselves. It was now the turn of the Hawázin and the Thaqíf to reel under their determined onslaught. The men of the Anṣár were the first to engage the enemy, but it was the men of Banú-Sulaym, still pagan scarcely a month before, who drove the Hawázin from the field. Málik Ibn 'Awf made good his escape and reached the safety of aṭ-Ṭá'if. The forebodings of the aged Durayd came only too true. The Hawázin lost all. The Thaqíf sustained heavy casualties, some of their best men dying around their standard. The battle of Ḥunayn was fought on 31 January 630.

The disposal of the enormous booty posed many problems. Muḥammad was very generous towards the leading men of Mecca, His former enemies. They came to be regarded as a class

[4] Ibn-Hishám names them as 'Alí, Abú-Bakr, 'Umar, 'Abbás and his son Faḍl, Abú-Sufyán Ibn al-Ḥárith, a cousin of the Prophet and his son Ja'far, Rabí'ah Ibn al-Ḥárith, brother of the said Abú-Sufyán, Usámah Ibn Zayd, and Ayman Ibn Umm-Ayman Ibn 'Ubayd.

by themselves—people whose hearts the Prophet had sought to win. Ṣafwán, because he was still an idolater, had no right to the spoils of war. But he had served the Prophet faithfully since the day he was pardoned. Muḥammad found him marvelling at the size of the capture and gave him all the animals there around him. Ṣafwán was so overcome that he spontaneously uttered the words: 'I bear witness that there is no God but God. I bear witness that Muḥammad is His Apostle.' 'Ikrimah, the son of Abú-Jahl, was also now totally transformed. He had spent a great deal of money to bring about the downfall of Muḥammad, he said, but would spend as much, if not more, to exalt His Faith. In later years, 'Ikrimah died in Syria while fighting the Byzantines.

Muḥammad went on from Wádí Ḥunayn to besiege aṭ-Ṭá'if, the stronghold of the people of Thaqíf. This was the delectable town He had visited, so many years before, in the hope of finding refuge. Instead He had suffered wounds in aṭ-Ṭá'if, both of the body and the spirit, and had been hounded out. The Thaqíf were, for the moment, well entrenched, and Muḥammad came to the conclusion that it was sheer waste of time and men to prolong the siege, because it was certain that, isolated, Ṭá'if could not hold out indefinitely and would submit to Him of its own accord. After a fortnight Muḥammad marched away. In the meantime Málik Ibn 'Awf, who was a fugitive inside Ṭá'if, had begun negotiations for his own surrender. On the way back from the siege, a man rode his camel close to the Prophet's, in a narrow space, and Muḥammad was injured in the ankle. He hit the man with his whip to drive him away, but the next day sent for him and handsomely compensated him for that lash, which, He declared, was unwarranted. Within the next few months, before Ṭá'if recognized the supremacy of the Prophet, elsewhere other events of mighty import came to pass.

The booty and the prisoners taken at Ḥunayn had been gathered together at al-Ji'ránah, to which the Prophet now repaired. He spent the last days of February and the first days of March there to attend to the consequences of His victory at Ḥunayn. The clan of His foster-mother, some members of which had been rash enough to join the league against Him, came to ask for clemency and for the restoration of their property. Among the prisoners taken from the Banú-Sa'd was a woman, Shaymá, whose husband had died in the battle. She claimed to be the daughter of Ḥalímah, Muḥammad's foster-mother. Muḥammad was greatly moved by the remembrance of His years of childhood in the desert. Shaymá and her relatives were all set free and given ample gifts, to their great satisfaction. But the matter of the disposal of the spoils and the distribution of rewards and recompenses was complicated and long drawn out. In the midst of it all Málik Ibn 'Awf came out of Ṭá'if and announced his conversion to Islám. Although defeated, he also expected and received his meed. There were others of the leading men of Hawázin, who, having embraced Islám, had to be considered. In His attempt to do justice to the tribe of His foster-mother, Muḥammad had to appeal to the Muslims to give to Him the women and children whom they held captive. The clans of Banú-Tamím and the Fuzárah were, at first, unwilling to comply. 'Abbás Ibn Mirdás of the Banú-Sulaym also objected, but the rest of that clan overruled their leader. This 'Abbás groaned at the paucity of his own share. Muḥammad told 'Alí to shut the mouth of the son of Mirdás. 'Abbás thought that the Prophet had ordered the cutting out of his tongue, and was mightily surprised when he learned that he was to be given more of the spoils.

Meccans, polytheists till late, such as Abú-Sufyán, the Umayyad, and his sons, and Suhayl Ibn 'Amr and Ḥakím Ibn Ḥizám, had received so much of the bounty of the Prophet that some of the young men among the Medinites showed discontent. Muḥammad had to speak to them to pacify them. Once all the dispositions had been made, Muḥammad returned to Mecca, performed the minor pilgrimage, entrusted the administration of Mecca to a young man of the House of Umayyah, named 'Aṭṭáb, and left Mu'ádh Ibn Jabal with him to teach the people the practices of Islám. Then He departed for Medina.

The eighth year of the Hijrah was now drawing to its close. Strangely, at Marr-aẓ-Ẓahrán, Muḥammad was surrounded by a clamorous group of Bedouins who had not been at Ḥunayn and yet demanded their share of the booty. They even went to the length of pushing the Prophet against a tree and pulling off His cloak. Soon after the Prophet's return to Medina, His daughter, Zaynab, died. It will be recalled that she was the wife of Abu'l-'Áṣ, the favourite nephew of Khadíjah, and was rejoined to her husband when he was converted to Islám. They had a son and a daughter. The son died before his fifteenth year. The daughter was married to 'Alí, after the passing of Fáṭimah, whose wish it was.

The ninth year of the Hijrah opened on 20 April 630. Several months later in the early autumn of that year, the Prophet led an expedition to Tabúk, far in the north. News had come that hostile forces were gathering in those regions. It is not clear whether the potential enemies were the Christian Arabs of the north, or Greeks of Byzantium. Sir John Glubb, well acquainted as he is with the area in question, writes: 'The weather in the Hejaz was still oppressively hot, water and grazing were scarce, and the movements of a large force would be extremely difficult. Perhaps also memories of the disaster at Mota [Mu'tah] deprived many men of the wish to face the Byzantines again.

'It is not plain from the surviving accounts why the Apostle of God insisted on carrying out the expedition at this unfavourable season, when a delay of two months would have introduced easier conditions. It is true that a merchant is said to have come from the north and reported that a large Byzantine force had assembled at Tebook.

'This suggestion seems to be extremely improbable. Tebook itself was divided by two hundred miles of desert from the nearest Byzantine garrison and it would have been quite impossible for a force of Byzantine regular troops to reach Tebook in the late summer, or indeed at any time of year. Even if by "Byzantines", the Arab tribes of the area are intended, the same difficulties would have confronted them as were experienced by the Muslims —lack of water or grazing at the end of the summer.'[5]

There are strong and clear indications that a fairly large number of the Muslims were chary of taking the long road to Tabúk. Several verses in the ninth súrah—*Súrata't-Tawbah* ('Repentance') —highlight this strange reluctance on the part of the Muslims: 'O ye who believe! What is wrong with you that when you are told to go forth in the path of God, you stay where you are tenaciously? Are ye contented with the life of this world in preference to life in the world to come? And yet, as compared with the world to come the life of this world is meagre.' (v. 38.) Even when the Prophet returned from Tabúk, there were men who went up to Him to say that they had absented themselves from that expedition and begged for forgiveness. Muḥammad had led His men

[5] *The Life and Times of Muhammad*, p. 333.

against greater odds in the past, but such recalcitrance had not been noticeable, except in the case of the Munáfiqún (Dissemblers). In this instance 'Abdu'lláh Ibn Ubayy camped outside Medina, but did not remain with the expedition and returned home. No battles were fought during the long march to Tabúk and back.

Khálid Ibn al-Walíd, ordered to Dúmata'l-Jandal, made a prisoner of Ukaydir Ibn 'Abdu'l-Malik, of the dynasty of Kindah. Ukaydir was a Christian. He agreed to pay poll-tax and placed himself and his people under the protection of Islám. The ruler of Aylah, named Yuḥannah (John) Ibn Rúbah, who was also a Christian, met the Prophet at Tabúk and submitted to Him on similar terms. And so also did the Christians of Jarbá' and Adhruḥ. Muḥammad stopped for ten days at Tabúk and then returned to Medina. 'Uthmán Ibn 'Affán contributed so generously to the expenses of this expedition, which was the Prophet's last, that He gave him particular praise. 'O God!' He said, 'Be Thou well content with him.' Whatever the reason for the march to Tabúk, it established the supremacy of Islám among people and in territories that had been subject to Byzantium.

Before Muḥammad left for Tabúk, a number of Medinites asked Him to visit a mosque which they claimed to have built for the sick and disabled. Muḥammad told them that He was on the point of departure, but on His return He would come to pray at their mosque. But now, at Dhí-Awán, within hailing distance of Medina, Muḥammad sent ahead three men of the Anṣár to burn down that mosque. Súrah ix, 108 obviously refers to this doomed mosque which, it is said, had been constructed by the partisans of Abú-'Ámir the Hermit:

> And those who have taken a mosque in opposition
> and unbelief, and to divide the believers,
> and as a place of ambush for those who fought
> God and His Messenger aforetime—they will swear
> 'We desired nothing but good'; and God testifies
> they are truly liars.[6]

Ibn-Hishám gives the names of the twelve men responsible for the erection of the mosque, but makes no mention of a link with Abú-'Ámir. According to Ibn al-Athír, Abú-'Ámir died, shortly afterwards, in Ethiopia.

[6] Translation by A. J. Arberry.

A strange feature of that ninth year of the Hijrah seems to have been the recrudescence of activity by a variety of people, all of whom are designated as the Munáfiqún. Yet they could not have been all of the same mind, the same intent, the same sympathies. The convoluted ways of 'Abdu'lláh Ibn Ubayy and his supporters had been evident ever since Muḥammad had come to Yathrib from Mecca. He had blown hot and cold on several occasions, the last being when he encamped close to the Prophet's quarters and then abandoned the expedition to Tabúk. Not long after the Prophet's return from Tabúk, 'Abdu'lláh Ibn Ubayy was taken ill. Muḥammad sat by his sick-bed and granted his wish to have one of His own shirts to serve as a shroud. And when the Son of Ubayy died Muḥammad, in person, performed the burial rites. It is said that 'Umar protested vigorously, declaring that the dead man was an enemy of God and should not have received the honours accorded to him. With 'Abdu'lláh Ibn Ubayy there died also the hopes of those who had followed his whims over the course of years. It will be remembered that at Uḥud three hundred men followed him when he deserted.

Ibn-Hishám and others tell us of another group of the critics of the Prophet, who used to gather in the house of a Jew named Suwaylim, but apart from the fact that his house was set alight by a Muslim, little is known about him and his associates. Then we have the story of that other band of the Munáfiqún, the people who built a mosque to the detriment of Islám, not for its glorification. Shí'ah bigots have conjured up still another group of the Munáfiqún, through sheer imagination. Their list includes the names of Abú-Bakr, 'Umar, 'Uthmán, Abú-'Ubaydah Ibn al-Jarráḥ, Khálid Ibn al-Walíd, Ṭalḥah Ibn 'Ubaydu'lláh and Sa'd Ibn Abí-Waqqáṣ, who, they have alleged, attempted the life of Muḥammad twice, once on His return from Tabúk, and a second time the following year, on His return from His last pilgrimage to Mecca. These lunatic statements apart, that ninth year of the Hijrah did witness a surprising stir amongst the various factions of the so-called 'false Muslims'.

In vivid contrast stands another feature of the year nine: the growing size and frequency of deputations coming from all over the peninsula to declare their allegiance to the Prophet. Indeed, so remarkable was the movement towards Medina that the ninth year has become known as the 'Year of Deputations'. 'Urwah Ibn

Mas'úd of the Thaqíf came from Ṭá'if, in December 630, to talk of peace. He was totally won over to the side of the Prophet and became a Muslim. With his newly-found faith and zeal, he went back to Ṭá'if to proselytize his compatriots. But opposition there was still strong and 'Urwah was murdered. Shortly afterwards, the Thaqíf realized that they could not withstand the rising tide of Islám any longer. Bedouins, all around them, were making their way to Medina to submit to Muḥammad. As the Prophet had foreseen, Ṭá'if could not exist in isolation. A deputation consisting of six men, one from each clan, took the same road that many others were taking. The Prophet granted them their requests save one. They wished to keep their idol, al-Lát, for three years. On that issue there could be no compromise. So, the delegation asked for the favour of retaining al-Lát for one more year. Again they were refused. Then they asked for six months' grace, and even one month. Every time the Prophet's reply was a categorical no. In the end they saw the futility of their plea. Muḥammad commissioned Abú-Sufyán, the Umayyad, and Mughayrah Ibn Shu'bah to accompany the *Wafd* (Deputation) back to Ṭá'if to destroy their cherished idol. Mughayrah, himself a man from Ṭá'if, toppled al-Lát with the blow of an axe.

Aṭ-Ṭá'if like Mecca came peacefully into the fold of Islám.

16

The Farewell

THE number of deputations was fast increasing. Professor Montgomery Watt writes: '. . . From the time of Muḥammad's return to Medina from Ḥunayn the trickle of such deputations became a stream. The strain on Muḥammad and his advisers must have been great. There were dozens of tribes and sub-tribes and smaller groups. Within a group of whatever size there were usually at least two factions or rival subdivisions. If a deputation came to Medina from a tribe, as often as not it was from one section of a tribe trying to steal a march on another section. To deal with such deputations tactfully Muḥammad must have had an extensive knowledge of the internal politics of the various groups. Not for nothing is Abú-Bakr, his chief lieutenant, said to have been an expert on genealogy, which included a knowledge of the relation to one another of the subdivisions of any group. That things went so smoothly says much for Muḥammad's wisdom in handling these affairs.'[1]

The deputation of the Banú-Tamím who came from the heart of Najd, headed by such prominent men as 'Uṭárid Ibn Ḥájib and Aqra' Ibn Ḥábis, challenged Muḥammad to a recitation and poetry contest. The Prophet had never composed a line of poetry. He was not a poet, He always maintained; the Qur'án was the Word of God revealed to Him. But His opponents had tried to picture Him as a versifier, passing off His brave show of eloquence as revelations from God. Arabs possessed a very rich poetry, although of limited range. They were apt to break into verse—resonant, mellifluous, exaggerated—at every turn of their fortune. There are sheafs of excellent poems, either by His people or His foes, commemorating the battles of the Prophet. Now, when challenged to a contest He accepted it, listened patiently to

[1] *Muhammad, Prophet and Statesman*, p. 213.

their oratory and then told His poet, Ḥassán Ibn Thábit of the Anṣár, to match their eloquence. These men of Najd were content with what they heard and admitted the superiority of the Prophet's champions. Muḥammad gave them suitable gifts and sent them home.

The tribe of the Banú-Sa'd Ibn Bakr sent a man named Ḍimám Ibn Tha'labah to the Prophet to investigate His Cause. Ḍimám boldly entered the Prophet's mosque and walked up to a group of people, amongst whom Muḥammad was sitting, and enquired which of them was the son of 'Abdu'l-Muṭṭalib. Muḥammad said that He was, and Ḍimám, to make certain, asked whether He was Muḥammad. Having ascertained this, Ḍimám addressed the Prophet: 'O Son of 'Abdu'l-Muṭṭalib! I shall speak to you with force and vehemence. Do not be offended.' Then he put a string of questions to the Prophet, the gist of which was whether Muḥammad truly claimed to be sent by God with those beliefs, practices and ordinances which He had propounded, and whether He would swear and stand by what He had said. Having received positive answers to all his questions, Ḍimám declared himself a Muslim, went back to his tribe, told them to do away with their idols and brought the Banú-Sa'd Ibn Bakr into the fold of Islám.

Ḥátim of the Ṭayy was renowned for his generosity. Today, after the lapse of fourteen hundred years, his name still stands throughout the world of Islám as a byword for that quality, both materially and in the realm of the mind and the spirit. In the course of centuries historians, chroniclers, story-tellers and poets have lavishly used his name. By the year ten of the Hijrah, which opened 9 April 631, Ḥátim was dead and his son, 'Adí, remained unreconciled to Islám. 'Alí had already led a small force into the territory of the Ṭayy, had demolished their temple and destroyed their idol called Fils. 'Adí, himself a Christian, had fled to Syria, but his sister had been captured and taken to Medina. Muḥammad treated her in the way that befitted the daughter of Ḥátim. She was sent back to her people, well escorted and endowed. Overpowered by the magnanimity of Muḥammad, she travelled to Syria in search of her brother and persuaded him to go to Medina and make his peace with the Prophet. At Medina, 'Adí went straight into the presence of Muḥammad, but, as soon as he disclosed his identity, the Prophet arose and walked out towards

His house. 'Adí followed Him. On the way an old woman, with a petition to make and a problem to resolve, stopped the Prophet and held him in a very long conversation. Muḥammad's meekness, patience and loving-kindness towards her left a deep impression on the son of Ḥátim. In His home, Muḥammad offered the best seat He had to 'Adí and chose to sit on bare earth Himself. 'Adí, who had come to make his peace with the Prophet, and to offer to pay the poll-tax demanded of the People of the Book, instead offered Muḥammad his undying devotion. In future years he was to play a distinguished part in the affairs of Islám.

The Prophet had good reason to be pleased with the tribe of Ḥátim. One of its leading men, Zayda'l-Khayl—Zayd of the Horses—who was both chivalrous and brave, had come earlier to test the validity of the position of Muḥammad and of His Faith. In the end Zayd and a large number of His people accepted Islám. Muḥammad called this singularly outstanding man Zayda'l-Khayr—Zayd of Goodness (or Zayd the Good)—and remarked that his sterling qualities excelled even the glowing accounts which had reached Him. Sadly, Zayd did not have long to live after his conversion.

Deputations also came to Medina from Yemen, then in an unsettled state following the death of Bádhán, who had held it in the name of the Sásánian monarch but had been converted to Islám. In Yemen lived the descendants of 'Abd-Kulál and other illustrious Ḥimyarite rulers. The Prophet sent 'Alí and Khálid Ibn al-Walíd, each at the head of a force, to stabilize the situation. Mu'ádh Ibn Jabal, whom the Prophet chose on many occasions to teach various groups of people the principles and practices of Islám, was also sent on that errand to Yemen. With the deputation of the Banú-Bajílah, whose haunts were in the interior of Yemen, came Jarír Ibn 'Abdu'lláh, whom Muḥammad held in high regard. Jarír succeeded in demolishing a famed pagan temple in Yemen.

The Christians of Najrán, living to the north of Yemen, were well aware of the fact that Islám was now sweeping over Arabia. From far and wide, even from the island of Baḥrayn, subject to Sásánian rule, deputations were making their way to Medina. Then came emissaries from Muḥammad to Najrán, and the priests and dignitaries of the town gathered together to take counsel and to debate the issue. There was a strong tendency in that meeting to form a confederacy with neighbours such as the Madhḥij and the Sabá, to defy Muḥammad, for they found it hard to place themselves under His protection and pay the poll-tax. It is recorded that a very old man (well over a hundred years old), named Ḥuṣayn Ibn Alqamah, of the Banú-Bakr Ibn Wá'il, who was a Muslim in secret, warned that assemblage not to let their passions guide them, but to consider their situation calmly. At first his sober words induced an inflammatory harangue from the chieftain of Banu'l-Ḥárith Ibn Ka'b, but in the end he gave way to reason. It was decided to send a deputation to Medina to parley with Muḥammad. In Medina, there was still talk of offering a challenge to the Prophet, but finally these Christians of Najrán submitted to the inevitable and made a pact with Him instead. It seems that they even requested Muḥammad to send them a governor, and the Prophet appointed Abú-'Ubaydah Ibn al-Jarráḥ to that office.

Included in the deputation of the people of al-Yamámah was one named Musaylimah, who ostensibly became a Muslim. But on his return to Yamámah he claimed that he, too, was a messenger of God and had the same status as Muḥammad. He began a letter to the Prophet with these words: 'From Musaylimah, the Apostle of God, to Muḥammad, the Apostle of God,' and invited Muḥammad to divide the world between them. Muḥammad's reply was to the point: 'From Muḥammad, the Apostle of God, to Musaylimah, the liar.' As will be seen, after the passing of the Prophet, Musaylimah and the people of Yamámah rose up, in unison with others, to break the power of Islám, but they failed.

In March 631, when the season of pilgrimage arrived, Muḥammad decided not to undertake the journey to Mecca. Certain customs lingering from the past, and apparently still in vogue, seem to have ordered His decision. He appointed Abú-Bakr to lead the pilgrims, and entrusted 'Alí with the task of conveying to them certain recent revelations concerning the idolaters. After a period of grace, idolaters were not to be admitted any longer into the Ka'bah. Authorities such as Ibn-Hishám, aṭ-Ṭabarí and Ibn-al-Athír have maintained that Abú-Bakr kept his position as the leader of the pilgrims, whereas some Shí'ah apologists have taken the view that 'Alí could not have been asked to function under Abú-Bakr. The argument is specious and childish, but is indicative of a rift intentionally deepened and hardened centuries later, which did not exist in early years.

The extent of the Prophet's supremacy, established by the close of the tenth year of the Hijrah, can be seen in the diversity of commissions that He gave for the collecton of revenues: 'Alí to Najrán, Zíyád Ibn Labíd of the Anṣár to Ḥaḍramút, Muhájir Ibn Abí-Umayyah to San'á' in Yemen, al-'Alá Ibn al-Ḥaḍramí to Baḥrayn.

Muḥammad's pilgrimage in the spring of 632 is known as the 'Farewell Pilgrimage': it was His last, for no more than three months of life were left to Him. His sermon during that pilgrimage indicated this, when He told His people that He would never again meet them in the same place. He particularly emphasized the fraternity of the Muslim community. All the blood-feuds of the past He unequivocally expunged from the body-politic. He affirmed the right of private property, but condemned usury. The months of the year He declared to be twelve, four of them being interdicted[2] months: Rajab, Dhu'l-Qa'dah, Dhu'l-Ḥijjah and Muḥarram; thus the old system of including an additional intercalary month was definitely abolished. (Revelations contained in the Qur'án had already made that provision.) 'You have rights over your women and they have rights over you,' the Prophet declared, and the vast congregation was exhorted to put behind them all vainglory. 'O people,' said Muḥammad, 'your God is one God, your fathers are one; you are all of Adam and Adam is of earth. In the sight of God he is more worthy who is more devoted to Him.' Fear of God and devotion to Him were the measure of the worth of a man, not his lineage and ancestry, not the glories of the group to which he might belong.

And when Muḥammad came to the end of His sermon He asked His audience whether He had not given them all the guidance they needed, told them all that needed telling, whether He had not completed the mission entrusted to Him. With one voice they replied: 'By God! Thou hast.' Muḥammad then lifted His face heavenwards and exclaimed: 'O God! bear Thou witness.' The rites of pilgrimage which the world of Islám has observed down the years are exactly those performed by the Prophet during the Farewell Pilgrimage. Muḥammad stayed ten days in Mecca, and then left His native town for the last time.

Shí'ah tradition has it that on the way back to Medina, at urgent

[2] Months in which raids and warfare were forbidden (or rather, placed under taboo).

bidding received from God, Muḥammad made, all of a sudden, a forced halt by the pool of Khum, a most inconvenient place; had a pulpit raised with saddles, and from this announced 'Alí as His successor, requiring the large body of Muslims who were with Him to pledge their loyalty to 'Alí. One can look in vain in other sources for any reference to this episode, which looms large in the writings of the Shí'ahs. They preserve total silence.

17

The Passing of the Prophet

THE eleventh year of the Hijrah, which opened on 29 March 632, witnessed the passing of the Prophet. On His arrival back in Medina, Muḥammad began to prepare for an expedition deep into the Byzantine territory. This was to redress the débâcle at Mu'tah, which resulted in the death of Zayd Ibn al-Ḥárithah. Now, Muḥammad gave command of the force He was raising to Usámah, the son of Zayd. Usámah, however, was but a beardless youth, inexperienced and untested, and Muḥammad had put under his command veterans such as Abú-Bakr, 'Umar, 'Uthmán, Abú-'Ubaydah Ibn al-Jarráḥ and Sa'd Ibn Abí-Waqqáṣ. Some felt slighted and there were muted complaints. Preparations became slow and time-consuming. From the pulpit in His mosque Muḥammad urged haste and praised both Zayd and Usámah. Then He fell suddenly ill.

Shortly before, Muḥammad had gone out, in the dead of night, to pray for the dead buried at Baqí'. One of His freedmen, who accompanied Him to the graveyard, has related that the Prophet's communion was prolonged and intense. Another night, He had gone to Uḥud where He had lost Ḥamzah, His much-loved uncle, to pray over the graves of His followers who fell there. It has been suggested that He caught a chill during one of those nocturnal visits.

Shí'ah apologists have hinted that Muḥammad's insistence on the rapid departure of the force under Usámah was due to the fact that He knew of the imminence of His passing, and wished men of the calibre of Abú-Bakr and 'Umar to be well away from Medina so that 'Alí, His appointed successor, could quietly assume office, free of hindrance and opposition. Although the Prophet undoubtedly wished to expedite the departure of Usámah's force, His sudden illness naturally caused considerable delay. And when Muḥammad found it impossible to lead the congregational prayers in the mosque, it was Abú-Bakr, enrolled in that force, whom He asked to deputize for Him. The Prophet's living quarters opened on to the mosque, and as He lay on His sick-bed, in the room that was 'Á'ishah's, He could hear all that transpired there. One day it was the voice of 'Umar that reached His ears, instead of Abú-Bakr's, and He sent word immediately that no substitution was permitted. Muḥammad did again go into the mosque, but not unaided, to lead the congregation in prayer while seated.

Here again Shí'ah commentators interject grave doubts. They maintain that since Muḥammad was lying ill in 'Á'ishah's apartment, she was able to keep her father, Abú-Bakr, fully informed of the Prophet's condition. 'Alí had been leading the people in prayer, instructed to do so by the Prophet Himself, but as he was much occupied with attendance upon Muḥammad, 'Á'ishah suggested to her father the idea of deputizing for the Prophet. When apprised of Abú-Bakr's action, Muḥammad rose from His sick-bed and, supported by 'Alí and Faḍl, the son of His uncle, 'Abbás, went into the mosque and brushed Abú-Bakr aside. Muḥammad, they state, could not walk and had to be dragged along. It is alleged that Muḥammad denounced Abú-Bakr from the pulpit, at the close of prayer. Needless to say, such authorities as Ibn-Hishám, aṭ-Ṭabarí, al-Wáqidí and Ibn al-Athír report otherwise. According to Ibn al-Athír, Muḥammad sat down beside Abú-Bakr, who led the congregation.

By all accounts Muḥammad suffered from severe headache and high fever. The day that Usámah came to take his leave, the Prophet was unable to speak. Strangely, there are contradictory views about the nature of Muḥammad's illness and its duration. Could it have been pneumonia? It has been stated that Muḥammad Himself ascribed His malady to the effects of the poison administered to Him by the Jewish woman at Khaybar, thus suggesting that Muḥammad died a martyr's death. Whatever the circumstances, it was soon evident that the Prophet's illness might prove fatal, which was, most probably, the reason why Usámah's expedition failed to depart.

One day Muḥammad had fallen into a coma, and the women present at His bed-side thought of a remedy. With the aid of

'Abbás, His uncle, a few drops of an unspecified oil were poured into His nostrils. This restorative helped, but, it is reported, Muḥammad did not approve of the treatment. He himself, when His fever was very high, ordered a remedy. From seven different wells seven vessels were filled with water and poured over Him. As a result, His fever subsided for a while.

There are indications that the Anṣár felt particularly anxious regarding their fate after the passing of the Prophet. To reassure them, it is related, Muḥammad had 'Alí and Faḍl, His cousins, help Him to His pulpit in the mosque, to deliver a sermon. He specially exhorted the Muhájirún to treat the Anṣár with great consideration. The Anṣár, He said, had thrown their homes open to them, had given them succour when they were in dire need, had shared with them all their wordly goods.

There seems to be some agreement that one day towards the end, Muḥammad asked for writing material to be brought, so that He might dictate His last wishes. What exactly happened next is obscured by disputation. Obviously the Prophet was in extremity, because the Shí'ah tradition holds that 'Umar said: 'The man is delirious, the Book of God sufficeth us.' It is also claimed that after 'Umar's intervention there was such a clamour in the sick-room that Muḥammad told everyone to leave at once. The question arises, if the Prophet had, by the pool of Khum, appointed 'Alí as His successor and told His followers present to pledge loyalty to 'Alí, what need was there for Him to dictate His last wishes? Sunnís and Shí'ahs alike maintain that during the period of His illness, Muḥammad, either aided or unaided, entered His mosque and spoke from His pulpit. Furthermore, it will be recalled that, at the close of His last sermon in Mecca, Muḥammad asked the people whether He had completed His mission, to which they replied that He had.

There is also general agreement that on the day Muḥammad passed away, He, to the surprise of His followers, appeared in the mosque at the hour of the dawn prayer, smiled at them, told them to go ahead with their devotions and lingered there a while. Abú-Bakr, it is related, noticing the sudden turn towards recovery that the Prophet's illness had taken, asked His permission to go and visit his family at Sunḥ, a quarter on the further side of Medina.

But within a few hours, at noon, Muḥammad passed away.

He had returned to His room, meticulously cleaned His teeth, and sought repose once again on His bed, resting His head against 'Á'ishah's breast. In a moment He was gone, with the name of God on His lips. It was a Monday in late May or early June.

Historians and chroniclers have not agreed on a definite date. Professor Montgomery Watt mentions 8 June 632, which corresponds to Rabí'-al-Awwal 13th, of the eleventh year of the Hijrah. That is the date given by Ibn-al-Athír. On the other hand, Shí'ahs commemorate the passing of the Prophet on Ṣafar 28th, which corresponds to May 25th. Monday is the common ground of agreement.

18

What Muḥammad Taught

OVER and above everything else, Muḥammad taught the oneness and transcendence of God.

'Say, God is one God, the Eternal God. He begetteth not, neither is He begotten; and there is not anyone like unto Him.' That is súrah cxii of the Qur'án—*Súrat al-I*<u>*kh*</u>*láṣ* ('Sincerity')—which is part of the everyday prayer of every devout Muslim. He repeats it five times a day. It brooks of no compromise. The statement is plain, unambiguous, decisive. The opening of súrah xxv—*Súrat al-Furqán*—underlines the statement that God 'begetteth not': 'Blessed be He Who hath sent His verses [*Furqán*[1]] unto His servant [Muḥammad] that he may be a warner unto all beings. He to Whom belongeth the Kingdom of the Heavens and the Earth, hath not taken a son unto Himself and hath no partner in the Kingdom. He created all things and disposed of all things as He willed.' And the first súrah—*Súrat al-Fátiḥah* ('The Opening')—which is also an ingredient of the *ṣalát*, the daily obligatory prayer, reads: 'In the Name of God, the Merciful, the Compassionate—Praise be to God, the Lord of all the Worlds, the All-Merciful, the All-Compassionate, the Master of the Day of Judgement; Thee alone do we worship, Thee alone do we ask for help. Guide us unto the straight path, the path of those to whom Thou givest of Thy bounty, not of those who anger Thee, not of those who go astray.'

'God is the Light of the heavens and the earth' declares súrah xxiv—*Súrat an-Núr* ('Light'):

> the likeness of His Light is as a niche
> wherein is a lamp
> (the lamp in a glass,

[1] *Furqán* is another name for the Qur'án.

the glass as it were a glittering star)
kindled from a Blessed Tree,
an olive that is neither of the East nor of the West
whose oil wellnigh would shine, even if no fire touched it;
Light upon Light;
(God guides to His Light whom He will.)
(And God strikes similitudes for men,
and God has knowledge of everything.)[2]

(v. 35.)

Scholars can argue, as much as they may, about the antecedents of 'Alláh', but none of their arguments has any relevance whatsoever to the 'All-Compassionate', 'All-Merciful', 'All-Powerful', 'All-Embracing' Godhead proclaimed by Muḥammad, whose Messenger He claimed to be. This God is the Creator of the Universe, independent of time and place, well beyond the grasp of the minds of men, supreme over all. He is nowhere and yet He is everywhere. 'God's is the East and the West; whithersoever ye turn, there is the Face of God; God is All-Embracing, All-Knowing', declares the Qur'án (ii, 109). He is transcendent, never incarnated and yet, 'We indeed created man,' the Qur'án again declares, 'And We know what his soul whispers within him, and we are nearer to him than the jugular vein.' (Súrah l, 15—*Qáf*.)

'God—there is no God but He, the Living, the Self-Subsistent. Slumber seizeth Him not, neither sleep; to Him belongeth whatever is in Heavens and on Earth. Who is he that can intercede with Him, but by His leave? He knoweth that which is past, and that which is to come unto them, and they shall not comprehend anything of His knowledge, but so far as He pleaseth. His Throne is extended over heaven and earth, and the preservation of both is no burden unto Him. He is the High, the Mighty.'[3] (Súrah ii, 256—*al-Baqarah*, 'The Cow'.)

It is a far, far cry from some obscure deity of pagan Arabia, carved in stone, to the Omnipotent Shaper and Ruler of the Universe.

The life of a devout Muslim is theocentric. As Muḥammad taught him, he must be conscious every moment of his life that he has his being in God, that he is moved by the Will of God, from Him he comes and to Him he will return.

[2] Translation by A. J. Arberry.
[3] Translation by George Sale (slightly modified).

Then Muḥammad taught the succession of the Messengers of God. He revealed a majestic procession, down the ages, from Adam to His own Person:

'Say, "We believe in God, and in that which has been sent down to us, and sent down to Abraham and Ishmael and Isaac and Jacob and the Tribes, and that which was given to Moses and Jesus and the Prophets from their Lord; we make no distinction between any of them, and to Him we submit.' (Súrah ii, 130.)

God chose Adam and Noah
and the House of Abraham
and the House of 'Imrán[4]
above all beings, the
seed of one another;
God hears, and knows.[5]

(Súrah iii, 30—*Ál-'Imrán*,
'The House of 'Imrán'.)

'We formerly delivered the Book of the Law unto Moses and caused Messengers to succeed him, and We gave Jesus the son of Mary evident signs and confirmed him with the Holy Spirit. Do ye therefore, whenever a Messenger cometh unto you with that which your souls desire not, proudly reject him, and accuse some of imposture, and slay others?'[6] (Súrah ii, 81.)

Indeed, We sent forth among every nation
a Messenger, saying: 'Serve you God,
and eschew idols.' Then some of them
God guided, and some were justly disposed
to error. So journey in the land,
and behold how was the end of them
that cried lies.[7]

(Súrah xvi, 38—*an-Naḥl*, 'The Bee'.)

The promise and the warning of the advent of a Day of Judgement and Reckoning—the Day of Resurrection—is another constant and recurring theme of the Qur'án.

'O Lord, Thou shalt assuredly bring mankind together on a

[4] The father of Moses (H.M.B.).
[5] Translation by A. J. Arberry.
[6] Translation by George Sale (slightly modified).
[7] Translation by A. J. Arberry.

day, of which there can be no doubt. God does not fail His promise.' (Súrah iii, 7—'The House of 'Imrán'.)

These three principles—recognition of the unity, the oneness, the transcendence of God; recognition of the Messengership of Muḥammad (which by its very nature entails belief, as well, in all the Messengers of the past); belief in the Day of Resurrection—are accepted by all Muslims, of whatever persuasion, as pillars of their Faith; to which Shí'ahs add the Imámate (belief in the legitimate and hereditary succession to the Prophet), and the Justness of God. Sunnís, who maintain that Muḥammad did not appoint 'Alí, His cousin and son-in-law, to succeed Him, and that an elective procedure had to be followed to find a head for the realm of Islám, reject the principle of the Imámate and further question why, since Justice or Justness is one of the many attributes of God, the belief in this particular attribute should be made a principle of the Faith, and not any of the others. As we shall see, there are sound historical reasons for this choice made by the Shí'ahs.

Subsidiaries of the Faith comprise *ṣalát*—prescribed obligatory prayer, to be said five times a day (before sunrise, at noon, in the afternoon, at sunset, in the evening); *ṣawm*—fasting during the lunar month of Ramaḍán, from dawn to dusk; *ḥajj*—pilgrimage, once in a lifetime, to the city of Mecca, by all who can afford the journey, the main rites to be performed on the tenth day of the lunar month of Dhu'l-Ḥijjah (the last month of the Muslim calendar); *zakát*—specified payments to the Common Treasury. Shí'ahs add to these payments *khums* (one fifth), which are offerings to the Imám and, in his absence, to those who deputize for him. *Zakát* is a prescription of the Qur'án, but not *khums*. *Jihád* (Holy War) is also a subsidiary of the Faith. In the days of the Prophet and in the years immediately following, this Holy War was directed against pagans and idolaters—the polytheists—and was undertaken in defence of the realm of Islám. With the passage of centuries the sense of *jihád* was obscured and lost. On numerous occasions *jihád*, when declared by a leader in a position of authority, was disregarded or ignored, the most notable case being the rescript of the Sulṭán of the Ottoman Empire, during the First World War.

The Faith of the Arabian Prophet must never be designated as Muhammadanism. It is Islám: the religion of submission to the

Will of God, and it was not imposed by the sword. Súrah ii, 257 declares:

> No compulsion is there in religion.
> Rectitude has become clear from error.
> So whosoever disbelieves in idols
> and believes in God, has laid hold of
> the most firm handle, unbreaking; God is
> All-hearing, All-knowing.[8]

And verse 172 of the same súrah imparts the essence of the Faith taught by Muḥammad:

> It is not piety, that you turn your faces
> to the East and to the West.
> True piety is this:
> to believe in God, and the Last Day,
> the angels, the Book, and the Prophets,
> to give of one's substance, however cherished,
> to kinsmen, and orphans,
> the needy, the traveller, beggars,
> and to ransom the slave,
> to perform the prayer [*ṣalát*], to pay the alms [*ẓakát*].
> And they who fulfil their covenant
> when they have engaged in a covenant,
> and endure with fortitude
> misfortune, hardship and peril,
> these are they who are true in their faith,
> these are the truly godfearing.[8]

[8] Translation by A. J. Arberry.

Postscript

SUCH were the antecedents, the life, the mission, the labours, the achievements of Muḥammad, the Apostle of God. He totally transformed the fortunes of a loosely-associated group of tribes and made of them a single, resolute nation. He banished idolatry from Arabia. From His time Arabia and her people came into the full light of history.

As long as He bore no responsibility for presiding over the fortunes of men, Muḥammad, in the face of constant abuse, vilification, physical assault and injury, did not raise a finger to defend Himself. But as soon as the destinies and the security of His followers and indeed of a whole town came to rest in His hands, He acted as a ruler should, with tact and forbearance, with wisdom and justice. It was His duty to halt the aggressor, to counter the moves of the adversary, to neutralize the efforts of the enemy, and if need be to order his elimination. He had no other choice in a largely lawless land. At al-Ḥudaybíyyah, while engaged in negotiating a truce with the implacable idolaters, Muḥammad gave way to Suhayl Ibn ʻAmr, the Meccan envoy, and instructed the scribe to delete the expression, 'Muḥammad the Apostle of God' from the draft treaty and refer to Him simply as 'Muḥammad Ibn ʻAbdi'lláh'. Even more, He acceded to the demand that a Meccan, who had embraced Islám and gone to Medina, against the wishes of his people, should be returned to Mecca. But in the matter of the worship of idols, of joining partners with the Supreme Creator of the Universe, Muḥammad never compromised, never yielded an inch.

It is untrue to say (as it has been said again and again by those who would denigrate Muḥammad) that Islám was the religion of the sword. It was months after the fall of Mecca that Ṣafwán Ibn Umayyah, who had been outlawed and subsequently pardoned by Muḥammad, declared his allegiance to Islám, entirely of his own choosing. Throughout the long years that ʻAbdu'lláh

Ibn Ubayy and his associates paid only lip-service to Muḥammad and tried to thwart His purpose, never was any force used to wrest a declaration of total allegiance from them. 'Adí, the son of the celebrated Ḥátim, went to Medina in two minds whether to give recognition to the prophethood of Muḥammad or not; he was accorded the honours due to a son of such a renowned father, and became a Muslim under no threat or pressure. That great work of Sir Thomas Arnold, *The Preaching of Islam*, admirably recounts the story of the spread of the Faith of Muḥammad.

Another malicious lie which the detractors of Muḥammad have never tired of reiterating concerns His marriages. In the first instance it should be borne in mind that as long as Khadíjah lived (who was much older than Muḥammad) the Prophet took no other wife. Arabs were polygamous and there existed no deterrent to Muḥammad, should he have wished to marry a woman younger than Khadíjah in her lifetime. Yet He remained monogamous in the prime of His youth. And after Khadíjah had died He did not rush immediately into fresh matrimony. The story of his later marriages, already related, proves conclusively that the marriages of the Prophet were not those of a voluptuary, as alleged oftentimes by detractors.

The record of the life of Muḥammad, cleared of encumbrances laid on it by ignorant Muslims of past times, speaks for itself. The Apostle of God is vindicated by His achievements—brilliant, unassailable and enduring.

PART II
The Course of Islám

19

The Succession

THE Prophet lay dead. As the news spread, confusion prevailed. ‘Umar, in his headstrong way, refused to countenance the fact that Muḥammad had passed out of this world. With drawn sword he stood in the thoroughfare defying anyone who dared to assert the fact of the Prophet’s death, until the gentle Abú-Bakr, wise and calm, arrived at the scene and pacified him. Hearing the shattering news, Abú-Bakr hurried to his daughter’s house, approached the mortal remains of the Prophet, pulled aside the robe that covered Him and put his lips thrice on Muḥammad’s forehead. ‘Greater art Thou,’ he said, ‘than the measure of praise, greater than the reach of lamentation. Were it within our power, we would have offered our lives for Thy life.’ Striving to restrain his tears, he added: ‘Were it not that Thou hast forbidden us to weep over the dead, streams of tears would have rained from our eyes as we wept.’ Then, after admonishing ‘Umar, he ascended the pulpit that had been Muḥammad’s, as the people, bewildered and dazed, gathered round him, and he addressed them thus:

‘Whoever worshipped the person of Muḥammad, let him know that Muḥammad hath died; and whoever worshipped God, let him know that God doth not die. Muḥammad was the Messenger of God, and other Prophets too, before Him, left this world. Muḥammad has gone from our midst; but keep your faith in Him and worship God. Should you rebel and break your faith, the loser will not be God.’

‘Umar submitted, and those who had gathered, understanding what had befallen them, dispersed. But dire winds of discord were already blowing.

‘Alí, whose right it was to assume the fallen mantle of authority, was engaged, with others of the Prophet’s close relatives, in preparing His funeral. For the time, the succession lay unguarded and open to seizure. Sa'd Ibn 'Ubádah, the leader of the Khazraj, though feeble and bed-ridden, decided to make a bid for the prize. Unable to walk, his people carried him on a litter to their place of assemblage. Others of the Medinites gathered there too, including men of Khazraj and of Aws, such as Usayd, the son of Ḥuḍayr, and Bashír, the son of Sa'd, who were envious of the Khazrajites. Although there was no one in their own ranks of sufficient standing to put forward as a rival claimant, they would not accept the Khazrajite leader as their ruler. Therefore, from the outset, they opposed the very idea that a man of Medina, and an Anṣár, could ever succeed the Prophet. Throughout that fateful day they reiterated, time and again, that Muḥammad had come from Mecca and was descended from the Quraysh; of necessity and by reason of kinship, His successor must be a man of the Quraysh. Those of the Anṣár, who supported Sa'd Ibn 'Ubádah, maintained as stoutly that the Meccans had persecuted the Prophet, that relatively few of them had believed in Him, that the prominent men of Mecca had plotted and would have put Him to death had they not offered Him refuge in Medina. They had given Muḥammad unquestioned allegiance, and He had found peace amongst them. The very designation which He had given them testified that their assistance had assured His victory. They had ungrudgingly shared their homes with the Muhájirún who, driven into exile, had arrived destitute at their doors. Such deeds, they claimed, entitled one of the Anṣár to hold the station of vicar of the Prophet. But this assumption was fraught with incalculable danger.

None, least of all of the Muhájirún, could dispute that the record of the Anṣár was noble and heroic. In opening their city to Muḥammad and declaring their determination to follow Him at all times, they had dared greatly, for they had thrown a bold and unmistakable challenge to the whole of Arabia. In the darkest hours they had stood firm and unflinching by the side of the Prophet. All this was evident. Nevertheless, the tribes and clans of Arabia considered the people of Aws and Khazraj as no greater than themselves; they could never accept a successor to the Prophet chosen from the ranks of the Anṣár.

Abú-Bakr was well aware of the impending perils, and that nothing less than the unity of Islám was at stake. As soon as the news of the gathering of the Anṣár reached him, he hastened to the meeting-place, accompanied by 'Umar and Abú-'Ubaydah, the son of al-Jarráḥ, another Qurayshite who commanded great respect. Now the argument was truly joined, and in the ensuing confusion the claims of 'Alí were forgotten.

Muḥammad had left neither a will nor any other document to specify a successor. But he had mentioned orally that His cousin and son-in-law should succeed Him. 'Alí was young. There were much older men in the ranks of the Muslims, prominent, well-tested and experienced, who believed that their age coupled with their services gave them a valid claim. There were also many leading figures among the Muslims—Muhájirún and Anṣár alike—who for a variety of reasons were hostile towards 'Alí. Thus it was that at the gathering assembled on the very day of the Prophet's death, whatever rights 'Alí did possess were, with no warrant of authority, entirely ignored. If voices were raised on his behalf they fell on deaf ears.

In spite of strong support, the claims of the Khazrajite leader, at whose instance that gathering had taken place, made little headway. The Aws, the other clan of the Anṣár, would under no circumstances countenance them. Furthermore, the intervention of Abú-Bakr and his words of warning had introduced a new element. As the ranks of the Anṣár fell into disarray, Abú-Bakr stepped forward, took the hands of 'Umar and Abú-'Ubaydah and said: 'Here are two honourable men; choose either of them that he may rule over you, and I shall be the first to pledge my loyalty to him.' But 'Umar and Abú-'Ubaydah refused to accept nomination and addressed Abú-Bakr: 'You are to be preferred over us—you, who were the companion of the Messenger of God when He journeyed from Mecca.' Next, 'Umar stretched forth the hand of Abú-Bakr and touched it with his own, as a sign of homage and a pledge of fealty. (The action was known as *bay'ah* and was the custom then and for centuries to come.) Abú-'Ubaydah followed suit. Then came Bashír Ibn Sa'd, the leader of the Awsites, who had struggled to defeat the Khazrajite pretender. In the rush that ensued, as men hastened to join their fellows in pledging their fealty to Abú-Bakr, Sa'd Ibn 'Ubádah lay deserted and helpless on his litter, and was almost trampled to death. Yet pride would not permit him to render homage to Abú-Bakr. To his last day, not far off, he persisted in his refusal. There can be no doubt that his success would have set Mecca against Medina, and unbridgable rifts would have disfigured the body-politic, at a time when Arabia was reverting to anarchy.

Indeed, the desert was astir once again. Deluded men and even a woman were claiming to be messengers of God. And with the Prophet's passing they became even bolder, gaining adherents. There was Maslamah or Musaylimah (the little Maslamah) in Yamámah, al-Aswad[1] in Yemen, Ṭulayḥah[2] (the little Ṭalḥah) amongst the powerful tribe of Banú-Asad. The lone woman impostor was Sajáḥ, said to have belonged originally to a Christian denomination, who had come into Arabia from the north. She commanded allegiance among the Banú-Taghlib, and when Musaylimah married her, their combined forces seemed formidable.

Apart from these self-appointed prophets and their substantial following, many tribes throughout the peninsula were seeking their old and discarded gods. Even beyond Arabia the people of Baḥrayn were once more reverting to idolatry. Mecca, however, remained firm, while once again Medina stood out as the citadel of Islám. It was because of this sudden reversion to anarchy and idolatry that 'Alí recognized and pledged his fealty to Abú-Bakr. Schism had to be prevented. For 'Alí the supreme necessity of preserving the unity of Islám, of stemming the tide of secession, took precedence over the assertion of his own rights. It is sad that some Shí'ah apologists have lost sight of this fundamental fact, in their attempts to denigrate the immediate successors of Muḥammad.

The Rightly-Guided Caliphs
(*al-Khulafá' ar-Ráshidín – Khulafá' Ráshidún*)
A.D. 632–61

1. Abú-Bakr Ibn Abí-Quḥáfah (632–34)
2. 'Umar Ibn al-Khaṭṭáb (634–44)
3. 'Uthmán Ibn 'Affán (644–56)
4. 'Alí Ibn Abí-Ṭálib (656–61)

ABÚ-BAKR IBN ABÍ-QUḤÁFAH (A.D. 632–34)

Abú-Bakr's first act was to send into Byzantine territory the expedition which the Prophet Himself had organized during the last days of His life. The leader, appointed by the Prophet, was the youth Usámah, the son of that Zayd who had lost his life at Mu'tah. Now Usámah was to undertake the same errand as his

[1] It is believed that he was killed prior to the passing of the Prophet.

[2] Again, as in the case of Musaylimah, contemptuously called that.

father and engage in battle the same people. Although the presence of Usámah's force was much needed in Medina, Abú-Bakr insisted on carrying out the Prophet's plan. Usámah's dash into Roman domains, although not productive of glittering success, had positive results, unlike the débâcle which met his father's foray. But he did not pursue the advantage gained, because of the urgent need to bring insurrection within Arabia to an end. Abú-Bakr gave the task of pacification to Khálid Ibn al-Walíd, whose generalship was exemplary, but whose ways were extremely harsh. Khálid succeeded brilliantly and his feat served as a prelude to the dazzling victories which he was to win in the realms of the Sásánids and the Byzantines.

Within a year of the passing of the Prophet, Muslim armies were moving northwards. At first the principalities—those tributaries to the two great Empires—were engaged, but soon the Muslims came face to face with the Romans and the Persians themselves. Why did the Arabs, within such a short time, erupt from their homeland to challenge the might of the civilized world? Many reasons have been advanced, among them the fervid desire to spread the new Faith, love of conquest and love of plunder. But no single reason serves as sufficient explanation. It was the combination of a number of factors that made the armies of Islám march into lands beyond the confines of their peninsula. The energetic and highly successful campaigns to discipline and pacify the rebellious and turbulent tribes had created an efficient military force which required an extension of its activities. It had also profoundly affected the clans to the north, who stood between the Muslims of Arabia and the declining Empires. It is well to mark the action of al-Muthanná, the son of Ḥárith, a chieftain of the tribe of Banú-Shaybán. Noticing the altered situation, both within Arabia and in the Sásánid realms, al-Muthanná decided, in 633, to lay hold of the fertile region of Sawád, in the central area of Mesopotamia. He declared himself a Muslim, invaded the Sásánid territory, and then asked Medina for help. That help took some time to arrive. In the meantime, Khálid had forced Ḥírah to submit. Thus conflicts grew and engagements widened by degrees. Given on the one hand the resurgent, vigorous faith of the Muslims, and on the other the overweening pride and arrogance of two war-weary, exhausted and effete Empires, the outcome was inevitable.

Abú-Bakr had to endure initial set-backs and did not live to witness the resounding triumphs of his armies. He died on 23 August 634, when he had been Caliph (*khalífatu*[3] *Rasúli'lláh*—the vicar or successor of the Messenger of God) for two years and two months. On his death-bed Abú-Bakr appointed 'Umar to succeed him, an act which nullified the elective principle upon which his own position had been based. Abú-Bakr was a good and just ruler, a man of deep piety. But his accession to the seat of authority and the manner in which he named his successor were unrelated to any specific command of the Prophet.

'UMAR IBN AL-KHAṬṬÁB (A.D. 634–44)

'Umar was stern but just. He had always resented Khálid's high-handed treatment of adversaries and before long took from Khálid his command in Syria, putting Abú-'Ubaydah, the son of al-Jarráḥ, at the head of the armies facing the forces of Heraclius. But before this change, Khálid, still in command, made a swift and triumphal march through Syria to take the Byzantines from the rear near Damascus, which, after a six-months' siege, opened its gates in September 635. Khálid also fought the great battle of Yarmúk[4] when, on a very hot day in August 636, the Byzantines suffered their most crushing defeat. Jacobite Christians contributed to this profound humiliation of Byzantium. Heraclius received at Antioch the news of that total disaster. He knew then that all was lost and that Syria could not be regained. After attending a service of intercession in the cathedral, he dejectedly took the road to the coast and boarded a ship for Constantinople. As he gazed on the land he was leaving he broke out in anguished lamentation: 'Farewell, a long farewell to Syria. What an excellent country is this for the enemy!'[5] He had only recently wrenched that fair land from the grasp of the Persians. This visitation of the uncouth warriors of Arabia he deemed to be Heaven's judgement upon him, for had he not incestuously married his niece?

On the Persian front Sa'd, the son of Abú-Waqqáṣ, had been given command. The battle of Qádisíyyah, in June 637, opened the way to Ctesiphon, the metropolis of the Sásánid Empire.

[3] The term *khalífah* appears only twice in the Qur'án (ii, 28 and xxxviii, 25), in different contexts. And in neither case does it indicate successorship to the Prophet.

[4] The Yarmúk is a tributary of the river Jordan.

[5] See Hitti, *History of the Arabs*, p. 152.

Already, Yazdigird III, the last of the Sásánians, had fled to the Persian uplands. There followed the battle of Jalúlá' at the end of the same year, which made the Arabs masters of the whole of Mesopotamia. Finally, in 641, the battle of Nihávand[6] ended all hope for the Sásánian monarch. He was treacherously murdered, a decade later, at Marv in the far reaches of Khurásán.

Meanwhile, Jerusalem had come under siege with other Syrian cities and held out longer than most. When the Arabs could no longer be resisted, the Patriarch, Sophronius, sent word to Abú-'Ubaydah that the city would surrender, but to no one save the Caliph. 'Umar came, and entered Jerusalem in February 638. Although the victor, he was dressed in a simple, travel-stained robe of wool, while the vanquished were arrayed in the utmost finery. It is related that the Patriarch, struck by the contrast, observed that he could now see why Muslims won battles while they lost them. At 'Umar's request, Sophronius took him to the Church of the Holy Sepulchre, to see the places sacred to the Christians. 'Umar was still inside the church when the hour of prayer overtook him. He asked the Patriarch where he could put down his mat to pray. But when told he might pray where he stood, 'Umar preferred to go to the porch, since were he to pray within the church, Muslims might, in years to come, claim the spot as their own and thus encroach upon the rights of the Christians. 'Umar's foresight was fully justified. The porch where he prayed was, in future years, appropriated by Muslims for that very reason. But the Church of the Holy Sepulchre remained inviolate.

A year after the fall of Jerusalem, an epidemic, variously described as cholera or bubonic plague, swept over Syria and Palestine, taking a heavy toll. Among its victims was the Arab commander and administrator, Abú-'Ubaydah. Then 'Umar took a decision which was to have incalculable consequences and change the face and the destiny of Islám. Two sons of the notorious Abú-Sufyán, the head of the House of Umayyah, named Yazíd and Mu'áwíyah, had minor commands on the Byzantine front where they had achieved remarkable successes. On the death of Abú-'Ubaydah, 'Umar appointed Yazíd to his post, and when Yazíd died he gave the command to Mu'áwíyah. This ambitious man, who became the administrator of Syria, was not devoid of

[6] Near Ecbatana, the present-day Hamadán.

virtues. In the Prophet's lifetime, he had been one of His scribes. He had courage, unlimited patience (which the Arabs call *ḥilm*), ability of a high order and a keen sense of governance. He showed remarkable tolerance towards the non-Muslims in his province and later in his empire. But he was also treacherous, unprincipled and indifferent to moral law in the pursuit of power.

By the end of the year 639 the great city of Antioch had also fallen and Muslim armies held sway over an area extending from the borders of Anatolia to the borders of Egypt. The Muslim commander who had wrested the southern regions of Palestine from the Byzantines was 'Amr, the son of al-'Áṣ. Now he wished to push quickly into Egypt, but the Caliph was cautious and would not sanction further exploits. When 'Amr obtained qualified approval for his plan, he moved in with only four thousand men, a small number for such an undertaking. But the Copts of Egypt, like the Jacobites of Syria, were also Monophysites, and hated Cyrus,[7] the Patriarch of Alexandria, who was their virtual ruler. The Son of al-'Áṣ achieved brilliant successes from the very start of his Egyptian campaign, and the Caliph sent him reinforcements under the command of az-Zubayr, the son of al-'Awwám. The famous city of Alexandria was a much coveted prize. 'Amr laid siege to it with twenty thousand men. Within its mighty ramparts and fortifications there were more than twice that number of Byzantine troops. Furthermore, Alexandria was a powerful naval base and the Muslims had no ships at all. Amidst the city's spectacular and magnificent buildings, which 'Amr and his warriors viewed with wonderment, stood two granite needles of the fifteenth century B.C. (wrongly ascribed to Cleopatra in recent times). One of them stands today by the Thames in the heart of London, and the other in Central Park, New York.

The detested Patriarch opened negotiations with the Muslims and Heraclius, horrified, dismissed him. However, Heraclius died in February 641 and his grandson, Constans II, sent Cyrus back to Egypt, whereupon the Patriarch proceeded to conclude a treaty with the Son of al-'Áṣ. Alexandria thus passed into the hands of the Muslims, without a battle being fought for its mastery. 'Amr was beside himself with joy. 'I have captured a city,' he wrote to 'Umar, 'from the description of which I shall refrain. Suffice it to say that I have seized therein 4000 villas with

[7] The Arabs call him Maqawqis.

4000 baths, 40,000 poll-tax-paying Jews and four hundred places of entertainment for the royalty.'[8] 'Umar sent for some dates and bread, and thus celebrated the occasion with the bearer of 'Amr's letter.

Four years later, Constans made an attempt to regain Alexandria. An Armenian general, named Manuel, sailed with a large fleet; he overpowered and put to death the small Muslim garrison left in the city. 'Amr, who had in the meantime been recalled from Egypt, was sent back with great dispatch, and the Armenian Manuel, finding the Copts both apathetic and uncooperative, considered it futile to fight the Arabs and sailed back to Constantinople.

A legend has grown up throughout the centuries that 'Amr, by order of the Caliph, consigned the renowned library of Alexandria to flames. It is pure legend. Emperor Theodosius the Great had destroyed that library long before, in his zealous efforts to stamp out pagan thought.

'UTHMÁN IBN 'AFFÁN (A.D. 644–56)

'Umar was struck down, in November 644, by the dagger of a slave, whose name has come down as Abú-Lu'lu', also as Fírúz of Daylam. Who his assassin really was—whether Persian or Ethiopian, Muslim, Christian or Mazdean—has remained in the realm of conjecture. Even his fate is uncertain. Did he commit suicide when cornered? We do not know. Some Shí'ah apologists have maintained that he was a Shí'ah, devoted to the cause of 'Alí, for no better reason than that none but an adherent of 'Alí could have wished to be rid of 'Umar. They have asserted that the assassin made his way to Írán and lived, to the end of his days, amongst people of the same persuasion as himself. Even a grave in Káshán has been pointed out as his, and has become a revered shrine.

'Umar's arrangement for the succession was yet another departure from the procedure which gave Abú-Bakr rulership in Islám. He decreed that six men should be candidates for the office of the Caliphate, and that those six should choose one of themselves for elevation to that office. They were: 'Alí, 'Uthmán, 'Abda'r-Raḥmán Ibn 'Awf, Sa'd, the conqueror of Ctesiphon, Ṭalḥah Ibn 'Ubaydu'lláh, and az-Zubayr, the son of al-'Awwám.

[8] ibid., pp. 164–5.

All were Qurayshites. But 'Umar commissioned Abú-Ṭalḥah, one of the Anṣár, to keep watch over their deliberations. His son, 'Abdu'lláh, was to attend the meeting of the six, but with no voice in the election. They were to conclude their work within three days, and should they divide evenly, the group of three which included 'Abda'r-Raḥmán was to prevail.

The deliberations of the six followed a labyrinthine course and 'Uthmán Ibn 'Affán was elected.[9]

'Uthmán was an Umayyad, and in the words of Syed Ameer Ali: 'His election proved in the end the ruin of Islám'.[10] Whereas 'Umar was just and impartial, not sparing his own son when the law demanded penalties, 'Uthmán was inclined to favouritism. Nepotism became the hall-mark of his feeble administration. He was past his seventieth year when he attained the supreme office, and was weak and impressionable. Umayyads and their clients swarmed round him, receiving not only civil and military commands, but also money and riches from the treasury. The most conspiratorial of them was Marwán Ibn al-Ḥakam, a cousin of the Caliph. 'Affán, the father of 'Uthmán, and al-Ḥakam were brothers. Muḥammad had expelled Marwán and his father from Medina, and neither of them was allowed by Abú-Bakr and 'Umar to return. Now, under 'Uthmán, Marwán wielded great power. He became the Caliph's chief scribe and counsellor and 'Uthmán lavished money on him.

During the Caliphate of 'Uthmán, which lasted until 656, Muslims reached the borders of the Caucasus, pushed on to the frontiers of India, crossed the Oxus into the plains beyond, and conquered the whole of the northern littoral of the Persian Gulf and the Sea of 'Ummán (Oman). In the Mediterranean they took Cyprus; in North Africa, Tripolitania. It was a vast dominion which 'Uthmán's uncertain hands administered: an amalgam of the eastern domains of Byzantium (with the exception of Anatolia), and the lands of the Íránian Sásánids. As the yoke of his governors pressed harder and harder upon the peoples of these countries, those who raised their voices in complaint were not primarily the indigenous inhabitants of these regions, but Arabs,

[9] Some Western writers have, in recent years, questioned this traditional account of the elevation of 'Uthmán to the office of the Caliphate, but no credible alternative has been suggested.

[10] *A Short History of the Saracens*, p. 46.

who, in the wake of conquest, had built new cities and founded new homes: cities such as Fusṭáṭ in Egypt, and Baṣrah and Kúfah in 'Iráq. Their bitter complaints were of no avail. Marwán was at the helm. Eventually they could no longer tolerate the wretchedness of their plight, and sent deputations from 'Iráq and Egypt to Medina to plead with the Caliph. In reality they were rebels. While the iron hand of Mu'áwíyah as well as his tact and diplomacy kept Damascus quiet, the deputation from Egypt complained vociferously against its governor, 'Abdu'lláh Ibn Sa'd,[11] because he was not only tyrannical but erratic as well. 'Uthmán, besieged in his house, gave way. He appointed Muḥammad, a son of Abú-Bakr, governor of Egypt, and handed his decree to the deputation. Rejoiced, the members of the deputation and their new governor set out for Egypt. They had not gone far when they sighted a camel-driver speeding in their direction. He turned out to be in the service of the Caliph, and a letter was discovered on him, bearing the Caliph's seal and addressed to the replaced governor in Egypt, 'Abdu'lláh Ibn Sa'd. It was an instruction to disregard the decree which the deputation held, and to behead the newly-appointed governor together with the rebel ringleaders. Maddened with fury the deputation hastened back to Medina, where 'Uthmán, presented with evidence of his own perfidy, denied any knowledge of it. His word can be accepted, for Marwán held the Caliph's seal and always wrote on his behalf.

The situation was now highly charged and distinctly menacing. The men of Baṣrah, Kúfah and Fusṭáṭ took their case to 'Alí, seeking his aid and counsel. 'Alí was greatly perturbed and went to 'Uthmán. The words he addressed to 'Uthmán at that hour of peril have been preserved:

'The people who are behind me have made me their envoy and mediator between thee and them. By God I do not know what to tell thee. I know nothing of which thou canst be ignorant. Neither can I guide thee to anything which is not known to thee. Verily, thou knowest what we do know. We did not precede thee in coming upon anything to inform thee of it, nor did we find anything in seclusion to bear thee its tidings. Thou hast seen what we did see, and hast heard what we did hear. Thou didst keep company with the Messenger of God as we kept company with Him.

[11] He was 'Uthmán's foster-brother and had incurred the Prophet's grave displeasure.

Neither the Son[12] of Abú-Quḥáfah, nor the Son[13] of al-Khaṭṭáb was better placed to act righteously, because thine is a closer kinship to the Messenger of God. To thee was given His daughter in wedlock, whereas theirs was not this bounty. Then, beware, beware of thy station, and take heed thereof. By God, perception cometh not from the blinded, nor doth knowledge from ignorance. The path is clear and the standards of faith are firmly established. Then know thou that of God's servants the best in His sight is that just leader, well-guided, who guideth well, he who upholdeth the precept that is perspicuous, and effaceth the innovation which is obscure. Verily, traditions and precepts that are right are evident and have signs to indicate them. And innovations are discernible and have signs to indicate them. And the worst of men in the sight of God is that leader who is tyrannical and misguided, by whom people are misguided, he who effaceth the accepted precept and reviveth the discarded innovation. For I did hear the Messenger of God, upon whom and His House be peace, say: On the Day of Resurrection, they shall bring forth the tyrannical ruler, bereft of helper and plea, and him shall they cast into the fire of hell, there to remain wandering as wandereth the millstone, then to be enclosed in its depths. I abjure thee by God not to be that leader who needs be slain amongst this people, because it has been said [by the Prophet] that a leader shall be slain amongst this people, by the reason of which the gateway shall be opened upon conflict and contention in their midst, which shall endure until the Day of Resurrection, and that which pertains unto them shall be concealed from the people, and mischief shall persist amongst them; wrong they shall not distinguish from right, and buffeted they shall be by storms. Take care not to be subservient to Marwán, the son of al-Ḥakam, lest he beguile thee and move thee whichever way he wisheth, thou who art crowned by age and advancing years.'

These words of admonition can be found in the celebrated history of Ibn al-Athír[14] entitled *Kámil*[15] (Perfect), and, more significantly, in the compendium of Discourses and Letters of 'Alí—entitled *Nahju'l-Balaghah* (The Perspicuous Path). Indicative of

[12] Abú-Bakr.

[13] 'Umar.

[14] 'Izzi'd-Dín Ibn al-Athír (d. A.D. 1234).

[15] The full title of this great work is *Kitábu'l-Kámil fi't-Táríkh* (The Perfect Book of Chronicles).

the relationship that existed between 'Alí and the first three successors of the Prophet, his words contradict the assertions of some S͟hí'ah apologists who present a picture of constant, unrelieved animosity.

However, 'Ut͟hmán was old and weak and Marwán thoroughly dominated him. 'Alí tried time and again to lower the tension. His eldest son, Ḥasan, was often by 'Ut͟hmán's side offering him any help that was possible. Other notables of Medina abandoned the Caliph to his fate, nor could 'Alí stem the tide of hostility directed against him. 'Á'is͟hah, the daughter of Abú-Bakr and the widow of the Prophet, left for Mecca to participate in the rites of the pilgrimage, not concealing the fact that she disapproved of the Caliph. Rebels offered 'Ut͟hmán the choice of abdication, which he valiantly rejected. In the end the besiegers, notably from Egypt, rushed the Caliph's house. Although his retinue put up some resistance, this could not be sustained because no force of any size was available to buttress their efforts. 'Ut͟hmán was indeed deserted. He sat calmly reading the Qur'án, when he was stabbed to death, and his blood crimsoned the pages of the Holy Book. His wife, Ná'ilah,[16] who tried to shield her husband, had her fingers severed. It was 17 June 656, and 'Ut͟hmán was eighty-two years old. Marwán, though badly wounded, escaped with his life. Then all was chaos. Rebels joined by some of the Medinites would not even allow the slain Caliph a decent burial and his body lay exposed to the whims and insults of every passer-by.

The murder of 'Ut͟hmán was a grievous blow from which Islám never recovered. The door was flung wide to dissension. Compared with what was to follow, the menace posed by impostors and the resurgent idolatry in Arabia of three decades before, paled into insignificance.

'ALÍ IBN ABÍ-ṬÁLIB (A.D. 656–61)

There was now no one to rule over the Muslims and no accepted procedure for obtaining a ruler. 'Alí—whose efforts to make 'Ut͟hmán change his ways and to protect him from the fury of his adversaries had borne no result—had retired to his house, away from the pandemonium that prevailed. In the midst of the total breakdown of authority a few remembered that Abú-Bakr had succeeded the Prophet by public acclamation. But to whom

[16] She had been a Jacobite Christian of the tribe of Banú-Kalb.

could they turn of those now left? Of the six men whom 'Umar chose, 'Alí, az-Zubayr, Ṭalḥah and Sa'd had survived 'Uthmán, and 'Alí towered over the other three. His claims were particularly pressed, in the Prophet's mosque, by 'Ammár, the son of Yásir, always his faithful supporter. 'Ammár had governed Kúfah in the days of 'Umar and had suffered humiliation in the days of 'Uthmán. For five days, while a motley group talked and talked, 'Alí held aloof from their deliberations. At last, having agreed that no one but 'Alí could be their ruler, they hurried to his house and asked him to stretch forth his hands for them to pledge their fealty. But 'Alí replied:

'O people! Leave me and choose someone other than me. That which faces me is an undertaking fraught with grave issues: hearts will waver, minds will falter, horizons will be dimmed, the right path will be obscured. And know this that if I respond to your call, I shall command you according to my own lights. I shall not give ear to anything which may be said, nor shall I heed any rebuke. If you pass me over and have another man to command you I shall be as one of you, and it might be that I shall listen to him and obey him more readily than you. It is better for you that I be your counsellor rather than your ruler.'

But the congregation would have none other. So 'Alí accepted their offer, but would receive their pledge of fealty only in the Prophet's mosque, that all might see and also proclaim their allegiance.

In the Prophet's mosque the multitudes hailed him, and one by one they touched his hand, all save a handful. Among these recalcitrants were Sa'd, the son of Abú-Waqqáṣ; 'Abdu'lláh, the son of 'Umar; Usámah, the son of Zayd; and Ḥassán, the son of Thábit, who had been the poet serving the Prophet. 'Alí did not force them to compromise their consciences. The next day he ascended the Prophet's pulpit and addressed the congregation in these words:

'When the Messenger of God passed away, people decided that Abú-Bakr should be their caliph, and then Abú-Bakr gave the caliphate to 'Umar who followed his path, and when his own time came 'Umar chose six men that they might take counsel. They conferred the caliphate upon 'Uthmán, but he acted in a manner that made you repudiate him, and he was besieged and slain. Then you came to me and called me. Indeed I am one of you.

What profiteth me profiteth you and what weigheth upon me weigheth upon you. God indeed joined you to righteousness, but mischief raised its head like a dark night. None can withstand this ordeal save those who are well-fortuned and who know the truth thereof. Verily, I guide you in the way of your Prophet. If you remain firm at my side I will keep you in the ways that He ordained. And God is the best of helpers. My worth in the sight of the Messenger of God, after His passing, is the same as it was in His lifetime. Then, do what you are told to do, and refrain from what you are forbidden to do. Do not be rash, and tarry until I have expounded matters unto you. We have reason to abhor anything which is abhorred. And God, above us in His Heaven, is the All-Knowing. Verily, I was reluctant to rule over the people of Muḥammad until you all agreed upon it, because I heard the Messenger of God say: "Whosoever takes hold of the government of this people after Me, I stand at the place of judgement and angels will open the book wherein his deeds are recorded; if found to have been just God will grant him salvation, and if found to have been a tyrant, he will be cast away." '

These words of 'Alí merit pondering.

The author of *A Short History of the Saracens* writes:

'The husband of Fâtima [Fáṭimah] united in his person the hereditary right with that of election. "One would have thought," says a French historian,[17] "that all would have bowed before this glory so pure and grand; but it was not to be." From the beginning he was beset with the hostility of the Oumeyades [Umayyads]. With the honesty of purpose which always distinguished him, and disregarding all advice for temporising, immediately on his accession he gave orders for the dismissal of the corrupt governors appointed by Osmân ['U<u>th</u>mán], the resumption of the fiefs and estates that had been bestowed, at public loss, by an aged Caliph upon his principal favourites, and the distribution of the revenues in accordance with the rules laid down by Omar ['Umar].'[18]

But the first foe 'Alí was to meet was not the governor of Syria, who had refused to accept his dismissal and had made his province independent of Medina. Mu'áwíyah, crafty as ever, was attempting to sow seeds of dissension in the very heart of Islám, in the cities

[17] Emmanuel Sédillot, 1777–1832. (H.M.B.)
[18] p. 49.

that had witnessed the Prophet's labours and triumph. Soon the cry was raised that 'U<u>th</u>mán should be avenged. And strangely enough, some of those who were vociferous in demanding condign punishment for the murderers of the late Caliph were guilty either of having encouraged and fomented the rebellion which led to that tragedy, or of having done nothing at all to avert it. Ṭalḥah and az-Zubayr were two of these, whose opposition to 'U<u>th</u>mán was well known. Both were men of means and influence and both were elderly. They coveted the governorships of Baṣrah and Kúfah, but 'Alí refused to heed their expectations. Disappointed, they abjured their pledge of allegiance and, having found a pretext for leaving Medina, betook themselves to Mecca. There they joined forces with 'Á'i<u>sh</u>ah, who was loudly lamenting the death of 'U<u>th</u>mán and accusing 'Alí of having the blood of his predecessor on his hands. But Mecca did not provide a favourable clime for rebellion, and so, with what following they could muster, they marched on Baṣrah. The governor, appointed by 'Alí, was defeated and the victors put to death a sizeable number of the people of Baṣrah, whom they dubbed the murderers of 'U<u>th</u>mán. It was true that Baṣrah had sent a contingent to Medina to demand redress from the aged Caliph, but so had the people of Kúfah and of Fusṭáṭ. The uprising which resulted in the death of 'U<u>th</u>mán was widely based.

In Damascus, Mu'áwíyah had the blood-soaked shirt of 'U<u>th</u>mán[19] and the severed fingers of Ná'ilah put on display in the mosque, and constantly harangued the people to demand the punishment of those responsible for the death of the third caliph.

Abú-Músa'l A<u>sh</u>'arí (or Abú-Músá al-A<u>sh</u>'arí, of whom more will be heard) was the governor of Kúfah; at first, he tried hard to destroy support for 'Alí, but as emissaries went back and forth he began shifting his position to neutrality, exhorting people to keep clear of internecine war in the Islamic domains and not to shed the blood of their brethren. While Ṭalḥah and az-Zubayr were establishing their power in Baṣrah, the neighbouring Kúfah was, thus, in a state of uncertainty and turmoil. At last, 'Alí had to send his eldest son, Ḥasan, to pacify Kúfah, which was done without a clash of arms. Abú-Músá withdrew from the city and went into

[19] In Persian, *Piráhan-i-'U<u>th</u>mán*—the Shirt of 'U<u>th</u>mán—has become proverbial for 'vain pretext'.

seclusion, although, as we shall see, he was brought out at a later date with unfortunate results. 'Alí was loath to settle the issue with the violators on the battlefield. Instead, he sent them letters, messages, missions and intermediaries, but they would not desist and were bent on fighting it out. Even when the two sides faced each other in battle array and the opposing archers were attacking his men, 'Alí would not order an assault. At the last minute az-Zubayr turned away, but the battle had already been joined. Az-Zubayr was killed by one whom he trusted. When his severed head was taken to 'Alí by the murderer, with the hope of obtaining a substantial reward, 'Alí wept and had him driven away. Ṭalḥah, too, met his death. Shí'ah writers have ascribed his death to Marwán, maintaining that the Umayyad, who chanced to be present, found an opportunity in the thick of the battle to avenge 'Uthmán. Sunní apologists have asserted that Ṭalḥah, in his death throes, asked the man who was tending him to deputize for 'Alí and receive his renewed pledge of allegiance, but Shí'ah apologists reject this claim.

These contentions indicate how deep the rift was to become in the course of time.

This battle, which took place in front of Baṣrah in December 656, is known as the battle of Jamal (Camel), because throughout the combat 'Á'ishah sat in a howdah on the back of a camel, in the midst of her army. Her camel became a focus for warriors who stood round it, holding its rein. When it was mortally wounded and went down, the battle was over. 'Alí left 'Á'ishah in the care of her brother, Muḥammad, and she was sent to Medina with a retinue and every mark of respect.

A delicate engagement had been won. Those who had repudiated their pledges had met defeat and were either slain or scattered. But only three decades after the passing of the Prophet, His followers—men who had known and loved, served and defended Him—were fighting one another. The sword had once again become the arbiter and the peace which Muḥammad had given His people was irretrievably lost. Christendom had already suffered the same fate, on the morrow of Rome's submission to the Faith of Christ, and for three centuries Christians had been fighting each other.

If the instigators of the battle of the Camel had been guilty of violation, Mu'áwíyah and his supporters in Damascus had never given their allegiance to 'Alí and their ranks were wide open to all types of malcontents. Moreover, they were better based and had greater resources at their command. Circumstances were now forcing 'Alí to abandon the fastness of the Arabian peninsula and the cradle of Islám as the seat of his caliphate. He needed to be with his army and nearer in person to the disaffected areas. Thus, he chose Kúfah to be his capital city.

Apart from neutrals of Abú-Músá's kind, there must have been many Muslims, who, horrified by the spectacle of civil war, felt uneasy and doubtful. What, they must have thought, had happened that, within the space of one year, the unity of a theocracy extending from the Hindú-Kush to the southern shores of the Mediterranean lay shattered, seemingly beyond any hope of repair? 'Alí, for his part, was exerting every effort to avoid resort to the arbitrament of the sword, and to help his adversaries realize how damaging their rebellion was. But he would not compound felony, would not compromise with the fundamentals of his faith and practice. Mu'áwíyah, on the other hand, cared only for dominion and power; chicanery, deceit and treachery were his effective weapons. 'Alí used his authority to serve the ends of justice; Mu'áwíyah used his power to aggrandize himself and enrich his accomplices. How could these forces, such poles apart, be reconciled? And all the while, the Umayyads cried out to avenge the blood of 'Uthmán. Many must have been beguiled by this travesty of truth, others simply bewildered.

'Alí approached Mu'áwíyah just as he had Ṭalḥah and az-Zubayr, by sending him letters, messages and emissaries. But Mu'áwíyah was adamant, until 'Alí, his own men growing restive, reluctantly concluded that another battle would have to be fought. As Mu'áwíyah had already started to move towards 'Iráq, with a heavy heart 'Alí crossed the Euphrates. The two armies met at Ṣiffín, in May 657. In the ranks of the loyalists, who stood by 'Alí, were many who had stood by the side of the Prophet, decades before, on the day of Badr. Twenty-five of those veterans fell on this battlefield. Khuzaymah, the son of Thábit, whom the Prophet had called Dhu'sh-Shahádatayn (Equal to Two Witnesses), such being His high regard for the man's truthfulness, also fought under 'Alí's banner and died at Ṣiffín. Qays Ibn Sa'd Ibn 'Ubádah was another prominent figure amongst the Anṣár who rallied to 'Alí's cause. It will be remembered that it was his father who first made the bid to succeed Muḥammad. Then both Qays and Khuzaymah had advocated the primacy of the Anṣár. Now, nothing could weaken them in their devotion to the House of the Prophet. Still another fervent champion in 'Alí's ranks, also one of the Anṣár and a companion of the Prophet, was Abú-Ayyúb, who at Ṣiffín fought bravely and outlived the carnage and the horrendous times that followed, to take part, during the reign of Mu'áwíyah, in the siege of Constantinople and to be buried under its walls. Only two men of any standing amongst the Anṣár had gone over to Mu'áwíyah.

'Alí had done everything possible to prevent the disaster of war, but Mu'áwíyah continued unyielding. Finally 'Alí threw him a challenge. Would he meet 'Alí alone in the field? Let them try their strength, decide the issue by their combat, and spare the lives of thousands. Again, Mu'áwíyah's response was negative. Historians' estimates of casualties in the ensuing battle vary widely, but there can be no doubt that thousands perished on both sides. Among them was the venerable 'Ammár Ibn Yásir, a devoted follower of 'Alí, who may well have been ninety years old. Yet he spurred his horse into the thick of the battle and his death greatly saddened 'Alí.

On July 26th Mu'áwíyah faced defeat, for he had suffered heavy losses in the night's fighting and his army was collapsing. Once again he resorted to deceit to save the day. His mentor was 'Amr Ibn al-'Áṣ, the conqueror of Egypt, the governorship of which he had lost and was now craving. A selected number of men were instructed to hoist copies of the Qur'án on their lances, march to the forefront of the troops and invite 'Alí's supporters to accept the judgement of the Holy Book. Many of the leaders of 'Alí's army had been killed; now the two who were most prominent took diametrically opposed attitudes. The warrior Málik Ibn Ḥárith, entitled al-Ashtar, of the tribe of Banú-Nakha', whom the Umayyads had particular reason to detest, favoured the continuation of fighting. Ash'ath Ibn Qays, of the tribe of al-Kindah, a Ḥimyarite, who had had a chequered career, stood firmly for an end to it. Ranged with him were many of the 'Pietists', those men whose scarred foreheads testified to the many hours during which they would prostrate themselves on rough earth, and falling on their knees bring their heads low in prayer. These 'Pietists', or 'Reciters of the Qur'án', pressed 'Alí to submit to the Umayyad ruse, even threatening him with death. 'Alí warned them: 'I am the living Qur'án amongst you; these men who now come to you with copies of the Holy Book raised on their spears have been sent by conspirators; they have no regard for truth and the command of the Qur'án and their sole objective is to gain time for their nefarious designs. Do not be deceived by them.' But the more 'Alí entreated the 'Reciters of the Qur'án' the more stubborn they grew. When 'Alí was forced that day to send word to Málik to stop pursuing the Syrians, Islám received yet another damaging blow.

But how was it all to end? An uneasy truce ruled, yet no solution was in sight. Ash'ath asked and received 'Alí's permission to meet Mu'áwíyah and ascertain the Syrians' wishes. He returned with the news that Mu'áwíyah proposed the appointment of two men, one from each side, with full powers of arbitration. It was the solution they all hoped for, he joyfully assured 'Alí. But 'Alí knew that here again a devious mind was at work. To accept arbitration implied that valid and reasonable doubt existed about his position. Yet, his rights apart, his election to the Caliphate had had the same validity as that of Abú-Bakr, and Mu'áwíyah had no reason to question it. The murder of 'Uthmán had already created a grave situation; to make the election of the Caliph the subject of review and reconsideration would inject another element of danger into the body-politic. But again 'Alí found large numbers of his own men insisting on the acceptance of Mu'áwíyah's terms. 'Amr, the son of al-'Áṣ, the *éminence grise* of the Umayyad faction, was named by Mu'áwíyah to represent them. 'Alí named his cousin, 'Abdu'lláh Ibn 'Abbás, a man renowned for his knowledge and perspicacity. Ash'ath intervened a third time, insisting that Abú-Músá al-Ash'arí be their man. Only perversity could have dictated so strange a choice, for Abú-Músá had tried with all the eloquence at his command to prevent the people of Kúfah from supporting 'Alí. Failing, he had withdrawn to a corner of Syria in the domain of the Umayyads. He was not even at Ṣiffín, nor was he known particularly for his intelligence. 'Alí told the howling mob that Abú-Músá did not have his confidence, that he was no match for 'Amr who could easily outwit him. But Ash'ath, being a man of Ḥimyar, wanted a Ḥimyarite to speak for his side, and Abú-Músá was a Ḥimyarite. 'Abdu'lláh Ibn 'Abbás, on the other hand, was a Muḍarite, as was 'Amr.

Rivalry between the people of Muḍar and the people of Ḥimyar was to plague Islám for several generations. It inflicted deep wounds as far away as Bactria (Afghánistán), Sicily and Spain, until the passage of centuries made the distinction meaningless. Muḍarites were said to be descendants of Ishmael. Ḥimyarites claimed descent from Qaḥṭan, whose son Ya'rib was supposed to have given his name to the peninsula. These two great divisions each contained a variety of subdivisions, clans and tribes, the Quraysh of Mecca being Muḍarites.

So Ash'ath and his supporters had their way and Abú-Músá was appointed. Thus peace was guaranteed for an entire year, while the arbiters would go to Dúmata'l-Jandal, in the vicinity of Medina, and there decide the issue. 'Alí returned to Kúfah and Mu'áwíyah returned to Damascus. And now those very men, the 'Pietists', 'Reciters of the Qur'án', who had forced 'Alí to submit to arbitration though he knew it to be wrong and unwarranted, began to shout: 'Arbitration belongs to no one save God, it is not thine, 'Alí'. And they urged 'Alí to admit his error in accepting arbitration, declare his repentance, denounce the truce, and resume the fighting immediately!

Meanwhile, 'Amr was plying Abú-Músá with flattery and praise, inching his way into Abú-Músá's favour. Finally he placed his ace. Was not 'Uthmán murdered unjustly, he asked. Abú-Músá agreed. Would it not, therefore, be conducive to the welfare of the Muslims if both 'Alí and Mu'áwíyah, around whom the entire edifice of contention had been built, retired, so that the people, unhindered, could make their own choice? Abú-Músá applauded the suggestion and agreement was reached between them. When the time came to announce their decision, 'Amr played still further on Abú-Músá's vanity. 'You,' he told him, 'must speak first; your station demands it; I must take second place to you, not precede you.' Inflated with pride, Abú-Músá stood up to deliver his disastrous verdict that he and his co-adjudicator had decided to depose both 'Alí and Mu'áwíyah. To drive his point home he pulled his ring off his finger and declared: 'Thus, as I take off this ring, I depose 'Alí.' 'Amr followed him, confirmed the decision by his revered colleague, and then to the wretched Abú-Músá's bewilderment and discomfiture, said: 'Now as I put this ring back on my finger, I reinstate Mu'áwíyah. He is your Caliph.' Then bedlam broke loose.

The pious men, 'Reciters of the Qur'án', raised anew their fierce and constant cry: 'Government is God's, not thine, 'Alí.[20] Why did you go to arbitration; why, 'Alí, did you appoint Abú-Músá to represent us?' Their fickleness and bigotry, which knew no bounds, created a perilous situation. Ash'ath was cowed. Málik was dead from poison. In Egypt, Mu'áwíyah's minions overcame Muḥammad Ibn Abú-Bakr, who was bravely loyal to 'Alí to the last, and barbarously put him to death. That master of perfidy, 'Amr Ibn al-'Áṣ now had his reward: Mu'áwíyah gave him Egypt to govern. Busr Ibn Urṭát, another of Mu'áwíyah's able but brutal lieutenants, led a raiding party into Arabia, humbled the two holy cities—most sacred to Islám—and ranged as far down as Yemen, everywhere spreading terror. Nor could the menace posed by the 'Reciters of the Qur'án' be overlooked, for they had now taken to murder. In their tortured minds all other Muslims, 'Alí and his supporters in particular, seemed as infidels deserving death. Twelve thousand of them, grouped at Nahrawán, not far from the Persian uplands, stood ready to launch a surprise attack. 'Alí, at the end of the year-long truce, was preparing to march once again against Syria, but perforce had to meet the frenzied zealots. Following his established practice, he first sent them letters, messages and emissaries to explain the enormity of their error, and to beg them not to run headlong into disaster. But their retort was always the same: 'Government is God's, not thine, 'Alí.' However, an appreciable number of them withdrew from the field before the rest fought and were annihilated. They are known as *Khawárij*: 'Outsiders' or 'Seceders'. The Khawárij (Khárijites in English) did not die out with their total rout in Nahrawán. For long they remained a thorn in the side of Islamic society, particularly in North Africa and the Persian Gulf littoral. Eventually they subdivided into a number of sects, recognizing and revering Abú-Bakr and 'Umar as rightful heirs to the Prophet, but detesting and cursing all who came after them. One of their subdivisions called Azáriqih (after the founder, Náfi' Ibn Azraq) dominated for a time parts of southern Írán, bearing close resemblance to similar groups of pietists in Christendom: the Montanists and the Donatists. As centuries went by, the burning zeal which drove them from aberration to aberration,

[20] Only these words are an exact quotation.

from atrocity to atrocity, was stilled. Today their remnants are found in the Ibáḍí sect of 'Ummán (Oman).

Next, three of the Kh̲árijites took counsel together,[21] possibly in Mecca, and decided to kill 'Alí, Mu'áwíyah and 'Amr, in Kúfah, Damascus and Fusṭáṭ respectively, all in the course of one night, the 19th of Ramaḍán in the year 40 A.H. (27 January 661). That night 'Amr was taken ill and sent a deputy to the mosque in his stead, to lead the congregation in prayer. The deputy fell to the assassin's sword. In Damascus, Mu'áwíyah escaped with injuries from which he soon recovered. But in Kúfah, 'Abda'r-Raḥmán Ibn Muljam, with his accomplices, succeeded in his purpose. 'Alí was mortally wounded. Two days later, this cousin and son-in-law of Muḥammad, the second to believe in Him at the tender age of thirteen; 'Alí, the first Imám of the Sh̲í'ites, and the fourth and last of the Caliphs known as *'ar-Rás̲h̲idín'* (or *'ar-Rás̲h̲idún'*—the Rightly-Guided); 'Alí, most just, most compassionate, most eloquent of men, died. The blow which, that winter dawn, the poisoned sword of the Son of Muljam dealt to 'Alí was another blow from which Islám did not recover. The door was now flung open to the calamitous rule of the House of Umayyah.

The people of Kúfah rallied to Ḥasan, the eldest son of 'Alí, but Kúfah was not Medina, the City of the Prophet; and the men of Kúfah, who rendered homage to Ḥasan, were not of the same rank and station as the concourse of the Companions of the Prophet, who gave their allegiance to his father in Muḥammad's mosque. Moreover, there was a quality of instability in the society of Kúfah which made itself felt as soon as Mu'áwíyah moved his army into 'Iráq. Ḥasan was at Ctesiphon when false news of reverses threw his troops into disorder. Further effort was useless, anarchy threatened, and Ḥasan found that no course was possible save coming to terms with Mu'áwíyah. He abdicated. The Umayyad pretender was to occupy the seat of the Caliphate as long as he lived, when it would revert to the House of 'Alí, and go to Ḥusayn, his younger son. Once the treaty was signed Ḥasan took the road to Medina, to end his days in the proximity of the tomb of his Grandfather.

According to the great historian, aṭ-Ṭabarí,[22] Mu'áwíyah wrote

[21] Professor Philip Hitti throws doubt on this traditional account, 'all of which', he comments, 'sounds too dramatic to be true'. (*History of the Arabs*, p. 182.)

[22] Abú-Ja'far Muḥammad Ibn Jarír aṭ-Ṭabarí, A.D. 839–923, the renowned author of an encyclopaedic history and an equally vast exegesis of the Qur'án.

to Ḥasan that he was aware of Ḥasan's superior claims to the Caliphate as a descendant of Muḥammad, and would himself pledge his fealty to him, were he certain that Ḥasan had the right qualities to govern. With that letter, Ṭabarí states, Mu'áwíyah sent a blank sheet which he had signed, that Ḥasan might write in whatever he wished.

Kúfah's glory was short-lived. Henceforth Damascus ranked as the metropolis. The theocracy which had arisen in Medina entered the first stage of its development as a temporal empire based on cities and lands that had borne the burden of other such empires in the past.

On the very day that Muḥammad passed out of this mortal world and before His body was laid to rest, winds of dissension blew through the edifice of His Faith. Having created a coherent nation out of an agglomerate of contending, restless tribes, and having founded a state with a framework of laws, it is inconceivable that He would not have envisaged who should succeed Him. Moses had conferred authority upon Joshua, Christ had put the keys of Heaven and Earth in the hands of Peter; yet neither of them had in His lifetime established a realm demanding an administration. But this was exactly what Muḥammad had done. Of His four immediate successors, each one of whom, as we have seen, reached that position by a different avenue, only the first, Abú-Bakr, died a natural death. 'Umar and 'Alí were both assassinated and 'Uthmán fell before the murderous onslaught of a demented mob. The appalling circumstances attending the death of 'Uthmán opened wide the way for usurpers. Mu'áwíyah, the extremely able but totally unprincipled champion of the House of Umayyah, challenged 'Alí and won in the end. The contest between 'Alí and Mu'áwíyah was responsible for the rise of the Pietists—the Khawárij—and the awakening of blind fanaticism. 'Alí fell a victim to the sword of one such fanatic. The stance of the Khawárij and their repeated depredations, through the ensuing years, could result only in anarchy and harsh suppression. Syed Ameer Ali writes: 'Had Ali been accepted to the Headship of Islâm, the birth of those disastrous pretensions that led to so much bloodshed in the Moslem world would have been averted.'[23]

Christianity had fared no better. Although Simon Bar-Jonah

[23] *A Short History of the Saracens*, p. 21.

was the disciple chosen by Christ to be the rock (Peter) upon which He would build His church, it was not Peter, but James, the brother of Jesus, still much attached to Judaism, who became the recognized head of the Christian community in Jerusalem. Upon his martyrdom in the year 62, he was succeeded by Simeon, the son of Mary Cleophas and cousin to Jesus; Simeon was crucified in the reign of Trajan. When the fervent zeal of Saul of Tarsus encountered chilling winds of opposition, they blew from the community of Jerusalem over which James presided. And when Peter reached Rome (if he ever did), it was the star of Paul that was then in the ascendant. Although Peter is hailed as the first Bishop of Rome, it was Paul who steered Christian action, and it was the Pauline doctrine that prevailed. Christendom, too, produced its fiery and unreasoning pietists. The great Tertullian joined the extremists of his day and raged against the Church. The Donatists, last of that brand, continued to pillage and murder—in particular, slaying monks and priests—even as late as the seventh century.

In Christendom and in the domains of Islám, the sword became and remained the final arbiter. But despite the feuds and the bitter struggles of potentates, despite the carnage caused by the caliphs and the sulṭáns of Islám and the monarchs and rulers of Christian nations, so overwhelming was the power of the spirit released by Jesus of Nazareth and the Arabian Prophet that their Faiths reared and sustained civilizations of untold splendour. We cannot avoid the horrendous chronicles of fratricidal warfare, nor overlook the stained records of oppression, tyranny and intolerance. Of such stuff is history made. Over them, however, shines the devotion of countless millions, who, through suffering, led mankind in its unceasing march to view more spacious horizons.

20

The Yoke of the House of Umayyah

> The persecutors of Mahomet usurped the
> inheritance of his children, and the
> champions of idolatry became the
> supreme heads of his religion and empire.
>
> EDWARD GIBBON

UMAYYADS were usurpers and tyrants. They broke many bonds and promises. They widened divisions and accentuated dissensions. But a few exceptions stand out in their lines.

Their founder, Mu'áwíyah, had qualities of strength which recommended him to his contemporaries and to posterity. He was a very efficient administrator who could be forbearing if the interests of his government demanded it. He was capable of generosity and showed wisdom and intelligence of a high order. But he was also vindictive, treacherous and exacting. One author has characterized him in these words: 'Astute, unscrupulous, and pitiless, the first Caliph of the Ommayas shrank from no crime necessary to secure his position. Murder was his accustomed mode of removing a formidable opponent.'[1] One notable case was the murder of 'Abda'r-Raḥmán, the son of the renowned Khálid who, in the days of Abú-Bakr, had invaded Syria and scored notable victories. 'Abda'r-Raḥmán had faithfully served Mu'áwíyah over the years, but because he was fast gaining public respect, Mu'áwíyah could not tolerate him.

Richard Dozy (1820–83), the Dutch orientalist, rightly maintains that the Umayyads, once having power, nurtured the same hatreds and feuds as had moved earlier generations. They were not truly reconciled to the defeat of their forbears, and their innate antipathy to Islám showed itself when, in the guise of heirs to the Prophet, they set out to desecrate much that was sacred.

[1] Cited by Ameer Ali, ibid., pp. 71–2, from Osborn, *Islam under the Arabs*.

V THE DOME OF THE ROCK

in Jerusalem (687–91) was built by the Umayyad Caliph ‘Abdu’l-Malik and stands, with the Aqṣá Mosque, on the third most holy site of Islám.

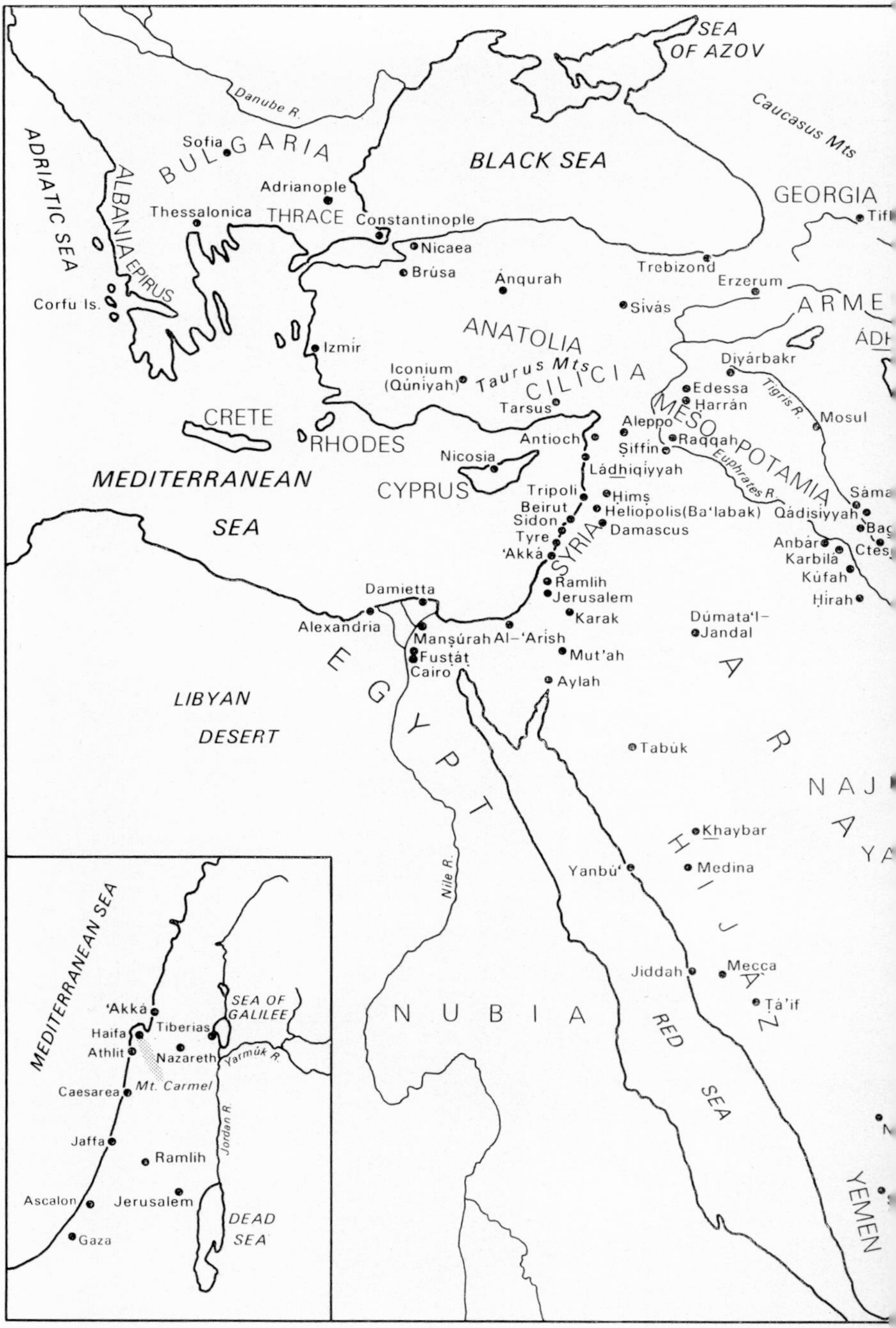

SEA OF AZOV
Danube R.
Caucasus Mts
ADRIATIC SEA
Sofia
BULGARIA
BLACK SEA
ALBANIA
Adrianople
GEORGIA
Thessalonica
THRACE
Constantinople
EPIRUS
Nicaea
Brúsa
Ánqurah
Trebizond
Erzerum
Corfu Is.
Sivás
ANATOLIA
Izmir
Iconium
(Qúniyah)
Taurus Mts
CILICIA
Diyárbakr
Edessa
Harrán
Tigris R.
Tarsus
Mosul
CRETE
Aleppo
RHODES
Antioch
Ṣiffin
Raqqah
MESOPOTAMIA
Euphrates R.
Nicosia
Ládhiqiyyah
MEDITERRANEAN
CYPRUS
Tripoli
Hims
SEA
Beirut
Sidon
Heliopolis(Ba'labak)
Qádisiyyah
Damascus
Tyre
'Akká
SYRIA
Anbár
Karbilá
Kúfah
Ramlih
Damietta
Jerusalem
Ḥirah
Karak
Dúmata'l-
Jandal
Alexandria
Manṣúrah
Al-'Arish
Fusṭáṭ
Cairo
Mut'ah
EGYPT
Aylah
LIBYAN
DESERT
ARABIA
Tabúk
NAJ
Khaybar
HIJAZ
Yanbú'
Medina
Nile R.
Jiddah
Mecca
Ṭá'if
NUBIA
RED SEA
YEMEN
MEDITERRANEAN SEA
SEA OF GALILEE
'Akká
Haifa
Tiberias
Athlit
Nazareth
Yarmúk R.
Mt. Carmel
Caesarea
Jordan R.
Jaffa
Ramlih
Jerusalem
Ascalon
DEAD SEA
Gaza

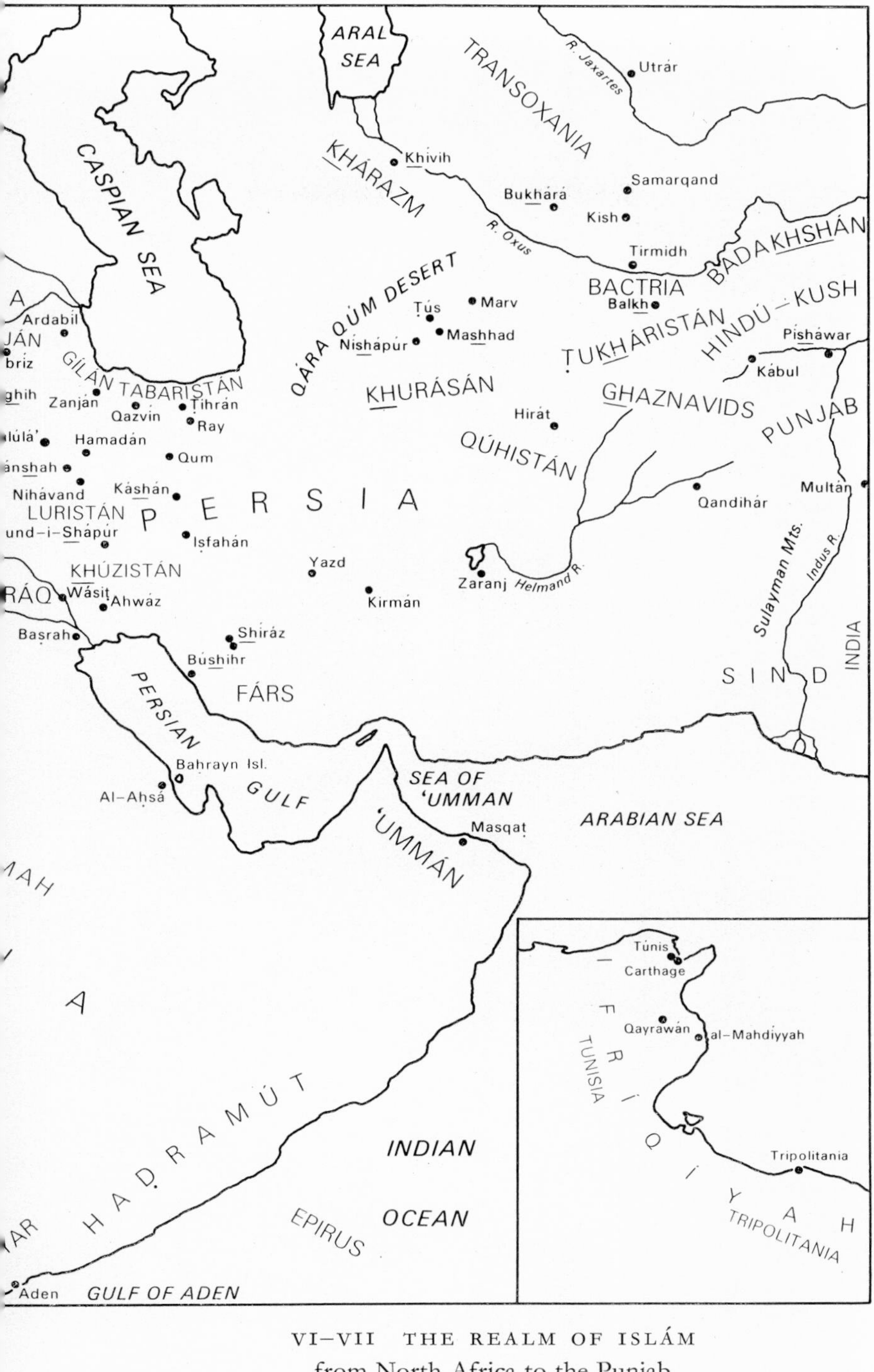

VI–VII THE REALM OF ISLÁM

from North Africa to the Punjab
A Guide to Place Names in Part II

VIII THE MOSQUE OF THE PROPHET IN MEDINA
built about 708 during the Caliphate of al-Walíd I,
incorporating materials from many parts of the world.

The expansion of Muslim domains had come to a halt at the close of 'Uthmán's rule and remained static during the Caliphate of 'Alí, but under Mu'áwíyah it was again resumed. In Asia, Hirát, Kábul and Bukhárá were conquered, while in North Africa Muslims drew nearer to the Atlantic. In the year 669, a Muslim army attacked the very heart of the Byzantine Empire; a decade later, on Mu'áwíyah's death, their fleet withdrew, leaving Constantinople still impregnable.

The Umayyad Caliphs
A.D. 661–750

1. Mu'áwíyah I (661–80)
2. Yazíd I (680–83)
3. Mu'áwíyah II (683–84)
4. Marwán I (684–85)
5. 'Abdu'l-Malik (685–705)
6. Al-Walíd I (705–15)
7. Sulaymán (715–17)
8. 'Umar (717–20)
9. Yazíd II (720–24)
10. Hishám (724–43)
11. Al-Walíd II (743–44)
12. Yazíd III (744)
13. Ibráhím (744)
14. Marwán II al-Ḥimár (744–50)

Mughírah, whom Mu'áwíyah had appointed governor of Kúfah, was extremely hostile to the cause of the House of 'Alí. 'Umar had given him office, but he had been dismissed under a cloud, believing that 'Alí had been responsible. During 'Alí's Caliphate he remained on the periphery of public life, as 'Alí had placed no reliance in him. However, once established as a confidant of Mu'áwíyah, he began to plant in the latter's mind the germ of a new idea. It would be his final act of revenge. Already he had lent himself to Mu'áwíyah's disastrous scheme of fabricating traditions ascribed to Muḥammad, maligning and denigrating 'Alí. And why, he suggested, need Mu'áwíyah be bound by his treaty with Ḥasan, since, by ignoring the rights of Ḥusayn, he could make the rulership of Islám hereditary in his own family? Mu'áwíyah took this idea to an elder, Aḥnaf, the son of Qays, one who was greatly respected and had served the Umayyads well. Aḥnaf expressed his emphatic disapproval and refused to countenance such a flagrant breach of trust. But Mughírah's promptings proved the stronger. Indeed Mu'áwíyah, who had struggled for many years to establish his own power, was loath to deny to his progeny a prize which he, himself, held so incontestably and cherished so dearly. And so Yazíd, his son, was proclaimed the heir apparent. But mere proclamation was not enough. Mu'áwíyah had to obtain the consent of a multitude of people. To quote Ameer Ali once again, Mu'áwíyah never permitted 'any human or divine ordinances to interfere with the prosecution of his plans or ambitions— . . .'[2] He flattered, threatened, bribed, until he succeeded in winning over deputations from many clans and tribes. However, in the City of the Prophet, five men, prominent both by reason of their lineage and by their own standing in the community, refused to give their assent or pledge their personal allegiance. These were Ḥusayn, the son of 'Alí, whose rights Yazíd would usurp; 'Abdu'lláh, the son of 'Abbás, the Prophet's cousin and 'Alí's faithful lieutenant; 'Abdu'lláh, the son of az-Zubayr—his mother was a daughter of Abú-Bakr—who had desired the caliphate for himself since the days of his father's rebellion against 'Alí; 'Abdu'lláh, the son of 'Umar, who had declined to side with either 'Alí or Mu'áwíyah; and 'Abda'r-Raḥmán, the son of Abú-Bakr, elderly and retired from public life. Both Abú-Bakr's and 'Umar's sons believed that they had more valid claims to the caliphate than the profligate son of Mu'áwíyah. Nothing could shake the resolve of these five dissenters, not even Mu'áwíyah's visit to the holy cities and his success in enlisting substantial support amongst their inhabitants.

A passing reference was made earlier[3] to a nefarious scheme which Mu'áwíyah calculated would bring 'Alí into disrepute and besmirch his memory. Mu'áwíyah had already instituted a daily ritual of cursing 'Alí from the pulpit. Next, he bribed some of his minions, who had known the Prophet and had been with Him, to engage in blasphemous forgery. These despicable men, such as Mughírah and Abú-Hurayrah, opened the field, under Mu'áwíyah's direction, to the corruption of doctrine, text, belief and practice. Their deeds were heinous, but their lies can, on the whole, be easily detected. Unfortunately they had their imitators, until faked traditions flooded an eager market. In this a number of Shí'ah apologists must bear their share of blame. There is a vast corpus[4] of genuine traditions that have come down from the

[2] ibid., p. 82.

[3] See p. 191.

[4] The four great compilations of traditions are: the Ṣaḥíḥ of al-Bukhárí (d. 870); the Ṣaḥíḥ of Muslim, a native of Níshápúr in the province of Khurásán (d. 875); the

Prophet and from His descendants—the Imáms of the Legitimists, the Shí'ahs—but there are also a great many which are spurious, some blasphemous, others only ridiculous. Incitement to forgery is yet another misdeed of the founder of the Umayyad dynasty.

Mu'áwíyah died in 680. Although Yazíd's succession was assured, Muslims in the holy cities as well as in Kúfah were having second thoughts. 'Abda'r-Raḥmán, the son of Abú-Bakr, was dead, and 'Abdu'lláh, the son of 'Umar, although highly esteemed, lacked the calibre to pose any danger or become the mainspring of revolt. Only Ḥusayn and 'Abdu'lláh Ibn az-Zubayr could attract a following large enough to oppose Yazíd and cause concern. Walíd, the governor of Medina, was therefore instructed to force them to submit, whereupon both men quietly moved from Medina to Mecca, where the Umayyad power was weak and the populace determined to disown the tyrant of Damascus. The people of Kúfah wrote to Ḥusayn to offer their allegiance; they urged him to hasten to their city and sent Háni, the son of 'Urwah, to plead on their behalf. 'Abdu'lláh Ibn 'Abbás, wise with years, advised caution. 'Abdu'lláh Ibn az-Zubayr, who wanted Ḥusayn out of Ḥijáz so that he might have the cradle of Islám entirely to himself, advised immediate departure. Ḥusayn took a middle course. He sent his cousin Muslim, the son of 'Aqíl and grandson of Abú-Ṭálib, to take the pulse of Kúfah. Even during the lifetime of Mu'áwíyah the leaders of that city had invited him to assume the reins of government. But Ḥusayn, honouring the treaty which his brother had concluded, would not contest Mu'áwíyah's rule under any circumstance. It was not Ḥusayn who broke that treaty, but Mu'áwíyah. His death, followed by Yazíd's reign, released Ḥusayn from any further obligation to abide by the system which Mu'áwíyah had designed.

Nu'mán Ibn Bashír, the governor of Kúfah, was an unhappy man. He held office under Yazíd, yet he was loath to ruin the chances of the House of the Prophet. Therefore he took no action against Muslim, who moved freely about Kúfah. Thousands thronged to Muslim and pledged their allegiance to Ḥusayn. Yazíd immediately dismissed the reluctant governor and sent a monster of a man to take his place. The new governor, 'Ubaydu'l-láh Ibn Zíyád, was one who would use any means to attain his

Ṣaḥíḥ of at-Tirmidhí (d. 892); and the Ṣaḥíḥ of an-Nisá'í (d. 914). Aṣ-Ṣaḥíḥ means the 'Genuine'.

ends. He killed mercilessly. Both Muslim and Hání were decapitated, and their corpses were subjected to indignities. The fickle men of Kúfah, forgetting their vows and protestations, just melted away. By then, Ḥusayn had left Mecca and was on his way to Kúfah, accompanied by the members of his family and a number of devoted adherents. When the news of Muslim's death reached him, he spurned the road back which might have led to safety and resumed his march. Estimates vary, but it is certain that his entourage, women and the very young excepted, was barely seventy in number. 'Ubaydu'lláh dispatched a force of four thousand men, under 'Umar Ibn Sa'd, to bar his way. 'Umar's father was that Sa'd who had humbled the might of the Sásánids, at the battle of Qádisíyyah in June 637. Qádisíyyah, where Sa'd gained his laurels, was by the Euphrates; and now on the banks of the same river, at Karbilá, his son stood in the path of the grandson of the Prophet. Ḥusayn had not come to fight, but he would not accept abject surrender. He suggested to 'Umar three possible courses which he, Ḥusayn, might take: to return to Medina and hold vigil by the side of the tomb of his Grandfather; to go to a frontier-line of the domains of Islám and help to keep at bay enemies without; to proceed to Damascus and hold parley in person with Yazíd. 'Umar did not want the blood of the Prophet's grandson on his hands, and urged the tyrant in Kúfah to come to terms with Ḥusayn. But 'Ubaydu'lláh would have none of the options and insisted that Ḥusayn should either acknowledge publicly and on the spot the supremacy of Yazíd, or be carried a prisoner to Kúfah. A second time 'Umar pleaded with 'Ubaydu'l-láh, begging him to relent. But the governor would not yield an inch; instead he sent Shimr Ibn Dhi'l-Jawshan, famed for his piety and attachment to devotional exercise, to replace 'Umar, whom he considered half-hearted and procrastinating, and to deal with Ḥusayn. Shimr's arrival convinced 'Umar that combat was the only alternative, since the grandson of the Prophet would never submit to the dictates of 'Ubaydu'lláh. Denied access to the water of the Euphrates and called upon to surrender, Ḥusayn knew that death was his only exit. The heroic men who were with him he freed from their allegiance, that they might leave him to his fate but save their own lives. The enemy, he said, desired solely to humiliate and destroy him, not to harm them. But not a single man defected, although they also knew that they could win only the crown of martyrdom. Ḥusayn then appealed to his opponents to spare the women and children the horror of thirst and slaughter, to deal with him alone; but the pious S͟himr and the timorous ‘Umar turned deaf ears to his plea.

It was the year 680 in the month of October, which corresponded that year to the month of Muḥarram, the first of the lunar calendar of the Muslims. The year after Hijrah was 61.

If it be asked why this detailed attention to dates, the answer lies in the enormity of the event. It was a watershed, an unparalleled disaster which unleashed passions not again to be contained. From Karbilá a wave of horror swept over the world of Islám which has never receded, and Muḥarram 10th—the ‘*Ás͟húrá*—is a date never to be forgotten.

The first act on that morning of Muḥarram 10th was a deed of unexpected bravery. Ḥurr, the cavalry commander who had first arrested Ḥusayn's march to Kúfah, forcing him to halt a score of miles away, was no longer able to still his pangs of conscience. He, with thirty others, broke ranks and joined the small band standing unflinchingly around the grandson of the Prophet. These men excelled in individual combat, but the massed onslaught of the enemy mowed them down. That day the House of Muḥammad suffered heavily, for many of the slain were related to the Prophet: amongst them were Ḥusayn's eldest son, together with his brothers, his nephews, and his cousins. Ḥusayn, at last, was the sole survivor; as the sun moved westward he sat at the door of his tent with an infant in his arms. He was wounded, an arrow pierced his jaw, and another transfixed his child. And he was now alone, but for the women and children and the only son left to him—a youth who languished in high fever on his bed, unable to stir. Warriors dared not approach the grandson of the Prophet, until S͟himr, apprehensive that the one person he had been especially sent to destroy might escape the doom envisaged for him, once again took control, upbraiding his bewildered men for dereliction of duty and charging them with cowardice. So Ḥusayn was cut down by thirty-three strokes of swords and lances, and decapitated by S͟himr. His clothes were torn from him and his naked body was trampled to pulp by the hooves of horses. While S͟himr saw to the decapitation of all the slain, others were busy gathering booty and driving the women and children before them. S͟himr, victorious and jubilant, carried the head of

Ḥusayn to Kúfah and laid it before 'Ubaydu'lláh, who, with rough humour, brought down his cane on its mouth. At this, an old man sitting nearby cried out in horror and pain: 'Alas, on these lips have I seen the lips of the Apostle of God!'

'In a distant age and climate,' says Gibbon, 'the tragic scene of the death of Hosein will awaken the sympathy of the coldest reader.' [5]

The captives were taken across the inhospitable waste of the Syrian desert to the capital city of the Umayyads. With the heads of the slain raised on lances preceding them, they were ushered into Damascus and paraded in the streets. Men and women, misguided, misinformed, misled, thronged the route to the palace of Yazíd and heaped abuse upon them. 'You are seceders,' they shouted; 'you have put yourselves outside the pale.' 'Alí, the only surviving son of Ḥusayn who had escaped the massacre because he was fever-ridden, replied: 'Nay, by God, we are His servants who believed in Him and His proofs. Through us the gladsome visage of Faith was revealed and the signs of the merciful God shone forth.' But the people retorted: 'Did you not forbid what God made lawful; did you not make lawful what God forbade?' And 'Alí answered: 'Nay, we were the first to follow the commandments of God. We are the root of this Cause and its origin. We are the sign of God, His word amidst mankind.'

It is related that when Yazíd faced the captives, and beheld the head of Ḥusayn, he wept at the sight of the stark reality before him, bitterly blaming the Son of Zíyád for the tragedy of Karbilá.

But Yazíd would not censure, let alone dismiss, his lieutenant in 'Iráq, because the security of his throne depended upon the strong arm of 'Ubaydu'lláh. Ample proof of Yazíd's own viciousness is provided by the events of the next two years of his reign, which he personally shaped through another monstrous instrument: Muslim, the son of 'Uqbah, who gained the title 'the accursed murderer'.

'Alí, the son of Ḥusayn, was sent to Medina; as soon as the inhabitants of the holy cities came to learn the full story of the wicked deeds of the Umayyads, their latent unrest erupted into violence. Only one man in the cradle of Islám, 'Abdu'lláh Ibn az-Zubayr, could turn the situation to his own advantage. When

[5] *The History of the Decline and Fall of the Roman Empire*, vol. v, pp. 462–3.

Yazíd heard that Medina was on the point of revolt, he hurriedly dispatched a new governor to calm the fears of the Medinites, but he could do no more than obtain agreement that a deputation should go to Damascus to hear what the Caliph had to say. This visit was disastrous for the cause of the Umayyads. The members of the deputation were aghast at what they saw in Damascus and, on their return, vociferously denounced it. Open revolt flared up, Yazíd's authority was defied, allegiance to him renounced, and his governor was expelled. Members and clients of the clan of Umayyah found themselves besieged in their homes. But the angry and outraged men of Medina had no one of sufficient stature to lead them. When Yazíd sent an army under Muslim Ibn 'Uqbah[6] to quash their rebellion, the result was a foregone conclusion. Nevertheless, the Medinites refused to submit to the power of Yazíd and marched out to meet the Syrians. In August 683, battle was joined at Ḥarrah, not far from the city of the Prophet. Muslim was a butcher, but a good general. He outflanked the Medinites and surrounded them. Eighty of the remaining companions of Muḥammad and seven hundred 'Readers' of the Qur'án (those who knew by heart the whole of the sacred text) died when Medina fell. The city of the Prophet was given over to rapine; the barbarity displayed and the desecration wrought was past belief. Not even the mosque of the Prophet was spared, and its precincts became a stable-yard. Many more were put to the sword within the enclave of Medina while others fled the city. Those who escaped death were forced to hail Yazíd not only as their caliph, but their master and liege. Whoever resisted this indignity was branded. Only the surviving sons of Ḥusayn and 'Ali Ibn 'Abdu'lláh Ibn 'Abbás[7] were exempted from subjection to this humiliation. Medina never recovered from this assault, which took place just over fifty years after the passing of the Prophet.

After the sack and degradation of Medina, Muslim Ibn 'Uqbah turned southwards to invest Mecca, where 'Abdu'lláh Ibn az-Zubayr held sway. He did not reach it, for within three days he was dead. He is reported to have said on his death-bed that two things had made him happy: uttering the creed of his Faith and

[6] Muslim's father, 'Uqbah Ibn Náfi', had commanded the army of North Africa and was killed fighting the Berbers.

[7] This 'Abbás was the uncle of the Prophet.

ravishing Medina. 'The accursed murderer' was succeeded in his command by Ḥuṣayn Ibn Numayr, who invested Mecca and inflicted severe damage upon it. The most sacred fane, the Ka'bah, crumbled under the weight of the stones hurtling down from the Syrians' mangonels and the roof caught fire. The shame brought upon Islám by the House of Umayyah had come full circle. Nothing remained undefiled. At this juncture Yazíd died. He was thirty-eight years old and had ruled for forty-four months.

Those European writers who have tried to whitewash Yazíd have ignored the fact that he was a very bad ruler. Obviously he had certain merits. He appreciated music and wrote good verse, rode well and distinguished himself in the hunting field. He was fond of open spaces and loved the freedom of the desert. In appearance he was extremely handsome. But he was very cruel and treacherous and cared little for the Faith over which he presided.

Yazíd's sickly son, aged only thirteen, succeeded his father as Mu'áwíyah II. It was apparent that he disliked the power thrust upon him as his birthright, and he died soon after his accession. His brother, Khálid, was too young; and Marwán, the son of al-Ḥakam, now an old man, was prepared to go to Mecca and acknowledge 'Abdu'lláh Ibn az-Zubayr as the rightful caliph of Islám. But before he could do this, another contender reached Damascus and prevailed upon Marwán not to take the road to Mecca. This was 'Ubaydu'lláh, son of Zíyád, who had failed to secure the caliphate for himself in 'Iráq, and had fled the territory he had governed. So Marwán proclaimed himself Caliph and received the acclamation of the Syrians.

Supporters of Ibn-az-Zubayr were by then threatening Damascus. Marwán went out with six thousand men to meet them at Marj Ráhiṭ, in the vicinity of the capital. A battle ensued and Marwán emerged victorious. This was in July 684. Next he marched upon Egypt and conquered it; thus he held Syria and Egypt as Mu'áwíyah had done in the beginning. Ḥijáz and 'Iráq, however, owed allegiance to 'Abdu'lláh Ibn az-Zubayr, as they had to 'Alí. Marwán had insinuated his way into the supreme office by making promises to Yazíd's widow, which he did not intend to keep. He married her to silence her, but had no intention of handing over the caliphate to her son, Khálid. This office he had promised to a cousin, 'Amr, who had helped him to power, but meant to disappoint him, as well. It was his own son, ʻAbdu'l-Malik, whom he named to succeed him. At this, Khálid's mother had had enough, particularly as Marwán added insult to injury by holding him up to ridicule. That night Marwán was smothered in his sleep. Throughout his long life of more than eighty years Marwán had consistently played an ignoble part in the affairs of Islám. Sunnís do not recognize Marwán, because ʻAbdu'lláh Ibn az-Zubayr was, during the same period, in possession of the holy cities. Incidentally, Khálid, the dispossessed son of Yazíd, lived to be an erudite scholar and writer of note.

ʻAbdu'l-Malik took up the reins of government in Damascus, but his position was far from secure. ʻUbaydu'lláh had been given the task of regaining ʻIráq, and was building up a force for that purpose. But Kúfah was, by then, in great turmoil. Ever since the martyrdom of Ḥusayn those who had deserted his cause, not daring to stand by their pledges to him, had timidly kept to their homes, but they were overcome by remorse and shame. They resolved to redeem themselves. As long as ʻUbaydu'lláh ruled over them, they had little opportunity to take counsel together and plan an uprising, except in strict secrecy. But when ʻUbaydu'lláh's bid for the caliphate failed and he fled to Damascus, these men who called themselves *at-Tá'ibín*—the Penitents—found the chance to organize themselves into a fighting force. Their immediate object was to storm Damascus. ʻAbdu'lláh Ibn az-Zubayr had the same end in view and they considered joining hands. ʻAbdu'lláh's governor in Kúfah put no obstacle in their way, since their common purpose was to destroy the Umayyads. The Penitents, however, were as rudderless as the Medinites who fought the battle of Ḥarrah. Their leader, Sulaymán Ibn Ṣurad, had only one thought: to hurl himself and his people against the hordes of the ungodly to atone for their cowardice. After weeping throughout one night by the tomb of Ḥusayn, they rushed across the desert, refusing to combine forces with the supporters of Ibn-az-Zubayr, who, after their rout at Marj Ráhiṭ, had taken refuge within the walls of Qirqísíyá (the ancient Circesium). Dashing headlong into battle at a place called ʻAyna'l-Wardah, they met and were cut down by a force far superior to their own, which was under the command of an experienced warrior, Ḥuṣayn Ibn Numayr, he who had invested Mecca. Some, who were persuaded by Rifáʻah, the son of Shaddád, to save their lives, managed to beat a retreat into the desert. Others plunged deeper into the mêlée, totally oblivious of the consequences, and were slaughtered to the last man. Even those who had sought the safety of the desert wished to return and immolate themselves. One did, caught up with the triumphant Syrians within sight of Damascus, and died. The bedraggled remnants of the Penitents of Kúfah, who dragged themselves back to their own region, came upon their compatriots from Baṣrah and Madá'in (Ctesiphon) who were moving towards Syria, and told them their sorry tale. Broken in spirit, they all dispersed. But already a new champion of the House of the Prophet had appeared on the scene. His name was Mukhtár. To understand his position, it is necessary to see what had been happening, meanwhile, in Medina.

Following the sack of Medina, 'Alí II, the son of Ḥusayn—who is generally known as Zaynu'l-'Ábidín (the Adornment of the Devout), and who is the fourth Imám of the Shí'ahs—left the city and went into seclusion. His uncle, a younger son of 'Alí (the first Imám), known as Ibna'l-Ḥanafíyyah, or just the Ḥanafíyyah—referring to the tribal origin of his mother—put forth the claim that after his brother, Ḥusayn, the Imámate devolved upon him. Whether he stood by that claim to the end of his days or not is a moot point. Some Shí'ah writers have maintained that Muḥammad the Ḥanafíyyah eventually acknowledged that the Imámate belonged by right to his nephew. However, a sect known as the Kaysáníyyah grew up around his claim. That over a long period he considered himself the rightful Imám is shown by the fact that during the season of pilgrimage,[8] in A.D. 688, eight years after the martyrdom of Ḥusayn, four men led their followers at Mecca through the prescribed rites. One of these was Muḥammad the Ḥanafite; the others were 'Abdu'lláh Ibn az-Zubayr, who held Mecca; 'Abdu'l-Malik, who ruled from Damascus; and Najdah, the Khárijite chieftain. The Kaysáníyyah believe that the Ḥanafite has not died, but has taken his abode in a cave in the neighbourhood of Mecca, and in the fullness of time will emerge to establish the rule of righteousness.

Mukhtár, who raised the standard of revolt in the year 685, with the declared intention of avenging the death of Ḥusayn,

[8] This was a period of truce.

called upon the people in the name of Muḥammad al-Ḥanafíyyah. 'Alí II, Zaynu'l-'Ábidín, the fourth Imám, had no connection at all with Mukhtár, and there was even a time when the Ḥanafite would not lend him his authority. Because Mukhtár succeeded where the Penitents had failed some of the Shí'ah apologists have idolized him. He put to death both the murderous Shimr and 'Umar, the son of Sa'd. 'Ubaydu'lláh, the son of Zíyád, also perished. But Mukhtár, in spite of his impeccable declarations, was an adventurer. Sponsoring the cause of the House of 'Alí would obviously win him support in 'Iráq, particularly in the wake of the disaster which had overtaken the first attempt at bringing the butchers of Karbilá to book. There are indications that Mukhtár once tried to switch his loyalty to 'Abdu'lláh, the son of az-Zubayr, who, although an implacable opponent of the detested Umayyads, had no love for the House of 'Alí.

When the Arabs made their first moves against the Sásánid Empire, during the early days of the Caliphate of 'Umar, a Muslim commander on that front was Abú-'Ubaydah, the son of Mas'úd of the Banú-Thaqíf. He was killed in the battle of the Bridge near Ḥírah, in November 634. Mukhtár was a son of this Abú-'Ubaydah. At first he carried everything before him. Centring his power on Kúfah, he established some semblance of authority over a portion of the Íránian uplands. But at Kúfah itself his position was precarious, particularly as it had become known that the letters which he purported to have received from members of the House of the Prophet were not genuine. Many of his supporters were non-Arab Muslims who were called *Mawálí* or the 'Clients'. 'Alí, the first Imám, had never allowed any distinction between the Arab and non-Arab elements amongst the Muslims, nor had Abú-Bakr or 'Umar. One of the stalwart adherents of 'Alí was the celebrated Salmán, the Persian companion of the Prophet. The Umayyads, on the other hand, although not suppressing the non-Arabs, were decidedly selective. Mu'áwíyah had non-Muslims in his service, Christians as well as Jews, who served him well and were treated well. But of the Muslims, the Mawálí stood little chance of advancement under Mu'áwíyah and his immediate successors. Another factor which counted in favour of the House of 'Alí amongst the Persian Mawálí was the fact that a daughter of Yazdigird III, the last Sásánid monarch, was married to Ḥusayn, the third and martyred Imám; and 'Alí II,

Imám Zaynu'l-'Ábidín, was thus of Íránian lineage. When Mukhtár's rule was challenged, the non-Arabs suffered at the hands of the Arabs. Mukhtár overcame his opponents, and it was then that he put to death all the men who stood guilty of offences at Karbilá. Kúfah was subdued, but danger loomed large in the north as 'Ubaydu'lláh, the son of Zíyád, drew near with an Umayyad army. The redoubtable Ibráhím, son of Málik—the loyal and brave general of 'Alí, the fourth Caliph—was sent at the head of a considerable force to stop the Syrian army. The two armies met outside Mosul. Not only 'Ubaydu'lláh Ibn Zíyád, but also the infamous Ḥuṣayn Ibn Numayr, who had wrecked the Ka'bah, lost their lives, and the Syrians were routed. This was the high-water mark of Mukhtár's success. The year was 686.

Mukhtár had next to contend with 'Abdu'lláh, son of az-Zubayr, and 'Abdu'lláh's formidable brother, Muṣ'ab. While 'Abdu'lláh kept to the fastness of Mecca, Muṣ'ab roamed the land and fought the battles. In April 687 he defeated Mukhtár, who met his death bravely when emerging from the besieged castle of Kúfah with drawn sword to give battle to the foe. The rise and fall of Mukhtár, like a meteor in its brilliance and doom, presaged many similar careers in the course of Islamic history. He was then in his sixty-seventh year. But more tragic even than his death was the massacre of his men, who surrendered in a vain hope of clemency. Muslim shed the blood of brother Muslim even after the struggle had ceased. The man responsible for this barbarity was Muhallab, the son of Abú-Ṣufrah, who had previously overthrown the Khárijites in Baṣrah with similar severity.

The shame of fratricide, for which the Umayyads must in a large measure bear the onus, remained a permanent blot on the polity of Islám, just as it disfigured the polity of Christendom. 'Abdu'l-Malik, the son of Marwán, who after the death of Mukhtár was the sole contender left to face 'Abdu'lláh Ibn az-Zubayr, now went to the length of killing his cousin, 'Amr, with his own hands, in full view of his sons and courtiers, while 'Amr's partisans were gathered outside the Caliph's palace. 'Amr's severed head was hurled down into their midst. Cowed into submission, they went home. It will be remembered that Marwán had employed the ruse of a confidence trickster with this ill-used cousin.

Divisions and wars amongst the Muslims persuaded the Byzantines that the time was ripe for reclaiming some of their lost territories. As ‘Abdu’l-Malik was more concerned to settle the issue with the sons of az-Zubayr than fight the Byzantines, he undertook to pay them a yearly tribute, and the heirs of the great Constantine preferred gold to military glory. Then ‘Abdu’l-Malik led his men eastwards. Muṣ‘ab was the adversary he wished to meet rather than his brother, who remained immured in Mecca. Once again Ibráhím, the son of Málik, was in the vanguard of an army challenging the might of the Umayyads. He had accepted service under Muṣ‘ab because for him the enemy was forever the House of Umayyah. He gained a brilliant victory, but fell on the battlefield. Other commanders in Muṣ‘ab’s army had already sold out to ‘Abdu’l-Malik. ‘Ísá, the young son of Muṣ‘ab, appalled by such betrayal and too proud to accept the proffered terms of the enemy, dashed into the very midst of the massed ranks of the Syrians. He was killed while his father looked on helplessly. Next, Muṣ‘ab himself was stabbed to death, the murderer shouting: ‘Revenge for Mukhtár’. An oft-told tale relates that as ‘Abdu’l-Malik sat in the citadel of Kúfah to receive the homage of the notables of that city, whose loyalties had shifted many times within the span of a single decade, he had in front of him the severed head of Muṣ‘ab. A Muslim of an earlier generation is reputed to have warned the Umayyad to beware the strange turns of fortune. ‘In this very chamber,’ he said, ‘I saw the head of Ḥusayn laid before ‘Ubaydu’lláh, and then it was the head of ‘Ubaydu’lláh that Mukhtár had placed before him; in a short while Muṣ‘ab had the head of Mukhtár brought to him, and now I behold the head of Muṣ‘ab at your feet.’ It is said that ‘Abdu’l-Malik had that chamber pulled down, lest one day his own head should lie on a platter there in front of another potentate. It was the latter half of the year 691 which witnessed the re-establishment of Umayyad rule in ‘Iráq and Írán.

The time had now come to deal with ‘Abdu’lláh Ibn az-Zubayr, still secluded in the holy city of Mecca. ‘Abdu’l-Malik entrusted this task to one whose name has become synonymous with horrific tyranny, al-Ḥajjáj Ibn Yúsuf of the tribe of Banú-Thaqíf. Mukhtár had been a scion of the same tribe. The siege of Mecca took the best part of the year 692, during which rocks from mangonels set on the surrounding hills rained down upon it. Food became scarce while the Umayyad army feasted. ‘Abdu’lláh’s men, even two of his sons, began deserting him. When all hope was lost, 'Abdu'lláh turned to his aged mother, Asmá', for advice as to what to do. She was that daughter of Abú-Bakr, who, seven decades before, had carried food in the dead of night to the Prophet and her father, as they lay hidden in a cave close by the city. So much had happened, so much changed, during those seventy years, that for Asmá' the world she once knew had ceased to exist. Her advice, at this hour of peril, was simple: 'If you believe your cause to be just, keep on; otherwise, surrender.' How could the son of az-Zubayr now renounce a claim which he had nurtured for so long? Many years before, when his father had quailed at the thought of opposing 'Alí, he had steeled his resolve. He could not surrender. So he walked out of the city, sword in hand, going on and on until the hail of stones brought him down. He was decapitated and his body was impaled. Ḥajjáj had no regard for valour. So once again Mecca was invested, the holiest city of Islám desecrated. At long last the House of Umayyah held undisputed sway; and 'Abdu'l-Malik, the treacherous son of a treacherous father, was supreme in the world of Islám.

The symbol of 'Abdu'l-Malik's power was Ḥajjáj, who for twenty-two years terrorized Arabia and 'Iráq and Persia. Without taking into account those who died in battles which he conducted or engineered, it is estimated that the number of people who suffered death at the instance of this infamous tyrant was 120,000. 'Abda'r-Raḥmán, the grandson of al-As͟h'at͟h,[9] was leading an army against Rutbíl, the non-Muslim ruler of Kábul, when Ḥajjáj grossly insulted him for his slow progress. He was so incensed that he led his army all the way back to Kúfah to overthrow Ḥajjáj, as well as the Caliph in Damascus. The inhabitants of Kúfah, true to their tradition, rallied to his banner. But it was not only the fickleness of the people of Kúfah that provided 'Abda'r-Raḥmán with massive support. Ḥajjáj, who had no love for non-Arab Muslims (nor for the Arabs, for that matter), had ordained that they should pay the same poll-tax (*jizyah*) as the *D͟himmís*—that is, the people of the Book enjoying the protection of Islám. This was because of his concern at the falling revenues, caused by decrease in the number of the D͟himmís, while the number of the Mawális was increasing. The Mawálí, recently

[9] The commander in 'Alí's army, who, at Ṣiffín, insisted that 'Alí should cease fighting Mu'áwíyah and enter into a truce.

converted to Islám, therefore joined the forces of 'Abda'r-Raḥmán, because of the exactions of tax-collectors. So widespread was the revolt that the Caliph was ready to parley with the rebel leader. However, the battle went against 'Abda'r-Raḥmán, and he fled for asylum to the ruler of Kábul. Rutbíl had no hesitation in putting him to death, and making a gift of his head to Ḥajjáj. Although insurrection did not cease, the rebellion of 'Abda'r-Raḥmán was the only upheaval of appreciable magnitude during the rule of the House of Umayyah, until the birth of that movement which brought about their downfall.

Through the remaining years of the Caliphate of 'Abdu'l-Malik Muslim armies gained remarkable victories in North Africa. Káhinah, a woman chieftain of the Berbers, who had held up the Muslim advance, was at last defeated and, sad to say, her head was carried away as a trophy. This repugnant custom of parading severed heads, which the Umayyads revived, has persisted right to the present day. Christendom, too, was once similarly afflicted. In the year 705, 'Abdu'l-Malik was succeeded by his son, al-Walíd I, and a new commander, the celebrated Músá Ibn Nuṣayr, was appointed to North Africa. Músá brought under control the area that we know today as Morocco, extended the Muslim Empire to the waters of the Atlantic, and even looked beyond to another continent, venturing to send men to cross the sea to an unknown land. Byzantine power was totally swept out of Africa.

It cannot be doubted that 'Abdu'l-Malik gave Islám the system of government and the administrative structure which it needed to control its vast domains. He created departments of state, appointed officials to conduct them, and introduced a system of accounting in Arabic for the exchequer and other governmental records. The Caliph himself became a monarch. These changes had a profound effect on society, and dependence on non-Arabs and non-Muslims decreased.

'Abdu'l-Malik, having had the people of Íránian origin ranged time and again against him and his House, had reason enough to dislike them. One day he entered the Mosque of 'Umar,[10] which stands on the site of the Temple of Solomon, to see how the

[10] Both the Dome of the Rock (*Qubbata'ṣ-Ṣakhrah*), erroneously styled the Mosque of 'Umar by Europeans, and the Aqṣá Mosque (*al-Masjid-al-Aqṣá*), close by, were built by 'Abdu'l-Malik. The enclave (most sacred to the Muslims after the holy sites of Mecca and Medina) within which these two mosques stand, is known as *al-Ḥaram ash-Sharíf*—the Noble Sanctuary.

beliefs and practices of the Faith were being taught. To his disgust and astonishment he found that most of the teachers there were Mawálí of Íránian descent. He called the leading men of Quraysh into a conclave to upbraid and chide them for this. 'You made so light of this faith of Islám,' he told them, 'that the sons of Furs[11] came to override you. I have never seen the like of these people. From earliest times until the appearance of Islám they reigned, and not for an instant had they any need of us. Today we rule over them, and not for an instant are we not in need of them.' Another shock awaited 'Abdu'l-Malik when he learned that in many towns and cities of the far-flung Muslim Empire, men in authority, both judges and administrators, were Mawálí. The process could not be entirely reversed, but it could be retarded. It is paradoxical that the same order, which provided the Empire with organs of government and stability, sowed the seeds of disruption. Stress on Arabism awakened the racial pride of the conquered peoples, and particularly of the Íránians. The Dihgáns or Dihqáns of the Íránian plateau, who were owners of huge estates, in order to safeguard their inheritance and keep their possessions had thrown in their lot with the conquerors, whether they had embraced Islám or not. Although they had not remained uniformly immune from expropriation they were not, in general, found in the ranks of malcontents and dissidents and contenders with the Umayyad power. These came from classes below them. It should be emphasized that the Sásánid polity had sustained a rigid caste system not unlike that which still besets Hindu society. Of course the Faith of the Prophet Muḥammad could not countenance such a stratification of society, but Umayyad tyranny and arrogance certainly bred racism and unmerited privilege.

The reign of al-Walíd I (A.D. 705–15) marked the zenith of the fortunes of the House of Umayyah. Músá, the son of Nuṣayr, who governed the whole stretch of North Africa from the borders of Egypt to the Atlantic, having received the Caliph's conditional approval to dispatch an exploratory expedition across the narrow straits that opened into the western sea, and having mounted a raid to ascertain the possibilities of success, decided to extend further the domains of Islám. He gave the task of exploring the unknown to his freedman, Ṭáriq Ibn Zíyád. The name of Ṭáriq is enshrined in the name of the Rock where, in April 711, he

[11] The name that the Arabs applied to Írán.

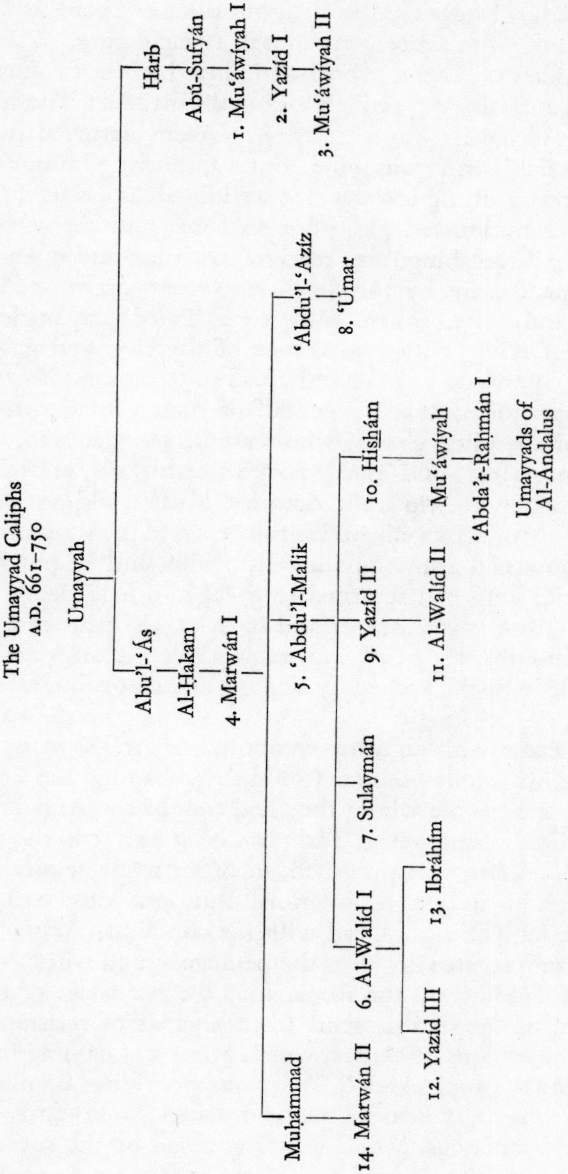
The Umayyad Caliphs
A.D. 661–750
Umayyah
Ḥarb
Abu'l-'Áṣ
Abú-Sufyán
Al-Ḥakam
1. Mu'áwiyah I
4. Marwán I
2. Yazíd I
3. Mu'áwiyah II
Muḥammad
5. 'Abdu'l-Malik
'Abdu'l-'Azíz
14. Marwán II
6. Al-Walíd I
7. Sulaymán
9. Yazíd II
10. Hishám
8. 'Umar
12. Yazíd III
13. Ibráhím
11. Al-Walíd II
Mu'áwiyah
'Abda'r-Raḥmán I
Umayyads of Al-Andalus

landed and established his command: Gibraltar—Jabal Ṭáriq, or Mount Ṭáriq. Roderick, the Visigoth ruler of Spain, had traitors in his army, who were sons of the former king, Witiza. And Count Julian of Ceuta, who had induced Músá to attempt the conquest of Spain, was actively aiding the invaders. The encounter with the Visigoths was ghastly. Renegades betrayed their king and Roderick's army was wiped out. Of the king himself nothing was ever seen. Roderick was not well liked, and once he and his army were annihilated Ṭáriq not only met with feeble resistance but, more astonishing, was received with joy and open arms by many, particularly by the Jews who were oppressed by both Church and State. When Ṭáriq took Toledo he made Oppas, brother of King Witiza, governor of the city, and gave him a garrison composed of Jews and Muslims to buttress his authority. Serfs also rejoiced at the downfall of their Christian overlords. Meanwhile, leading clerics, who were no less detested, made for Rome and safety; and Ṭáriq moved northwards, entirely on his own authority, to win fresh victories. Músá could not allow him all the glory of achievement. He too crosssed the straits into Spain with a powerful army. Seville fell to him, and he pushed on to find Ṭáriq, who had returned to greet him in Toledo, far from pleased. Ṭáriq was a Berber and most of his men were Berbers. Within months, they had won remarkable victories and given a strife-ridden Spain, racked by tyranny and extortion, a new social fabric.

Músá came with an army composed of Arabs, many of them boasting illustrious descent. Could they abandon the field to the Berbers, the people whom they had fought for years and tamed and civilized? Moreoever, Ṭáriq had been a slave in the service of Músá. So, Ṭáriq was punished, in order to be reminded of his origin and his duty to his overlord. But once Músá had made his point he let Ṭáriq go ahead with his conquests. With his freedmen he moved steadily over the peninsula, and within two years from his landing on the Rock, they were masters of the entire kingdom of the Goths, apart from pockets of resistance in the remote mountains of Galicia which Músá was hammering. In the south, Músá's son, 'Abdu'l-'Azíz, was providing a sound system of government, when summons reached Músá and Ṭáriq to repair to Damascus. Walíd was frightened by the success of his viceroy, but when Músá and Ṭáriq reached the capital Walíd was on his death-bed. Sulaymán, his brother, succeeded him, and Sulaymán would not forgive slights. Músá was publicly degraded, mulcted of his wealth, and sent to end his days in a village near Medina. But the cruellest blow was yet to come, when Sulaymán sent hired assassins to Spain to murder 'Abdu'l-'Azíz and send his head to his aged father. Ṭáriq was sent back to Africa to a menial task. Thus did the Umayyads flourish.

Sulaymán's reign was glittering but short, a bare two years. His successor was his cousin, 'Umar Ibn 'Abdu'l-'Azíz Ibn Marwán—the shining light of the House of Umayyah. He stood apart from all the monarchs of the dynasty founded by Mu'áwíyah and Marwán, with the exception of Mu'áwíyah II, who was a sickly youth and died very young. 'Umar Ibn 'Abdu'l-'Azíz was just, merciful and discriminating. He put an end to the ritual of cursing 'Alí, the first Imám and the fourth Caliph, which Mu'áwíyah had instituted. Unlike his immediate predecessors, 'Umar attached more importance to the well-being of his Faith than to the state of the exchequer and other financial considerations. He ordained that anyone who had embraced Islám must be exempted immediately from the payment of the poll-tax. His officials were alarmed, and one of them wrote to the Caliph from Egypt that should the trend continue there, before long not a single Christian would be left and the financial loss would be incalculable. 'Umar replied that he would be delighted, remarking that God sent His Prophet as His Apostle amongst men, not as a collector of taxes. The governor in Khurásán was even more perturbed, because so many Persians had come into the Faith to escape the payment of the poll-tax, but had not bothered to be circumcised. The Caliph's answer was simple and terse: 'God sent the Prophet to reveal true faith to men, not to circumcise them.'

Ironically, the policy pursued by this honest and just Caliph led to fresh troubles. The treasury suffered, the Arab element smarted, and soon his liberal policy was reversed by his successors.

About a year after 'Umar's accession his forces in Spain crossed the Pyrenees into France and captured Narbonne. Two years later, 'Umar Ibn 'Abdu'l-'Azíz died, at the age of thirty-nine, and the caliphate reverted to the sons of 'Abdu'l-Malik. Yazíd II, who reigned till 724, did nothing of note, but Hishám, the last son of 'Abdu'l-Malik to reign, whose rule lasted nineteen years, provided a new measure of stability by careful administration and attention to his finances. So attentive was he to his accounts that he was considered niggardly. It was in his days that Muslim expansion into the heart of Europe was stemmed, and the tide began slowly to recede.

In October 732, a hundred years after the passing of the Prophet, Charles Martel defeated the Muslims at Poitiers, near Tours. 'Abda'r-Raḥmán, the Arab commander, lost his life on that fateful battlefield. The Muslim débâcle was not due wholly to the prowess of Frankish arms. Internal dissensions made a major contribution to that defeat. The Berbers were also restive, and Khárijite agitation was rife in the Berber homeland. Indeed, at one time, it seemed as if North Africa from Qayrawán[12] to the Atlantic was slipping from the grip of the Umayyads. The battle of Tours, although it was not an engagement of vast proportions or a titanic trial of strength, became a landmark in the history of the world, but the victorious Franks were too exhausted to follow up its immediate advantages.

It was also during the reign of Hishám that another clash occurred between the House of 'Alí and the House of Umayyah. Zayd, a son of the fourth Imám, went to Damascus to seek redress. He was insulted and denied elementary justice. His pride bruised and his sensibilities outraged, Zayd made his way to Kúfah, the notorious home of the fickle and the malcontent, to attempt a stand against the tyranny of the Umayyads. His relatives warned him not to put his reliance upon the word of the people of Kúfah. More than twenty thousand had pledged him their support, but when he showed his hand his following melted away and only some three hundred remained faithful to him. Zayd was killed, but his opponents did not allow his death to close this sad chapter. They searched for his grave, found it, disinterred his body, decapitated it to present his head to the Caliph, had the corpse stretched on a cross, then burned it and threw away the ashes. A fresh wave of horror swept over the land. Zayd's son, Yaḥyá, a boy barely seventeen years of age, fled to Khurásán to find refuge. He was imprisoned, and when set free was so hounded that he had to turn and fight. Both Yaḥyá and his brother perished, and for months their bodies were left hanging upon gibbets. By then Khurásán was seething with unrest, but the focal point of revolt was not the House of 'Alí.

[12] A famous city in Tunisia, regarded as holy.

In A.D. 712 the Imámate had passed from 'Alí II, the fourth Imám, to his son Muḥammad, known as al-Báqir. After him, in A.D. 734, his mantle rested on his son Ja'far, who was surnamed aṣ-Ṣádiq—the Truthful. The sixth Imám, like his father and grandfather, resided in Medina and kept aloof from plots and intrigues. The fame of his immense learning was well spread, and round him gathered earnest disciples—not only from the ranks of those who believed in his apostolic succession. Although he wished Zayd well and supported him when Zayd was only pressing a law-suit, he gave his uncle no encouragement to resort to insurrection. There came a break, and Zaydís became a distinct sect standing apart from the Shí'ites. To this day they are centred in Yemen.

But the revolt which shattered the power of the Umayyads stemmed from the House of 'Abbás. Muḥammad al-Ḥanafíyyah, the son of 'Alí, the first Imám—whose mother was not Fáṭimah, the daughter of the Prophet—entertained claims which, after his death, his son, Abú-Háshim upheld. It is said that Abú-Háshim was poisoned on the instructions of Sulaymán, the Umayyad caliph. However, before he died he transferred the authority which he claimed to Muḥammad, the great-grandson of 'Abbás, the Prophet's uncle.[13] This Muḥammad lived in Syria, in a village named Ḥumaymah, whence, in the reign of 'Umar Ibn 'Abdu'l-'Azíz, a deputation came to acknowledge Muḥammad and to offer him allegiance. That was the beginning of the movement which destroyed the Umayyads.

[13] Muḥammad was the son of 'Alí, the son of 'Abdu'lláh, whose father was 'Abbás, the uncle of the Prophet.

21

Revolt and its Roots

THE revolt which broke the Umayyads was essentially the revolt of the non-Arab Muslim. Previous attempts at dispossessing the usurpers, although supported by non-Arabs, had had only leaders of distinguished Arab descent at the helm. The movement which thrived on the magic of its name, the Háshimite, achieved its objective, in spite of initial failure, under directors of non-Arab lineage. Most prominent in the Háshimite movement were the Mawálí, whom the Umayyads had spurned.

As the first century of the Hijrah drew to its close, expectations ran high that with the passage of a hundred years the hand of Providence would bring low those who wielded power not rightly theirs, and that the legitimacy of power would be restored. This belief was widespread and firmly held. So it was that in the first year of the new century, Ḥayyán the Druggist, Abú-'Ikrimah the Saddler, Maysarata'l-'Abdí and Muḥammad the son of Khunays—men of humble pursuits and no particular renown—made their way to an obscure village of Syria, where Muḥammad, the head of the House of 'Abbás, had a modest establishment.[1] He received their homage unobtrusively, after which they went away to fire others with their zeal. Hence they and their like were known as the *du'át* (callers),[2] in other words, missionaries. Calling, as they did, upon the people to rally to the cause of the House of Háshim, they could enlist the sympathies of supporters of the House of 'Alí. Because Khurásán was an area badly disaffected, they brought their persuasion to bear particularly on that province. The governor, hearing of their dubious activities, summoned them and demanded to know what they were doing in his domain. They were merchants, they said, mindful of their own business; where-

[1] See p. 211.

[2] Plural of *dá'í*—the 'one who calls'.

upon they were released and continued to travel throughout Khurásán in that guise. In due course they repaired to the Syrian village to give the great-grandson of 'Abbás (the uncle of the Prophet) the tidings that the ground had been well and truly laid for revolt.

As long as Hishám, the son of 'Abdu'l-Malik, reigned the Háshimite movement had to remain underground. Hishám's rule was partly beneficent and his grasp was firm. Abú-'Ikrimah and Ḥayyán lost their lives because hostile propaganda was traced to them. The 'missionaries' were then cautioned not to show their colours until the person who was wooed had taken a solemn and binding oath. And so the work went on in stealth. The death of Hishám, in 743, brought to the throne a man so profligate that even the partisans of the House of Umayyah shuddered in horror. He was al-Walíd, the son of Yazíd II. Hishám dreaded his nephew's succession and tried to debar him from the throne. He planned to bequeath the caliphate to a son of his own. But Yazíd II had laid the notables of his court under an oath of allegiance to al-Wálid; thus his inheritance was assured and his accession inevitable. Al-Walíd II was a drunkard, who, when in his cups, dared even to practise archery on a copy of the Qur'án. As yet, the protagonists of the Háshimite cause were not strong enough to channel popular disgust and topple the Umayyads from their seat of power. But Yazíd, the son of Walíd I, led the people of Damascus against his cousin and brought about his death after a reign of little over fifteen months. Yazíd III was by far a better ruler, but the House of Umayyah itself had become a divided house. Marwán Ibn Muḥammad, a great-grandson of Marwán I, and a seasoned soldier who had earned the nickname of al-Ḥimár (the Ass) because of his stamina and reserves of endurance, had lived away from the court, fighting battles on the periphery of Muslim domains or governing outlying provinces.[3] Now he moved with his army towards the capital and declared that the caliphate rightly belonged to the two sons of the murdered Walíd. Yazíd III had no desire to fight his own kinsman. When he died within six months of his accession, his brother, Ibráhím, assumed the Caliphate, and Marwán pressed forward. The force which

[3] Marwán had defeated the Khazars, a Turkish clan in the area of the Caspian Sea, who preferred to embrace Judaism so as to be free of obligations to the Muslims and Christians around them.

Damascus could muster under the command of Sulaymán, a son of the Caliph Hishám, was routed. Ibráhím had to flee, after a rule of only two months, although he returned later to offer his submission to Marwán. However, before abandoning the capital, he ordered the death of the two boys, sons of Walíd II, who languished in prison. By the end of November 744, Marwán the Ass occupied the seat of the Caliphate.

Marwán II was in the saddle, but the whole Empire was in turmoil, and the members of the House of Umayyah had fallen out amongst themselves. Contesting with one another for power, they had butchered their innocent kinsmen in cold blood. The Khárijites were astir once again, and Mecca, Medina and Kúfah fell to them. Old enmities between Ḥimyarites (Yemenites) and Muḍarites (Qaysites) were reawakened. Marwán favoured the Muḍarites, but southern Írán declared for the Ḥimyarites and refused to recognize Marwán. The strangest spectacle of all was the defection of Sulaymán, the son of the Caliph Hishám. At first acknowledging the overlordship of Marwán, he suddenly moved to gain the caliphate, then unexpectedly joined forces with the Khárijites, the inveterate foes of the House of Umayyah. Marwán had fought and won many battles, but now it seemed he was facing impossible odds. Nevertheless, he laid siege to the Khárijites in Mosul, where a young kinsman of his own named Mu'áwíyah, a nephew of the renegade Sulaymán, fell into his hands. Mu'áwíyah's plea for his life met with disdain; he was led out and, within sight of both armies, had his hands chopped and his head struck off. Eventually, the Khárijites were defeated in 'Iráq and in the Arabian peninsula, and once again they went to ground in the broad lands of the Íránian plateau.

Whether advanced age, after years in the field, was telling on Marwán, or for a cause unknown, the Caliph did not pursue his advantage to subdue the people of the plateau, left the affairs of the administration to his two sons, 'Abdu'l-Malik and 'Abdu'lláh, and sought respite in the fortress of Ḥarrán in the northern confines of Syria. Damascus with its ornate palaces and luxuries was abhorrent to him. Now was the moment for the partisans of the House of the Prophet to arise.

On the death in 743 of Muḥammad Ibn 'Alí, head of the House of 'Abbás, his son, Ibráhím, had succeeded him. His supporters—

with their well-planned organization, fully equipped with secret cells and furtive missionaries—were active but supremely discreet. The *du'át* or *dá'ís* spoke on behalf of the *Ahla'l-Bayt*—'People of the House', meaning the House of the Prophet. In the minds of many, the 'House' could be none but the House of 'Alí, whereas the Dá'ís, without saying so, were really paving the way for the advent of the House of 'Abbás.

While Marwán II had been fighting in Syria and 'Iráq to consolidate his position, a remarkable man, one of the most remarkable of all time, had appeared on the scene in Khurásán. He was a native of that province which was the nursery of the 'Abbásid movement. Friend and foe agree that this man, Abú-Muslim, possessed such singleness of mind, such firmness of resolve, such mastery of his faculties and emotions that neither success nor defeat, neither joy nor sorrow, could affect his demeanour or deflect him from his purpose. For him the end always justified the means. The triumph of the 'Abbásid cause owed its stratagem, its impetus and achievement more to him than to any other human being. Yet, as late as the year 742, he had been a menial servitor in the Castle of Kúfah, seeing to the needs of the prisoners—partisans of the House of the Prophet—whom the governor of Kúfah had put under arrest. While attending them, Abú-Muslim was attracted by their talk, showed sympathy towards their cause and wept over their plight. Bukayr, a prominent member of the pro-'Abbásid hierarchy, who happened to be in Kúfah, witnessed this young Persian's zeal for the Háshimite cause, and bought him from the authorities for four hundred dínárs. Within a few years, Abú-Muslim rose to become the acknowledged leader of the Messianic movement in his homeland. But he bided his time until the middle of the year 747. Then having received orders from Ibráhím (generally known as Ibráhím the Imám) to mobilize his forces, Abú-Muslim directed his men to come into the open, dressed in black, and to side publicly with the Ḥimyarites against the governor of Khurásán, Naṣr Ibn Sayyár, who was a Muḍarite. Henceforth they became known as the '*Musawwidah*'—the Black-robed—and black became the colour of their banner and the colour of the House of 'Abbás. (The Prophet's standard had been black.)

Naṣr, an octogenarian, was well aware of the dangers threatening the very existence of the Umayyads. He sent warning after warning to the Caliph, and the verses which in despair he addressed to Marwán have deservedly attained high fame.

> I see amidst the embers the glow of fire, and it wants but little to burst into a blaze,
> And if the wise ones of the people quench it not, its fuel will be corpses and skulls.
> Verily fire is kindled by two sticks, and verily words are the beginning of warfare.
> And I cry in amazement, 'Would that I knew whether the House of Umayya were awake or asleep!'.[4]

His pleas went unanswered until he was routed, had to abandon his province and retire to Ray (ancient Rhages),[5] to see Abú-Muslim proclaimed the ruler of Khurásán. By the year 748, Abú-Muslim stood supreme in the Eastern Marches. When Marwán moved to send aid to the hard-pressed Naṣr, it was too late.

While Khurásán was bursting into rebellion, a letter from Ibráhím to Abú-Muslim fell into the hands of Marwán. Until then the Umayyad Caliph had no knowledge at all that this scion of the House of 'Abbás, who lived quietly in a Syrian village, was the fount-head of the forces which threatened his life and his throne. Not only did Marwán and his men not know of the position which Ibráhím the Imám occupied; there were very few among the hundreds of thousands of Ibráhím's own avowed adherents who had any intimation of his identity. Upon discovering the prime mover of the revolt, Marwán had Ibráhím taken to the fortress of Ḥarrán, where he was poisoned. The 'Abbásid succession, at Ibráhím's death, devolved upon his young brother, Abu'l-'Abbás 'Abdu'lláh, who came to be known, before long, as as-Saffáḥ, the Shedder of Blood. Abu'l-'Abbás and his brother, Abú-Ja'far al-Manṣúr, together with other prominent members of his family, fled to 'Iráq. There they were given sanctuary at Kúfah, unbeknown to the governor, Yazíd Ibn Hubayrah, who was a bulwark of the Umayyad power and had shattered the forces of the Khárijites. It was Abú-Salmah Ḥafṣ Ibn Sulaymán, a

[4] Browne, *A Literary History of Persia*, vol. I, p. 241. Translation by E. G. Browne.
[5] Its ruins are close to Ṭihrán.

Persian and a native of Hamadán, who provided safety at Kúfah for the 'Abbásid fugitives.

Abú-Salmah, who was later to become the first vizier (*wazír*) in the Empire of Islám, was originally an adherent of the House of 'Alí. He wrote to three of the most outstanding members of that House, inviting them to put themselves at the head of the anti-Umayyad movement. His first choice was the sixth Imám of the Shí'ite persuasion, Ja'far-aṣ-Ṣádiq; his second, 'Abdu'lláh-al-Maḥḍ, a grandson of Ḥasan, the second Imám; and his third, 'Umar-al-Ashraf, a son of Zaynu'l-'Ábidín 'Alí II, the fourth Imám. Ja'far-aṣ-Ṣádiq not only left Abú-Salmah's letter unanswered and refused to associate himself by word or deed with schemes of violent action, but also prevailed upon his kinsmen to do the same, asking his uncle, 'Umar-al-Ashraf, what he knew of the people of Khurásán to cause him to put trust in them. Abú-Salmah and his collaborators, whose sympathies lay with the House of 'Alí, were, however, too deeply committed to rebellion to be able to pull back. Perforce, they cast in their lot with the House of 'Abbás. Abú-Muslim, too, attempted to win the support of Imám Ja'far-aṣ-Ṣádiq, only to learn in no uncertain terms that the Imám stood above all contention.

So it was that the army of Khurásán set out to strike at the heart of the Umayyad power. Abú-Muslim himself remained in Khurásán, giving the command to an Arab general, Qaḥṭabah, the son of Shabíb. It must not be assumed that this army was wholly composed of the Mawálí, or non-Arabs, for many Arabs, particularly of the Ḥimyarite faction, marched behind the Black Standard. These Arabs were mostly people with Persian forbears, who knew no homeland but the highlands of the Íránian plateau. Already the process of assimilation had begun. In Syria the Arabs had almost absorbed the local population, but in Írán the reverse had occurred.

Qaḥṭabah moved steadily westwards. The aged Naṣr left Ray and died soon after; no aid had reached him from Marwán. In May 749, the army of Khurásán captured Nihávand, the scene of that great battle and victory, Fatḥ-al-Futuḥ (Victory of Victories), which, in the year 641, had sealed the fate of the Sásánid Empire. Then Qaḥṭabah descended onto the plains of 'Iráq, bypassing the Umayyad forces under the command of Yazíd Ibn Hubayrah, the governor of Kúfah. Battle was joined in August, and although

Qaḥṭabah was killed, his army won the day. Yazíd withdrew to Wásiṭ,[6] and Kúfah fell to Ḥasan, Qaḥṭabah's son. The city which, time and again, had defied the Umayyads, sometimes bravely, sometimes timorously and sometimes treacherously, was free from the rule of the 'accursed'. Many were the Shí'ites of the House of 'Alí in Kúfah who rejoiced and looked for a descendant of 'Alí to come forth and ascend the pulpit in the mosque. They had a rude awakening, for it was not a scion of the House of 'Alí who made his appearance, but Abu'l-'Abbás 'Abdu'lláh, the head of the House of 'Abbás, who came out of hiding and rode in great pomp to the mosque associated with 'Alí, the first Imám and the fourth Caliph. Abu'l-'Abbás led the congregation in prayer and then addressed the people. The iniquities of the Umayyads, he said, condemned them out of hand, and now the House of Háshim, the House of the Prophet, had come to wipe out all traces of their transgressions, to let the light of religion shine, to cover the face of the earth with justice and equity and righteousness. His uncle, Dáwúd, following him, made the pronouncement that the House of the Prophet would hold the reins of affairs and keep the sacred trust until the Last Day, to be handed over to Jesus, the Son of Mary, on his second coming. The bewildered people of Kúfah had no choice but to make their way to the Mosque of 'Alí, there to swear fealty to the head of the House of 'Abbás.

The next battle, which finally shattered the power of the Umayyads, was fought in January 750 on the banks of the river Záb, which runs into the Tigris about eighty miles to the south of Mosul. Another army had by then reached 'Iráq from Khurásán, also under the command of an Arab general, 'Abdu'l-Malik of the Ḥimyarite tribe of Azd. Here Marwán, at last, took to the field in person. He was decisively beaten. The battle of Záb changed the course of the Empire of Islám. City after city opened its gates to the 'Abbásids. Only at Damascus was some resistance shown. 'Abdu'lláh, the uncle of Abu'l-'Abbás, overran it, put many to the sword, and raised the black banner of his House on the citadel where Mu'áwíyah, almost a century before, had first laid his plans to build himself a kingdom. Marwán the Ass became a wanderer, tried to recoup his fortunes in Egypt, but one night was surprised in a church and killed. Those Umayyads who

[6] As its name 'In-between' indicated, this was a town built mid-way between Baṣrah and Kúfah, by Ḥajjáj.

had escaped with their lives in Damascus, ostensibly amnestied, were called to a banquet by 'Abdu'lláh, the uncle of Abu'l-'Abbás, who had been appointed governor of Syria by his nephew. As-Saffáḥ had ordered him to exterminate the Umayyads. When they came to the banquet and sat down, they were set upon and slaughtered. Some ninety of them perished. Dawúd, another uncle of Abu'l-'Abbás (he who had spoken in the mosque of Kúfah), was given the holy cities of Arabia to govern, and there too the scions of the House of Umayyah were to be destroyed. Swift and ghastly retribution overtook them, guilty and innocent alike, and the graves of their caliphs in Damascus were desecrated. But the grave of 'Umar Ibn 'Abdu'l-'Azíz, the just and compassionate caliph, was spared.

Yazíd Ibn Hubayrah, the Umayyad general who had lost the battle for Kúfah and fled to the safety of Wásiṭ, agreed, after a month of siege, to surrender to Abú-Ja'far, the brother of the Caliph, having received solemn assurance of safety for himself, his family and his men. But as-Saffáḥ would have none of it and instructed his brother to kill the son of Hubayrah. Not daring to disobey the Caliph, Abú-Ja'far had to break his bond. Even Abú-Salmah, the first vizier of the world of Islám, who had made Kúfah safe for the 'Abbásid fugitives and had proclaimed as-Saffáḥ caliph on the day of victory, did not survive the blood bath with which the 'Abbásids inaugurated their reign. No wonder that the poet, Abu'l-'Aṭṭár, wished for the return of the 'oppression' of the House of Marwán and the consignment of the 'justice' of the House of 'Abbás to the nether world. It is said that Abú-Muslim could not tolerate a rival and encompassed Abú-Salmah's death. Be that as it may, the assassination of Abú-Salmah had the blessing of as-Saffáḥ.

A modern Íránian historian[7] has written:

'These people of Khurásán, who (after the death of Muḥammad Bin[8] 'Alí, the Imám, in the year 124 [A.D. 742]), turned their garb into black, and became known as the Musawwidah, were mostly the Dihqáns [land owners] of that region and the descendants of the nobility of Írán. They, at last, with the aid of Abú-Muslim of Khurásán and Abú-Salmah Ḥafṣ Bin Sulaymán-i-Khallál of Hamadán, brought down the rule of the Umayyads in

[7] The late 'Abbás Iqbál Áshtíyání.

[8] The same as Ibn (the son of). (H.M.B.)

the year 132 of Hijrah; and at the battle of the Záb, proved the dominance of the Íránian element over the Arab, and proclaimed the inauguration of a new era in the history of the Islamic caliphate and civilization.'[9]

Historians have differed over the truth of this bold assertion and will continue to differ. But a few facts are ascertainable. There were, as we have seen, Arabs in the ranks and at the head of the anti-Umayyad forces. Others of the Mawálí, besides Persians, joined the anti-Umayyad movement. But, as the above-quoted historian states, it was the men of Khurásán, a province profoundly Íránian in spite of the large influx of Arab settlers, who took up arms to overthrow the Umayyads, and it was the strategy and tactics of Abú-Salmah and Abú-Muslim which achieved that end. Abú-Muslim had at his elbow, as close adviser and collaborator, an eminent Persian, Khálid, the son of Barmak, the forbear of the celebrated family of the Barmecides. It can also be pointed out that another close adviser of Abú-Muslim was Muḥammad al-Ash'ath, a man of illustrious Arab descent, whose grandfather, 'Abda'r-Raḥmán, had contended with the cruel Ḥajjáj and the Caliph 'Abdu'l-Malik. Another fact is of paramount importance. The advent of the 'Abbásids meant the extinction of the Byzantine successor-state in Syria. The centre of the Muslim Empire shifted eastwards to 'Iráq, where formerly the Sásánids of Írán had had their famed metropolis. This transference of the fulcrum of power brought the 'Abbásid Caliphate into proximity with its Persian supporters, who subsequently rose to high positions in the administration and service of the state. As-Saffáḥ, although raised to power in Kúfah, had no love for it and chose Anbár, on the Euphrates, as his capital. His reign was short-lived; he died of small-pox in 754, and his brother, Abú-Ja'far al-Manṣúr, succeeded him.[10]

[9] *Khánidán-i-Nawbakhtí*, p. 65 (Jep 41).

[10] Because of the strict attention he paid to the accounting of money, Abú-Ja'far Manṣúr became known as ad-Dawánaqí.

22

Ferment of Thought and Belief

ALMOST all Western scholars have concluded that Muḥammad did not name His successor, and that the mode of election, which created the office of the caliph and enabled Abú-Bakr to assume the caliphate, was in line with the normal traditions of the people of Arabia. It is a fact that the Prophet did not leave a written testament. It is also a fact that the Qur'án is silent on the question of succession. Some apologists have alleged that there were verses in the Qur'án which extolled 'Alí, but these were suppressed by 'Uthmán, when he confiscated the divergent versions[1] of the Qur'án, and sanctioned the text that had been confided to the care of Ḥafṣah, a widow of the Prophet, by 'Umar, her father. This assertion is manifestly untenable. There is no indication at all that either 'Alí, or any other of the Imáms, ever contested, by a single word, the authenticity of the text which 'Uthmán adopted. The 'tradition' which has been labelled 'democratic', and cited to provide the legal basis for the institution of the caliphate, if it ever existed, must have had only a tenuous hold on the people. It was not in evidence in subsequent decades. Arabs were certainly not unacquainted with the hereditary principle. They had their own monarchs, and chieftainships were decided by processes of selection and not election.

Unlike Christ, Muḥammad had, in His lifetime, founded a society subject to the prescriptions of His Revelation. Scholars in the West have dwelt on the theme that Muḥammad was fundamentally a preacher, thereby inferring that He was not particularly concerned with administration which had to be contrived by those who came after Him. The society which the Prophet brought into being was still an infant when He passed away, and obviously required organs of government to serve its needs as it

[1] Four versions are known to have existed.

grew. It is absurd to imagine that Muḥammad, who had created a totally new polity, had no thought for its future administration.

When the inordinate ambition of Sa'd Ibn 'Ubádah, the Khazrajite leader, precipitated a crisis which was resolved by the elevation of Abú-Bakr to the rulership of the Islamic society, there were a few men who stoutly maintained that the position of command amongst the Muslims had been specifically conferred upon 'Alí by the Prophet. Of their number were 'Ammár Ibn Yásir; Miqdid Ibn al-Aswad; Abú-Dharr al-Ghifárí; Salmán the Persian; az-Zubayr Ibn al-'Awwám, whose mother was the daughter of 'Abdu'l-Muṭṭalib;[2] Khálid Ibn Sa'íd, who was a prominent member of the House of Umayyah and cousin to 'Uthmán and Marwán. But 'Alí himself, considering the unity of Islám to be of prime importance, agreed to acknowledge Abú-Bakr; and those who regarded him as the rightful successor to the Prophet followed his example. It was in later times that they came to be reckoned as the first of the Shí'ahs. Shí'ah means a 'faction', and this term was applied to the adherents of the House of 'Alí, although, for a while, the partisans of the House of 'Abbás were also known as Shí'ahs. The majority of the Muslims, who accept as correct the elevation of Abú-Bakr to the office of the caliphate, are known as the people of *Sunnah*—'Tradition'—or Sunnís. But it must be emphasized that in the early days such terms and divisions were unknown. Even after the rebellion of Ṭalḥah and az-Zubayr and open defiance by Mu'áwíyah, no sectarian line was drawn in the community of Islám. The first decisive rift on points of belief and practice came with the defection of the Khárijites from the ranks of the supporters of 'Alí. A combination of bigoted pietism, frustrated idealism and blind obduracy gave the Khárijites a doctrine that would never brook toleration, and made them a menace which Islamic society, in its turn, could not tolerate.

The secession of the Khárijites was linked with the ruses of Mu'áwíyah, and it was Mu'áwíyah's disregard of his pledged word and the subsequent disaster of Karbilá which created rifts and divisions. We have seen that 'Alí II, Zaynu'l-'Ábidín, the son of the martyred Ḥusayn, withdrew from the world around him, choosing

[2] Thus az-Zubayr was a cousin of 'Alí. His separation from him, when 'Alí was at last the ruler, stands out in strange contrast.

to live in strict seclusion. However, there were adherents of the House of 'Alí who regarded him as heir to the Prophet, the immaculate Imám. Imám means the 'Leader'. The person who leads the congregation in the mosque, in prayer, is called the imám. The fourth, the fifth and the sixth Imáms all lived in Medina or close to it, and took no part whatever in the affairs of the Empire. Imám Ja'far aṣ-Ṣádiq, the sixth Imám, had a circle of students drawn from many backgrounds. His discourses were not concerned with matters which agitated the minds of the discontented. The position which the Imáms held was purely spiritual, and in no way temporal. As we have seen, Imám Ja'far aṣ-Ṣádiq refused to lend his name to the movement against the Umayyads, which was increasingly gathering momentum, but very different was the conduct of other members of the House of 'Alí. Muḥammad al-Ḥanafíyyah stood with 'Abdu'l-Malik, the Damascene caliph, and Ibn-az-Zubayr, the Meccan ruler, at the head of their respective adherents during the season of pilgrimage, proclaiming by this act his claim to a seat of authority. Based on his assumptions the Shí'ah sect of the Kaysáníyyah came into existence, and the Imámate of his line passed to the House of 'Abbás.

The next division occurred as a result of the stand which Zayd, a son of the fourth Imám, took against the Umayyads. The Zaydís have greater affinities with the Sunnís, but they are classed as a Shí'ah sect. From A.D. 864 to 928 a Zaydí kingdom had an independent entity in Ṭabaristán,[3] but with its fall the sect seems to have died out there, to flourish only in Yemen.

Belief of an entirely different kind, which was at variance with the fundamentals of Islám, had been gaining ground from early times. It originated with a man named 'Abdu'lláh, who stated that 'Alí was God incarnate. 'Alí himself had this 'Abdu'lláh put to death, but the strange belief persisted and manifested itself in a variety of cults. Some of these went to the length of repudiating Muḥammad, for having usurped, as they said, the station of 'Alí. The Angel Gabriel, others of them maintained, made a mistake when he came to Earth as the bearer of revelation from God: to 'Alí he should have gone, not to Muḥammad. Most of these cults, collectively called *Ghulát* (those who exaggerate or the Extremists), have faded out with the passage of time. Only two esoteric sects,

[3] In Írán by the Caspian Sea, comprising parts of the provinces of Gílán and Mázindarán.

which can be traced back to them, have survived the extravagances of their progenitors, and have settled down to a quiet, meditative existence: the Nuṣayrís of northern Syria and the *Ahl-i-Ḥaqq*[4] of Írán. In their day, the G͟hulát, because of their particular and peculiar attachment to 'Alí or his descendants, not only caused confusion and heart-searching amongst devoted S͟hí'ahs, but brought also upon the head of the S͟hí'ahs much adverse and undeservedly bitter comment from rival denominations. However, notions of 'Return', 'Reincarnation', 'Transmigration', 'Anthropomorphism' and the like, which the G͟hulát had taken over from pre-Islamic cults and schools of thought, were passed by them in diverse ways to others in Islamic society.

Thus in spite of active disengagement by the Imáms of the House of 'Alí and their discouragement of fissiparous tendencies, a number of cults and sects, some politically-oriented, some nightmarishly inventive, were forming round the House of the Prophet; but the bulk of the Muslims, who provided the backbone of the Umayyad power, were inclined to move in step with the kaleidoscopic turns of fortune. They argued that any man raised to power by the consensus of general support should be acknowledged as the rightful ruler of the people, whoever he might be; and that the fate of the transgressor ought not to be dragged into debate, but left to the Day of Judgement, when all would be made clear. They were for a quiet life, undisturbed by partisan passions and speculations. Their attitude towards passing sentence on the state of a Muslim earned them the designation *Murji'a*—'those who postpone'. This problem, as to whether a Muslim placed himself beyond the pale by committing a sin, was made the subject of fierce controversy, and was, as will be seen, bound up with the fundamental appraisement of values and beliefs. At one end of the spectrum were the Murji'a, and at the other the Azáriqih, a powerful group of K͟harijites who condemned any Muslim to apostasy for any act deemed sinful, relegating him to the ranks of idolaters who richly deserved the penalty of death in this world and consignment to hell-fire in the next. His wives and children were also to be put to death. They even considered any non-Muslim who had been guilty of a sin, no matter how

---

[4] 'The People of Truth'—the name which they apply to themselves. Others have called them '*Alíyu'lláhí*—those who equate 'Alí with God. They are known for their tolerance, charity and compassion.

trivial, to be equally an idolater. To this category they assigned both 'Alí and Mu'áwíyah.

The Christian Church, as briefly mentioned before, has also had its share of similar crises. Tertullian (*c.* 155–222), one of the greatest apologists of the Christian Faith, who had battled with heathens, Jews, Marcionites and Gnostics alike, and was the first to formulate the doctrine of Trinity, broke away from the Church about A.D. 220 and joined the Montanists, because Pope Calixtus (Callistus) refused to turn his back on those Christians who had fallen short of grace. Then he mounted a virulent campaign against the Church. He and the Pope both died about the same time. Following the persecutions initiated by Diocletian in 303, the sect of Donatists sprang up, which waged war against those Christians who had handed over copies of the Scriptures to their persecutors. They dubbed such Christians *Traditores*,[5] and set about slaying priests and monks.

Eventually, from the masses of the Murji'ites, who after the downfall of the Umayyads lost both their designation and *raison-d'être*, the people of *Sunnah* emerged, under the tutelage of four eminent jurisconsults: Abú-Ḥanífah Nu'mán Ibn Thábit (d. 767), Málik Ibn Anas of Medina (715–95), Muḥammad Ibn Idrís ash-Sháfi'í (787–820), Aḥmad Ibn Ḥanbal (d. 855). All have the appellation of Imám. Their schools of jurisprudence are known after them, respectively, as the Ḥanafí, the Málikí, the Sháfi'í and the Ḥanbalí. The most liberal and tolerant was the Ḥanafí school, the most orthodox and unbending, the Ḥanbalí. Later we shall examine the distinctive features of these four great schools.

From the early days of the Islamic society the question of free will began to exercise and perplex the minds of men. A tradition, the authenticity of which is very much doubted, was circulating to the effect that Muḥammad had said: 'The proponents of free will are the Magians of my people'. Opposed to free will is rigidly-enforced predestination. Those who maintained that man is chained to a fate decided for him by Providence, incapable of free choice, were known as *Mujabbirah* or *Jabríyyah*—'believers inforceful fate'. When we speak of a river flowing, they said, we are speaking figuratively, because the river, in truth, has no will of its own to flow. By the same token when we ascribe action to man, it is figurative.

[5] The word 'traitor' is thereby derived.

During the Caliphate of ʻAbdu'l-Malik, there lived a man named Maʻbad Ibn ʻAbdu'lláh al-Juhaní, who knew intimately an Íránian, Sanbúyih by name. It is not at all clear who this Persian was, nor whether he was a Mazdean, a Manichaean, or a convert to Islám. It is claimed that he came from the nobility of Írán. From him Maʻbad learned a great deal, and one idea which Sanbúyih implanted in his mind was that man is invested with free will. A German scholar, Alfred von Kremer, has posed the thesis that the notion of free will, and similar notions which later came into prominence, were hammered out by Christian theologians in Damascus, particularly by St. John the Damascene. However, there is agreement that Maʻbad learned his ideas from a Persian. We shall see later the significance of this injection of ideas from Persian sources. Maʻbad, then, challenged the Jabríyyah. ʻAbdu'l-Malik had him put to death in 699, although it may have been Ḥajjáj who ordered his death. Whichever the case, the Umayyads would have no truck with new ideas at all. Later others took up where Maʻbad had been silenced. Not long after, Ghaylán the Damascene, Jaʻd Ibn Dirham and Yúnus al-Aswárí were talking and spreading the same doctrine of free will, quoting verses from the Qur'án in support of their view. Yúnus belonged to the Asávirih, a Persian group of noble descent who had settled in Baṣrah. It has been hinted by some historians that this Yúnus and Sanbúyih, the mentor of Maʻbad, were the same person. Once again the Umayyad Caliph and his agents intervened. Hishám sent Ghaylán to his death, and Khálid[6] Ibn ʻAbdu'lláh al-Qasrí, the governor of ʻIráq, condemned Jaʻd to the gallows. By then the orthodox were thoroughly alarmed. The Qadaríyyah—proponents of the doctrine of free will—were denounced, and it was proclaimed that a true Muslim should not salute the Qadaríyyah, should not participate in the prescribed prayer at their funerals, nor even visit their sick.

The scene was now set for the birth of one of the most outstanding intellectual movements in the realm of Islám, indeed in the whole domain of thought, which had wide repercussions and paved the way for the advent of the golden age of the Islamic civilization.

In Baṣrah there lived and taught one revered for his knowledge,

[6] Khálid later suffered humiliation at the hands of Hishám for misappropriation of funds.

wisdom and piety. In his youth he had been a disciple of 'Alí, the first Imám. But in time he broke off all connection with the House of the Prophet, and outlived all the tribulations which overtook 'Iráq. Ḥasan al-Baṣrí died during the reign of Hishám, at the age of eighty-seven. His large circle of pupils and disciples included both the recluse and man of action. At a later stage Ṣúfís put forth a dubious claim to him. When the status of the sinner had become a burning question in more senses than one, and the Khárijites had divided into three groups over the theory which had severe practical application, Ḥasan al-Baṣrí declared that anyone who committed a major sin was a hypocrite, and a hypocrite was worse than a heathen who openly confessed his unbelief. Abú-Ḥudhayfah Wáṣil Ibn 'Aṭá', a Persian disciple of Ḥasan al-Baṣrí, had become familiar with the views of the so-called[7] Qadaríyyah and could not accept his teacher's dogmatic assertion. The perpetrator of a major sin, Wáṣil maintained, was neither of the category of unbelievers, nor of the rank of true believers; he stood somewhere between. The story goes that Wáṣil took some of the pupils of Ḥasan aside, to another part of the mosque, to expound his ideas to them. Ḥasan pointed him out to others and said: *'I'tazala 'an-ná'*—'he has taken himself away from us'. Hence, the name *Mu'tazilah* (Seceders) was given to the school of thought founded by Wáṣil Ibn 'Aṭá' with the collaboration of 'Amr Ibn 'Ubayd, another Persian disciple of Ḥasan al-Baṣrí. Gradually it developed into the semblance of a religious denomination. The ideas of the Mu'tazilite school not only found widespread acceptance in their totality, but fertilized the thoughts of others as well. At the very outset, the tables were turned on orthodoxy, because Yazíd III, the Umayyad Caliph, whose reign was no longer than six months, readily assented to the five points which Wáṣil Ibn 'Aṭá' and 'Amr Ibn 'Ubayd formulated as the basis of their belief.

The Mu'tazilah preferred to be known as the 'People of Unity and Justice', since these qualities formed the bedrock of Mu'tazilite doctrine. God is Just, He does not bind human beings to a wheel turning inexorably, endlessly, dragging men in spite of themselves to the bliss of heaven or the torture of hell-fire. Men are endowed with free will, which betokens justice. All power

[7] 'So-called' because they themselves, having in mind the spurious tradition ascribed to the Prophet, rejected the label of Qadaríyyah. (See p. 225.)

comes from God, but man determines the use that power is put to, because God, although omnipotent and capable of forcing human beings to act, does not do so. God is not corporeal, not an essence, not an element, not an 'accident', rather the Creator of all and above any concept of limitation. The particular stress laid upon the unity and the transcendence of God carried with it the refutation of two points in orthodox belief. The orthodox maintained that the attributes of God were coeval with Him, and the Qur'án was 'uncreate'. The Mu'tazilites retorted that making even abstract notions part of the Godhead or equivalent to Him was *shirk* (joining partners with God); as for the Qur'án, how could it be co-existent with God? Ja'd, who had been put to death, had said the same of the Qur'án. Not only was the notion of the Holy Book being 'uncreate' tantamount to joining partners with God, it would impose, as well, total rigidity on law and society, leading to a social pattern forever frozen and immutable.

Before long, Mu'tazilites too had their own divisions. While controversy about the status of sinners faded into the background, a battle, heated, vigorous and merciless, raged over the pre-existence of the Qur'án. Had it not been for the political upheavals which had begun to rack Islamic society, the sudden emergence of the Mu'tazilite school would have produced yet more violent reaction, and caused more immediate mutations in patterns of thought. In the event, a few decades had to elapse before the Mu'tazilite catalyst could work effectively; but dividing lines were already appearing. Mu'tazilite thought was close to the Shí'ah doctrine taking shape under the guidance of the sixth Imám, but, of course, there were points of difference. Mu'tazilites were not particularly concerned with the question of the caliphate. On the other hand, the spiritual authority of the Imám had become a cardinal principle of Shí'ah belief. Until the latter part of the eighth century (the middle of the second century of Hijrah) this principle remained unargued and largely unexpressed, although belief in it was implicit in adherence to the rights of the House of 'Alí. But as soon as controversy and argument on a rational plane came into vogue, the learned amongst the Shí'ites took to the pen. Mu'tazilites had been pioneers in this field, and now through the diligence and the literary ability of these two groups, the Mu'tazilah and the Shí'ah, *'Ilma'l-Kalám* (Scholastic Theology) was developed and became an integral part of the culture of Islamic society. It is interesting to note that none of the apostolic Imáms ever wrote or compiled a book. But their prayers, discourses, aphorisms and directives have been gathered into books, the most famous of which are *Nahju'l-Balághah*, the eloquent discourses and letters of 'Alí, the first Imám; and *Sahífatu's-Sajjádíyyah*, the moving prayers of 'Alí II, the fourth Imám.

Every group, every school of thought, every denomination, naturally went to the Qur'án to find evidence for its own viewpoint. In the Holy Book there are verses that speak of beholding the visage of the Lord. Mu'tazilites, with their vehement emphasis on the incorporeality of God, could not admit that the Qur'án promised men the possibility of encountering God face to face. Such a supposition was sheer blasphemy to them. Their opponents, while allowing that God could not have human form, and therefore the face of God could not be a human face, insisted that the wording of the Qur'án must be taken literally: people must one day gaze on God. Argument over these incompatibilities was fierce and relentless.

It is claimed that Muslims were the first to write on the history and philosophy of religions and creeds. The pantheon of the ancient world of Greece and Rome did not lend itself to doctrinal and philosophical treatment. Jews, who were custodians of monotheistic thought, had a horror of everything they considered pagan, and, in spite of the fact that their thought was undoubtedly influenced by the Faith of Zoroaster, had too little interest in other systems of belief to write about them. Christians, harrowed by persecution, in need of constructing a framework of organization which their Founder had not given them, in constant battle with heresy, perforce holding aloof from intimate contact with followers of other Faiths except when attempting to preach the Gospel, had neither the leisure nor the inclination to write about any religion other than their own. And much of what they wrote was in refutation of creeds and heresies which seemed to threaten the infant Faith they were nurturing in face of immense odds. Patristic writings were concerned with the statement and restatement of the gradually developing creed, which might be termed the official viewpoint of a church burgeoning into an institution.

And when Christians turned to consider other Faiths, the Jews had discreetly retired behind the protective barriers of racial separateness; moreover, Islám was militantly at their door. Although converts could still break into the citadel of Judaism, as the Turkish Khazars of the Caspian area did at a later date, Jewish proselytizing had reached its end, particularly in the Mediterranean basin where the Faith of Israel had grown and flourished. Christians, dominant in the lands where the Jews had suffered, forgetting or ignoring the counsel of their tolerant Master, were making life heavily burdensome for them, driving them into a closed world of their own, where they were always at the mercy of their oppressors. Intellectual communication between Jews and Christians was impossible. Wherever Muslims overcame Christians, notably in Spain, the Jews welcomed them as deliverers. And Judaism, throughout the expanse of Europe, turned more devoutly and eagerly and haughtily than ever before to Messianic hope.

Christian treatment of Islám in book lore belongs to the period when the peak of Islamic civilization had passed. The recrudescence of a vengeful Christianity in Spain coming in the wake of Muslim decline and demoralization; the arrival of Turkish bigots on the Islamic scene which made Islám in the West synonymous with the detested religion of the Turk, and the name of Muḥammad eponymous for idols and false gods in the form of Maumet and Mammet and Mahound; the degeneracy of Byzantium accelerated by its defeat (Manzikert, A.D. 1071) at the hands of Alp-Arslán, the Saljúq (Seljuk) monarch, and by the repeated depredations of fellow-Christians from the West, who, in the guise of Crusaders, sought land, money and fortune; the bitter hatreds which the Crusaders engendered and which ricocheted all round—all these were factors which gravely distorted the image of the Faith of Muḥammad. When Christians came to write about Islám they were terribly handicapped.

Muslims, it seems, were the first to undertake a systematic and scholarly study of the Faiths of mankind. But two reservations ought to be made. Their studies were not comprehensive enough, and when they came to deal with divisions within their own ranks they were seldom fair. However, the breadth of the vision and understanding of Muslim writers can be gauged by their reference to the Scriptures of the Jews, Christians and Sabeans, in the great encyclopaedic work, *al-Fihrist* (The Index), by Muḥammad Ibn

Isḥáq, known as Ibna'n-Nadím (Ibn an-Nadím) who flourished in the tenth century of the Christian era and composed his celebrated book in A.D. 987–8. Section II of the First Discourse, which deals with the Scriptures of other Faiths, is thus introduced by Ibna'n-Nadím: 'On the names of Books of the Law revealed to the different sects of Muslims and the different sects of those who follow them'.[8] All Faiths are of Islám.

In another chapter we shall come back to the theme of this chapter on the ferment of thought, idea and belief. But later developments can best be understood in the light of events associated with the caliphate of the 'Abbásids. We must now turn, therefore, to the year A.D. 754, when Abú-Ja'far al-Manṣúr succeeded his brother, as-Saffáḥ.

[8] Browne, *A Literary History of Persia*, vol. I, p. 384.

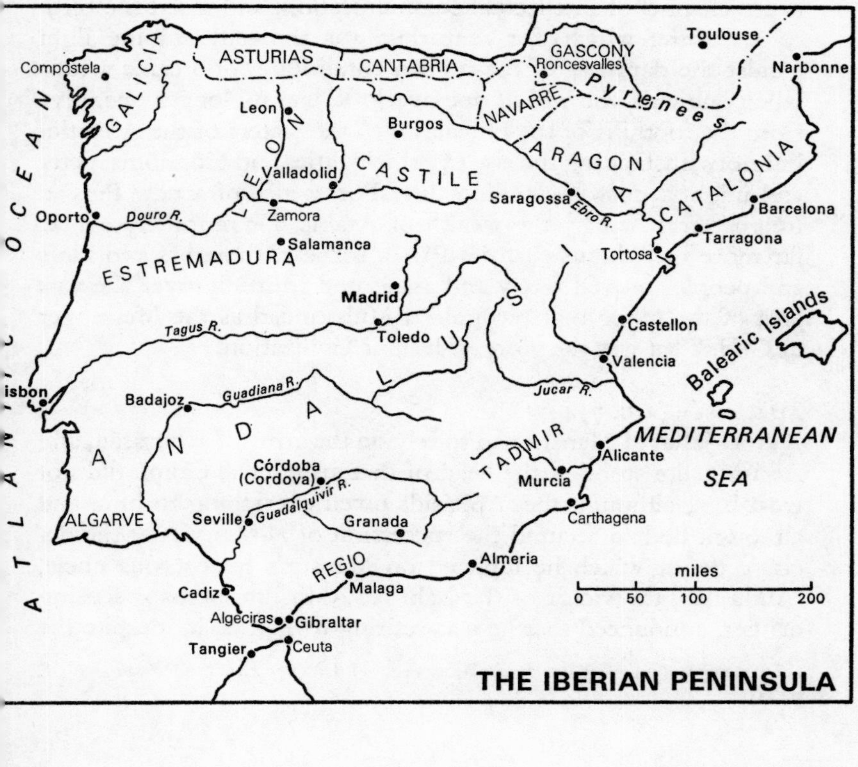

THE IBERIAN PENINSULA

23

The New Society

IT is true that 'Abbásids waded 'through seas of blood'[1] to supreme power. But it is also true that their triumph dealt the death-blow to racialism entrenched under the Umayyads. The face of Islamic society changed perceptibly. This change eventually destroyed the hegemony of the Empire of Islám. It produced a belated reaction, sterile and vainglorious, amongst non-Arabs against Arab pride. But over and above everything else, it opened every channel of intellectual communication, and aided the birth of a culture, which, for centuries, was the only shining light amidst the darkness of the human condition. Soon came a time when one writ, the will of one overlord, was no longer operative from the foothills of the Himalayas to the waters of the Atlantic; but notwithstanding the rise of principalities and kingdoms, petty and mighty, notwithstanding the efflorescence of a new Persian tongue, enriched by the wealth of Arabic, far more expressive, far more mellifluous than its Pársík forbear, thoughts and ideas and peoples moved freely and associated fruitfully over the vast area of the globe that recognized Muḥammad as the Messenger of God. That was the glory of Islamic civilization.

AL-MANṢÚR (A.D. 754–75)

Abú-Ja'far al-Manṣúr had to rely on the army of Khurásán, and Abú-Muslim stood at the head of that army. The Caliph did not trust him, although the 'Abbásids owed everything to him, and although he had secured the succession of al-Manṣúr by the decisive defeat which he inflicted on Manṣúr's treacherous uncle, 'Abdu'lláh, the victor of the Záb. Abú-Muslim, perhaps sensing danger, announced that he was retiring to Khurásán, despite the

[1] An expression used by E. G. Browne in *A Literary History of Persia*, vol. I, p. 245.

fact that the Caliph had offered him the governorship of Syria, and had summoned him to his presence. Then, Manṣúr enticed him with solemn assurances; but once Abú-Muslim was entrapped within the Caliph's palace, he was rushed upon and stabbed to death. Thus died the man who was known as Amín-u-Ál-i-Muḥammad (the Trusted One of the House of Muḥammad). Manṣúr must have felt secure to have dared to encompass the

The ʻAbbásid Caliphs
A.D. 750–861

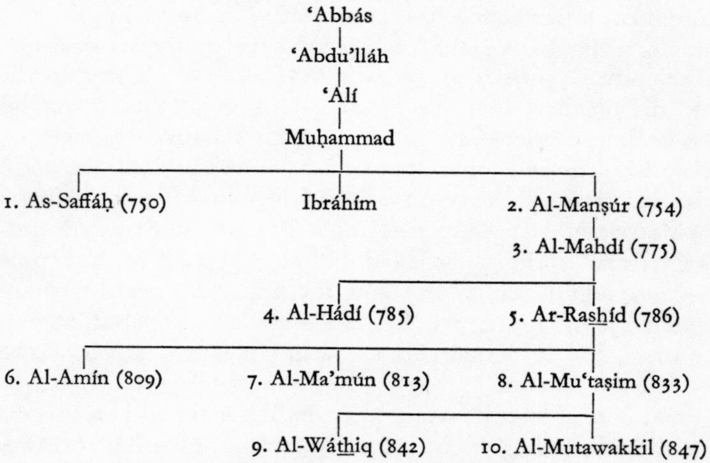

Dates are those of accession to the Caliphate.

death of so powerful a man. Undoubtedly Abú-Muslim had raised legions of enemies amongst the Arabs, and from the Persians, as well. Manṣúr counted on their support, and he was proved right.

Violent death plucked Abú-Muslim away at the prime of his life and achievement, in the year 755; and the mode and manner of his death provided the milieu for his apotheosis. Before long a sect variously called Muslimíyyah or Khurramíyyah was flourishing. They believed that Abú-Muslim had not died, but had turned into a dove when imperilled by Manṣúr's treachery. He had flown away, they maintained, to take his abode in celestial realms, from which he would emerge at the appointed time to rule the world with justice.

People who were disenchanted and disillusioned with the 'Abbásids were many. The rise of the Muslimíyyah group foreshadowed the appearance of many more of various guises, forms and pretences. But before we turn to the story of the heresiarchs and the founders of new movements, four points ought to be made and stressed. Firstly, both Abu'l-'Abbás as-Saffáḥ and Abú-Ja'far al-Manṣúr had belied the promise which their propagandists had made on their behalf and in their names. Manṣúr was chiefly responsible for making the division between legitimists and defenders of consensus marked and permanent. He dogged and persecuted the House of 'Alí. So badly did he treat the descendants of Ḥasan, the second Imám, that two of them—Muḥammad, known as an-Nafs' az-Zakíyyah (The Pure Soul), and his brother, Ibráhím—fearing to present themselves before the Caliph, challenged whether Manṣúr's assurances were of the same kind he had given to his uncle, 'Abdu'lláh, and to Abú-Muslim. Perforce, they raised the banner of revolt, Muḥammad in Medina and Ibráhím in Kúfah. Both were defeated and lost their lives, while their aged father, 'Abdu'lláh, was publicly flogged; and he had been one of the three prominent members of the House of 'Alí, to whom Abú-Salmah had offered, in the first instance, the leadership of the anti-Umayyad movement. Syed Ameer Ali writes:

'. . . Saffâh's cruelty was due to vindictive frenzy; his successor's bloodshed sprang from calculation. Cold-blooded, calculating, and unscrupulous, he spared none whom he thought in the least dangerous to himself or his dynasty. His treatment of the descendants of the Caliph Ali forms the darkest page in Abbasside history. Suyûti[2] says that "Mansûr was the first who occasioned dissensions between the Abbassides and Alides, for before that they were united." '[3]

Strangely enough, one of the new groups that sprang up, called the Ráwandíyyah, believed in the divinity of Manṣúr himself, and by its devious antics endangered his life. Manṣúr dealt with it as harshly as he dealt with others.

The second point which needs to be emphasized is that much is unknown about many of these groups and movements. Nothing

[2] Jalálu'd-Dín as-Suyúṭí (1445–1505), was a distinguished historian and writer on many subjects, such as philology, philosophy, law and tradition. (H.M.B.)

[3] *A Short History of the Saracens*, p. 213.

of their writings, if there were any, has survived, nor have they left any adherents to tell us the truth about their beliefs, no matter how mistaken and deluded. Thirdly, a good deal of what has been written about them is slanted and distorted. Some commentators have written with evident malice, some purely for the purpose of refuting them, while others, having no particular interest to seek out the truth, have recorded mere hearsay. It is astonishing that writers of high eminence such as Shahristání, the author of *Kitábu'l-Milal-W'an-Niḥal* (Book of Religions and Philosophical Sects) considered all of them to have been from the same stable.[4] Niẓámu'l-Mulk, the distinguished vizier (vazír) of Malik-Sháh, the Saljúqid monarch, takes the same view and writes with exceeding hostility. He was an able administrator, a man of highest integrity, a devoted servant of the realm, but when he came to evaluate, judge and narrate the rise and spread of tenets which were heretical and repulsive to him, he did not deign to check his data, confused his terms and nomenclature, and sadly failed to do justice to historical truth.[5]

The last point that ought to be borne in mind is the fact that, contrary to popular belief, Islám was not forced upon recalcitrant subject races at the point of the sword; for decades vast numbers in conquered lands remained in the fold of their existing affiliations. The entire area north of the Elburz (Alburz) range on the shores of the Caspian was still Mazdean in the reign of Manṣúr. Side by side with the followers of Zoroaster lived, although under cover, people who cherished the memory and the teachings of Mání[6] and Mazdak.[7] Manichaeans, who had already played havoc in the Christian camp, were even more numerous. Gnosticism in its later manifestations had its roots in Manichaean thought. The great St. Augustine, Bishop of Hippo, had, in his youth, trodden that path. To a greater extent the followers of Mání, to a lesser extent those of Mazdak, contributed to the upheavals that came in the wake of the murder of Abú-Muslim.

[4] Muḥammad Ibn 'Abdu'l-Karím ash-Shahristání flourished in the twelfth century A.D.

[5] In the *Siyásat-Námih*, his famous polemic on the art of government.

[6] Mání, an Íránian, attempted a synthesis of Christian and Mazdean Faiths. He was put to death by the Sásánian monarch, Bahrám I (A.D. 273–76).

[7] Mazdak was put to death by Chosroes I, in A.D. 529. What he really taught is veiled in falsifications. It is said that he advocated the communal sharing of wealth and wives. He certainly mounted devastating attacks on the Mazdean priesthood. Zoroastrians, Christians and Muslims alike have done their best to denigrate him.

Close upon his murder, the Empire of Islám experienced a novel type of uprising. From the assassination of 'Uthmán to the accession of Manṣúr, rebellions were initiated and fostered by people proud to call themselves Muslim. Now, a man named Sinbádh, who has been described as 'the Magian', led a revolt. From his home in Níshápúr, in the province of Khurásán, he moved west to Ray. The startling fact is that Abú-Muslim had succeeded in winning the affection of the Mazdeans. Sinbádh, having announced his intention to avenge Abú-Muslim's death, gathered round him a motley of men: Muslim and non-Muslim, the discontented and the disillusioned. His stand lasted no more than seventy days, and had already been suppressed when one named Isḥáq (and called 'the Turk' for no reason at all), preached in Transoxania a religion in which both Zoroaster and Abú-Muslim featured. Again, little that is reliable is known about him. He failed as Sinbádh had, and as Yúsuf al-Barm did after him, a man about whom still less is known.

A legend, quoted by Niẓámu'l-Mulk, assumed that following the death of Mazdak, his wife, supposedly named Khurramah, fled from Ctesiphon to Ray and preached his religion in its environs. Hence the label of Khurramíyyah [8] accorded to the partisans of Abú-Muslim. Ray was contiguous with the areas of Ṭabaristán and Daylamán (present-day Mázindarán and Gílán), the inhabitants of which, even after embracing Islám, continued to be at variance with the caliphate of the 'Abbásids and its tenets. The very name Daylamán became synonymous with heterodoxy and heresy. Eventually from the Daylamán land arose the first powerful Shí'ah dynasty: the Buwayhids (A.D. 932–1062).

There had also been a pseudo-prophet, sprung from the loins of the Mazdeans. It seems that one Biháfarídh, the son of Máhfurúdhín, had accepted Islám under the guidance and influence of Abú-Muslim, but afterwards had reverted to his own claim. One authority makes Abú-Muslim responsible for his death. Mazdeans, according to Shahristání, detested him. His doctrines, so far as is known, had affinity with those of the Ghulát.

The influence of Neo-Platonism and Indian thought was becoming increasingly felt. The development of *Taṣawwuf* or Ṣúfíism, at a later age, also owed much to Neo-Platonism.

[8] Others have stated that Khurramah was a locality in Ádharbáyján.

Al-Andalus and North Africa

While Írán was showing disenchantment with the 'Abbásid deliverers, a bold bid to dismember the Empire was meeting with unexpected success at the western extremity of Islamic domains. 'Abda'r-Raḥmán, a grandson of the Caliph Hishám, had escaped with his life in the holocaust which overtook the House of Umayyah. Across the long trail of North Africa, he found his way to the safety of al-Andalus. Yúsuf al-Fahrí, the Arab governor of Spain, was a Muḍarite, and the Ḥimyarites were only too willing to lend their support to the fugitive Umayyad prince, in order to oust their governor. 'Abda'r-Raḥmán was soon in possession of an army, and had no difficulty in occupying Seville. In May 756, he defeated Yúsuf al-Fahrí, and the way was open to Cordova. It still took some years before 'Abda'r-Raḥmán could firmly establish his authority, but Spain was irretrievably lost to the 'Abbásids, and the Umayyad caliphate was reborn in a far-off land. It is interesting to note that as late as 777 some of the leading figures amongst the Arabs of Spain, in their hatred of 'Abda'r-Raḥmán, resorted to the great Charlemagne and offered him help, should he come to conquer their adopted country. One of them was a son-in-law of Yúsuf al-Fahrí, another the governor of Barcelona, and a third a descendant of Sa'd Ibn 'Ubádah, the Khazrajite chief who had hoped to become the successor to the Prophet. In fact, it was the latter, Ḥusayn Ibn Yaḥyá, who realized, at the eleventh hour, how appalling their conduct was, and refused to hand Saragossa over to Charlemagne, when the Emperor of the Franks arrived at its gates. Charlemagne was preparing to take Saragossa by a long siege, but news came that Wittekind, the Saxon king, whom he had defeated and driven to Denmark, had returned to lead his people once again. The Emperor had to raise the siege and make posthaste for the Rhineland. In the defiles of the Pyrenees, at Roncesvalles (Roncevaux) his rear-guard was isolated and annihilated. The sound of Roland's horn did not reach those who had gone ahead. It is claimed that the Basques were responsible for the massacre. Muslims claim responsibility too. Perhaps both had a hand in achieving a minor victory, which, in 778, gave the world the legend of Roland and his song.

'Abda'r-Raḥmán concluded a treaty with Charlemagne, and when he died, two years later, leaving the throne to his saintly son, Ḥishám, the fair land of al-Andalus was at peace.

North Africa, from the borders of Egypt to the Atlantic, also went through tumultuous years, following the downfall of the Umayyads in the East. Berber spirit of freedom and Khárijite zeal and intransigence kept the area on the boil. Eventually, by the year 800, three independent principalities, and one more, self-governing but owing allegiance to the 'Abbásid Caliph, occupied the area. At the western end, where we find Morocco today, was the Idrísid Kingdom of Maghrib. Its founder, Idrís, was a brother of Muḥammad, 'the Pure Soul', a descendant of 'Alí. Finding life in Medina intolerable under the 'Abbásids, he fled in 788 to the furthermost boundary of Islám, and the Berbers gave him a home and a haven. The long arm of the 'Abbásids reached him even there. He was poisoned by an emissary who posed as a physician. Although his son, Idrís II, was born after his death, the Berbers nurtured him as their ruler. The other two independent principalities, both Khárijite in faith, were also inhabited by Berbers. They were situated around the foothills of the Atlas mountains. One was centred on the town of Sijilmásah on the edge of the Sahara, an important trading-post to which valuable merchandise came from the coastal regions of West Africa. Guinea was so named because Arabs called it *Balad al-Ghina'*—the Land of Riches. The other Khárijite principality, extending to the waters of the Mediterranean, was founded by a Persian named Ibn-Rustam. The province called Ifríqíyah (Africa), which became self-governing under Ibráhím Ibn al-Aghlab in the year 800, covered the territories which we know today as Libya and Tunisia and parts of Algeria. Thus in the first fifty years of the 'Abbásid Caliphate a large portion of the Empire of Islám tore itself away from the body of the empire.

A task which occupied much of Manṣúr's time and attention was the search for a capital. To Damascus he would not go, and the town of Anbár on the Euphrates, chosen by his brother as the seat of his government, was not suitable. Manṣúr decided to have a capital built. He reconnoitred for an ideal site, found it by the Tigris, and supervised in person the construction of the new metropolis which he called *Dára's-Salám*—the Abode of Peace. It was to become known as Baghdád, derived from the Persian

IX THE GREAT MOSQUE OF DAMASCUS

built by al-Walíd I (705–15), is an Umayyad reconstruction of the Cathedral of St. John. Its mosaics surpass in beauty and fantasy any which survive from Roman or Byzantine art.

X THE GREAT MOSQUE OF CORDOVA

begun by ‘Abda’r-Raḥmán I in 785, was several times enlarged until, in the fifteenth century, it became a Christian church. Its hexafoil arches in two tiers were an innovation in Islamic architecture.

name of a village that stood where Manṣúr built his capital. The site which the Caliph chose was near Madá'in (Ctesiphon), and Manṣúr decided to pull down the buildings of the Sásánian monarchs, and use their materials in the construction of his own city. He asked the opinion of Khálid the Barmecide. Khálid advised against it, and Manṣúr told him that being a Persian, he did not wish to see the glories of his kings removed. He went ahead with his project, but found the cost of demolition excessive. It is related that Khálid then advised him not to desist, because people would remark that the Caliph was incapable of pulling down what the monarchs of yore had built. Baghdád was a magnificent creation. The depredations of centuries yet far distant, the descent of Mongol hordes in the thirteenth century on the domains of Islám, the battles which were fought by kings and chieftains in and around 'the Abode of Peace', and the pathetic misrule of the Ottoman Turks who eventually became the masters of Arab lands—all combined to obliterate the beauties and the grandeur of that Baghdád which Manṣúr and his successors brought into being. Establishing his capital where he did, the second 'Abbásid Caliph showed perspicacity of a high order. He began the construction of Baghdád in the year 763.

In the year 757, a Persian, 'Abdu'lláh Ibn al-Muqaffa', was put to a painful death by the order of Manṣúr. Ibn-al-Muqaffa' had once had access to the person of the Caliph, and had suggested to him that he should undertake a detailed examination of the various schools of jurists in the diverse parts of his far-flung Empire, to try to introduce some measure of uniformity and co-ordination. Manṣúr declined to interfere with the work and the formulae of the jurists, who maintained that diversity, both of theory and administration, was God's bounty to man.

The real name of 'Abdu'lláh Ibn al-Muqaffa' was Dádhbih, and his father's name Dádhjushras. He was a native of the province of Fárs, well-versed and well-informed, a master of Arabic which was not his mother tongue. Ibn-al-Muqaffa' outwardly professed Islám and welcomed the advent of the 'Abbásids. Secretly he was a devout Manichaean. It became his lifelong task to diffuse the doctrines of his arcane Faith. It could not be done openly, but he found the right milieu: translating such texts as scholars would deem useful. Ibn-al-Muqaffa' was also intensely patriotic and anxious to keep alive in the minds of his compatriots the thought of the achievements of their forefathers. The language which the Íránians used in the days of the Sásánians was undergoing profound change and would soon become unfamiliar. The Persian we know today was evolving from it, chiefly in the province of Khurásán. Arabic had become the language of learning, of commerce and of communication. Ibn-al-Muqaffa', proficient in these languages, put his hand to translation with a vengeance. He translated the Fables of Bídpáy (or the *Kalílah-wa-Dimnah*),[9] amending it, adding to it a chapter here, allusions there, to present under a cloak his own personal beliefs. He translated other Íránian texts as well, all of which are lost. Not even his translations of them have survived except the *Kalílah-wa-Dimnah* (Kalílah and Dimnah). He went even further and rendered into Arabic works of Marcion and Bardesane.[10] Ibn-al-Muqaffa' paid with his life for his devotion to the religion of Mání, but so subtly had he served it that before long it was gaining adherents in unexpected quarters, and the term *Zindíq*[11] (plural: *Zanádiqah*) had passed into common usage, by which a Manichaean was meant. Arabs too were embracing the religion of Mání and the doctrines of Marcion (Arabic: Marqíyún) and Bardesane (Arabic: Ibn-Dayṣán), and following poets such as Muṭí' Ibn Ayás and Ṣáliḥ Ibn 'Abdu'l-Quddús, and writers such as Ḥammád al-'Ajrad and Yaḥyá Ibn Zíyád. In the reign of the celebrated Hárún ar-Rashíd, an officer was specifically appointed with the title of aṣ-Ṣáḥiba's-Zanádiqah (the Controller of Heresy) to seek out the Zindíqs and destroy them. The Caliph Mahdí, Hárún's father, is reported to have said that no book of the Zindíqs ever came into his hands that could not be traced to 'Abdu'lláh Ibn al-Muqaffa'.

As it happened, the proliferation of Zindíq literature coincided with the dissemination of Greek thought and philosophy, again through copious translations. These translations were undertaken with the approval and even under the patronage of the Caliphs. Mu'tazilites and others who were engaged in rational argument

[9] It is believed to have been brought originally from India, in the days of Chosroes I. However, Ibn-al-Muqaffa' has been suspected of having compiled the book himself.

[10] Bardesane (A.D. 154–222) or Bar-Daisan was a Parthian born in Edessa. He embraced Christianity in 179 and battled with the Gnostics, but was eventually declared heretical by the Church. Later Christian apologists have sprung to his defence. His disciples could be found as far away as China.

[11] From the Persian word: *Zandík*, meaning the 'follower of Zand'. In 1842, it appeared in English in this form: Zendic.

welcomed and used the store of knowledge thus opened up. But the orthodox had no taste for Greek philosophy, and tried to equate it with the thoughts of the Zindíqs. A result of this verbal inaccuracy was the draining of the original meaning from the term 'Zindíq'. It was used wildly and indiscriminately to such an extent that the hunt for the Manichaeans and the Marcionites became confused. The efflorescence of a new culture, the shapings of a new society, and fresh controversies, all helped to play down the impact of Manichaeanism and halt the search for its adherents. Manichaeanism did not die out. It went underground and lived on, an esoteric sect thriving on secrecy.[12] But its imprint on Islamic society was unmistakable.

AL-MAHDÍ (A.D. 775–85)

Manṣúr managed to set aside the order of succession laid down by his brother, and disinherited his nephew, 'Isá Ibn Músá, who had played a conspicuous part in defeating the pretenders of the House of 'Alí. And so, when he died in 775, his son, Muḥammad al-Mahdí followed him into the seat of the caliphate. Al-Mahdí's reign had its quota of rebellions and civil disturbances, and Khurásán continued to be a hotbed of unrest. The uprising of Yúsuf al-Barm was a minor affair, but of greater proportion and harder to defeat were the insurrection and the pretensions of the 'Veiled Prophet of Khurásán'. This is how al-Muqanna' (the Veiled One) appears in Thomas Moore's *Lalla Rookh*. Veiled he was, and the incarnation of the Divine he claimed to be. Háshim, the son of Ḥakím,[13] was a native of Marv, and had connections with the followers of Abú-Muslim. Because the 'Abbásids sported black garments as the emblem of their House, this impostor ordered his followers to don pure white and hoist white standards. Thus they gained the name *al-Mubayyaḍah*—the White Clad. There had also been the Red Clads—*al-Muḥammirah*—who were identified with the Khurramíyyah. But why did Háshim hide his face behind a veil? According to his detractors, because he was repulsive of countenance, and according to himself, because

[12] The author recalls meeting a Welshman in London in the late thirties, who was very much interested in the mystical aspects of religion. One day he mentioned that he was a Manichaean. To the author's eager queries he would only say that their order consisted of several grades, and that he had not sufficiently progressed to reach higher echelons and higher mysteries.

[13] Authorities differ over his name and that of his father.

human eyes could not bear to gaze at his resplendent visage. In his case, too, there is a good deal of confusion and reliable data is meagre. He must have been a man of considerable learning, because there is general agreement that he had contrived an artificial moon, which issued forth from a well at night to illumine the countryside. 'The Moon of Nakhshab'[14] has lived on in literature. The end of the 'Veiled Prophet of Khurásán' is also wrapped in mystery. Hitler seems to have emulated his stratagem of disappearance. The body of Al-Muqanna' was not found when the forces of the Caliph Mahdí entered his stronghold. Some of his close associates, too, were not to be found. Whether immolated in fire, or dissolved in a tank of corrosives, as Thomas Moore imagined, al-Muqanna' had left a legend behind. He had gone the way of Abú-Muslim and would come back in the fullness of time.

In Mahdí's reign the hunt for the Zindíqs began, but more lustre was shed on his reign by his patronage of learning. The victories which his son, Hárún, won against the Byzantines, were noteworthy as well, and Hárún imposed an annual tribute on the Empress Irene. Mahdí's rule lasted ten years. He was succeeded by his eldest son, Músá al-Hádí. Mahdí had decreed that his second son, Hárún, should inherit the Caliphate, but Hádí tried immediately to change the order of succession in favour of his own son, and to further his design he threw Yaḥyá Ibn Khálid, the Barmecide, into prison. Yaḥyá was the champion and the protector of Hárún, and had been a second father to him. But Hádí lived not more than a year and, in 786, the most famous and the most glamorous of all the 'Abbásids ascended the throne. Hárún ar-Rashíd was only twenty-two years old, but had already proved his worth on the battlefield, and had shown considerable wisdom and forbearance when subjected to his brother's taunts and persuasion to divest himself of his right. He left the affairs of his government in the hands of Yaḥyá the Barmecide (*al-Barmakí*) to do as he wished. The process begun under Manṣúr which had brought more and more of the Persians into the administration of the Empire, tilting the scale to the disadvantage of the Arabs, gathered momentum with the rapid rise of the House of Barmak. When Yaḥyá was too old to fulfil his functions as vizier, his place was taken by Ja'far, his son, whom we also meet in the pages of the *Arabian Nights*. Another son of Yaḥyá, named Faḍl, also held

[14] *Máh-i-Nakhshab*, in Persian.

high office, and others of the Barmecides (Barmakids) occupied important posts. In all probability, they were devout adherents of the Imáms of the House of 'Alí, and yet they served the 'Abbásid Caliphs faithfully. They did their best to extend protection to the descendants of 'Alí, wherever required. There were also other Shí'ites in the ranks of the government, who served both the interests of their persuasion and the interests of the State.

HÁRÚN AR-RASHÍD (A.D. 786–809)

The reign of Hárún is considered to have marked the zenith of the Golden Age of Islám. In another chapter we shall examine the rise and the development of the Islamic civilization and note its contributions to the world at large. Here it suffices to say that Hárún ar-Rashíd furthered, by his patronage, the growth of that civilization; but it was left to his son, 'Abdu'lláh al-Ma'mún, to become personally involved in discussions and exchanges that widened the horizons of the minds of the people.

In the year 800, Hárún reached an understanding with Ibráhím Ibn al-Aghlab that was to set a precedent of mighty consequences. In effect, it was that should Ibráhím succeed in calming the disturbed province of Ifríqíyah, without asking the Caliph to aid him with troops, he could hold its government in perpetuity, and Ibráhím would, in return, unreservedly acknowledge the overlordship of the Caliph. Ibráhím did succeed, and founded a dynasty that ruled Ifríqíyah for a century.

The brilliance of Hárún's reign was overshadowed by his erratic and unjustified attitude towards Músa'l-Káẓim (Músá al-Káẓim), the seventh Imám of the main body of the Shí'ites. We have noted, on several occasions, the total withdrawal of Ja'far aṣ-Ṣádiq, the sixth Imám, from all temporal commitments, in spite of contradictions in the behaviour of many members of his family. Although it was apparent to the Caliph Manṣúr that Imám Ja'far aṣ-Ṣádiq would never, in any way, contest his power and authority, he held the sixth Imám in suspicion and under surveillance. After the passing of this Imám, in 765, there came another break in the ranks of the Shí'ahs. The Imám had first named his eldest son, Ismá'íl, to succeed him. For reasons which are not clear, he revoked the appointment and gave the succession to his next son, Músá, whose mother was a slave. Ismá'íl died in the lifetime of his father, and notwithstanding the fact that his body was shown to the populace, just before his burial, the legend was born and believed that Ismá'íl had retreated from the world and would come forth as the expected Mahdí—the Deliverer—at a time decreed by God. But there were others who maintained that the Imámate had passed to his son, Muḥammad, and that this Muḥammad was the seventh Imám and the Mahdí of latter days. Mahdí—'the One Who Is Guided'—or Mihdí, is the name applied by Shí'ahs and Sunnís alike to the One whose appearance, in the fullness of time, is expected by them, the promise of whose advent is enshrined in Scripture and Tradition.

With the claim made for Muḥammad, the son of Ismá'íl, came the cleavage that produced the most powerful branching of the main Shí'ah persuasion. The Ismá'ílíyyah sect is one of the most maligned in the world. It was, at one time, a very effective force in the body-politic—a militant group which made many enemies and inflicted deep injuries on its adversaries, had amazing turns of fortune, suffered from splintering and from the excesses of its zealots, and established one of the most enlightened, tolerant and benign regimes in Islám. Its meteoric rise will be considered later.

Although the breaking away of the Ismá'ílís proved to be the most significant, the passing of the sixth Imám caused other schisms, of lesser magnitude, amongst the Shí'ahs. A group called the Náwúsíyyah denied the obvious: the death of the Imám, and asserted his corporeal disappearance. He was the Mahdí to come, they claimed. A second group gave their allegiance to 'Abdu'lláh, known as al-Afṭaḥ, another son of Imám Ja'far aṣ-Ṣádiq. Hence they were called the Afṭaḥíyyah. Still others looked to Muḥammad, another son of the sixth Imám, as his successor. But the greater number of the adherents of Ja'far aṣ-Ṣádiq upheld the Imámate of his son, Músa'l-Káẓim, who followed in the footsteps of his father and remained completely detached from temporal concerns. Hárún was uneasy, however, and had the Imám brought from Medina to Baghdád and handed into the charge of Sindí Ibn Sháhik, the governor of the metropolitan prison. Imám Músa'l-Káẓim was lodged in the house of Sindí's sister, where he was kept a prisoner, and in all probability poisoned. He passed away in 799. Immediately, a number of the Shí'ites declared that Músa'l-Káẓim had not suffered death, but had retired behind a veil, to issue forth at the time decreed, as the Mahdí. The notion of corporeal disappearance or occultation had become contagious. Abú-Muslim had flown away as a dove, Muḥammad al-Ḥanafíyyah was awaiting the appointed time in a cave near Mecca, 'the Veiled Prophet of Khurásán' was coming back. Subsequent to the passing of the seventh Imám, his adherents divided into five groups. The majority hailed his eldest son, 'Alí ar-Riḍá, the eighth Imám. It is said that the man responsible for introducing the idea of occultation was 'Umar, the second Caliph. Refusing to accept (as he did at first) the fact of the mortality of the Prophet, he kept repeating, *qad ghába Rasúlu'lláh*—'Verily, the Messenger of God has gone from our sight'.

Another blot on the reign of Hárún was his treachery towards the House of Barmak. From the day Abú-Muslim unfurled the black standard in Khurásán the House of Barmak had served the 'Abbásids faithfully. Hárún owed his life, his education, his throne to Yaḥyá the Barmecide. There must have been many an occasion when the loyalty of the members of this House was severely tested by the unjust, inhumane deeds of the 'Abbásid caliphs. Yet they never betrayed their trust. The first seventeen years of the reign of Hárún were particularly distinguished by the good administration of the Barmecides. A legend has been fostered to the effect that Hárún, being extremely fond of the company of Ja'far, his vizier, and 'Abbásah, his own sister, and wishing to have both in his company at the same time, sought a way out of the dilemma, and arranged a marriage between them with the injunction that their marriage should never be consummated. When he went on pilgrimage to Mecca, in the year 802, he accidentally discovered that Ja'far and 'Abbásah had disobeyed him and a child had been born to them. He cloaked his wrath until he was back in Baghdád, and then vented it on the Barmecides. No less an authority than Ibn-Khaldún[15] vehemently repudiates this legend. Incidentally, on that pilgrimage Hárún was accompanied by his sons, Muḥammad al-Amín and 'Abdu'l-láh al-Ma'mún, whom he required to pledge in the 'House of God'[16] to abide by the plan he had devised for the succession.

No one knows truly why Hárún ar-Rashíd destroyed the people who wished and served him so well. Glimmers of truth can be

[15] The fourteenth-century historian ranking amongst the greatest in the world.
[16] '*Baytu'lláh*'—the Ka'bah.

discerned in some of the reasons advanced, but that is all. Ja'far was beheaded and indignities were heaped on his corpse. The aged Yaḥyá and his other sons, Faḍl and Músá, were thrown into prison and their vast properties were confiscated. All the Barmakís were shorn of office. Yaḥyá and Faḍl died in prison. People bitterly mourned the downfall of the House of Barmak, because the Barmakís had been generous and just, but even those who mourned them were punished. The House of Barmak was destroyed in the year 803.

Nicephorus, the Byzantine Emperor, who had deposed the Empress Irene, wrote imperiously to Hárún ar-Ras͟hīd, not only refusing to pay the annual tribute, but demanding back all that Irene had paid. Hárún was incensed, wrote back calling Nicephorus the 'Roman dog', took the field in person in the year 805, and decisively defeated and humiliated the vainglorious Emperor of Byzantium. Hárún came back from Asia Minor with thousands of slaves and much booty. He might have been able to take Constantinople, had he tried, but he was not interested in conquest. The crusading spirit of early years had abated and Hárún had no quarrel with Christians. He and Charlemagne sent gifts to each other and exchanged envoys. Hárún ar-Ras͟híd had reigned for twenty-three years, and was not more than forty-five years old, but he was worn out and weary. Nearly six years had passed since the time he had cruelly dispensed with those who would, as the years advanced, have stood him in good stead. He had abandoned Bag͟hdád and had made his home in the Syrian town of Raqqah on the Euphrates. But K͟hurásán, turbulent as ever and suffering from the misrule of its governor, called him. He was forced to undertake the long journey, which taxed him greatly, and he died at Ṭús, in March 809. He was buried in the same city. History has few ironies to compare with this, as we shall see.

AL-AMÍN (A.D. 809–13)

According to Hárún's dispositions, the throne was now Amín's, and Ma'mún, left autonomous in the governorate of K͟hurásán and other realms of the East, was to succeed him. Ma'mún, who was at Marv, the capital of K͟hurásán, declared his submission and all seemed well. However, Ma'mún's mother was a Persian, and his entourage almost totally Persian, whereas Amín's mother was Zubaydah, a princess of the House of 'Abbás. Amín's vizier was

Faḍl Ibn Rabí', of renowned Arab descent, a well-known opponent of the Barmakids in the past and of cosmopolitanism at all times. Contemplating with horror the prospect of Ma'mún ruling over the concourse of the faithful, Faḍl began to plant in the mind of the weak, impressionable Amín the germ of an idea, by no means novel: Amín should set aside his father's will, and name his own son the heir-apparent. Amín demurred at first, but his mother was no less insistent. The first step he took in response to his mother and his vizier was to dispossess another younger brother Mu't-amin, to whom Hárún had given the governorship of Jazírah.[17] Next, he began to intervene in the affairs of Ma'mún's domains, though he was expressly forbidden to do so by his father. Ma'mún was inclined to extemporize, but his Persian vizier, also named Faḍl, the son of Sahl, warned him of impending dangers. Once again an army took the road to the west from Khurásán, under the command of Ṭáhir, the son of Ḥusayn, another Persian, to meet Amín's army moving towards Khurásán, under 'Alí Ibn 'Ísá Ibn Máhán, the discredited ex-governor of that province. Amín's general was killed and his army routed. Ṭáhir captured a town here and there until he reached the gates of Baghdád. Under siege Amín showed total ineptitude. The civil war went on from 811 to 813, and when it was over Amín was dead. It was tragic that his reign should have ended in that fashion, because fresh suspicions were engendered and the Arab element was further pushed from the centre of affairs.

AL-MA'MÚN (A.D. 813–33)

Ma'mún would certainly have spared his brother's life had he been there in person to receive his surrender, but he lingered on in Khurásán, screened from the outside world by his vizier. Ḥasan, a brother of Faḍl Ibn Sahl, was dispatched to 'Iráq as governor, and Ṭáhir (who is known as Dhu'l-Yamínayn, the Ambidextrous) was ordered away to Raqqah. But the whole area west of the Íránian plateau was now in great turmoil. In Syria, a scion of the House of Umayyah rose in revolt. Members of the House of 'Alí and their kinsmen followed suit in the holy cities of Mecca and Medina, in Yemen, in Kúfah and Baṣrah. In Baghdád, Manṣúr, the son of al-Mahdí, an uncle of Ma'mún, was proclaimed Caliph, but he refused the honour and agreed to serve

[17] The area bounded by the northern reaches of the Euphrates and the Tigris.

as a deputy-governor for his nephew. Ḥasan Ibn Sahl fled to Wásiṭ. All this while, Ma'mún had no knowledge of what was transpiring beyond Persia. In the year 815, he called the eighth Imám, 'Alí Ibn Músa'r-Riḍá (generally known as Imám Riḍá) from Medina to Khurásán, and offered him succession to the throne. Oaths of allegiance were taken, the black standard of the 'Abbásids was discarded and the green of the House of 'Alí was made the colour of the Empire. The 'Abbásids in Baghdád were outraged and set about searching for another caliph. Manṣúr would not be one, but another uncle of Ma'mún, Ibráhím, obliged. However, he was a man of no consequence, and Baghdád fell into disorder. The city had suffered much in the last months of Amín's reign and many of its fine buildings had been torn down. Now robbers and brigands and blackmailers infested its streets and markets. Nor was the surrounding country immune from such depredations. No tax could be collected. Soldiers could not be paid.

At last the heir-apparent, 'Alí Ibn Músa'r-Riḍá, opened Ma'mún's eyes to the realities of the situation. Ma'mún woke up as from a dream. More than four years after his accession to the throne, he moved out of Marv, in the direction of Baghdád. Just then, in February 818, the vizier, Faḍl Ibn Sahl, who, for purposes of his own, had kept Ma'mún in the dark, was stabbed to death in his bath. The assassins were put to death. Some historians have imputed the murder of Faḍl to Ma'mún's instigation. Others refute this allegation. It is not in keeping with what we know of Ma'mún's character to have compounded a felony of that nature. He could easily have dismissed his vizier. Ḥasan, the brother of Faḍl, continued in the service of the Caliph. At a later date, Ma'mún married his daughter, Púrán. The éclat of the nuptials was truly dazzling. The account faithfully recorded by the historians is an index to the scale of wealth in the court of the 'Abbásids. Europe of the time in its wildest dream could not have known anything approaching it. Yet, Ma'mún led a simple life. He wore a robe until it nearly fell apart.

Ma'mún halted at Ṭús, where his father lay buried. There, in October, his heir-apparent passed away. Imám 'Alí Ibn Músa'r-Riḍá had partaken of grapes just before his death occurred. It looked certain that he had been poisoned. Again suspicion has rested on Ma'mún, and again it is difficult to reconcile such a heinous deed with his character. There were others amongst the 'Abbásids who hated to see the caliphate pass to the House of 'Alí. Around the magnificent tomb of the eighth Imám has sprung up the city of Mashhad (Meshed)—the crown of Khurásán. Ṭús has long been forgotten.[18] Other splendorous cities of Khurásán have suffered eclipse. But Mashhad flourishes, the cynosure of the devout Shí'ah. The pilgrim prostrates himself at the Shrine of Imám Riḍá, and pauses to cast a glance at the grave of Hárún, close by. Throughout the centuries, he has accompanied that glance with execration. Such has been the fate of the resplendent Caliph of the *Arabian Nights*.

The passing of the eighth Imám caused further rifts amongst the Shí'ahs. The majority gave their allegiance to his son, Muḥammad, known as al-Jawád (the Generous) and at-Taqí (the Pious).

Ma'mún's journey to Baghdád was unhurried, and it was not until September 819 that he entered the city which both he and his father had neglected. He was dressed in green and the green standard led his cavalcade. But very soon all that changed, and the black colour of the House of 'Abbás was restored. Under Ma'mún, Baghdád took a new lease of life. Its wounds were healed, and it became truly a centre for liberal learning, a forum for rational discussion. Here the Mu'tazilites came into their own; they surrounded the Caliph and the most eminent amongst them, Aḥmad Ibn Abí-Du'ád, was held in high regard by Ma'mún. In the next reign, he was elevated to the office of chief justice. Abú-Isḥáq Ibráhím Ibn al-Sayyár an-Naẓẓám and Abu'l-Hudhayl Muḥammad Ibn al-Hudhayl al-'Alláf, Mu'tazilite scholars of high repute, were the Caliph's constant companions. At the start, Ma'mún made no attempt to impose the Mu'tazilite doctrines which he embraced on those who rejected them. Indeed, his favourite saying was that he liked a position to be gained and superiority established by argument and sound proof, and not by the use of force; because once force was removed, the superior position could disappear with it, whereas supremacy based on sound proof remained inviolable and immovable. But towards the end of his reign, the controversy over the nature of the Qur'án had reached such a high pitch that Ma'mún was swayed into promulgating the Mu'tazilite belief by compulsion. When away on his

[18] The name Mashhad has replaced the name Ṭús, because the tomb of Imám Riḍá is situated there. Mashhad means the place of martyrdom.

wars with the Byzantines, he sent a decree to the governor of Baghdád, instructing him to test the views of all the judges and theologians of note, and make them declare that only the Mu'tazilite doctrine was valid and true. The tolerant had in turn become the intolerant. All the outstanding judges and theologians of Baghdád submitted to the inevitable, except Aḥmad Ibn Ḥanbal, the last of the four great Sunní jurisconsults. He stuck steadfastly to the orthodox view, and only Ma'mún's timely death saved him.

From the year 830 to 833, Ma'mún led his armies thrice into Byzantine territory. For years, as far back as the days of Ma'mún's sojourn in Marv, another Persian heresiarch, named Bábak, had been terrorizing areas in the neighbourhood of Ṭabaristán. His haunts were the ravines of the Elburz (Alburz) range, where he had his hunting-ground and stronghold. Our knowledge of his antecedents is meagre and cannot be trusted in every respect. As usual, it is said of him that he was a Khurramí (whatever that may mean), that he claimed to be God incarnate, that he taught transmigration. What is certain is that he had a large following, that he broke several generals sent against him and formed an alliance with the Byzantines. Bábak was still infesting Northern Írán, when death came suddenly upon the Caliph in the vicinity of Tarsus. He had already humbled the Greeks of Byzantium.

AL-MU'TAṢIM (A.D. 833–42)

Ma'mún was succeeded by his brother, Muḥammad, who took the title of al-Mu'taṣim-Bi'lláh.[19] He is referred to as al-Mu'taṣim. Although he kept the Empire together, overcame rebellions and defeated the Byzantines, his reign marked the decline of 'Abbásid power. He abandoned Baghdád and moved his capital to Sámarrá, which he built as a garrison town, in 836, well to the north of Manṣúr's city. Mu'taṣim's new capital was manned by Turkish troops. These Turks were for the most part freed slaves, brought originally from Transoxania. But as Mu'taṣim and his immediate successors put their whole trust in the protection afforded by the Turks, they sought them out in their homelands

[19] All the 'Abbásids from al-Manṣúr onwards adopted an official title, by which they are known. Until al-Mu'taṣim adopted his, which in full means 'He Who Is Steadfast in God', these titles were simple in construction and meaning, but, as time went on, they became, with some exceptions, rather involved.

to offer service in the Caliph's army. Their officers attained high rank and had palaces to live in at Sámarrá, which was given the additional name of *Surra-Man-Ra'á* (Anyone Who Sees It Is Delighted). They became professional soldiers, and knew nothing but soldiery. At first al-Mu'taṣim was strong enough, and they subdued enough, for him to enforce his bidding. But once becoming sure of themselves, they tried their strength and, discovering it, set about to make a mockery of the Caliph and the Caliphate. They succeeded only too well.

At last in 838, Ḥaydar al-Afshín, a renowned general serving Mu'taṣim, got the better of Bábak, not in the open field but through a ruse, and took him captive. The treatment that Bábak received in Surra-Man-Ra'á was savage, but he himself had done nothing but create havoc and engage in slaughter.

Afshín was of princely descent, his ancestors having ruled Transoxania, and he was not a Turk, but an Íránian. Witnessing the rise of the Ṭáhirids[20] in Khurásán as hereditary rulers, envy and jealousy possessed him. In Ṭabaristán, Mázyár, another prince of illustrious lineage, unconverted like Afshín to the Faith of the Arabs, was in revolt, chafing at the imperiousness of 'Abdu'lláh the Ṭáhirid. Afshín made advances, in secret, to the Prince of Ṭabaristán. Mázyár lost his battle, and Afshín's dealings with him became known. For a long while the corpses of Bábak, Mázyár and Afshín remained gibbetted in a row in the garrison city, open to public gaze.

In A.D. 835, the third year of the reign of Mu'taṣim, Imám Muḥammad at-Taqí, the ninth Imám, passed away while visiting the Caliph. He was accompanied on that visit by his wife, Ummu'l-Faḍl, who was a daughter of Ma'mún. It has been asserted that his death was engineered by his wife and her uncle, and effected by poison. He was buried beside his grandfather, the seventh Imám, round whose shrine the town of Káẓimayn (or Káẓimíyyah) stands today. His son, 'Alí IV, entitled both an-Naqí (the Distinguished) and al-Hádí (the Guide), was hailed as the tenth Imám by his adherents.

[20] Ṭáhir Ibn Ḥusayn, the Ambidextrous, was given the viceroyalty of Khurásán by Ma'mún in the year 820. He died two years later, to be succeeded first by one son, Ṭalḥah, and then by another, 'Abdu'lláh.

AL-WÁTHIQ (A.D. 842–47)

Mu'taṣim died, seven years later, in A.D. 842. Victorious in his campaigns, he ruled with a firm hand, but his harshness was mollified by the liberalism of his Chief Justice, the Mu'tazilite Ibn-Abí-Du'ád. His son Hárún, bearing the title of al-Wáthiq-Bi'lláh (He Who Has His Trust in God), was benevolent and learned, and well-disposed towards the House of 'Alí. It has even been said that he was a Shí'ah. In his short reign of less than six years he tried to rekindle the flame that had nearly gone out a decade before. The last three years of Ma'mún's reign had been spent on wars with Byzantium. Mu'taṣim had little learning of his own, and was much occupied with wars and rebellions. Wáthiq, by contrast, was an accomplished poet and musician, intensely interested in science, and his court at Sámarrá was open to all who had anything to offer in the field of learning and culture. He left the affairs of state in the hands of Ibn-Abí-Du'ád and Muḥammad Ibn 'Abdi'l-Malik az-Zayyát, and he fought no wars. Thus the Mu'tazilites were strongly entrenched. In one respect Wáthiq particularly emulated his father. He added to his Turkish retinue and soldiers. With the death of Wáthiq died all that had been good and beneficent and splendorous in the 'Abbásid dispensation. The curtain came down upon its glory.

AL-MUTAWAKKIL (A.D. 847–61)

Wáthiq's brother, Ja'far, entitled al-Mutawakkil-u-'Al'-Alláh (He Who Puts His Reliance in God), who succeeded him in August 847, has been called 'The Nero of the Arabs': an epithet richly deserved. The orthodox have lauded him just as they have tried to besmirch the character of Wáthiq. Mutawakkil put Muḥammad az-Zayyát to death, threw Ibn-Abí-Du'ád into prison, interdicted rational argument, gave power to men narrow in mind and small in their sympathies. He showed particular venom towards the House of 'Alí. His parvanimity was reflected in all he did. The Shrine of the martyred Ḥusayn was levelled to the ground, the earth was ploughed, the river was let loose on the site, pilgrimage to Karbilá was forbidden. A jester in his court used to tie a large pillow to his midriff, and strut about in a grotesque manner, pretending to be 'Alí, the first Imám and the fourth Caliph. This was the depth of degradation that Mutawakkil touched. And this is the man whom the orthodox have extolled for his devotion to religion. The non-Muslims too—Jews, Christians, Sabeans and Mazdeans alike—were dealt heavy blows by Mutawakkil. They were barred from offices they had hitherto held. They had to humble and humiliate themselves in diverse ways, wear clothes and badges that set them apart. Their places of worship were desecrated and destroyed.

Mutawakkil was killed in December 861, at the instance of his Turkish general, Bughá. With his death, the effective power of the ʻAbbásids also expired. Occasionally a caliph would show a semblance of authority and no more. Power was in other hands. The Turks, having once tasted the fruits of success, would not peacefully give up the positions which they had attained, and killed one caliph after another. The person of the caliph was no longer sacrosanct. He could be made and unmade to suit the ends of contenders for power. And the Empire steadily declined, while independent kingdoms and emirates and principalities within it multiplied.

To end this chapter we shall note that the tenth Imám, ʻAlí an-Naqí, passed away in 868; his son, Ḥasan II, surnamed al-ʻAskarí,[21] succeeded him.

[21] The origin of this surname is from the fact that Imám Ḥasan II lived all his life in Sámarrá which was a garrison town. *Askar* means 'army'. He and his father have adjacent shrines in Sámarrá.

24

Divisions of Thought and Belief

'THE apostolical Imâm Hassan al-Aaskari died in the year 260 A.H.,[1] during the reign of Mutamid.[2] Upon his death the Imâmate devolved upon his son Mohammed, surnamed *al-Mahdi* (the Conducted), the last Imâm of the Shiahs. The story of these Imâms of the House of Mohammed is intensely pathetic. The father of Hassan was deported from Medîna to Sâmarra by the tyrant Mutawakkil, and detained there until his death. Similarly Hassan was kept a prisoner by the jealousy of Mutawakkil's successors. His infant son, barely five years of age, pining for his father, entered in search of him a cavern not far from their dwelling. From this cavern the child never returned. The pathos of this calamity culminated in the hope—the expectation—which fill the hearts of Hassan's followers, that the child may return to relieve a sorrowing and sinful world of its burden of sin and oppression. So late as the fourteenth century, when Ibn Khaldûn was writing his great work, the Shiahs were wont to assemble at eventide at the entrance of the cavern and supplicate the missing child to return to them. After waiting for a considerable time, they departed to their homes, disappointed and sorrowful. This, says Ibn Khaldûn, was a daily occurrence. When they were told it was hardly possible he could be alive, they answered that as the prophet Khizr was alive, why should not their Imâm be alive too? Upon this, Ibn Khaldûn remarks that the belief about Khizr being alive was an irrational superstition. The Imâm is therefore called the *Muntazzar* [Munṭaẓar], the Expected One,—the *Hujja* [Ḥujjah or Ḥujjat] or the Proof (of the Truth), and the *Kâim* [Qá'im], the living.'

[1] A.D. 873. (H.M.B.)

[2] Al-Mu'tamid-u-'Al'-Alláh (870–92), the fifteenth Caliph of the House of 'Abbás. (H.M.B.)

The author of the lines above quoted, taken from *A Short History of the Saracens* (p. 295), is Syed Ameer Ali, the most prominent and erudite Shí'ah Indian of recent times. He died in 1928, a member of the Judicial Committee of the Privy Council. However, anyone who might be called an orthodox Shí'ah would not present the case of the twelfth Imám in this manner.

Equally divergent from the orthodox view is this more recent statement:

'After the death of the eleventh Imam his son succeeded him. The twelfth Imam is known by several titles, of which one of the best known is the Arabic title Imam Zaman [Imám-i-Zamán], the Imam of all time. According to Shi'a, the twelfth Imam, who was born in the year 255 (A.D. 869), is still living; but he is invisible. As the Prophet and others prophesied, when the earth is full of cruelty he will appear and bring justice.

'After he became Imam he learned that the Caliph planned to kill him, so he disappeared. The disappearance is known as the absence, and the Imam Zaman had two absences—the short absence and the long absence. For sixty-nine years the twelfth Imam spent his time in hiding, communicating through four great Shi'ites, and through them guiding the people and answering their questions. As this was a short time and communication was carried on during this time, it is known as the short absence. The men through whom he communicated were known as the ambassadors, or specifically appointed deputies. During this time there were four ambassadors who guided the Shi'ites, and it was the fourth ambassador who was assigned the duty of giving the people the news of the Imam's bodily death through a letter from the Imam. The Imam said that after his bodily death no one was to be the Imam's ambassador and that there would be a long absence. And this took place.'[3]

When the eleventh Imám, Ḥasan al-'Askarí, passed away, it was obvious that he had no children. His brother, Ja'far, whom the Shí'ahs have styled *al-Kadhdháb* (The Liar) asserted that the Imám had died childless. A slave of the Imám, named Ṣayqal, claimed that she was with child. The 'Abbásid Caliph had her removed to his own palace, to be kept under close surveillance.

[3] 'Shi'a' by Mahmood Shehabi, University of Tehran, p. 201 of ISLAM: THE STRAIGHT PATH—Islam Interpreted by Muslims, edited by Kenneth W. Morgan. Copyright © 1958, The Ronald Press Company, New York.

The wives of the Caliph and of the Chief Justice, Ibn-Abi'sh-Shawárib, watched over her. Eventually her claim was found to be fictitious. But for years the poor woman was fought over by various factions. Ja'far, who had from the start assailed her veracity, made matters worse by persecuting her in diverse ways. She was abducted from the palace of the Caliph Mu'tamid, when Ya'qúb-i-Layth-i-Ṣaffár,[4] the Persian claimant to the Íránian uplands, was approaching Baghdád with a large force. Ya'qúb had succeeded in establishing an independent kingdom which stretched across Írán; and it is clear that he had Shí'ah tendencies.

In the meantime another dispute had broken out between Ja'far and the mother of the eleventh Imám over his property. Once the Caliph was satisfied that there was no child to inherit from the Imám, he decided, after a bitter litigation which lasted seven years, that both the brother and the mother of Imám Ḥasan al-'Askarí should be his heirs. More than twenty years later, quarrels over Ṣayqal were still raging so fiercely that the Caliph al-Mu'taḍid, the nephew and successor to al-Mu'tamid, ordered her removal, once again, into protective custody. She languished in the palace until her death in the reign of al-Muqtadir, the next Caliph, who himself had Shí'ah leanings, and whose viziers were followers or partisans of the Imáms of the House of 'Alí.

Whether this woman's name was Ṣayqal or not is a moot point. The importance of the nomenclature lies in the fact that the 'Twelvers', who constitute the majority of the Shí'ahs, maintain that she was the mother of the twelfth Imám: Muḥammad, the son of Imám Ḥasan al-'Askarí. Rayḥanah, Súsan and Narjis are other names by which she is known. A legend has it that Narjis was the daughter of an emperor of Byzantium. Greek slaves, male or female, were not uncommon in Muslim lands. The mother of the Caliph al-Wáthiq was Greek.

But to return to the day when the eleventh Imám passed away: there was bewilderment in the ranks of his followers, and authorities agree that no less than fourteen groups were formed amongst them. The meticulous and reliable Mas'údí,[5] who wrote not long after in the tenth century A.D., put their number at twenty. Only two of them demand consideration—one, due to the turmoil it caused, and the other because it formulated the doctrine that held

[4] Reigned A.D. 867–79.

[5] Abu'l-Ḥasan 'Alí (d. A.D. 957), author of two highly-reputed works.

the field, becoming the recognized belief of the vast majority of the upholders of the Imámate.

Ja'far is said to have claimed the Imámate for himself. Whether he had a large following or not is a matter of conjecture. It is also problematical whether he ever thought that his claim could be considered seriously. There is no shred of evidence that his brother had ever named him to don the mantle of the Imámate. Today there is not a single soul amongst the Shí'ahs who reveres Ja'far as the twelfth Imám. But overshadowing any claim which Ja'far laid to the spiritual station or wordly goods of his brother was his fierce contention with that body of the Shí'ahs who maintained that the twelfth Imám lived, hidden from the eyes of men. Through thick and thin he asserted that his brother had died without issue. However, there was an eminent follower of the eleventh Imám, Abú-'Amr 'Uthmán Ibn Sa'íd al-'Umarí, who claimed that Muḥammad, the five-year-old son of the deceased Imám, had chosen to withdraw from the sight of men, and that he himself had been invested with authority to act as his deputy, and establish a link between the infant twelfth Imám and the body of the faithful. He stated that epistles from the Hidden Imám were transmitted through him. The ensuing confusion amongst the Shí'ahs can be well imagined. Abú-'Amr 'Uthmán was succeeded by his son, Abú-Ja'far Muḥammad, who stood firmly by the assertion that the office of 'deputy' had the sanction of the Imám, with whom he held communication by means which he could not and would not divulge. These two deputies, father and son, held sway for wellnigh forty-five years, during which time the controversies did not abate.

The 'Abbásid Caliphate was now far gone into decline. The Caliph al-Muqtadir, who succeeded to the throne in the year 908, was well-disposed towards the Shí'ahs; he was also hopelessly incompetent. He had Shí'ah ministers, and his court was manned by prominent Shí'ahs. The third deputy of the Hidden Imám, Abu'l-Qásim Ḥusayn Ibn Rúḥ, came from an eminent Persian family, the House of Nawbakht, whose members were highly influential in governmental and academic circles. In the opening years of Muqtadir's caliphate, he lived in Baghdád in circumstances of affluence, surrounded by his disciples, a revered figure in the capital of the 'Abbásids. Next, we find him a fugitive and, later on, a prisoner. Turns of fortune, on such a scale, had lost their oddity. The strange whims and the capricious nature of Muqtadir, who every now and then was wont to change all his ministers and courtiers, were undoubtedly responsible for the incarceration of Ḥusayn Ibn Rúḥ. It has been assumed that he was accused of withholding and evading certain governmental dues. But that was a common enough accusation constantly brought against officials who had fallen out of favour.

Now we hear of a certain Abú-Ja'far Muḥammad Ibn 'Alí, a native of the village of Shalmaghán, in the region of Wásiṭ, therefore known as ash-Shalmaghání. It becomes clear amidst the confusion of biased accounts and vitriolic attacks on his reputation that Shalmaghání was a close confidant of Ḥusayn Ibn Rúḥ, who, in the period of the latter's enforced seclusion, maintained contact for him with his people. Apparently, during the same period, he withdrew his support from the third deputy of the Hidden Imám and preached a doctrine which it is impossible to ascertain, except for one fact, that he would no longer give credence to the belief that Muḥammad, the infant son of the eleventh Imám, lived in a corporeal body, away from the sight of men. However, even trustworthy commentators and historians, not to mention those whom he had directly challenged, have laid at his door charges from which the rational mind flinches. It is suggested that Shalmaghání claimed to be God incarnate, while community of wives, that hoary favourite of calumniators, is included in the list of gross deviations attributed to his supporters. From what is known of Shalmaghání's antecedents, it is impossible to accept as true what has been said of him, unless one concedes at the same time that he had lost his senses. This was the man whose books the Twelvers studied for knowledge of their own doctrines, and to learn how to defend them. His adversaries denounced him before the Sunní doctors of law, their own avowed opponents, and thus they encompassed his destruction. For a while Shalmaghání enjoyed the protection of the Amír Náṣiri'd-Dawlah, the Ḥamdánid ruler of Mosul (A.D. 929–69). But disturbances there drove him to Baghdád, where he was discovered and arrested. During the Caliphate of ar-Ráḍí (A.D. 934–40), Shalmaghání and Ibráhím Ibn Abí-'Awn, one of his prominent supporters, were put to death and their bodies were consigned to the flames.

Another 'deviant' whom the Twelvers destroyed during this

period was the highly-famed or notorious (depending on one's viewpoint) Ḥusayn Ibn Manṣúr al-Ḥalláj, whom the Ṣúfís extolled in a later age. Ḥalláj was a native of Bayḍá in the province of Fárs, of Persian (Magian) descent. By all accounts he was a devoted Shí'ah. Again, in his case, we come up against imponderables and it is almost impossible to separate fact from fiction. Certain it is that Ḥalláj took a stand which put him beyond the pale. It is also certain that his deviation consisted of choosing 'the mystic way'. For the rest, one has to resort to conjecture because contradictions abound. Ṣúfí leaders and poets who, in subsequent years, waxed eloquent in his praise, totally ignored the question of the Imámate and deputyship of the Hidden Imám, on which Shí'ah scholastics have based their condemnation of Ḥalláj.

These words of Ḥalláj: '*Ana'l-Ḥaqq*'—'I am the Truth' (i.e. God)—have come ringing down the ages, to be intoned ecstatically by some, or quoted with horror by others. Ḥáfiẓ, the greatest lyric poet of Írán, more than four hundred years later, exonerated Ḥalláj: 'That friend, who adorned the gallows, died for the crime of revealing secrets'. The giants among the Ṣúfí poets, including Jaláli'd-Dín-i-Rúmí (thirteenth century),[6] the greatest of them all, have unfailingly sung his praise. But there can be no doubt that Ḥalláj, who by some accounts was a man bereft of learning and much too boastful, posed a menace to the security and the integrity of the Twelvers. Otherwise he would not have been denounced with such vehemence. As mentioned before, the third deputy of the Hidden Imám was a member of the eminent Shí'ah House of Nawbakht. Over several generations, the Nawbakhtís had established themselves in the favour of the caliphs of the House of 'Abbás. They had been exceedingly wise and cautious. Unostentatiously they had helped many who shared their beliefs to find positions of trust in the court. Now Ḥalláj was threatening to nullify the patient work of decades. His challenge to the third deputy of the Hidden Imám was a challenge to the House of Nawbakht, which, in turn, was a challenge to the security of the Shí'ah brotherhood—a small group of legitimists, overwhelmed and hemmed in by the might of the vast multitudes

[6] He was a native of Balkh and lived in Asia Minor (hence styled Rúmí), being highly esteemed by the Saljúq rulers. His great work, entitled *Mathnaví*, remains peerless in its quality, range, volume, intensity, depth and rapture.

of Muslims who did not believe in the primacy of 'Alí and the Imáms of his House. Shí'ahs, no matter how pervasive their influence, had no standing in the courts of law. Within these precincts only four systems of jurisprudence, and no others, were recognized: the Ḥanafí, the Sháfi'í, the Málikí and the Ḥanbalí, all pillars of the Sunní orthodoxy.[7] About the time the Twelvers had to face the question of the occultation of the twelfth Imám, a doctor of law, Abú-Bakr Muḥammad Ibn Dáwúd, a native of Iṣfahán, devised a fifth system to which the name Ẓáhirí (Literalist) was given.[8] Jurists among the Twelvers and jurists who had accepted the fifth system of jurisprudence arrived at an understanding, which made it possible for the Twelvers to carry the new label and obtain a measure of civic recognition.

It is a fact that the leader of the Ẓáhirí school issued a verdict against the very troublesome Ḥalláj, and condemned him to death. Did the Twelvers make an appeal to Abú-Bakr Muḥammad Ibn Dáwúd, and induce him to pronounce against Ḥalláj? Most probably they did. In any case, Abú-Sahl, a prominent member of the House of Nawbakht, whom Ḥalláj had tried unsuccessfully to win over to his view, was on friendly terms with the Caliph Muqtadir's celebrated vizier, Ibn-al-Furát, who himself had Shí'ite tendencies. The fate of Ḥalláj was thus sealed. He fled to Ahváz, in south-west Írán, but the Caliph's men traced and arrested him. After languishing for eight years in a Baghdád prison, he was subjected to a prolonged and protracted trial. The death sentence was eventually confirmed; and Ḥusayn Ibn Manṣúr al-Ḥalláj became one of the most celebrated martyrs of all time. Was he an illiterate impostor, a mere adventurer? Was

[7] Differences between the four Sunní schools of jurisprudence lie in the varying degrees of emphasis put on the four sources of the Law. These sources consist of the text (i.e. the Qur'án), supreme at all times; the *Sunnah* (practices and traditions attributed to the Prophet); the *Ijmá'al-Ummah* (consensus of opinion); and the *Qíyás* (analogy). The Ḥanafí school of 'Iráq became dominant in areas which eventually formed the enclave of the Ottoman Empire, as well as in India and Central Asia. The Málikí school of Medina came to flourish in North Africa, particularly Morocco. The ultra-orthodox Ḥanbalí school captured the ground in Central Arabia, which, in recent times, has become the stronghold of the Wahhábís. The Sháfi'ite school of Egypt established itself in Lower Egypt, Palestine, western and southern regions of Arabia, parts of India, and in the islands comprising present-day Indonesia. It has been estimated that today there are 180 million Ḥanafís, 105 million Sháfi'ís, 50 million Málikís and 5 million Ḥanbalís.

[8] This school of jurisprudence did not endure, nor did the Twelvers remain associated with it for long. The Málikite school eclipsed it in North Africa.

he a clear-sighted mystic? Was he a victim of circumstances beyond anyone's control? Who knows?

The fourth and last deputy of the Hidden Imám was Abu'l-Ḥusayn 'Alí Ibn Muḥammad as-Sámarrí, who held office for a bare three years and died in the year 941. He did not name a successor, but stated that he was the last deputy, that after him no direct link would be maintained between the Imám and his people. His own death, he said, would inaugurate the period of major occultation, whose length no man could gauge or guess, and during which the world would be deprived of the direct personal guidance of the Imám. In the fullness of time, Muḥammad, the son of Ḥasan al-'Askarí (the eleventh Imám), would step forth to regenerate the world and restore righteousness to it. He would be the Qá'im (He Who Arises), the Mihdí (Mahdí—the Rightly-Guided), whose advent was promised by the Prophet.

Now, but for a brief interlude, the curtain descends on the Twelvers.

From the coastal regions of the Caspian, the home and hunting-ground of the Daylamites, emerged the family of Buwayh (Búyih) —Shí'ah and Twelvers by persuasion. In Írán, three brothers of the family, 'Alí, Ḥasan and Aḥmad, built a kingdom out of the ruins of the realms of the Ṣaffárids (A.D. 873–900) and the Sámánids (A.D. 875–999). Those two dynasties of Persian descent had brought to an end the direct rule of the Caliph on the Íránian plateau. The youngest brother, Aḥmad, marched on Baghdád and entered the 'Abbásid metropolis in the year 945. The Caliph, al-Mustakfí, the twenty-second of his line, was helpless, and although he conferred the title of Mu'izzi'd-Dawlih (He Who Gives Might to the State) on the Daylamite conqueror, and made no effort to assert his own authority, he was soon deposed.[9] However, another caliph of the House of 'Abbás had to be installed in the same office, although the Daylamites were Shí'ahs, in no way bound by allegiance to a Sunní Caliph. The stark fact was that the vast majority of Muslims could not and would not forgo an institution which had been firmly established on the morrow of the passing of the Prophet. And the Imámate, which the Twelvers upheld, had reached its apogee in the major occultation of the

[9] At the same time 'Alí, the eldest of the three brothers, was given the title, 'Imádi'd-Dawlih (the Mainstay of the State), and the next brother received the title, Rukni'd-Dawlih (the Pillar of the State).

twelfth Imám. The successful Shí'ite polity, which flourished in North Africa and was about to capture Egypt, was heretical in the eyes of the Twelvers, for it was founded on the belief that Ismá'íl and his line inherited primacy from Ja'far aṣ-Ṣádiq, the sixth Imám. The House of Buwayh could not possibly acknowledge the Fáṭimid Caliphs of North Africa. And so the Muslim world from the borders of Egypt to Central Asia was presented with a Sunní Caliph commanding fealty by the choice, dictate and toleration of powerful Shí'ite overlords.

For a hundred years the Buwayhids dominated Baghdád and the Caliph was their puppet. The great Maḥmúd of Ghaznah (reigned A.D. 998–1030), the monarch who extinguished the Sámánid rule in Khurásán, and with the sword took Islám to India, overcame the Buwayhids in Ray, but Baghdád remained in their hands. Sulṭán Maḥmúd was a Turk, the descendant of a slave whose father had risen to high office under the Sámánids and had served them faithfully. Under his patronage Persian poetry flourished. Firdawsí, the epic poet of Írán, whose work is unmatched, dedicated his celebrated *Sháh-Námih* (The Book of Kings) to him. Later, he fell out with Sulṭán Maḥmúd and satirized him savagely, partly because of the Sulṭán's miserly reward, but chiefly because of Maḥmúd's fanaticism.[10] He was an exceedingly fanatical Sunní, but apart from rendering homage to the 'Abbásid caliphate in the same way mediaeval Christian monarchs would and did *vis-à-vis* the Supreme Pontiff in Rome, Maḥmúd of Ghaznah did nothing to restore the temporal power of the House of 'Abbás. Should he have found it imperative, Maḥmúd would not have hesitated to overthrow a caliph, and replace him with another more agreeable to his own purposes. But he was not subjected to that test of loyalty, although he once showed his peevishness over the matter of a title.

The Saljúqs (A.D. 1038–1194), also Turks and also fanatically Sunní, came in the wake of the Ghaznavids (977–1186). Their empire extended from Transoxania to the heart of Asia Minor. In the middle of the eleventh century, the Saljúqs terminated the paradox of a Sunní Commander of the Faithful (*Amíra'l-Mu'minín*)

[10] Although the great scientist Abú-Rayḥán-i-Bírúní stayed with Sulṭán Maḥmúd, served him and accompanied him to India, the equally great Abú-'Alí Ibn-i-Síná (Avicenna) could not abide the narrow-mindedness of Sulṭán Maḥmúd and shunned his court.

nestling under the wings of a S͟hí'ah potentate by their defeat of the Buwayhids in Bag͟hdád. Thus they restored a measure of dignity to the office of the caliph, but also made it evident that power resided with them and they meant to exercise it.

With the extinction of the Buwayhids, the brief interlude ended for the Twelvers. Henceforth, almost total obscurity surrounded them until the Ṣafavids (the 'Great Sophy' of the Elizabethans) rose to power in Írán, half a millenium later. True, there were principalities, groupings and individuals of that persuasion, who occasionally showed their colours; but with rare exceptions, the range of their influence in the body-politic was negligible, and the general rule for the Twelvers was *taqíyyah* (prudential concealment of opinion).

In Egypt, however, the star of the Fáṭimids was shining brightly. Theirs was one of the most enlightened regimes that the world has ever known. And the Ismá'ílís or the Seveners are one of the most maligned group of people.

25

The Bright Star of the Fáṭimids

IN recent years when a sudden awareness of the use of cannabis has caused new panic, and the media of communication have vied with one another to provide information (at times half truth, on occasions erroneous), two men in Britain, eminent in their disciplines, were heard to denounce the drug by resting their case on the 'abominable practices of the Assassins'. The word 'Assassin' is understood to be a corruption of the Arabic term '*ḥashsháshín*'—users of ḥashísh—of which their adversaries accused Ismá'ílís: users of the drug *en masse*. Today that palpable lie is perpetuated unashamedly in the Western world! There was a time when the Ismá'ílís struck terror into the hearts of their foes. But their practices were no more abominable than those of the world around them, Islamic and Christian alike. If they engaged in the reprehensible act of eliminating their antagonists, their adversaries also killed and destroyed in the exercise of power. The Crusaders who suffered at the hands of the followers of 'the Old Man of the Mountain' were only receiving their meed. Furthermore, the number of those who fell by the dagger of the so-called 'Assassins' has been grossly exaggerated. However, a clear distinction must be made between the extremists known as the Qarámiṭah or the Carmathians, and the other Seveners.

As we have seen, a considerable number of the followers of the sixth Imám, Ja'far aṣ-Ṣádiq, refused to recognize the Imámate of his son, Músá, and stoutly maintained that the rightful Imám was Muḥammad, the son of Ismá'íl, who was the eldest son of the sixth Imám, and had predeceased his father. Their belief and firm stand marked the appearance of the Ismá'ílí order, which proved, in the long run, to be the most effective and the most significant breakaway group of the Shí'ah branch of Islám—its largest offshoot. So far the historical record is clear, but thereafter we run into myth, legend and fabrication.

The celebrated Niẓámu'l-Mulk, vizier to Malik-Sháh the Saljúqid, makes out that the Ismá'ílí movement had nothing to do with the descendants of Muḥammad himself, that it was the product of the wiles of a native of Ahváz, named 'Abdu'lláh Ibn Maymún, and the cupidity of a freedman of Muḥammad, named Mubárak. This Mubárak, Niẓámu'l-Mulk states, was an accomplished calligrapher, excelling in a style known as *muqarmaṭ*. For that reason he was entitled Muqarmaṭwayh. Thus the appellation Qarmaṭí (pl. Qarámiṭah) and its westernized form, Carmathian, are derived from the name of the style of calligraphy which Mubárak used competently.[1] According to Niẓámu'l-Mulk, after the death of Muḥammad Ibn Ismá'íl, his freedman, Mubárak, was beguiled by the man of Ahváz into believing that he, 'Abdu'lláh, son of Maymún, had been entrusted with the secrets and the esoteric doctrines of Mubárak's master. In that fashion, these two devised a new heresy between them. From that starting point Niẓámu'l-Mulk builds up a story of successors to the two men, and relates an amazing account of their reverses and their conquests: one section active in Transoxania and Khurásán and the inevitable Daylam territory, and another turning its attention to Syria and Egypt. At times the great Niẓámu'l-Mulk hopelessly confuses his terms. And he maintains that the one who appeared in North Africa, in the territory of the Aghlabids, called himself 'Abdu'lláh Ibn al-Ḥusayn and was, in fact, Sa'íd, a grandson of that crafty native of Ahváz: 'Abdu'lláh Ibn Maymún al-Qaddáh (the Oculist).

Niẓámu'l-Mulk was a contemporary of the formidable Ḥasan-i-Ṣabbáḥ, and in deadly conflict with him. The imagination of Western romantics was once captured by the story of this Ḥasan, said to have been a fellow-student of Niẓámu'l-Mulk (whose name was also Ḥasan) and 'Umar-i-Khayyám.[2] Though bright and accomplished, they were poor and penniless, and made a pact that whichever of them first achieved wealth and position would amply share the benefits of his good fortune with the other two. It made a good tale, but was pure moonshine. This story went on to suggest that Abú-'Alí Ḥasan Ibn 'Alí, having become the mighty and all-powerful Niẓámu'l-Mulk and risen high in the

[1] Others have ascribed the origin of 'Qarmaṭ' to the nickname of Ḥamdán Ibn al-Ash'ath, who was so called because of his short body and legs. Ḥamdán was a lieutenant of 'Abdu'lláh Ibn Maymún.

[2] Omar Khayyám.

service of the great Saljúqs—Alp-Arslán and his son Malik-Sháh, remembered the two friends of his youth. 'Umar, the retiring poet, scientist and sceptic, was content with enough to keep him in his modest way of living; the other Ḥasan was overwhelmingly ambitious. He was given a place in the court, but he coveted the highest seat of authority, bit the hands that fed him, betrayed Niẓámu'l-Mulk, fled the court and rose in rebellion.

Indeed Ḥasan-i-Ṣabbáḥ, who was of the Ismá'ílí persuasion, challenged the might of the Sunní Saljúqs, and in the gorges and on the heights of the Elburz mountains founded a realm and a refuge from which to sally forth and effect the utmost damage to the reputation and the solidarity of the Saljúqid Empire. And Niẓámu'l-Mulk was a very staunch, a very prejudiced Sunní. Even more he was an Ash'arí, a believer in the discipline of Abu'l-Ḥasan al-Ash'arí, whose role in the development of Islamic theology we shall duly examine. Suffice it to say here that al-Ash'arí introduced a rigidity of thought and belief into Islamic society which blighted both mind and spirit. Niẓámu'l-Mulk was

The Relationship of the Caliphates

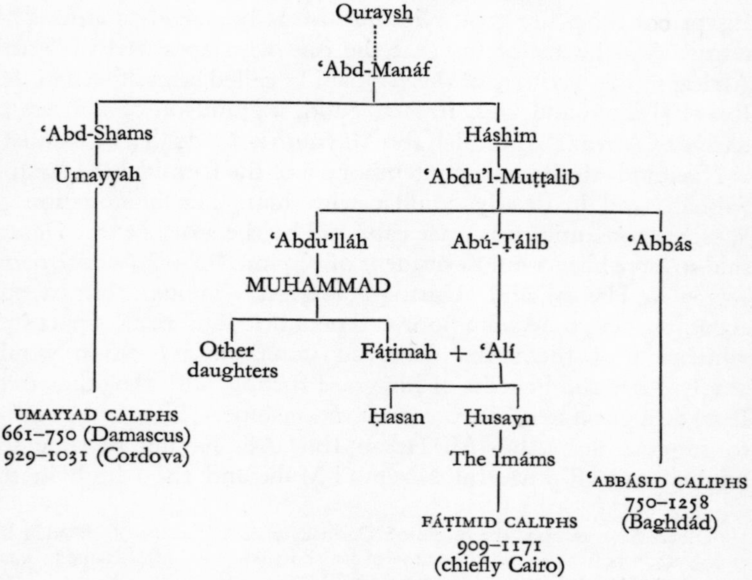

Dates are A.D. The chief seats of the three Caliphates are shown.

a great, an able and sagacious servant of the State, but he could not escape the coils of his own prejudices. What is surprising, however, is the easy acceptance by eminent orientalists of some of these stories woven around the origins of the Ismá'ílís and the Fáṭimid caliphs, who upheld and promulgated the tenets of the Ismá'ílí Faith.

In the year A.D. 909 a man, who called himself 'Ubaydu'lláh al-Mahdí, reached North Africa from Syria and proclaimed that he was a descendant of Muḥammad Ibn Ismá'íl, the grandson of the sixth Imám. He is the same man whom Niẓámu'l-Mulk identified as Sa'íd, the grandson of 'Abdu'lláh Ibn Maymún of Ahváz. He went to Egypt on the assurance of his *dá'í* (missionary), Abú-'Abdu'lláh ash-Shí'í, that the moment was ripe for his arrival. In this, the Ismá'ílís were following almost the same pattern as that set by the 'Abbásids, some two hundred years before, when their *dá'ís*, or *du'át*, were constantly moving from region to region and secretly calling upon people to rise and support the House of 'Alí. The supremacy the Ismá'ílís questioned was that of a Sunní caliph, for the 'Abbásids had lost their temporal power almost completely. Yet their spiritual overlordship was so well entrenched that even the Buwayhids of the Daylam territory, Twelvers though they were, could not dispense with it.

The Turks, who as soldiers and officers in the service of the 'Abbásids had reduced the caliphs of Baghdád to impotence, had also injected an element of obstinate fanaticism into the body politic. Of course the rebels, the heresiarchs and the pretenders who had tried to overthrow the 'Abbásids in the past, were also intensely fanatical, but theirs was a fanaticism of a different sort, one of desperation. The kind of fanaticism with which the polity of Islám became imbued, and which a man of the calibre of Niẓámu'l-Mulk betrayed in his writings, took its source from those great and single-minded warriors who came flooding in from the territories beyond the river Oxus. This was the fanaticism which would make the life of the Christian pilgrim so onerous, rouse the Supreme Pontiff to utter his call for action, drive Europe into frenzy, and give the younger sons of feudal lords and impoverished knights of France and Italy their pretext to seek fame and fortune under the cloak of an unmistakably devout desire to free the city of Christ's death and triumph from the impious grasp of the infidel. Neither the Arabs at the height of their racism, nor the Persians at their hour of revenge, had known and exercised the kind of fanaticism that the Turks now presented to the Islamic society.

'Ubaydu'lláh al-Mahdí, in that year 909, was throwing down his gauntlet to the whole Sunní confraternity which swarmed over the realm of Islám. Since the Twelvers considered him a heretic in any case, it was immaterial to them whether he was a scion of the House of 'Alí, a Fáṭimid, or not. Moreover, Shí'ahs had found positions of influence and trust in the courts of the 'Abbásid caliphs and maintained their precarious existence, nay even thrived, under the shadow of the protection thus procured; and this in spite of the fact that the death of every single one of the Imáms, from the sixth to the eleventh, and the reason for the minor occultation of the twelfth, were imputed by their scholastics and apologists to the malice of these very rulers.

In an Islamic world shaped and ordered by Sunní discipline, the rebellion of the militant Ismá'ílís could only inflict injuries upon the Sunní polity. Therefore, only fierce reaction to 'Ubaydu'lláh al-Mahdí could be expected from the Sunnís. It must not be assumed, however, that the Twelvers did not add some quota of denunciation. And there were also the Khárijite Rustamids of Táhart in North Africa, although early Khárijite passions were by now stilled. For them it was immaterial whether the newcomer to their continent was a descendant of the sixth Imám or not, for they had decided long ago that 'Alí, the progenitor of all the Imáms, was an inmate of hell. Then there were the Idrísids of Fez, Shí'ites of sorts, but their influence upon the affairs of Islám was nil.

The Umayyads of Andalus and the 'Abbásids of Baghdád declared that they had examined the pedigree and scrutinized the parentage of 'Ubaydu'lláh al-Mahdí, and had satisfied themselves that his claim was false; he was none other than a descendant of 'Abdu'lláh Ibn Maymún, the oculist of Ahváz. Since then, historians in the East and the West have clung to the pronouncement of these Sunní caliphs of Andalus and Baghdád. Even Ibn-Khaldún, who accepted the genuineness of 'Ubaydu'lláh's claim, refers to the dynasty he founded as 'Ubaydíyyún, rather than Fáṭimíyyún, scions of the daughter of the Prophet. It is said that 'Aḍudi'd-Dawlih (reigned 949–83), the son of Mu'izzi'd-Dawlih and the greatest of the Buwayhids, made investigations and reached conclusions similar to those of the Sunní caliphs. But 'Aḍudi'd-Dawlih was a Twelver and the parentage of al-Mahdí could not have swayed him one way or the other.[3]

In the event, 'Ubaydu'lláh overcame both the Aghlabids and the Rustamids and made the Idrísids his tributaries.

Sunní bitterness against the Fáṭimids must also be regarded in another context, that of events preceding the arrival of 'Ubaydu'l-láh at Ifríqíyyah, and to these we must give due attention.

In the year 869 the Negroes who had been brought over from East Africa to work the saltpetre mines on the Euphrates broke into bloody rebellion. They were led by a man of obscure origin, named 'Alí Ibn Muḥammad, who claimed to be an Alawí, that is, a descendant of the first Imám; but apparently, before long, he showed certain Khárijite tendencies. This 'Alí Ibn Muḥammad became known as aṣ-Ṣáḥiba'z-Zanj (the Master of the Zanj). (Zanj is the arabicized form of the Persian word Zangí—Negro.) For fourteen years these Negroes successfully fought off the armies of the 'Abbásid caliphs. They could not be dislodged from the marshlands; and they killed mercilessly and indiscriminately. They ranged as far as Ahváz and Wásiṭ, ravaging both these towns and Baṣrah as well. At last al-Muwaffaq, the brother of the Caliph al-Mu'tamid, took the field, and defeated the Ṣáḥiba'z-Zanj.

In the ninth century A.D. the town of Jannáb stood on the Íránian shores of the Persian Gulf, where the town of Ganávih stands today, close to the port of Búshihr (Bushire). A native of this town, Abú-Sa'íd Ḥasan al-Jannábí, a miller by trade, established in the year 899 a principality of his own on the opposite shore of the Persian Gulf, and made al-Aḥsá his capital. At one time, he had been closely associated with Ḥamdán Qarmaṭ, that lieutenant of 'Abdu'lláh Ibn Maymún whose nickname is said to have been the origin of the term Qarmaṭí or Carmathian. To Ḥamdán is also attributed the founding of the Báṭiní sect, which is only another name for the Ismá'ílís. It is assumed that the

[3] No one has ever been able to refute conclusively the claim made by the Fáṭimids. Their opponents, by deliberate proliferation of names, attempted to make an unclear situation even more confused. It must be said, however, that the Fáṭimids could not produce documentary evidence to establish their claim beyond any shadow of doubt. And a further question to pose is whether it would have been possible to produce such documentary evidence.

Qarmaṭís, or the Carmathians, branched from the Báṭinís. Al-Jannábí and his supporters had also had some connection with the rebellious Negroes of the Lower Euphrates and their mysterious leader. But whoever al-Jannábí and his Carmathian supporters may have been, and whatever the position he held as a religious guide and mentor, there is certainly a wide gulf separating them from the Ismá'ílís who rose to prominence in North Africa and established the Fáṭimid Caliphate. Could they be even accounted Muslims when it is an established fact that the Carmathians under Abú-Ṭáhir Sulaymán, the son of al-Jannábí, overran Mecca in the year 930, and wrenched apart the sacred *Ḥajar al-Aswad*—the Black Stone—from the structure of the Ka'bah? Every Muslim sect and denomination has held the Black Stone in awe and reverence. For decades, these Carmathians based on Baḥrayn and the Arabian shore of the Persian Gulf terrorized the realm of Islám as far away as Khurásán, killing, as the Khárijites of earlier generations and the Negroes of the Lower Euphrates had done before, indiscriminately and ruthlessly. Professor Hitti writes: 'The Qarmaṭian [Carmathian] movement with its communistic, revolutionary tendencies developed into a most malignant growth in the body politic of Islám.' [4]

Náṣir-i-Khusraw (11th century), hailed as one of the greatest of the great classical poets of Persia, was a native of Balkh, holding a minor office in Marv, under the Saljúqs. Feeling dissatisfied with his life, and having had a vision of the Prophet in a dream, he gave up his post, set out on pilgrimage to Mecca, and decided to roam at leisure over the realm of Islám. He was to see the Carmathians at close quarters, berating them for having led the people away from Islám. But he first visited Egypt. Jawhar, the Fáṭimid general, had, in the year 969, captured Fusṭáṭ, and ousted the last of the Ikhshídids, the Turkish rulers of Egypt, who, themselves, had overthrown the Ṭúlúnids in 935. The founder of the Ṭúlúnid dynasty, Aḥmad Ibn Ṭúlún, also a Turk, whose magnificent mosque still graces the capital of Egypt, had made himself independent of Baghdád, during the tormented years of the rise of the Ṣáḥib'az-Zanj. While based on the province of Ifríqíyyah, the Fáṭimids had built themselves a capital which they had named al-Mahdíyyah. Becoming at last the masters of Egypt, they set

[4] *History of the Arabs*, p. 445.

XI ARCADES OF THE MOSQUE OF IBN-ṬÚLÚN

in Cairo (876–79), one of the earliest examples of extensive use of the pointed arch, nearly three centuries before its adoption by Gothic architects.

XII THE UNIVERSITY MOSQUE OF AL-AZHAR

was founded in Cairo about 970, in the reign of the fourth Fáṭimid Caliph. Despite later additions, it remains an early and monumental example of the Egyptian architectural style.

about constructing a new capital: al-Qáhirih—the All-Victorious—a city of world fame, which is Cairo.

It was his visit to Cairo and what he witnessed there which made the sensitive, discerning Persian poet acclaim the Ismá'ílí doctrines with zeal and fervour—such zeal and fervour that he was elevated, before long, to the high position of the Ḥujjat (Proof) of Khurásán. The Ismá'ílí hierarchy had several grades. The self-effacing *dá'í* served under a *Ḥujjat*. The testimony of Násir-i-Khusraw is fortunately preserved in the record of his travels, and is of prime importance. Náṣir-i-Khusraw, who was in Cairo during the reign of al-Mustanṣir,[5] the eighth of the Fáṭimid caliphs, found a country thoroughly at peace with itself and with the whole world.

In a lucid, enchanting language, Náṣir-i-Khusraw describes the condition of Egypt. He was particularly impressed by the soundness of the administration and the prosperity of the people. The army, nearly a quarter of a million strong, he found to be composed of men of many nations and races, with weapons peculiar to them and with commanders of their own ethnic groups: Arab, Persian, Turk, Negro and others. These men had their regular dues, and no exaction was ever levied by them or their superiors on the population. The court was frequented by princes of Georgia and Daylam and Turkistán, by poets and jurisconsults, by men of high learning and accomplishments, who all received their apportionments regularly from the Treasury. In the bazars, tradesmen did not have recourse to false claims, and their customers trusted their word. When any one of them broke the code, he was put on the back of a camel and made to go through the streets, ringing a bell and announcing that he had broken the rules of trading and deserved opprobrium. The inhabitants of Egypt, Náṣir-i-Khusraw goes on to relate, knew that the Sulṭán did not covet their goods and would not give ear to calumniators. He writes: 'Then I met a Christian, who was one of the wealthiest in Egypt, and it was said that the worth of his ships and properties was immeasurable. One year the waters of the Nile proved insufficient and the price of corn went up. The vizier called on this Christian and told him: "The year is bad and the Sulṭán is very much concerned about the plight of the people. How much corn can you give us, either to be paid for or on a lending basis?"

[5] Al-Mustanṣir had a long reign, from 1036 to 1094.

The Christian replied: "August be the fortunes of the Sulṭán and the Vizier; I have as much corn as to provide Egypt with bread for six years." At this time there were, no doubt, five times as many people in Egypt as in Níshábúr,[6] and whoever is acquainted with measures would know how great must be a man's holdings to have that much corn. How secure must be the governed and how just must be the Sulṭán, that in their day there could be such conditions and such wealth; neither would the ruler tyrannize over and impose on anyone, nor would the subject keep anything hidden and concealed.'

Náṣir-i-Khusraw recalls that he had seen the grandeur of the court of such mighty kings as Maḥmúd of Ghaznah and his son, Mas'úd, and wished to witness the court of al-Mustanṣir. One of the officials took him there on the concluding day of Ramaḍán, the month of fasting, to see the preparations made for the following day: the Festival of al-Fiṭr. And he gives a dazzling description of the scene.

Náṣir-i-Khusraw travelled south as far as the boundaries of Nubia, then turned towards the Red Sea, took ship to Arabia, and went once again on pilgrimage to Mecca. Thence he proceeded to the further coast and the domain of the Carmathians. They disgusted him. He returned, after more journeyings, to his home. His travels had taken seven years, and he was now raised to an exalted station in the ranks of the Ismá'ílís. Before long he met with such fierce persecution that he had to seek refuge, first in Mázindarán, and then in Ṭukháristán and Badakhshán, in the region of the river Oxus. The Amír of Badakhshán, Abu'l-Ma'álí 'Alí Ibn Asad Ibn al-Ḥárith, himself a poet and a savant, became an adherent of the Ismá'ílí doctrine, and gave the fugitive Ḥujjat of Khurásán sanctuary—to end his days in peace.

The French historian, Guyard, writes: 'The (Isma'ílí) doctrines were publicly taught at Cairo in universities richly endowed and provided with libraries, where crowds assembled to listen to the most distinguished professors. The principle of the sect being that men must be converted by persuasion, the greatest tolerance was shown towards other creeds. Mu'izz (the fourth Fáṭimid Caliph, reigned A.D. 952–75) permitted Christians to dispute openly with his doctors, a thing hitherto unheard of; and Severus, the celebrated bishop of Ushmúnayn, availed himself

[6] Níshápúr.

of this authorisation. Out of the funds of the Treasury Mu'izz rebuilt the ruined church of St. Mercurius at Fusṭáṭ, which the Christians had never hitherto been permitted to restore. Certain Musulmán fanatics endeavoured to prevent this, and on the day when the first stone was laid a Shaykh, leaping down amongst the foundations, swore that he would die rather than suffer the church to be rebuilt. Mu'izz, being informed of what was taking place, caused this man to be buried under the stones, and only spared his life at the instance of the Patriarch Ephrem . . .'[7]

Another French historian, Renée Dussaud, in his *Histoire et Religion des Nosairis* (Paris 1900), remarks: '. . . the disappearance of the Fáṭimids, who brought about the triumph of the Ismá'ílí religion in Egypt, concludes an era of prosperity, splendour, and toleration such as the East will never again enjoy.'[8]

Gustave E. von Grunebaum writes: 'The documents found in the *genizah*, the "archives" of a Jewish synagogue in Cairo, mainly of the ninth to twelfth century and the most extensive collection of their kind from mediaeval Islam, give an impressive picture of the economic activity of the time; they throw a light too on the situation in the Jewish community, whose position under the Fāṭimids was more favourable than at any time in the first thousand years of Muslim history.' Next, von Grunebaum makes this strange comment: 'Their treatment went far beyond mere tolerance and probably arose in part from the indifference of the inner circle of the Ismā'īlīs towards the externals of religions, an attitude which facilitated their foreign propaganda in non-Muslim circles and created a suitable psychological climate for the peace concluded in 1040 with the Byzantium.'[9]

It is now an established fact that al-Ḥákim, the sixth Fáṭimid caliph (reigned 996–1021), made extravagant claims. He declared, it is said, that he was God incarnate. The origin of the Druzes is usually traced back to him, and it is assumed that the Druzes revere al-Ḥákim as the Deity. But here we enter the realm of speculation. Al-Ḥákim was not a very good ruler. Christians and Jews suffered at his hands, whereas they had held high offices in

[7] Cited by Browne, *A Literary History of Persia*, vol. I, p. 399, footnote, from *Un grand Maître des Assassins*.

[8] ibid., p. 395, translated by E. G. Browne.

[9] *Classical Islam*, p. 147.

the state under his predecessors. Yet he had remarkable achievements to his credit, such as the institution of a great library.

C. E. Bosworth tells us that 'Egypt and Cairo enjoyed under the Fāṭimids an economic prosperity and cultural vitality which eclipsed those of contemporary Iraq and Baghdad. Trade links were maintained with the non-Islamic world, including India and the Christian Mediterranean countries . . . It is from the workshops of Egypt at this time, too, that some of the finest products of Islamic art were turned out.'[10]

The world-famed theological college of al-Azhar in Cairo, which flourishes to this day, was founded by the Fáṭimids. From it well-trained *dá'ís* went forth to other Islamic lands. Fáṭimids made no attempt to impose their own beliefs on the people of Egypt, who, by and large, remained Sunní. The cultural standards of Cairo were considerable, surpassing, at times, those of Bag͟hdád. No distinction was ever made (apart from the interval when al-Ḥákim reigned) between the diverse Faiths and ethnic entities, in the common search for knowledge and the common effort to widen horizons of learning. The orthodox grip, which, in the Eastern domains of the realm of Islám, threatened time and again to fetter thought and knowledge, was absent in the Fáṭimid Egypt, which had also extended its power over Palestine and Syria.

Then, after the long reign of al-Mustanṣir, a serious cleavage appeared in the Ismá'ílí community. He had named his eldest son, Nizár, to succeed him, but the army put the next son, al-Musta'lí, on the throne, and Nizár died in prison. It was outside Egypt that Nizár's cause found supporters, chiefly in Írán and Syria. Ḥasan-i-Ṣabbáḥ, who in the year 1090 had seized the Castle of Alamút, in the heart of the Elburz range, and had established an Ismá'ílí principality, surrounded on all sides by the Saljúq domains, was a supporter of Nizár. When al-Mustanṣir died, the Fáṭimid territory to the north of Egypt had dwindled to the limits of Ascalon ('Asqalán) and Jerusalem had gone to the Turks.

[10] *The Islamic Dynasties*, p. 48.

26

Ṣúfís and Ṣúfíism

MUCH has been said and written about the Muslim mystics, styled Ṣúfís, which is sheer nonsense. Of the diverse ethnic elements within the polity of Islám, Íránians eventually became more prominent in unfolding and promulgating the tenets of Ṣúfíism, albeit Arabs, both in early and latter days, and Turks also, at a later period, produced eminent Ṣúfís. Some of the ardent reformers and iconoclasts of modern times in Írán have gone to the absurd length of blaming Ṣúfís and Ṣúfí thought for every conceivable ill that befell their land and their culture. Whereas in the Western world, jaded as it is by crass materialism, anything and everything carrying the label of Ṣúfí has been acclaimed by the eager and the bemused as the quintessence of wisdom and spirituality. Such Persian poets of unsurpassed eloquence as Sa'dí (thirteenth century) and Ḥáfiẓ (fourteenth century) have been hailed erroneously as Ṣúfís. Even stranger has been the attempt to make of 'Umar Khayyám a Ṣúfí 'guide'. It would have amused mightily this versatile mathematician-astronomer of Níshápúr. Alas for western acolytes Ṣúfíism has never been what many of them have imagined it to be.

Fantastic theories put forth by earlier occidental scholars, to explain the nomenclature of these mystics, have all been discounted. It is now established beyond doubt that the word Ṣúfí is derived from *ṣúf*, which is the Arabic word for 'wool'. The immediate successors of the Prophet, who lived frugal lives, wore garbs of rough wool. For that matter John the Baptist had 'raiment of camel's hair'. 'Umar Ibn al-Khaṭṭáb, the second Caliph, was particularly noted for the coarseness of his garment. Jámí (fifteenth century), the last of the outstanding Ṣúfí poets of Persia, states that the term 'Ṣúfí' was first applied, in the eighth century, to a Syrian named Abú-Háshim. Why he, specifically, was called a

'Ṣúfí' we do not know. Was being a man of great piety, detached from the world, synonymous with being a Ṣúfí? The great Ṣúfí poet, Farídi'd-Dín-i-'Aṭṭár (twelfth century), in his 'Memorial of Saints' (*Ta<u>dh</u>kiratu'l-Awlíyá'*), seems to indicate by implication that men very different in their outlook all have a niche in his gallery of the elect—men such as Uways, who died fighting for 'Alí, the first Imám and the fourth Caliph, at the battle of Ṣiffín; and Ḥasan al-Baṣrí, who gave no support to 'Alí at all, and whose disciple, Wáṣil Ibn 'Aṭá', founded the Mu'tazilite school; and Ja'far aṣ-Ṣádiq, the sixth Imám; and Aḥmad Ibn Ḥanbal, whose school of jurisprudence is the most rigid of the four Sunní disciplines, and whose intolerance is most marked. There can be no doubt that 'Aṭṭár himself was a mystic, and that many among his 'Saints' were undoubtedly delineators of the mystic path. But, can it not be argued that, by casting his net so wide, Farídi'd-Dín-i-'Aṭṭár was doing no more than making his choice of saints from a long list of men whose lives were considered to have been exemplary, and their thoughts and precepts to have been sublime? Nevertheless, Ṣúfíism, both by name and practice, belongs to a later age.

Ṣúfíism or *Taṣawwuf*, as the appellation is in the original, did certainly have a beginning which cannot be pinpointed. For whatever influences were at work to mould the thought of early Muslim mystics, those who are regarded as the pioneers of Ṣúfíism were a number of men and a most remarkable woman, who were repelled by the worldliness which had come upon people in high places. They were quiet, gentle and self-effacing, not firebrands like the <u>Kh</u>árijites. To such a man as Sufyán a<u>th</u>-<u>Th</u>awrí (d. 777) the pomp and luxury of the Umayyads and the 'Abbásids were anathema. He chose a life of seclusion, to pray and meditate, but not to establish a new school of thought or a new discipline. The word 'Ṣúfí' has become a portmanteau word, but not all Ṣúfís have been of the same genre. Wide indeed is the gulf which separates that remarkable woman, Rábi'ah (eighth century), from a mystic such as Báyazíd-i-Bisṭámí (ninth century). She it was who prayed thus: 'O God! Were I to worship Thee for the fear of Hell, consign me to that Hell, and were I to worship Thee in expectation of Paradise, deny me that Paradise, but if I worship Thee for Thine own sake, withhold not from me the Eternal Beauty.' And it was Báyazíd who exclaimed: 'Verily, I am God, there is no God but me.' There is a like contrast between Fuḍayl Ibn 'Iyáḍ, who, in the middle of the eighth century, gave utterance to such thoughts: 'He who fears God, all things fear him; and he who does not fear God, fears everything'; and Ḥalláj, who said: 'I am the Truth'.

It must be stressed that the Prophet had repudiated asceticism as practised by Christian monks. 'There is no asceticism in Islám,' is a saying of Muḥammad, generally accepted. But mortification of the flesh is not the same as detachment from the world. The people of the calibre of Ibráhím-i-Adham and Sufyán ath-Thawrí did not fly to the desert, as Christian monks had done before, once the fever of other-worldliness had gripped them. They were devout Muslims and had no code of worship or mode of conduct other than those followed by everybody else. They cherished no esoteric beliefs, did not attempt to create a new discipline, to systematize a way of living, to express views at variance with those commonly held. Ḥasan al-Baṣrí was a teacher with his pupils and disciples but, apart from aphorisms ascribed to him, nothing has come down to indicate any innovation. But the way Wáṣil Ibn 'Aṭá' broke away from his circle points out that Ḥasan held what might be termed orthodox views. The men who thought little of the vanities of the world and preferred a life of contemplation and quiet worship were not monks and hermits. No Muslim monastery is known ever to have existed. And when eventually 'Retreats' and 'Hermitages' were established they bore little resemblance to Christian monasteries. What was the extent, if any, of the influence of Christian mysticism on the development of Islamic mystic thought? This is a vast and uncertain area of conjecture.

Sometime or other, groups of people emerged who considered themselves 'Treaders' of the 'Path' (*Ṭaríqat*), who adopted a distinct style called *Taṣawwuf*, and who inaugurated and perpetuated certain spiritual disciplines. None can give a definite date and say when it all happened. It was a gradual and imperceptible process. Although Ṣúfís have attempted to trace their tradition back to the Prophet Himself, their thesis is manifestly untenable. Apart from being Muslims, the only common denominator of the inaugurators of Ṣúfí disciplines was the very broad aim of God-seeking. They never were, nor could ever be a cohesive body. They reacted, at different times and in diverse ways, to their environment and to the climate of thought. The view prevalent in the Western world, amongst the devotees of mysticism, that the Ṣúfís formed a large and compact group of enlightened Muslims, does not stand up to investigation.

Those high-minded and God-fearing men who detached themselves from the concerns of the world around them, in the two centuries that followed the passing of the Prophet, went their individual ways. They could certainly find comfort and encouragement for their attitude in the Qur'án, and in the life, the sayings and the precepts of the Prophet. But that is not the same as claiming that Muḥammad Himself had formulated the Ṣúfí doctrine. Málik-i-Dínár and Ibráhím-i-Adham and Sufyán ath-Thawrí made no such claims. In any case the word Ṣúfí meant nothing to them. However, once the orthodox ties were loosened and liberal thought permeated Islamic society, the alien influences that came pouring in included Indian pantheism and Greek Neo-Platonism. As we have seen already, the Zindíqs, that is to say the Manichaeans as well as the Marcionites and the proponents of the views of Bardesane (Ibn-Dayṣán), were also active. Their beliefs could not but find receptive minds, if not multitudes of converts. Some orientalists—notably Edward Granville Browne, who had a marked antipathy towards matters Indian in the earlier years of his distinguished career—have rejected the suggestion that Indian thought could have seeped through to the Muslims in the formative years of Islamic civilization. They point out that it was not until the eleventh century that the great Abú-Rayḥán-i-Bírúní (al-Bírúní)[1] made a detailed and painstaking study of India and her peoples to write his famous treatise on that subcontinent. By then Ṣúfí doctrines were well formulated and well established. But this argument does not hold water. The coming of Islám had not blocked the communication and interchange between Írán and India which had always flowed through a number of channels.

Another view, as exemplified by Professor Zaehner's rigid insistence on clear-cut definitions and exact differentiations between 'nature mysticism' and 'spiritual mysticism', 'monistic' and 'theistic' mystics, is also questionable.[2] In the seething cauldron of thought, Christian or Muslim, many ingredients were admixed.

[1] This is the name by which his compatriots, the Persians, know him. Arabs know him as Abú-Rayḥán Muḥammad Ibn Aḥmad al-Bírúní.

[2] In *Mysticism—Sacred and Profane* (Oxford University Press, 1957) Prof. R. C. Zaehner brought his great erudition and vast knowledge to defeat Aldous Huxley's thesis in *The Door of Perception*. He used a sledge-hammer to crack a tiny nut.

Of course it is possible to decide on a particular line of mystic experience as the only true one, as Professor Zaehner very ably does, and show how unsound and unreliable all the others are, particularly when one can find solid support among the findings of Freud and Jung. Some scholars do not give enough attention to the environment, the climate of thought and the political and social conditions by which people are surrounded, when dreaming weird dreams and experiencing ecstasies, 'sacred and profane'. True, one can be caught in the Marxist trap of economic determinism, and accept with too great a fervour the mechanistic orderings of overzealous economists and highly imaginative sociologists.

It is strange to say that if a man finds himself in harmony with the beauties of nature, truly sees God in nature, his is not a true spiritual experience, but mere 'nature mysticism'. The celebrated Sa'dí of Shíráz, who, although labelled Ṣúfí by zealots, was as much a Ṣúfí (taking another poet at random) as Lord Byron, wrote these lines:

> Green leaves of trees in the sight of the sagacious;
> Each one is a book that bears the knowledge of God.

The reaction of the early Muslim mystics, such as Ibráhím-i-Adham and Aḥmad Ibn Khiḍrawayh and Dhu'n-Nún of Egypt, as we have already remarked, was against luxury-loving and worldliness which riches of an empire naturally engendered. But when the Mu'tazilite peak had passed and dissensions had appeared amongst them; when the intolerance of the Ḥanbalites and the bigotries of the Ash'arites began to throttle thought and blunt the edge of feeling; when uncouth Turks made a mockery of the heritage of Hárún and Ma'mún; when such a fanatical Caliph as Mutawakkil could evoke paeans of praise—it was time for another reaction. In the field of rational thought, the Ikhwán-aṣ-Ṣafá (Brethren of Purity) came forth to redress the balance, and in the realm of metaphysics it fell to the Ṣúfís to restore the joy of belief.

The first poet of calibre, who wrote, in Persian, verse which can be termed mystic, was Abú-Sa'íd Ibn Abi'l-Khayr. He flourished in Khurásán in the eleventh century. Báyazíd-i-Bisṭámí (whose grandfather was a Mazdean) and Junayd-i-Baghdádí, both Persians, had already, in the course of the previous century, made a discipline of mysticism. Báyazíd had spoken wildly of Deity and himself, had uttered words which, mingled with the accruing legends of following centuries, can be construed in a variety of ways. But the point to note is that whereas earlier mystics had quietism as their keynote, their successors had ecstasy as their theme. Their aim was to escape from the rigidity imposed on Islamic society.

It cannot be overstressed that no matter what exaggerations and profligacies were given currency, throughout the centuries, in the name of Ṣúfí thought and practice, such shining lights in the firmament of Ṣúfíism as Saná'í (twelfth century), the first of the great Persian mystic poets; Farídi'd-Dín-i-'Aṭṭár (d. 1230); the celebrated Arab poet, 'Umar Ibn al-Fáriḍ (d. 1235) of Egypt; the illustrious Andalusian, Muḥyí'd-Dín Ibn al-'Arabí (d. 1240);[3] and the incomparable Jaláli'd-Dín-i-Rúmí (d. 1273), never deviated from the discipline of Islám. The story is told of Rúmí, who, riding through the town one day surrounded by his disciples, encountered a Greek who was a Christian. The Greek, overawed by Rúmí's procession, fell prostrate on the ground to render his homage. Rúmí immediately dismounted and did the same. The Christian, still more overwhelmed, repeated his act of homage, which Rúmí reciprocated. Why, a disciple asked, did a man of his station bring himself so low as to put his forehead to the ground before a Christian? Rúmí replied that were the Christian's humility not matched by a Muslim's, Muḥammad would have been shamed before Jesus.

The earliest work, in Persian, on *Taṣawwuf* that has come down to us is *Kashfu'l-Maḥjúb* by 'Alí Ibn 'Uthmán al-Jullábí al-Hujwírí. It was excellently translated into English by Professor Reynold Nicholson and published in 1911. In his preface the translator writes: 'I conjecture, then, that the author died between 465 and 469 A.H. [A.D. 1072–3]. His birth may be placed in the last decade of the tenth or the first decade of the eleventh century of our era, and he must have been in the prime of youth when Sultan Maḥmúd died in 421 A.H. (1030 A.D.).'

Thus, by the time the very orthodox and fanatical Maḥmúd of Ghaznah died, Ṣúfíism had been so established and consolidated, possessing its own arcane terminology, that a whole book could be written about it in modern Persian, a language itself young and

[3] Author of two outstanding books on mysticism: *Futúḥáta'l-Makkíyyah* and *Fuṣuṣu'l-Ḥikam*. Ibn-al-'Arabí has been called the greatest of all Islamic mystics.

fast developing. It behoves anyone particularly interested in the evolution of mysticism within the Islamic fold to read Hujwírí's book with diligence and patience (it is not an instant manual nor an easy book to read), and discard a good many of the volumes written in the West. Unfortunately, the West has been subjected to a spate of useless, misleading and even dangerous literature on the subject of Ṣúfíism. Of course this is not meant to cast a slur on the works of such eminent authorities as Reynold Nicholson, A. J. Arberry and Father Cyprian Rice.

Another outstanding service (unequalled in the vast range of western oriental studies) rendered by Reynold Aleyn Nicholson to a proper appraisal and understanding of Islamic mysticism, was the correction and editing of the text and the translation into English of Jaláli'd-Dín-i-Rúmí's monumental *Mat͟hnaví*, a work to which he devoted decades of his life, 'which occupied him day and night into the small hours when the silence of Cambridge is only disturbed by the mad periodic chiming of clocks'.[4] Rúmí has justly been hailed as the greatest mystic poet of all time. A. J. Arberry, who sat at the feet of Reynold Nicholson, in his turn made invaluable contributions to the study of Islamic mysticism. His translation of the mystical odes of Ibn-al-Fáriḍ is particularly noteworthy.

A few quotations from Hujwírí's book in Nicholson's translation will clarify many misunderstandings and will show how Ṣúfíism looked to a devotee in the years of its efflorescence. Even when Hujwírí was writing his book the legend had grown that the birth of Ṣúfíism was conterminous with the birth and the growth of Islám itself.

'Knowledge of the Divine Essence involves recognition, on the part of one who is reasonable and has reached puberty, that God exists externally by His essence, that He is infinite and not bounded by space, that His essence is not the cause of evil, that none of His creatures is like unto Him, that He had neither wife nor child, and that He is the Creator and Sustainer of all that your imagination and intellect can conceive.' (p. 14.)

'Knowledge of the Divine Attributes requires you to know that God has attributes existing in Himself, which are not He nor a part of Him, but exist in Him and subsist by Him, e.g. Knowledge, Power, Life, Will, Hearing, Sight, Speech, etc.' (p. 14.)

[4] Arberry, *Oriental Essays*, pp. 224–5.

'Knowledge of the Divine Actions is your knowledge that God is the Creator of mankind and all of their actions, that He brought the non-existent universe into being, that He predestines good and evil and creates all that is beneficial and injurious.' (pp. 14–15.)

'Knowledge of the Law involves your knowing that God has sent us Apostles with miracles of an extraordinary nature; that our Apostle, Muḥammad (on whom be peace!) is a true Messenger, who performed many miracles, and that whatever he has told us concerning the Unseen and the Visible is entirely true.' (p. 15.)

'Muḥammad b. [Ibn] Faḍl al-Balkhí says: "Knowledge is of three kinds—*from* God, *with* God and *of* God." Knowledge *of* God is the science of Gnosis (*'ilm-i ma'rifat*), whereby He is known to all His prophets and saints. It cannot be acquired by ordinary means, but is the result of Divine guidance and information. Knowledge *from* God is the science of the Sacred Law (*'ilm-i sharí'at*) which He has commanded and made obligatory upon us. Knowledge *with* God is the science of the "stations" and the "Path" and the degrees of the saints. Gnosis is unsound without acceptance of the Law, and the Law is not practised rightly unless the "stations" are manifested. Abú 'Alí Thaqafí [native of Níshápúr, died 328 A.H.] says: . . . "Knowledge is the life of the heart, which delivers it from the death of ignorance: it is the light of the eye of faith, which saves it from the darkness of infidelity".' (pp. 16–17.)

And here is a perceptive comment by Nicholson:

'When speaking of the various current theories as to the origin of Ṣúfiism, I said that in my opinion they all contained a measure of truth. No single cause will account for a phenomenon so widely spread and so diverse in its manifestations. Ṣúfiism has always been thoroughly eclectic, absorbing and transmuting whatever "broken lights" fell across its path, and consequently it gained adherents amongst men of the most opposite views—theists and pantheists, Mu'tazilites and Scholastics, philosophers and divines. We have seen what it owed to Greece, but the Perso-Indian elements are not to be ignored. Although the theory "that it must be regarded as the reaction of the Aryan mind against a Semitic religion imposed on it by force" is inadmissible—Dhu'l-Nún, for example, was a Copt or Nubian—the fact remains that there was at the time a powerful anti-Semitic reaction, which expressed itself, more or less consciously, in Ṣúfís of Persian race. Again, the literary influence of

India upon Muḥammadan thought before 1000 A.D. was greatly inferior to that of Greece, as any one can see by turning over the pages of the *Fihrist*; but Indian religious ideas must have penetrated into Khurásán and Eastern Persia at a much earlier period.'[5]

Finally, this comment of Father Cyprian Rice ought to be noted: 'This Ṣūfi movement was not itself an order or a sect. Many confraternities, based on Ṣūfi principles and ideals, did arise in course of time and, in a number of cases, still survive, although the times are against them.'[6]

We have seen how the Mu'tazilites, at the height of their power, deviated from their noble principles, abused their power and replaced persuasion by brutal force; how the tolerant became intolerant in the face of obstinate intolerance. Imám Aḥmad Ibn Ḥanbal almost died, while tortured to give his assent to Mu'tazilite doctrines. And when the brief reign of al-Wáthiq, which had heralded a brighter dawn of liberalism, ended in 847, dark days of orthodox reaction came in with the accession of al-Mutawakkil, and the Mu'tazilites paid the penalty of their intemperance. Henceforth, their influence was steadily on the wane, but still greater humiliation awaited them. Ḥanbalites, now holding the field, made life unbearable in Baghdád. They even went to the length of denying aṭ-Ṭabarí burial according to the rites of Islám. Al-Ash'arí's renunciation of Mu'tazilite beliefs and his fierce attacks on them was the worst blow.

Abu'l-Ḥasan 'Alí Ibn Ismá'íl al-Ash'arí (873–4 to 935–6) was a descendant of that Abú-Músá who allowed 'Amr Ibn al-'Áṣ to dupe him in the matter of arbitrating between 'Alí and Mu'áwíyah. He is a highly controversial figure. Up to his fortieth year he was a disciple of the Mu'tazilite leader, al-Jubbá'í (d. 915). Then he broke away and from the pulpit of a mosque in Baṣrah declared it to be his intention to expose the falsity of Mu'tazilite doctrines. He carried out that intention with a vengeance. His polemical output, in condemnation of Mu'tazilite beliefs, was enormous. The Qur'án, he asserted, was uncreated; it had existed coeval with God. This asseveration particularly pleased the followers of Aḥmad Ibn Ḥanbal. Al-Ash'arí's categorical insistence that all the allegorical verses of the Qur'án bore literal truth, and ought to be accepted as such, *bilá kayf* (without asking how), was

[5] *A Literary History of the Arabs*, pp. 389–90.
[6] *The Persian Ṣūfis*, p. 19.

certainly an impediment to free thought and speculation. Although the so-called scholastic theology of the As͟h'arí school gained ascendance over the Mu'tazilite system, it must not be assumed that it received universal acceptance immediately. S͟hí'ahs of various denominations were decidedly opposed to the orthodoxy of al-As͟h'arí and there were still powerful survivors and pockets of resistance amongst the Mu'tazilites. Ibn-al-At͟hír relates that as late as 456 A.H. (A.D. 1063–4) 'Amídu'l-Mulk al-Kundurí, the vizier of the Saljúqid Alp-Arslán, with the approval of the king, ordered that the Ráfiḍís[7] (S͟hí'ahs) as well as the As͟h'arís should be publicly denounced from the pulpits of K͟hurásán. As a result, prominent As͟h'arís such as Abu'l-Qásim al-Qus͟hayrí and the Imám al-Ḥaramayn Abu'l-Ma'álí al-Juwayní migrated from the province. However, the next vizier of the Saljúqs, the celebrated Niẓámu'l-Mulk, was a dedicated and unrelenting As͟h'arí, hence his particular antipathy to the Ismá'ílís. It was to promote the As͟h'arí school that Niẓámu'l-Mulk established his famous college, the Niẓámíyyah of Bag͟hdád.

Resistance to the rigidities of the Ḥanbalí jurisprudence and the As͟h'arí theology led to the formation, in the middle of the tenth century, of a fraternity known as the Ik͟hwán aṣ-Ṣafá—Brethren of Purity or Sincerity. The Society originated in Baṣrah and then a branch sprang up in Bag͟hdád. These Brethren were encyclopaedists and tractarians, and issued fifty-two tracts (*Rasá'il*) in all, covering a wide field: ethics, mathematics, astronomy, geography, philosophy, music—prerequisites of knowledge for any cultivated and cultured man. The fifty-second *risálah* sums up the ideals, the aims and the intents of the previous fifty-one. There is still a good deal of mystery surrounding these Brethren. Who were they? It is obvious that they were men out of sympathy with the prevailing moods and views of the day—Mu'tazilites, S͟hí'ites (Ismá'ílís in particular), free-thinkers, perhaps Manichaeans and even other brands of Zindíqs. Two outstanding men, whom orthodoxy has severely condemned as heretics—Abú-Ḥayyán at-Tawḥídí and the most celebrated Syrian poet, Abu'l-'Alá al-Ma'arrí—have been named as associates of the Brethren. Names of a number of lesser men have come down to us as the authors of those *rasá'il*: Zayd Ibn Rifá'ah, Abu'l-Ḥasan 'Alí Ibn Hárún az-Zanjání,

[7] This term which means 'deserters' or 'those who have cast away' was generally applied to the S͟hí'ahs by the Sunnís.

Abú-Sulaymán Muḥammad Ibn Naṣr al-Bustí known as al-Maqdasí, and Abú-Aḥmad al-Mihrajání.

However, soon the rise of the Buwayhids changed or at least modified the climate of thought. But before long Maḥmúd of Ghaznah became all too powerful, and he was a fanatical upholder of extreme orthodoxy. Despite Maḥmúd's machinations Ibn-Síná (Avicenna) managed dexterously to keep out of the way and the clutches of the Ghaznavid monarch, although Abú-Rayḥán-i-Bírúní, another great savant, accepted service under him.

The works and thoughts of the Ikhwán aṣ-Ṣafá were introduced to al-Andalus (Spain) by Abu'l-Qásim Muslim Ibn Muḥammad al-Majríṭí (d. 1004–5), a native of Madrid, whence they exerted influence over the West.

The scholastic theology of Abu'l-Ḥasan al-Ash'arí would have kept Islám within a very rigid mould, had it not been for the spiritual odyssey of one man—Abú-Ḥámid Muḥammad al-Ghazálí of Ṭús (1058–1111), whom the West knew as Algazel. Although al-Ghazálí has had his detractors as well as balanced and learned critics, it is impossible to exaggerate the position that he came to occupy (and still occupies) in bringing together the various strands of Islamic religious thought to form a broad, generally acceptable pattern.

Al-Ghazálí was well-versed in scholastic theology. He was a lecturer at the Niẓámíyyah College of Baghdád, appointed by Niẓámu'l-Mulk himself. Furthermore, al-Ghazálí was well acquainted with the works of Muslim philosophers, which means with the Aristotelian and Neo-Platonic thought. He had a good knowledge of Christian Scriptures, good enough to write a refutation of St. John's Gospel. He taught for four years, but as time went on he became restless. Theology no longer satisfied the yearnings of his soul. In his remarkable autobiography *al-Munqidh Min aḍ-Ḍalál* (Deliverance from Error), which has been likened in some respects to St. Augustine's Confessions, al-Ghazálí writes:

'Ever since I was under twenty (now I am over fifty) . . . I have not ceased to investigate every dogma or belief. No Bāṭinite [8] did I come across without desiring to investigate his esotericism; no Ẓáhirite, without wishing to acquire the gist of his literalism;

[8] Ismá'ílí. (H.M.B.)

no philosopher,[9] without wanting to learn the essence of his philosophy; no dialectical theologian (*mutakallim*), without striving to ascertain the object of his dialectics and theology; no Sufi, without coveting to probe the secret of his Sufism; no ascetic, without trying to delve into the origin of his asceticism; no atheistic *zindīq*, without groping for the causes of his bold atheism and *zindīqism*. Such was the unquenchable thirst of my soul for investigation from the early days of my youth, an instinct and a temperament implanted in me by God through no choice of mine.'[10]

Al-Ghazálí almost lost his faith—all was darkness with no glimmer of light. Theology and philosophy were equally barren, verbal dexterity and intellectual arrogance were equally futile, disputation and labyrinthine reasoning were equally unavailing. He gave up his post in Baghdád. Wracked in soul and mind and body, he went wandering over the face of the earth. Then he turned to mysticism, to Ṣúfí life and practice. And his soul found peace. He went back to Baghdád after a long absence, and wrote his monumental works: *Iḥyá' 'Ulúmi'd-Dín* (The Revivification of the Sciences of Religion) in Arabic and *Kímíyáy-i-Sa'ádat* (The Alchemy of Felicity) in Persian. He also wrote *Maqáṣid al-Falásifah* (The Intentions of the Philosophers), *Taháfut al-Falásifah* (The Inconsistency of the Philosophers) and *al-Iqtiṣád Fi'l-I'tiqád* (The Golden Mean in Belief). Al-Ghazálí brought the *Sharí'at* (Religious Law) and the *Ṭaríqat* (The Mystic Path) together, harmonized philosophy with religious belief, and ironed out the rigidities of the Ash'arí and the Ḥanbalí systems. Henceforth, the Ṣúfí path, cleared of extravagances, became respectable, philosophy could be countenanced by the theologian, and jurisprudence (*fiqh*) found its proper level. Latin translations of al-Ghazálí's works made a deep impression on European thought, and it is claimed that St. Thomas Aquinas was influenced by them.

[9] Neo-Platonist. (P. K. Hitti.)
[10] Cited by Hitti, *History of the Arabs*, pp. 431–2.

27

The Civilization of Islám

'ARAB scholars were studying Aristotle,' writes Professor Philip Hitti, 'when Charlemagne and his lords were learning to write their names. Scientists in Cordova, with their seventeen great libraries, one alone of which included more than 400,000 volumes, enjoyed luxurious baths at a time when washing the body was considered a dangerous custom at the University of Oxford.'[1]

Endless argument has gone on as to the correct name of the civilization that grew up in the wake of the establishment of the Faith of Muḥammad. It has been called Arab. It has been called Saracenic. Persians have boasted that they civilized the Arabs and led the way into a new era. Even the grammarians and the philologists and the lexicographers who told the Arabs what their language was like, how it was constructed, what its possibilities were, and what it could convey, were Persians, the compatriots of those great and learned men have exclaimed triumphantly. Turks, who came into the realm of Islám decades later, have, in their moments of unbridled nationalistic fervour, claimed as their own all and sundry who blazed the trail (Zoroaster included). Indeed, al-Fárábí, one of the most illustrious and formidable figures in the galaxy of pioneers, was a Turk. But he seems to have been a solitary figure in the early days. To Arabs must certainly belong the pride of having released the impetus and the dynamic which a new civilization must needs have; of providing a language immeasurably rich in its achievement and its potential to link men of diverse nations and backgrounds in common purpose and pursuit and common understanding. Again in the words of Professor Philip Hitti: 'Few peoples in history seem to have been as susceptible to the influence of the word, spoken or written, as the "sons of Arabic", the Arabs' favourite designation of

[1] *The Arabs*, p. 2.

themselves. It was only in the field of verbal expression that pre-Islamic Arabians distinguished themselves. The extent to which they developed their language is surprising; it was out of proportion to the development of their political, social, and economic institutions. How illiterate camel breeders living in scattered tribes, with no political cohesion to unite them, could develop a refined, richly worded means of expression remains a mystery.'[2]

Arabs must not forget, however, that it was not 'Arabism' in any way which moulded and shaped the Islamic civilization. Persians too must not forget that when the Arabs conquered them and brought them the gift of Islám they were decadent, that culturally they were spent, and socially were slaves of a caste system, that the Sásánian dynasty was no longer fit to govern. They must also not forget that many of them (in earlier years) still looked back to a dead past for comfort and some of them tried wantonly to wreck rather than to build.

But modern vauntings and tendencies apart, the haughtiness and the race-consciousness of the Arabs, at its height when the House of Umayyah ruled, led to the rise of a movement, chiefly literary, which aimed at denigrating the Arabs and glorifying non-Arabs, particularly the Persians. Those who followed that line were called the Shu'úbíyyah, deriving their name from a verse in the Qur'án: 'O people! Verily we have created you from a male and a female, and have made you nations and tribes that you may know that the noblest of you in the sight of God is he that feareth God the most. Verily, God is the All-Knowing, the Best-Informed.' (Súrah xlix, 13.) *Shu'úb* is the plural of *sha'b*, the word which Arabs use today in the sense of 'nation'. It was believed that in the Qur'ánic verse the term *qabá'il* (tribes) indicated 'Arabs' and *shu'úb* referred to others. Of course the modern notion of 'nation' did not then exist.

The Caliph Hishám ordered his men to throw Ismá'íl Ibn Yásár into a pool, because he had expressed in a poem his pride in his ancestors. At the other end of the scale was Abú-Tammám, another poet, taken to task by the vizier for likening the Caliph al-Mu'taṣim to Ḥátim (celebrated for his generosity). He was asked: 'Dare you compare the Commander of the Faithful with those uncouth Arabs?' Abú-Dulaf al-'Ijlí, a courtier attending al-Ma'mún and al-Mu'taṣim, had no hesitation in extolling his own

[2] *Islam, A Way of Life*, p. 25.

style as *Kisrawí* (like unto Chosroes). Since Arabs were renowned and praised for their hospitality, books began to appear commending miserliness. These were called the 'Books of Misers' (*al-Kitábu'l-Bukhalá'*). One such book was written by a librarian in the service of al-Ma'mún, another by the celebrated al-Jáḥiẓ (d. 839), a master of graceful Arabic prose, who was also a prominent Mu'tazilite. On the other hand Zamakhsharí (d. 1144), the last eminent Mu'tazilite, noted for his commentary on the Qur'án, and himself a Persian, thanks God in his introduction to his great work for being free from the proclivities of the Shu'úbís. Such historians of the first rank as al-Baládhurí (d. 892) and Ibn-Qutaybah, a contemporary of the former but of Íránian descent, parted company with the Shu'úbís; whereas a man as accomplished as al-Bírúní (d. 1048), hailed as the greatest of the savants of his age, leaned towards them.

Shu'úbí philologists went to the length of challenging the power of Arabic. The historian Ḥamzah of Iṣfahán (d. circa 961), a profoundly learned man whose contribution to knowledge is indisputable, was ingeniously, but also childishly, inventive in finding origins for Arabic words in Persian. His devious etymology is similar in its infantilism to Mírzá Áqá Khán-i-Kirmání's[3] flights of fancy, in the nineteenth century, who found the origin of the French word *histoire* in the Persian word *ustuvár*, the meaning of which is 'firm'. Shu'úbism never became a political force in the earlier centuries, but endured in different guises, and could be encountered in later times.

The civilization of Islám was neither Arab, nor Persian, nor Syriac. It had all those elements within its fold, and many more: Egypto-Coptic, Indian, Greek, Spaniard, Berber and Turkish. Jews, Christians, Muslims, Mazdeans, Sabeans, even Pagans, were equally proud to bear its burden and rear its structure. Never before in the experience of mankind had monotheistic thought and pagan speculation found a congenial home in which to exist side by side, neither infringing on the other, neither sanctioning the other, neither assimilating the other. Centuries later, when the pagan thought of ancient Greece trickled back to the West, through the medium of Islamic culture and Arabic translation, the first reaction of the Church was to repudiate and denounce it. Then the genius and the logic of St. Thomas Aquinas gave birth

[3] He was put to death in Tabríz, in July 1896.

to the system known as Scholasticism, which, in spite of its great and undoubted merits, carried one serious defect, inasmuch as it accorded the sanction and the approval of the Church to a science which was bound to suffer from the ravages of time. Aristotelian and Pythagorean theorems were thrown into a rigid, immutable cast. This was the reason why Roger Bacon was frowned on, Copernicus was not favoured and Galileo was persecuted. On the other hand, when, in the years of decline in Islamic lands, new science was condemned, the culprit was the conglomeration of myths and superstitions, not an officially-blessed Aristotelian system.

The Umayyads, despite their dislike for non-Arab elements in Islamic society, did not differentiate on grounds of creed. Christians and Jews, if they had any outstanding talent to offer, found posts under the Caliphs, although not in the area of government. They gravitated towards arts and sciences. Art, in those early years, was represented solely by poetry, and the science which was eminently desirable was medicine. However, these disciplines had strict, immediate and practical application. Poetry was amatory and laudatory and pleased the Caliph and his court. It was also a double-edged weapon. In Arabic poetry the abstract was relatively meagre but Arab wit was extremely mordant.

The Prophet is quoted as saying that science has two aspects: the science of religions and the science of human bodies. The latter is of course medicine. Galen and Hippocrates[4] stood supreme in that field. Shí'ahs and Mu'tazilites, as we have already seen, had pioneered in the area of scholastic theology. Healing provided by medicine is always in demand. Disciples of Galen were naturally well-received, no matter what their creed. But search for new horizons, either in the science of healing or any other, did not characterize the period of Umayyad rule. Theological argument was then gathering momentum, and the establishment of the organs of government was of prime importance.

Arabs had already produced in the very early years of Islám a distinguished physician, in the person of al-Ḥárith Ibn Kaladah, who has been styled 'the doctor of the Arabians'. Al-Ḥárith, who lived on to the days of 'Umar, the second Caliph, received his training in Persia. He was married to a sister of Áminah, the mother of the Prophet, and so his son, an-Naḍr, another physician

[4] Jálínús and Buqráṭ in Arabic.

of high merit, was a cousin of Muḥammad. During the reign of Marwán I, a Persian Jew named Másarjawayh translated a book on medicine from Syriac into Arabic. It was the very first of a long line of translations that opened the way for the advent of Islamic civilization and shed lustre upon it.

Although many of the eminent translators were not Muslims, they who set themselves to the pursuit of learning had the words of the Prophet Himself to guide and inspire them. 'Seek knowledge from the cradle to the grave', 'Seek knowledge be it even in China', 'The ink from the pen of the scholar is more worthy than the blood of the martyr', 'He who leaves his home in search of knowledge, walks in the path of God' were clear, unhedged, emphatic statements by Muḥammad. And the Qur'án had declared: 'Are they equal: those who know and those who know not?' (Súrah xxxix, 12.)

Baghdád became the cynosure of the world of savants when the Caliph al-Ma'mún established his House of Wisdom (*al-Bayt al-Ḥikmah*). Men came to Baghdád to partake of the liberality of the Caliph and to converse on themes close to their hearts. Al-Ma'mún's astronomers computed the circumference of the earth and concluded that it must be a globe. But many years before al-Ma'mún threw open his court to the savants, listened to their discourses and became an active partner in their discussions, men of learning had reached Baghdád and enjoyed the patronage of the Caliph. An early arrival was that of Júrjís (George) Ibn Bakhtíshú', a Nestorian Christian, who was in charge of the hospital at Jund-i-Shápúr.[5] When Nestorians were finding it hard to practise their Faith in Byzantium, Chosroes I, the Sásánian monarch, who had his trials of strength with Justinian, gave them refuge, instituted a College of medicine and philosophy in Jund-i-Shápúr (in the province of Khúzistán), and appointed a number of the learned amongst the Nestorians to staff it. Al-Ḥárith Ibn Kaladah had been trained in that institution.

The Caliph al-Manṣúr summoned Júrjís to Baghdád in the year 765, to attend him during an illness which had proved beyond the competence of his own physicians to cure. Júrjís remained in the 'Abbásid capital, still a Nestorian. His son, Bakhtíshú', and the latter's son, Jibrá'íl (Gabriel) rose to great eminence under al-Manṣúr's successors, and indeed, for some two hundred and

[5] Or Gundishápúr.

fifty years, the gifted descendants of Júrjís Ibn Bakhtíshú' dominated the medical scene in Baghdád.

Some six years after the arrival of Júrjís from Jund-i-Shápúr, an Indian came to Baghdád with a book on astronomy—a *Siddhánta*.[6] The Caliph wished it to be translated. Muhammad Ibn Ibráhím al-Fazárí undertook the task, and earned the distinction of being the first astronomer in the realm of Islám. The celebrated Muhammad Ibn Músá al-Khárazmí, at the bidding of al-Ma'mún, took the work of al-Fazárí a stage further, brought together the Indian and the Greek disciplines of astronomy, and produced the Astronomical Tables (*Zíj*), based on al-Fazárí's, which gained great fame. Abú 'Abdu'lláh Muhammad Ibn Jábir Ibn Sinán al-Battání (d. 929), known in the West as Albategnius, was the author of another set of Astronomical Tables, which in its Latin version provided the groundwork of astronomy in Europe for several centuries. The pioneering work and the contributions of al-Khárazmí cannot be overrated. He was a Persian and a native of Baghdád. Although his part in the development of astronomy was significant, far more important was his work in the field of mathematics. It was he who adopted Indian numerals and made use of zero, which facilitated calculation to an extent hitherto unknown and prepared the way for great scientific advance. The word 'zero' comes from the Arabic *ṣifr* which means 'empty'. In all probability either he or some other savant in the area of the Islamic civilization evolved the very concept of zero. When the Indian numerals reached the Western world, to oust the Roman, they came to be known as 'Arabic numerals'. Al-Khárazmí was also the originator of algebra, which attained its highest development within the pale of the Islamic civilization, at the hands of the celebrated 'Umar Khayyám. 'Algebra' comes from the Arabic word '*al-Jabr*', meaning the renovation of something broken. Trigonometry, both plane and spherical, is another branch of mathematics that owes its inception to the scientists of the Islamic civilization. The term 'sine' (L. *sinus*), used in trigonometry, is the Latin translation of the Arabic word '*jayb*' which means an 'opening'.

The following list of the names of stars and scientific terms, by no means exhaustive, will suffice to indicate the measure of the indebtedness of Western civilization to the civilization of Islám:

[6] *Sindhind* in Arabic.

Stars: Betelgeuse—*Bayt al-Jawzá'* (The House of Twins); Altair —*aṭ-Ṭá'ir* (The Flyer); Pherkad—*Farqad* (Calf); Acrab—*'Aqrab* (Scorpion); Algedi—*al-Jadí* (Kid).

Scientific Terms: Alembics—*al-Inbíq*; Alkali—*al-Qilí*; Arsenic— Zarníkẖ; Azimuth—*as-Sumút*; Nadir—*Naẓír*; Zenith—*Samt ar-ra's.*

Al-Ḵhárazmí, whose name appeared in Europe as Algorism or Algorithm, signifying decimal notation, made use primarily of Indian sources. But by then, Greek sources were being copiously translated into Arabic and made available to scholars. For over a hundred years translators transmitted in Arabic to the world of Islám gems of Greek philosophy and science, which Christian Europe had neglected and even repudiated. Many of these works were first translated into Syriac and then into Arabic. Those eminent translators came mainly from two groupings of people: the Nestorian Christians and the pagans of Ḥarrán (who eventually claimed to be Sabeans and people of the Book). Christians of the Jacobite persuasion also contributed their share. So did the Jews. And so did the Muslims.

Ḥunayn Ibn Isḥáq (809–73), known to the West as Joannitius, is hailed as the doyen of that distinguished host of translators. He was a Nestorian from Ḥírah, and served under the physician Jibrá'íl Ibn Baḵhtíshú', in Baghdád, rising eventually to such eminence in the field of medicine as to obtain appointment as the Caliph's personal physician. But before al-Mutawakkil accorded him that highly-coveted honour, Ḥunayn was, under al-Ma'mún, the director of the Caliph's Academy and his duties entailed the work of translation. He wrote in Syriac, and his son, Isḥáq, who was a better master of the language, rendered his Syriac translations into Arabic. Ḥunayn had other able assistants, including his nephew, Ḥubaysh. Befitting his high standing in his profession, Ḥunayn turned his attention, in particular, to the works of Galen and Hippocrates, but he also translated Plato's *Republic* and Aristotle's *Categories* and *Physics*. The originals of seven books on Anatomy by Galen are irretrievably lost, but Ḥunayn's work has saved them from total loss. It is sad to relate that a man of the calibre of Ḥunayn committed suicide, because Bishop Theodosius excommunicated him.

The man who led the field amongst the pagans of Ḥarrán was Thábit Ibn Qurrah (836–901), who even amended and improved the translation of Euclid made by Ḥunayn. Sinán (d. 943), the son of Th́ábit, proved as talented a translator as his father, and this tradition of excellence continued within the family of Th́ábit Ibn Qurrah. Two grandsons, one named after him and another named Ibráhím, as well as a great-grandson, Abu'l-Faraj, made noteworthy contributions, both as translators and savants. Qusṭá Ibn Lúqá (Costa, son of Luke, d. 922), a Christian of Ba'labakk, was another accomplished translator.

No matter how significant, important and far-reaching the pioneering work of Ḥunayn Ibn Isḥáq was in the area of translation, one must not overlook his stature as a physician and his own original contributions to learning, particularly in the sphere of medicine. It is said that he wrote nearly a hundred books, mostly on his own subject. His *Ten Treatises on the Eye* (*al-'Ashr Maqálát Fi'l-'Ayn*) is considered to be the oldest systematic work extant on ophthalmology. He was also the author of *Questions on the Eye*. Ḥunayn scientifically explained the structure of the eye and the brain and the connection between the two. He also gave an accurate description of the prevalent diseases of the eye and remedies available.

As we have seen, the Jews and the Christians were the first to gain distinction in the discipline of medicine. But it was not long before Muslims came to attain equal eminence. 'Alí Ibn Sahl Rabbán aṭ-Ṭabarí, a Persian Christian from the shores of the Caspian Sea, embraced Islám during the reign of al-Mutawakkil and while attached to his court wrote, in the year 850, an encyclopaedia, which he termed *Firdaws al-Ḥikmah* (The Paradise of Wisdom). Dealing chiefly with medicine, 'Alí aṭ-Ṭabarí treated in that book of astronomy and philosophy as well. The hold of the savants of the world of Islám on the science of medicine and the art of healing was astonishing, a hold which they maintained for several centuries and which was consolidated in the Western world by the medium of the Latin translations of their works and by the rise of institutions in the West modelled on theirs.

Anyone entering the chapel of Princeton University should not be surprised to find on a window panel the figure of a turbaned oriental holding a scroll on which Arabic characters are inscribed. This figure represents Abú-Bakr Muḥammad Ibn Zakaríyyá' ar-Rází (865–925), known as Rhazes in the West, a Persian, native of the city of Ray, considered by an impressive body of authoritative opinion to have been the greatest of all the physicians of Islamic civilization. The inscription on his parchment is the title of his *magnum opus*: *Kitáb al-Ḥáwí*, which translated into Latin was given the title of *Continens*, signifying that the whole science of medicine was contained therein. And in the great hall of the Medical School of the University of Paris, amongst the portraits of the eminent men of science, one encounters Rhazes and also Abú-'Alí Ibn Síná (980–1037), whom the West knows as Avicenna, another formidable figure of the civilization of Islám. Avicenna was also a Persian, a native of Balkh. These portraits, placed as they are in a venerable and ancient institution, itself raised on the pattern of Islám's distinguished centres of learning, bear witness to the high regard which the West has had for those benefactors of the world of humanity.

Ar-Rází composed another all-embracing medical work in ten volumes, which he named *Kitáb aṭ-Ṭib al-Manṣúrí* (The Book of Manṣúrí on Medicine), after the Sámánid Amír, Manṣúr Ibn Isḥáq. *Liber Almansoris* is the title of its rendition into Latin, which was published in Milan, in the latter part of the fifteenth century. Even in recent years sections from *Kitáb al-Manṣúrí* have appeared in both French and German versions. Ar-Rází's particular distinction lies in the fact that he was the first physician to give an accurate clinical description of smallpox and measles. His monograph on the subject, entitled *al-Judarí w'al-Ḥaṣbah*, was printed as late as 1848, in London, in an English translation by W. A. Greenhill.

Ar-Rází was a profound philosopher and alchemist as well. His alchemy laid the foundations of modern chemistry. *Sirr al-Asrár* (The Mystery of Mysteries, *Secretum Secrotorum* in Latin), his book on alchemy, has the great merit of dispensing with legend, to rely on laboratory techniques and clear scientific analysis. He used instruments and methods previously unknown. In this field ar-Rází was preceded by Jábir Ibn Ḥayyán (Geber to the West). Although Jábir was primarily an alchemist, it was he who first crossed the borderline from the murkiness of his ancient craft to the clarity of scientific precision. Jábir was a native of the city of Ṭús and rose to fame in Baghdád. There he enjoyed the patronage of the House of Barmak and became a follower of the sixth Imám, Ja'far aṣ-Ṣádiq. The fall of the Barmecides forced Jábir to abandon Baghdád for Kúfah. It is believed that he died in his native city in the year 815. Many are the works attributed to Jábir Ibn Ḥayyán, but modern research has indicated that Ismá'ílí scholars of a later period had a hand in composing many of them. Translated into Latin, Jábir's works had a certain vogue in the West and were even preferred to ar-Rází's *Book of Mysteries*.

We shall return later to examine the standing and the achievements of both ar-Rází and Avicenna as thinkers and philosophers. However, great as ar-Rází's attainments were in the field of medicine, it was the *al-Qánún fi'ṭ-Ṭibb* (Canon of Medicine), the encyclopaedic work of Avicenna, which, over several centuries, set the standard of medical knowledge in both the East and the West. In the course of the last three decades of the fifteenth century, Avicenna's *Canon*, consisting of five books, was printed fifteen times in its Latin version. And in the seventeenth century it was still used in the universities of the West.

The genius of Shaykhu'r-Ra'ís Abú-'Alí Ibn Síná, was a rarity amongst men. By the age of eighteen he had mastered all that was to be learnt of human knowledge. Barely twenty years old, he was ministering to the sick, writing tomes and treatises, instructing pupils. Saná'í, a leading mystic Persian poet of the twelfth century prays fervently that God may grant him, at all times, such wisdom and understanding as would excite envy in the soul of Abú-'Alí Ibn Síná. And the poet who thus prayed was himself held in such high regard that the great Jaláli'd-Dín-i-Rúmí wrote: ''Aṭṭár [7] was the light and Saná'í his two eyes; we came following their trail.'

Avicenna went on to become a king's [8] minister. During the day he transacted affairs of state. At night he taught and wrote. And he wrote the greatest of his works without using any notes or books of reference, totally impromptu. The range of his writings is breath-taking. He wrote on all branches of science, on music, logic, metaphysics, mysticism, philology and prosody.

The Prophet Himself, as we have seen, had focused attention on the art of healing. The blind fanaticism of the Byzantines which caused the closure, in 489, of the school maintained by the Nestorians in Edessa, and made Justinian ban, in 529, the school kept in Athens by the Neo-Platonic philosophers, redounded to the advantage of the Sásánians and enriched their colleges and insti-

[7] Farídi'd-Dín-i-'Aṭṭár, see p. 276.

[8] Shamsi'd-Dawlih, the Buwayhid ruler in Hamadán.

tutions at Jund-i-Sháápúr[9] by the inflow of Christian expatriates who were received with open arms. These flourishing establishments in the south-west corner of Írán, in the land of ancient Elam and the cradle of the Achaemenians, which soon became part of the realm of Islám, greatly benefited both the study and the practice of medicine amongst the Muslims. Next, the rise of eminent disciples of the art of healing, Jewish, Christian, Mazdean and Muslim, within the realm of Islám, induced favourable conditions for the rapid development and extension of institutions where the means of healing could be dispensed with efficiency. When in the West the practice of medicine was still primitive, over the realm of Islám, hospitals known by the Persian designation of *Bímáristán* (Home for the Sick) were appearing, all well ordered and systematized.

These hospitals had ample endowments for their maintenance. The *Bímáristán* of Baghdád, one of the largest, was named al-Aḍudí, after its founder and benefactor, Aḍudi'd-Dawlih, the most renowned of the Buwayhid rulers. Al-'Atíq of Cairo had the great Ṣaláḥi'd-Dín al-Ayyúbí (Saladin) as its founder. In the midst of all his battles and preoccupations, that remarkable man, whose generosity of spirit and liberality never flagged, found time to attend to the establishment of a *bímáristán*. The *bímáristáns* had separate wards for various branches of medicine such as internal diseases, ophthalmology and orthopaedics; and there were further divisions for specific ailments, such as fevers, diarrhoea and diverse afflictions of the mind. Furthermore, the *bímáristáns* had well-equipped departments of pharmacy, under competent heads, to provide the patients with all their needs. The freedom which the physicians enjoyed in carrying out useful experiments was phenomenal. Physicians wrote down the accounts of their clinical observations and the results of their experiments to which the public at large had full access.

Allied to the art of healing is the knowledge of drugs, the discovery of new substances which have remedial qualities and experimentation with them—which is pharmacology. This science too was diligently pursued with outstanding results. A book by Abú-Rayḥán al-Bírúní[10] ought to be mentioned in this connection. This is *Kitáb al-Ṣaydal fí'ṭ-Ṭibb* (The Book of Drugs in Medicine). It is a pharmacopeia which richly details the advances made.

[9] Gundisháápúr. [10] Abú-Rayḥán-i-Bírúní.

Many of the substances, included in Abú-Rayḥán's book, were naturally superseded in later times, but this fact does not detract from the value of the work of those pharmacologists of the realm of Islám.

Abú-Rayḥán (973–1048) was himself a man of considerable achievement. Familiar with Sanskrit, Syriac and Hebrew, he drew upon several sources to enrich his own keen and precise observations in the field of natural sciences. In three profound volumes he surveyed systems of calendars throughout the ages, dealt with the rotation of the earth on its own axis, worked out latitudes and longitudes and systematized all that was known of the various branches of mathematics and astronomy and astrology. Accompanying the Ghaznavid conquerors to India, he fell in love with the spirit of that land, prolonged his stay, and wrote the first comprehensive book about India.

As already remarked, a significant contribution by the savants of the Islamic civilization was the use they made of laboratory techniques and the invention of instruments which facilitated measurements and computations. The three sons of Músá Ibn Shákir—Muḥammad, Aḥmad and Ḥasan—set up an observatory in their own home in Baghdád, which rivalled the observatory that the Caliph al-Ma'mún had built in the capital. These enterprising men took the young Ḥunayn Ibn Isḥáq under their wing and sent him to search in other lands for manuscripts, the works of ancient Greece. Al-Ma'mún did the same, sending his emissaries to seek out manuscripts. The learned sons of Músá Ibn Shákir also took part in the delicate and important operations (already referred to) which aimed at measuring and determining the size of the earth and its circumference, taking it for granted that the earth was round. Jund-i-Shápúr had achieved the further distinction of possessing the first observation post, equipped with adequate and up-to-date instruments, to take measurements of the earth and the stars. Next the honour fell to al-Ma'mún to extend the scope of celestial observations; and it was as an adjunct to his Bayt al-Ḥikmah—the House of Wisdom—that the first observatory was established in Baghdád. Later, on a hill close to Damascus, this enlightened Caliph raised a second observatory. The Buwayhid rulers were no less enthusiastic in promoting astronomical studies. Rukni'd-Dawlih, in Ray, and Sharafi'd-Dawlih, in Baghdád, gave their patronage to celebrated astronomers and provided them with observatories. Of the invaluable contributions made to astronomical knowledge throughout the realm of Islám, in places as far apart as Shíráz and Samarqand, the work of al-Battání (Albategnius to the West), noted earlier, and of 'Umar Khayyám, ought to be particularly underlined. Al-Battání came from Ḥarrán—the home of pagans who paraded as Sabeans. Al-Battání was Sabean before his conversion to Islám. He dominated the closing decades of the ninth and the opening decades of the tenth century. Al-Battání carried a good deal further the work of Ptolemy and corrected some of his calculations. 'Umar, whom Edward Fitzgerald has immortalized in his brilliant renderings of the *Rubá'íyyát*, was by far a greater mathematician and astronomer than poet.[11] The whole of Khayyám's quatrains, which are of uncertain number, pale into insignificance beside the scientific work of this sage of Níshápúr. Under the patronage of the Saljúqid Jaláli'd-Dín Malik-Sháh and Niẓámu'l-Mulk, that monarch's highly accomplished minister, Khayyám, with the assistance of other astronomers working in the observatory provided for them, devised a new calendar, which Írán has now officially adopted. Named Táríkh-i-Jalálí, after the Saljúq king, it is much more accurate than the Gregorian Calendar. The latter goes wrong by one day in 3330 years, whereas Khayyám's calendar makes that error only in 5000 years.

The science of optics, which, in later times, came to have close association with astronomy, was also assiduously cultivated by the savants of the realm of Islám. The name that stands out most prominently in this connection is that of Ibn-al-Haytham (Alhazen in the West). It has been said that ar-Rází, Abú-Naṣr al-Fárábí, Abú-'Alí Ibn Síná and Ibn-al-Haytham were the four pillars sustaining the edifice of the civilization of Islám. Ar-Rází and Avicenna, as we have seen, were Persians, al-Fárábí was a Turk and Ibn-al-Haytham (Ḥasan Ibnal-Haytham) was an Arab of Baṣrah. But one must not forget the paramount importance of the pioneering work of Abú-Yúsuf Ya'qúb Ibn Isḥáq al-Kindí (801–73), hailed as the 'Philosopher of the Arabs'. In the words of Professor Hitti: 'The harmonization of Greek philosophy with Islam begun by al-Kindi, an Arab, was continued by al-Fārābi, a Turk,

[11] Recent attempts to decry Fitzgerald's translation, and to make of Khayyám a Ṣúfí *murshid* are risible.

and completed in the East by ibn-Sīna, a Persian.'[12] More of al-Kindí's works have survived in Latin rendering than in their original Arabic, thanks to the labours of Gerard of Cremona (1114–87), the most prolific and the most accurate of a host of Latin translators of works in Arabic.

Al-Kindí's book on optics, translated into Latin under the title of *De Aspectibus*, which undoubtedly influenced Roger Bacon (1214–94), had the final word on the subject until Ibn-al-Hay<u>th</u>am began his investigation and experiments, and wrote on 'Light' and its properties. We shall come back to the work and the achievement of al-Kindí, al-Fárábí and Ibn-Síná, the three who did more than any others to promote the knowledge and the understanding of music. These Muslim savants looked at music as a branch of mathematics.

Ibn-al-Hay<u>th</u>am had an early failure which nearly caused him to lose his life. Al-Ḥákim (reigned 996–1021), the Fáṭimid Caliph in whose service Ibn-al-Hay<u>th</u>am had enrolled, commissioned him to devise a system of controlling the annual rise of the waters of the Nile. He failed, and just escaped with his life.

Ibn-al-Hay<u>th</u>am can be rightly acclaimed as the progenitor of the art of photography and ultimately the cinematograph, for it was he who first demonstrated the principle of the camera-obscura during an eclipse. However, it took three centuries before another Muslim scientist, Kamáli'd-Dín al-Fárisí (d. 1320), took that principle and its application a stage further. Ibn-al-Hay<u>th</u>am's work on optics provides another vivid example of the attention to observation and experiment which the savants of the Islamic civilization increasingly displayed. He used a variety of lenses and mirrors for his experiments, and studied the refraction of light. His investigation of the atmospheric refraction enabled him to measure the height of the atmosphere. Ibn-al-Hay<u>th</u>am's book, *Kitáb al-Manáẓir* (The Book of Optics), had a wide range of influence in the West.

Yet another instance of the considerable success of the Muslim scientists, in developing new instruments and gaining fresh insight and knowledge by their use, is provided by Bírúní's determination of a number of specific gravities.

We hear of those three indefatigable sons of Músá Ibn <u>Sh</u>ákir writing the first book about mechanics, in the year 860, which

[12] *History of the Arabs*, p. 371.

contained descriptions of various appliances then in common use. Some of the items described are not particularly remarkable, but there are also a number, new to the experience of mankind and exceedingly effective.

Although instituting libraries, open to scholars, was not a measure specific to the civilization of Islám and had impressive precedents in Hellenistic and pre-Hellenistic times, the scope, the range and the number of libraries within the realm of Islám greatly added to the splendours of that civilization.

From al-Ma'mún's Bayt al-Ḥikmah came many of the great advances of Islamic civilization. And it was the library attached to this House of Wisdom which became the model institution. Al-Mu'taḍid (892–902), the sixteenth caliph of the House of 'Abbás, opened an academy in his newly-built palace, fully equipped with books and all other appurtenances of learning, staffed by competent teachers to serve the needs of the students. Incidentally, this Caliph had a Christian at the head of his department for the army. In Baghdád, men of ample means, collectors of books who owned sizeable libraries, were not tardy in emulating the caliphs and providing the student and the scholar with every amenity.

When Avicenna was summoned to attend the Sámánid Amír Núḥ II (976–97), who lay seriously ill, he was given the freedom of the royal library. 'I entered a building,' he writes in his short autobiography, 'that had many rooms. In these, trunkfuls of books rested on top of one another. In one room there were books on linguistics and poetry; in another, books on jurisprudence and so on. I looked up the catalogue of the books of the Greeks, and asked for those I required. I found books there even the names of which are unknown to most men, compositions that I had not encountered before and have not encountered since. I read those books and realized what the position of each author was in various branches of knowledge. Thus by the time I had reached my eighteenth year I had mastered all those sciences. My memory was better then, but now I am more experienced. My knowledge is exactly what I garnered in those days.' That peerless library of the Sámánid ruler had a sad fate. His rebellious troops set fire to it, and Avicenna's enemies averred that it was he who was responsible for that act of arson, in order to deny others the benefits of the royal collection.

Mosul possessed a Dár al-'Ilm (House of Knowledge), established by its citizens, which had a fine library. Scholars pursued their studies there free of charge. They were even given all the paper they required. The Buwayhid ruler, 'Aḍudi'd-Dawlih, founded in Shíráz a Khizánat-al-Kutub (Treasury of Books), well known and well organized. Ray boasted a vast Bayt-al-Kutub (House of Books), the catalogue of which, alone, was in ten volumes. The Fáṭimid al-Ḥákim established a library in Cairo, the Dár-al-Ḥikmah (Home of Wisdom), which excelled all the rest because of the opulence of material and facilities, and the munificence of the benefactor. Not only were there well-paid, deeply-versed librarians at the service of the public, but those who wished to follow a line of study were given a stipend to enable them to concentrate on their work. Thus, literary pursuits were encouraged from Bukhárá and Marv and Khárazm, at one end of the realm of Islám, to Cairo and Fusṭáṭ and Qayrawán and the magnificent institutions of Moorish Spain, at the other, culminating in the superb library of Cordova, founded by the Umayyad Caliph, al-Ḥakam II (961–76), which housed 400,000 volumes, with a catalogue in forty-four volumes.

AL-ANDALUS

Moorish Spain provides a dazzling example of the civilizing power of Islám. Out of the desolate Visigothic wilderness, rampant with hate and oppression, Muslims fashioned a land of peace and plenty, brought equity and justice and tolerance to reign, and lit a torch of culture in the fair land of al-Andalus that illumined the continent. When their political fabric gave way to accumulating stresses, that brilliant torch blazed the brighter, overshadowing the darkness of internal disorder and anarchy. And when the Christian reconquest was completed and only the architectural glories of al-Andalus remained, then bigotry, intolerance and the Inquisition held dominance over Spain. Flushed with victory, the Christian conquerors sailed across the Atlantic in search of their El Dorado, destroyed ancient civilizations, built an empire and gathered riches, but Spain never again rose to the heights she had attained under the Muslims. Her eclipse in the course of the subsequent centuries provides a salutary lesson.

We discontinued the story of Moorish Spain at the point when 'Abda'r-Raḥmán, a scion of the Umayyads of Damascus, escaped from the 'Abbásid blood-bath and established himself as the master of al-Andalus.[13] The Emirate set up by him, although naturally independent of the 'Abbásids who had exterminated his family, was not a rival to their dominion. 'Abda'r-Raḥmán did not claim the title of caliph. His mother was a Berber, which won for him the whole-hearted support of those natives of North Africa who constituted the majority of the Muslims in al-Andalus. Arabs, though not too numerous, held the reins of power. They were of two factions: Yemenites or Ḥimyarites and Muḍarites or Qaysites. The latter opposed 'Abda'r-Raḥmán, while the Ḥimyarites rallied to him. For the *Muwalladún*, that is the Spanish Muslims, it was immaterial who the new ruler was and what claims he had to that position. The Umayyad Amír of al-Andalus was wise, patient and efficient, a contrast to the last members of his family, occupants of the seat of authority in Damascus. But he had been severely tested in the crucible of adversity.

'Abda'r-Raḥmán ruled al-Andalus from 756 to 788. His death in that year did not shake the foundations which he had laid, and by the time 'Abda'r-Raḥmán II came to the throne in 822, the Umayyad Emirate was well consolidated.[14] The second 'Abda'r-Raḥmán reigned for thirty years over a land tranquil and prosperous, but the following six decades were turbulent ones in the life of al-Andalus. The three Amírs who succeeded 'Abda'r-Raḥmán II were weak, and at least one of them, 'Abdu'lláh (888–912), was rather subservient to Málikite jurists. Unruly notables were many, the most dangerous and the most powerful of whom was Ibn-Ḥafṣún, a Spanish Muslim, one of the Muwalladún. Eventually, Ibn-Ḥafṣún went to the Christian fold, although there was a time when it seemed that he was prepared to acknowledge the supremacy of the Fáṭimid Caliphs. His conversion caused many to abandon him, but he and his sons after him were, for years, a source of grave embarrassment to the State, a pernicious force to be reckoned with. In those decades of instability the cultural life of al-Andalus did not suffer decline. On the contrary it gained further strength. The celebrated musician, Ziryáb, came from Bag͟hdád during those years, to set up a vigorous tradition of his art in al-Andalus. The talented poet, Ibn-'Abd-Rabbih (860–940), whose great fame rests on his compilation of a literary

[13] See p. 237.

[14] 'Abda'r-Raḥmán I was succeeded by his son His͟hám I (788–96), whose son al-Ḥakam I (796–822) was the father of 'Abda'r-Raḥmán II.

encyclopaedia, *al-'Iqd al-Faríd* (The Peerless Necklace), also flourished at this time.

'Abda'r-Raḥmán III (912–61), a grandson of 'Abdu'lláh, succeeded him at the age of twenty-one. His long reign and the shorter one of his son, al-Ḥakam II, covering between them the best part of the tenth century, witnessed the zenith of Umayyad power in Spain and constituted the golden age of al-Andalus. Father and son were both patrons of learning, and to their courts came savants and poets and artists, men of many talents, to bask in the sunshine of their liberality. Al-Ḥakam II, who founded the great library of Cordova, the greatest in the realm of Islám, was himself a scholar, a man of deep erudition. In the days of this father and son al-Andalus could boast of four hundred flourishing towns and cities, seventeen colleges and universities, and seventy well-stocked libraries. Cordova alone had six hundred mosques, nine hundred public baths and eighty schools.

'Abda'r-Raḥmán III found himself confronted by the menace of the rising power of the Fáṭimids, which, for a while, extended over the whole of North Africa, reaching the environs of Spain. And a time came when all that was left to 'Abda'r-Raḥmán of his North African possessions were the two cities of Ceuta and Tangier. But once the Fáṭimids turned to the East to conquer Egypt and then move southwards, their pressure on North Africa eased considerably, and 'Abda'r-Raḥmán's successors regained much of the lost territory. However, to safeguard his position in al-Andalus, 'Abda'r-Raḥmán, in the year 929, proclaimed himself Caliph and also Amíra'l-Mu'minín (Commander of the Faithful), styling himself An-Náṣir Li-Díni'lláh (Defender of the Faith of God). The 'Abbásid Caliphate was, by then, only a pale ghost of what it had been, and by establishing another Sunní Caliphate, 'Abda'r-Raḥmán provided a bastion to ward off the onslaught of the Fáṭimids.

When al-Ḥakam died his son, Hishám, was a minor, and soon intrigue developed around him. In the contest for power a certain Ibn-Abí-'Ámir emerged the victor and ruled wisely in the name of the boy-Caliph. He took the title of al-Manṣúr (the Victorious). After him his son, 'Abdu'l-Malik, entitled al-Muẓaffar (the Triumphant), guided the destinies of the Umayyad Caliphate with similar wisdom and circumspection. Unfortunately he had only six years as the administrator of the state, and died in 1008, in circumstances that have remained obscure and unexplained. His younger brother, 'Abda'r-Raḥmán, entitled al-Ma'mún, who succeeded him, was foolish and possessed of vaulting ambition. He forced Hishám to transfer the Caliphate to him. This event caused the Umayyads to revolt. Six of them occupied the throne in quick succession. There were also three members of a half-Berber family, the Ḥammúdids, who donned the mantle of caliph. By the year 1031 the Caliphate was extinct and al-Andalus plunged into total anarchy. Out of that welter gradually a number of petty kingdoms took shape, the most brilliant of which was the Kingdom of Seville, founded by a judge, the Qáḍí Muḥammad Ibn 'Abbád. And yet in that maelstrom arts flourished and poetical expression bloomed afresh. The Qáḍí's son, al-Mu'taḍid, and his grandson al-Mu'tamid, kings of Seville, were both eloquent poets.

The petty kingdoms into which al-Andalus had split were ruled by three ethnic groups: Berbers, Andalusians (a fusion of Arab and Spanish stock) and the Ṣaqálibah, that is to say Slavs (a composite group, newcomers to al-Andalus). The breakdown of the unified al-Andalus gave ample scope and opportunity to the Christian principalities of Castile and Leon, Aragon and Navarre, outgrowths of the mountain fastnesses of northern Spain, to make further and further inroads into Muslim domains. This was the time when the legend of El Cid was born. Cid is the same as Sayyid in Arabic, which means lord and master. The celebrated Cid—Rodrigo Diaz de Vivar—was a Castilian nobleman who broke away from Alfonso VI of Castile, in or around 1081, and entered the service of the Muslim ruler of Saragossa. His reward was dominion over Valencia, a town almost entirely inhabited by Muslims. In 1085, the same Alfonso VI wrested the very important centre of Toledo from the Muslims, and the much-praised city never again reverted to them. Then it was that al-Mu'tamid of Seville decided to seek aid from the Berbers of North Africa to stem the onrush of the Christians.

North Africa, at this point, was in the grip of *al-Murábiṭún*: a body of the Ṣanhájah tribes of the Berbers. A certain 'Abdu'lláh Ibn Yásín, invited by an elder of the Ṣanhájah to teach his people and meeting with opposition, had retired to an island on the River Niger. There disciples had rallied to him and from his *ribáṭ* (cloister) a religious revival had ensued. Hence the name *al-Murábiṭún* given to his body of disciples, which in European languages has become Almoravids. When al-Mu'tamid's plea for help reached North Africa the Amír of al-Murábiṭún was a man named Yúsuf Ibn Táshufín. Yúsuf was the founder of the renowned city of Marákish (Marrákesh). He responded to al-Mu'tamid's call, led his warriors into Spain, inflicted a crushing defeat on Alfonso at Zalláqah (near Badajoz) and returned to North Africa. However, the chronic disunity of al-Andalus allowed Alfonso to retrieve the situation, and before long the Málikite jurists who held sway in al-Andalus, as well as al-Mu'tamid and other potentates, were begging Yúsuf to return. This time, having repelled Alfonso once again, he stayed and took over the petty kingdoms, one by one. In a short while, al-Mu'tamid, the accomplished poet-king of Seville, found himself a prisoner in Yúsuf's hands. Al-Andalus had three Almoravid rulers (who had the title of Amíra'l-Muslimín—the Commander of the Muslims) from 1090 to 1145. But then the Almoravid kingdom crashed. The rot set in with the fall of Saragossa to Alfonso I of Aragon in 1118.[15] Next, in 1133, Alfonso VII of Castile found himself in a position to take the offensive. Popular discontent, rumbling for a while, broke into open revolt in 1144, and the Almoravid rule could not survive the convulsion.

In the meantime, North Africa was swept by yet another religious revival: that of al-Muwaḥḥidún (Unitarians), or Almohads in European jargon. Exponents of the new religious outlook were the Maṣmúdah group of Berber tribes. The Muwaḥḥidún apparently had Ẓáhirite tendencies which made the dominant Málikite jurists of al-Andalus detest them. Matters were made even worse when Ibn-Túmart, the fount-head of the new movement, claimed in about the year 1121 to be no less a person than the Mahdí—the Deliverer. But the Murábiṭún, backed though they were by the Málikites, were fast losing ground. The Muwaḥḥidún conquered the city of Marákish in 1147, and soon they spread over al-Andalus.

Ibn-Túmart died on the battlefield in 1130. He had, in his lifetime, given the command over his people to 'Abdu'l-Mu'min, the most distinguished of his lieutenants. 'Abdu'l-Mu'min intended to invade al-Andalus, but it was left to Abú-Ya'qúb Yúsuf I, his son who succeeded him in 1163, to cross the sea.

[15] It is interesting to note that this was the year when, as predicted by astrologers, many rulers died. See pp. 322–3.

Abú-Ya'qúb Yúsuf went so far as to lay siege to Toledo, a daring but unsuccessful enterprise. Still pursuing his campaigns against the Christians, he was fatally wounded while besieging a fortress near Lisbon. His death, in 1184, was a great loss, as he was both a just and efficient ruler. Abú-Yúsuf Ya'qúb, his son, had to call a halt to the military operations in al-Andalus, because there were urgent matters in Algeria to engage his attention. But when he could turn once again to the almost constant struggle against the Christians, this third Caliph of the Almohads heavily defeated Alfonso VIII of Castile, at Alarcos in 1195, nearly half-way between Toledo and Cordova. Within four years of his signal victory, Abú-Yúsuf Ya'qúb was dead, to be succeeded by a son, Muḥammad (entitled an-Náṣir), who was unequal to the tasks which lay ahead. On the other hand, smarting under the serious reverse at Alarcos, the Christian camp was particularly active and agitated. Ecclesiastics took the matter hard, preached a Crusade, and began to mend fences between the contending Christian principalities. A herculean effort was demanded to turn the tide. It all bore fruit, because in the year 1212, Leon, Castile, Aragon and Navarre, making common cause, crushed the army of Muḥammad an-Náṣir at Las Navas de Tolosa. This defeat spelled the end of the rule of Almohads in al-Andalus. Abú-Ya'qúb Yúsuf II, who succeeded his father a year later, at the age of fifteen, carried on precariously for ten years, and when he died in 1223, the power of al-Muwaḥḥidún died with him.

Leon and Castile were united in 1230 and the Castilian Ferdinand III vigorously pressed his advantage over the almost leaderless and broken Muslims. He conquered Cordova in 1236 and Seville in 1248. It seemed then that the end had come for Muslim rule in Spain, but a man of Medinite origin, Muḥammad Ibn Yúsuf Ibn Naṣr had carved out, in the year 1235, a kingdom for himself round the city of Granada. This Naṣrid kingdom endured to the end of the 15th century.

The amazing vitality of the Islamic civilization in al-Andalus is evidenced by the fact that not only did it not wilt and wither when exposed to the harsh strains of encroachment from without and disorders from within, but it became even more productive, more fruitful. The *joie de vivre* which pervades the work of the poets and the men of belles-lettres in those decades of darkening horizons, such as Ibn-Ḥazm (994–1064), Ibn-Zaydún (1003–70) and Ibn-

Khafájah (1050–1139), is unbelievable. Ibn-Ḥazm, who composed *The Ring of the Dove* (*Ṭawqa'l-Ḥamámah*),[16] a book on love, was a theologian. When hemmed in within the enclave of Granada, Muslim genius defiantly gave birth to the wonder and the beauty which is the Alhambra: Al-Ḥamrá'—the Red Palace. And three of the most brilliant minds of any age belong to this period: Ibn-Rushd (1128–98), whom the West knows as Averroes, hailed as the greatest philosopher of Islám; Muḥyí'd-Dín Ibn al-'Arabí (1165–1240), perhaps the greatest of all the Muslim mystics; and Ibn-Khaldún (1332–1406), the most penetrating of all the Muslim historians.

Ibn-Ṭufayl (c. 1105–85), Abubacer in the West, was another noted philosopher of al-Andalus. He it was who, befriending Ibn-Rushd, took him to the court of Abú-Ya'qúb Yúsuf. Ibn-Ṭufayl was Abú-Ya'qúb Yúsuf's personal physician and eventually became his vizier. The book on which Ibn-Ṭufayl's fame rests is the story of *Ḥayy Ibn Yaqẓán* (The Living Son of the Awake). Avicenna had also written a treatise bearing the same title.[17] Whereas Avicenna, philosopher *par excellence*, had a purely mystic theme to unfold, Ibn-Ṭufayl expounded a philosophic theme in the allegorical story of Ḥayy, who is nurtured on a desert island by a gazelle. Ḥayy by his own contemplation, and not by human instruction, becomes aware of the world around him, of nature and its laws, and finally attains belief in God, the Creator of all things. Another young man, who has decided to withdraw from the world to pass his time in meditation and contemplation, comes to Ḥayy's desert island. They meet and talk and find themselves in agreement, having reached the same conclusion by different routes. The Latin translation [18] of Ibn-Ṭufayl's allegory, entitled *Philosophus Autodidactus*, had a profound influence in the West. Indeed, the inspiration of Daniel Defoe's *Robinson Crusoe* can be traced to the influence of Ibn-Ṭufayl's book. *Risálatu Ḥayy Ibn Yaqẓán* has been translated into the main European languages time and again.

The effect of the works of the philosophers of Islám on the minds of the Europeans was such that Dante would not consign Avicenna, Averroes and Saladin to Hades. He placed them in limbo.

[16] Translated by A. J. Arberry (1953).
[17] He wrote this during a short imprisonment.
[18] In the latter part of the fifteenth century.

Professor Arberry states in the introduction to his translation of the treatise on self-discipline by ar-Rází—*The Spiritual Physick of Rhazes*[19]—that in the field of natural sciences the influence which the works of ar-Rází exerted in the West was perhaps unmatched, but in the realm of philosophy his views went largely unnoticed because they were considered heretical. Even Abú-Rayḥán-i-Bírúní, who devoted a monograph to the works of ar-Rází and listed 164 books, was highly critical of his philosophy. Among others, Ibn-Ḥazm wrote to refute it.

As noted before, the three great figures who substantially shaped the discipline of philosophy in the realm of Islám were al-Kindí, al-Fárábí and Ibn-Síná (Avicenna)—an Arab, a Turk and a Persian. And they were men who were polymaths. They shone and excelled in many fields, including mathematics and medicine. They, like the Greeks on whose philosophy their minds were nurtured, treated music as a branch of mathematics, and wrote brilliantly and authoritatively on that theme. At least one of them, Abú-Naṣr al-Fárábí, was himself an accomplished performer and is reputed to have invented new instruments. They took their theorems of music and sound and their computations beyond the stage reached by the Greeks and borrowed the word *Músíqí* (Music) from them. Unfortunately much of what al-Kindí wrote has been lost. But we still have some of his writings on music. Al-Fárábí's most famous work is *Kitáb al-Músíqá al-Kabír* (The Great Book of Music). Avicenna devoted long sections of his encyclopaedic work *ash-Shifá'* (Cure) to music.

Although there is not a single verse condemnatory of music in the whole text of the Qur'án, all the four Sunní schools of jurisprudence forbade it, a ban which was largely ignored. The Caliphs—Umayyads and 'Abbásids alike—led the way in keeping alive the glorious tradition of Arab song (*ghiná'*). *Kitáb al-Aghání* (The Book of Songs), in twenty-one volumes, by Abu'l-Faraj al-Iṣfahání (*c.* 897–967) shows how very rich that tradition was. We read of later developments and of the superb players, Ibráhím al-Mawṣilí and his son Isḥáq, Persian by descent, who adorned the courts of the 'Abbásids from the days of Hárún ar-Rashíd to the days of al-Mutawakkil; and of Ziryáb, their brilliant pupil, who went to al-Andalus and left an indelible mark on the culture of Spain. The Persian and Indian musical heritages, both

[19] The Wisdom of the East Series (London, John Murray).

immensely rich, not to speak of the invaluable contributions from the Greeks, which the great philosophers discovered and developed, added to the immense vigour and the bewitching beauty of Arab song, producing new forms and new instruments. We are told that the musical powers of Abú-Naṣr al-Fárábí could wring the hearts of his audience. At one moment, he could induce tears of sorrow, at another transports of sheer delight and ecstasy. He could make the audience fall into slumber or leap for joy.

The story is often told of the blind poet Rúdakí (d. 940), the most eloquent of the pioneers of Persian poetry, and the Sámánid ruler, Naṣr Ibn Aḥmad (914–43). Amír Naṣr had his capital in Bukhárá. It was customary for him to spend the summer elsewhere and return in the winter. One year he visited Hirát and was so enchanted by its beauties and the bounteous gifts of nature there that he prolonged his sojourn into winter and beyond. His retinue, chafing at separation from their homes and families, begged the blind poet, who was an accomplished minstrel as well, to incline the Amír to return to his capital. One morning Rúdakí took up his harp, and began to sing to the Amír:

> The Jú-yi-Múliyán we call to mind,
> We long for those dear friends long left behind.
> The sands of Oxus, toilsome though they be,
> Beneath my feet were soft as silk to me.
> Glad at the friends' return, the Oxus deep
> Up to our girths in laughing waves shall leap.
> Long live Bukhárá! Be thou of good cheer!
> Joyous towards thee hasteth our Amír!
> The Moon's the Prince, Bukhárá is the sky;
> O Sky, the Moon shall light thee by and by!
> Bukhárá is the Mead, the Cypress he;
> Receive at last, O Mead, thy Cypress-tree![20]
>
> (Translation by E. G. Browne)

So moved was Naṣr Ibn Aḥmad that, not even waiting for his riding-boots to be brought to him, he mounted his horse and set his face towards Bukhárá; nor did he stop until he had reached his capital.

Orthodoxy failed utterly to banish all that joy and exhilaration and when the Ṣúfís not only gave their approval, but went further

[20] Cited by Browne, *A Literary History of Persia*, vol. I, p. 16.

to add positive encouragement, the triumph of the proponents of music was well-assured. The celebrated Egyptian Ṣúfí, Dhu'n-Nún, a model of piety, declared that when one listens to music with the ear of the spirit one is drawn nearer to God; it is only when one listens purely sensuously that one falls into error. Finally, the verdict of the great Abú-Ḥámid Muḥammad al-Ghazálí left no doubt that the opinion of the jurisconsults could not prevail.

In its hour of political decline, when at the same time the realm of Islám was exposed in the East to the intolerable strains of the Crusades and was soon to be rocked to its foundation by the onrush of the Mongols, al-Andalus did not bow to adversity. Furthermore, it became the channel for the bright gifts of the civilization of Islám to pass to a Europe still engirdled by the gloom and obscurantism of the Middle Ages. To her renowned universities still came students and scholars from the West, as they had done in the past. One of these scholars, a brilliant Frenchman, Gerbert of Aurillac, ascended the papal throne as Sylvester II in 999. And those flourishing universities of al-Andalus became models for the great universities that were to be raised in Christendom: Pisa, Paris, Oxford. Even those Christian rulers who were struggling to reconquer Spain were appreciative of the boon of Islamic culture. King Alfonso X of Castile and Leon, enchanted by the excellence of that culture, commissioned the translation into Spanish of the famous tale of *Kalílah-wa-Dimnah.* This book, it will be recalled, was the medium by which that master of stratagem, the Persian 'Abdu'lláh Ibn al-Muqaffa', tried subtly to disseminate his Manichaean beliefs.

Two new poetical forms which had had their beginnings most probably in the eastern areas of the realm of Islám, both originating from popular songs, had attained literary status and reached perfection in al-Andalus. These were the *muwashshaḥ* and the *zajal* (provider of cheer), and of the two the latter, in particular, had a characteristic Andalusian flavour. Ibn-Quzmán (Abenguzman), who lived into the second half of the twelfth century, became the exponent of *zajal*, and as he was a minstrel moving from place to place with his song, *zajal* verse became widely known, evoking a ready response from Spanish-speaking Christians. The Castilian popular style of *villancico* was greatly influenced by the *zajal* verse, and since this Castilian verse form features much in Christmas songs, *zajal* left a permanent mark on the life of Spain.

France was next to be affected by it, resulting in the rise of Provençal poetry. Arab bards, too, following the example of Ibn-Quzmán, moved from Spain into France and then into Italy, taking with them a variety of new musical instruments. Two such instruments especially, the lute and the rebec, greatly helped the musical development of the western world. The rebec was a stringed instrument, the precursor of the viol. Troubadours of France and Italy learned their art from those Arab minstrels and *zajal* singers and emulated their example.

SIX GREAT MEN

Al-Kindí

Abú-Yúsuf Ya'qúb Ibn Isḥáq al-Kindí (801–73), 'the Philosopher of the Arabs', was of noble descent, a scion of that Ash'ath Ibn Qays, the Ḥimyarite chief who failed 'Alí, the fourth Caliph, at Ṣiffín. A man of considerable means, al-Kindí could employ some of the ablest men to assist him in his researches and studies.

It ought to be emphasized that the Aristotle whom these savants of the realm of Islám came to know was not the Aristotle of the Hellenic, but of the Hellenistic age, shrouded in the Neo-Platonism of the Syrian Porphyry.

Mu'tazilite writings, so impregnated with Greek thought, led al-Kindí to turn to Aristotle and to philosophy. He reached the conclusion that philosophy is all-comprehensive, comprising every branch of knowledge, and that religion and philosophy are not competitive. Religion, the product of prophetic Revelation, is accepted by faith, whereas philosophy is apprehended by reason. However, certain issues were left unresolved. One was the question of resurrection. A Muslim believed that resurrection was of the body, and so did a Christian. The Neo-Platonist maintained that resurrection was of the soul. Al-Kindí did not attempt a synthesis. But he would not agree with Aristotle that matter and time had no beginning. And he followed the Mu'tazilite line, asserting that certain verses of the Qur'án were allegorical and need not be taken literally. Al-Kindí's pioneering work made the Islamic civilization conversant with Greek philosophy.

Ar-Rází

The next outstanding philosopher, ar-Rází, struck another trail, as we have seen, which put him at odds with contemporary thought. Because he repudiated the whole concept of prophetic Revelation, he became isolated. As a scientist and physician his word carried great weight. As a philosopher he was either denounced or wholly ignored.

Al-Fárábí

Abú-Naṣr al-Fárábí (872–950) was a Turk and a Ṣúfí, attending the court of Sayfi'd-Dawlih 'Alí Ibn Ḥamdán, the Shí'ite ruler of Aleppo. So vast was his learning and so accomplished was he that to him was given the title of Mu'allim-i-Thání (the Second Teacher), the first being Aristotle. Although it was his commentary which, on Ibn-Síná's own admission, enabled the latter to comprehend the complexities of Aristotle's *Metaphysics*, al-Fárábí devoted the greater part of his philosophical speculation to civics and the art of government. He achieved fame with his *Risálah fí Ará' Ahli'l-Madínata'l-Fáḍilah* (A Treatise on the Opinions of the People of the Superior—or the Virtuous—City), and *as-Síyásat-al-Madaníyyah* (The Politics of Civilization); the former after the manner of Plato's *Republic*, and the latter in a similar vein to Aristotle's *Politics*. Needless to say that the *Madínata'l-Fáḍilah*—the Superior or the Virtuous City—is none other than Utopia. According to the doctrine of Emanation, Neo-Platonic in origin, the universe is hierarchical. There is the Supreme Being, All-Perfect, at the very summit. From Him a lower tier of beings originate or emanate, and they, in turn, give existence to the next grade. This process is continued until the lowest grade of existence is reached. Al-Fárábí causes his Utopia to be similarly structured. There is the Head whom none can or will command, and there are those at the very base who command none. Qualities required of that Head are such as to make of him almost a superman—in other words the Philosopher-King of whom Henry St. John, Viscount Bolingbroke, was dreaming in eighteenth-century Britain. Al-Fárábí also envisages a situation in which no single person has all the required qualities, but two or more persons collectively possess them; then there would be a presidium to command the 'Superior City'; and should *Ḥikmat* (Wisdom, or Philosophy) be absent from the sum total of those excellences, the Utopia would be deprived of true Headship. In developing the theme of his Utopia, al-Fárábí nowhere and in no way denies the necessity and the validity of prophetic Revelation.

On the contrary he affirms the need for it. Al-Fárábí also wrote a commentary on Aristotle's *Organon*, which Roger Bacon found very useful.

Ibn-Síná

Thus we pass on to the next colossal figure: Shaykhu'r-Ra'ís Abú-'Alí Ḥusayn Ibn 'Abdu'lláh Ibn Síná, a Persian, originally a native of Balkh, who was born thirty years after the death of the Túránian al-Fárábí. His father, an official serving the Sámánid monarchs, was an Ismá'ílí, but Ismá'ílí doctrines did not prove attractive to the son. We have already noted his precocious genius, his astonishing memory, his immense erudition and his vast output. As in the discipline of medicine, so in the field of philosophy Ibn-Síná outshone all. His philosophic system, neither Aristotelian nor Platonic, neither Stoic nor Neo-Platonic, came to dominate the thought of the East and left visible marks on brilliant intellects in the West, notably the leading scholastics, Albertus Magnus and Thomas Aquinas. Ibn-Síná could not give full assent to any single one of the Greek schools. He chose carefully the Greek ideas he would adopt to synthesize with various strands of thought found in the Islamic milieu. While he agreed with Aristotle that matter was ancient and eternal, he took the concept of emanation from the Neo-Platonists. He inclined towards the Mu'tazilah, maintained that man is possessed of free will, and rejected the rigidity of predestination. He also refuted the belief in the resurrection of the body and brought upon himself the wrath of theologians. Central to his theme was the necessity of the existence of God. The only essential being was the Being of God, supreme and transcendent. And from His all-encompassing will and knowledge emanated every other being, whose existence was possible but not essential. The office of the Prophet-Revelator was also needed to give direction to the affairs of men. The welfare of the state depended upon it. The part which the philosopher played was secondary to that of the Prophet. He, himself, despite the depth of his philosophic insight and the vastness of his knowledge, had, as an administrator and statesman, failed time and again. His attainments had proved insufficient. For him there was no Philosopher-King. The precepts of religion had to be expressed in symbolic terms. The language of the philosopher was incomprehensible to the majority of men.

It seems an aberration that whereas Ibn-Síná had given his encyclopaedic work on medicine the title of *al-Qánún* (Canon, or Law)[21] he accorded the title of *ash-Shifá'* (Cure, or Remedy) to his equally encyclopaedic work on philosophy, which treats of all branches of knowledge, including music. A recension of the same work, a shorter version, he named *an-Najáḥ* (Deliverance). And apart from the aforementioned *Ḥayy Ibn Yaqẓán*, in another work *al-Ishárát wa't-Tanbíhát* (Directions and Warnings) Ibn-Síná turned his attention to mysticism and the inner life—the life of the spirit. He traced three stages on the mystic path: first, that of the *Záhid* (the Ascetic), next that of the *'Ábid* (the Worshipper), and finally that of the *'Árif* (Gnostic).

With Ibn-Síná, philosophical speculation in the East reached its climactic point. Those who followed him either took from him their guide-lines or adumbrated on the basis of what he had propounded. Such was the case with Shihábi'd-Dín Yaḥyá as-Suhrawardí, known as Shaykha'l-Ishráq. Suhrawardí was put to death in Aleppo, in 1191, by order of the Ayyúbite al-Malik aẓ-Ẓáhir, the son of Ṣaláḥi'd-Dín (Saladin), for alleged pantheistic views. He developed his *Ḥikmata'l-Ishráq* (Philosophy of Illumination) from the statements of Ibn-Síná on *Ishráq*. This doctrine of Illumination has its origin in Neo-Platonism.

Ibn-Rushd

In al-Andalus the star of Ibn-Rushd was yet to rise. Abu'l-Walíd Muḥammad Ibn Aḥmad Ibn Rushd (Averroes), a native of Cordova, belonged to a family renowned for its jurists and theologians. Both his father and grandfather occupied the office of Qáḍí (Judge). He studied medicine and jurisprudence; while practising medicine he also served the state in the same manner as his father and grandfather. As we have seen, it was Ibn-Ṭufayl who introduced him to the Muwaḥḥid ruler, Abú-Ya'qúb Yúsuf I. In 1182 he was given the post of Court physician in succession to Ibn-Ṭufayl. The King also appointed him Chief Justice, first of Seville and afterwards of Cordova, and wished him to write a treatise on philosophy. Royal favours continued in the reign of

[21] It is of interest that three centuries prior to the discovery in Europe of the pulmonary circulation of the blood, Abu'l-Ḥasan 'Alí Ibn-an-Nafís (d. 1228), the dean of the hospital established in Cairo by the Mamlúk ruler, Qaláwún, gave a description of that vital bodily process, in his commentary on Ibn-Síná's *al-Qánún*.

al-Manṣúr, the son of Abú-Ya'qúb Yúsuf. However, in 1194, at the instigation of the Málikite theologians, who still dominated the scene and whose support the king badly needed, Ibn-Rushd, then sixty years old, was shorn of office and exiled. His books were burnt. Although al-Manṣúr soon made amends and gave him the office of judge in North Africa, Ibn-Rushd had received a severe blow. He died at his post within a few years, in the closing weeks of 1198. At a later date his remains were taken to Cordova.

Ibn-Rushd was the last and possibly the greatest of those giant figures who bestrode the arena of philosophy in the realm of Islám. He wrote thirty-eight commentaries on philosophy. Of these only twenty-eight have survived in Arabic. More exist in Hebrew and Latin translations. In addition to his scientific works, the most notable of which is *al-Kulliyyát fi'ṭ-Ṭibb* (Generalities of Medicine), he wrote a book to demonstrate that religion and philosophy were not and need not be contradictory and that there is an essential harmony between them; to this he gave the name of *Faṣl al-Maqál* (The Decisive Treatise).

When Ibn-Rushd received his commission from the king, he made a survey of the sources available to him. Soon realizing that the Aristotle handed down to the scholars of the realm of Islám was not the genuine philosopher of the Hellenic Age, he set about to dispel the obscurities caused by Neo-Platonism. For the first time Aristotle emerged as he had been, and when the commentaries of Ibn-Rushd were put into Latin the Western world came to know the true Aristotle. The profound effect of this discovery was reflected in the Thomism of St. Thomas Aquinas.

Ibn-Rushd like Ibn-Síná maintained that matter was ancient and eternal. Likewise he rejected belief in corporeal resurrection and predestination. But unlike Ibn-Síná he could visualize a Philosopher-King in the manner of Plato, and had no use for the theory of Emanation. He saw creation as a continuous process, never-ending, and the social structure as the creation of the Prophet-Revelator and Legislator. He, himself, had been successful as a judge and jurist. Therefore, he could endorse the participation of the philosopher in the work of government. He could not let al-Ghazálí's strictures on philosophers remain unanswered, and adopting the same word which al-Ghazálí had used to criticize the philosophers, he composed his *at-Tahâfut-at-Tahâfut* (The Inconsistency of the Inconsistency) to examine al-Ghazálí's objections point by point and to indicate where the true philosopher stands.

Averroism was at first hailed universally in the West and found its way into the universities. But then the Church took fright, the cry of heresy went up and, in 1231, Pope Gregory IX condemned it. However, Averroism had taken root in a Europe just awakening, and could not be dislodged. The name may have been forgotten with the passage of centuries but the liberalizing influence remained.

Ibn-Khaldún

It remains now to have a look, no matter how briefly, at the work of another outstanding figure of al-Andalus, before bringing to a close this chapter of glorious achievement in the realm of Islám. 'Abda'r-Raḥmán Ibn Khaldún (1332–1406) was born and bred in Tunisia, but his origins were in al-Andalus, and the culture of al-Andalus was his spiritual home, the source of his inspiration.

Ibn-Khaldún spent many years in the service of various rulers—in Fás, in Granada, in Cairo—and thus gained valuable experience of the affairs of men. He negotiated with the Castilians on behalf of Granada, and he met Tamerlane—'the scourge of God'—on behalf of Egypt. This mighty conqueror showed him every mark of respect. Ibn-Khaldún is rightly honoured for his wisdom and insight, judgement and discernment. He is the first historian ever to look for forces that shape history. That has brought him renown as the first sociologist. His history of the Arabs, Persians and Berbers has a very long title in Arabic.[22] The introductory volume, know as the *Muqaddimah* (Prolegomena) has run to three massive volumes in its excellent English translation by Franz Rosenthal.[23] In this Prolegomena Ibn-Khaldún probes diligently into the processes of history, examining with care such factors as climate and geographical position, ethical, moral and spiritual values, and the masterly sweep is truly superb. Ibn-Khaldún is undoubtedly the greatest of all the historians of the realm of Islám and one of the greatest intellects of all history.

[22] *Kitáb al-'Ibár Wa Díwán al-Mubtadá Wa'l-Khabar fí Ayyám al-'Arab Wa'l-'Ajam Wa'l-Barbar* (Book of Instructive Examples and Register of Subject and Predicate Dealing with the History of the Arabs, Persians and Berbers).

[23] Published by Routledge and Kegan Paul, London, 1958.

28

The Crusades

THE Saljúqs restored, to a very large extent, the hegemony of the Islamic Empire. They rescued the Sunní 'Abbásid caliphs of Baghdád from the feeble grasp of the Shí'ah Buwayhids, who like so many similar dynasties had swiftly gone into decline. And in 1071 Alp-Arslán broke the Byzantines in the battle of Manzikert (Maládhkirt) and Emperor Romanus Diogenes fell into his hands. Not only were the Byzantine inroads into the realm of Islám halted, but the uplands of Asia Minor were opened to the Saljúqs. Malik-Sháh, the son of Alp-Arslán, had a brilliant reign, but died when only thirty-seven years old, in 1092; and the feuds and jealousies within the circle of his own family, which he, with the wise counsel of Niẓámu'l-Mulk, had kept in check, tore the Saljúq Empire asunder. Niẓámu'l-Mulk had already fallen from the high office which he had held with distinction and competence for many years, and had soon after died by the dagger of an Ismá'ílí, a follower of Ḥasan-i-Ṣabbáḥ.[1] His assassination preceded the death of Malik-Sháh by a matter of weeks.

The territory over which Malik-Sháh, the Saljúqid, ruled was extensive and far-flung. When his army crossed the river Oxus to complete the conquest of Turkistán, the boatmen, who ferried his troops to the other bank of the river, came to him to complain that the vizier had made their dues payable from the revenues of Antioch. To the Sulṭán's remonstrances Niẓámu'l-Mulk replied that he had done so to register the fact of the vastness of the Empire. 'But this description of his limits,' Gibbon remarks, 'was unjust and parsimonious: beyond the Oxus, he reduced to his obedience the cities of Bochara [Bukhárá], Carizme [Khárazm] and Samarcand [Samarqand] and crushed each rebellious slave, or independent savage, who dared to resist. Malek passed the

[1] Ḥasan-i-Ṣabbáḥ died in the year 1124.

Sihon [Sayḥún] or Jaxartes, the last boundary of Persian civilization: the lords of Turkestan yielded to his supremacy; his name was inserted on the coins, and in the prayers, of Cashgar,[2] a Tartar Kingdom on the extreme borders of China. From the Chinese frontier, he stretched his immediate jurisdiction or feudatory sway to the west and south, as far as the mountains of Georgia, the neighbourhood of Constantinople, the holy city of Jerusalem, and the spicy groves of Arabia Felix.'[3] Gibbon also relates the story of Malik-Sháh's visit to the shrine of Imám Riḍá, at Ṭús, on the eve of a battle he had to fight with a rebellious brother. 'As the Sultan rose from the ground,' writes Gibbon, 'he asked his vizir Nizam, who had knelt beside him, what had been the object of his secret petition: "That your arms may be crowned with victory," was the prudent and most probably the sincere answer of the minister. "For my part," replied the generous Malek, "I implored the Lord of Hosts that he would take from me my life and crown, if my brother be more worthy than myself to reign over the Moslems." '[4] Such was the measure of the single-mindedness of this devout Turk. And also, such was the fanatical intensity of the will to power of the descendants of Saljúq, the Turkish seeker after fortune, that with the death of Malik-Sháh the immense empire, which he bequeathed to his successors, could not endure the strains to which it was subjected. What followed is a sad story of fragmentation, of shrinking principalities, of desperate intrigues, of fratricidal struggles within the House of Saljúq, and of the moving in of fresh barbarians from the East. In the meantime, Crusaders no less uncouth had come from the West: some truly devout, inflamed with the love of Christ, many merciless, possessed by greed. The fall of Jerusalem to the Franks, on 15 July 1099, changed the face of both the East and the West.

The Crusaders had come upon Jerusalem on Tuesday, 7 June 1099. Its ramparts and fortifications disallowed an immediate assault. Iftikhári'd-Dawlih, the Muslim commander in the Holy City, knew that he could not reasonably expect any rescue operation from the Muslim principalities of the region. Antioch and

[2] Káshghar, situated in the present-day Chinese province of Sinkiang.
[3] Gibbon, *The History of the Decline and Fall of the Roman Empire*, vol. 6, p. 262.
[4] ibid., pp. 261–2.

Edessa had been captured by the Crusaders, the first by Bohemond, the Norman lord from Southern Italy, and the second by Baldwin of Boulogne. The leaders of the Crusaders, Godfrey de Bouillon, Duke of Lower Lorraine,[5] Bohemond[6] of Taranto, his nephew Tancred,[7] Baldwin of Boulogne,[8] and Raymond of Saint-Gilles, Count of Toulouse, were disunited, even warring amongst themselves. The Byzantine Emperor Alexius distrusted them all, and was trying hard to prevent them from obtaining permanent possession of cities taken back from the Saljúqs in Asia Minor, towns such as Nicaea and Iconium.[9] The rulers of Muslim principalities were also at loggerheads, one with the other, and their ranks had fallen into disarray. When the Crusaders were preparing to march on Nicaea, the Saljúq, Qílích-Arslán I (reigned 1092–1107) went away to fight Amír Ghází Gumushtigín (reigned 1084–1134), the Dánishmindid Prince of Eastern Anatolia. Another Saljúqid, Tutush, the brother of Malik-Sháh, held Aleppo and Damascus, and had grave problems of his own to contend with. But in the first days of July news reached the Crusaders that Egypt had sent a force to fight them. Thus time was precious.

A tight ring was thrown around Jerusalem with siege towers and mangonels, and the night of July 13th to 14th was chosen for a concerted attack to reduce the defences of the Holy City. The battle that ensued was truly desperate. The assailants sustained enormous losses, and the defenders, at first, stood their ground well. Let the able pen of Sir Steven Runciman picture Jerusalem in mid-July 1099:

'. . . By the evening of the 14th Raymond's men had succeeded in wheeling their tower over the ditch against the wall. But the defence was fierce; for it seems that Iftikhar himself commanded in this sector. Raymond could not establish a foothold on the wall itself. Next morning Godfrey's tower closed in on the north wall, close to the present Gate of Flowers. Godfrey and his brother, Eustace of Boulogne, commanded from the upper storey. About midday they succeeded in making a bridge from the tower to the

[5] Elected ruler of Jerusalem, after its fall, he assumed the title *Advocatus Sancti Sepulchri*: the Dedicated Defender of the Holy Sepulchre. He died on 18 July 1100.

[6] Prince of Antioch.

[7] Prince of Galilee, Regent of Antioch.

[8] Count of Edessa, who succeeded Godfrey de Bouillon as King of Jerusalem; he was known as King Baldwin I.

[9] Qúníyah, the modern Konya.

top of the wall; and two Flemish knights, Litold and Gilbert of Tournai, led the pick of the Lotharingian army across, followed soon by Godfrey himself. Once a sector of the wall was captured, scaling ladders enabled many more of the assailants to climb into the city. While Godfrey remained on the wall encouraging the newcomers and sending men to open the Gate of the Column to the main forces of the Crusade, Tancred and his men, who had been close behind the Lorrainers, penetrated deep into the city streets. The Moslems, seeing their defences broken, fled towards the Haram es-Sherif,[10] the Temple area, where the Dome of the Rock and the Mosque of al-Aqṣá stood, intending to use the latter as their last fortress. But they had no time to put it into a state of defence. As they crowded in and up on the roof, Tancred was upon them. Hastily they surrendered to him, promising a heavy ransom, and took his banner to display it over the mosque. He had already desecrated and pillaged the Dome of the Rock. Meanwhile the inhabitants of the city fled back in confusion towards the southern quarters, where Iftikhar was still holding out against Raymond. Early in the afternoon he realized that all was lost. He withdrew into the Tower of David, which he offered to hand over to Raymond with a great sum of treasure in return for his life and the lives of his bodyguard. Raymond accepted the terms and occupied the Tower. Iftikhar and his men were safely escorted out of the city and permitted to join the Moslem garrison of Ascalon.

'They were the only Moslems in Jerusalem to save their lives. The Crusaders, maddened by so great a victory after such suffering, rushed through the streets and into the houses and mosques killing all that they met, men, women and children alike. All that afternoon and all through the night the massacre continued. Tancred's banner was no protection to the refugees in the mosque of al-Aqsa. Early next morning a band of Crusaders forced an entry into the mosque and slew everyone. When Raymond of Aguilers later that morning went to visit the Temple area he had to pick his way through corpses and blood that reached up to his knees.

'The Jews of Jerusalem fled in a body to their chief synagogue. But they were held to have aided the Moslems; and no mercy was shown to them. The building was set on fire and they were all burnt within.

'The massacre at Jerusalem profoundly impressed all the world.

[10] Ḥaram ash-Sharíf (The Sacred or Noble Sanctuary).

No one can say how many victims it involved; but it emptied Jerusalem of its Moslem and Jewish inhabitants. Many even of the Christians were horrified by what had been done; and amongst the Moslems, who had been ready hitherto to accept the Franks as another factor in the tangled politics of the time, there was henceforward a clear determination that the Franks must be driven out. It was this bloodthirsty proof of Christian fanaticism that recreated the fanaticism of Islam. When, later, wiser Latins in the East sought to find some basis on which Christian and Moslem could work together, the memory of the massacre stood always in their way.'[11]

The Fáṭimid power was now on the wane. For another half century the Ismá'ílí caliphs of Cairo exercised varying degrees of authority, but in the meantime their viziers were becoming stronger and more powerful. And whilst the Crusaders, in the opening years of the twelfth century, were consolidating their position, conquering more cities in the realm of Islám, Muslim principalities, in their neighbourhood, were unstable, until the Zangids of Mosul appeared on the scene. Haifa fell to Tancred and Daimbert of Pisa in July 1100. In the same year Caesarea was conquered. 'Akká (Acre)[12] fell to King Baldwin in 1104 and Beirut in 1110. Tripoli had gone to the Franks the previous year, after a long siege. Count Raymond of Saint-Gilles (whom Arabs call Sanjil, also Ibn-Sanjil), one of the most assiduous and most ambitious leaders of the Crusaders, who instituted the siege, did not live to witness the fulfilment of his cherished wish. Two Saljúq brothers, Riḍván and Duqáq, sons of Tutush, held Aleppo and Damascus, respectively. They were disunited and their conflicts led to the extinction of Saljúqid power in Syria. The Saljúqs of Rúm (Asia Minor) were contained for the time being, powerless in the face of a resurgent Christendom. Emperor Alexius I, Comnenus, of Byzantium, was particularly vigilant and concerned, trying to wrest as much as possible, both from the Muslims and from the Crusaders. In the year 1117, there were two eclipses of the moon: one in June and one in December, and on the sixteenth of December the aurora borealis was seen in Palestine. It was said that these omens in the skies foreshadowed the deaths of rulers. True enough, many of them died in the following year, among them: Pope

[11] *A History of the Crusades*, vol. I, pp. 285–7 (Penguin edn.).

[12] Also St. Jean d'Acre.

Paschal II, of Ravenna (January 21st); King Baldwin I (April 2nd); Sulṭán Muḥammad, the Saljúqid monarch of Írán (April 5th); al-Mustaẓhir, the 'Abbásid Caliph (August 6th); the Emperor Alexius (August 15th). The weakened state of the Saljúqs, and the rise of new principalities in places as far apart as Kh̲árazm, Fárs, Ád̲h̲arbáyján and Mosul, all under potentates of Turkish origin, provided a new lease of life for the 'Abbásid power in Bag̲h̲dád, short-lived though it was. Sulṭán Sanjar (reigned 1118–57), the youngest son of Malik-S̲h̲áh, revived, for a while, the moribund kingdom of the Saljúqids in Írán; but in the end he met total disaster, by falling into the hands of the barbarous G̲h̲uzz Turkamáns, and spent four years in bondage. On the ruins of the Saljúq domains the K̲h̲árazms̲h̲áhs of Transoxania built another kingdom which comprised a large section of the Íránian plateau, as well as parts of northern India: it flourished until C̲h̲ingíz and his Mongol hordes swept over it and destroyed all.

In the western stretches of the realm of Islám, the rise of the Zangids posed, for the first time, a serious threat to the Crusaders, who had initially carried all before them. 'Imádi'd-Dín Zangí was appointed Governor of Mosul, in the year 1127, by Sulṭán Maḥmúd II, the Saljúqid overlord of 'Iráq. He was also given the office of Atábig, guardian of the sons of the Sulṭán. These various Atábigs (or Atábaks) whom the later Saljúq rulers, in pursuit of their own internecine struggles, placed in high positions, eventually made themselves the masters, and carved out principalities from the domains of the Saljúqids. Such was the case in Mosul, in Fárs and in Ád̲h̲arbáyján. 'Imádi'd-Dín in Mosul soon became a power to be reckoned with. He extended the area under his control, captured Aleppo and waged war against both the Byzantines and the Franks. In 1144 he took away Edessa (ar-Ruhá) from Count Jocelyn II. The loss of Edessa led to the Second Crusade at the head of which marched Louis VII of France and Conrad III of Germany. Damascus was invested but could not be taken by storm, and the Second Crusade petered out. 'Imádi'd-Dín Zangí was murdered in 1146, and his enlarged domains were partitioned between his sons. Sayfi'd-Dín G̲h̲ází kept the original principality and Núri'd-Dín Maḥmúd had the Syrian portion. Aleppo was his capital. Núri'd-Dín was a much more competent ruler than his father. He conquered Damascus, overran the whole of the Crusaders' principality of Edessa, and even made inroads into their principality of Antioch. Bohemond III of Antioch fell into his hands, and so did Raymond III of Tripoli. Raymond remained Núri'd-Dín's prisoner for nine years. But both these Frankish rulers, being heavily ransomed, were eventually freed.

Núri'd-Dín had in his service a Kurdish warrior named Shírkúh, who, encouraged by his master, turned his attention to Egypt, where the Fáṭimid Caliphate was in its death throes. In 1169, Shírkúh, having gained notable victories both on the field of battle and in the field of diplomacy, was appointed vizier to the weak Fáṭimid Caliph, al-'Áḍid (reigned 1160–71). The previous vizier, Shávar, had made an alliance against Shírkúh with King Amalric of Jerusalem, the successor of King Baldwin III (reigned 1131–62). The Kurdish contestant won, but died the same year. His nephew, al-Malik an-Náṣir[13] Ṣaláḥi'd-Dín (Saladin), son of Ayyúb, took his uncle's place. In less than two years, Saladin brought the Fáṭimid rule to its end, and restored Egypt to Sunní orthodoxy and allegiance to the 'Abbásids of Baghdád. Kurds had always been staunch Sunnís, and few amongst them had ever shown any sympathy for the Shí'ite cause. Thus in 1171 one of the most liberal and enlightened régimes that the realm of Islám had ever known passed into limbo.

In 1174 both the redoubtable Núri'd-Dín Maḥmúd and King Amalric died. Whereupon Saladin declared Egypt independent of the Zangids and set about to deprive them of Syria. He needed control over Syria in order to destroy the Crusader's kingdom of Jerusalem, which, next to the total overthrow of the Fáṭimid heterodoxy, had been his objective. And so he set about to dispossess Núri'd-Dín's eleven-year-old son, Ismá'íl, of his patrimony. Ismá'íl died in 1181. During this period of Ayyúbid entrenchment in Syria, Túrán-Sháh, a brother of Saladin, overran Yemen (Yaman) and Saladin's writ was extended to the twin holy cities of Arabia. Before long his domains became contiguous with the borders of Írán. However, in the course of the twelfth century, a new force, potent and effective, though operating from a very narrow base, had made its presence thoroughly felt in Syria and its environs. This force was the outstretched arm of the Ismá'ílís of Alamút, who had gained a small, but well-defended

[13] This title signifies the monarch who dispenses victory.

territory in the heart of the mountains of northern Syria. Muslims and Franks alike had experienced the impact of that force. Not only had the Fáṭimid Caliph, al-Amír, died by the dagger of an Ismá'ílí in 1130; Raymond II of Tripoli had suffered the same fate in 1152. The life of Núri'd-Dín was attempted once, and that of Saladin twice. Saladin, therefore, decided to extirpate the heretics with one blow. Rá<u>sh</u>idi'd-Dín Sinán, who had earned the sobriquet of the 'Old Man of the Mountain' (<u>Sh</u>ay<u>kh</u>-al-Jabal), found himself, in 1176, besieged at his stronghold of Maṣyád by Saladin's army. Sinán had succeeded in throwing off the tutelage of the masters of Alamút and could, on his own choosing, come to terms with Saladin. He solemnly promised the Ayyúbid Sulṭán not to cross his path again, a promise which he kept; and Saladin raised the siege.

King Baldwin IV of Jerusalem, who had succeeded his father at the age of thirteen, was very brave and courageous, but he suffered from leprosy and the ravages of that dreaded disease were increasingly disabling him. As late as November 1177 he had inflicted a severe defeat on Saladin, in the neighbourhood of Ramlih, which had sent the Ayyúbid monarch fleeing into Egypt. Six years later, Baldwin's condition had sadly deteriorated. His physical miseries apart, his mother, his sister Sibylla, and Guy of Lusignan, Sibylla's husband (freshly arrived from Europe), made his life even harder to bear. Disorders encompassed the bedridden king. Nearly totally blind, hands and feet useless and rotting, in the last years of his life Baldwin was plagued by rank disobedience as well, almost amounting to rebellion. Guy, whom he had dismissed from his side, sat defiantly at Ascalon. The King had a treaty with Saladin, a two-year truce, concluded in May 1180. The treacherous conduct of Reynald of Châtillon, Prince of Antioch and Lord of Oultrejourdain (the area beyond the Dead Sea and the river Jordan, with its capital at Karak), led to the breakdown of the truce. Reynald was a man who had no regard for any pact, treaty, or promise. He raided whenever and wherever he could, and even entertained plans for assaults on Mecca and Medina. His acts of blatant piracy in the Red Sea were numerous. Muslim trading vessels, rich with merchandise, fell to him, and a pilgrim-ship with all its inmates went down before his onslaught. Saladin took a solemn oath to slay him with his own hands.

On 11 May 1182, Saladin marched out of Egypt for the last

time. As a bystander foretold, he would never return to the country which had given him the substance of his power. Saladin was not yet ready, however, to take the kingdom of Jerusalem by storm. Christian ranks were disunited, but so were the Muslim ranks, and each side had allies amongst the ranks of their opponents. Aleppo was still to be conquered, and King Baldwin could still take the field. He even attempted the capture of Damascus at the close of the year 1182. But soon Baldwin could no longer rise from his bed and died in March 1185, no more than twenty-four years old, having named his nephew, a mere child, to succeed him. Count Raymond of Tripoli, although reluctant at first, had accepted the regency. However, the eight-year-old Baldwin V died in 'Akká, in August 1186. Thus the kingdom of Jerusalem came at last to Guy of Lusignan, a foolish, vainglorious man. During those few years Saladin had consolidated his position considerably in Syria and its neighbourhood. He had won Aleppo from the Zangid, 'Imádi'd-Dín, and overawed other potentates, Muslim and Christian alike. Both Bohemond III of Antioch and Raymond III of Tripoli reaffirmed the truce with Saladin, and King Guy accepted it. Once again it was Reynald of Châtillon who broke the truce.

Saladin was now ready to take the kingdom of Jerusalem by storm. A few miles from Tiberias and the Sea of Galilee lie the heights known as the Horns of Ḥaṭṭín or Ḥiṭṭín. Miscalculation and a desire to save Tiberias brought King Guy and his army onto those heights. On 3 July 1187 they bivouacked for the night, unable to go further. But no water could be found nor was there protection from the intense heat. Below them Saladin kept watch. His men had shade, water and comfort, while the Christians were thirsty, weary and exposed. When Saladin closed in on July 4th few of them escaped. The King, his princes, barons, knights and troopers were all made captive. Reynald was amongst them and Saladin, after recounting to Reynald all his misdeeds, with one stroke of his sword decapitated the Lord of Oultrejourdain to fulfil his oath. King Guy, on the other hand, was treated with respect, for one king does not slay another, Saladin told him. The next day Tiberias fell, 'Akká opened its gates on July 10th, and Jerusalem capitulated on October 2nd. Saladin proved most generous at the hour of his supreme victory. He freed King Guy, the princes, barons and knights (save the

Templars and the Hospitallers[14]), together with thousands of other captives. The Emperor Isaac Angelus of Byzantium sent a deputation to congratulate Saladin, and to ask that the Church of the Holy Sepulchre be returned to the care and the rites of the Greek Orthodox Church. Saladin complied with the wish of the Emperor. Not only did he give Christians their liberties; Jews were encouraged by him to go back to Jerusalem (after the lapse of nearly a century) and settle there.

The news of the loss of Jerusalem jolted Europe to action and the Third Crusade (1189–92) was set afoot. Warring kings and princes buried their hatchets, for the time being, and marched eastwards. Frederick Barbarossa of Germany was in the vanguard, but was drowned while crossing a river in Cilicia, when the greater number of his soldiery gave up and retraced their steps to Europe. Then came Richard Coeur-de-Lion of England and Philip Augustus of France, who were deadly enemies. Richard scored a great success at the very start, by conquering Cyprus for Christendom before setting foot in the Holy Land.

In the meantime, Saladin had systematically advanced to reduce one Frankish stronghold after another; from Lá<u>dh</u>iqíyyah (Laodicea, Latakia) in the north to Ṣafad and Karak in the south, he swept over them all. By the end of 1189, all that remained to the soldiers of the Cross were (apart from isolated castles and a few minor towns) Tyre, Tripoli and Antioch. Had Saladin gone straight from 'Akká to Tyre in 1187, he would have gained that glittering prize as well. But by the time he reached the walls of Tyre, much had happened. Conrad of Montferrat had arrived from Europe to take charge of the city's defences. Saladin caused the old Marquis, his father, to be brought from Damascus and shown to him, threatening his death if Tyre did not surrender. Conrad's sense of honour and his zeal for the cause proved the stronger: he refused to surrender Tyre. Saladin's sense of honour prompted him to match Conrad's magnificent stand: Conrad's aged father was not put to death. Saladin's second attempt to overcome the resistance in Tyre was disastrous. He lost ships, and his army, battle-weary and in need of rest and recuperation, had to be disbanded.

The Franks, reinforced with some of the men whom Barbarossa

[14] These were put to the sword at Ḥiṭṭín. Only the Grand Master of the Temple was spared.

had led, and strengthened by the arrival of the advance army of Philip Augustus, found a golden opportunity to wrest back 'Akká from Saladin. King Guy, who had promised on his release to go back to Europe, and never again to fight Saladin, appeared at the head of the investing forces. He was joined by Richard of England, of whom it has been said: '. . . He was a bad son, a bad husband and a bad king, but a gallant and splendid soldier';[15] both chivalrous and romantic, he entertained notions of marriages that would bind his House to the House of Saladin. He and Saladin exchanged gifts but no meeting ever took place between them. The siege of 'Akká was long and hard. The Christians found it impossible to break through its defences, while Saladin was unable to give substantial aid to the besieged Muslims. The siege lasted from 27 August 1189 to 12 July 1191. At last the brave defenders of 'Akká had to surrender. Although gravely shaken, Saladin would not repudiate the pledge given on his behalf by the garrison of 'Akká. There were further battles and skirmishes along the coast, during which Jaffa was taken and re-taken, but it was obvious that the Third Crusade, having achieved the establishment of yet another Frankish kingdom in the Holy Land (destined to last for a century), was already a spent force. Fresh quarrels had broken out among its protagonists. Philip Augustus abandoned his post in the fight for the Cross—a deed which amounted to high treason in Richard's eyes—and promising Richard not to encroach on his possessions, went back to France. Once there he promptly ignored his promise.

The English king himself had been too long absent from his kingdom and had pressing problems that required his early return. Still entertaining his romantic notions he knighted a son of al-Malik-al-'Ádil, a brother of Saladin. Then Conrad of Montferrat was assassinated in 'Akká, in all probability on the direct orders of Sinán, the Old Man of the Mountain. Guy of Lusignan who coveted the kingship of 'Akká was denied it; instead, Henry of Champagne, nephew of both Richard and the King of France, became the ruler of the new kingdom. Richard made arrangements that Cyprus might go to Guy, the ex-king of Jerusalem, as a consolation prize; Guy was at last out of the Holy Land, and happy. After protracted negotiations a peace treaty was signed between Richard and Saladin, in September 1192. Cities on the

[15] Runciman, ibid., vol. III, p. 75. (Cased edn.)

coast, from ʻAkká to Jaffa, were all that the Third Crusade had gained for the Cross. Richard sailed away, only to be shipwrecked and to fall captive to Duke Leopold of Austria, who hated him and considered him guilty of the murder of Conrad. Saladin, who had only a few months to live, would not now turn over the Church of the Holy Sepulchre to the Greek rite. He himself would decide the apportionment between the Latins, the Greeks and other Christians, and not let any sect assume a dominant position. After decades of warfare Saladin was greatly wearied, but before going to Damascus which was to be his capital, he journeyed from Jerusalem to Beirut, to reach a settlement with Bohemond. Then he went to Damascus, and there died on 3 March 1193, at the age of fifty-four. His mausoleum stands there today, awesome and revered. Al-Malikan-Náṣir Ṣaláḥi'd-Dín was one of the greatest leaders of men in the whole range of the history of mankind. His nobility of character and his generosity were exemplary.

29

Islám at Bay

TIMÚJIN, the son of a petty Mongol chieftain, was a boy in his early teens when his father died. For many years he had to fight to secure his patrimony; but he achieved even more, for he united the tribes of Mongolia under his own rule. In the year 1206, by general acclaim, Timújin took the name and title of Chingíz Khán.[1] Next, he set about extending his empire eastwards, and eventually conquered northern China.[2] By then (1215), he was nearly fifty years of age—he was born in 1167—and had been campaigning since the age of thirteen. To his west lay the empire of the kings of Khárazm—the Khárazmsháhs.

At one time in Transoxania, the Qarákhaṭá'í or the Gúrkhhánívyih kingdom, together with the smaller principality of the Ál-i-Kháqán or the Ál-i-Afrásíyáb (based on Samarqand) formed buffer states which separated the territory of Chingíz Khán from the domains of the Khárazmsháhs. Their Turkish rulers were renowned for their justice and patronage of learning and poetry, but Sulṭán 'Alái'd-Dín Muḥammad, the Khárazmsháh, wantonly destroyed them. Thus his frontiers became contiguous with the frontiers of the Mongols.

Chingíz Khán apprised Sulṭán 'Alái'd-Dín Muḥammad of the fact that he had overrun China, and was now a mighty and powerful ruler; but he was weary of warfare and wanted to be at peace with his western neighbour. He hoped that trade between his people and those of Khárazm would flourish. Though somewhat riled that Chingíz Khán had addressed him as his son, 'Alái'd-Dín Muḥammad responded appropriately to this expression of

[1] Variously written in English as Jenghiz and Genghiz, it means the Perfect Warrior.

[2] The Chin Empire. The Sung Empire of southern China was overrun in 1279, during the reign of the famous Qubiláy Qá'án (Kubla Khan).

good will. However, when four Muslim traders from Mongolia arrived at Utrár, a frontier town, its avaricious governor, coveting their riches, accused them of espionage, threw them into prison, robbed them of their possessions and, to compound his felony, put them to death. Chingíz was naturally furious, but he kept calm and sent a deputation to the court of the Khárazmsháh to obtain redress. The arrogant Sulṭán Muḥammad responded stupidly and abominably by executing the head of the deputation and sending back the rest to Chingíz Khán with their beards shaved off. Chingíz moved quickly to avenge the blood of innocent people and the insult so grotesquely rendered to his own person. His Mongol hordes descended mercilessly upon the realm of Islám.

The first to taste the wrath of Chingíz was the governor of Utrár, who had murdered harmless merchants for the love of silver and gold. Molten silver was poured down his throat.

The distinguished Arab historian, Ibn-al-Athír (d. 1234), was a witness to the horrors of the Mongol invasion, but when writing his great history, *al-Kámil at-Tawáríkh*, he could not, at first, bring himself to make any record of it.

'For years,' he wrote, 'I drew back from mentioning this event. So horrendous did I find it that I could not mention it. Whenever I took a step forward to deal with it, the sheer horror made me take another step backwards . . . How I wish that I had never been born, or that prior to the descent of this calamity I had been taken away from this world—no trace left of me. Notwithstanding, my friends persuaded me not to leave this episode unrecorded. I hesitated, but then I saw that no good purpose would be served by omitting it. Let me say, then, that what is entailed is describing the most dire of all disasters, the most catastrophic of all calamities which befell all men and Muslims in particular. Should anyone claim that since the day God created man to the present time this world had never witnessed a tragedy of such dimension, he would have spoken the very word of truth.'

Such was the reaction of a level-headed historian to the enormity of the misfortune which overtook the realm of Islám.

Yáqút al-Ḥamawí (d. A.D. 1220), the greatest of Muslim geographers, who was of Greek parentage, was engulfed by the onrush of the Mongols and narrowly escaped with his life from the city of Marv. According to Ibn-al-Athír, 700,000 perished in this one city, while 'Aṭá-Malik-i-Juvayní[3] (d. 1283) put the figure at 1,300,000. Yáqút endured much hardship before he reached the city of Mosul. There he wrote these lines to the vizier[4] of the ruler of Aleppo:

'Great was the number of its pious men who outshone their peers in their nobility. Numerous were its jurists whose deeds shielded the integrity of Islám. Evidence of its science and learning is inscribed on the scroll of time. The excellence of its authors shed glory on religion and upon the world. Their works have reached far-away lands. None was there of sound judgement and sound knowledge who did not but rise like unto the sun from that region of Khurásán. And none was there, worthy and true, who would not but choose that horizon for the setting of his star, a year to dwell there and be counted amongst its denizens. Their children were as stalwart men, their youth heroes, their aged the élite of the world. The proofs of their accomplishments and the evidences of their glory exist for all to see. Then there is every reason to wonder why the king, who ruled over such cities and towns, turned his back on them and left them to their fate.'

Indeed the behaviour of 'Aláí'd-Dín Muḥammad-i-Khárazm-sháh was inexplicable. He insulted Chingíz Khán in the grossest manner, provoking the Mongol ruler to the white-heat of fury; and then he not only neglected the defence of the region that lay in the path of the Mongol hordes, but ran away—from town to town, from city to city—until, abandoned by his officers and officials, he took refuge in a small island in the Caspian Sea, leaving a disrupted empire that had once extended from the Ural Mountains to the Persian Gulf and from the Indus to the Euphrates, to his brave, courageous, but ill-starred son, Jaláli'd-Dín. Yáqút may have been carried away by his rhetoric, his grief, and the recollection of his own past and privations. But, in truth, that area of the East which comprised Transoxania, Khurásán and the present day Afghánistán, was a region teeming with populous, prosperous and renowned cities, such as Samarqand, Bukhárá, Gurganj, Ṭús, Níshápúr, Tirmidh, Marv, Balkh, Bámyán and Hirát. It was there that modern Persian was formed. From that

[3] Author of *Táríkh-i-Jahángushá*, translated by John Andrew Boyle under the title of *The History of the World-Conqueror*. 'Atá-Malik-i-Juvayní was a high official in the service of the descendants of Chingíz Khán.

[4] Jamáli'd-Dín 'Alí ash-Shaybání al-Qiftí.

region arose such men as Abú-Muslim, Firdawsí, Abú-'Alí Ibn Síná (Avicenna), Fárábí, Khayyám, Ghazálí, Faríd'id-Dín-i-'Aṭṭár and Jaláli'd-Dín-i-Rúmí.

Chingíz destroyed those flourishing cities and, literally, millions lost their lives. The entire population of Hirát was put to the sword in a massacre which lasted for several days. The scale of the havoc wrought by the Mongols in the Eastern Marches of the realm of Islám can be measured by the story told of a man who found a hiding-place in a minaret, and, when the invaders left a wrecked city behind them, all he could utter was: 'They came, they killed, they burned, they went'. Jaláli'd-Dín, the last of the Khárazmsháhs, had his back to the Indus when Chingíz, at the head of his army, closed upon him. His mother and his wife, dreading captivity, pleaded to be thrown into the river. At first Jaláli'd-Dín flinched from such a dire deed, but consented at the last moment. And then, riding his third horse (two others had been killed under him), he leapt into the waters of the fast-flowing river from a considerable height, and gained the safety of the other shore. Chingíz watched this daring feat with amazement and admiration, and stopped his men from pursuing the last of the Khárazmsháhs. But he did not spare the young children of Jaláli'd-Dín and even an infant was murdered.

In India, Jaláli'd-Dín had to face the opposition of both the ruler of Sind and Shamsi'd-Dín Iltamish of Delhi. He subdued them, then turning to the Íránian plateau, held off the Mongols for a while, but not before they had flattened Ray and Hamadán. The ancient city of Ray (Rhages) was dealt such a savage blow that it disappeared for ever from the map.[5] Surprisingly, an 'Abbásid force also stemmed the tide on the borders of 'Iráq. Meanwhile, Chingíz himself had returned to Mongolia, where he died in 1227. His army had already broken the resistance of the Russians, though it had not pressed home its advantage. The ill-fated Jaláli'd-Dín's temporary successes brought fresh hordes from Mongolia, who ranged as far as the Caucasus and invaded Georgia. Jaláli'd-Dín, fleeing before them, as well as from the Ayyúbids, his fellow-Muslims, met his death on a solitary mountain-top, at the hands of a Kurd who nursed a grudge against him. Apart from the province of Fárs, the Íránian plateau passed

[5] In recent years a township, adjacent to Ṭihrán, has been named Shahr-i-Ray. It is not the ancient city.

firmly under the rule of the heirs of Chingíz Khán. Although the 'Abbásid preserve of 'Iráq held out for a while longer, Islám was at bay.

The Franks were also on the move, regaining Jerusalem not as the consequence of a pitched battle, but as the result of the fratricidal contests of the Ayyúbids. Al-Malik al-Kámil Náṣiri'd-Dín (reigned 1218–38), the ruler of Egypt, ceded to Emperor Frederick II Jerusalem, Bethlehem and a corridor linking them with the sea. Just at that time (1229), the Hohenstaufen Emperor was excommunicated by Pope Gregory IX, ostensibly because he had not embarked on a crusade at an earlier date. The Muslims were pained and horrified, the Christians embarrassed and uneasy. To hand over Jerusalem was rank treachery in the eyes of Muslims, although they had retained full possession of the Ḥaram ash-Sharíf.[6] As for the Christians, that an excommunicated Emperor should gain mastery over the Holy City was quite inadmissible, although many of them owed no allegiance to the Pope. But so confused and contradictory were the affairs and the behaviour of the Muslim Ayyúbid and Saljúqid potentates, and the Franks of Outremer and other Christians of the East, that the quiet deal between the Sulṭán of Egypt and the Hohenstaufen Emperor did not seem entirely out of place. Before long Al-Malik al-Kámil died, Emperor Frederick was forgiven and restored to favour, and new patterns emerged. Strange cross-currents, futile alliances and ruinous counter-alliances, battles between Muslim and Muslim, Christian and Christian, proceeded apace until the year 1244, when the Khárazmian army, left leaderless by the cruel death of Sulṭán Jalálí'd-Dín, and roaming over the vast stretches of northern 'Iráq and northern Syria, plundering and pillaging as they went, raced towards Damascus. Finding it hard to reduce, they wheeled to overrun Tiberias and Nablus, and storm Jerusalem, where the Christians received no mercy at their hands. These soldiers, being desperate, put their loyalty at the disposal of the highest bidder. When they found al-Malik aṣ-Ṣáliḥ Najmi'd-Dín (reigned 1240–49), the Ayyúbid ruler of Egypt, ungrateful for services they had rendered him and refusing them entry into Egypt, they changed sides in assaults on Damascus, and were overwhelmed in the vicinity of Ba'labakk (Baalbek) by al-Malik aṣ-Ṣáliḥ's army, which had been sent to relieve pressure on the

[6] See p. 205n.

besieged city. They deserved a better fate, for they had wrested Jerusalem back from the Franks, who never again possessed the Holy City. Instead, they were denied a home and were decimated, and their remnants retreated eastwards to enrol under the banner of the Mongols. It was a sad end for a group of men once led by the intrepid Jaláli'd-Dín.

The Mongols had had to call a halt while arrangements regarding the heritage of Chingíz Khán were discussed and settled. For the succession Chingíz had passed over his eldest son, Juchí,[7] who actually predeceased him, and his second son, Chaghatáy,[8] naming his third son, Uktáy,[9] to succeed to the overlordship of his empire, which extended from the waters of the Pacific to the headwaters of the Tigris, from the Indian Ocean to the Arctic. At the Assembly (Quriltáy) of the Mongol nobles, held conveniently soon, Uktáy offered to step down in favour of his elder brother, but the Quriltáy decided that Chingíz Khán's wishes should be honoured. Brothers of Chingíz, his other sons and the sons of Juchí had all had territories and principalities allotted to them, and they, one and all, pledged obedience to the overlord, who was now hailed as the Qá'án. Uktáy Qá'án proved to be a just and benevolent ruler, who sought to repair the grievous damage which his father had inflicted on a vast area of the globe. Following his death in 1241, there was an interregnum of five years before his son Gúyúk (Güyük) was elevated to his high office. Gúyúk reigned for only three years and, on his death in 1249, another period of regency intervened before a decision was reached for the overlordship to pass to the line of Tuluy, the fourth son of Chingíz Khán. Mingú (Möngke) Qá'án, the son of Tuluy, was also a remarkable ruler. He realized as his grandfather had, when he apportioned various territories to the members of his family, that such a vast empire as that of the Mongols could not be ruled directly from a central point, although there must be a powerful overlord to whom the separate administrations would bear ultimate allegiance. At the same Assembly which raised him to overlordship, Mingú commissioned his brothers Húlágú (Hülegü) and Qubiláy[10] (who eventually succeeded him in 1260) to com-

[7] Variants: Jochi, Tushi, Júji.
[8] Variants: Chaghatai, Jagatai.
[9] Variants: Ögetei, Ogodai, Ögedei, Ögedey.
[10] Kubla Khan of Coleridge's famous poem.

plete the conquest of Írán and China and consolidate Mongol power therein. Húlágú went to Írán and Qubiláy to China.

In Írán the hold of the Mongols had somehow slackened. Húlágú was particularly instructed to destroy the power of the Ismá'ílís[11] and to bring the 'Abbásid caliph in Baghdád to heel. But on leading a considerable force into Írán, he found conditions considerably altered. The descendants of Chingíz Khán had become aware and enamoured of the gifts of civilization. Qaraqurum, in Mongolia, which three or four decades earlier had been an unknown, isolated spot for tribes to congregate, had now become an imperial seat, attracting men of science and learning, poets and artists of many kinds.

Húlágú wrote to the rulers of principalities and emirates, such as the Zangids of Fárs, who had preserved their independence, that he intended to attack the strongholds of the Ismá'ílís, and he asked for their co-operation. Atábak Abú-Bakr of Fárs sent Sa'd, his son and successor, to meet the Mongol Prince, offering him homage and support. Submission and offers of support came also from Sulṭán 'Izzi'd-Dín and Sulṭán Rukni'd-Dín, the rival Muslim potentates of Anatolia. Húlágú moved by easy stages. Before he reached Khurásán, Kit-Búqá, his celebrated Nestorian general, was already in the field. Gird-Kúh, the famous Ismá'ílí stronghold in Qúhistán (Kúhistán) successfully resisted the assault of the Mongols, but the city of Tún in Khurásán was reduced and its inhabitants slaughtered. It was now the summer of 1256 and Húlágú had opened negotiations with the Ismá'ílí 'Grand Master', Rukni'd-Dín Khur-Sháh. The Ismá'ílí leader was expected to deliver himself to the mercy of the Mongols. In his impregnable castle of Maymún-Diz, Khur-Sháh had with him a number of learned men, honoured prisoners who were not Ismá'ílís. The most prominent of them was Khájih Naṣíri'd-Dín-i-Ṭúsí, a philosopher and scientist, of no mean accomplishment, and of the Ithná-'Asharíyyah (Twelver) affiliation. These men advised Khur-Sháh to send one of his brothers to the encampment of Húlágú, in token of his submission. Accordingly Shahansháh was sent; Húlágú received him with proper honours, but was far from satisfied. His prime purpose was to obtain the dismantling of all the Ismá'ílí fortifications. Rukni'd-Dín Khur-Sháh was

[11] Ismá'ílis had been responsible for the murder of Chaghatáy, the second son of Chingíz.

well aware of the might of the Mongols. He could not possibly meet them in the open, nor could he withstand a long siege. Yet he much feared that once his castles and battlements had been made inoperative, his future and the future of his people would be at stake. Nor was he wrong in his assumptions. So, he began to temporize. While fervent in expressing his submission to the great overlord in Qaraqurum, he asked for time. Could he have a year's grace before pulling down the fortifications of Maymún-Diz? Would Húlágú Khán agree to leave the castles of Alamút and Lanbasar untouched? Húlágú now demanded that Khur-Sháh come before him in person. Meanwhile, he was relentlessly drawing nearer to Maymún-Diz. The castle of Sháhdíz had to be reduced and Maymún-Diz encircled and attacked before Khur-Sháh yielded to the inevitable, and, receiving assurances that he and his family would be safe, abandoned his strongly-fortified castle. The extinction of Ismá'ílí power took place in November 1256.

Húlágú kept his promise, because as long as Rukni'd-Dín Khur-Sháh was his highly honoured and revered prisoner, he could (and did) use him to persuade all the Ismá'ílí castles to surrender. Alamút and Lanbasar put up some resistance but were soon overwhelmed. 'Aṭá-Malik-i-Juvayní managed to save part of the great library and some of the astronomical instruments that were lodged in Alamút. As soon as the Ismá'ílí strongholds were overthrown Húlágú allowed Rukni'd-Dín Khur-Sháh to go to Qaraqurum, but it was a long and futile journey, for the overlord had no use for him. Somewhere he was put to death, as was every member of his family and every Ismá'ílí held by the Mongols. Such was the tragic end of the amazing handiwork of the dedicated and single-minded Ḥasan-i-Ṣabbáḥ.

Flushed with victory, Húlágú now turned his attention to the next objective set by his brother: the overthrow of the 'Abbásids. Even before Lanbasar had fallen Húlágú was moving westwards. He had as a close personal adviser the same Naṣíri'd-Dín-i-Ṭúsí whom the Ismá'ílís had forcibly detained in order to benefit by his vast store of knowledge. Naṣíri'd-Dín, an Ithná-'Asharí (Twelver) Shí'ah, who could have no love either for the Ismá'ílís or the Sunní caliph, brushed aside with sound reasoning and faultless logic all the forebodings about attacking Baghdád and dispensing with the 'Abbásid caliphate. Húlágú had been told that such action would result in natural and supernatural calamities. To Húlágú's query Naṣíri'd-Dín replied simply that nothing would happen except that he, Húlágú, would replace the Caliph as the ruler of Baghdád.

Al-Musta'ṣim-Bi'lláh, the thirty-seventh caliph of the House of 'Abbás, had been elevated to the Caliphate in 1242. He was weak and vacillating, unlike his great-grandfather, the formidable an-Náṣir-li-Díni'lláh (1180–1225), who had, in the course of his long tenure of the Caliphate, restored some semblance of authority to the institution which he represented and had added considerably to the material power of his state. When Húlágú requested support in his campaign against the Ismá'ílís, Musta'ṣim failed to respond, although he should have welcomed the move; and to Húlágú's summons he turned a deaf ear, replying in contemptuous terms. Húlágú hoped to play the same game with Musta'ṣim as he had with the last of the Ismá'ílí rulers: to lure him out of Baghdád. But Musta'ṣim seemed unimpressed, and once again counselled Húlágú to go back the way he had come. Even the news of the fall of Kirmánsháh and the massacre of its inhabitants, followed by the descent of the Mongols from the Íránian plateau onto the plains of 'Iráq, did not disconcert the Caliph. However, when his army was routed and had its back to land which was being inundated by the waters pouring through the dyke destroyed by the Mongols,[12] with Baghdád invested and under attack, Musta'ṣim found that he had no choice but to negotiate surrender terms. It is claimed that Musta'ṣim was beguiled and betrayed by his vizier, Ibn-al-Alqamí, who, like Naṣíri'd-Dín-i-Ṭúsí, was of the Ithná-'Asharí Shí'ah persuasion, and proof is provided by the fact that Húlágú gave him the same office he had held under Musta'ṣim. On 10 February 1258, Musta'ṣim and his three sons walked into the camp of Húlágú, who received them well. At Húlágú's bidding, the fallen Caliph sent word to the people of Baghdád to give up the struggle and come out of their barricades. They did so, only to find the Mongols waiting to cut them down. For seven days, Baghdád, the renowned city of Manṣúr, of Hárún and Ma'mún, was delivered to carnage and looting. Then Húlágú withdrew from the humbled and ravished Dár-as-Salám (the Abode of Peace) to a village on the road to

[12] The Mongols wrecked the irrigation system of 'Iráq which had remained intact for centuries.

Írán. There Musta'ṣim was put to death. The very thought of shedding the blood of the Caliph was horrendous to many in the service of the Íl-Khán,[13] although in the past caliphs had been murdered without ado. In any case, it is doubtful if Húlágú would have had any qualms in that respect. However, the manner of Musta'ṣim's death was itself horrific, for, to prevent shedding his blood he was put within the folds of a carpet and rolled and kicked until dead. No doubt a shudder went through the realm of Islám at the news. In far-away Shíráz, where Mongols had not yet set foot, the famed poet Sa'dí bewailed the fall of the House of 'Abbás. Heaven has every cause, he said, to rain tears of blood on the earth, and he called out to the Prophet not to delay until the Day of Resurrection, rather to rise up then to witness the calamity that had overtaken the world. Yet, Atábak Abú-Bakr, the Sulghurid, whose patronage the poet enjoyed and whose court he adorned, had to go posthaste to Marághih in Ádharbáyján,[14] to renew his pledge of submission, offer felicitations and express his delight at the brilliant success of the Mongol arms. And so did Sulṭán Rukni'd-Dín Qilich-Arslán IV, the Saljúqid ruler of Rúm (Anatolia), as well as Badri'd-Dín Lu'lu' of Mosul, then in his nineties, who had wrested power from the descendants of 'Imádi'd-Dín Zangí in 1222, and had loyally accepted the suzerainty of Húlágú Khán. Neither Abú-Bakr of Fárs or Badri'd-Dín of Mosul had long to live; the former died in 1260 and the latter the following year. Abú-Bakr's son, Sa'd, fell ill, while on his way home from Húlágú's camp, and died twelve days after his father. Sa'd's son, Muḥammad, a minor, fell from a roof and died. Saljúq-Sháh, a nephew of Atábak Abú-Bakr, proved to be a headstrong and incompetent ruler, arousing Húlágú's ire and, as a consequence, losing his throne and his life. The last of the Sulghurids was a daughter of Sa'd, married to a son of Húlágú. Thus the last independent principality in Írán passed into the possession of the Mongols. In Mosul, Ṣáliḥ, the son of Badri'd-Dín, also brought upon himself the wrath of Húlágú, and he too lost his life. Thus the whole of northern 'Iráq was added to the Mongol domains.

Although the conquest of Syria was a goal which Húlágú

[13] The title applied to Húlágú and his successors.

[14] Húlágú had chosen Marághih for his capital; there Naṣíri'd-Dín-i-Ṭúsí built for him an observatory which attained well-deserved fame.

achieved initially, very soon the whole enterprise turned to failure. When the Mongols overthrew the ‘Abbásids, Ayyúbids still ruled in Damascus and Aleppo, but in Egypt the Mamlúk Turks had treacherously murdered the Ayyúbid Túrán-Sh͟áh, bringing to an end the reign of the descendants of Saladin. In September 1259, Húlágú set out from Ád͟harbáyján for the west. As he and his general moved in the direction of Syria, famous cities such as Diyárbakr, Mayyáfáriqín, Ámid, Edessa, Naṣíbín and Ḥarrán fell to them. The Kurds were the chief sufferers in this steady advance of the Mongol army until Aleppo was reached. King Hethoum of Little Armenia (who had gone in person to Qaraqurum to offer homage) and his son-in-law, Bohemond VI of Antioch and Tripoli, joined Húlágú in besieging Aleppo. The city was taken within six days, followed by six days of rapine and slaughter. The Armenian king himself set fire to Aleppo's main mosque. Al-Malik an-Náṣir Ṣaláḥi'd-Dín Yúsuf escaped towards Egypt, but he was captured by the Mongols and Damascus surrendered without a battle. Carrying their advance as far as Gaza, the Mongols were poised to invade Egypt when news reached Húlágú that Uktáy Qá'án was dead. He decided to return immediately to Írán. Before turning back, Húlágú sent an envoy to Sayfi'd-Dín Qutuz, the Mamlúk ruler of Egypt, calling upon him to submit to Mongol suzerainty. Qutuz had murdered Aybak, the first of the Mamlúks, and seized the throne. Now, he put Húlágú's envoy to death. Whereas the Franks of Antioch and the Armenians had rallied to Húlágú and may even have encouraged him to invade Syria and restore Jerusalem to the Christians, the Franks of ‘Akká and other cities of the coast let the Mamlúk army pass by without hindrance and provided it with victuals. They were Latins and the Mongol commander, the renowned Kit-Búqá, was a Nestorian.[15] Furthermore, they knew of the arrogance and brutality of the Mongols and preferred Muslims to them. They were yet to learn of the brutality of the Mamlúks.

On 3 September 1260, the Mongol army was destroyed at ‘Ayn Jálút (the Pools of Goliath) near Nazareth. The brave Nestorian fought to the last, but was captured and beheaded. Rukni'd-Dín Baybars, the victorious Mamlúk general, now killed Qutuz, his own monarch, took his place and cleared Syria of the Mongols.

[15] Both the mother of Húlágú and the step-mother of Abáqá, Húlágú's son and successor, were ardent Nestorians.

Húlágú's return to Írán looks to have been pointless. If he had hoped to gain the overlordship, his brother Qubiláy had already secured that position and exercised it, having conquered the whole of southern China, no longer from Qaraqurum but from Khán-Báligh—the City of the Kháns (Peking). The great distance between his capital and western Asia contributed to the loosening of control over the descendants of Húlágú in Írán, who became independent and were known as the Íl-Kháns. Moreover, while the Mongols in western Asia embraced Islám, the Mongols in China and Mongolia itself became Buddhists. The descendants of 'Kubla Khan' in China ruled there until 1368 as the Yüan dynasty, Chinese for all intents and purposes. The Ming dynasty replaced them.

At Tabríz, Húlágú heard of the disaster that had overtaken his army at 'Ayn Jálút. He had just given the governorship of Damascus to the Ayyúbid al-Malik an-Náṣir, who had shown himself happy and contented to serve under the Mongols. Incensed and suspecting treachery, Húlágú sent a small force in pursuit of the Ayyúbid, now on his way to Syria. Al-Malik an-Náṣir and all his followers were killed. The only survivor of that party was the astronomer, Muḥíyyi'd-Dín al-Maghribí, who was spared because his science and accomplishment were highly valued. Húlágú made a second attempt to conquer Syria; that too ended in failure. The Mongols drove as far as Ḥimṣ, but Húlágú was not with his army which suffered a decisive defeat, on December 10th, at the hands of the Mamlúks. Thus the Mongols remained barred from Syria and their westward expansion into Islamic lands was definitely checked. The Franks, who had previously displayed benevolence towards the Mamlúks, soon began to reel under the hammer blows of Rukni'd-Dín Baybars and longed for relief from any quarter. Húlágú, however, had a more urgent problem on his hands than making a third attempt to invade Syria. He was threatened in the north, from the Caucasus, by the Golden Horde, whom the Muslim historians call Qipcháq.[16] Their ruler, Berke, was a cousin of Húlágú, a descendant of the eldest son of Chingíz Khán. Berke had become a Muslim, and it is claimed that Húlágú's attack on Baghdád and the death of Musta'ṣim aroused his hostility. On the other hand, there is also the fact that princes of the House of Jochi had been put to death in

[16] Eastern Mongols, from the valley of the Volga.

Írán. Whatever the reasons for this fratricidal struggle, Berke posed a serious menace. At first Húlágú achieved victory over the Golden Horde, but an army under the command of his son, Abáqá, sent to pursue the enemy, was routed by Berke himself, and Abáqá just managed to escape with his life. Sad and disheartened, Húlágú turned back to Tabríz. He died in February 1265, on the shores of Lake Urúmíyyih (now Riḍá'íyyih), not yet fifty years of age. The war with the Golden Horde continued into the reign of Abáqá, who had also to meet invasion on his north-eastern frontier by the descendants of Chaghatáy, the second son of Chingíz Khán.

Abáqá's reign (1265–82) was thus interspersed with warfare. Berke's death, not long after the death of Húlágú, brought the war with the Golden Horde to a close. The aggression from Transoxania was also eventually contained, but not before Bukhárá had been overrun and destroyed, a tragic fate for a renowned city which had suffered grievously, half a century before, at the hands of the great-grandfather of these contestants. Baráq of the House of Chaghatáy had inflicted a similar punishment on the city of Níshápúr, in Khurásán, which had also been totally devastated, decades before, by the armies of Chingíz.

The famous castle of Gird-Kúh opened its gates, in 1271, after a siege which had lasted eighteen years. This victory of Mongol arms was a minor affair, but it did mark the final liquidation of all Ismá'ílí power in Írán. The Saljúqs of Rúm had accepted (as we have already seen) the Mongol suzerainty, and preserved their independence, although there was a Mongol garrison stationed in Anatolia. Internal disturbances forced Kay-Káwús II, one of the two rival Saljúq sulṭáns, into exile. The other, Qilich-Arslán IV was sent to his death by the vizier, Mu'ínid-Dín-i-Parvánih. In collusion with the usurper, Baybars invaded Anatolia in 1277, massacred the Mongols and swiftly returned to Egypt. Incensed by the perfidy of the people of Rúm, Abáqá marched into Anatolia, put many to the sword, ordered the execution of Mu'íni'd-Dín-i-Parvánih (who was tried and found guilty), and would have entered Syria from the north but for the onset of winter. Abáqá's wish was to obtain support from the Franks and the Christian rulers of Europe to fight the Mamlúks, just as the Christians had hoped for Mongol support against these Muslims. His preparations for an attack on Syria were badly impeded by yet another excursion into his territories, on the part of his Chaghatáy cousins, this time from the south-east, in the region of Fárs and Kirmán. Having dealt with the marauders and despairing of any aid from the potentates of Europe, he committed a force of forty thousand men to the invasion of Syria, under the command of his young brother, Mangú-Tímúr, who had hardly any experience of generalship. Georgians and Armenians added their support. But, once again, the attempt to penetrate into Syria and to hold it failed. In October 1281, in the vicinity of Ḥimṣ, the Mongol army suffered a crushing defeat. The days of Outremer were numbered.

We have now to go back with the years to obtain a picture of the affairs of Outremer, the attitudes and the mentality of the Mongol conquerors, the tide of fortunes involved in abortive Crusades, the entanglements and divisions of Christian Europe, and to note how these factors contributed to the increase and consolidation of Mamlúk power, the enfeeblement of Christian endeavour, the failure to cement a working alliance between the Mongols and the Christians of the West, and finally to the liquidation of Outremer at the close of the thirteenth century.

30

Islám Ascendant

PROFESSOR PHILIP HITTI writes:

'Hard pressed between the mounted archers of the wild Mongols in the east and the mailed knights of the Crusaders on the west, Islam in the early part of the thirteenth century seemed for ever lost. How different was the situation in the last part of the same century! The last Crusader had by that time been driven into the sea. The seventh of the Īl-Khāns,[1] many of whom had been flirting with Christianity, had finally recognized Islam as the state religion—a dazzling victory for the faith of Muḥammad. Just as in the case of the Saljūqs, the religion of the Moslems had conquered where their arms had failed. Less than half a century after Hūlāgu's merciless attempt at the destruction of Islamic culture, his great-grandson Ghāzān, as a devout Moslem, was consecrating much time and energy to the revivification of that same culture.'[2]

When Saladin died in 1193 at the early age of fifty-four, the unity which he had forged betwixt the Muslims in western Asia and Egypt was shattered. He had too many scheming and foolish sons, who plotted and counter-plotted and, unlike their father who never broke his word, made promises and alliances, only to break them at a suitable moment. As Sir Steven Runciman remarks: '. . . the tragedy of medieval Islam was its lack of permanent institutions, to carry on authority after a leader's death. The Caliphate was the only institution to have an existence transcending that of its holders; and the Caliph was now politically impotent. Nor was Saladin Caliph. He was a Kurd of no great family who commanded the obedience of the Moslem world

[1] Gházán (1295–1304) embraced Islám and took the name Maḥmúd. His career is dealt with in the next chapter.

[2] *History of the Arabs*, p. 488.

only by the force of his personality.'[3] And now it was the personality of Saladin's brother, al-Malik al-'Ádil Sayfi'd-Dín (1200–18),[4] who held his heritage together. If the Ayyúbids had their squabbles, so did the Saljúqids of Rúm, the Franks of Outremer, and the Armenians of Cilicia. Matters were no better in Byzantium, where Emperor Isaac Angelus was deposed, blinded and thrown into prison, together with his son, young Alexius. A brother of Isaac, also named Alexius, took his place as Emperor Alexius III. In 1201, the deposed emperor's son escaped from prison and made his way to Europe, to the court of his brother-in-law, Duke Philip of Swabia.

In Europe, Pope Innocent III (1198–1216) was preaching yet another Crusade. As long as Henry VI, the Hohenstaufen emperor, son of Barbarossa, lived, Celestine III, Innocent's predecessor was chary of promoting a fourth Crusade, because he rightly feared that Henry would dominate it. Henry was on the way to becoming the most powerful potentate in Christendom, and that was not to the liking of Rome. He had already dispatched German troops to the Holy Land, whose presence added to the bewildering confusion of Outremer and its kaleidoscopic relations with the Ayyúbids and Saljúqids. The fact is that the Franks in the East were happy as they were, and did not welcome the arrival of large bands of knights and warriors from Europe.

Henry died in September 1197 at the age of thirty-two. On hearing of the Emperor's death the German Crusaders went home. They had, however, wrested Beirut from the control of a Muslim who was universally detested, and left behind a legacy: the institution of Teutonic Knights. This made a situation already complicated by the presence of Knights Templars and Knights Hospitallers even more complex and unpredictable. One constant factor was the mutual antipathy of these two orders. Although they remained loyal to the Latin Church, their alliances and partisanships were ever-changing. The Hospitallers were even in league with the Ismá'ílís of the Old Man of the Mountain. The Teutonic Knights, on the other hand, could always be counted upon to follow the lead of the Hohenstaufens, even if in opposition to Rome.

With the opening of the new century, the Pope's efforts at

[3] Runciman, *A History of the Crusades*, vol. III, pp. 78–9. (Cased edn.)
[4] He was called Safadin (Saphadin) by Europeans.

mounting a Crusade were beginning to bring results. At first the leading figure of the Fourth Crusade was Tibald of Champagne, but he died in March 1201, and the leadership fell to a man whom the Pope did not trust, Boniface of Montferrat, a grandee from northern Italy who was a friend and supporter of the Hohenstaufens. Young Alexius made a successful attempt to enlist the sympathies of Boniface, through Duke Philip, his sister's husband, brother of Emperor Henry VI. Pope Celestine's negotiations with Byzantium had not led to reunion. Now Alexius promised that should the Crusaders help him to oust his uncle, he would end the schism, bring the Greek Church into communion with Rome, and replenish the coffers of the Crusaders.

Richard Coeur-de-Lion, who was killed in 1199, had maintained that the Crusaders should first invade Egypt, in order to open a way to success in the Holy Land. It was decided to follow his advice. The Crusaders had no means of maritime transport other than that obtainable from the seafarers of Italy. Venice would provide them with the ships they required but, having close and very profitable trading relations with Egypt, was by no means prepared to lend assistance to an invasion of this realm of the Ayyúbids. The Crusaders assembled at Venice to set out for Egypt, but they did not have the money their leaders had agreed to pay the ship-owners of Venice. Enforced idleness, their mounting debts, and the continual Venetian demands became very irksome and began to tax the patience of the Crusaders. Boniface and the Doge of Venice provided a way out.

Boniface had spent the previous winter at the court of Duke Philip, where the young Alexius was angling for help. The Hohenstaufens hated Byzantium, chiefly because they could not bear to have rivals; it was a hatred which Enrico Dandolo, the aged Doge of Venice, shared. He and Boniface made secret arrangements and concealed them from others. The Crusaders were given ships, but instead of sailing for Egypt they were taken across the Adriatic to Zara on the Dalmatian coast. Although the town belonged to the Roman Catholic King of Hungary, Zara was taken and sacked, thus confirming the worst fears of Innocent III. He was powerless, however, to divert the course which the Fourth Crusade was taking. He excommunicated them all, but relented later when he realized that the Venetians had duped them. Only Venice was left under interdiction. The wily Doge cared not at all, since a force intended to capture Jerusalem for the glory of the Cross had secured for him a firm foothold on the other side of the Adriatic; he had every reason to be content. Even better prospects were now in view: a march on Byzantium. Young Alexius had joined the Crusaders, and in July 1203, Constantinople was attacked and captured.

Alexius III fled to Thrace. Blind Isaac was brought out of prison and made co-ruler with his son, who took the title of Emperor Alexius IV. But it soon became apparent that the young Alexius could not keep his promises, while the Venetians were making exorbitant demands. At last the people of Constantinople rose in revolt. Alexius IV was strangled, his father died a few days after him, and Alexius Murzuphlus, a son-in-law of Alexius III, was hailed Emperor Alexius V. A sad and curious casualty was the statue of Athena, a work by Phidias. It was smashed because some of the outraged citizens of Constantinople thought that it seemed to be inviting the Franks to come into the imperial city.

Alexius V was competent and would have governed well, but the Crusaders (and the Venetians in particular) were determined to destroy the Greek character of the Empire, and to replace it with a Latin régime. Who was to be the fortunate Latin emperor? Philip of Swabia was half a continent away, and in any case he had other ambitions and problems of his own. Boniface of Montferrat, who had made a mockery of the Crusade, was not the Venetians' choice, although the Doge was willing to support his candidature, because Boniface had friendly relations with the Genoese. The intense rivalry between the Italian city-states—Venice, Genoa and Pisa—was a baneful influence which dogged the fortunes of the Franks of Outremer and led to bitter hostilities and much bloodshed. Six Venetians and six of the Crusaders were given the task of choosing a Latin emperor. Byzantium was divided between this Latin emperor, the Venetians and the knights of the Crusade—the major portion being allotted to the conquerors. Appalled by their misfortunes the Byzantines made a last desperate effort to retrieve the situation, but it failed. Their soldiery had lost heart. Alexius V fled to Thrace, to join his father-in-law. Another son-in-law of Alexius III, Theodore Lascaris, escaped with the Patriarch, other prelates and members of the nobility to the mainland of Asia, where he established an empire based on Nicaea, which was truly Byzantine.

What happened in Constantinople, in the wake of the occupation of the city, was barbaric, shameful and criminal in the highest degree. For almost a thousand years, this proud city of Constantine the Great had harboured and preserved priceless gems of art and the finest products of culture and learning. Now that the Franks had triumphed Constantinople was delivered to unbridled rapine and total anarchy. Nothing and no one was spared. All things, sacred and profane, were desecrated. Nuns were raped, churches were looted, drunken orgies were staged in the basilica of St. Sophia, libraries were ransacked, houses were wrecked. The civilized Venetians knew the value of the precious objects they plundered and took them with care to their city, where one finds them today. Others, uncouth and ignorant, just trampled on icons and images, pictures and manuscripts.

Then Baldwin IX, Count of Flanders and Hainault, was made Emperor of the Latin Romania. But his reign was short-lived. The following year, in the battle of Adrianople, he was defeated by the Bulgars and the Greeks, who carried him into captivity. His brother, Henry, took his place. This emasculated kingdom had a shadowy existence till 1261. Then the Nicaean Emperor overthrew it. In the north of Anatolia, on the shores of the Black Sea, another Greek empire based on Trebizond arose, which endured for two hundred and fifty years; it was established by Alexius Comnenus, another prince of Byzantium. In the Balkans, another scion of the Byzantine emperors raised himself to power in Epirus and destroyed the kingdom of Thessalonica, which Boniface of Montferrat had salvaged for himself and his heirs. Venetians took the islands of Crete and Corfu and a port or two in Greece. The Greek Church was not reunited with Rome. The Papal legate absolved the Crusaders from the pursuit of their original objective. No help reached Outremer, apart from a few insignificant contingents that had refused to embark on the Byzantine adventure.

Pope Innocent III was mortified, for he had indeed raised a monster to torment other Christians. Yet, before long, the Pope was endeavouring to promote a fifth Crusade.

Meanwhile, there had been the tragic episode of the Children's Crusade. Thousands of children from France and Germany headed for seaports to take ship to the Holy Land. Very few ever returned home and hundreds died as they trudged along the roads that led to the coast. Those who reached Marseilles were given ships, but the ship-masters took them to Egypt and sold them. Al-Malik al-Kámil, it is reputed, bought a number of them to have as teachers of languages, interpreters and secretaries. He did not force them to become Muslims. In Germany, bereaved and infuriated parents hanged the father of Nicolas, the boy who had led their children away.

In Europe the star of Frederick II of Hohenstaufen was rising. Innocent III died in 1216. His successor, Honorius III, had feelings of affection for Frederick because the Emperor had once been his pupil. Where Innocent was stern Honorius was forbearing. While energetically pursuing the work of the late Pope to set the Fifth Crusade in motion, Honorius gave Frederick every latitude.

Affairs of both camps, Christian and Muslim, were highly convoluted. Their twists are well illustrated by incidents which centred round the principality of Antioch. In 1206, King Leo of Little Armenia raided the territory which Bohemond IV of Antioch claimed as his own. At the same time the Ayyúbids of Egypt attacked Tripoli, a riposte against hostile acts committed by the Knights of the Hospital. Bohemond asked the Saljúqs of Rúm to help him punish the Armenians. Pope Innocent turned to the Ayyúbids of Aleppo to save Antioch from the depredations of Greeks. Seven years later, Raymond, the eighteen-year-old son of Bohemond IV, was murdered by the Ismá'ílís of Syria, who were in league with the Hospitallers. The Patriarch, Albert of Jerusalem, had also fallen foul of the Hospital, and Ismá'ílís eliminated him as well. Bohemond, supported by the Knights of the Temple, besieged a castle of the Ismá'ílís. Sworn enemies of the Sunní Ayyúbids, the Ismá'ílís besought the help of the Ayyúbid al-Malik aẓ-Ẓáhir of Aleppo, who appealed in turn to his uncle, al-'Ádil of Egypt.

Al-Malik al-'Ádil Sayfi'd-Dín was now old and tired. He had no desire for confrontation with any opponent, Christian or Muslim. He had long been at peace with the Kingdom of Acre[5] and had amicable relations with the European seafarers, particularly with the Venetians. Large numbers of Italians lived and traded in Egypt, where al-'Ádil had been a tolerant and enlightened ruler. The Franks of Outremer also did not favour the prospect of future

[5] 'Akká was known in the West by this name.

conflicts under the banner of the Cross. However, Innocent III had raised the call for a fresh Crusade, and now Pope Honorius was in full cry, despite the tergiversations of his former pupil, who wanted to make his own power-base strong and secure before embarking on adventures overseas.

King Andrew of Hungary and Duke Leopold VI of Austria had both taken the Cross but, having arrived with their armies at Spalato in Dalmatia during the summer of 1217, found themselves faced with the same problem which had daunted and tried the patience of earlier Crusaders: a shortage of shipping. With the bulk of troops left behind in Spalato, Andrew and Leopold arrived at Acre in the autumn, and King Hugh of Cyprus joined them there. They had no overall command. King John of Acre (John of Brienne) was keen on dislodging al-'Ádil's garrison from their fort on Mount Tabor. These Muslim warriors were too close for comfort. Others had no interest in the mountain which, it was claimed, was the scene of the Transfiguration. Troops from Acre, even aided by the Templars, could not capture the fort, but shortly afterwards al-'Ádil, himself, ordered his men away. A fort on Mount Tabor was really of no use to him.

King Andrew, having obtained some holy relics, including the head of St. Stephen, and having lost some of his men in a blizzard on the heights of Lebanon, felt that it was time to return home, which he did. He marched away to Cilicia and reached Constantinople under the protection of the Saljúqs of Rúm. Duke Leopold was in dire financial straits and stayed behind. He and King John of Acre, together with the Grand Masters of the Temple, the Hospital and the Teutons, sailed in Frisian ships to Egypt, in May 1218, at the head of their combined forces. Richard Coeur-de-Lion's advice had not gone unheeded. Initially, they were successful and captured the fort of Damietta (Dimyáṭ).

Al-Malik al-'Ádil was in Damascus when he heard of the loss his army had sustained in Egypt. His younger son had wrested Caesarea from the Franks, but that did not compensate for the reverse in Egypt. At the end of August the saddened al-'Ádil died in Damascus, as had his brother, the great Ṣaláḥi'd-Dín (Saladin). Al-Malik al-Kámil Náṣiri'd-Dín, his eldest son, took over Egypt, and the younger son, al-Malik al-Mu'aẓẓam Sharafi'd-Dín, took over Syria. The Frisian ships had returned home, but others brought fresh contingents from Europe, which included French counts, bishops, and English lords—the Earls of Chester, Arundel, Derby and Winchester. But the personage of highest rank amongst the new arrivals, the Spanish Cardinal Pelagius, the Papal legate, soon proved that his presence there was not at all a blessing. King John, now that Andrew of Hungary had left and Hugh of Cyprus had died, claimed the right to supreme command, but the Cardinal would not have it; as representative of Honorius he believed he should lead. Fortunately for the Crusaders, al-Kámil had serious problems and disloyalties to contend with. He retreated and al-ʻÁdilíyyah fell to the Crusaders. Although his brother, al-Muʻaẓẓam, had been tardy to come up with help, he arrived at last to strengthen the Muslim position. Although Crusaders occupied the fort, the town of Damietta was still held by the Muslims, but daily their position was becoming less and less tenable. Finding themselves bogged down, the Crusaders began to lose heart. The Grand Master of the Temple was killed. Duke Leopold had had enough and returned home, as did many others. King John and Cardinal Pelagius continued to dispute. There was still no sign of the Emperor Frederick.

It was now the year 1219. St. Francis of Assisi arrived to watch the fighting and was allowed by the Cardinal to visit the ruler of Egypt. Al-Kámil treated St. Francis with the esteem due to a holy man and he was escorted back with respect to the Christian camp. Then a short truce intervened, but not before the Crusaders' army had been nearly destroyed. Al-Kámil and his brother were both aware of the weakness of their own position and offered peace terms. They were willing to cede Jerusalem, Bethlehem and Nazareth to the Christians, should the Crusaders withdraw from Egypt. King John proposed acceptance and the nobility of Outremer, France, Germany and England supported him. But Cardinal Pelagius refused to treat with infidels, and the Knights of the Temple, the Hospital and the Teutonic order also opposed the conclusion of a peace treaty. Their objection, however, was not theological but practical. In their view Jerusalem could not be defended without the castles of Oultrejourdain. Thus the stalemate continued into yet another winter of misery. Damietta, now peopled by a few thousand starvelings who were helplessly awaiting death, was at last taken by the Crusaders. But bitter quarrels arose over the division of the plentiful spoils. The Italians revolted and had to be put down by the Templars.

The legend of Prester John, the zealous and brave Christian warrior-king, who stood poised in Central Asia to come to the aid of the Crusaders, was at this time much cherished, but it was Chingíz Khán that Central Asia produced, not Prester John.

King John went back to Acre, but returned in a sullen mood in July 1221. In the meantime the Emperor Frederick had made a move. He sent Duke Louis of Bavaria with a sizeable force. The Cardinal, hearing the good news of the Emperor Frederick's impending departure from Europe, rejected once again al-Kámil's peace offer, and ignoring King John's sound advice, moved his forces far inland, at a time when the Nile was rising. The rest of the story is soon told. Frederick did not come. Floods completed the débâcle of the Crusaders' army. In September 1221 Pelagius was forced to capitulate. Both he and King John surrendered as hostages. John went back to Acre, but Pelagius did not return to Europe, going instead to Antioch and Little Armenia, where he failed to resolve the conflicts of the Christians and excommunicated Bohemond IV. The repercussions of the Fifth Crusade were disastrous for the Christians of Egypt; even al-Kámil's generosity could not save them from the anger of the Muslims. And when it came to handing over the True Cross to the Papal legate no one knew where it was.

Honorius III died in 1227 and was succeeded as Pope by Gregory IX, a stern disciplinarian. He had no particular affection for the Emperor Frederick and would stand no nonsense. He excommunicated the Emperor at a time when Frederick really intended to honour his vows, and excommunicated him a second time for going to the Holy Land while still under an interdict. It was a deliciously farcical situation, and although (as we saw in the previous chapter) Frederick did get Jerusalem and Bethlehem for the Christians, he managed to stir up enough trouble in Cyprus and Outremer to shake these Frankish outposts in western Asia to their foundations.

King John of Acre held his position and his title by virtue of having married in 1210 Queen Maria, the ruler of the kingdom of Acre. Maria died after giving birth to a daughter, named Isabella, but known as Yolanda. Although keeping the title of king, John was, in fact, the regent for her daughter. Yolanda, at the end of the Fifth Crusade, was nearing the age when she would rule in person, and it was urgent to find her a suitable husband. John of Brienne, an obscure Frenchman, had found himself a spouse in Queen Maria by the good offices of King Philip Augustus. Now he went to Europe, in the company of Cardinal Pelagius, in search of a husband for his daughter. The Pope expressed his warm approval of marriage between the Emperor Frederick and Yolanda. The King of France was not at all pleased with the prospect, but died before the marriage took place in 1225. As soon as Yolanda was married the Emperor made it plain to his father-in-law that there was no longer a place for 'King John' in Outremer. Despite John's appeal, Honorius could do no more for the ex-king than offer him a post in Tuscany. Soon after, a much more attractive and dignified position became available to John of Brienne. The child-Emperor of Romania, Baldwin II, needed a regent, and John was chosen. He was then almost eighty. His four-year-old daughter, Maria, (by his Armenian wife[6]), was married to the child-Emperor. John made certain that no matter what happened in future, he would keep the title of 'Emperor' till his death. He lived on until 1237.

In April 1228, Yolanda gave birth to a son and died within a week, not yet seventeen years of age. The infant, Conrad, was now the rightful ruler of Acre, and the Emperor, his father, held exactly the same position as had John of Brienne during Yolanda's minority. Frederick was now going to the Holy Land, in earnest. It was lucky for him that the news of the Queen's death had not reached Outremer. Otherwise the notables of Acre might have chosen another regent.

The bickerings, the bitter conflicts, the battles of Christians and Muslims in western Asia and Egypt provided the right background for the functioning of the Emperor's dark genius. Frederick was indeed brilliant, he spoke several languages fluently, one of which was Arabic, but he was cold and calculating, cruel and treacherous. The Saljúqids and the Ayyúbids were, as usual, at each other's throat. Christians sought help from one or the other in their own quarrels. In 1226, Bohemond IV of Antioch asked the Saljúqid Sulṭán Kayqubád to aid him against the Armenians, by invading Cilicia. The Ayyúbids were, once again, showing signs of a serious split in their ranks. Al-Malik al-Mu'aẓẓam had aided his brother to defeat the Crusaders, but once the

[6] She too was dead by 1225. It was rumoured that she had tried to poison Yolanda, and John, discovering it, gave her a severe beating which led to her death.

danger had passed, relations between him and al-Kámil became strained. Therefore al-Kámil entered into secret negotiations with Frederick before the Emperor sailed for the East. Frederick was non-committal. And al-Mu'aẓẓam refused to fall in with the suggestion of ceding Jerusalem to the Christians, a course of action which he had twice proposed during the Fifth Crusade. But al-Mu'aẓẓam died in 1227 and his brothers, al-Kámil and al-Ashraf, combined after some wrangling to deprive their nephew, al-Malik an-Náṣir Ṣaláḥi'd-Dín Dáwúd, of his patrimony.

Al-Malik al-Kámil was at last in a position to hand Jerusalem to the Emperor Frederick. A peace treaty was signed which (as we have seen) pleased nobody except its authors. Frederick entered Jerusalem on 17 March 1229. The Muslims, in deference to him, had decided that *mu'adhdhins* should not raise the call to prayer while he was in the city. Frederick said that he had come to hear the *adhán*. When he entered the Ḥaram ash-Sharíf he saw that a Christian monk was following him. He chased out the poor monk, and then declared that any Christian, who entered the holy places of Islám without obtaining permission from the Muslims, should be put to death.

For all his achievements Frederick had set many a hornet's nest buzzing, and apart from the Teutonic Knights, he found little support in Outremer. Knights of the Temple were particularly offensive. The Emperor thought that he would punish them by capturing Athlit, their stronghold by the sea, round the spur of Mount Carmel. But it was too heavily fortified and well defended. Frederick's partiality towards the Pisans had angered the Venetians and the Genoese. His conduct towards the Family of Ibelin whose head, John the Lord of Beirut, was one of the most powerful and highly respected magnates of Outremer, amounted to frenzied persecution. When he left Acre to embark for Cyprus, crowds turned out to hurl abuse and offal at him as he walked down the Street of Butchers to the harbour. He had hardly reached Europe, in the late spring of 1229, when Cyprus erupted into civil war as a direct result of his policies. The mainland was also affected, especially after the arrival, in 1231, of Marshal Filangieri with the title of Imperial Legate and a powerful force. Meanwhile, in 1230, Frederick had come to terms with the Pope. Peace with Gregory IX added considerably to his stature in Outremer. The Templars and the Hospitallers could no longer oppose him. But the struggles with the Ibelins and others dragged on, to weaken the position of the Christians.

If Christians were enormously harming themselves, so were the Muslims. Jaláli'd-Dín, the last of the Khárazmsháhs, went down to defeat before the Ayyúbite al-Malik al-Ashraf. The Ayyúbites, after the death of al-Kámil in 1238, resumed their quarrels; and as they fought amongst themselves, al-Kámil's treaty with Frederick expired. Pope Gregory, following in the footsteps of his predecessors, now began to preach another Crusade. Frederick had no intention of going yet again to the Holy Land. Nor did the Kings of France and England wish to be involved. It fell to Tibald, King of Navarre, to assume command. Many noblemen took the Cross at the same time. This Crusade, too, was not devoid of grotesque episodes. Frederick would have nothing to do with it. Being the regent for his son, Conrad, and concerned with the affairs of Outremer, he considered such interference highly impertinent. In Acre Tibald found divided counsel. Finally it was decided to attack Egypt. Jealousies and futile rivalries led, in the vicinity of Gaza, to foolhardy action. The Christian army was so badly mauled that retreat to Acre became inevitable. Now, the Ayyúbid an-Náṣir of Karak took action against Jerusalem, in reprisal for the assault by the Count of Brittany, who had waylaid a caravan belonging to the Muslims and seized a very large herd of cattle and sheep. An-Náṣir demolished whatever fortifications Jerusalem had, and went back to Karak. Next, the Ayyúbid Amír of Hamá sought the help of the Crusaders to thwart his kinsmen of Aleppo and Ḥimṣ. Then, the Ayyúbid Prince of Damascus, fearing the designs of his relatives in Egypt and Karak, agreed to hand over to the Christians the castles of Ṣafad and Beaufort, in return for their protection. Muslims who held Beaufort refused to cede it and al-Malik aṣ-Ṣáliḥ 'Imádi'd-Dín had to come from Damascus to eject them. Knights of the Temple came into possession of Ṣafad. This was too much for the Knights of the Hospital. So they made common cause with al-Malik aṣ-Ṣáliḥ Najmi'd-Dín Ayyúb of Egypt and obtained Ascalon as their prize. Tibald approved of this alignment, which scandalized the noblemen of the kingdom of Acre. Tibald could stand it no more and sailed away.

The next Crusade was led by a saint: Louis IX of France, whom the Church of Rome has canonized. King Louis reached Egypt in

1249. During the decade which separated Tibald's Crusade from King Louis's, the Franks of Outremer and the Ayyúbids of Egypt and Syria had persisted with their ruinous dog-fights, and Jerusalem had been retaken by the Kháarazmian army. In all those years Conrad, the rightful ruler of the kingdom of Acre, never visited Outremer. Conrad was also the heir of the Emperor Frederick and his patrimony in Europe was by far the more attractive. Frederick's disgust with the Franks of the East apart, he had need of his son in Europe, to whom he had already given the rulership of Germany. King Louis had indeed a saintly character, but he had two hot-headed and impetuous brothers, Robert of Artois and Charles, who did irreparable damage to the fortunes of Louis as a soldier of the Cross.

News of the eruption of the Mongols into the realm of Islám had been received with glee in Europe. But there came a time when Europe felt apprehensive. In 1240, Mongols invaded Ukraine and captured Kiev, slaying its inhabitants and destroying its heritage of art. As they penetrated into Poland, Hungary and Silesia and reached the Adriatic, Pope Gregory appealed to the Emperor Frederick and to the Kings of France and England to join forces and halt the Mongols. However, the death of Uktáy Qá'án intervened and the Mongol armies retired from Europe. After the death of Gregory IX in 1241, his successor, Innocent IV, had high hopes of enlisting Mongol support against the followers of Muḥammad. The legend of Prester John was, once again, current and fervently believed. Pope Innocent sent envoys, in 1245, to the Great Khán. They acquitted themselves well of the duties of their mission, and Güyük, who had just been raised to the overlordship of the Mongols, treated them amiably. Nestorianism dominated Christian belief in Central Asia and the Great Khán was served by a substantial number of Nestorian officials and counsellors. Güyük wrote to the Pope that he and all the princes of Europe should come to his capital, to acknowledge him as their suzerain and the Ruler of the World.

Now, when King Louis reached Cyprus in 1248, two Nestorians arrived at Nicosia, on behalf of a Mongol general. Louis immediately responded. A Dominican mission set out with gifts to try and forge an alliance against the Muslims of Egypt and Syria. They were under the illusion that the overlord of the Mongols was ready to embrace the Christian Faith, and so they included in the gifts they carried a portable chapel with all its appurtenances. By the time they reached Qaraqurum, Güyük had died and his widow was regent. She accepted King Louis's gifts as offerings of a vassal. The affairs of the Mongol Empire, however, would not allow at that moment the dispatch of an effective force to aid the vassal, who was told to keep sending gifts every year.

In Cyprus, King Louis came up against the intractable problem of shipping. As in the past, Venetians were unwilling to provide ships for the invasion of Egypt. Louis expected the Genoese to supply the ships he required. But just then the Genoese and the Pisans went to war, up and down the Syrian coast, and the Genoese fared badly. Louis's problems were multifarious. Suitors came from the mainland asking for his help. Maria of Brienne, now the empress of Romania, was one of them. She wanted protection because of the threatening attitude of the emperor of Nicaea. King Louis had come to fight the infidels, not to aid one Christian monarch against another.

Al-Malik aṣ-Ṣáliḥ Najmi'd-Dín Ayyúb was a dying man. He hurried to Egypt from Syria. King Louis had little difficulty in capturing Damietta. When the waters of the Nile subsided he moved on towards Cairo. Najmi'd-Dín Ayyúb was in Manṣúrah—the Victorious—the city built by al-Kámil to mark his victory and the failure of the Fifth Crusade. (He had been carried there in a litter and had died there.) Grave dangers were in the offing because the Sulṭán's heir, al-Malik al-Mu'aẓẓam Túrán-Sháh, was far away in the Jazírah. Shajarat-ad-Durr, the widow of Najmi'd-Dín Ayyúb, succeeded in concealing the news of her husband's death, and held the country together until Túrán-Sháh reached Egypt in February 1250. In the meantime, King Louis had crossed the canal that separated his army from the Egyptian camp at Manṣúrah; but the rashness of Robert of Artois in a premature bid to capture Manṣúrah (which cost him his own life) had greatly weakened Louis's position.[7] He was bogged down before Manṣúrah, his food ships were intercepted, and shortage of food, the unhealthy climate and raging disease were taking heavy toll of his army. Louis realized that there was no hope of further advance and all that could now be achieved was to contrive, in

[7] Robert had disregarded his brother's strict orders and impetuously brushed aside sound advice given him by the Templars and the English.

some way, an orderly retreat to Damietta. Unfortunately, the King fell ill, his retreating army was continuously harassed, treachery raised its hideous head, and the entire army capitulated on false orders. As a result, Louis himself fell into the hands of the enemy and was carried to Manṣúrah where he was put in chains. The disaster for the Christians was complete and unmitigated, but now the prestige of Frederick brought the defeated Crusaders some measure of relief. The ruler of Egypt was demanding the cession of all the territories held by the Franks in Syria, to which King Louis replied that he could not give away what was not his, for those lands belonged to Conrad, the son of the Emperor Frederick. The demand was never again made.

Negotiations for the restoration of Damietta and the ransom to be paid were almost completed when nemesis overtook the vain-glorious Túrán-Sháh, virtually the last of the Ayyúbids of Egypt. Made arrogant by unexpected victory, he insulted his stepmother who had saved the throne for him, and used abusive language to the Mamlúks, his élite and loyal corps of Turkish and Circassian slaves. On 2 May 1250, he was murdered by Rukni'd-Dín Baybars, who was destined to play a central role in the affairs of Islám in future years. Túrán-Sháh had ruled for only a few months. Had he been more moderate his reign might have been truly remarkable. As it was, it spelled the end for the House of the great Ṣaláḥi'd-Dín.

By the common consent of the Mamlúks, one of them, 'Izzi'd-Dín Aybak, assumed the regency and married Shajarat-ad-Durr. An infant named Músá, cousin to Túrán-Sháh was proclaimed co-ruler, but no one knows what happened to him. Amidst these convulsions King Louis suffered horribly. When freed he refused to return to France. Let anyone go who wished, but he would remain in Outremer, for his presence was needed to help put its affairs in order. His own force had been destroyed, but even more serious was the fact that Outremer's military resources had been exhausted. Whereas Frederick had been brusque and unyielding, Louis was tactful and forbearing. His brothers and the nobility of France left him, which in all probability aided his endeavours at conciliation. He restored a large measure of peace and tranquillity to the Frankish outposts in the East, although soon after his return to France, fighting broke out between the Italian seafarers. Both the Mamlúk 'Izzi'd-Dín Aybak of Egypt and the Ayyúbid al-Malik an-Náṣir II Ṣaláḥi'd-Dín Yúsuf of Damascus had become very much aware of the menace posed by the Mongols. They concluded pacts with King Louis, as did the Ismá'ílís of Syria. Moreover, although deadly enemies, the Mamlúks and the Ayyúbids gave ear to the plea of the 'Abbásid Caliph and resolved to live in peace.

In Europe, the Emperor Frederick had again succeeded in putting himself under papal interdict. His attacks on the papal states in Italy had forced Innocent IV to excommunicate him and also to abandon Rome. Frederick's stormy career ended in December 1250. Conrad, who succeeded him, died in May 1254 after a brief reign, when his son, Conradin, was an infant. At last, conditions in France left King Louis no choice but to go home. That was in April 1254. In 1256 open war broke out in Acre between the Genoese and the Venetians over the possession of the monastery of St. Sabas. Pisans supported the Genoese, while in Tyre Philip of Montfort took action against the Venetians. The Teutonic Knights and Knights of the Temple sided with the Venetians, but the Hospitallers stood with the Genoese. The whole of Outremer was dragged into the bitter strife of the Italians, which assumed much wider proportions, by involving the rights of Queen Plaisance of Cyprus as regent for Conradin. Plaisance's own son, King Hugh, was only five years old and Conradin was about the same age. The Queen was sister to Bohemond VI of Antioch and Tripoli, who tried to keep aloof, although his sympathy was for the Venetians. He accompanied his sister to Acre and was inevitably drawn into the foray. Finally an appeal was made to Pope Alexander IV, who had succeeded Innocent IV on the latter's death in 1254. Summoning representatives of the Italian city-states to attend and hear his verdict, Alexander demanded an immediate armistice, and an elaborate peace plan was drawn up. Before it could be put into effect, the Genoese were decisively defeated in a fierce sea battle off Acre and had to pull out.

In 1259, the Pope dispatched a legate to Outremer to seek a solution to the conflict which had undone all the good work of King Louis. It was agreed that the Genoese should have their colony and establishments in Tyre and keep away from Acre. The Pisans and Venetians would establish themselves in Acre. Smarting under defeat, the Genoese took their vengeance by putting their fleet and services at the disposal of Michael Palaeologus, the emperor of Nicaea. With their aid Constantinople was captured in 1261 and Romania ceased to be.

Over the years, King Louis had watched from afar the sad deterioration in the condition of Outremer; and he had never put away the thought of making yet another effort to recover Jerusalem. By 1270 his preparations for yet another Crusade were complete. Whether he would have succeeded, had he avoided past errors, is a matter of conjecture. The fact is that he unwisely allowed himself to be seriously misled by his brother, Charles of Anjou, and was landed in yet another disaster. Charles was the very antithesis of King Louis. His rise to power had its origins in the traditional hostility betwixt the Papacy and the House of Hohenstaufen. Four years after the death of Conrad, Sicily, which was an appanage of the Papal States, was taken over by his half-brother, Manfred. Pope Urban IV, who succeeded Alexander IV in 1261, began to look round to choose a prince who would wrest Sicily from Manfred. King Louis had come to believe that a Hohenstaufen on the throne of Sicily would impede his Crusade, on which he had set his heart. Urban's choice fell on Charles of Anjou. King Louis endorsed the choice and provided financial aid. Manfred was defeated and killed. Now Charles of Anjou showed his true colours. His ambition knew no bounds, so much so that Clement IV, who had succeeded Urban in 1265, took fright. Poor Conradin, dispossessed in his early childhood, tried to win back the Italian territories which his grandfather had conquered. He failed, fell into the hands of Charles of Anjou and was beheaded. He was only sixteen, and with his death the House of Hohenstaufen became extinct.

Charles was now dreaming of dominance over Europe. He detested the Byzantines and in his estimation the recapture of Constantinople had much greater priority than the recapture of Jerusalem. The force which his brother had raised, Charles reckoned, could well serve his own ends. He presented his brother with the tale that the Amír (Emir) of Túnis was on the point of declaring for Christ. A call there, on the way to the Holy Land, would clinch matters. The ruler of Túnis, however, had no desire to change his religion, and the French army, soon ravaged by disease, could not fight. Louis himself died in Tunisia on 25 August 1270 and was buried by the ruins of Carthage.

We have seen that King Louis had hopes of an alliance with the Mongols against the Muslims. But the hauteur of the Mongols made impossible such alliances with European monarchs. Even the Pope, as we have seen, was summoned to Mongolia to render homage to the Great Khán. But it was different with such Christian rulers as Hethoum of Little Armenia. For them, recognizing Mongol suzerainty did not mean a lowering of status, and Mongol protection would give them the kind of security they needed. Thus, Hethoum made his way to Qaraqurum, but the Franks, while witnessing with alarm the displays of strength and ruthlessness by Baybars of Egypt, remained sceptical of putting their trust in the Mongols. Baybars was ranging now over Syria. In 1263 he overran Nazareth and demolished the Church of the Virgin. In 1265 he captured and destroyed Caesarea and Haifa, with their citadels. Those of the inhabitants of Haifa unable to make good their escape were put to the sword. In 1266 it was the turn of Ṣafad and Toron. Despite the promise of safe conduct the Templars of Ṣafad were all put to death. Next, Baybars murdered every Christian he could find, right up to the gates of Acre. In the same year another Mamlúk force erupted into Cilicia and almost destroyed the Armenian kingdom. And so it went on, with another show of force outside Acre in 1267. Beaufort and Antioch fell the following year. Antioch, the oldest of the principalities established by the Crusaders, had been governed by Christians for more than a century and a half. Its loss was a tremendous blow to the Franks of Outremer. The behaviour of the victors in Antioch was appalling and boded ill for the future. It is true to say that massacre and destruction reduced a fine, flourishing city to total obscurity and insignificance, from which Antioch has never recovered.

The death of King Louis dimmed the hopes of Outremer. Charles of Anjou had his eyes on other goals and maintained good relations with Rukni'd-Dín Baybars. The Venetians as well as the Genoese were also on excellent terms with the Mamlúks, a fact which astounded Edward, the son and heir of King Henry III of England, when he reached the Holy Land in May 1271. Edward had set out from England to join King Louis; although the latter's death and the consequent abandonment of the Crusade by the French army were dispiriting, he decided to go on to the Holy Land. With the small force at Edward's command and Outremer's paucity of resources, Baybars felt in no way threatened. Only a short time before Edward's arrival at Acre, Egyptians had, at long last, captured the fortress of Karak, which had successfully defied onslaughts in the past. Edward needed massive aid, either from Europe or from the Mongols. He sent three English emissaries to Abáqá—Reginald Russell, Godfrey Welles and John Parker—and the Íl-Khán promised his support. But occupied as he was with repelling the attacks of his own kinsmen, all Abáqá could do was to send some ten thousand men from Anatolia to harass the Mamlúks in northern Syria. Baybars was in Damascus with a considerable force, and the small Mongol detachment was no match for him. In addition to his military gifts, Baybars was also a proficient and very successful diplomat. He not only established friendly relations with Charles of Anjou, but also negotiated treaties with James of Aragon and Alfonso of Seville, and in Asia won the Golden Horde and the newly-restored Byzantium to his side. In Constantinople Michael Palaeologus rebuilt a mosque which the Franks had destroyed. Moreover, the Italian seafarers were conducting a profitable trade with Egypt.

Prince Edward soon reached the conclusion that his sojourn in Outremer was useless. A peace treaty with Baybars was signed at Caesarea, in May 1272, which guaranteed Outremer another ten years and ten months of existence. When on the point of leaving for England, Edward was stabbed with a poisoned dagger at the instigation of Baybars, although the Mamlúk monarch dissociated himself from the act which was attributed to the Assassins. By the time Edward reached home, Henry III had died.

Charles of Anjou was now a very powerful potentate in Europe; for four years his intrigues blocked the election of a successor to Pope Clement IV. When, in 1272, Gregory X ascended the throne of St. Peter, he at once began to review the possibilities of organizing another Crusade. Despite Europe's lack of enthusiasm for a holy war, and the discouraging reports he was receiving from well-informed sources, Gregory convened in Lyons, in 1274, a council to consider the situation and map out a policy. Charles of Anjou would have no part of it. The Byzantine Emperor sent representatives because he greatly feared Charles's designs. Neither King Philip III of France, who had nearly died in Tunisia, nor King Edward I, so recently returned from Outremer, attended the council. Gregory X died two years later and the deliberations of his council proved abortive.

Now it was Abáqá's turn to ask, but in vain, for assistance from the monarchs of Europe. He sent emissaries to the Council of Lyons, wrote to Edward of England and Philip of France, but received no firm response. Charles of Anjou was hostile towards the Mongols because they were on friendly terms with the Byzantines. Able to put pressure on the Curia, he blocked all manner of aid to Abáqá. The Íl-Khán, as we have seen, then attempted the conquest of Syria unaided and failed; he died shortly after in 1282.

Meanwhile, Rukni'd-Dín Baybars, the scourge of Outremer, had died in July 1277. His son was a weakling; not until three years later, when Sayfi'd-Dín Qalá'ún came from Syria and took over the government, did the Mamlúks march again. In Írán Abáqá was succeeded by his brother, Takúdár, who, on becoming a Christian, had taken Nicholas as his name. After his accession he was converted to Islám and assumed the name Aḥmad. The Mongols, however, were not yet ready to countenance a Muslim as their ruler; so within two years, Arghún, the son of Abáqá, revolted and deposed his uncle, putting him to death. Takúdár had been trying to establish amicable relations with the Mamlúks, but, with Arghún on the throne, old enmities were revived. Arghún sought unsuccessfully, time and again, to obtain aid and support from the Pope and monarchs of Europe.

The very year of Abáqá's death witnessed an event of prime importance in the Mediterranean, known in history as the Sicilian Vespers. The people of Sicily, unbearably angered and humiliated by the haughtiness and insolence of their French masters, burst into revolt and killed them mercilessly. Peter of Aragon, whose wife, Constance, was the daughter of Manfred of Hohenstaufen, was offered the kingdom of Sicily. Thus Charles of Anjou lost his power-base and his efforts to retrieve his fortune were fruitless. Byzantium (which had incited the rebellion) felt immensely relieved of the anxieties which had weighed heavily on it since its rebirth, while the Mamlúks, although in friendly relationship with King Charles, were not unhappy to see some curtailment of this imperious man's unbounded ambition. The disappearance of a powerful Christian kingdom to the north of them could have been, also, a source of satisfaction.

The loss of Sicily to the Aragonese incensed Pope Martin IV

(1281–85), a Frenchman who was intensely proud of his native land and its royal dynasty, and was the patron and champion of Charles of Anjou. He excommunicated the King of Aragon, the Emperor of Constantinople (who, in any case, no longer felt obliged to be deferential towards the Pope), the Sicilians, the anti-Angevin Italians, and called for a Crusade against the Aragonese. King Philip of France, attached to his uncle as he was, set about preparing to invade Aragon, although he had hardly shown any zeal for a Crusade to rescue the Holy Land. It ought to be noted that Pope Martin owed his position to the manoeuvrings of Charles of Anjou. Repeated efforts to reverse the state of affairs in Sicily were not successful, but the Papacy remained strongly committed to the Angevin cause. King Charles was now in poor and declining health; his son and heir, Charles of Salerno, had been captured; and the movement to force Aragon into submission was slow, although King Philip had massed a considerable force. Then death intervened to remove the chief protagonists from the scene. Charles of Anjou died in January 1285, Pope Martin IV (who had so ardently promoted the Angevin cause and had damaged the prestige of his supreme office) died in March, Philip of France in October, and Peter of Aragon in November. But Sicily would not know peace for decades.

Sayfi'd-Dín Qalá'ún of Egypt did not live to see the total extinction of Outremer, although he hastened it and was about to deal the final blow when he died in 1290. The monarch who wished to save Outremer, and even restore Jerusalem to the Christians, was Arghún, the Íl-Khán of Írán. But he knew that he could not accomplish his purpose without aid from Europe. While jealousies and rivalries racked Outremer, and the Angevin cause continued to cast its baleful spell over the Pope and the Curia, Arghún was sending a stream of letters, missions and envoys to Europe, to plead for help against the Mamlúks. But if Edward of England had ever truly intended to go back to the Holy Land, the conquest of Wales and Scotland had now become his objective to the exclusion of all else. Kings of France, Philip III (Phillipe le Hardi) and his son, Philip IV (Phillipe le Bel, d. 1314), were wholly occupied with other pursuits. And the Popes, Honorius IV (1285–87) and Nicholas IV (1288–92) were involved in the failed projects of their predecessors.

Shamsi'd-Dín-i-Juvayní, the Ṣáḥib-Díván (brother of the

historian, 'Aṭá-Malik-i-Juvayní), who, in the service of the Mongols, has been compared with Niẓámu'l-Mulk in the service of the Saljúqs, had been put to death in the third month of Arghún's reign. Shamsi'd-Dín had indeed served Húlágú and Abáqá with great distinction and unquestionable fidelity. Arghún had as his vizier a noted Jewish physician, Sa'di'd-Dawlih of Abhar. And a man very close to the Íl-Khán, a loyal counsellor, was the Nestorian Catholicus,[8] Már Yahbhalla, who hailed from the Chinese Turkistán. This Turkish Catholicus was urging Arghún to deliver Jerusalem from the oppression of the Turkish Mamlúks. Arghún wrote to Pope Honorius, who left his letter unanswered. Two years later, in 1287, Rabbán Sauma, a Chinese Nestorian priest, was sent to the courts of Europe. The Byzantine Emperor, Andronicus, although giving him a splendid welcome, had little to offer. In Rome, Honorius was dead and the next Pope had not been elected. Cardinals engaged the Nestorian prelate in theological disputations which taxed his patience. In France, the youthful Philip IV accorded him a regal welcome, and appointed Gobert d'Helleville to accompany him back to Írán. Edward of England also received him with great warmth in Bordeaux. When he returned to Rome, Nicholas IV had been raised to the Papal throne. Rabbán Sauma had the honour of celebrating Mass in the presence of the College of Cardinals and receiving Communion from the person of the Pope. Nicholas declared the Nestorian Catholicus to be the Patriarch of the East, and sent him highly-valued gifts which included holy relics. But, despite the honours showered upon him, the Chinese prelate returned with a heavy heart to the court of the Íl-Khán. There was no definite promise of material aid that he could convey to Arghún. Nevertheless, the Íl-Khán did not give up the attempt to persuade Christian monarchs to fight for the Cross. Buscarel of Gisolf, a Genoese, long resident in Mongol domains, was sent to the courts of Europe in 1289. A year later, the same man was dispatched in the company of two Christian Mongols. It was all of no avail. No aid came from Europe. Arghún died in 1291, and in the same year Outremer perished.

The rulership of the Kingdom of Acre had passed to the strikingly handsome kings of Cyprus. But they were terribly handicapped in that they could not reside permanently in Acre, since

[8] In Arabic Játhlíq.

Cyprus was their base. Nor would their nobility stay long in Outremer. Furthermore, partisans of King Charles were numerous in Acre and the Orders of Chivalry were vacillating. King Hugh came in 1283 to claim the crown of Acre. Mishaps plagued him, his nobles returned to Cyprus and he died in Tyre in March 1284. His heir, John, was an ailing seventeen-year-old youth, who had only one more year to live. After him the next son of King Hugh came to the throne—Henry, only fourteen years old, the last Christian ruler of Acre. In the meantime Qalá'ún had wrested the stronghold of Marqab from the Hospitallers; he had already extended the truce with Acre for another ten years. In 1286, King Henry, now fifteen, arrived at Acre amidst jubilation but also some opposition. His sojourn in Outremer was short. Following his return to Cyprus war broke out between the seafarers of Pisa and Genoa, and immense damage was done to the waning fortunes of Outremer. A natural catastrophe in 1287 further ruined Outremer's chance of survival. An earthquake struck Lattakieh (Ládhiqíyyah). Its fortifications suffered considerably, and Qalá'ún captured the port with little difficulty. Next, Tripoli fell to him in 1289, in the following circumstances. He had been invited by some of the Venetians to take action there against the Genoese, but at the last minute the Venetians as well as the Genoese sailed away. So did Amalric, brother of King Henry, and the Countess Lucia, sister of Bohemond VII of Antioch. It was Lucia's arrangements with the Genoese which had infuriated the Venetians. So Tripoli was totally destroyed and its inhabitants massacred. Another Tripoli would arise in future years, but diminished and insignificant, as in the case of Antioch.

For ten years Qalá'ún had honoured his truce with King Henry and Acre was flourishing and enjoying a period of calm. Muslim merchants and farmers thronged its market. Then came a band of Italians as Crusaders. They were riotous and unruly, and one day in a drunken brawl they set upon the Muslim visitors and murdered them all, taking anyone bearded for a Muslim. Thus many Christians were slain as well. The commune of Acre was aghast and Qalá'ún was livid with rage. He might have been pacified, had the government of Acre been wise enough to hand over to him those of the culprits whom it had caught and imprisoned. Instead, Qalá'ún left Cairo in November 1290, to extirpate the

II (A) A COVERED BOWL
m East Persia, about A.D. 1200.
Bronze inlaid with silver.
inches wide by $8\frac{1}{2}$ inches high.

(B) AN ASTROLABE
used for navigation, engraved and inlaid with silver and copper. From Cairo, dated A.D. 1236 and signed by the astrolabist 'Abdu'l-Karím in 633 A.H.

Photo: Pope, A Survey of Persi

XIV THE MAUSOLEUM OF ULJÁYTÚ

octagonal in form and crowned by a great dome, was built (1305–13) to dominate the imperial city of Sulṭáníyyih. Today it stands in solitary grandeur in lush meadows near Zanján.

Franks of Outremer. Within a few days he was dead, but before dying he laid a mandate on Khalíl, his son, to complete his purpose. Before setting out from Cairo, in March 1291, al-Malik al-Ashraf Ṣaláḥi'd-Dín Khalíl declined to parley with the envoys from Acre, and cast them into prison where they died. On April 5th, he encamped in front of Acre. King Henry first dispatched his brother, Amalric, and then arrived himself from Cyprus with a pitiably small force—all that he could commandeer. In response to urgent appeals some men had come from Europe, but far too few; Edward I had sent only a tiny contingent of English. On the other hand, the army of al-Malik al-Ashraf was truly formidable. With the odds obviously much against them, the warriors of Acre nevertheless fought bravely. Henry and Amalric stayed to the very end, having sent the women, children and the old to Cyprus. Yet Henry was, in the first instance, King of Cyprus. Regretfully, this young and courageous monarch, no more than twenty years old, took ship with Amalric.

By May 18th, Acre was in the hands of the Mamlúks, and the slaughter of the population went on apace. No one knows how many were killed, how many of the young were taken into slavery. The castle of the Templars which was built into the sea, on the south-west promontory of Acre, held out for another ten days. Its surrender would have been peacefully carried out but for the fact that the Mamlúk soldiery ran amuck and tried to seize the women and the youths; whereupon the Templars turned and murdered them. The last scene of that gruesome and bloody finale was the beheading of Peter of Sevrey, the Marshal of the Temple, and a few others who had gone under safe conduct to the tent of al-Malik al-Ashraf. Two thousand assailing Mamlúks, together with the defenders of the castle, were entombed under the debris of its massive walls which crashed in the thick of fighting. Al-Malik al-Ashraf had achieved his father's mandate with a vengeance.

Next to fall was Haifa, occupied on July 30th. Monasteries on Mount Carmel were set on fire and their monks were put to the sword. Tyre and Sidon and Beirut were easily overrun. Their warriors sailed away to Tortosa or to Cyprus. Their inhabitants, as many as could, took to the mountains, to live in destitution amongst the native Christians, for whom also the conquerors had no pity. The tolerance of the Fáṭimids and the Ayyúbids became memories of the past. Ravaged and ruined towns and devastated countryside, along the Syrian coast, bore witness for a long time to the ferocity and ruthlessness of the victorious Mamlúks, standing sentinel over the wreck of an experiment, which though nobly conceived, and spanning two hundred years, began and ended with incredible cruelty. It had evoked great piety and unrelieved infamy, great devotion and sordid greed. It had drawn within its orbit peoples of infinite diversity, who should have been reconciled by common aims and purposes, by shared sufferings, but who drew apart in bitterness. Thus fare the projects of the mighty, when touched by perversity and sullied by self-seeking.

At the time al-Malik al-Ashraf was moving out of Cairo to destroy Outremer, the monarch who would have saved it was on his death-bed. Arghún died on 10 March 1291, in his early thirties, and was succeeded by his brother, Gaykhátú. There was a brief clash between the armies of the two brothers, on the banks of the Euphrates, but neither side ventured to expand the area of hostilities. Gaykhátú might have had a longer and a peaceful reign, had it not been for his extravagances, his lavish way of living and his curt behaviour towards his cousin, Báydú. Sa‘di’d-Dawlih, the wise and moderate vizier of Arghún, had met the same fate as Shamsi’d-Dín-i-Juvayní, and had been executed by a group of conspirators. The young Íl-Khán was beset by the machinations of a number of disloyal and rebellious Amírs, whom he had treated with remarkable clemency. These very men declared for Báydú. They captured Gaykhátú in March 1295 and strangled him, when he was only twenty-four years old. Báydú, who was not involved in the intrigues leading to his cousin’s death, had ruled only a few months, when Gházán, the son of Arghún, challenged him for the throne and won. Before gaining it, prompted by Amír Nawrúz, a powerful Mongol nobleman, Gházán declared himself a Muslim. That event, a prominent landmark in the history of Islám, took place on 19 June 1295, in the beautiful Lár valley in the heart of the Elburz range. In October, Gházán reached Tabríz, the capital of his forefathers. He mounted the throne with clean hands, for Báydú, by his orders, had not been executed.

The new master of Írán took a new name, Maḥmúd, to indicate his conversion to the Faith of the Arabian Prophet.

31

The Changing Face of Islamic Society

OUTREMER was dead and five centuries were to pass before the people of Europe would become, once again, involved in the affairs of the realm of Islám. But it certainly must not be assumed that traffic between Europe and the Islamic world came to a halt with the death of Outremer. During those very years of bitter clash between Christendom and Islám, scholars such as Gerard of Cremona (1114–87) were quietly transmitting the learning of the Islamic world to the Christendom of the West, through their copious translations of outstanding works which the civilization of Islám had produced. This process went on into the fourteenth century, unaffected by the dislocations and upheavals of war. It is interesting to note that while Muslim Spain, the principal channel of cultural intercourse, was being fragmented and then diminished under Christian pressure, the transmission to the West of Islamic learning gathered speed.

Abáqá's descent on Anatolia in 1277 extinguished the rule of the Saljúqs of Rúm, although nominally, until 1307, there were Saljúqids on the throne, whose names were struck on coins. At the end of the thirteenth century, a Turkish chieftain, 'Uthmán, the son of Irṭughril, rose to eminence in Anatolia. Not much is known of the origins of this remarkable warrior, who, before long, found for himself a seat of power. We find his successor, Urkhán (reigned 1324–60) well established, with his capital at Brúsa (Bursa). 'Uthmán and Urkhán fought many battles with the Byzantines to consolidate and expand their domain. Such were the beginnings of the great Ottoman Empire of future years. In 1357 Urkhán ventured to cross the Dardanelles at Gallipoli, and under Murád I (reigned 1360–89) Adrianople, on the European mainland, became the capital of the Ottoman kingdom. This was no mean achievement.

The conversion of Gházán to Islám did not remove the causes of hostility between the Mamlúks and the Mongols and that hostility continued as long as the Íl-Kháns had the power and the substance to sustain it. Gházán was by nature a tolerant man. He soon put an end to excesses committed by fanatics, who had issued a decree ordering the demolition of the Buddhist, the Jewish and the Christian places of worship. This bore heavily on the Buddhists in particular, because they had only recently come to settle on alien soil. Buddhism had, for long, totally disappeared from the Íránian plateau, until the Mongols brought a variety of it with them. It disappeared again as soon as the Mongol nobility, *en masse*, embraced Islám. Jews and Christians suffered for the time being, but their Faiths were indigenous and survived. Eventually, Gházán went to the length of punishing those responsible for attacks on Christian churches in Tabríz. Possibly, one reason for Gházán's eager reversal to his natural tolerance towards Faiths other than his own was the disgrace and fall from power of the Amír Nawrúz, which led to his execution. Nawrúz had greatly helped Gházán to obtain the throne, but his arrogance and the discovery of his treasonable correspondence with the Mamlúks, in the days of Báydú, destroyed him and his family. Although it was true that he had appealed to the Mamlúks to come and overthrow the Íl-Khán, a good deal of the evidence brought against him consisted of forgeries.

Gházán had a far from peaceful reign. He had to contend with rebellions often engineered by members of his own family, with acts of disloyalty and misdemeanour in the high offices of state, which he dealt with brutally at times, and with his own ill-health, for though young he was a sick man. And the seething hostility between himself and the Mamlúks erupted into inconclusive war and invasion. Also, he intervened forcefully in the Saljúq principality of Rúm, by dismissing one puppet ruler and putting another in his place, who had soon to give way to the previous one.

That Gházán's conversion to Islám did not incline him to make common cause with other Muslim potentates against Christendom is further attested by his letter to the Pope and by the favourable reception which he gave to the envoy of the Byzantine Emperor. In April 1302 Gházán wrote to Boniface VIII (1294–1303) to the effect that he was preparing for the 'great work'[1]

[1] Fighting the Mamlúks.

which was to be his 'sole aim', and that the Pope and the Christian rulers of Europe should do the same and 'not fail to keep the rendezvous'.[2] Towards the end of the same year, an embassy came to him from the Emperor Andronicus II (1282–1328) to solicit his aid against the Ottomans. But Gh̲ázán was a devout Muslim. In the course of his campaigns and his wanderings around his Empire, he visited the shrine of Ḥusayn, the third Imám, at Karbilá, and the graves of the supporters of 'Alí, the first Imám and the fourth Caliph, who fell at Ṣiffín. He and his nobles gave up their Mongolian hats which were brimmed, hindering the performance of the daily prayers, and acquired turbans instead.

Under Gh̲ázán, Mongols invaded Syria three times. He was marshalling his forces for a fourth attempt when death overtook him in 1304. During his first incursion, his army cleared Syria of the Mamlúks (or so it was said); on the last day of the year 1299, in the meadows of Marj Ráhiṭ, the Damascenes came to greet him. There, more than six hundred years before, the Umayyad Marwán I had met and put to flight the partisans of 'Abdu'lláh Ibn az-Zubayr. But as soon as Gh̲ázán had completed his first conquest of Syria, he went back to 'Iráq, and his general, Qutlug̲h̲-S̲h̲áh, retreated in his wake. During the second attempt in 1300, floods immobilized both armies. Then Gh̲ázán called on the Mamlúk monarch, al-Malik an-Náṣir Náṣiri'd-Dín, to recognize him as his overlord; naturally, the Mamlúk refused. Gh̲ázán did not take part in the third invasion, which was led by Qutlug̲h̲-S̲h̲áh. This general, who stood high in the esteem of Gh̲ázán and had served him with distinction, suffered a decisive defeat and fled in haste. This precipitate flight so angered the Íl-K̲h̲án that he dismissed that seasoned campaigner from his presence.

Gh̲ázán died in the vicinity of Qazvín, at the age of thirty-three. He was a learned man himself and encouraged others in the pursuit of learning. It is said that he was conversant with many languages, including a language of Europe, possibly Latin. At the bidding of this monarch, the celebrated vizier, K̲h̲ájih Ras̲h̲ídi'd-Dín Faḍlu'lláh, a Jewish convert to Islám, began to compose in Persian his great encyclopaedic history, the *Jámi'u't-Tawárík̲h̲*. Gh̲ázán's reign inaugurated a cultural revival, at first imperceptible, which, in its plenitude, produced magnificent works of painting and architecture.

[2] Cited in *The Cambridge History of Iran*, vol. V, p. 391.

Gháhzán's successor was his brother, Uljáytú, named Nicholas when he embraced Christianity, and further renamed Muḥammad when he embraced Islám. He is known in the annals of Írán as Sulṭán Muḥammad-i-Khudá-Bandih[3] (or Khar-Bandih).[4] It is related that he was hesitant in choosing between the two Sunní schools of Ḥanafí and Sháfi'í. He therefore summoned an eminent representative of each to argue the case, that he might be better informed. Their disputation became so rancorous and abusive that the Íl-Khán was disgusted, and so were the members of his retinue, who urged him to abandon Islám and revert to the religion of his forefathers. Apparently those new converts were still wavering, but not so Uljáytú. He finally chose to be a Shí'ah—the first Shí'ah ruler in Írán and 'Iráq since the days of the Buwayhids.

Firm as Uljáytú remained in allegiance to his Faith, no less firm was he in his stand to continue the contest with the Mamlúks. He went on corresponding with Christian potentates, as his brother and his father had done before him, to obtain their support. He wrote a long letter to Philip IV (Phillipe le Bel) of France, but there is no evidence to show whether the French king ever received or answered it. Uljáytú's letter to Edward I of England was answered by Edward II, his son. The English king expressed his joy that the Íl-Khán was determined to destroy 'the abominable sect of Mahomet',[5] but for Edward it was a long way to the Holy Land and he faced other exigencies. (The Scots were still unruly and he had yet to fight the battle of Bannockburn.) Pope Clement IV (1305–14) was more responsive. He wrote to the Íl-Khán that when the time was opportune he and other potentates would send an army and inform him of the fact. But, of course, that information never came. Again, single-handed, the Mongols tried to dislodge the Mamlúks from Syria. Taking heart from the reports of some discontented Amírs, the Mongol army crossed the Euphrates and laid siege to Raḥbat ash-Shám. It was winter-time, victuals were hard to come by and the loss in manpower was great. Nothing could be done but to retire. Thus in January 1313, the very last attempt of the Mongols to beat the Mamlúks was foiled.

[3] Servant of God.
[4] Ass-herd.
[5] ibid., p. 402.

The Caspian province of Gílán had always defied the Mongols. Uljáytú decided to force the Gílakís into submission. There were initial successes, but in the end thick forests and bogs proved to be the undoing of the Mongol army, and Qutlugh-Sháh, who had been restored to favour, lost his life. His death brought the Amír Chubán (Chúpán) to the fore. He was destined to play a decisive part in the affairs of the Íl-Khåns.

Control from far distant Peking over the Empire of Chingíz Khán had long ceased to exist. As we have seen, the descendants of Chingíz had been fighting amongst themselves. During the reign of Uljáytú, prompted by the Emperor in China, a pact was made for the purpose of harnessing them in unity, which was short-lived. Internal developments in these kingdoms, ruled by the members of the House of Chingíz, had taken divergent courses, and as far as the Íl-Khåns were concerned the sun was almost setting on their fortunes.

The memorial of Uljáytú is his massive mausoleum, which, in its ruined state, inspires awe and admiration. In the lush meadows on the plains, in the north-west corner of 'Iráq-i-'Ajam, near the city of Zanján, Arghún had begun the construction of a city which Uljáytú, his son, completed, made his capital and named Sulṭáníyyih. That city is no more, but the majestic mausoleum remains, in solitary splendour, dominating the landscape.

Uljáytú, like his brother, died young. When the end came, in December 1316, he was thirty-six years old. His son and heir-apparent, Abú-Sa'íd, was a boy of twelve, far away from the capital at the time of Uljáytú's death. Two Amírs contended for his guardianship. However, it was to the Amír Chubán's care that his father had left him. Gradually, this Amír became the most powerful man in the realm, until Abú-Sa'íd resolved to be rid of him. The learned and accomplished Rashídi'd-Dín Faḍlu'lláh had voluntarily retired from the service of the State. Chubán sought him out and urged him to take up his office once again. The enemies of that eminent man now conspired to ruin him. It was rumoured that Uljáytú had been poisoned, and Rashídi'd-Dín was accused of having encompassed it. Chubán, who had brought him from retirement, did not lift a finger to protect him. Rashídi'd-Dín and his sixteen-year-old son, 'Izzi'd-Dín, who had been page to Uljáytú, were executed on flimsy charges. His head was carried round the streets of Tabríz and he was reviled as a Jew.

As Abú-Sa'íd grew up he became acutely aware that all power was in the hands of Chubán, and he naturally resented it. But there were rebellions to be put down and an invasion by the Golden Horde to repel, which the Amír managed most effectively. The young monarch displayed great bravery in combat, for which he gained the title of Bahádur (Valiant). Taymúr-Tásh, a son of Chubán, was Viceroy of Rúm. He too rebelled and claimed that he was the promised Mahdí. Chubán himself undertook the punitive expedition against him, whereupon Taymúr-Tásh offered his submission and was pardoned. He was very successful in containing the Byzantines and the Ottomans. Later, when his father fell from power, Taymúr-Tásh fled to Egypt. Al-Malik an-Náṣir Náṣiri'd-Dín received him most amiably, but, in the end, put him to death, in order to keep friendly relations with the Íl-Khán. Times had indeed changed.

The first member of Chubán's family to meet the wrath of the Íl-Khán was another son, Dimashq Khájih, governor of Ádharbáyján, who had been acting as the chief minister. It was alleged that Dimashq Khájih was involved in a plot with a wife of Uljáytú. His murder caused his father to rebel, who, in turn, was destroyed. This happened in 1327. Eight years later, while on his way to throw back another invasion by the Golden Horde, the thirty-year-old Íl-Khán died, in all probability by poison. Abú-Sa'íd Bahádur was both talented and courageous, but domination by the Amír Chubán and the Amír's relations had an adverse effect on him. It is worth recording that after the elimination of Dimashq Khájih, Abú-Sa'íd made Ghíyáthi'd-Dín, a son of Rashídi'd-Dín, his vizier; that high-minded and generous man did not take any action against those responsible for his father's execution. On the contrary, he overwhelmed them with his favour.

Abú-Sa'íd, like his predecessors, was very tolerant where other people's faith was concerned. He would not allow Armenians to be molested. In the second year of Abú-Sa'íd's reign, Pope John XXII (1316–34) established the Archbishopric of Sulṭáníyyih and gave it into the charge of Franco de Pérouse. He also appointed six suffragans. This new Archdiocese had for its domain the whole of the Íránian plateau. It speaks well for the tolerance shown to the Christians that, at the same time, bishops sent by Rome took up their posts in Izmír and Sívás. William (Guillaume)

Adam, the Bishop of Izmír, became the second Archbishop of Sulṭáníyyih. These arrangements from Rome were not to last. Turbulent times lay ahead.

Within a year of the death of Abú-Sa'íd, who had no heir-apparent, the kingdom of the Íl-Kháns broke up. Two protagonists, who contested for power in the Íl-Khánid realm, were Shaykh Ḥasan-i-Kúchik (the Lesser), son of Taymúr-Tásh, and Shaykh Ḥasan-i-Buzurg (the Greater). The latter had been disgraced in the reign of Abú-Sa'íd, but, restored to favour when his innocence was proved, he was sent to be Viceroy of Rúm. A series of puppets, descendants of Chingíz, were put up by Ḥasan-i-Kúchik and Ḥasan-i-Buzurg, and discarded at will. By the middle of the fourteenth century, the lands stretching from the confines of Hindú-Kush to the frontiers of Syria had been parcelled out between the Kurt Maliks of Hirát, the Sarbadárán of Khurásán, the Muẓaffarids of Shíráz, Iṣfahán and Kirmán (descendants of Mubárizi'd-Dín Muḥammad), the Chúpánids of Ádharbáyján (descendants of Shaykh Ḥasan-i-Kúchik) and the Jaláyirids of 'Iráq (descendants of Shaykh Ḥasan-i-Buzurg).

Now for the first time in that vast realm of Islám no kingdom or emirate could be considered all-powerful. Apart from the Banu'l-Aḥmar or the Naṣrids of Granada, who were tributaries to the kingdom of Castile, there were no Arab dynasties anywhere in control of a substantial part of the Islamic realm. With the growing power of the Ottomans and the still dominant position of the Mamlúks, Turks seemed destined to wield supreme authority over Islamic lands. Then arose a man whom Christopher Marlowe has well described as 'the Scourge of God'. He too was a Turk, a Tartar.

Amír Tímúr-i-Gúrkán, known generally in the West as Tamerlane, came from Transoxania. Kish or Shahr-i-Sabz (the Verdant City) was his native town. Wounded during one of his battles by an arrow, he was permanently lamed, and was known subsequently as Tímúr-i-Lang (Lame), which became, in due course, Tamerlane (or Tamburlaine) in English. He was born in the year of Abú-Sa'íd Bahádur's death, the last of the effective Íl-Kháns. Tímúr's early years resemble those of Chingíz Khán. His father died when he was young and Transoxania was as turbulent as Mongolia had been. The Chaghatáyid kingdom was in dissolution and when Tughluq-Tímúr came from Jatah to annex

Transoxania, its leading men joined forces to resist him. At the last minute Ḥájí Barlás, Tímúr's uncle, felt that he was not equal to the task and sought refuge in Khurásán. Young Tímúr, far from attempting to fight the invader, went to him and offered his submission, for which he was rewarded with the governorship of Transoxania. However, the situation was basically unstable, and there were many who craved for power. Tímúr's fortunes ebbed and flowed for several years; at one time he was a wanderer in the desert, looking for friends and allies. Time and again supposed friends turned against him. Even his uncle returned from Khurásán to stand in his way. His brother-in-law, Amír Ḥusayn, who was once a fellow wanderer with him, in the wastes of Transoxania, tried to snatch away the prize. Just as Chingíz had overcome all odds, so did Tímúr, and by the year 1369 he was master of the whole of Transoxania. Then he set out to reduce the neighbouring territories of Jatah to the east, Khárazm to the west and Badakhshán to the south. In 1381, he captured the fair city of Hirát.

The Memoirs (*Malfuẓát*) and the Institutes (*Taẓúk*) ascribed to his own pen are now rejected by scholars as forgeries. Yet they have a ring of authenticity and, even if written by someone else, they show Tímúr's valour, perseverance, total disregard of danger and superb generalship. Tímúr was possessed of those virtues, but he was also cruel, bloodthirsty and vindictive. This is what Professor Arnold Toynbee has written of him:

'Thus, besides forfeiting a Promised Land, Timur undid his own work of liberating his native country;[6] but the greatest of all his acts of destruction was committed against himself. He has succeeded in making his name immortal at the price of erasing from the minds of Posterity all memory of the deeds for which he might have been remembered for good. To how many people in either Christendom or Dār-al-Islām[7] to-day does Timur's name call up the image of a champion of Civilization against Barbarism, who led the clergy and people of his country to a hard-won victory at the end of a nineteen-years-long struggle for independence? To the vast majority of those to whom the name of Timur Lenk [Lang] or Tamerlane means anything at all, it commemorates a militarist who perpetrated as many horrors in the span of twenty-

[6] This refers to events of future decades. (H.M.B.)
[7] The realm of Islám. (H.M.B.)

four years as had been perpetrated in a century by a succession of Assyrian kings from Tiglath-Pileser III to Asshurbanipal inclusive. We think of the monster who razed Isfarā'in to the ground in 1381; built two thousand prisoners into a living mound, and then bricked them over, at Sabzawār in 1383; piled 5,000 human heads into minarets at Zirih in the same year; cast his Lūrī prisoners alive over precipices in 1386; massacred 70,000 people, and piled the heads of the slain into minarets, at Isfahān in 1387; massacred the garrison of Takrit, and piled their heads into minarets, in 1393; massacred 100,000 prisoners at Delhi in 1398; buried alive the 4,000 Christian soldiers of the garrison of Sivas after their capitulation in 1400; built twenty towers of skulls in Syria in 1400 and 1401;[8] and dealt with Baghdad in 1401 as he had dealt fourteen years earlier with Isfahān. In minds which know him only through such deeds, Timur has caused himself to be confounded with the ogres of the Steppe—a Chingis and an Attila and the like—against whom he had spent the better half of his life in waging a Holy War. The crack-brained megalomania of the homicidal madman whose one idea is to impress the imagination of Mankind with a sense of his military power by a hideous abuse of it is brilliantly conveyed in the hyperboles which the English poet Marlowe has placed in the mouth of his Tamburlaine:

I hold the Fates bound fast in yron chaines,
And with my hand turne Fortune's wheel about,
And sooner shall the Sun fall from his Spheare,
Than Tamburlaine be slaine or overcome. . . .
The God of war resignes his roume to me,
Meaning to make me Generall of the world;
Jove, viewing me in armes, looks pale and wan,
Fearing my power should pull him from his throne. . . .'[9]

Toynbee so deservedly and mercilessly castigates Tímúr, because in his view Tímúr became a victim of militarism and turned upon the realm of Islám, inflicting horrors of mass destruction upon it, instead of going beyond the area of Qipcháq to conquer and control the whole of the Eurasian Steppe and establish a 'Pan-Eurasian Islamic Empire'. Here we are not concerned

[8] Tímúr conquered Damascus in that year. (H.M.B.)
[9] *A Study of History*, vol. IV, pp. 500–1.

with what might have been, nor, particularly, with Professor Toynbee's views. The above quotation has been cited at length because it presents a forceful picture of the enormities committed by Tamerlane. Nevertheless it is salutary to ponder over the miseries which his bloody assaults brought on his fellow Muslims. And the nomads of the Eurasian Steppe, not very long after the death of the great conqueror, swept down over Khárazm and then Transoxania, dispossessing his heirs of their heritage. Professor Toynbee even suggests that had Tímúr gone on to push his frontiers inexorably northwards, there would be today an empire based on Samarqand controlling Moscow rather than the reverse.

While Tímúr was battling in the eastern limits of the realm of Islám, the Ottomans were advancing steadily at the expense of the Christians. Sofia was captured by them in 1382 and the whole of Bulgaria in 1393. By 1390 they had driven the Byzantines entirely out of Asia Minor. Murád I had been murdered, in 1389, to be succeeded by Báyazíd I, the Bajazet of Christopher Marlowe and other Western writers. The same year the Serbians received a heavy defeat at the hands of the Ottomans. In 1396, Báyazíd overwhelmed a Christian army at Nicopolis. The Emperor Manuel travelled to France and England, in the year 1400, to ask for help against Báyazíd. The Mamlúks had also been active. They overran the kingdom of Little Armenia (Cilicia) in 1375. Up to 1382, the Mamlúk rulers were Turks, originating mainly from Qipcháq, and are known as Baḥrís (Marines), because under the Ayyúbids, their quarters were on an island in the Nile. The next line of the Mamlúks, all Circassian (with two exceptions), are known as Burjís (Men of the Tower), because their barracks were originally in the citadel.

Tímúr sent envoys to al-Malik aẓ-Ẓáhir Sayfi'd-Dín Barqúq, whom the Burjí ruler wantonly put to death although their mission was innocent enough; and in the words of Professor Hitti:

'Like a cyclone Tīmūr swept over northern Syria in 1400. For three days Aleppo was given over to plunder. The heads of over twenty thousand of its Moslem inhabitants were built into mounds ten cubits high by twenty in circumference, with all the faces on the outside. The city's priceless schools and mosques of the Nūrid and Ayyūbid ages were destroyed, never to be rebuilt. Ḥamāh, Ḥimṣ and Ba'labakk fell in turn. The advance forces of the Egyptian army under Sultan Faraj were routed and Damascus captured (February, 1401). While the city was sacked the fire broke out . . . Of the Umayyad Mosque nothing was left but the walls. Of the Damascene scholars, skilled labourers and artisans the ablest were carried away by Tīmūr to his capital, Samarqand, there to implant Islamic sciences and to introduce certain industrial arts which have since been lost to the Syrian capital . . . Ibn Khaldūn[10] accompanied Faraj from Cairo and headed the Damascene mission which negotiated peace with Tīmūr.'[11]

Flushed with triumph in Syria, Tímúr made another assault on Baghdád to redress a wrong with vengeance, and then set out to challenge the Ottomans. At the battle of Ánqurah (modern Ankara), in 1402, he crushed them and made a prisoner of Báyazíd, who died the following year in captivity. Sulaymán I succeeded him. Tímúr himself died in Utrár in 1405. His tomb in Samarqand, Gúr-Amír, a magnificent structure, stands in good repair. At his death, his vast empire, larger than Chingíz Khán's, began to crumble. The fratricidal strifes of his progeny made it impossible for that empire to endure, quite apart from the fact that Tímúr had been almost continuously engaged in piling conquest upon conquest and had not consolidated his gains, although there were powerful men lurking about to seize the territories which he had made his own.

Tímúr's progeny (with one exception) were not very successful as rulers, but their petulance and self-destructive, senseless quarrels were overwhelmingly compensated by their brilliant talents. Their patronage of art and learning combined with their own achievements made those few decades a glorious period of renaissance. The most effective and successful of Tímúr's descendants (barring the Mughul Emperors of India, whose age is different, as is their story) was Sháhrukh, the conqueror's fourth son. Tímúr had named Pír-Muḥammad, the son of Jahángír, his eldest son, to succeed him, but he never came to the throne. Míránsháh, another son of Tímúr, controlled a substantial part of the Íránian plateau; Khalíl-Sulṭán, the son of Míránsháh, held Transoxania, and Sháhrukh was well established in Khurásán. Throughout Ádharbáyján and 'Iráq and into Anatolia, two Turkamán (Turkmen) factions subdued by Tímúr—the Aq-

[10] The great scholar and historian. (H.M.B.)
[11] *History of the Arabs*, p. 701.

Quyúnlú (White Sheep) and the Qará-Quyúnlú (Black Sheep)—were struggling for mastery. However, within four years of the conqueror's death, Sháhrukh was the acknowledged head of the House of Tímúr and obeyed as such (although insubordination was not lacking). He defeated Qará-Yúsuf of the Qará-Quyúnlú and held him at bay, later forcing Iskandar and Jahánsháh, sons of Qará-Yúsuf into submission.

Sháhrukh was the husband of Gawhar-Shád, whose name is immortalized by her resplendent mosque at Mashhad, of which the Shrine of the eighth Imám forms an integral part, and by the Theological College and mausoleum at Hirát, which even in their ruined condition are truly dazzling. In these buildings Islamic architecture and faience reached great heights. Báysunqur and Ulugh Beg were sons of Sháhrukh and Gawhar-Shád. The former lived in Hirát and the latter was given the viceroyalty of Transoxania by his father. Ulugh Beg was a learned astronomer. He had an observatory built in Samarqand, and gathered round him astronomers no less talented than himself. The set of Astronomical Tables which Ulugh Beg produced is described as 'the most accurate and complete which have been bequeathed by the East to the West'.[12] John Greaves, Savilian Professor of Astronomy at Oxford, published Ulugh Beg's Tables, in Latin, in 1665. The West was profoundly impressed. Báysunqur excelled in arts, calligraphy being his forte. His work is imprinted on the faience of his mother's mosque in Mashhad. An Englishman, who in disguise found his way into the court of the Mosque of Gawhar-Shád, has written:

'I hastened down the dark bazaar, found the dome where I turned to the left, and was greeted, on coming out into the court, by such a fanfare of colour and light that I stopped a moment, half blinded. It was as if someone had switched on another sun.

'The whole quadrangle was a garden of turquoise, pink, dark red, and dark blue, with touches of purple, green, and yellow, planted among paths of plain buff brick. Huge white arabesques whirled above the ivan[13] arches. The ivans themselves hid other gardens, shadier, fritillary-coloured. The great minarets beside the sanctuary, rising from bases encircled with Kufic the size of

[12] Sykes, *A History of Persia*, vol. II, p. 138.
[13] *Ayván*: portico, open gallery. (H.M.B.)

a boy, were bedizened with a network of jewelled lozenges. The swollen sea-green dome adorned with yellow tendrils appeared between them. At the opposite end glinted the top of a gold minaret. But in all this variety, the principle of union, the life-spark of the whole blazing apparition, was kindled by two great texts: the one, a frieze of white *suls*[14] writing powdered over a field of gentian blue along the skyline of the entire quadrangle; the other, a border of the same alphabet in daisy white and yellow on a sapphire field, interlaced with turquoise Kufic along its inner edge, and enclosing, in the form of a three-sided oblong, the arch of the main ivan between the minarets. The latter was actually designed, it says, by "Baisanghor, son of Shah Rukh, son of Timur Gurkani (Tamerlane), with hope in God, in the year 821 (A.D. 1418)." Baisanghor was a famous calligrapher; and being the son of Gohar Shad also, he celebrated his mother's munificence with an inscription whose glory explains for ever the joy felt by Islam in writing on the face of architecture.'[15]

Báysunqur brought together brilliant calligraphers and miniaturists in Hirát and personally directed and instructed them to make books and bindings, to paint and write and create works of unsurpassed beauty. Poets and musicians, too, found an honoured place in the court of Báysunqur. He died in the lifetime of his father, as a result of his intemperate drinking bouts. Ulugh Beg succeeded his father in 1447, but his reign was short-lived, for his wretched son, 'Abdu'l-Laṭíf, had him put to death. Six months later, 'Abdu'l-Laṭíf received his deserts, when he was assassinated. Thereafter the fortunes of the House of Tímúr rapidly declined, except for the long reign from 1470 to 1506 of Sulṭán Ḥusayn Mírzá Báyqará in Khurásán. Once again, Hirát became the cynosure of poets such as Jámí, the last great classical poet of Persia and an eminent exponent of Ṣúfiism; miniaturists such as the incomparable Bihzád; writers such as Mír-Khund, the industrious historian and author of the *Rawḍatu'ṣ-Ṣafá*,[16] and Mullá Ḥusayn-i-Vá'iẓ-i-Káshifí, author of the *Anvár-i-Suhaylí*

[14] Thulth. (H.M.B.)

[15] Byron, *The Road to Oxiana*, pp. 243–4 (Cape Paperback edn.).

[16] This work, which is in seven volumes, has been denigrated, but the view of Professor Arberry that it 'exercised a wholly baneful influence' (in *Classical Persian Literature*, Allen & Unwin, 1958, p. 390) is not justified. In the nineteenth century, Riḍá-Qulí Khán-i-Hidáyat wrote a Supplement to it, in three volumes, which is known as *Rawḍatu'ṣ-Ṣafáy-i-Náṣirí*.

(Lights of Canopus), a recension of the *Kalílah-wa-Dimnah* (The Fables of Bídpáy). Sulṭán Ḥusayn's minister, Amír 'Alí-Shír-i-Navá'í, was also a remarkable man, giving his patronage to all who deserved it, and is particularly renowed as a talented writer in Turkí and the promoter of that language.

It is sad to relate that because of the internecine struggles amongst the Tímúrids, Gawhar-Shád was put to death, when she was over eighty, by Abú-Sa'íd, a great-grandson of Tímúr. Abú-Sa'íd was the grandfather of Bábur, the founder of the Mughul Empire in India. He ruled over Transoxania and Khurásán until 1469, when he was defeated by Ḥasan Beg (Úzún Ḥasan) of the Aq-Quyúnlú and was handed over to Mírzá Yádgár Muḥammad, a grandson of Báysunqur, who had no hesitation in ordering his execution.

Ḥasan Beg, whose seat was at Diyárbakr in Anatolia, also defeated Jahánsháh and extinguished the power of the Qará-Quyúnlú. Jahánsháh had, for a while, extended his rule to the southern regions of Persia; but now the star of the Aq-Quyúnlú was in the ascendant. For nearly fifty years they held in their possession almost the whole of Írán (Khurásán excepted) and 'Iráq, as well as a part of eastern Anatolia.

The Ottomans had, in the meantime, recovered their territories, and at long last they achieved that victory which had eluded the Muslims for eight hundred years. In 1453 Sulṭán Muḥammad (Mehmet) II Fátiḥ (the Conqueror) captured Constantinople and a dream came true. Byzantium fell, never to rise again. The Basilica of St. Sophia became the Mosque of Ayá Súfíya. Today it is a museum.

Within half a century of being humbled, humiliated and nearly obliterated by Tímúr, the Ottomans had regained all they had lost in Europe and Asia, had won the defiant City of Constantine, and had begun their meteoric rise to imperial power.

By the opening years of the sixteenth century a series of events were to occur which would cause the fulcrum of civilization and the balance of world polity to move steadily westwards, away from the Mediterranean Basin—for two millenniums the main centre of world events; which would bring down a shutter on Central Asia, plunging it into an impenetrable darkness reminiscent of barbaric times, cutting off this vast area of the world from the significant currents of civilized life; and which would create a deep rift in the realm of Islám, such as it had not experienced before.

In January 1492, the last vestige of Islamic presence in Spain, once so dramatically and beneficently dominant, was removed by the action of Ferdinand and Isabella of Castile and Aragon. Abú-'Abdu'lláh (Boabdil of Western chroniclers and writers), the weak, scheming ruler of the Banu'l-Aḥmar, lost his tenuous grip on Granada. In October of the same year, Christopher Columbus, financed and equipped by the same Spanish monarchs, reached an island in the Antilles which he named San Salvador and which he thought was India. Europeans stood at the portals to a New World. By 1488, Bartholomew Diaz had rounded the Cape of Good Hope. In 1498, Vasco da Gama brought his ships into harbour at Calicut in India, John Cabot discovered Labrador and Columbus discovered South America. In 1499, a boy of thirteen named Ismá'íl, descended from Shaykh Ṣafíyyi'd-Dín, a revered Ṣúfí *murshid* (guide), set out to carve a kingdom for himself in Ádharbáyján. And in 1505, Uzbaks became the masters of Transoxania.

We shall examine these events in the next chapter, as they touched upon the fortunes of the realm of Islám.

32

Final Divisions

THE rapid growth of Ottoman power produced, not unreasonably, alarm and consternation in the West. As already mentioned, the Byzantine Emperor travelled to France and England in search of help. The West, alerted to a potential danger, looked to the East to find a possible ally against the Ottomans. The pattern was almost the same as in the days of the Crusaders, when descendants of Chingíz Khán were courted and fervent hopes expressed that Prester John would issue from the confines of Central Asia. Now there was Tímúr, and his remarkable story had reached the ears of the potentates of Europe. Henry III of Castile, son-in-law of John of Gaunt, sent an embassy, and two of Henry's envoys witnessed the defeat and capture of Báyazíd. Tímúr himself had written to Henry IV of England, brother-in-law of the enterprising King of Castile, with the purpose of fostering trade. The English King congratulated him on his victory over the Ottomans. But despite his friendship with the West, Tímúr expelled the Knights of St. John from Smyrna.

Tímúr, however, died shortly after his triumph in Asia Minor, and the Ottomans were soon back and menacing Europe. Venice, particularly, felt threatened. In the past she had been able to come to terms with the rulers of Egypt, be they Ayyúbids or Mamlúks. But making deals with the Ottomans—ever advancing, ever expanding their dominions—was not easy. In the latter part of the fifteenth century, Venice had become the leading maritime power in the Mediterranean; she had humbled Genoa and had a near monopoly of trade with Beirut and Alexandria. Her consuls were stationed in Damascus, Aleppo, Tripoli and Beirut. Wares and merchandise from the East came to Damascus, to be sent to the port of Beirut—spices, precious stones, Persian gums, silk goods, all highly valued in the West. Alexandria equalled Beirut as an important depot, particularly for spices and pepper which Europe badly needed to preserve its meat. To safeguard her interests, Venice was desperately trying to rally Western powers to form a common front against the Ottomans, but the response was hardly encouraging. So when Ḥasan Beg of the White Sheep made an approach to Venice, the Doge and his council were delighted. The tall (Ūzún) Ḥasan had backed the Prince of Karamania (Cilicia), only to be defeated by the Ottomans. Realizing that he needed naval help he turned to Venice. The Venetian leaders decided to reciprocate by sending an envoy to Diyárbakr. Ḥasan Beg was married to Theodora, daughter of an emperor of Trebizond. A sister of Theodora was married to the Duke of Archipelago. Caterino Zeno, a wealthy merchant of Venice, whose wife was a daughter of the Duke, was chosen to go to attend Ḥasan Beg and persuade him to mount an attack on Sulṭán Muḥammad the Conqueror. The Ottomans had extirpated the empire of Trebizond in 1461, and had wrested Negroponte from the Venetians in 1470.

Ḥasan Beg readily agreed to attack the Ottomans from the rear while the Venetian naval forces operated off the coast of Cilicia. However, attacks and counter-attacks by the White Sheep and the Ottomans proved equally futile; the war between Venice and the Ottomans, begun in 1463, dragged on until 1479, ending in the cession to the Ottomans of Lemnos and the Venetian holdings in Albania. In 1473, during a brief struggle between the forces of Muḥammad the Conqueror and Ḥasan Beg, the Venetians became masters of Cyprus. Now Caterino Zeno, representing Ḥasan Beg, visited European potentates to obtain their support against the Ottomans, but Zeno's mission failed, and the White Sheep ruler wisely decided not to embroil himself further. Nevertheless, in future decades both East and West continued to seek allies from each other's regions.

The net gain of these contacts was the settlement of a number of Persian metal-workers in Venice. Their craftsmanship and patterns profoundly affected this branch of art in Europe, reaching England from Germany. The designs and the finished products of goldsmiths of the reign of Queen Elizabeth reflect the influence of those Persians who went to live in Venice.

In the end it was not the dominance of the Ottomans which ruined Venetian trade, but Columbus's desire to reach India and

Vasco da Gama's successful journey to Calicut. Within a few years Venetian ships could not find enough pepper and spices in the depots of Beirut and Alexandria to take to Europe. Whereas in 1498 there was such an abundance of pepper in Alexandria that the Venetians had not sufficient cash to buy it all, four years later they had to search for the merchandise they required, while in Beirut they found no more than four bales of pepper. Portuguese merchants were now buying these goods at source and bringing them to Europe without payment of imposts *en route* or any other hindrance. It was a long journey by land from the source to ports on the Mediterranean and the dues extracted mounted up, particularly as the Ottomans within two decades swept over Syria and Egypt. The discovery of sea routes to the south, the east and the west created new maritime powers: the Spanish, Dutch and English.

THE RISE OF THE ṢAFAVIDS

And now we must turn to the amazing story of a boy of thirteen, who wrought unbelievable changes which diverted the course of history; who succeeded where both his father and grandfather not only had failed, but had lost their lives as well. This boy was the future renowned S͟háh Ismáʿíl-i-Ṣafaví. He had many faults, but right through the course of his career his courage and single-mindedness shone dazzlingly. His achievements, in a lifetime of no more than thirty-six years, testify to what one man can do, with firm resolve, to alter the affairs of mankind in directions not warranted or even demanded by the sociological and economic climate of his day—factors to which many historians, particularly those tied to notions of economic determinism, usually give priority.

It has been said that S͟háh Ismáʿíl represented the resurgence of the national spirit of Írán. This is manifestly untrue. Ismáʿíl himself was Turkish-speaking and wrote habitually in Turkish, whereas his inveterate opponent, Salím (Selim), the Ottoman ruler, wrote in Persian and composed Persian poems. Ismáʿíl's main support rested on the seven great Turkish tribes of Afs͟hár, Qájár, Takallú, Rúmlú, S͟hámlú, Ustájlú and D͟huʾl-Qadar. Collectively they bore a Turkish name: Qizil-Bás͟h (Red-Capped), by which for a long period the Ṣafavid power was known. A contemporary chronicler, bitterly hostile to S͟háh Ismáʿíl and his policy, speaks bitterly of 'the Qizil-Básh Turkmans'. For centuries, Írán had had a succession of rulers: the Ghaznavids, the Saljúqs, the Khárazmsháhís, the Atábaks of Fárs and Ádharbáyján, the Íl-Kháns, the Tímúrids (Gúrkánís), the Black Sheep and the White Sheep—alien conquerors all—who had been so thoroughly and completely assimilated that no one could think of them except in terms of the natives of the land. Even the Turkman White Sheep (Aq-Quyúnlú), whom Sháh Ismá'íl supplanted, were more thoroughly Persian than he.

Another theory which considers Shí'ism (so punctiliously and fanatically promulgated by Sháh Ismá'íl and imposed on a population averse to it) as the natural embodiment of the aspirations of the Íránians, is a theory not sustained by facts. The days when the call in the name of the House of the Prophet aroused the people of Írán were long since forgotten. In those times the racial preferences of the detested Umayyads weighed heavily on the Persians, and Abú-Muslim had raised his black standard in Khurásán to challenge their power. But in the fifteenth century of the Christian Era, Khurásán was Sunní to the core. The Tímúrid Sulṭán Ḥusayn Báyqará, despite his Shí'ah tendencies, had been dissuaded by his vizier, Amír 'Alí-Shír-i-Nává'í, from making a public profession. Uljáytú had found Shí'ah beliefs more acceptable because the argumentations of Sunní theologians had disgusted him, nearly leading him to abandon Islám altogether; yet he had not attempted to make others fall in line with him. At Tabríz, which Sháh Ismá'íl made his capital, even the Shí'ah divines of the city begged him, on the eve of his coronation, not to imperil his position by forcing the people to conform to Shí'ah beliefs, since two-thirds of the inhabitants of Tabríz were Sunní. Sháh Ismá'íl brushed aside their plea. It is certainly true that the people of the Caspian provinces beyond the Elburz range, and particularly the Daylam, because of their opposition to the caliphs, first of Damascus and then of Baghdád, had always had Shí'ah proclivities. But when Sháh Ismá'íl appeared on the scene, the principal centres of Shí'ism were in Ḥillah in 'Iráq, Jabal 'Ámil in Syria, Baḥrayn and al-Ḥasá. So short was Írán of Shí'ah divines that Sháh Ismá'íl had to bring a large number of them from Syria, at the same time putting to death prominent Sunní doctors of law who were Persian. No less a person than Sayfi'd-Dín Aḥmad-i-Taftázání, the Shaykhu'l-Islám of Hirát—great-grandson of the celebrated jurist and author Sa'di'd-Dín-i-Taftázání—suffered in this manner; and at Kázirún, in the province of Fárs, a number of Sunní clerics were made to pay the supreme penalty. Only in Káshán and Qum did the young Ismá'íl have an enthusiastic welcome, since their populations were overwhelmingly Shí'ah. Sháh Ismá'íl, by the exercise of his iron will, completely changed the religious environment of Persia. Professor Arnold Toynbee argues that the schismatic effect of Sháh Ismá'íl's policy on the nascent 'Iranic Society' (born after the demise of the 'Abbásid Caliphate) was such that the other powerful half which remained Sunní, represented by the Ottomans, recoiled upon its sister Islamic society, which Toynbee names the nascent 'Arabic Society', and absorbed it. Thus the 'Iranic Society' fell asunder and the 'Arabic Society' was destroyed. In Toynbee's view, until Sháh Ismá'íl appeared in the role of a militant divider, the Ottomans had no thought of expanding their domains southward or eastward; their sole objective was to regain territories they had lost as a result of defeat at the hands of Tímúr, and then to strike ever deeper westward into Christian lands. Toynbee's verdict is that Sháh Ismá'íl's bellicosity and aggressiveness triggered off the same fierce qualities in Sulṭán Salím.

So, let us start at the beginning and see who were Sháh Ismá'íl's forbears, and what happened to set a thirteen-year-old boy on his fate-laden and stormy career.

We have to begin with the renowned Shaykh Ṣafíyyi'd-Dín, who lived in the days when Outremer still existed, and pagan or Buddhist Íl-Kháns reigned over Írán. He died in 1334, at the age of eighty-five—one year before the death of Abú-Sa'íd Bahádur Khán, the last of the great Íl-Kháns, and one year before the birth of Tímúr. We cannot go further back than Shaykh Ṣafíyyi'd-Dín Isḥáq, because those who are named as his ancestors have left no mark at all on history, and also because we know now that the genealogy of Shaykh Ṣafíyyi'd-Dín is fabricated. Sháh Ismá'íl claimed descent from Músá al-Káẓim, the seventh Imám of the Twelvers, which reinforced his position as the defender and the promoter of the rights of the House of the Prophet. Modern research has shown, beyond any doubt, that despite the assertion of the author[1] of the *Silsilatu'n-Nasab-i-Ṣafavíyyih* (The Genealogy of the Ṣafavids) and other contemporary chroniclers of the

[1] Shaykh Ḥasan Ibn-i-Shaykh Abdál-i-Záhidí.

Ṣafavid period, Sháh Ismá'íl was not a descendant of the Prophet, and that Shaykh Ṣafíyyi'd-Dín was a Kurd, a Sunní and the head of a fraternity of Ṣúfís. That Shaykh Ṣafíyyi'd-Dín was a man of high eminence is particularly evidenced by a letter from the great minister of Gházán and Uljáytú, Rashídi'd-Dín Faḍlu'lláh, to his son, the governor of Ardabíl, enjoining him to act in such a way as to earn the good-pleasure and the gratitude of the illustrious Shaykh.

Ṣafíyyi'd-Dín's successor, Ṣadri'd-Dín Muḥammad, did nothing remarkable to recommend him to attention, but the latter's son, Khájih 'Alí, a contemporary of Tímúr, is particularly worthy of note, because he was decidedly the first of his line to change his allegiance from Sunní doctrines to the Shí'ah. And he was a man of sufficient stature to intercede with Tímúr for prisoners brought from Anatolia. These men and their descendants became ardently attached to the House of Shaykh Ṣafíyyi'd-Dín. Khájih 'Alí died in Syria and was succeeded by his son, Shaykh Ibráhím, better known as Shaykh Sháh, who did nothing out of the ordinary and, in turn, passed his mantle of authority to his youngest, Shaykh Junayd. By this time, the following of the Ṣafavids had greatly increased and they had assumed a military character. The famous Ḥasan Beg (Úzún Ḥasan) of the White Sheep married his sister, Khadíjah, to Junayd, a union which enhanced enormously the prestige of the Ṣafavid Superior. Amír Jahánsháh of the Black Sheep, who ruled over Ádharbáyján and 'Iráq, although growing apprehensive of the power wielded by Shaykh Junayd, turned his attention to Shírván in the Caucasus and died in the ensuing battle. Shaykh Ḥaydar, the son of Junayd, enjoyed the protection of his uncle, the White Sheep ruler; Ḥasan Beg gave his daughter in marriage to him. This lady, whose mother, Despina Khátún, was the daughter of Kalo Ioannes, the last Greek Emperor of Trebizond, has been variously named as Marta, Halímah, Bakí-Ághá and 'Álam-Sháh Bagum (Begum). Ismá'íl was the second son of this auspicious marriage. Contemporary Europeans have described him as being very handsome, fair of complexion with red hair.

Shaykh Ḥaydar was even more warlike than his father, a quality which Ismá'íl and his elder brother, Sulṭán-'Alí, inherited in full measure. It was Shaykh Ḥaydar who devised for his devout followers the headgear which made them feared and famous—a scarlet twelve-gored hat. When Ismá'íl was a year old, Ḥaydar too lost his life, fighting Shírván Sháh (the ruler of Shírván). As his grandfather, Ḥasan Beg, was dead, his uncle, Sulṭán Ya'qúb, sent him and his brothers to Fárs, in the care of its governor. The White Sheep ruler was now much alarmed, as the last Amír of the Black Sheep had been, by the growing strength of the Qizil-Básh, and he arranged to have his nephews, the three sons of Shaykh Ḥaydar, kept in a fortress in Fárs. After him, the family squabbles of the White Sheep led to the death of Sulṭán-'Alí on the battlefield and the flight of Ismá'íl and his younger brother to the Caspian province of Gílán, where Kár-Kiyá Mírzá 'Alí, the governor of Láhíján, was friendly and afforded them refuge. It was in this province that Shaykh Ṣafíyyi'd-Dín had found his *murshid* in the person of Táji'd-Dín Aḥmad, a Kurd known as Shaykh Záhid-i-Gílání, had married Shaykh Záhid's daughter, and had inherited from him the headship of that Ṣúfí order which he directed. In those days, the direction of the Shaykhs had been entirely spiritual, but, after three successive heads of the order had gone down fighting, to avenge their blood became a burning desire, and the martial spirit imparted to the Red-Caps transformed the erstwhile Ṣúfí fraternity into a considerable force of seasoned warriors who were biding their time. When Ismá'íl came out of the safety of Láhíján, at the age of thirteen, he was accompanied by only seven men, but by the time he reached Ardabíl, the home of his forefathers and their burial place, his entourage had greatly increased. However, he was not yet in a position to give battle, and when he was told to leave Ardabíl, he discreetly withdrew to the shores of the Caspian. Next year (A.D. 1500) he was back with an army and prepared to fight. His first act was to invade Shírván, to avenge the death of his father and grandfather. Farrukh-Yasár, the King of Shírván, was slain, and the extirpation of this long-reigning dynasty of Shírván-Sháhs, who claimed to be descendants of the Sásánian Chosroes I, was accompanied by repellent horrors. Next, Sháh Ismá'íl defeated Alvand Mírzá of the White Sheep and captured Tabríz, where he was crowned. Sulṭán Murád, son of Sulṭán Ya'qúb, who was Ismá'íl's cousin, held the central areas of Írán, but he too went down to defeat.

The Ottoman ruler, Báyazíd II, son of the conqueror of Constantinople, was peace-loving; he did not wish to make

Sháh Ismá'íl's fierce assault on the Sunnís a *casus belli.* In his attempts at conciliation he even sent an embassy, laden with presents, to congratulate Sháh Ismá'íl on his victories. Sháh Ismá'íl made suitable gestures in return, then went on to conquer 'Iráq and Akhlaṭ and Diyárbakr, to the very limits of the Ottoman domains. His pride was great when he gained possession of Karbilá, Najaf and other holy cities and sites held in reverence, particularly by the Shí'ahs. By now the Ottoman army had had enough of the docile, pacific Báyazíd. He was swept off his throne and his son, Salím, replaced him. At last, Sháh Ismá'íl was to meet his match.

The incident which sparked off the clash between the Ottomans and the Ṣafavids was the rebellion in 1514 of the Shí'ahs of Anatolia, led by a certain Sháh-Qulí (Techelles of Christopher Marlowe), which may or may not have been inspired and engineered by Sháh Ismá'íl. At first the rebels gained some ground, but their failure was inevitable without active help from the Ṣafavid monarch, which was not forthcoming. Salím put down the rebellion with ferocity and massacred the Shí'ahs. They were Turks, not Persians, and probably as many as forty thousand perished. The figure of sixty thousand has also been mentioned. No one knows for certain, as the majority of chroniclers and historians, both Sunní and Shí'ah, for purposes of their own, failed to register the fact of this rebellion or massacre. Salím, having got rid of troublesome elements in Anatolia and having consolidated his position, now turned his full attention to Ismá'íl. A letter written in April 1514, grossly abusive and imperious in tone, demanded repentance and recantation from the Ṣafavid; otherwise punitive action would be taken against him. Not content with that insulting missive, Salím wrote a second letter, even more abusive than the first, demanding the cession to him of the Ṣafavid domains. In the meantime Sháh Ismá'íl had established a secret accord with al-Malik al-Ashraf Qánṣúḥ al-Ghawrí (1501–17), the Mamlúk monarch. Qánṣúḥ was as much a stalwart Sunní as Salím, but he was alarmed by the latter's militancy. Ismá'íl, for his part, had no illusions that he could persuade Qánṣúḥ to become a Shí'ah, but it was politic to ally himself with the Mamlúk. As we shall see, Ismá'íl had already ruined the chances of the Tímúrid prince, Ẓahíri'd-Dín Bábur, in Transoxania, by making him declare allegiance to Shí'ah doctrines as a condition of military support. Qánṣúḥ had the foresight to realize that unless Salím was checked and the Portuguese were driven out of the Indian Ocean, Egypt stood in dire peril. So he prepared for innovations. Throughout the previous centuries, Egypt and Persia had been always in opposite camps. Now they were to be reconciled. The Venetian fleet had served Egypt well in the past, but now Egypt's transit trade had vanished and Venice was helpless. Qánṣúḥ was the protector of Mecca and Medina; he cast his eyes on the shores of Arabia to establish naval outposts to prevent Portugal from depriving Egypt of her lucrative transit trade.

Salím, as good as his word, invaded Persia. The Ottoman and the Ṣafavid armies met at Cháldirán, some sixty miles from Tabríz, on 22 August 1514. Ismá'íl's valour was exemplary but although Salím lost more men than Ismá'íl, his artillery prevailed. A dejected Ismá'íl (who, it is said, never regained his *joie de vivre*) had to withdraw and let his capital fall to the detested enemy. Salím lost no time in broadcasting far and wide the news of his victory, but he could not retain his gains. His Janissaries,[2] the backbone of his army, were not used to the conditions of north-western Írán and pined for south-eastern Europe. So Sulṭán Salím had to retreat, taking with him Prince Badí'u'z-Zamán Mírzá, son of Sulṭán Ḥusayn-i-Báyqará, the last Tímúrid ruler of Hirát, who had taken refuge with the Ṣafavid king. Within weeks a crestfallen Sháh Ismá'íl was back in Tabríz. The Mamlúk Qánṣúḥ was next on the move. He came out of Egypt accompanied by jurists and by al-Mutawakkil, the 'Abbásid nonentity, ostensibly to mediate between Salím and Ismá'íl; in fact, to bring aid to Ismá'íl against Salím. But the Ottoman ruler was aware of the intentions of the Mamlúk monarch, for his spies had done their work well. The Ottoman and the Mamlúk armies clashed at Marj Dábiq, north of Aleppo, on 24 August 1516. Qánṣúḥ, betrayed by Khá'ir Bey, the governor of Aleppo, was slain and Salím won the day. The battle of Marj Dábiq sealed the fate of the Mamlúks and also of the sham Caliphate. Salím entered Cairo in January 1517. His victory over the Mamlúks also meant gaining possession

[2] These were European Christians, forcibly converted to Islám at an early age, and drafted into an élite military corps. With the passage of years their morale deteriorated and they became unruly—a menace to the stability of the Empire. Sulṭán Maḥmúd II (1808–39) found that he had no alternative but to destroy them.

of the holy cities of Mecca and Medina, which raised him to high eminence in the realm of Islám. The wretched al-Mutawakkil was carried off to Constantinople, accused of peculation.

When Húlágú exterminated the Caliphate at Baghdád, Rukni'd-Dín Baybars installed an 'Abbásid in Cairo with the title of al-Mustanṣir, but gave his puppet Caliph scant support in the latter's foolish attempt to recover Baghdád. Al-Mustanṣir was killed and Baybars put another 'Abbásid in his place. Over the years the position of these 'Abbásids in Cairo bore no relation to fact. They were obscure if decorative figureheads in the Sunní kingdom, without power or authority. It has been claimed that Salím forced al-Mutawakkil to transfer the Caliphate to him. No document exists which would give credence to this claim. In any case, Sulṭán Salím did not need a legal document from one who had no power to exercise or give. Salím had achieved all that he desired; he had become master of Syria, Egypt, North Africa and the Arabian Peninsula but, above all, of the holy cities of Arabia—the cradle of Islám. He died in 1520, having reigned for less than nine years. In that short space of time he had wiped out Shí'ism in his domains and inflicted a resounding defeat on Sháh Ismá'íl —'that vile, impure, sinful, slanderous, reprehensible and bloodthirsty Ṣúfí-cub' (Salím's words)[3]—which shattered the confidence of the Ṣafavid, but proved a hollow victory for the Ottomans, as it thoroughly destroyed what Arnold Toynbee terms the 'Arabic Society'.

THE EASTERN MARCHES

Now we should turn to the story of Transoxania and to events in the Eastern Marches of the realm of Islám. The fate of Transoxania is deplored by Professor Toynbee, who holds Tímúr responsible for it. What eventually befell that area of the realm of Islám was indeed tragic; but could Tímúr have foreseen and forestalled the happenings of nearly a century after his death?

Shíbán was a grandson of Chingíz Khán. This youngest son of Jújí (Jochi) became the progenitor of the people whom we know as Uzbaks (Özbegs). The Giray Kháns of Crimea, who ruled there until 1783, were also descendants of Jújí. However, the people of Shíbán, who eventually became known as Shaybání, kept to western Siberia and were relatively isolated. These

[3] Quoted by Browne, *A Literary History of Persia*, vol. IV, pp. 73–4.

Shaybánís finally dispossessed the Tímúrids in Transoxania. Tímúr fought Tuqtamish, who had united the White Horde and the Golden Horde, all descendants of Chingíz Khán; and to punish him for his broken word and his rank treachery, forced him out of his capital on the river Volga, driving him to seek refuge in Lithuania. Tímúr went so far north in search of Tuqtamish that, according to Sharafi'd-Dín 'Alí Yazdí, in his *Ẓafar-Námih* (The Book of Victory), he came upon an area where sunset merged into sunrise. Tímúr scoured the vast expanse of Qipcháq; what more could he do? Professor Toynbee believes he should have tamed completely the nomads of the Eurasian Steppe. He did cow them into submission; but perhaps he should have been content to rule over the steppes instead of going west to conquer Shíráz and Baghdád, Damascus and Ankara. Be that as it may, the fact is that Tímúr's death signalled the break-up of his Empire. The in-fighting of his dynasty accelerated the process of dissolution, while nomads of the steppes descended upon his beloved Transoxania, until all that was left of his heritage was Khurásán and a part only of Transoxania.

Abu'l-Khayr the Shaybánid captured Khárazm in 1447, and at the turn of the century his grandson, Muḥammad Khán, also known as Shaybak Khán, drove the Tímúrids completely out of Transoxania. Toynbee writes: 'This fresh invasion of the Islamic World by a Eurasian Nomad horde within less than a century after the death of Timur Lenk[4] was a signal proof that Timur's life-work was utterly undone.'[5]

Shaybak Khán next invaded Khurásán in the year 1506 and Badí'u'z-Zamán Mírzá, the son of the renowned Sulṭán Ḥusayn-i-Báyqará, fled to the court of Sháh Ismá'íl. The Shaybánid conqueror was arrogant and overbearing, as witnessed by his letter to the Ṣafavid monarch. And he was a staunch Sunní. A clash between these two had to come sooner or later. When Shaybak Khán made a foray into the province of Kirmán, Sháh Ismá'íl moved against him. The engagement took place at Ṭáhir-Ábád, near the city of Marv, in December 1510. The Uzbaks were overwhelmed and Shaybak Khán lost his life on the battlefield. Ismá'íl had a drinking-goblet made of Shaybak's skull, set in gold, and sent the head stuffed with straw as a present to

[4] Tímúr-i-Lang. (H.M.B.)
[5] Toynbee, *A Study of History*, vol. I, p. 372.

Báyazíd II. A devotee took one of Shaybak's hands to Mázindarán, and found an opportunity to throw it onto the lap of Áqá Rustam-i-Rúz-Afzún, the ruler of that principality. It was a challenging and a symbolic act, for on one occasion the Mázindarání chieftain, refusing to submit to Sháh Ismá'íl, had exclaimed: 'my hand on the skirt of Shaybak Khán', and now the severed hand of the Shaybánid had come to rest on his own skirt. It is said that Áqá Rustam-i-Rúz-Afzún did not survive the shock of this encounter. Incidentally, the downfall of this principality brought to a close the long line of independent and semi-independent rulers and chieftains, based on the shores of the Caspian Sea, who had ruled since the early days of Islám when, well protected behind the fastness of the Elburz range, men of Daylam and Mázindarán and Ṭabaristán had defied the Arab conquerors and maintained the ways of their forefathers.

On the death of Shaybak Khán, Ẓahíri'd-Dín Bábur, the only remaining Tímúrid prince with a sizeable enough force to fight the Uzbaks, took the field to retrieve his fortunes, particularly his native city of Farghánah, to which he was greatly attached. But the Uzbaks were still too formidable and Bábur had to turn to Sháh Ismá'íl. The Ṣafavid made the supplying of aid conditional upon his public profession of the tenets of Shí'ah doctrine. Bábur readily acceded to Ismá'íl's demand. It brought him the support he needed but lost him the sympathy of the people of Transoxania, who, though preferring the Tímúrids to the Shaybánids, had yet greater regard for their own strong Sunní convictions. Bábur entered Samarqand, in October 1511, to occupy the throne of Tímúr, and the Uzbaks were cleared out of Transoxania. However, Bábur's triumph was short-lived, for the Uzbaks swiftly returned, and Bábur, defeated, had to abandon Samarqand after a reign of only eight months. Once again he appealed to Sháh Ismá'íl. This time the celebrated Amír-i-Kabír Najm II was ordered to his aid with a large army. They stormed the town of Qarshí and put multitudes to death, amongst them Banná'í, a well-known poet. But at Ghujduván, the Qizil-Básh army was overpowered, Najm was slain, and Bábur had to beat a second hasty retreat to Afghánistán. Faced with threats from Sulṭán Salím of the Ottomans, Sháh Ismá'íl dared not risk another incursion into Transoxania. Instead, he made peace with 'Ubaydu'lláh Khán, the Shaybánid, in 1513 and Bábur, giving up all hope of ever returning to his native land, turned eastwards to India in search of a kingdom. Although the struggle between the Persians and the Uzbaks was not at an end, as Professor Toynbee has pointed out: '. . . on this frontier, social conditions eventually relapsed so far towards barbarism that the opposing forces on either side of the barrier became incapable of waging formal wars like those which were fought periodically between the Safawis and the "Osmanlis"[6].'[7]

A final comment by Professor Toynbee on the transformation effected by the rise of the Ṣafavi power ought to be quoted in full:

'The most conspicuous tangible effect, which was not only immediate but was also enduring, was the abrupt and violent break-up of the former Iranic World into three separate fractions: one consisting of Transoxania and the Iranic "colonial" domain in India, the second consisting of Iran proper, and the third consisting of the other Iranic "colonial" domain which had been created by the Turkish conquests in Orthodox Christendom. These three fractions of the former Iranic World were prised asunder and held apart by two new frontiers: a new frontier between Iran and Transoxania which ran from the north-western face of the Hindu Kush northwards to the Qāra Qūm Desert or alternatively to the south-eastern corner of the Caspian Sea; and a new frontier between Iran and the Ottoman domain which ran from the southern face of the Caucasus southwards to the Syrian Desert or alternatively to the head of the Persian Gulf.

'Strictly, these two new frontiers were not fresh cuts but ancient wounds which had broken open and begun to bleed again along the lines of the old scars, under the stress of a tremendous social shock. The frontier which now divided the Safawī Empire from the Uzbeg Empire had once divided the Seleucid and Arsacid and Sasanian and Umayyad Empires in Iran from a series of Hellenic and barbarian principalities in the Oxus-Jaxartes Basin over a span of about a thousand years extending from the third century B.C. into the eighth century of the Christian Era. Similarly, the frontier which now divided the Safawī Empire from the Ottoman Empire had once divided the Arsacid and Sasanian Empires from the Roman Empire over a span of about seven hundred years extending from the last century B.C. into the seventh century of the Christian Era.'[8]

[6] The Ottomans. (H.M.B.) [7] ibid., p. 390. [8] ibid., pp. 388–9.

SULAYMÁN THE MAGNIFICENT AND ṬAHMÁSB I

Salím and Ismá'íl both died young: Selim I Yavuz, 'the Grim', in 1520 and Ismá'íl in 1524. Both their successors had long reigns: Sulaymán II Qánúní (the Law-Giver)—called in Europe 'the Magnificent'—till 1566, Ṭahmásb I, the Ṣafavid, till 1576. Their armies clashed and the Ottomans wrested 'Iráq from the Ṣafavids. In Europe, the pattern of past centuries recurred, with the Habsburg Emperor and Francis I of France at each other's throat, straining every nerve for supremacy; at the battle of Pavia in 1525 Charles scored a signal victory and captured Francis. The Ottomans hammered at the gates of Vienna, the French desired alliance with the Ottomans, and the Persians wanted help from the Habsburgs.

Sulaymán, soon after the accession of Ṭahmásb, wrote him a letter which was far from conciliatory. Sháh Ṭahmásb did not reply but sought the help of the Emperor Charles V, applying also to the King of Hungary. Sulaymán's armies were pressing hard upon the Emperor's domains. In 1529, Vienna was besieged by the Turks. Foiled in his attempt to capture Vienna and having made peace with Ferdinand of Bohemia, Sulaymán brought the full strength of his martial power to bear on the hapless Ṭahmásb, who had inherited his father's bigotry, but sadly lacked many of his better qualities. Tabríz was occupied in 1534, after which Sulaymán wheeled round to complete his conquest of 'Iráq. Everywhere the Qizil-Básh army seemed helpless. Even the depredations of the Uzbaks in Khurásán, throughout the long reign of Ṭahmásb, could be countered only feebly. The loss of the holy cities of 'Iráq must have been very galling to Sháh Ṭahmásb and his subjects, now imbued with Shí'ah zeal. In 1538, Sulaymán once again invaded Persia and once more occupied Tabríz. Nine years later, Ilqáṣ Mírzá, a brother of Ṭahmásb, rebelled and fled to obtain the protection and aid of Sulaymán the Magnificent. This time the Ottoman army advanced so deep into the heart of Írán as to capture Iṣfahán. Worsted time and again, Ṭahmásb sued for peace in 1554. The Ottoman Emperor, checked in Europe by Charles V who had pushed the Turkish army back along the line of the Danube, granted Ṭahmásb's request and peace was concluded a year later. Charles V had won against odds. France remained hostile despite Francis's humble and abject submission, which opened up Italy to the Austrians who held power there for three centuries. The Papacy was unfriendly, and Henry VIII and Edward VI of England were cool and obstructive. Yet Charles succeeded in warding off the danger posed by the conjoining of Sulaymán's fleet with the ships of the Muslim corsairs of North Africa; he occupied Túnis, and but for circumstances beyond his control would have gained Algeria as well. Nevertheless Hungary became an appanage of Turkey in 1541 and remained so until 1688.

Sulaymán was perhaps the greatest of all the Ottoman rulers, his father, Salím, and Muḥammad the Conqueror included. He too, like the last Mamlúk ruler, had seen the danger of Portuguese supremacy in the Indian Ocean, and his ships, operating from Arabian bases, tried to put an end to the activities of the Portuguese. By contrast with Sulṭán Sulaymán, the Ṣafavid Sháh Ṭahmásb cut a very poor figure. Just as Ilqáṣ, Ṭahmásb's brother, had sought refuge in the court of the Ottoman ruler, so Báyazíd, a son of Sulaymán, sought asylum in Qazvín, to which city Ṭahmásb had moved his capital. Ṭahmásb betrayed him unashamedly. Báyazíd and his four sons were handed over to Turkish envoys, for 400,000 pieces of gold; they were all put to death.

On the other hand, Ṭahmásb gave an amiable reception to the Mughul (or Mongol, a misnomer) ruler, Humáyún, who had to flee for his life when rebels unseated him in 1540. He had succeeded his father, Ẓahíri'd-Dín Bábur—founder of a new Tímúrid Empire in India—when his father died in 1530. Although much has been written to extol the generous treatment and aid he is said to have received from Sháh Ṭahmásb to regain his throne, in point of fact the Ṣafavid monarch was incapable of great effort. It took Humáyún nearly fifteen years to establish himself again in Delhi.

The episode of the visit to Qazvín in 1561 of the Englishman, Anthony Jenkinson, throws a lurid light on the bigotry and the shallowness of Sháh Ṭahmásb (written as Shaw Thomas by Jenkinson). Jenkinson was the representative of the Muscovy Company, which was seeking more opportunities for trade. Ivan the Terrible found his accomplishments so engaging that he sent him on a mission to the Uzbaks of Bukhárá. Although fanatical Sunnís, they gave Jenkinson every consideration. 'Abdu'lláh Khán, the Amír of Shírván, likewise held Jenkinson in high

Photo: Pope, A Survey of Persian Art

XV THE MOSQUE OF GAWHAR-SHÁD

at Mashhad (1405–18), resplendent in colour and calligraphy, is a supreme example of Islamic architecture and faience. The Shrine of the eighth Imám forms an integral part.

XVI THE ROYAL SQUARE, IṢFAHÁN

regard. But all that Sh̲áh Ṭahmásb had to tell Jenkinson was that Írán had no need or place for infidels such as he. Jenkinson wrote, quoting Ṭahmásb: 'O thou unbeleeuer, we have no neede to have friendship with the unbeleeuers, and so willed me to depart. I being glad thereof did reuerence and went my way, accompanied by many of his gentlemen and others, and after me followed a man with a Basanet of sand, sifting all the way that I had gone within the sayd pallace, even from the sayd Sophies sight unto the court gate.'[9] Jenkinson's life was saved by the intervention of the Amír of Sh̲írván; else he too might have been sold to the envoys of the Ottoman Emperor.

Threatened by the Turks and fearing the imminent loss of Cyprus, the Venetians sent an ambassador, Vincentio A. d'Allesandri, to Sh̲áh Ṭahmásb to invoke his aid. But Ṭahmásb had been beaten enough by the Ottomans and would not commit himself to any action. Thus ended his far from glorious reign. The description left by the same d'Allesandri shows how negligent Ṭahmásb had been of his duties towards his subjects, how derelict his country had become, and how impoverished were his people.

The next two monarchs, Ismá'íl II and Muḥammad, sons of Ṭahmásb, were both unfit to rule. The first was dissolute and highly eccentric, bent on destroying all the male members of his family in revenge for twenty-five years of incarceration in the lifetime of his father. He was found dying, in a drunken torpor, in the house of a boon companion. It must be said to his credit that he banned public reviling of 'Á'is̲h̲ah and the first three of the 'rightly-guided Caliphs'. Muḥammad, the next monarch, who had escaped the holocaust, was almost blind, and had a weak mind as well as a weak will. But the star of the Ṣafavids shone brightly again with the accession, in 1588, of Muḥammad's son, 'Abbás I, justly known as 'Abbás the Great. We shall presently deal with the story of his reign.

In the Ottoman Empire, after Sulaymán the Magnificent, the character and the personality of the occupants of the throne steadily declined, and we have to look far ahead to the nineteenth century to find another ruler of noteworthy calibre, Sulṭán Maḥmúd II (1808–39), who tried to drag his Empire into the new

[9] From Richard Hakluyt's *The Principal Navigations, Voyages, Traffiques and Discoveries of the English Nation.*

age.[10] Salím II, who succeeded Sulaymán the Magnificent, was a drunkard like Ismá'íl II of Írán. Aḥmad I (1603–17) was completely dominated by the women of the seraglio. Muṣṭafá I, Aḥmad's successor, was insane, and 'Uthmán II (1618–22) was killed by the Janissaries, because he intended and tried to have a hand in the governance of his Empire. Murád IV (1623–40) was the last Ottoman ruler to take the field. His intemperate habits led to his early death. On his death-bed he ordered the execution of his brother Ibráhím, so that the dynasty of 'Uthmán would have no one left as heir to the throne, and a Páshá, his favourite, could occupy with ease the seat of Sulaymán the Magnificent. His order was not carried out, but Murád was told that his brother was dead. Though almost in the throes of death he wished to rise from his couch to see the corpse, and had to be held down until he died. When members of the royal household went to hail Ibráhím as the new Sulṭán (1640–48) he was too terrified to open the door of his chamber. Ibráhím's excesses and extravagances were so great that even his mother, who wielded much power as Sulṭán Válidih (the Mother of the Sovereign), consented to his deposition. He was eventually murdered. Ibráhím's son Muḥammad, still a child, whom he had tried to kill, was then proclaimed Sulṭán. Soon a plot was hatched to put Sulaymán, another son of Ibráhím, on the throne. The exposure of this plot led to the murder of Ibráhím's aged mother. And so it went on.

The momentum of Ottoman power was maintained not by the Sulṭáns, but by a number of able and dedicated men who wielded power in their name. Princes of the blood grew up in the isolation of the seraglio, kept away from the outside world and its multifarious affairs, and when they emerged to mount the throne they stepped into an alien world. Salím III (1789–1807) was the first Sulṭán to escape that dreadful fate. He became acquainted with French culture, fell in love with it, and tried to set his countrymen on the path to reform. The early Ottoman rulers, up to the time of Sulaymán the Magnificent, were rovers and virile warriors, freely moving from place to place and ever on the alert; but as the seraglio was established and its ramifications multiplied, the future rulers of Turkey were entrapped.

The remarkable family of Kuprílí (or Kuprúlú) gave the Empire five capable grand viziers, the first of whom, Kuprílí

[10] Salím III was the first to initiate reforms.

Muḥammad, took up the direction of affairs in the early part of the reign of Muḥammad IV (1648–87). Turkey had failed to take full advantage of the disunities of European powers in the course of the Thirty Years War. However, in 1683 Qará Muṣṭafá, the grand vizier, renewed the effort to capture Vienna. Although the Habsburg Emperor fled, John III Sobieski of Poland took the Turkish army from the rear and caused it to retreat. This brilliant success brought about an alliance against the Ottomans, composed of Russia, Poland, Austria, the Papacy and Malta. The great retreat of the Turks from the heart of Europe had begun, and Hungary and Transylvania were lost in quick succession. The Ottomans solicited the help of France but le Roi Soleil[11] was elsewhere engaged. Throughout the eighteenth century, the fortunes of the Ottomans in south-eastern Europe fluctuated greatly. As late as 1739, Turkey defeated both Russia and Austria; Belgrade was reclaimed, and Russia had to pledge herself not to maintain a navy in the Sea of Azov or in the Black Sea. During the War of the Austrian Succession it was the turn of Turkey not to heed the pleas of France. But in 1768 Catherine the Second's demands on Poland brought Turkey into war with Russia, which proved disastrous for the Ottomans. The Treaty of Kuchuk Kaynárjí of 1774, which humbled Turkey, signalled the end of an era.

ʻABBÁS THE GREAT AND HIS SUCCESSORS

Now we should turn back to the reign of ʻAbbás the Great. The realm, of which ʻAbbás found himself the ruler in 1587, was in a sorry state. His elder brother, Ḥamzih Mírzá, had been assassinated at the age of eighteen; his father, Muḥammad, had been dethroned; his Qizil-Básh chiefs were at odds; famine and plague had swept over the land; Uzbaks continued to raid Khurásán; and Ottoman troops were in Tabríz and in occupation of Luristán and Khúzistán. It seemed that the whole structure of Ṣafavid power was disintegrating. The young monarch began by ridding himself of overbearing chieftains. Next, he made peace with the Ottomans in 1590. As he was in a weak position, he had to let the Turks remain in possession of Tabríz, Shírván, Georgia and Luristán. ʻAbbás considered it more urgent first to eliminate the Uzbak menace. Indeed, the Shaybánids had made considerable gains in all directions: they had occupied Káshghar to the east,

[11] Louis XIV.

Badakhshán and Balkh and Hirát in the south. The Qizil-Básh, who had served Sháh Ismá'íl well, had, within a few decades, become uncontrollable and turbulent. Sháh 'Abbás had to build up a new fighting force before he could restore the balance on either of his frontiers. To this end he raised a force composed of converted Georgians and Armenians. This new army resembled the Janissaries of Turkey, but only in the manner of recruitment. Secondly, Sháh 'Abbás called for loyal men from each of the seven Turkish tribes of the Qizil-Básh to enlist under his banner. Thus a composite tribe came into existence: the Sháh-Savan—Friends of the Sháh—which has preserved its entity. As luck would have it, the famous Sherley brothers, Sir Robert and Sir Anthony, with a retinue of twenty-six, arrived at Qazvín in 1598. One of the men accompanying the Sherleys was a cannon-founder. Full use was made of his skill and services. It should be remembered that the Turks excelled with their artillery.

The depredations of the Uzbaks reached a climax with the capture of the holy city of Mashhad and the massacre of its people. The Shrine of the eighth Imám was looted, and priceless treasures, offerings of the devout over the years, were lost. Then came a day when Sháh 'Abbás was ready to strike. In the year 1597, in the vicinity of Hirát, he inflicted a crushing defeat on the raiders. The Uzbaks were pushed back into Transoxania, and thereafter, for many years, Khurásán enjoyed peace and security. To set up a powerful barrier against the Uzbaks, Sháh 'Abbás settled a large number of Kurds in the northern regions of Khurásán, where their descendants live to this day.

Sháh 'Abbás was anxious to gain the support of the monarchs of Europe, before countering the aggression of the Ottomans. For that purpose he sent Sir Anthony Sherley as his envoy to the courts of Europe. The mission was not successful and Sir Anthony did not return to Írán. But Sir Robert stayed with the Ṣafavid monarch, and was greatly trusted. He held a high rank in the Sháh's army and took part in his campaigns against the Ottomans. These campaigns began in 1602 and continued for nearly a quarter of a century, in the course of which Sháh 'Abbás regained all the territories which the Turks had won, returning his frontiers to their positions in the days of Salím I and Ismá'íl I. Sháh 'Abbás was particularly gratified to have ended Ottoman domination over 'Iráq and Ádharbáyján, and to have retaken the holy cities and

Tabríz. However, 'Iráq was not to remain for long in the possession of the Persians.

Sháh 'Abbás, like his equally renowned contemporary, the Emperor Akbar of Mughul India, and totally unlike his grandfather Ṭahmásb, was free of religious prejudice except where it was directed, for reasons of state, against the Sunnís. He was also severe with other sects within Islám, considered to be heretical, such as the Nuqṭavís and the Ḥurúfís. While Carmelites were not only tolerated but welcomed, as long as they did not try to convert the Sháh, Ṣúfís were beginning to feel the cold wind of disapproval. And this was truly strange because Shaykh Ṣafíyyi'd-Dín and his descendants attained prominence as heads of a Ṣúfí order. Included in the mission that accompanied Sir Anthony Sherley were some Persians who became Christians and remained in Europe. One of these was Ulugh Beg, who made a name for himself as Don Juan of Persia. In the book he wrote about his native land he imparted to zealous Christians the false notion that Sháh 'Abbás, too, would embrace Christianity. The Carmelites arrived at Iṣfahán, the new capital of the Sháh, in 1607. Not long after, Father Paul Simon wrote to Pope Paul V (1605–21): 'All I can inform your Holiness is that the King of Persia is very powerful and no longer has need of Christian princes to help him.' Father John Thaddeus wrote later: 'As to the character of the King, at heart he is a Muslim and all he has done in the past is feigned.'[12] Nevertheless, he agreed to act as the envoy of Sháh 'Abbás to the Czar, the Pope and the King of Poland. At Astrakhán, thinking he was a spy, Russians imprisoned Father John and might have put him to death, were it not for the Sháh's strenuous efforts to obtain his release.

The glories of the capital which 'Abbás the Great created in Iṣfahán still stand, despite the deep wounds inflicted by ungenerous hands, to evoke wonder, awe and admiration. Sháh 'Abbás's vast building projects were not confined to the magnificent mosques and pavilions which he raised in Iṣfahán. He provided the country with a large number of beautiful and solidly built caravanserais, particularly on the roads leading to the holy city of Mashhad, and many of these have escaped destruction. In his time faience reached its perfection in Írán, as did calligraphy and the work of the miniaturist; and yet Persia became a cultural

[12] Waterfield, *Christians in Persia*, p. 65, for both quotations.

desert in the Ṣafavid era. Prose composition reached its nadir, original thought was banished, and poets such as 'Urfí of Shíráz and Ṣá'ib of Iṣfahán and Ṭálib-i-Ámulí took the road to more appreciative courts in India. It was the theologian who dominated the scene and the power of the divines increased immensely. The Majlisís, father and son—Mullá Muḥammad-Taqí and Mullá Muḥammad-Báqir—wrote extensively and overburdened Shí'ah doctrine and practice with dangerous fictions and trivialities. And the divines led the way to the downfall of the Ṣafavids, while Sháh 'Abbás himself contributed, in no small measure, to the eventual break-up of his Empire by introducing the same system which had bedevilled the princes of the blood in Turkey. His experiences of childhood and early youth were so bitter and he had suffered so much at the hands of unruly chieftains that he made it a pillar of his policy to keep men of power and influence at loggerheads, one against the other.

Although his first efforts at establishing connections with European powers had not been successful, Sháh 'Abbás still desired to have some relationship, particularly in the field of commerce. To that end he sent Sir Robert Sherley twice to Europe, in 1609 and 1623. The result was not very encouraging. One ought, however, to take into consideration the condition and the affairs of Europe in the opening decades of the seventeenth century. The bitter feuds and struggles of the Thirty Years War were ravaging Central Europe. Britain was ruled capriciously and indecisively by James I. France had a young and inexperienced king in Louis XIII, a sagacious administrator in the person of Richelieu, who was hated by powerful men, and was suffering a series of civil wars. Philip III of Spain and Portugal was greatly concerned with the Netherlands. And Sháh 'Abbás wanted to oust the Portuguese from the Island of Hurmuz at the entrance to the Persian Gulf. He succeeded in this in 1621, with the aid of the East India Company, which was only too glad to lend a hand. This company was created by Royal Charter, soon after the defeat of the Great Armada. The Portuguese, beaten and driven out of Hurmuz, took a fresh position at Masqaṭ (Muscat). But the Imám of 'Ummán (Oman) wrested Masqaṭ from them in 1650. Attempts to recapture Hurmuz were unsuccessful and Portuguese ascendancy in the Indian Ocean was at an end. The participation of the English in the conquest of Hurmuz added greatly to the stature of the East India Company. The Dutch who had come to replace the Portuguese did not last long in those waters, although according to Chardin they still had the bulk of Persian trade in 1666. Their possessions, however, fell to the British.

The gathering British strength in the Persian Gulf and the Arabian Sea was a prelude to far-reaching successes in the eighteenth century, which led, although unplanned, to the establishment of an empire in India. Incidentally, by the time the last Mughul Emperor, Bahádur Sháh, who was no more than a titular figure, was removed from the scene by the British after the Indian Mutiny of 1857, the descendants of Ẓahíri'd-Dín Bábur had long lost all power and were tributaries to the Mahrattas.

Sir Dodmore Cotton, the first British envoy to Írán, was appointed by King Charles I to accompany Sir Robert Sherley. They reached Persia early in 1628. Both Sir Dodmore and Sir Robert died in Qazvín in the same year, and Sháh 'Abbás followed them to the grave soon after—a brilliantly successful monarch, whose last years were embittered and saddled with appalling personal tragedies engendered by his own dark suspicions. The Ṣafavid power was now in decline; apart from the reign of 'Abbás II (1642–66), the great-grandson of 'Abbás the Great, who attempted to stop the rot, the story is of a long procession of disasters. Murád IV, the Ottoman ruler, took the field in person, seized Baghdád and occupied Tabríz. Hamadán also fell to the Turks. The damage done to those two Persian cities was enormous; nothing was spared, not even the trees. The famous Blue Mosque of Tabríz was rescued just in time by the intervention of the Muftí, who pointed out that the magnificent edifice had been raised by a Sunní. Such was the harvest of the aberrant policies of Sháh Ismá'íl. After the death of 'Abbás II at the age of thirty-five, the Ṣafavids slid swiftly toward doom and extinction. Men of competence were swept aside, the morale of the army sank, eunuchs of the Royal household became arbiters of government policies and appointments, the number of self-styled, ignorant clerics, wielding greater and greater power, increased alarmingly. Sháh Sulṭán Ḥusayn (1694–1722), a replica of Henry VI of England, fell a victim to his own piety and finally lost all will to govern. An ill-equipped army of Afgháns, under Maḥmúd, a Ghilzá'í chieftain, besieged Iṣfahán and forced Sháh Sulṭán

Ḥusayn to abdicate. That was virtually the end of the Ṣafavid rule. Russia and Turkey made a pact to share out parts of the Ṣafavid Empire.

The situation was saved by the meteoric rise of Nádir Sháh (1736–47) of the tribe of Afshár. He ousted the Afghláns and subdued them in their own land. The Russians withdrew discreetly, but the Ottomans fought for the mastery of the territories they had occupied. Nádir defeated them and went on to lay siege to Baghdád and Mosul. Nádir had served at first under Ṭahmásb II, the son of Sháh Sulṭán Ḥusayn, whom the Afghláns had put to death before evacuating Iṣfahán. Then at an opportune moment, in 1732, he deposed Ṭahmásb and made himself regent for ʻAbbás III, his son. Finally, on ʻAbbás's death in 1736, he assumed the kingship and tried to throw out the rigid Shíʻism of Shah Ismá'íl, proposing that Írán should have instead a discipline to be named Jaʻfarí, after the sixth Imám, which would rank with the four Sunní schools. But by then the handiwork of Sháh Ismáʻíl had become firmly entrenched and was immovable, while the Ottomans refused to recognize the validity of a fifth discipline. Nádir Sháh's crowning achievement was his victory over Muḥammad Sháh, the Mughul Emperor of India, and his occupation of Delhi. Realizing that he could not administer the Mughul Empire, he let Muḥammad Sháh keep his throne, but took away from him all the territory on the right bank of the river Indus; he returned home with spoils estimated to have been worth more than eighty-seven million pounds, including the Peacock Throne and two diamonds of world renown: the Kúh-i-Núr (Koh-i-Noor)[13] and the Daryáy-i-Núr.[14] The Mughul Empire was already tottering and Nádir Sháh dealt it a fatal blow. Although Nádir declared that anyone who dared to contend with Muḥammad Sháh (1719–48) would have to reckon with him, the protection thus afforded was of little value, since Nádir's own over-stretched empire began to disintegrate on the very day of his assassination. However, he scored one more remarkable achievement before his suspicions and resentments led to his murder: a victory over the Uzbaks which made him the master of Transoxania. This feat put him in line with the mighty conquerors of the past. But here too, by his own lights, he was generous with

[13] The Mountain of Light.
[14] The Sea of Light.

the conquered and returned Bukhárá to Abu'l-Fayḍ Khán, the Uzbak, and restored the border to the ancient frontier line of the river Oxus. On the other hand, with the Uzbak ruler of Khívih he was stern and unrelenting, because Ilbars Khán was guilty of putting Nádir's envoys to death. Now he and twenty of his chief men were executed. At this point in his career (1742) Nádir's character sadly deteriorated. Reverses in the upper reaches of the Caucasus, an attempt on his life in the forests of Mázindarán, the possession of the riches brought from India, and repeated rebellions within Írán, all combined to make of him an avaricious, distrustful and suspicious tyrant. He had the eyes of his own son, Riḍá-Qulí Mírzá, put out, and plotted the deaths of his Persian officers, relying more and more on the Afgháns and the Uzbaks in his service. One night in 1747, in Khurásán, a number of officers who included members of his own tribe ventured into his tent and murdered him. As the news spread his army disintegrated. Aḥmad Khán-i-Durrání, commander of Nádir's Afghán and Uzbak troops, gathered his men together, seized booty brought by Nádir from India including the Kúh-i-Núr, and marched away to Afghánistán, where he set up an independent kingdom based on Qandihár. Persia descended immediately into chaos.

Amongst the contenders for power, it was Karím Khán of the non-Turkish tribe of Zand who rose to eminence. Karím Khán had been a simple soldier in the army of Nádir Sháh. By the year 1750, he had overcome all the other chieftains and ruled over Írán, with the exception of Khurásán, for twenty-nine years. Having served under Nádir, this magnanimous man would not invade Khurásán because it was in the possession of Sháh-Rukh, the grandson of Nádir Sháh, a monarch whose 'bread he had eaten'. Nor would he assume the title of King, instead calling himself Vakílu'r-Ru'áyá—the Deputy of the People. He chose Shíráz for his capital and set about doing for it what 'Abbás the Great had done for Iṣfahán. His only foreign adventure consisted of an attack on Baṣrah, which his brother succeeded in taking from the Ottomans. The benevolent reign of this great man, who not only spared the lives of his opponents, but invited them into his court as advisers, brought Írán a peace it had not known for decades. Unhappily, his successors fell out among themselves and once again Persia became a centre of contention and anarchy. Luṭf-'Alí Khán, his valiant great-nephew, might have restored the fortunes of the Zands, but being young and inexperienced he was overcome by the brutal eunuch, Áqá Muḥammad Khán, the head of a clan of the Qájár tribe. The father of Áqá Muḥammad Khán had met his death by treachery, while engaged in trying his strength against the founder of the Zand dynasty. Karím Khán had treated his offspring with great generosity. But the eunuch king treated the last of the Zands abominably, and had him blinded and then put to death.

Áqá Muḥammad Khán (1779–97) salvaged Írán from chaos and confusion and held the Russians at bay in the Caucasus. During the reign of his nephew, Fatḥ-'Alí Sháh (1797–1834)—the highly uxorious monarch who was courted by Napoleon Bonaparte as well as the British—the Persians suffered a series of reverses at the hands of the Russians, which lost them the whole of the Caucasus. The Treaty of Turkumancháy (1828) brought those wars to an end, imposed capitulations on Írán, fixed the river Araxes as the frontier, and also brought an era to an end. It will be recalled that the Treaty of Kuchuk Kaynárjí (1774) dealt a similar blow to the Ottomans.

THE MUGHULS OF INDIA

In the course of the eighteenth century, Great Britain and France went to war time and again. These strifes and contentions centred around the ambitions of Louis XIV, in the early part of the century. Then, during the Wars of the Austrian Succession (1744–8), there were clashes in India between the British and the French which, though indecisive and of no great consequence, were highly symptomatic. After the elimination of the Portuguese and the Dutch as leading commercial figures, the position of the British East India Company was commensurately strengthened. But the French were also in the field. In order to survive, both British and French required friends and allies amongst the potentates of India, much in the same way as, in the New World, they sought the aid of Red Indian tribes.

India had never been one united realm; ethnic, linguistic, racial and religious differences precluded that. But from time to time a measure of order was imposed over the greater part of the subcontinent by one or other powerful entity. The Mughul Emperors achieved this, at least in the northern part of India. But the Mughul Empire, although it endured for more than two centuries, was basically unstable. After the struggles of Ẓahíri'd-Dín Bábur to found this empire, his son, Humáyún, as we have seen, had to flee for his life to Ṭahmásb in Persia, returning to Delhi only after fifteen years. And his son, Akbar, had also to fight for his throne.

Jaláli'd-Dín Akbar (1556–1605) is one of the most remarkable monarchs of all time, who almost united under his rule, by conquest, most of the subcontinent. But in the words of Laurence Binyon: 'His greater achievement as a ruler was to weld this collection of different states, different races, different religions, into a whole. It was accomplished by elaborate organisation—Akbar had an extraordinary genius for detail—still more by the settled policy which persuaded his subjects of the justice of their ruler. Akbar's conceptions were something new in the history of Asiatic conquerors. Though a foreigner, he identified himself with the India he had conquered. And much of his system was to be permanent. The principles and practice worked out by Akbar and his ministers were largely adopted into the English system of government.'[15]

Akbar loathed intolerance and longed for the day when Hindu and Muslim would join in one fraternity. He even wished for more—a universal Faith to which all religions would adhere. To that end he instituted a debating-house to which Zoroastrian, Jain, Hindu, Christian and Muslim (Shí'ah, Sunní and Ṣúfí) came to present their views. Akbar would sit for hours listening to their controversies, and sometimes himself participated in their discussions. Ridolfo Aquaviva, a Neapolitan, and Antonio Monseratte, a Spaniard, both learned Jesuits, had been sent from Goa at Akbar's invitation. They came not just to enlighten the Emperor; their true intent was to convert him. Akbar treated them as personal friends and lodged them in his palace. The orthodox were shocked, even scandalized, and from one end of the Empire to the other a plot was set afoot to rid the realm of this renegade monarch. The Jesuits, too, showed an intolerance which was anathema to Akbar, by denouncing the English as vile heretics when a letter reached him from Queen Elizabeth. Akbar assured them that he revered Christ and hoped that Christians would come and live in his domains. He would permit them to build their churches just as he had permitted the Hindus to build their temples. But the Jesuits were offended to be put on a par

[15] *Akbar*, pp. 8–9.

with idolaters. It seems that the Faith of the Pársís had a particular fascination for Akbar. He sent for a learned Dastúr,[16] whom he had met in Gujrát, to come and instruct him. Thereafter, Akbar kept a fire alight in his palace which was never to be extinguished, rendering solemn respect to the sun as a daily ritual.

The outraged Muslim plotters invited Muḥammad Ḥakím, Akbar's brother, who had his seat in Kábul, to rise for the vindication of their Faith. Even Sháh Manṣúr, a man whom Akbar had elevated from low rank to become the administrator of his finances, was in league with them. The correspondence which he carried on with Akbar's brother fell into the hands of the Emperor. Twice pardoned and reinstated, Sháh Manṣúr persisted in corresponding treasonably with Muḥammad Ḥakím, until Akbar had no alternative but to have him hanged, thereby losing for the Mughul Empire a very able administrator. The fact that many important offices of state were held by Hindus also riled the orthodox.

Akbar's three great friends and boon companions were Abu'l-Faḍl and Fayḍí, sons of Shaykh Mubárak—a liberal-minded theologian from whom Akbar had received advice and instruction—and Birbal, a Hindu. Abu'l-Faḍl was a scholar who became Akbar's minister and chronicler.[17] Fayḍí was a talented poet and became the Emperor's laureate. Birbal was an accomplished musician whose company delighted the Emperor. But Shaykh Mubárak and his sons were considered heretics by the orthodox. Such was the hatred felt for the liberal views of Fayḍí that a man named Faṣíḥ gave this line as the chronogram of the year of his death: 'When infidel Fayḍí died, Faṣíḥ said at the date of his death, "A dog departed from the world in a foul fashion" '.[18]

The Jesuits realized at last that Akbar would not declare himself a Christian, while Akbar, despairing of the contentions assailing his ears (although he still liked to listen to arguments and counter-arguments), decided to devise a syncretic system of belief which could appeal to Hindu and Muslim alike. He called it Dín-i-Iláhí—the Divine Faith—and presented it to his people, but it failed to win favour. Rajah Birbal, his close friend, accepted it, but soon he and Fayḍí were killed in action, and Abu'l-Faḍl was ambushed

[16] A Pársí priest.

[17] He wrote *Akbar-Námih* (The Book of Akbar) in Persian.

[18] Browne, *A Literary History of Persia*, vol. IV, p. 243.

and murdered, at the instigation of Salím, the Emperor's eldest son. Akbar, laden with sorrows, suddenly abandoned his magnificent new city, Fatehpur-Sikri. It still stands, unoccupied, in all its forgotten splendour. When Akbar himself was on his death-bed, entirely oblivious to the world and those around him, his lips were faintly uttering the name of God.

Salím had a Rajput mother, and Akbar had hoped that in his own person he would bring Hindu and Muslim together. But it was not to be; Salím rebelled against his father, the worst blow being his treachery in contriving the death of his father's trusted friend and counsellor. Nevertheless, on succeeding his father as the Emperor Jahángír (1605–27), he followed the same liberal policies and managed to hold his Empire together. His son, Sháhjahán (1628–58), who is immortalized by the world-famous Táj Maḥal, endeavoured to unite India and Transoxania and to create a vast Sunní Empire; it was a forlorn hope and a vain enterprise. His life ended in deep tragedy, when he was dethroned and imprisoned by Awrangzíb, his rebellious youngest son, who then, by various ruses, brought about the death of his three elder brothers and his nephews, and ascended the throne. Fratricide was no novelty in the Family of Tímúr. The Ṣafavids and the Ottomans were both afflicted by it. Murád III (1574–95) murdered his five younger brothers, while Muḥammad III (1595–1603) has an even more terrible record of murdering, at the start of his reign, nineteen of his brothers. Awrangzíb had a long and eventful reign. Although he departed from the liberalism of his predecessors, he could not dispense with the services of Hindus, nor could all his exertions halt the rising power of the Maráthás, in the person of their brilliant protagonist, Shíváji. Awrangzíb died in the year 1707, and although Shíváji was dead, too, the Maráthá Confederacy grew in strength and the Mughul Empire went into rapid decline. Both Hindu and Muslim principalities sprang up, in some cases making themselves totally independent of the Mughul Empire, in others acknowledging a merely formal and titular overlordship. Nádir Sháh's invasion was before long followed by repeated incursions on the part of Aḥmad Sháh-i-Durrání, who had founded a vigorous Afghán Kingdom. These invasions from the north further ruined the chances of the survival of the Mughul Empire.

THE RENEWAL OF EAST–WEST CONTACTS

The British East India Company, which began life as a chartered trading concern, was disposing of land and naval forces, unencumbered by the power of the State. The bitter conflicts of Britain and France led it step by step to supremacy in India. Finally, in June 1757, when the Seven Years War was raging in Europe, Robert Clive's dazzling victory over Suraju'd-Dawlih,[19] the Navváb (Nawab) of Bengal, at the battle of Plassey, ensured that the British, not the French, would found another Empire in India. Under Clive's direction, Major Coote chased the French as far as Benares. The Mughul Emperor, Sháh 'Álam II, who formally transferred Bengal, Behar and Orissa to the British in 1765, became eventually a pensioner of the East India Company. These widespread gains and successes of the East India Company induced William Pitt to bring it, in 1784, under the control of the Privy Council.

Again it was the British and the French, in the fresh context of the Revolution and the meteoric rise of Napoleon Bonaparte, who involved Europe more and more in the affairs of the various branches of the realm of Islám. In order to bring Britain to her knees, Napoleon planned an overland attack on India. He invaded Egypt in 1798, and in July of that year, at the battle of the Pyramids, destroyed the power of Murád Bey, the Circassian Mamlúk who held Egypt under the authority of the Sulṭán of Turkey. On July 25th, he triumphantly entered Cairo. Throughout the Crusades no Christian potentate had succeeded in breaching Cairo—the Victorious—and forcing it to submit to him. Next, Napoleon instituted a Council of State composed of Arab notabilities, and met them wearing turban and Egyptian dress. They heard from him what was almost a sermon on the ideals of the French Revolution. Bonaparte is reported to have said that he would be a Christian in France, a Muslim in the East. He had come not only with an army but with a host of brilliant scientists and savants: engineers to dig the Suez Canal, geologists, astronomers, mathematicians, mineralogists, chemists, physicists, zoologists, archaeologists, poets, painters, philologists and historians. Amongst them were the Comte Claude-Louis Berthollet, discoverer of the properties of chlorine and the inventor of the

[19] He was notorious for his cruelties and excesses.

method of using carbon to filter water; Baron Dominique-Vivant Denon, the renowned archaeologist; and Gaspard Monge, Comte de Péluse, one of the world's greatest mathematicians. Napoleon himself took on the vice-presidency of the Institut d'Égypte, under Gaspard Monge. After an abeyance of more than four hundred years, renewal of cultural contact between the East and the West, on the scale envisaged by Napoleon, was to have far-reaching results. But whereas in the past it was exclusively a case of transmittal and conveyance from the civilization of Islám to the West, now it was to be chiefly a transfer of the benefits of Western civilization to the realm of Islám.

In India (Napoleon's target), a beginning had also been made with cultural contacts and pursuits that were to widen greatly in scope in future years. Warren Hastings, the first Governor-General of British India (1773–85), was an accomplished Persian scholar. He founded, at his own expense, the famous Madrasa (Madrisah) or College in Calcutta for Islamic education, and planned an Indian Institute for London. Sir William Jones (1746–94), rightly hailed as the 'Founder' of modern orientalism, then judge of the Supreme Court of Judicature at Calcutta, established in 1784 the Asiatic Society of Bengal, with the active help of the Governor-General. Indeed, the employees of the East India Company were encouraged to gain deeper insight into the culture of the people around them. The Hon. Mountstuart Elphinstone (1779–1859), who went to India in the service of the Company at the age of sixteen, could in his early twenties read with profit and understanding the poems of such giants of Persian literature as Rúmí, Sa'dí and Ḥáfiẓ.

Napoleon's Egyptian adventure was not going smoothly. Nelson annihilated his fleet at Abúqír (Aboukir), on August 1st.[20] The following year (1799) he invaded Syria, but the Turkish garrison in 'Akká (Acre), directed by Sir Sidney Smith, one of Nelson's commanders, successfully resisted his attempts to storm the town. After a siege lasting two months, Napoleon gave up on May 20th, hurriedly left Syria, and inflicted a crushing defeat on the Turkish land forces at Abúqír on July 25th. Muṣṭafá Pá<u>sh</u>á, the Turkish commander, was captured and his casualties were enormous. But on August 22nd, Napoleon had to sail for France because the situation there had become threatening. Kléber

[20] This engagement has been misnamed 'the Battle of the Nile'.

remained in Egypt, much against his will, for he did not relish the prospect of being marooned. Yet, in March 1800, he defeated an army of Turks and Mamlúks at Heliopolis. Previously he had entered into negotiations with the Turks and Sir Sidney Smith, who were at al-'Aríṣh. They had come to a reasonable solution whereby the French would evacuate Egypt honourably. The British Government, however, refused to abide by this agreement and required the French to lay down their arms, which naturally Kléber rejected. In June 1800, Kléber was assassinated in Cairo and the command devolved on Beillard. In the meantime a British force sent from India landed in Egypt. By then Murád Bey had thrown in his lot with the French and was hurrying to Beillard's assistance, when plague struck him down. Negotiations were resumed with the British, who offered to provide transport for evacuation. By October 18th, the French troops were on their way to France, and the British force, which had arrived from India, also embarked for Europe. Suddenly there was a vacuum in Egypt. It gave Muḥammad-'Alí (later Páṣhá), an Albanian serving with the Turkish army which Napoleon routed at Abúqír, the chance to establish himself in Egypt, destroy the Mamlúks for good, and make himself virtually independent of Turkey. His career (1805–48) and his ambitions would provide in future years a fruitful source of friction between Great Britain and France.

Bonaparte, having overthrown the Directoire in France, assumed powers as the First Consul, detached Russia from the Second Coalition, inflicted a humiliating defeat on the Austrians at Marengo, shattered the Second Coalition, and then cast once again a longing glance on India. It was for Persia or Afghánistán (or both) to provide the corridor for the march of the French army to the desired land. The possibility of a combined Franco-Russian assault on India also loomed on the horizon. The Government of India was thoroughly alarmed and the Governor-General, the Marquis of Wellesley (1760–1842),[21] decided on immediate and energetic measures to put up an effective barrier against the French. It is said that Robert Clive secured India, Warren Hastings consolidated the British power, but it was Wellesley who turned the British supremacy into an Empire. Wellesley had no patience with the tiresome 'tradesmen in Leadenhall Street' who were his superiors, and he had young and able men under him to

[21] He was the brother of the Duke of Wellington.

accomplish his purpose: men such as Captain (later Colonel Sir John) Malcolm (1769–1833), the Hon. Mountstuart Elphinstone, Charles Theophilus (later Baron) Metcalfe (1785–1846), and Colonel (later General Sir) David Ochterlony (1758–1815). Malcolm, whose *The History of Persia* remained a standard book on the subject for decades,[22] was dispatched to Ṭihrán in 1800, where he successfully concluded a treaty with Ḥájí Ibráhím Khán, the I'timádu'd-Dawlih, the minister of Fatḥ-'Alí Sháh. As a reciprocal gesture, a Persian envoy, Ḥájí Khalíl Khán, was sent to Bombay.[23] Malcolm's mission provided all that was desired, but Ḥájí Ibráhím Khán, the minister who dealt with him, was disgraced and fell from power. When Persia lost Georgia to Russia, no help was forthcoming from London; but war broke out afresh between Russia and France, causing Napoleon's overtures to Fatḥ-'Alí Sháh to become more assiduous. In 1807, the Treaty of Finkenstein was signed between France and Persia, and General Gardanne, with seventy French officers, arrived at Ṭihrán to train the Persian army. Then, in the same year, Bonaparte met Alexander I at Tilsit and forgot his promises to Persia, although he still meant to confront the British in India and had it in mind to send his brother, Lucien, as his envoy to Persia. Fatḥ-'Alí Sháh was angered by the Treaty of Tilsit and became once again attentive to the British, who were apprehensive of the accord between Bonaparte and the Tsar. Wellesley had gone from India, but he had already done enough, with or against the Indian potentates, to ensure the rule of the British. His successor, Baron (later, first Earl of) Minto (1751–1814), was instructed to counter any possible move on the part of the French. Malcolm was again sent to Persia, in 1808, but did not proceed beyond Búshihr because he was told by the Persian authorities to negotiate with Ḥusayn-'Alí Mírzá, the Farmán-Farmá, a son of Fatḥ-'Alí Sháh and the Governor-General of Fárs. Malcolm felt insulted and promptly returned to India, proposing the immediate occupation of the island of Khárg in the Persian Gulf, close to the Persian coast. Although his proposal was accepted better counsels prevailed, and Malcolm set out on his third mission to Persia in 1810. The Government in London thought, at the same time, that they

[22] It was published in two volumes, in 1815.

[23] He was accidentally shot and killed, during a brawl between his servants and the Indian guard.

too should try their hand at the diplomatic game, and Sir Harford Jones reached Ṭihrán in due course. It both surprised and amused the Persians to find two British envoys, obviously at loggerheads with each other, soliciting their favours. Napoleon had by then become sufficiently discredited for General Gardanne to be sent home. A treaty was initialled with Great Britain, and an envoy was sent from Persia to London in the person of Mírzá Abu'l-Ḥasan Khán, whom James Morier has portrayed as Mirza Firouz.[24] But this treaty did not save Persia from defeat at the hands of the Russians.

Afghánistán, to which Mountstuart Elphinstone was sent in October 1808, was in a state of chaos. The members of the dynasty of Aḥmad Sháh-i-Durrání had fallen out amongst themselves. Elphinstone at no time went as far as Kábul, but met Sháh Shujá' in Písháwar (Peshawar). A treaty, which proved to be worthless, was concluded with the Afghán king. Sháh Shujá' was a fugitive from Kábul. However, as far as the French menace was concerned, it was obvious by the end of the first decade of the century that it was no more. Malcolm wrote a worthy book on *The History of Persia*; and Elphinstone wrote an excellent work, also in two volumes, entitled *An Account of the Kingdom of Caubul* [Kábul].

Napoleon fell from power and was gone, but his legacy remained.

[24] Morier's classic book, *The Adventures of Hajji Baba of Ispahan,* had a sequel with a similar title.

Epilogue

NAPOLEON's heritage was multifarious, and the impact of his initiative in the cultural field was indeed considerable and should by no means be overlooked. For the purposes of this epilogue, however, we are more concerned with the effect on the realm of Islám of the clashes of interest and the rivalries of European Powers.

The Treaty of Kuchuk Kaynárjí of 1774 had sown the seeds of what came to be known as the Eastern Question—a bone of contention amongst the Great Powers and a cause of despair. Forced to give Russia the right, however flimsy and tenuous, to protect the Greek Orthodox subjects of the Sulṭán, Turkey lost the freedom to be the sole arbiter within her own boundaries.

The Treaty of Turkumancháy of 1828 not only put an end to Persia's hopes in an area that had been an integral part of the realm of Islám for well over a thousand years, but it imposed capitulations[1] which severely restricted her jurisdiction in her own domain, eventually giving every Christian Power the right of intervention in judicial affairs and criminal cases—a right which could be and often was frequently abused.

Anglo-French conflicts led to British dominance in India and to the establishment of a new Empire in the subcontinent, with the inevitable consequence of the detachment of large territories from the realm of Islám. Fears for India, engendered by Napoleon's dreams and designs, did not die with Napoleon's empire, but found fresh life and menace in the real and imaginary schemes of Russia, which mesmerized successive governments in Britain. Nor did the tug-of-war in Egypt, between Britain and France, cease with the demise of Napoleon's empire, but went on to become more and more pronounced with the march of the nine-

[1] A system of extraterritorial rights.

teenth century. The area of rivalry amongst the old Powers and the new rising Powers in Europe eventually stretched right across the whole of North Africa.

The Caliphate, once a binding force in the realm of Islám even when divided into three ('Abbásid, Fáṭimid, Umayyad), now rested with the Ottomans. But their title to it was extremely dubious, and the attachment of the generality of Muslims to a Turkish Caliphate could not be taken for granted. Indeed, when put to the test it wilted. Strangely, it was the humiliating treaty of Kuchuk Kaynárjí which, for the first time in the domain of diplomacy, gave explicit recognition to the Turkish Caliphate.

A significant movement in the Sunní fold, which deliberately ignored the Caliphate of the Ottomans and seemed even directed against it, was the Wahhabí uprising. This occurred in the middle of the eighteenth century, within the Arabian peninsula which was divided into several principalities. Muḥammad Ibn 'Abd-i'l-Wahháb (1703–93), a native of Najd, having studied for long years in Baṣrah and Damascus, and having seen at close quarters the practices of his fellow Muslims, concluded that Islám needed to be cleansed of accretions. He returned to Najd, in middle life, and preached a strict puritanism that recalled the austerities and the overtones of Khárijite beliefs. The veneration and worship of holy places and relics and of holy men he regarded as idolatry. While favouring the Ḥanbalí school of jurisprudence, he rejected as spurious a large body of traditions. Of all the rulers of the disparate principalities of Arabia, it was Amír Muḥammad Ibn Sa'úd, based on Dar'íyyah, who responded to the call of Muḥammad Ibn 'Abd-i'l-Wahháb.

Muḥammad of Dar'íyyah died in 1765. By then he had established the authority of his House over the central and eastern areas of the peninsula. 'Abdu'l-'Azíz, his son, extended that power well beyond the confines of Najd and began to raid the caravans of pilgrims to Mecca. The Ottomans tried ineffectively to stop him. Amír 'Abdu'l-'Azíz simply widened the sphere of his operations. He sacked Karbilá in 1801 and a year later occupied Mecca. Mausoleums and tombs, the objects of veneration in both places, were demolished. Sa'úd, the son and successor of 'Abdu'l-'Azíz, added Medina to the Wahhábí conquests in 1804. The Ottoman Government was now thoroughly roused and ordered Muḥammad-'Alí Páshá, whom it had named Viceroy of Egypt, to stem the tide of Wahhábí expansion. In 1811, Amír Sa'úd was on his way to attack Baghdád when news reached him that Ṭúsún, the sixteen-year-old son of the Albanian potentate, had reached the coast of Ḥijáz with a sizeable force. He immediately returned to meet the Egyptians and defeated the young Ṭúsún, but both Mecca and Medina were lost to him. Next, Muḥammad-'Alí Páshá took the field in person, but he was no match for Sa'úd. In 1814, Ṭúsún once again commanded the army and was once again soundly beaten. It was the last of Sa'úd's victories; he died the same year.

Now the redoubtable Ibráhím Páshá, another son of Muḥammad-'Alí Páshá, took over command of the Egyptian army. By means of bribes, he won to his side a number of tribes, and in a series of campaigns overran Najd, besieged Dar'íyyah, forced it to capitulate in September 1818, and destroyed it completely. Amír 'Abdu'lláh, the son of Sa'úd, was sent a prisoner to Constantinople, where he was beheaded. For the time being the Wahhábí movement had been crushed, but not for long. Turkí, the son of 'Abdu'lláh, rose in 1824 to challenge the Egyptians and successfully recreated the Wahhábí State with his capital at Ríyáḍ. Ibráhím Páshá, at grips with Turkey for the mastery of Syria, had to withdraw the bulk of his troops from Najd, and the continuation of the new state was assured.

The four Sunní schools—Ḥanafí, Málikí, Sháfi'í and Ḥanbalí—have no clerical order. Their *muftís* and *faqíhs* and *qáḍís* are men well-versed in the law and have the same status as judges in secular courts. But it is otherwise in the Shí'ah fold. The Shí'ah (Twelver) divine speaks and delivers judgements in the name of the absent Imám—the Qá'im expected to come forth from his major occultation in the fullness of time. Therefore the power of the Shí'ah divine has been immense, and this power particularly accrued to him with the advent of the Ṣafavids in Írán. None of the four 'Gates' to the twelfth Imám, who were believed to be intermediaries between him and his people during his minor occultation, instituted a clerical order to perform a special function after them. Necessity led to the emergence of such an order, but how it happened and when exactly, in point of time, these divines began to make *ex cathedra* pronouncements cannot be ascertained.

Theoretically any Shí'ah of the Twelver persuasion is either a *mujtahid*, or a *muqallid*. The *mujtahid*, which literally means 'the person who strives', is the man whose attainments are such as to entitle him to be an authoritative divine. The way to become a *mujtahid* is to obtain a permit from a divine who already has that status. Of course there have been clerics, and many of them, who have not had the right of *ijtihád* (making *ex cathedra* pronouncements), but still have had functions to perform, such as leading the congregational prayer in the mosque and performing marriage and burial ceremonies. Serious differences of opinion between *mujtahids*, even some of the most prominent divines, have not been unknown. As to the *muqallid*, which literally means the 'imitator', not every Shí'ah of the Twelver persuasion has had to choose or has chosen a divine as guide and exemplar. Theory and practice have not generally coincided. Furthermore, the whole basis of *ijtihád* has not gone unchallenged. Mullá Muḥammad-Amír of Astarábád, who died during the reign of Sháh 'Abbás the Great, witnessing the growing power of the divines and disliking it, spoke out in protest and founded what came to be known as the Akhbárí school, in opposition to the *mujtahids* or the Uṣúlís. *Akhbár* means 'traditions' and *uṣúl* means 'principles'. The Akhbárís rest their case solely on the authority of traditions ascribed to the Prophet and the Imáms and accepted by all, whereas the Uṣúlís, who constitute the vast majority of the Twelvers, maintain that the *mujtahid* has the right, as the deputy of the Hidden Imám, to deduce principles from the Qur'án as well as the traditions, and to use *qiyás* or 'analogy' to make an authoritative statement. In the seventeenth and eighteenth centuries, the Akhbárí school did attain some prominence, but at the beginning of the reign of the Qájárs in Írán, a concerted effort was made by the *mujtahids* in general, and two divines in particular, Shaykh Ja'far-i-Najafí and Áqá Muḥammad-Báqir-i-Bihbahání,[2] to undermine the Akhbárí school. They were only too successful. Kirmán, where the Akhbárís had a stronghold, eventually yielded to the Shaykhís, whom we shall now consider as the next potent contenders with the Uṣúlís, though not altogether for the same

[2] The son of Áqá Muḥammad-Báqir, named Áqá Muḥammad-'Alí and known as Kirmánsháhí, because he lived in that town, attained fame or notoriety, depending on how one views his actions, as the persecutor of the Ṣúfís. Núr-'Alí Sháh, a well-known Ṣúfí *murshid*, was killed by his prescription.

reasons as the Akhbárís. Gradually, in the course of the nineteenth century, the Akhbárí school faded into insignificance, although not into total extinction. But before we turn to the Shaykhí school, the oft-told story of Mírzá Muḥammad-i-Níshápúrí is worth repeating.

Mírzá Muḥammad was an Akhbárí divine residing in 'Iráq. He was driven out by Shaykh Ja'far-i-Najafí. In Írán, he caught the ear of Fatḥ-'Alí Sháh, at a time when the Qájár monarch was reeling under a series of defeats at the hands of the Russians. The actions of General Tsitsianoff, a Georgian inspector in the Russian forces, were bitterly resented in Írán. Mírzá Muḥammad told Fatḥ-'Alí Sháh that should he, the Akhbárí divine, bring about the destruction of this detested general, whom Persians knew as Ishpukhtur (Inspector), the Sháh should, in return, suppress the *mujtahids* and put Akhbárís in their place. Apparently Fatḥ-'Alí Sháh agreed to this proposal and Mírzá Muḥammad retired to the precincts of the shrine of Sháh 'Abdu'l-'Aẓím (in the vicinity of the capital), engaged in an occult rite which ended with the decapitation of a wax image of 'Ishpukhtur', and then announced that the Georgian's head would be laid before the Sháh within forty days. It happened as Mírzá Muḥammad had promised. But the ministers of Fatḥ-'Alí Sháh dissuaded him from keeping his side of the bargain. The Akhbárí divine was told that it was not safe for him to remain in Írán, whereupon he returned to 'Iráq, foretelling his own death. At Káẓimayn, a mob, egged on by the *mujtahids*, broke into Mírzá Muḥammad's house and killed him, while he was reading from the Qur'án.

The founder of the Shaykhí school was Shaykh Aḥmad-i-Aḥsá'í (1743–1826), a native of Baḥrayn. He is known as al-Aḥsá'í, because his family, members of the ancient tribe of Banú-Ṣakhr, came from al-Aḥsá on the Arabian mainland. Shaykh Aḥmad was approaching middle age when he left his island home for the holy cities of 'Iráq, to disseminate amongst a larger circle of people certain views which he had come to hold. Established at Karbilá, he drew to himself a group of disciples, whose numbers gradually increased. The *mujtahids* of 'Iráq, with no voice of dissent, admitted him into their own ranks. His fame spread to Írán and Fatḥ-'Alí Sháh invited him to Ṭihrán. Shaykh Aḥmad chose, however, to take a southerly route, to visit Shíráz and Yazd and go on pilgrimage to the holy city of Mashhad. He resided in Yazd for several years. Although at no time did he identify himself with the Akhbárí school, attacks were mounted against him by the Uṣúlís. Later, he was specifically described and denounced as an Akhbárí, although his firmly-held opinions inclined him to neither side. Ḥájí Mullá Muḥammad-Taqí, a prominent divine of Qazvín,[3] refused to sit down to a meal with him, calling him an infidel. But Shaykh Aḥmad was held in high esteem by Fatḥ-'Alí Sháh, whose invitations became so insistent that the Shaykh finally yielded and journeyed to Ṭihrán, where he was shown every mark of respect. Then, in the company of Ḥájí Siyyid Káẓim-i-Rashtí (1793–1843), who succeeded him after his death, he went on to Kirmánsháh. Rukni'd-Dawlih, a son of Fatḥ-'Alí Sháh, was the governor of that city and had begged his father to let Shaykh Aḥmad be his guest; his premature death intervened and caused Shaykh Aḥmad's return to 'Iráq, after an absence of many years. Later, well advanced in years, he set out on pilgrimage to Mecca and Medina, where he died. In particular, Shaykh Aḥmad clashed with the Uṣúlí divines over two fundamental points of belief. He totally denied the possibility of corporeal resurrection, and he maintained that the *mi'ráj*, the Prophet's night journey to Heaven, was not a physical but a spiritual experience. Refutation of these two components of accepted doctrine, apart from anything else, was sufficient to damn him in the eyes of the orthodox. Despite his admirers in high places and a growing body of powerful support in the ranks of his compatriots, Shaykh Aḥmad was bitterly assailed by the Uṣúlí divines, and the clamour against his school increased in the days of his successor.

If sheer necessity caused the Shí'ah Twelvers to provide themselves with a clerical order to guide and protect them, the same process can be discerned in the evolution of ecclesiasticism in the Christian Faith. But before we examine this theme it should be stated that the nature of *ijtihád* within the Shí'ah fold has made for flexibility and catholicism, in contrast to the rigidities and extreme orthodoxies of such Sunní schools as the Málikí and the Ḥanbalí. In the secular field a parallel can be found in the two systems of Equity and Common and Statutary Law. It should also be noted that *ijamá'* (consensus), repudiated by the Shí'ah jurists, has been

[3] He is known as Shahíd-i-Thálith—the Third Martyr.

responsible for the acceptance, by the entire realm of Islám, of that version of the Qur'án which the third Caliph promulgated. No sect or division within Islám has ever taken the contrary view,[4] although it is known that other versions existed which 'Uthmán suppressed. By the same token and process a vast corpus of traditions has found universal recognition.

When Jesus was crucified, there were Christians nowhere but in Jerusalem. Peter was the chief of the Apostles. He was thus appointed by Jesus:

> When Jesus came into the coasts of Caesarea Philippi, he asked his disciples, saying, Whom do men say that I the Son of man am?
>
> And they said, Some say that thou art John the Baptist: some, Elias; and others, Jeremias, or one of the prophets.
>
> He saith unto them, But whom say ye that I am?
>
> And Simon Peter answered and said, Thou art the Christ, the Son of the living God.
>
> And Jesus answered and said unto him, Blessed art thou, Simon Bar-jo-na: for flesh and blood hath not revealed it unto thee, but my Father which is in heaven.
>
> And I say also unto thee, That thou art Peter, and upon this rock I will build my church; and the gates of hell shall not prevail against it.
>
> And I will give unto thee the keys of the kingdom of heaven: and whatsoever thou shalt bind on earth shall be bound in heaven: and whatsoever thou shalt loose on earth shall be loosed in heaven.
>
> (Matt. 16:13–19.)

The Apostles elected Matthias to fill the place of the fallen Judas. But it was not Peter who became the head of the community of the Nazarenes (or Nazoreans) in Jerusalem. That honour went to James, the brother of Jesus, who was put to death by the orders of Ananas, the High Priest, in the year 62. Simeon, the son of Mary Cleophas, succeeded James. Simeon was a cousin of Jesus and was in turn crucified, during the reign of Trajan, in the year 104 or 105. Between the date of his martyrdom and the year

[4] It is true that some Shí'ah apologists claim the deletion of specific verses referring to 'Alí, but there is no evidence to show that 'Alí himself or any other of the Imáms ever made or supported such a claim.

133, there were thirteen others who are named as the bishops of Jerusalem. Jews made a final effort under Bar-Kochba, in that year 133, to oust the Romans and gain their freedom, but Hadrian crushed them. Jerusalem was then totally destroyed and the Nazarene community ceased to exist.[5]

The Nazarenes were still anchored in their Jewish faith, adhering firmly to Jewish law. When Saul of Tarsus, with his burning faith in Christ, appeared on the scene, and wished to make it easier for the Gentiles to accept the Saviour, he came up against the relentless opposition of the Nazarenes. For James and Simeon and possibly some of their successors, the term 'bishop' (from Gr. *episkopos*), now applied to them in a specific sense, had no meaning, unless it might have had the connotation of 'overseer'. Naturally, when the gates were flung open by St. Paul and Gentiles poured in, the Jewishness of the Nazarenes was submerged and Apostolic churches were founded in major cities such as Rome and Alexandria. Although St. Peter is acknowledged as the first Bishop of Rome, the hand which raised and reared that Church was the hand of Paul, not of Peter. And the Church of Rome amongst the other Apostolic Churches came to have the position of *primus inter pares*. It was the rise of Islám and the victory of Arab arms, which wrested cities such as Antioch and Alexandria from Byzantium, that gave primacy to Rome. By then the organs of the church (*ecclesia*)[6] were well developed. There had been several oecumenical councils, beginning with the Council of Nicaea[7] in 325 which formulated the creed, proclaiming the doctrine of Trinity (first enunciated by Tertullian, who later, in 220, turned his back on the Church and joined the Montanists), and condemning the views of Bishop Arius. The Council of Nicaea, from which also emerged the form and contents of the New Testament, was followed, in 381, by the Council of Constantinople, convened by the Spanish Emperor, Theodosius the Great. It set the final seal on the creed, after years of struggle with Constantius, the son of Constantine the Great, who favoured Arianism; and it sent such men as Athanasius of Alexandria, Hosius of Cordova, Hilary of Poitiers and Liberius of Rome into

[5] During the first rising of the Jews, which ended with the triumph of Titus, in the year 67, this Christian community of Jerusalem had moved to Pella in Decapolis.

[6] Originally, '*ecclesia*' was the general assembly of Athenian citizens.

[7] Earlier, in 314, a Council had been convened at Arles by Constantine to consider the activities of the Donatists.

exile. Next, in 431, the Council of Ephesus condemned the Nestorians; the Council of Chalcedon, twenty years later, condemned both the Nestorians and the Monophysites or Jacobites; and the second Council of Constantinople, in 553, condemned the Monothelites. Others were yet to come to condemn the Iconoclasts and heresies similar to theirs.

The Nazarenes of Jerusalem, the Corinthians, the Colossians, the Ephesians, the Philippians and other Christian communities to whom Paul wrote his epistles were groupings of the faithful, for whom 'bishops' and 'deacons' were just 'overseers', 'supervisors' and 'administrators'. They had their 'presbyters' (elders), 'prophets' (people who prophesied what was to come and were eventually suppressed because of their frenzied extremism) and preachers. Every grouping of people, anywhere in the world, at any time, needs elders and supervisors. But it is a far cry from these to possessing authoritative prelates and decision-making councils. These came into being from sheer necessity, to act as shields against dissent and disorder, and hostile forces without and within.

Can it not be truly said that the great living religions of mankind, by the dictate of necessity, came to fashion and develop, as a bulwark, systems and institutions which neither the Founders nor the early converts had envisaged?

We have surveyed the story of the Faith of Muḥammad, the 'Arabian Prophet', up to the period of time when the Christian West had begun to hack at the realm of Islám, mulcting it of large sections to bring under its own domination; while the same onslaught was making the destinies of those parts of that realm which kept their sovereignty more and more dependent on the whims, the conflicts, the rivalries and the fears of the Powers of Europe. From the far stretches of the Pacific to the eastern edge of the Atlantic, the realm of Islám was under attack and was fast losing its independence of action. But here we must halt because the examination of the next turbulent chapter, leading eventually to the reversal of that process in recent decades, is a vast study which must also entail a close scrutiny of two World Wars which devastated Europe. Of course, Europe still exists, but the 'mighty Continent' which once dominated the world is no more.

Glossary

All Arabic and Persian terms are explained in the text on first usage, but this glossary includes terms fairly often repeated, or terms which the reader may frequently encounter elsewhere. Although they may be italicized in the text, it seems more practical not to do so here.

Abú	The father of. When preceded by Ibn it changes to Abí.
Adhán	The call to prayer by the mu'adhdhin.
Anṣár	The Helpers, the name given by Muḥammad to His followers in Medina.
Bashír	'He who gives glad tidings'. A term used in the Qur'án for Muḥammad.
Bímáristán	Home for the Sick; hospital.
Bint	The daughter of.
Byzantium	The Byzantine or Eastern Roman Empire, with its capital in Constantinople.
Caliph	From *khalífah*, meaning 'successor' or 'viceregent'; the supreme head of the realm of Islám from the time of the election of Abú-Bakr to succeed the Prophet, accepted by Sunnís. The institution is known as the Caliphate.
Clan	A subdivision of a tribe.
Coat of arms	Mail dress to the waist, as worn in ancient times, i.e., by Alexander the Great.
Dá'í (pl. Du'át)	'The one who calls'; a missionary.
Dhimmís	People of the Book (i.e., Jews and Christians) enjoying the protection of Islám, on payment of the poll-tax *(jizyah)*.
Ghazwah	Expeditions led by the Prophet.
Ghulát	'Those who exaggerate', or the Extremists; a collective name for the extremist sects of Shí'ah Islám.
Ḥadíth	A 'statement' or tradition describing some action or word of the Prophet, passed on through generations

	from the original eye-witness; the whole corpus of the *sunnah*. A term also used of the traditions of the Imáms.
Ḥajj	Pilgrimage to Mecca, once in a lifetime by those who can afford it, prescribed by Muḥammad to take place in the month of Dhu'l-Ḥijjah.
Ḥaníf	A monotheist; a term also applied to Muslims.
Hijrah	The Prophet's emigration to Medina. The Muslim calendar dates from this event in A.D. 622.
Ḥimyarites	People of Ḥimyar in Yemen, South Arabia, claiming descent from Qaḥṭan, whose son Ya'rib was thought to have given his name to the Arabian peninsula.
Ibn	The son of. Some authors use bin or b.
Imám	The legitimate and hereditary successor to the Prophet, from His House, accepted by Shí'ahs. The institution is known as the Imámate. From *imám*, one who leads the congregation in the mosque in prayer; the term is also used of the founders of the four schools of Sunní jurisprudence.
Islám	The religion of submission to the Will of God.
Jáhilíyyah	The days of 'ignorance' before the advent of Muḥammad.
Jihád	Holy war against pagans and idolaters.
Jiwár (Juwár)	'Protection', as extended by a clan to its members, or by powerful men to whomever they choose to protect.
Jizyah	Poll-tax or tithes, payable by non-Muslims in the realm of Islám.
Ka'bah	Literally, 'cube'. The ancient four-square sacred shrine in Mecca, chosen by Muḥammad as the *qiblih* of His Faith and the place of pilgrimage.
Khárijites	The Khawárij, meaning 'Seceders' or 'Outsiders', who withdrew their support from 'Alí during his contest with Mu'áwíyah, to form a separate sect which for long disturbed Islamic society, particularly in North Africa and the Persian Gulf littoral.
Mahdí (Mihdí)	'The One who is guided', a name used by both Shí'ahs and Sunnís for the One whose appearance they expect in the fullness of time.
Makkah	Mecca.
Mawálí	'Clients'; the non-Arab Muslims.
Mazdean	Zoroastrian.
Mi'ráj	The 'Ascent', the Prophet's night journey to Heaven.

Monophysite	One who believes that the human and divine in Christ constitute one single nature. This form of Christianity was introduced into South Arabia from Syria at an early date, and was also followed in Ethiopia and Egypt.
Mu'adhdhin	One who gives the call to prayer; muezzin in English.
Muḍarite	People of Muḍar, a North Arabian tribe which settled in 'Iráq before Muḥammad, claiming descent from Ishmael. The Quraysh of Mecca were Muḍarites.
Muhájirún	The Emigrants, the name given by Muḥammad to His followers who emigrated from Mecca to Medina.
Munáfiqún	Dissemblers who paid lip service to the Faith of Muḥammad, but derided it at every opportunity.
Murshid	'Guide'; a Ṣúfí spiritual guide or leader.
Muslim	A follower of the Faith of Muḥammad.
Mu'tazilite	The Mu'tazilah, or 'Seceders', a name given to the liberal school of thought founded by Wáṣil Ibn 'Aṭá' in collaboration with 'Amr Ibn 'Ubayd.
Nadhír	'He who warns.' A term used in the Qur'án for Muḥammad.
Neo-Platonist	One who accepted a combination of Platonic and Oriental thought, as developed by Plotinus, Porphyry, Proclus and others.
Nestorian	One who follows the teaching of Nestorius, patriarch of Constantinople (*c.* A.D. 428), that Christ had distinct divine and human persons.
Nuqabá' (sing. naqíb)	The 'leaders', a term applied to the twelve men of Medina whom Muḥammad chose as His apostles.
Qá'im	The twelfth, or absent, Imám, expected to come forth from his major occultation in the fullness of time.
Qiblih	The point toward which the Muslim turns while saying his daily obligatory prayers (Mecca).
Qur'án	The Holy Book of Islám, comprising the Revelation received at various times by Muḥammad during His ministry. It is also known as the Furqán.
Sacred months	The four months of Rajab, Dhu'l-Qa'dah, Dhu'l-Ḥijjah and Muḥarram during which raids and warfare were interdicted.
Ṣalát	Obligatory prayer prescribed by Muḥammad, to be said five times a day, before sunrise, at noon, in the afternoon, at sunset and in the evening.

Saríyyah	Expeditions led by others than the Prophet.
Sásánids	The ruling dynasty of the Persian or Sásánian Empire, A.D. 224–642.
Shí'ahs	Legitimists upholding the right of succession for the House of the Prophet.
Ṣúfí	A Muslim mystic. See ch. 26.
Sunnah	Practices and traditions attributed to the Prophet.
Sunnís	The majority of the Muslims who uphold the elective principle in the matter of succession to the Prophet. The people of *Sunnah*, or Tradition.
Súrah	A chapter of the Qur'án.
'Umrah	The lesser pilgrimage.
Yathrib	The name by which Medina was known before the Prophet's emigration (Hijrah).
Zindíq (pl. Zanádiqah)	A Manichaean, or follower of Mání, an Íránian who attempted a synthesis of the Christian and Mazdean (Zoroastrian) Faiths.

Select Bibliography

The page numbers given for references refer to the first edition cited, when two editions are mentioned.

Ahmad, Aziz. *An Intellectual History of Islam in India.* Edinburgh University Press, 1969.

Ameer Ali, Syed. *A Short History of the Saracens.* London: Macmillan and Co Ltd, 1949.

—— *The Spirit of Islam.* A History of the Evolution and Ideals of Islam with a Life of the Prophet. London: Methuen & Co Ltd, (University Paperbacks), 1965. London: Chatto and Windus Ltd (Cased edn.).

Arberry, Arthur J. *The Koran Interpreted.* London: George Allen & Unwin Ltd, 1955. (Also available from Oxford University Press in the World's Classics series and from Barnes & Noble, Inc, New York.)

—— *Oriental Essays.* Portraits of Seven Scholars. London: George Allen & Unwin Ltd, 1960.

Á<u>sh</u>tíyání, 'Abbás Iqbál. *<u>Kh</u>ánidán-i-Nawba<u>kh</u>tí* (The House of Nawba<u>kh</u>tí). Ṭihrán, 1932.

Binyon, Laurence. *Akbar.* London: Peter Davies Ltd, 1932.

Bosworth, Clifford Edmund. *The Islamic Dynasties.* A chronological and genealogical handbook. Edinburgh University Press, 1967. Chicago: Aldine Publishing Company.

Browne, Edward G. *A Literary History of Persia*, vols. I and IV. London: Cambridge University Press, re-issue 1928.

Byron, Robert. *The Road to Oxiana.* London: Jonathan Cape Ltd (Paper edn.), 1937.

Cambridge History of Iran, The, vol. V. Cambridge University Press, 1968.

Cambridge History of Islam, The, vols. I and II. Cambridge University Press, 1971.

Dermenghem, Émile. *The Life of Mahomet.* London: George Routledge & Sons, 1930.

EDWARDES, MICHAEL. *Glorious Sahibs*. Eyre & Spottiswoode, 1968.

GIBBON, EDWARD. *The Decline and Fall of the Roman Empire*. Oxford University Press, 1920. (World's Classics series.)

GLUBB, JOHN BAGOT (Lieutenant General Sir John Glubb). *The Course of Empire*. London: Hodder & Stoughton Ltd, 1965.

—— *The Empire of the Arabs*. London: Hodder & Stoughton Ltd, 1963.

—— *The Life and Times of Muhammad*. London: Hodder and Stoughton Ltd, 1970.

GRUNEBAUM, G. E. VON. *Classical Islam*. A History 600–1258. Trans. by Katherine Watson. London: George Allen & Unwin Ltd, 1970. Chicago: Aldine Publishing Company.

GUILLAUME, ALFRED. *The Traditions of Islam*. An Introduction to the study of the Hadith Literature. Oxford: Clarendon Press, 1924.

HITTI, PHILIP K. *The Arabs: A Short History*. Princeton University Press, 1943.

—— *History of the Arabs*. London: Macmillan and Co Ltd, 10th edn. 1970. New York: St. Martin's Press, Inc.

—— *Islam. A Way of Life*. Minneapolis: The University of Minnesota Press, 1970. London: Oxford University Press, 1970.

HUJWIRI, 'ALI B. 'Uthman Al-Jullabi Al-Hujwiri. *The Kashf Al-Maḥjûb*. The Oldest Persian Treatise on Ṣúfiism. Trans. by Reynold A. Nicholson. London: Luzac & Co, 1936. (This is vol. XVII of the E. J. W. Gibb Memorial Series.)

JUVAINI, 'ALA-AD-DIN 'ATA-MALIK. *The History of the World-Conqueror*. Trans. from the text of Mirza Muhammad Qazvini by John Andrew Boyle. Manchester University Press, 1958.

The Korân. Translated into English from the original Arabic by George Sale. London: Frederick Warne and Co Ltd, first published 1734.

The Legacy of Islam. Edited by Joseph Schacht with C. E. Bosworth. London: Oxford University Press, 1974.

LE STRANGE, GUY. *The Lands of the Eastern Caliphate*. Mesopotamia, Persia and Central Asia from the Moslem conquest to the time of Timur. Cambridge University Press, 1905. London: Frank Cass & Co Ltd, 1966.

LEVY, REUBEN. *An Introduction to the Sociology of Islam*. (in two vols.) London: Williams & Norgate Ltd, 1931.

LEWIS, BERNARD. *The Arabs in History*. London: Hutchinson University Library, rev. edn. 1958.

MORGAN, KENNETH W. (Ed.). *Islam: The Straight Path*. Islam Interpreted by Muslims. New York: The Ronald Press Company, 1958.

NICHOLSON, REYNOLD A. *A Literary History of the Arabs*. Cambridge University Press (Paper edn.), 1969.

PRESCOTT, H. F. M. *Friar Felix at Large*. A Fifteenth-Century Pilgrimage to the Holy Land. New Haven: Yale University Press, 1960. (Yale Paperbound edn.)

RICE, CYPRIAN, O. P. *The Persian Ṣūfis*. London: George Allen & Unwin Ltd, 1964.

RUNCIMAN, STEVEN. *A History of the Crusades*, vol. I, *The First Crusade*; vol. II, *The Kingdom of Acre*. London: Peregrine Books (Penguin), 1971. London: Cambridge University Press (cased edns.), 1951 and 1954.

SHABAN, M. A. *The 'Abbasid Revolution*. Cambridge University Press, 1970.

SYKES, BRIGADIER-GENERAL SIR PERCY. *A History of Persia*, vol. II. London: Macmillan and Co Ltd, 1930.

TOYNBEE, ARNOLD J. *A Study of History*. vol. I (1934), vol. IV (1939). London: Oxford University Press.

WATERFIELD, ROBIN E. *Christians in Persia*. London: George Allen & Unwin Ltd, 1973. (Also available from Barnes & Noble, Inc, New York.)

WATT, W. MONTGOMERY. *A History of Islamic Spain*. Edinburgh University Press, 1965.

—— *Muhammad, Prophet and Statesman*. Oxford University Press, (Oxford Paperbacks), 1964.

—— *Muslim Intellectual*. A Study of Al-Ghazali. Edinburgh University Press, 1971.

——*What is Islam?* London and Harlow: Longman, Green and Co Ltd, 1968. Beirut: Librairie du Liban, 1968.

Index

Index

Titles of books and some Arabic words are italicized. Bold figures indicate main references. Footnotes are indicated by n after the page number.